THOREAU'S SEASONS

Thoreau's Seasons

RICHARD LEBEAUX

The University of Massachusetts Press
Amherst, 1984

Copyright © 1984 by The University of Massachusetts Press
All rights reserved   Printed in the United States of America
Publication of this book was assisted by the American Council of Learned Societies under
a grant from the Andrew W. Mellon Foundation.
Library of Congress Cataloging in Publication Data appear on the last printed page of
this book.

Grateful acknowledgment is made to the following publishers and authors for permission to
reprint material under copyright.
Basic Books, Inc., from Robert Jay Lifton, *The Broken Connection,* © 1979 by Robert Jay
Lifton.
E. P. Dutton, Inc. and Bantam Books, Inc., from Gail Sheehy, *Passages: Predictable Crises of
Adult Life,* © 1974, 1976 by Gail Sheehy. All rights reserved.
Twayne Publishers, G. K. Hall & Co., Boston, from Richard Lebeaux, " 'Sugar Maple Man':
Middle-Aged Thoreau's Generativity Crisis," in *Studies in the American Renaissance 1981,*
ed. Joel Myerson, © 1981.
Walter Harding, from his *The Days of Henry Thoreau* (1965; New York: Dover Publica-
tions, 1982).
New York University Press, from *The Correspondence of Henry David Thoreau,* ed. Walter
Harding and Carl Bode, © 1958 by New York University.
W. W. Norton & Co., Inc., from Henry David Thoreau, *Cape Cod,* arranged with notes by
Dudley C. Lunt, © 1951 by W. W. Norton & Co., Inc., © renewed 1979 by Dudley C. Lunt.
Alfred A. Knopf, Inc., from Daniel J. Levinson, *The Seasons of a Man's Life,* © 1978 by
Daniel J. Levinson.

For Rachel and Ellen

Contents

Acknowledgments

I have been sounding Thoreau for well over a decade now, seeking to fathom (as he expressed it in *Walden*) his "depth and concealed bottom." Many people have helped make my soundings for this book possible and, I believe, more sound. As the Notes make clear, I am indebted to a long chain of Thoreau scholars and students of human life and development.

I owe a special debt of gratitude to Walter Harding, not only for *The Days of Henry Thoreau*, the invaluable biography that decisively launched my own expedition into Thoreau, but also for encouraging me to continue beyond *Young Man Thoreau*. As part of a conference he organized at the State University College of New York at Geneseo in 1978, he gave me an opportunity to reflect on the "later" Thoreau and provided me with my first public forum for trying out some of my ideas. In addition, I am very fortunate to have had Professor Harding as the consulting editor for this book. Certainly he has helped to strengthen it, most particularly by making it more accurate. Another person to whom I am especially indebted is Leone Stein, until recently Director of the University of Massachusetts Press, who believed in me and supported this project from its inception, and who supplied me with sage advice and with a valuable, sensitive reading of the manuscript. Robert Sayre's reactions to the manuscript were extremely thoughtful and perceptive, and Leo Marx responded helpfully to my ideas and parts of this work at different stages. I also very much appreciate the suggestions and guidance of Richard Martin, Pam Campbell, and other members of the staff of the University of Massachusetts Press.

Others who have aided with their encouragement, support, and counsel at various stages include Thomas Blanding, John Callahan, Raymond Gozzi, Michael Meyer, Caroline Moseley, Joel Myerson, Richard Noland,

Michael Reed, Edmund Schofield, William Shurr, and Paul Wright. I wish
also to thank Henry Silverman, Chairperson of the Department of American Thought and Language at Michigan State, for his support and genuine interest, as well as my many valued friends and dedicated colleagues,
present and former, in the department who—despite the heavy demands
of their own teaching, paper evaluating, and writing—were concerned,
encouraging, and willing to act generously as sounding boards for my
ideas. Students in all my classes have provided me with a continuing adult
education and with responses to my viewpoints on many issues; they have,
I am certain, made their contribution to this book.

Indispensable was the help and solid advice of Elizabeth Witherell,
Editor-in-Chief of *The Writings of Henry D. Thoreau*, who facilitated
immensely my research at the Thoreau Textual Center at Princeton University (now relocated at the University of California at Santa Barbara),
furnished me with transcriptions and proofs from the center, and gave me
permission to quote from some of their materials. Carolyn Kappes of the
Textual Center also helped make my research at Princeton more productive and pleasant. Surely all scholars and readers of Thoreau, including me,
are indebted to the thorough, painstaking work of the Textual Center and
to Princeton University Press for publishing authoritative texts of Thoreau's writings. I wish, furthermore, to acknowledge gratefully the Henry
E. Huntington Library, San Marino, California, for granting me permission to quote from unpublished transcriptions at the Thoreau Textual
Center of HM 13182, which will later appear as part of the Princeton Edition of *Journal 3: 1848–1851* and from those portions of HM 924 that
constitute the "First Version of *Walden*" that appeared, as determined by
J. Lyndon Shanley, in *The Making of Walden*, published by the University
of Chicago Press (1957). Thanks are also due to the American Antiquarian
Society, Worcester, Massachusetts, for allowing me to examine and quote
from Ruth Hallingby Frost's unpublished typescript, "Thoreau's Worcester Associations." Mrs. Anne McGrath, Curator of the Thoreau Lyceum,
has always been more than willing to aid me with my research over the
years.

For financial support of this project, I am grateful for the assistance
of a year-long Fellowship from the American Council of Learned Societies,
made possible by a grant from the National Endowment for the Humanities. Also appreciated was the help provided by a one-term research
leave and yearly All-University Research Grants from Michigan State
University.

Much of the writing of this book coincided felicitously with the birth
and infancy of my daughter Rachel. I will always treasure the experience of

having nurtured both "babies" during the same period and of having seen them both grow.

I wish, finally, to express my deepest gratitude to my wife, Ellen, who has shared with me many seasons.

East Lansing, Michigan
August 1983

Preface

THIS book continues essentially where *Young Man Thoreau* left off. It concentrates primarily on the period from the beginning of Thoreau's Walden experiment in 1845 to his death in 1862. I hope that readers will refer back to *Young Man Thoreau* for a detailed, in-depth consideration of Thoreau in the pre-Walden years. But while this book is a continuation of —and seeks to maintain continuity with—the previous volume, it has been my aim to make it a self-contained experience for readers and a work that stands on its own as an exploration of Thoreau's life and writings.

Among the purposes of the first chapter are to provide a bridge linking the previous book to this one and to introduce readers to *Thoreau's Seasons*. In the course of interpreting Thoreau's significant first book, *A Week on the Concord and Merrimack Rivers*—a work that in its evolution spanned the pre-Walden, Walden, and early post-Walden years—as, in part, a "Picture of Human Life" and of Thoreau's life, I have taken the opportunity to review some of the key discoveries of *Young Man Thoreau* that serve as a foundation for this book; to furnish a preliminary sense of the Walden experience that will be examined intensively in the second chapter; and to give readers a preview and overview of the challenges and crises Thoreau would face in the post-Walden years that will be the focus of subsequent chapters. Moreover, the first chapter seeks to acquaint, or reacquaint, readers with approaches, especially Eriksonian psychology, that were important in *Young Man Thoreau* and to introduce other viewpoints, particularly on the life cycle and adult development, vital to this book. My intention has been to integrate these perspectives in such ways as to come to, and reflect, my own understanding and envisioning of adult development as well as of Thoreau.

One central belief that I share with many recent students of the life cycle is that people develop, and have the capacity for growth, throughout life, even if they remain strongly influenced by what has happened in, and how they have "handled," earlier developmental stages. Although, as *Young Man Thoreau* shows, Thoreau was critically influenced by his childhood, adolescent, and early adult experience in the years before he went to Walden, he was also decisively shaped by the events and experiences of the 1845–1862 period and by the necessity of coming to terms, as we all must, with issues and crises integral to adult phases of the life cycle. In the process, Thoreau and his art grew, though not without difficulties and setbacks, and often with and through struggle. That he went through such struggle, that he carried with him from his past burdens, conflicts, and shortcomings—as well as undeniable gifts, and virtues that often revealed an ability to convert weaknesses into strengths—make Thoreau and his accomplishments, in my view, all the more human, understandable, remarkable, and instructive.

This book draws extensively on Thoreau's voluminous writings (including the formidable *Journal* that became, as he once put it, a "meteorological journal of the mind") and the biographical evidence in order to explore the "several lives" within Thoreau's life; to trace his evolving conceptions of self, art, and life; and—especially by examining them in pertinent biographical, psychological, sociocultural, and historical contexts— to illuminate the writings themselves. As the book's title suggests, the seasons—natural and human—emerged as a most apt and fruitful way to envision Thoreau and the life cycle. I sensed early the fitness of the seasons and natural imagery as prisms through which to perceive a man who was himself so closely and vitally connected to nature. Coming at an important formative stage of my own thinking and research, such recent studies as Daniel Levinson's *The Seasons of a Man's Life*—in addition to providing significant models of, and meditations on, the life cycle—further alerted me to the potential of that ages-old metaphor of the seasons as it was applicable to my interpretation of Thoreau and human development, and to Thoreau's own perspectives. My research solidly confirmed this potential: in the long process of reading and rereading Thoreau, and seeking to arrive at an understanding and characterization of him from *my* angle of vision (which included the seasonal angle, among others), I was struck over and over again by just how seriously and freshly *he* regarded the seasons, and natural phenomena in general, as a means by which to comprehend and characterize his own life and human life, and as a medium through which to communicate his thoughts, feelings, moods, and vision. As the research proceeded, I was also even further heartened and enlightened by the suggestive organic (and mythic) imagery used by such humanistic psychologists as William Bridges in *Transitions*. By the time I was earnestly into the writing, and the book was taking its present shape, I became more and more drawn to *Thoreau's Seasons* as an appropriate and evocative title. As this book makes abundantly clear, nature was by no means the only focus of Thoreau's life, thinking, and writing. He was, for instance, a man involved in, and influenced by, relationships—often problematic, to be sure—with family, friends, community, a former mentor (Emerson), a would-be career adviser and sponsor (Greeley), disciples, and others; who cared about, and responded to, what he saw as the disappointing, disturbing directions in which his society and country were moving; and who was galvanized by such urgent issues of his time as the fate of the Indians, the Mexican War, slavery, the John Brown affair, and both the prospect and reality of the Civil War. However, it is also quite clear that nature's seasons and phenomena did provide Thoreau with absolutely essential and critical occasions, images, metaphors, and analogies for his profound grappling—conscious and unconscious—with the crucial personal, artistic, social, political, and human concerns that confronted him in the 1845–1862 period.

I continue to believe, as I indicated in *Young Man Thoreau*, that Thoreau has very considerable limitations as one who can suggest solutions to our contemporary dilemmas, including those pertaining to human relationships and "social facts"; the need to acknowledge the importance of human dependence and interdependence as well as independence; gender, sex roles, and sexuality; and the imperative for sensitivity, care, and compassion among people, diverse groups and peoples, and nations. But I am even more convinced than previously that he speaks eloquently to us today, living as we do in a world in which many are, usually with good reason, troubled; in which people are often denied, or restricted in, opportunities for growth and authenticity; in which some are denied decent work and even those necessities of life basic to survival; in which human beings, those extraordinary creatures with such capacity for constructive and creative action, are both an endangered and endangering species, threatening not only themselves but also those other species and wonders with which they share this planet.

In the course of my study of and long-term relationship with Thoreau —as well as in the process of living my own life, thinking about it, and pondering the life cycle—I believe that I have learned much. For instance, I have come more keenly to realize that I, too, have led "several lives" and have "several more lives to live," that I have gone, and will go, through many more seasons. In considering how Thoreau sought to come to terms with aging and death, I also have had to reckon more fully with my own aging and mortality. Moreover, reading Thoreau, and going through the seasons with him, has, among other things, further sensitized me to how keeping in touch with nature, and contemplating the correspondences between nature and the human experience, can be edifying, inspiring, calming, and healing. As it has been for me in working on *Thoreau's Seasons*, so certainly do I hope it will be for those reading it: that the book will lead readers to reflect not only on Thoreau's seasons but also on their own.

Abbreviations

The following abbreviations are used in citing sources in the text.

C   *The Correspondence of Henry David Thoreau*. Edited by Walter Harding and Carl Bode. New York: New York University Press, 1958.

CC   *Cape Cod*. Edited by Dudley Lunt. New York: Bramhall House, 1951.

CP   *Collected Poems of Henry Thoreau*. Edited by Carl Bode. Baltimore: Johns Hopkins Press, 1964.

EEM   *Early Essays and Miscellanies*. Edited by Joseph J. Moldenhauer and Edwin Moser, with Alexander C. Kern. Princeton: Princeton University Press, 1975.

E   *Excursions*. 1863. Reprint. New York: Corinth Books, 1962.

H   *Huckleberries*. Edited by Leo Stoller. 1970. Reprinted in *The Natural History Essays*. Salt Lake City: Peregrine Smith, 1980.

J   *The Journal of Henry D. Thoreau*. Edited by Bradford Torrey and Francis H. Allen. 1906. Reprint (14 vols. in 2). New York: Dover Publications, 1962.

JMN   *The Journals and Miscellaneous Notebooks of Ralph Waldo Emerson*. Edited by William H. Gilman et al. Cambridge: Harvard University Press, 1960– .

L   *The Letters of Ralph Waldo Emerson*. Edited by Ralph Rusk. New York: Columbia University Press, 1939.

MW   *The Maine Woods*. Edited by Joseph J. Moldenhauer. Princeton: Princeton University Press, 1972.

PJ   *Journal 1: 1837–1844, Journal 2: 1842–1848,* and *Journal 3:*

1848–1851 (forthcoming): *The Writings of Henry D. Thoreau.* Edited by John C. Broderick et al. Princeton: Princeton University Press, 1981– . Since the page proofs were not yet available, I have not included page number references in the text for *Journal 3.*

RP   *Reform Papers.* Edited by Wendell Glick. Princeton: Princeton University Press, 1973.

W   *Walden.* Edited by J. Lyndon Shanley. Princeton: Princeton University Press, 1971.

THOREAU'S SEASONS

1 Week of a Man's Life

$\mathcal{F}$ROM August 31 to September 13, 1839, the Thoreau brothers, Henry and John, took a trip during a vacation from the school they ran together.[1] It consisted of voyaging on the Concord and Merrimack rivers and hiking in the White Mountains. No doubt from the very moment the excursion itself ended and thus became subject to the transforming powers of memory, need, imagination, and composition, it began to take on new meanings for Henry Thoreau, then twenty-two years old and an aspiring writer. A long period of artistic gestation commenced where the two-week experience left off, as is evident in his 1839–42 journal. Originally he conceived of the trip as the basis for an essay combining travel and natural history; he apparently first thought of entitling it "Memoirs of a Tour—A Chit-chat with Nature" and then considered "Merrimack & Musketaquid" as a possible title.[2] But after the watershed event of John's death from lockjaw in 1842—and his own near-fatal case of "sympathetic" lockjaw—Thoreau's conception of the significance and implications of the trip, and of the art that would render it, was dramatically, profoundly transfigured. Imbued now with an urgent sense of mission, he started to work on a book that would be not only a richly detailed and allusive re-creation primarily of the week he had spent with John on the rivers but also a worthy memorial to the elder brother he had loved and lost.

Clearly, what had once been the "Memoirs of a Tour" was evolving into a tour de force, and there was yet another dimension emerging by the time he began to work on the book. It is suggested by a remark in one draft of his travel essay, "A Walk to Wachusett," composed in the months after John's death: "though a 'Journey of a Day,' we meant that it should be a

'Picture of Human Life.'" Through all the expansions and revisions of *A Week*—in his "Long Book" of 1842–44, at Walden Pond where an important part of the "private business" he transacted was the writing of the bulk of the book, and in the two years after he left the pond[3]—it is certain that Thoreau, with his perspective tested, stretched, and deepened by his encounter with death and, thus, with life's parameters, was at least to some degree mindful of the underlying theme and organizing principle he had enunciated in the "Wachusett" draft. Though ostensibly writing about the "journey of a week," he meant too that it should be a "Picture of Human Life."[4]

Thoreau had been an alert and enthusiastic, if still somewhat derivative and informal, student of the passages of the seasons. Indeed, his first recorded essay, written when he was eleven or twelve,[5] was called "The Seasons";[6] his first recorded book review was of William Howitt's *Book of the Seasons; or, A Calendar of Nature;*[7] and he was well acquainted with James Thomson's *The Seasons* (J, I: 467–68). And Emerson's *Nature,* a powerful inspiration and influence, had proclaimed that "particular natural facts are symbols of particular spiritual facts" and that "Nature is the symbol of the spirit." Emerson, moreover, had inquired in *Nature,* "But is there no intent of an analogy between man's life and the seasons?"[8] Therefore, it is not surprising that Thoreau, intensely interested in the nature of life as well as in the life of nature, was, as he worked on *A Week* (and partly, no doubt, as a result of further perceptions generated by the composing process itself as well as his other experiences), becoming increasingly sensitive to and sophisticated about what might be called the human seasons.[9] In the years that followed *A Week* and the stay at Walden, his understanding of both natural and human seasons would grow deeper and be revised and refined, as his journal, *Walden,* and his later essays would attest. In "A Walk to Wachusett," a one-day journey could serve as an analogy for human life, and in the *Journal* and *Walden* his exploration of life would revolve particularly around the seasons and, to some extent, the days. In *A Week,* Thoreau used not only the day and the seasons—most especially the transition from summer to autumn—but also the days of the week, the details of the trip itself, and the digressions that flow—not always smoothly —from the trip to create a work that may be interpreted as containing remarkably suggestive perspectives on the human journey (and of the virtues associated with different phases) and that may be perceived, in fact, as having many points of correspondence with the insights and discoveries of more recent students of the life cycle.[10] Without, of course, reducing *A Week*—a work composed of several strands—to life-cycle concerns, without suggesting that Thoreau was always fully conscious of these concerns

or saw them in the exact way or terms to be proposed here, it can nevertheless be argued that a "Picture of Human Life" is embedded in the text, that
it invites fruitful contemplation and the sort of emphasis and interpretation that follow, and that it is one significant theme and thread of continuity in his book.

But *A Week* is not only a generalized "Picture of Human Life"; it is
also very much a self-portrait, an idealized but nonetheless revealing version of Thoreau's own autobiography—past, present, and future—in
which he suggests how he has personally dealt, is dealing, and hopes to
deal with issues rooted in the life cycle and in which he seeks—and needs—
to affirm his own ideals and ego ideal. As such, it represents in part, as he
intimates in "Sunday," the transmutation of the "raw materials of biography and history" into a personal "mythology" (60).[11] This is not to say
that Thoreau ignores entirely the harsh realities of life, even if he often
tends to downplay these realities and underestimate the pain and severity
of the challenges posed by life. After all, even myths have more than their
share of trials and crises. Thoreau himself says in "Sunday," after observing that even Christ "taught mankind but imperfectly how to live": "Even
here we have a sort of living to get, and must buffet it somewhat longer.
There are various tough problems yet to solve, and we must make shift to
live, betwixt spirit and matter, such a human life as we can" (73–74).
Written largely in the buoyant and relatively stable sojourn at the pond, at
once a period of moratorium and settling down, of withdrawal and commitment, which temporarily and partially resolved his conflicts, *A Week*
characteristically reflects a confidence, assurance, and optimism he did not
have before Walden, and would seldom have after leaving the pond. As recently as January 16, 1843, he had described himself as a "diseased bun-
dle of nerves standing between time and eternity like a withered leaf that
still hangs shivering on its stem" (PJ, 1:447).

If Thoreau reconstructs and recovers his past, interprets his present,
and peers into his future in an idealized way that reflects his needs and state
of mind, particularly but by no means exclusively while he was at the
pond, he nevertheless reveals much, both wittingly and unwittingly, consciously and unconsciously, about the actual man. There are evasions,
denials, glossings over, and revisions of historical reality—which are
themselves revealing—and, despite the attempts to weave a safe and seam-
less web, conflict, ambivalence, anxiety, and guilt sometimes do break
through. It must also be recognized, however, that in *A Week* Thoreau
shows considerable insight and even wisdom concerning human life and
his own life. And, to the extent that he envisioned his future, he displays an
unusual, if still limited, prescience about the issues and challenges he

would face, as must all people in one way or another, from young adulthood to the end of life. In the process of reading *A Week* as a version of Thoreau's past, present, and future—as well as of the life cycle in general —we are afforded the opportunity to backtrack on his life, pick up the trail where *Young Man Thoreau* left off (with Thoreau going to Walden), and look ahead, all the while making use of those approaches and perspectives central to *this* book's picture of Thoreau's life and human life.

The toughest, most disturbing problem with which Thoreau struggled to come to terms in *A Week*—frequently in an indirect, subterranean, unconscious manner—centered around the painful loss of his brother, three years his senior.[12] John's death, and the circumstances that surrounded it, had been traumatizing and had precipitated a crisis that Thoreau almost did not survive. The book is in part an affectionate elegy to John; the epigraph invokes his brother as Muse: "Where'er thou sail'st who sailed with me,/Though now thou climbest loftier mounts,/And fairer rivers dost ascend,/Be thou my Muse, my Brother" (3). Though, perhaps partly due to the conventions of elegy and partly due to the pain it would conjure, John is never referred to by name in the text, his presence pervades and casts shadows over it, and *A Week* represents a profound attempt to work through the grief and guilt associated with John's tragically premature demise.[13] Thoreau's relationship with his brother had been characterized by deep ambivalence. Although he ardently loved and respected John—saw himself as having an Indian camaraderie with his brother, an avid student of Indian lore and fellow gatherer of arrowheads, to whom he had referred as "brother sachem—Hopeful—of Hopewell" in a November 1837 letter (c, 16–18)[14]—he also found himself in a hostility-engendering and guilt-provoking competition with him for family, community, and student approval. And at the time of the Concord-Merrimack trip, while they were teaching together and before John's fragile health forced him to leave his teaching duties (leading Thoreau to close down their school), they were both courting Ellen Sewall. We cannot be sure if they ever directly acknowledged their rivalry—Thoreau was no doubt reticent in discussing these matters openly—but one piece of information indicates that an alarming "crisis," quite possibly linked to their competition for Ellen, took place during their river voyage. Before John's death but after Ellen had turned down both brothers, Margaret Fuller (editor of the soon-to-be-defunct *Dial*) wrote Thoreau on October 18, 1841, "The pencilled paper Mr. E[merson] put into my hands I have taken the liberty to copy it. You expressed one day my own opinion that the moment such a crisis is passed we may speak of it. There is no need of artificial delicacy, of secrecy, it keeps its own secret; it cannot be made false. Thus you will not be sorry that I have seen the paper. Will you not send me some other records of the good week" (C, 57). These comments, which appear as a postscript to a letter evaluating Thoreau's "Wachusett" poem—in which he apostrophized the mountain and declared, "May I approve myself thy worthy brother!" (CP, 50)—suggest that even the "good week" had its dark side and that the trip came to be associated not only with brotherly love but also with fraternal competition. In his journal, accounts of the trip were interspersed and juxtaposed with veiled references to the courtship of Ellen, ambivalent discussions of friendship and success, shadowy references to a "difference with a Friend." Well before John's death, then, he had experienced considerable anxiety about his falling-out with his brother.

After John's death, catastrophic and arbitrary enough in its own right to prompt unsettling questions and rage, the sense of alienation from his brother and the suspicion, on some deep level, that he had competed with, felt hostility toward, and hurt John, even wished to do away with him, and now had survived and thus "defeated" him compounded a grief that would have been powerful in any case and aroused intense remorse and all but unbearable guilt. These emotions were manifested in the psychosomatic attack of lockjaw, which almost resulted in a literal sharing and duplicating of his brother's fate, and then in the shock, near paralysis, numbness, denial, and depression that plagued him in the ensuing months. Due both to cultural constraints on men and to his own character, Thoreau was unable to mourn openly and unabashedly; yet he needed desperately to perform "grief work," which would involve placating the inward foes of guilt and anxiety, gaining reconciliation with his brother, and keeping him alive in significant ways. *A Week*, then, would be the work of an uncomfortable survivor. Survival guilt, explains Robert Lifton, "may in part reflect the psychic death one did literally undergo—the extreme stasis or numbing accompanying one's inactivation in the face of death and threat —and the related sense that subsequent assumption of vitality in the absence of true enactment (mostly in the form of preventing the dead from dying) is wrong." Death guilt "ultimately stems from a sense that until such enactment is achieved, one has no right to be alive."[15] Writing about the trip with John provided Thoreau with just such a form of urgently needed enactment; it was with this sense of exigency that he went to Walden Pond. He made his first journal entry at the pond on July 5, 1845, the anniversary of his brother's birth.[16] In dedicating himself to purification at Walden, and in writing *A Week*, Thoreau did manage to accomplish some crucial grief work, but, as would become all too evident in the post-

Walden years, he was not able fully or conclusively to assuage his grief and guilt. He would continue to be haunted; the Muse was also a ghost.

Erik Erikson writes of the necessity of a "ground plan" for epigenetic growth: "Anything that grows has a *ground plan* and . . . out of this ground plan the *parts* emerge, each part having its time of special ascendancy until all parts have arisen to form a functioning whole."[17] In *A Week,* the ground plan is the Concord River itself (and later the Merrimack), "an emblem of all progress" (12). It is from the daily movement up and down the rivers and from the events and observations along the way that Thoreau selects to stress—the embarkings and disembarkings, the human and natural scenes on the rivers and along the banks, the distant landscapes, the obstacles and interruptions and interpolations generated, to some degree organically, by the flowing of the river and the narrative—that the reader sees emerging different parts, modalities, and issues linked to phases or stages of life in "special ascendancy." Each phase is *built on* the previous ones and thus exerts a cumulative impact on the developing whole. By allowing the river's course in large part to define and circumscribe his journey, Thoreau will discover, as Erikson says, that "if we will only learn to live and let live, the plan for growth is all there."[18] For him, as for the fisherman he describes in "Saturday," "Human life is . . . very much like a river" (24).

With the river as ground plan, as a template for growth, it is appropriate that, before the particular "days" begin, Thoreau has a prologue, "Concord River." This river, he tells us, was called by the Indians "Musketaquid," or "Grass-ground River" (5), and it is on *this* "ground," with this ground plan, that he is most comfortable and comforted. Lifton says, "The survivor must look backward as well as forward in time. His tendency to claim a personal 'golden age' prior to the death encounter can, it is true, distort, but also may serve as a source of life-sustaining imagery."[19] In grounding his work in the "Grass-ground River" (the grass itself and the mud and slow current suggesting something primal and primordial), Thoreau strives to reclaim in imagination the "golden age" of the watery, protective womb and of the sustaining breast; he speaks in the prologue of the rivers "bearing [the traveller] on their bosoms" (12) and of "launching" himself on the "bosom" of the river (13). Moreover, he seeks to recover, to return to, the golden age before the white man "supplanted the Indian" —back to the time before his brother's death; back to the time, idyllic in retrospect, when he and John were, as he often liked to imagine, inseparable "Indian braves," before his disturbing rivalries with John for the affections of Ellen Sewall, students, community, and parents; and even further back to a time before oedipal competition. Going to Walden was itself part of the attempt to recapture that golden age.

The survivor, in order to "be forward-looking, to be receptive to experience that propels . . . to the future . . . must assemble those image-feelings available to [him] . . . that can assert, however tenuously, the continuity of life."[20] John's death was an overwhelming loss for Thoreau, an unexpected ending that he experienced as an abrupt "break in the continuity of things."[21] The ancient and enduring Concord River and the nature of which it is a part become crucial means and symbols of continuity for Thoreau amidst the realities of sudden loss, drastic change, and mutability. While traveling on the Concord and its extension, the Merrimack, he never has to leave (unless he *chooses* to) the "womb" and "breast" of the river, which keeps him firmly connected to his native Concord and all its reassuring memories and associations. The river, then, represents a mother to Thoreau, "an all-enveloping world-image tying past, present, and future together in a convincing pattern of providence."[22] Although the river promises him the opportunity for "distant enterprise and adventure" (12), he can maintain his dependence upon the mothering, life-sustaining river. As will be discussed later, Walden Pond—where he wrote so much of *A Week*—was analogous to the river in that it provided him with another image of motherly womb and breast and of continuity; and at Walden too he could see himself as embarked on an independent and adventurous initiative while simultaneously remaining dependent upon the pond, as well as on his real mother, who lived, in fact, only a short distance away. The Walden experience, like the river trip, was both a moratorium, a non-threatening mode of strategic withdrawal, and an arena of commitment to heroic enterprises.

There is, to be sure, an impression and undertone of loss, of the elegiac, in Thoreau's perception of the Concord River—and, for that matter, throughout the journey; we early get the sense of separation from the womb, breast, and full security offered by the mother and of a powerful urge to return eventually. The intimation of loss is quite strong in *A Week,* as it is in so many of Thoreau's writings—not only the loss of his brother but also the lost Eden of the prerivalry and preoedipal past, of youth and childhood, of the womb, of the golden age of the Indian and, in *Walden,* of the Greeks. But the loss is mitigated by Thoreau's trusting attachment to river and nature. He understands that trust—in nature and in the river, which is its tributary—is absolutely essential to the success of his developmental voyage.[23] "To the human infant," Erikson says, "his mother *is* nature."[24] For Thoreau, nature is his mother, in which he can put his complete trust; it is an alternative to his actual mother, who threatened his sense of independence and identity. His trust in this substitute mother apparently firmly established, he resolves finally to "launch" himself on the river's "bosom," and "float whither it would bear" him (13).

Emerging from the moist womb of the morning and of a long, drizzling rain, the Thoreau brothers in "Saturday" launch their boat with a "vigorous shove." Yet "Saturday" in some ways remains in a transitional, semiembryonic modality—the river, the "placid current of our dreams" (19–20), still amniotic ocean, ontogeny recapitulating phylogeny, gills appearing before lungs, as well as route to future adventures. The boat is compared to "an amphibious animal" (16), half fish and half bird. Thoreau identifies partly with the fisherman (associated with faint memories and "pleasures of my earliest youth" [23]) but even more with the fish (linked to "dim visions" from childhood of "miraculous draughts of fishes, and heaps uncountable by the river-side" [34]). James Russell Lowell, in his review of *A Week,* even commented on Thoreau's capacity to "recreate the sensation of that part of his embryonic life which he passed as a fish."[25] While discussing the fish in the river, he seems to become a fish himself; he is at one with, rather than the predator of, the faithful, vulnerable shad, "armed only with innocence and a just cause" (37), who are much like helpless, trusting infants, who have acquired the virtue taking root in life's first stage, "hope," the "ontogenetic basis of faith."[26] Thoreau recognizes the "virtue" of these vulnerable fishes, threatened not just by other animals but also by the encroachments of civilization and industrialization, *as* "faith." He avers that, whatever the perils, these fish (and he himself) will "ere long have thy way up the rivers, up all the rivers of the globe, if I am not mistaken" (37–38). At the end of "Saturday," he affirms his faith in "nature's health or *sound* state" and drifts off into an infantlike or even fetal sleep, an archetypal "time before speech or verbal memory"[27] where "all sounds were denied entrance to our ears" (42).

"Sunday" opens with the journey still in its infancy. The brothers row through a thick morning fog that finally dissipates with the sunlight. This Sunday morning is quiet and gentle and has more of the "auroral rosy" and "white" than of the "yellow light" in it, "as if it dated from earlier than the fall of man, and still preserved a heathenish integrity" (43). But this "natural Sabbath" (46), this dawn after Creation, still moist with amniotic dews and mother's milk, must—not without reluctance—be left behind. "The impressions which the morning makes," Thoreau remarks wistfully, "vanish with its dews, and not even the most 'persevering mortal' can preserve the memory of its freshness to mid-day" (43–44). In passing the numerous islands, the Thoreau brothers "gave names to them," suggesting the process whereby infants are named and eventually become "namers," thrust irrevocably into the world of language and other forms of human symbolization. Also, in the manner of young children who are still learning to differentiate between the safe breast and the otherness of the land upon which they must soon walk and fend for themselves, they are unclear, confused about "whether the water floated the land, or the land held the water in its bosom" (45). Thoreau observes the "gold and silver minnows" that "swept by as if moved by one mind . . . and yet preserving the form of their battalion unchanged, as if they were still embraced by the transparent membrane which held the spawn." This "young band of brethren and sisters," still attached in significant ways to their mothers, are like young children gradually learning to stand on their own feet, in the process of "trying their new fins" (49).

The brothers' arrival at the village of Billerica seems to mark a conclusive emergence from self-absorption and security to a recognition of the social and of separateness, bringing particularly to the fore issues of "autonomy vs. shame, doubt"[28] and the emergence of "will" as a virtue,[29] which are rooted in early childhood. Thoreau's own discomfort with the social world symbolized by Billerica may be gauged by his remark that the village is decaying and that "if you would know of its early youth, ask those old gray rocks in the pasture" (50). Contact with the civil can be dangerous, and Thoreau displays clear preference for the "wildness" of the Indians and the "purity" of the preagricultural era to the white man's "civilization"—with its stultifying political, educational, and religious institutions—"yielding obedience to authority" (53). What he says about the "taming" of animals surely has implications for children, and the adults they become, who are all too easily broken by the imposition of rigid standards and training. "We would not," he observes, "always be soothing and taming nature, breaking the horse and ox, but sometimes ride the horse wild and chase the buffalo" (56). He mocks the "virtues" of civilized people, which are merely, he claims, "good manners" (55). The Indian, on the other hand, he sees as the archetypal "willed" being: "Steel and blankets are strong temptations; but the Indian does well to continue Indian" (56).

Passing in "Sunday" from the sluggish, if more primal and nurturing, Concord River to the faster-flowing Merrimack, Thoreau must prepare to go against the current and to battle against the currents of social pressures and expectations. Like young children who, engaged in a clash of wills with elders for bodily control and a broader autonomy, are acutely vulnerable to humiliation, so must he seek to steel himself against shaming. Sometimes this requires fighting fire with fire. Thus the Thoreau brothers stare down one of the "impudent" young men who "leaned . . . over the rails [of a bridge] to pry into our concerns": "we caught the eye of the most forward, and looked at him till he was visibly discomfited. Not that there was any peculiar efficacy in our look, but rather a sense of shame left in him which disarmed him." As Thoreau well knew from his battles for autonomy in his family and community, the susceptibility to shame experienced by young children remains a potent threat to the adult; it is therefore "wonderful," he observes, "how we get about the streets without being wounded by these delicate and glancing weapons" of people's stares (63).

It is at this juncture, appropriately, that the issue of religion is raised. On this sunny Sunday, "the people coming out of church paused to look at us from above, and, apparently, so strong is custom, indulged in some heathenish comparisons." Thoreau, buttressed by his abiding faith in nature and the presence of his comrade-in-arms, affirms his resistance to public opprobrium by proclaiming defiantly that "we were the truest observers of this sunny day" (63). In rejecting conventional religion, he asserts his will; even more specifically, he is able to deal with his own struggle for autonomy with his culture, community, and parents—especially his mother. Orthodox religion is associated with the bonds of societal—and, by extension, parental and maternal—strictness and repression: "I presume that there is not less *religion* than formerly. If the *ligature* is found to be loosened in one part, it is always drawn the tighter in another" (64). The sources of genuine faith, he suggests, are not to be found in untrustworthy "creeds" (78) imparted through socialization; rather, true faith bypasses the false "goddess," the orthodoxy imposed by mother and culture, and establishes an umbilical link with nature and the "god" immanent in nature. Indeed, Thoreau explicitly connects orthodox Christianity, which has "dreamed a sad dream," with the mother, who "tells her falsehoods to her child, but thank Heaven, the child does not grow up in its parent's shadow. Our mother's faith has not grown with her experience" (77).

Yet, however much he wished to deny it, Thoreau *had* grown up in the shadow of his extraordinary, strong-willed, sharp-tongued, and dynamic mother.[30] By contrast, his father, John Sr., was relatively quiet, meek, unambitious, and less than successful as a merchant, storekeeper, and pencil maker. Cynthia was exceedingly liberated for her day; but she was, it can be argued, to some degree frustrated by the limitations imposed upon her by the culture and by her dependence on male figures, especially her "unambitious" husband, to define her status. Both of Henry's parents were upstanding and respectable citizens, but his mother, who operated a boardinghouse in the family home, seemed more bent on upward mobility and social prestige. Thoreau was a devoted son and in many ways the apple of his mother's eye; even when he was an adult, she would refer to him as "my Henry" or "my David Henry."[31] She encouraged him to feel special and groomed him for future success and greatness by sending him— rather than his brother—to Harvard (where her own father, a more formidable figure to her in many respects than her husband, had gone). To some extent she lived through her son, and Thoreau was put in the position of justifying her. He was, in fact, greatly influenced by Cynthia, who transmitted to him her love of nature, didacticism, reformist inclinations, outspokenness, and sharp wit. However, Thoreau was uncomfortable with his heavy dependence upon her, and his rebelliousness as an adolescent and young adult, his embrace of transcendentalism, and his "signing off" from the Unitarian church (in which his mother was an active member) in 1841 were part of an ongoing, militant struggle to get out from under his mother's shadow. As he perceived it, it was not only literally but figuratively that his father lived "in the shadow of his wife, who towered a full head above him." Because he *was* so dependent upon his mother and feared she could control his life—prospects especially threatening in a culture that celebrated a bold, independent, adventurous frontiersman stereotype of masculinity and harbored misogynist attitudes toward women who took charge—he had to assert his autonomy all the more radically and defiantly. It is not surprising that both Cynthia and Aunt Maria would be upset with his critique of conventional religion in "Sunday."[32]

Thoreau warns in "Sunday" of the dangers of a tyrannical conscience, regarded as "instinct bred in the house"—with all its cultural, domestic, and maternal associations—an "unnatural breeding in and in" which could "monopolize the whole of our lives. . . . I have seen some whose consciences, owing undoubtedly to former indulgence, had grown to be as irritable as spoilt children, and at length gave them no peace" (74–75). The cure—one he prescribed to liberate himself, nicknamed "the judge" when he was still a boy by Samuel Hoar[33]—was to "Turn it out doors,/Into the moors." But even this medicine did not always work.

If the development of conscience can be traced back in part to the vulnerability to shame and doubt, it is even more decisively linked to "initiative vs. guilt," a conflict emerging during the phallic stage, when oedipal issues first become prominent,[34] issues that Thoreau both faces and shrinks from in "Sunday" and with which he continued to struggle during his adult life. Clearly he had been caught early in a classical oedipal bind, burdened with the suspicion that he had competed for his "strong" (and unconsciously seductive) mother and won her away from his "weak" father —these "strong" and "weak" labels, of course, largely reflect the oppressive gender stereotyping of the culture from which Thoreau, sadly, was far from immune and by which he himself was victimized. The competition with his beloved brother, and then John's death, served to exacerbate severely his oedipal conflicts.

His focus in "Sunday" on the Indians in some ways permits regression to a less threatening preoedipal stage. It is understandable that Thoreau, for whom nature was a purifying alternative to his real mother—and other women—with respect to whom he had not fully resolved his oedipal feelings, was more comfortable with what he saw as the Indian's relationship to nature. "The Indian's intercourse with Nature," he says, "is at least such as admits of the greatest independence of each. If he is somewhat of a stranger in her midst, the gardener is too much of a familiar. There is something vulgar and foul in the latter's closeness to his mistress, something noble and cleanly in the former's distance" (56). In lamenting the supplanting of Indians by the white man, Thoreau seeks to identify himself as an ally, rather than the oedipal rival, of the brother-Indian he sees himself as having survived (and perhaps the father he sees himself as having displaced in some significant way). Therefore, he is able to forswear any initiative, laden with guilt, to do away with his fellow Indian brave. It is perhaps only by such guilt-avoiding mechanisms that he is ultimately able to accept for the moment, not without sorrow and ambivalence, the displacement of the Indians by the white man, the wild by the civil, as epigenetic necessities. As he observes, "Every one finds by his own experience, as well as in history, that the era in which men cultivate the apple, and the amenities of the garden, is essentially different from that of the hunter and forest life, and neither can displace the other without loss." Only in this context can Thoreau allow himself the phallic, aggressive imagery that immediately follows: "I would at least strike my spade into the earth with such careless freedom but accuracy as the woodpecker his bill into a tree" (54).

Upon returning to the narrative after his discussion of religion, Thoreau notes that the brothers are permitted entrance to the Merrimack through the Middlesex locks, not by a threatening, castrating figure who would bar the way for initiative but by a "serene and liberal-minded man, who came quietly from his book" (79). This approving father figure, whose "duties . . . did not require him to open the locks on Sundays," provides them with "the freedom of the Merrimack" and thus allows them to make their first forays into the "novelties" (109) of the wider world; they "now felt fairly launched on the ocean-stream of [their] voyage" (79–80). At this point, in the intrusive mode linked to the phallic stage, the brothers enter the state of New Hampshire. The Merrimack River itself, Thoreau informs us, was formed by the flowing together—a sort of sexual union— of two rivers. He speaks fondly of the fish that "penetrate up the innumerable rivers of our coast in the spring, even to the interior lakes" (89). The aggressive imagery of entrance and penetration is, however, tempered somewhat by Thoreau's subsequent discussion of the virtues of literature and poetry which, though they in some regard even "make us dangerous to existing institutions" (96), also offer the opportunity to achieve "memorable success" without the guilt accompanying competition and excessive ambition. The poet need not compete with or depend upon anyone; he "should be as vigorous as a sugar maple, with sap enough to maintain his own verdure. . . . He hibernates in this world, and feeds on his own marrow" (99). The only competition with which Thoreau appears to be fully comfortable are "the peaceful games of the Lyceum" (100).

Clearly, his discomfort with conventional success and competition (which, of course, may be questioned in their own right) stemmed in part from his reluctance to surpass his father, a man "far too honest and scarcely sufficiently energetic for this exacting yet not over scrupulous world of ours."[35] In one sense, he no doubt identified with John Sr., which made it difficult to contemplate succeeding in an increasingly dog-eat-dog world. In another sense, surpassing his father could further compound oedipal guilt. The rivalry with, and demise of, John Jr. immeasurably reinforced his fear and avoidance of standard versions of success. With his gifts and ambivalence, it is understandable that he turned to writing as a profession, since in America it rarely led to material success or security. Yet he did harbor notions and visions of "greatness," and these ambitions, combined with the need most have for some sort of social recognition and validation, would assert themselves in connection with the dream, not always easily suppressed or repressed, of establishing a literary career that would, like Emerson's, provide a substantial measure of success and acclaim.

Thoreau's ambivalence about purposeful initiative—a central virtue emerging from the oedipal phase[36]—is further suggested by his willingness to forswear aggressive pursuit of valued goals. "We do not," he says, "directly go about the execution of the purpose that thrills us, but shut our doors behind us, and ramble with prepared mind, as if the half were already done" (108). The recounting of a dream with which he concludes "Sunday" reveals even more fully his inability to dissociate enterprise from guilt and anxiety and his need to escape the demons conjured by the oedipal phase and sibling rivalry. In the dream, Thoreau is the sailor who "was visited . . . this night by the Evil Destinies, and all those powers that are hostile to human life, which constrain and oppress the minds of men, and make their path seem difficult and narrow, and beset with dangers, so that the most innocent and worthy enterprises appear insolent and a tempting of fate, and the gods go not with us. But the other [John] happily passed a serene and even ambrosial or immortal night. . . . and his cheerful spirit soothed and reassured his brother, for whenever they meet, the Good Genius is sure to prevail" (116). Thus does Thoreau, who was in fact competing with John for Ellen Sewall at the very time of their trip together, seek absolution and reassurance of his brother's blessings on his "innocent and worthy enterprises."

"Monday" begins with the declaration that "all men, having reinforced their bodies and their souls with sleep, and cast aside doubt and fear, were invited to unattempted adventures" (117). Somewhat like a school-age child who has confronted (if not entirely cast aside) doubt and fear and who now, in the work of play and the play of work, is ready to take on the challenges of developing a sense of industry[37] and mastery, so does Thoreau turn attention to these issues in the first section of "Monday." He witnesses the bustle and busyness that mark the first day of the workweek; the "countrymen, recruited by their day of rest, were already stirring, and had begun to cross the ferry on the business of the week. The ferry was as busy as a beaver dam, and all the world seemed anxious to get across the Merrimack." He observes with obvious disdain that "many of these Monday men are ministers, no doubt. . . . Good religious men, with the love of men in their hearts, and the means to pay their toll in their pockets" (118–19). Thoreau questions the value and authenticity of much conventional work—with its unreflective hurriedness and harriedness, its hollow routines, its materialistic emphasis. Life's "unattempted adventures" are not, he suggests, undertaken by those who travel on ferries. While the workers must pay a toll for the ferry ride—and the work does indeed exact a heavy toll in his view—he need not pay any toll and instead rows "leisurely along through Tyngsboro'" (119). Unlike the frenetic, impatient ferry travelers, Thoreau and his brother have the time to rest in the shade, eat a melon, and ponder at their leisure "the lapse of the river and of human life" (124). Of course, there is such a virtue as genuine "competence."[38] Even the Thoreau brothers must gain competence in order to navigate the difficult turns in the river. Certainly those who "first built the barns, and cleared the land . . . had some valor," and hard, honest toil and craftsmanship—virtues Thoreau saw as growing scarcer with the rise of the commercial and industrial in the 1830s and 1840s—are to be appreciated. There are, he contends, "many skilful apprentices, but few master workmen. . . . unless we do more than simply learn the trade of our time, we are but apprentices, and not yet masters of the art of life" (125). To gain true mastery, and avoid inferiority and mediocrity,[39] one must learn the virtues of leisure, play (and play of the mind), and waiting; leisure and play, far from being wasted time, are central to gaining mastery of the art of living. Vacation is a necessary prelude to finding a vocation. "There are moments," says Thoreau, "when all anxiety and stated toil are becalmed in the infinite leisure and repose of nature. All laborers must have their nooning, and at this season of the day, we are all, more or less, Asiatics, and give over all work and reform" (125–26). Faced, as life's noon approaches, with the potentially oppressive demands of the world of work, "The hero . . . will know how to wait, as well as to make haste. All good abides with him who waiteth *wisely;* we shall sooner overtake the dawn by remaining here than by hurrying over the hills of the west" (128–29).

Thoreau wished to perceive himself as one such hero. After his graduation from Harvard in 1837, he had resisted pressures and rejected opportunities to establish rapidly a conventional career so that he might discover his true vocation and thus ultimately gain mastery of the "art of life."[40] During adolescence and young adulthood when one is seeking to gain a sense of incipient identity and vocation and is experiencing some degree of identity confusion, one searches most urgently for people and world views to believe in.[41] This quest had special immediacy for Thoreau, whose father, virtuous gentleman though he was, had not provided him with a strong male model. However much he may have loved him, he may also have resented him, unconsciously at least, for his relative submissiveness and his inability to protect him from dependence on his mother. John Sr. may, in fact, have provided Thoreau with a blueprint for what to avoid: economic entanglements and the threat of indebtedness; inability fully to control the circumstances of one's life; commitments, including marriage and children, that might endanger one's autonomy and life choices. Moreover, his culture and community had let him down, offering more choices than they once had but only very circumscribed opportunities for idealistic, sensitive, and gifted young people like himself.[42] Although the ultimate task incumbent upon him was, thus, to become father to himself (it was symptomatic that he began signing his name "Henry David" rather than his given "David Henry" soon after graduation from college), he needed first, as do so many youth and young adults, to find and ally himself with transitional father substitutes and an ideology compatible with the self's needs and providing an all-inclusive world view.[43] By far his most influential father surrogate and identity sponsor was, of course, Emerson, the great and controversial literary figure then living so providentially in Concord. The master, Emerson, put Thoreau, the novice, under his wing and even envisioned him as his heir apparent, his "American Scholar" in the flesh.

Thoreau does not mention Emerson by name in *A Week;* indeed, when he wrote the bulk of the book he believed that he was at least in the process of taking wing on his own, and by the time he finished the book he had become disillusioned with him. But, in "Monday," Thoreau does invoke some of the masterworks, and the ideologies they espoused, which had, like Emerson himself, given legitimacy to the moratorium he so vitally needed and helped crystallize his emergent sense of identity. Before affirming his ideological loyalties, however, he expresses his distaste for what he considers the false ideologies of his day. "I love man-kind," he claims, "but I hate the institutions of the dead unkind" (131). Political institutions especially come under fire here, but he also attacks the love of country and religion as an "infirmity of noble minds [that] marks the gradual decay of youthful hope and faith. It is the allowed infidelity of the age" (133). By contrast, such works as the Bhagavad-Gita and the Laws of Menu, with their call to purity, patience, and spiritual discipline, merit fidelity, a virtue that takes root particularly in adolescence and young adulthood.[44] "Vast and cosmogonal" (143) Eastern philosophy—which may be taken in part as a shorthand for transcendentalism, which drew so heavily from the oriental world view and which was Thoreau's most crucial frame of reference —has taught him that the "things immediate to be done are very trivial. I could postpone them all to hear this locust sing" (140). Occidental philosophy, on the other hand, "says forsake not your calling, outrage no institution, use no violence, rend no bonds, the State is thy parent. Its virtue or manhood is wholly filial" (141). While he praises such figures as Goethe, "a few Hebrews," and Shakespeare, it is the oriental philosophers who are the true "fathers of modern thinking" (143), the fathers and mentors to whom he can freely pledge utter loyalty.

In the midst of these reflections, Thoreau and his brother come upon some boatmen, who "appeared to be green hands from far among the hills, who had taken this means to get to the seaboard, and see the world." Although these youths are embarked on a classic form of moratorium, Thoreau perceives them as having already surrendered to "the private interests of the landsman"; they "were ready to mess with mankind, reserving only the till of the chest to themselves." Having staked so much of his evolving identity on being a "traveller in Concord"—independent, adventurous, and marginal but still close to and dependent upon home—he sees little value in shipping out to see the world (or, another classic American version, lighting out for the Territory) and wonders "what is wanting to human life here, that these men should make such haste to the antipodes?" (145). However, even if his concept of a constructive moratorium involves more an inward than an outward quest, he continues to use imagery of geographical exploration. Upon seeing a bass tree, he is reminded that "we had reached a strange land for us," just as the spiritual explorer may feel he is a stranger in a strange land. The Thoreau brothers pass a "small desert" (146) between Tyngsboro and Hudson and see the remnants and relics of the vanishing Indian past. In the distance they sight Uncannunuc, "the most conspicuous mountain in these parts" (162), and it is apparent that mountains will have to be climbed, further challenges met, before the high ground of identity can be reached. In the poem "Wachusett," inserted in this section, Thoreau expresses his wish to be the "worthy brother" of the mountain which, though never leaving its native ground, is a "western pioneer / Who know'st not shame nor fear" (163–65). The brothers pass by a "wild and antiquated looking grave-yard" (169), by the village of Nashua, and then go into the wilderness again. Camping in the forest by the riverside at night, Thoreau hears the sound of a distant drummer, whose "music afforded us a prime and leisure hour, and we now felt that we were in season wholly" (173), and this leads into the poem, "Now chiefly is my natal hour, / And only now my prime of life" (174). At the end of "Monday," with the drumbeat resonating in his ears, indifferent to the high winds buffeting the area, Thoreau goes to sleep, resolved to be the "champion" of "Heaven" (178) who will march to the beat of a different drummer and enter his prime.

"Tuesday" begins in a fog, which suggests the confusion one may experience during a period given over to moratorium and exploration. But buoyed by their faith "that there is a bright day behind it" (179), the brothers push resolutely into the mist. It is at this point, appropriately, that Thoreau chooses to leave behind for the moment his brother and the reassuring river-mother to re-create an 1844 excursion he made to Mount Saddleback (Greylock) in the Berkshires. He seems impelled here to adopt a framework and strategy—a gap in the river narrative[45]—that stresses his belief in the essential aloneness of the process whereby one insists on a moratorium and ultimately establishes unique selfhood, an aloneness magnified and further defined in his case by his brother's death. The recounting of the ascent of Saddleback furnishes him, it appears, with an extended, if partial, analogy of his own solitary, protracted, and heroic moratorium, culminating with the achievement of authentic identity at Walden.

As he commences his expedition up the mountain, he gradually casts off distracting or cumbersome influences. Early in his route up a "long and spacious valley," Thoreau, who had come close to buying the Hollowell farm in 1841, notices a few scattered farms. A stream on which there is a mill (which suggests the industrial and commercial influences he is abandoning) is compared to "a road for the pilgrim to enter upon who would climb to the gates of heaven." With its "uneven earth" and inspiring vistas, "one could not imagine a more noble position for a farm house than this vale afforded" (181). One of Thoreau's earlier versions of a Walden-type experience consisted, as he wrote in 1841, of the "dream of looking abroad summer and winter, with free gaze, from some mountain-side" (c, 45). By now he is determined to "find [his] own route up the steep, as the shorter and more adventurous way." At the second-to-last house, he comes upon "a frank and hospitable young woman . . . with lively, sparkling eyes and full of interest in that lower world from which I had come" (182); this attractive young woman may perhaps be taken as representing potential romantic partners, including Ellen Sewall, who he recognizes must be renounced if he aspires to reach the summit. At the last house he meets a man who wonders what he has to sell and who gives him some advice about how to reach the mountaintop; but Thoreau rejects the counsel of this would-be mentor: "I was more used to woods and mountains than he, and went through his cow-yard, while he, looking at the sun, shouted after me that I should not get to the top that night" (183). At some point during the 1842–45 period, Thoreau had begun to realize that he would eventually have to go beyond his mentors, particularly Emerson, who, for all his philosophizing, knew less about "woods and mountains" than he and who had no doubt started to put up warning signs concerning his drive and ability to sell his literary wares. Thoreau recognized that he would have to reach the summit in his own time and on his own terms.

During his moratorium, when, as William Bridges puts it, one is in a "forest-dweller stage," withdrawing from the world's business and going into the "solitude of the forest for a time of reflection and study,"[46] Thoreau learned—though not without pain and not as fully as he *thought* he had—to trust his own time and find his own way. As he says, "Even country people, I have observed, magnify the difficulty of travelling in the forest, especially among mountains. They seem to lack their usual common sense in this. I have climbed several higher mountains without guide or path, and have found, as might be expected, that it takes only more time and patience commonly than to travel the smoothest highway" (183). Some may feel confused and lost during the "forest-dweller stage," but Thoreau advises, "If a person lost would conclude that after all he is not lost, he is not beside himself, but standing in his own old shoes on the very spot where he is . . . but the places that have known him, *they* are lost,— how much anxiety and danger would vanish" (184).

Contradicting the warning given by the last man he met (and thus proving him wrong), Thoreau does reach the summit by nightfall. But since he is thirsty, he must descend the mountain a way to a moist spot where he digs a well, "which was soon filled with pure cold water" (185). Living at Walden Pond, sometimes described by him as a "well," also required a walk—albeit a much shorter one—down a hill to quench thirst. And, of course, the purity and coldness of Walden had also served to quench a spiritual thirst. Having discovered this pure well, he again climbs to the summit, where the old Williams College observatory is located; at the top he can see the stars and universe with increased clarity. In preparing for the cold night, as he was to prepare for the winter at the pond, he constructs a makeshift version of the Walden hut by gathering "a pile of wood and lay[ing] down a board against the side" (186) of the observatory. But as the night grows even colder—the price he must pay for being on the summit[47]—he "at length encased [himself] completely in boards," settled in, and slept "comfortably" and peacefully.

With the dawn's arrival, Thoreau finds himself enveloped in an "ocean of mist," which "shut out every vestige of the earth." It is a strange and brave new world that he has attained, "an undulating country of clouds." "It was such a country," he says, "as we might see in dreams, with all the delights of paradise. . . . As there was wanting the symbol, so there was not the substance of impurity, no spot nor stain. It was a favor for which to be forever silent to be shown this vision." Having left the familiar world behind, Thoreau feels blessed, purified, reborn on this mountaintop, as he had felt when he arrived at Walden and achieved a new and liberating sense of identity. Still shrouded by mist, the earth "had passed away like the phantom of a shadow . . . and this new platform was gained. As I had climbed above storm and cloud, so by successive days' journeys I might reach the region of eternal day beyond the tapering shadow of the earth" (188–89). Walden had represented a "peak experience" for Thoreau, the attainment of a higher plateau than he had ever reached before; from and on this "new platform" and podium he could speak with a passion and authority he had only dreamed of in the pre-Walden years. It is a July day on Saddleback, just as it had been July 4 when he had moved into his Walden dwelling. In his first journal entry at Walden on July 5, he had written, "My house makes me think of some mountain houses I have seen, which seemed to have a fresher auroral atmosphere about them, as I fancy of the halls of Olympus" (PJ, 2:155). The imagery and tone of his exhilarated response to the Saddleback sunrise is strikingly similar: "When its own sun began to rise on this pure world, I found myself a dweller in the dazzling halls of Aurora . . . playing with the rosy fingers of the Dawn" (189).

The sense of unsullied purity and invigoration does not last, however.

While, Thoreau remarks, "'Heaven's sun'" never "stained himself," "my private sun did stain himself," and before noon, his "virtue wavering," he "sank down again into that 'forlorn world' from which the celestial Sun had hid his visage" (189–90). Here Thoreau seems to be commenting on the inconstant nature of inspiration and sense of congruence with the ego ideal, even at Walden and certainly when, as is inevitable, one's Walden must be left behind. Hoping eventually to scale "new and higher mountains, the Catskills," and thus "climb to heaven again," he descends the mountain and before long finds himself "in the region of cloud and drizzling rain," where "the inhabitants affirmed that it had been a cloudy and drizzling day wholly" (190). This section was not fully developed until at least the second draft of *A Week*, written at the pond in 1847,[48] which suggests that the prospect of leaving Walden was already on his mind, if not a fait accompli. In any event, he does anticipate, albeit incompletely, some of the challenges and trials such "forest-dwellers" and mountain climbers as he must face when they find themselves "sojourner[s] in civilized life again" (w, 3).

Upon returning to his brother and the Merrimack, he stresses the necessity for one who has descended from the summit to keep in touch with the Edenic sources of purity and rejuvenation that were so accessible on the peak. "So near along life's streams," he says, "are the fountains of innocence and youth making fertile its sandy margin; and the voyageur will do well to replenish his vessels often at these uncontaminated sources" (193). Thoreau would himself return again and again to Walden Pond and the Walden experience in a sometimes desperate attempt to "replenish his vessels." So many young men, eager to be accepted as adults and make names for themselves, acquire a veneer of politeness, deference, and even obsequiousness; Thoreau—seeking to affirm that he is not such a young man—takes pains, in describing a "rude Apollo of a man" he meets at the Cromwell's Falls locks, to make a distinction between false and authentic civility, which "does not result from any hasty and artificial polishing ... but grows naturally in characters of the right grain and quality, through a long fronting of men and events." Compelled to remind himself of the need to maintain a "core or sapwood" (201) of inviolable identity, Thoreau briefly goes back to another episode of his 1844 Berkshire excursion, his encounter with a "rude and uncivil" man named Rice from whom he rented a room for the night. Though Rice had "no artificial covering to his ill humors," he was "earthy" and had "good soil in him, and even a long-suffering Saxon probity at bottom." The next morning, when he offered him breakfast and lit the lamp, Thoreau was impressed and moved by a "gleam of true hospitality and ancient civility ... from his bleared and moist eyes" (207). Rice may be taken, in this context, as a validating identity model, a reassuring reminder that one need not sacrifice one's sharp-edged "genius" and authenticity as one becomes involved again in "civilized life." What Thoreau could not entirely foresee or face squarely was the extent to which his sense of authenticity would be jeopardized and compromised after his return to Concord.

By this time in "Tuesday," the brothers are "fairly in the stream of this week's commerce" and start "to meet with boats more frequently" (209), and Thoreau is prompted to consider issues related to occupation, the assumption of social responsibilities, stability, and settling down.[49] In this context, he discusses those occupations—boatman, farmer, boatbuilder—he finds preferable to more "modern" ways of earning a living. In the "noontide" of life, young adults may subordinate everything else to their endeavors to consolidate their positions in society. "Men," Thoreau notes, "are as busy as the brooks or bees, and postpone every thing to their busy-ness" (218). He does find something legitimate in the need for a sense of solidity and stability—an urge that, in part, had led him to Walden and that would also contribute to his decision to leave the pond. He suggests that this stability is provided by nature, though for many it comes through occupation and marriage. "The routine which is in the sunshine and the finest days," he says, "commends itself to us by its . . . apparent solidity and necessity. . . . If there were but one erect and solid standing tree in the woods, all creatures would go to rub against it and make sure of their footing" (217). Thoreau does not acknowledge directly or recognize that, even for him, an increasingly important way to make sure of his footing, settle down, was to gain a foothold in a vocation—writing. Upon reaching some falls in Bedford, the brothers meet a young stonemason, working on solid ground with solid things, who wishes to accompany them, but he is too firmly embedded to accompany a man like Thoreau who is so intent on becoming his own person.[50] But, as if to concede that even the adventurous require some form of stability, the chapter concludes with the brothers, unable to "fix" their "tent firmly" (234) on a rock above the falls, needing and eventually finding solid dry land upon which to pitch their tent for the night and settle in.

"Wednesday" opens with the discovery by Thoreau and his brother that they had pitched their tent directly in the masons' path to their boats, a situation that suggests the inescapability of the social and the inevitability of conflict. Indeed, the inscription for "Wednesday" is a quote from Charles Cotton, "Man is man's foe and destiny" (235). In this most "social" of A *Week*'s chapters, issues of "intimacy vs. isolation,"[51] which become especially pressing matters in young adulthood, are preeminent.

Much early discussion revolves around houses that "in the noon of these days" they approached to "get a glass of water and make some acquaintance with their inhabitants" (241–42). These humble, unassuming houses, "homely and sincere, in which a hearth was still the essential part"—not unlike the Walden hut—meet with a generally favorable response from Thoreau. But the "graves of the aborigines" and Indian ruins in the town of Bedford, celebrated for "hops and for its fine domestic manufactures" (237), evoke a more ambivalent response to the social; he is reminded by the "scars" of the past that the white man's commercial and industrial culture is based on the supplantation of the Indian. His own life, he says in a poem, "is like a stroll upon the beach," and he has "but few companions on the shore" (241). Viewing an island from the boat, Thoreau, uncomfortable with intimacy and drawn to the life of a latter-day Robinson Crusoe, indicates how "an island always pleases my imagination. . . . I have a fancy for building my hut on one" (243). The description of how, at Amoskeag Falls, "the river is divided into many separate torrents and trickling rills by the rocks, and its volume is so much reduced by the drain of the canals that it does not fill its bed" (246–47), may be taken as a metaphor for the way human inspiration and potential may be dissipated and fragmented by social entanglements. Similarly, Thoreau's account of how "pot-holes" on rocky islands in the river are formed can be interpreted as analogous to the cumulatively entrapping ruts of social involvement:

> A stone which the current has washed down, meeting with obstacles, revolves as on a pivot where it lies, gradually sinking in the course of centuries deeper and deeper into the rock, and in new freshets receiving the aid of fresh stones which are drawn into this trap and doomed to revolve there for an indefinite period, doing Sisyphus-like penance for stony sins, until they either wear out, or wear through the bottom of their prison, or else are released through some revolution of nature. (247)

As the journey proceeds, the land is "very barren of men again," and the brothers glimpse Uncannunuc Mountain; before long they have passed through the locks and "gradually overtook and passed each boat in succession until [they] had the river to [themselves] again" (258–59). The threat of the social has been left behind—for the moment.

At this point, however, Thoreau inserts a long exposition on friendship. There had been ample discussion of this subject in the 1845 first draft of "Wednesday"; in 1847–48 he worked on "an essay or lecture on Friendship" (C, 204), which substantially expanded upon the first draft and which was eventually incorporated into the final version of *A Week*.[52] Thus the book's treatment of friendship draws not only on the long period of crisis related to his brother (and on his journal entries of those pre-Walden years) but also on the post-Walden era when Thoreau was seeking to consolidate his writing career and when his friendship with Emerson was becoming increasingly strained and ambivalent.[53] In "Wednesday" he attempts to come to terms with his relationship with John, John's death, and the opportunities and dangers of intimacy, issues in which emotions concerning Emerson as well as his brother no doubt seeped in. Thoreau acknowledges early in the friendship section, "Our fates at least are social. . . . as the web of destiny is woven we are fulled, and we are cast more and more into the centre" (264). He reviews, though in an indirect and disjointed manner, many significant interpersonal landmarks: for instance, his friendship (with homoerotic overtones) with Edmund Sewall (Ellen's brother, who had been a student at the Thoreau brothers' school) in the poem, "Lately, alas, I knew a gentle boy" (260–61); his brother's proposal to Ellen ("I heard that an engagement was entered into between a certain youth and a maiden, and then I heard that it was broken off, but I did not know the reason in either case" [293]); and, of course, John's death ("Even the death of friends will inspire us as much as their lives" [286]). There is a relatively brief consideration of the relationship between the sexes, though Thoreau concludes—as he had concluded with regard to his own relationships with women—that friendship "is no respecter of sex; and perhaps it is more rare between the sexes, than between two of the same sex" (271).

A major portion of the friendship essay is devoted to grief work. It is clear that thoughts of his brother infuse what sometimes seems to be an abstract discussion, as is movingly suggested by his claim that "my friend is . . . my real brother. I see his nature groping yonder so like mine. We do not live far apart. Have not the fates associated us in many ways?" (284). By expressing closeness to Indians, he seeks to assure reconciliation with, closeness to, his brother.[54] He extols, for instance, the virtues of the friendship between Wawatam, an Indian, and Henry, a fur trader: "The stern imperturbable warrior, after fasting, solitude, and mortification of the body, comes to the white man's lodge, and affirms that he is the white brother whom he saw in his dream, and adopts him henceforth. He buries the hatchet as it regards his friend, and they hunt and feast and make maple-sugar together" (274–75).[55] Another way to "bury the hatchet" and assert intimacy with his brother—indeed, to keep him alive in a way—was to associate him with the nature he so dearly loved. "As surely," he writes, "as . . . the manifold influences of nature survive during the term of our natural life, so surely my Friend shall forever be my Friend, and reflect a ray of God to me, and time shall foster and adorn and consecrate our

Friendship. . . . As I love nature, as I love singing birds, and gleaming stubble, and flowing rivers, and morning and evening, and summer and winter, I love thee my Friend" (285). Thoreau gains solace, moreover, from the realization that a friend who has died is enshrined in the memories of the living; as he writes in a passage that draws on his 1842 journal, "their memories will be incrusted over with sublime and pleasing thoughts, as monuments of other men are overgrown with moss; for our Friends have no place in the graveyard" (286). As he was quite aware, *A Week* itself was a way to honor his brother's memory and keep at least his spirit alive, thus denying and defying death through the power of the word.

If, however, the essay is a poignant expression of his love, it also has a gloomy side that embodies and suggests his ambivalence about interpersonal intimacy, unquestionably deepened by his experiences after leaving Walden. "We have nothing to fear from our foes," he notes, "but we have no ally against our Friends, those ruthless Vandals" (287). Since we love them and take to heart their opinions and expectations of us, our friends can hurt us severely; and to the extent that we feel hostility toward those we also love, we are doomed to be threatened by the "inward foes" of guilt and anxiety. Friendship, which all men dream of, is a "drama . . . enacted daily," which is "always a tragedy" (264). Thoreau, who was highly idealistic—perhaps impossibly and self-defeatingly so—in his standards of friendship, observes that "there may be the sternest tragedy in the relation of two who are more than usually innocent and true to their highest instincts" (276). While he contends that "the only danger in Friendship is that it will end," it is evident that there are other dangers that flow from human flaws. "In human intercourse the tragedy begins," he indicates, "not when there is misunderstanding about words, but when silence is not understood" (277–78). Furthermore, suspicion breeds suspicion, and friendship is always threatened because "every one has a devil in him that is capable of any crime in the long run" (284). It can be surmised that Thoreau's curiously abstract and impersonal concept of genuine friendship— which "is not so kind as is imagined" and "has not much human blood in it, but consists with a certain disregard for men and their erections, the Christian duties and humanities, while it purifies the air like electricity" (275–76)—emerged from his deep sense of vulnerability to the tortured feelings friendship can evoke and the threats it posed to his ego ideal. Thoreau's self-protective strategy tended to be "distantiation"—the "readiness to fortify one's territory of intimacy and solidarity,"[56] as he did so successfully and archetypically at "Walled In" Pond. There, by and large, he managed to insulate himself from the danger. And, of course, the prospect of sexual intimacy, burdened as it was with undercurrents of oedipal and sibling rivalry and loss of control, made it much safer to take nature as a bride.

The final paragraphs of "Wednesday" put into relief Thoreau's ambivalence about friendship—his exalted, romantic dream of friendship all too often threatening to become a nightmare. He recounts Wednesday night's dream of a "difference with a Friend," which draws heavily, it appears, from a dream he had in January 1841 in the aftermath of the rivalry with John for Ellen.[57] The "difference with a Friend," he says, "had not ceased to give me pain, though I had no cause to blame myself. But in my dream ideal justice was at length done me for his suspicions, and I received that compensation which I had never obtained in my waking hours. I was unspeakably soothed and rejoiced, even after I awoke" (296–97). Such a troubling dream is no accident, for "in dreams we but act a part which must have been learned and rehearsed in our waking hours. If this meanness has not its foundation in us, why are we grieved at it?" Surely these comments reflect Thoreau's sense that intimacy is a double-edged sword and that our "suspicion" and "meanness," our anxiety and guilt, can be evoked most harshly when we have differences with those to whom we are close, as was so true for him regarding his brother and Emerson. At the end of "Wednesday," he observes, "We bless and curse ourselves" (297); for him the prospect of human love and intimacy was, and would be, both blessing and curse.

At the beginning of "Thursday," the "faint deliberate and ominous sound of raindrops" (298) appears to signal not only the fading of summer and the approach of autumn but also the loss of youth and the imminence of middle age. The Thoreau brothers' discovery that they have pitched their tent "on the very spot which a few summers before had been occupied by a party of Penobscots" suggests the increased sensitivity of people moving into middle age to their place in an inevitable succession of generations. Looming on the horizon is the "dark conical eminence called the Hooksett Pinnacle, a landmark to boatmen." With the Pinnacle and Uncannunuc in sight, Thoreau recognizes that "this was the limit of our voyage, for a few hours more in the rain would have taken us to the last of the locks, and our boat was too heavy to be dragged around the long and numerous rapids which would occur" (299). Similarly, persons making the transition to middle age, having attained a certain pinnacle of achievement, grow more cognizant of the limitations and finiteness of their voyage. Even those things that have "worked" or helped in the journey upstream can become burdensome and must be discarded. The task of midlife "individuation"[58] requires an even more decisive, unequivocal casting off of deference to, and reliance on, former mentors and pat answers, just as Thoreau suggests in his poem, "My books I'd fain cast off" (301–2). The further sloughing off of reliance on mentors and books would indeed become a task for Thoreau after *A Week* was published, as he came to realize that his quest for authenticity and autonomy was still unfinished business rather than something conclusively achieved. From the top of Hooksett Pinnacle, he is able to get his most comprehensive view of the river he has traveled on thus far, suggesting also the tendency and capacity of those nearing or in middle age to review and reappraise—survey the landscape of—the lives they have led, struggling to develop broader, more inclusive perspectives.

William Bridges describes the "transitions of life's afternoon" as a kind of "homing process." This "homeward journey of life's second half," like Odysseus's prolonged and obstacle-fraught homecoming, demands that we "unlearn the whole style of mastering the world that we used to take us through the first half of life"; "that we resist the longings to abandon the developmental journey and refuse the invitation to stay forever at some attractive stopping-place"; and "that we recognize it will take real effort to regain the inward 'home.'"[59] The brothers will soon be prepared to begin this homeward journey, one that Thoreau would also undertake as he made the transition to middle age. However, the brothers first spend some time in Concord, New Hampshire, which they insist on calling "*New* Concord . . . to distinguish it from our native town." "This," says Thoreau, "would have been the proper place to conclude our voyage, uniting Concord with Concord by these meandering rivers, but our boat was moored some miles below its port" (303). He is aware, as are many people in late young adulthood and early middle age, of having reached a new plateau, both distant from and connected to previous generations and parents. But there are tasks and transformations, mountains to climb, beyond New Concord; and eventually one must make the challenging journey toward home. In many respects the most original—and hazardous—part of the adventure still lies ahead. At least up to this juncture, as Thoreau remarks, "Go where we will on the *surface* of things, men have been there before us" (303).

As summer begins to fade into autumn, one is again venturing into an uncleared forest, a wilderness—though the journey is at least as much an inner as an outer one. "The frontiers," Thoreau declares, "are not east or west, north or south, but wherever a man *fronts* a fact. . . . there is an unsettled wilderness between him and Canada, between him and the setting sun, or, further still, between him and *it*." In this fateful transitional period or crisis, one is once more a "forest dweller," as one was during the earlier period of identity crisis. Like the Thoreau brothers, who now "trod the unyielding land like pilgrims" (304), one must relinquish the safety and reassurance of the river, risk confrontation with life's mysteries, tragedies, and intractabilities, and accept again the challenge of climbing mountains. Thoreau's mode of traveling, he insists, "is no pastime, but it is as serious as the grave, or any other part of the human journey, and it requires a long probation to be broken into it." Only those travelers bent on authenticity, "to whom travelling is life for the legs, and death too, at last," who have truly opened themselves to the pain and potentialities of mortal life, can be, as Thoreau puts it, "born again on the road, and earn a passport from the elements, the principal powers that be for him." As Thoreau would learn firsthand after he left Walden and as he moved toward middle age, one must undergo a metamorphosis, shed one's thick skin, give painful birth to oneself all over again, in order finally to gain health and wholeness. The traveler "shall experience at last that old threat of his mother fulfilled, that he shall be skinned alive. His sores shall gradually deepen themselves that they may heal inwardly, while he gives no rest to the sole of his foot, and at night weariness must be his pillow, that so he may acquire experience against his rainy days" (306). Only then is one able, as the Thoreau brothers are able, to inhale "the free air of Unappropriated Land," revitalize oneself again at the "uncontaminated sources" of one's dreams, and reach new, heretofore unimagined, heights of authenticity. "Thus," Thoreau observes in recounting the brothers' expedition into the wilderness, "in fair days as well as foul, we had traced up the river to which our native stream is a tributary, until from the Merrimack it became the Pemigewasset that leaped by our side, and when we had passed its fountain-head, the wild Amonoosuck, whose puny channel was crossed at a stride, guiding us toward its distant source among the mountains, and at length, without its guidance, we were enabled to reach the summit of AGIOCOCHOOK" (314).[60] But even Thoreau, for all his prescience, could not fully foresee the enormous difficulties and dangers he would encounter in his personal quest for "Unappropriated Land" in the post-Walden years.

As middle age nears, "generativity"—the "concern for establishing and guiding the next generation"—and its counterpart, "stagnation," become insistent and overriding issues. While generativity often revolves around childbearing and child rearing (which help provide a sense of continuity with the future), there are people who, "from misfortune or because of special and genuine gifts in other directions, do not apply their drive to offspring of their own, but to other altruistic concerns and creativity. . . . And indeed, the concept of generativity is meant to include productivity and creativity."[61] Emerging in "Thursday" is Thoreau's own rapidly burgeoning commitment to, and dependence on, alternative and compensatory forms of generativity, which he anticipated would assume even greater significance to him in the future. Upon returning to Hooksett after a week of hiking and mountain climbing in the wilderness, the brothers note that it is already harvest time, and their first act is to buy a watermelon, which turns out to be ripe. But the focus on "ripeness" is evident even before the account of the trek to Agiocochook, in the essay on the poet Aulus Persius Flaccus, the sort of person, Thoreau remarks, to be contemplated when in the "barren society of . . . travellers." He stresses in his discussion the monumental, enduring quality of the artist's life (which can itself be an immortal work of art generated by the artist). At one point he observes that "the divinest poem, or the life of a great man, is the severest satire" (309), and later he comments that the "life of a wise man is most of all extemporaneous, for he lives out of an eternity which includes all time" (311–12). Toward the end of "Thursday," Thoreau speaks of the "man of Genius, who may at the same time be, indeed commonly is, an Artist," as the prototypical generative man, an "originator . . . who produces a perfect work in obedience to laws yet unexplored" (328). A poem he characterizes as a form of ripeness passed without mediation from the artist to those who are receptive to it. It is "one undivided unimpeded expression fallen ripe into literature, and it is undividedly and unimpededly received by those for whom it was matured" (329).

The story of Hannah Dustan is, among other things, an exploration of generativity issues and suggests Thoreau's ambivalence toward parenting, and especially toward his iron-willed, resourceful, indomitable mother.[62] Indeed, immediately after the Dustan narrative, he shows how, by tracing the matriarchal succession of generations back through the ages, "the lives of but sixty old women . . . say of a century each, strung together, are sufficient to reach over the whole ground. Taking hold of hands they would span the interval from Eve to my own mother" (325). Dustan is in one sense the admirable, nurturing parent who protects her offspring from the Indians who capture them, even if she is unable to prevent her infant from having his "brains dashed out against the apple-tree" (323–24). Yet she is also the killer of Indians, with whose wildness and independence Thoreau identified closely. Thus Dustan can be seen as an enemy, an all-too-dominating figure who was able to stamp out the wild virtues associated with Indians.[63] Moreover, to the extent that he identifies with the "favorite boy" Indian who was spared by Dustan or the "English boy" saved by her (and himself a killer of Indians), there may well be an element of survival guilt. He may have seen himself as having somehow been implicated in his brother-Indian's death, at some level conspiring with his mother and aspiring to be the one remaining "favorite boy." His view of parents as both protectors and potential destroyers could well have contributed to his own reluctance to become a parent and his embrace of less problematic (for him) forms of generativity. The Dustan narrative also suggests that, despite his celebration of the Indians, his allegiance was divided between the Indians and those who, only partly out of self-defense, have sought to vanquish them. Thus American expansionism had both positive and disquieting implications for him.

As "Thursday" draws to a close at the beginning of harvest season, the Thoreau brothers embark from Hooksett on their return voyage. If the trip has to this point been primarily linear in its forward sequence of growth and progress, it now begins to take on a kind of circularity. The brothers' task, "as the season was further advanced" (315), is to make their way home; their homing instinct, a deeply felt yearning to get back, is aided by "the wind from the north," a wind that registers the inevitability of winter. As they plunge quickly downstream, they are able to review "many a fair bank and islet on which [their] eyes rested in the upward passage," and carried by the inexorable northern wind toward home, they seek a new maturity, a new sense of equanimity: "All the world reposes in beauty to him who preserves equipoise in his life, and moves serenely on his path without secret violence" (317). It is a state of mind Thoreau would often find hard to come by in his later years. Having learned, with the "afternoon . . . far advanced" (320), what his "proper work" is, the "forms of beauty fall naturally around the path" (318) of the mellowing, ripening individual. That night the brothers pitch their tent "in a spot in the northern end of the Merrimack" and, reminded by the wind rustling in their ears that they "lay on the bank of the Merrimack, and not in [their] chamber at home," they sense "a great haste and preparation throughout nature" and become aware of the "new drapery which was to adorn the trees" (332–33).

Thursday night, Thoreau notes, "was the turning point in the season," and the brothers wake up on Friday to discover that it is now unmistakably autumn. Just as one passes, by often imperceptible but accumulating increments, into the latter phases of one's own life cycle—middle age and beyond—so, as Thoreau says with apparent acceptance, "summer passes into autumn in some unimaginable point of time, like the turning of a leaf" (334). The brothers shove off into the fog and "sweep downward with the rushing river, keeping a sharp look-out for rocks" (335), keenly cognizant of their vulnerability to mortal dangers. Having confirmed by continued observation that "the Fall had commenced" (335), they are imbued with a heightened sense of the preciousness of time at this stage of the odyssey; with the wind's help, they "lost not a moment of the forenoon by delays, but from early morning until noon were continuously dropping downward" (339). Knowing now what is truly important, they are determined not to be distracted by the petty or transient sights along the banks but rather give themselves over to timeless reflections: "the thoughts of autumn coursed as steadily through our minds, and we observed less what was passing on the shore, than the dateless impressions and associations which the season awakened" (348–49).

In the latter stages of the life cycle, and in "Friday," not only generativity issues but also "integrity vs. despair" are paramount concerns. Integrity involves the "acceptance of one's one and only life cycle . . . as something that had to be and that, by necessity, permitted of no substitutions."[64] It would be an issue to which Thoreau would devote much energy in his final years. In the course of painting a Brueghelesque portrait of Concord's "autumnal festival," the annual cattle show, he expresses a fatherly "love" for the farmers, "those sons of earth every mother's son of them" (337). He acknowledges, furthermore, that although "there are many crooked and crabbled specimens of humanity among them, run all to thorn and rind, and crowded out of shape by adverse circumstances . . . yet fear not that the race will fail or waver in them; like the crabs which grow in hedges, they furnish the stocks of sweet and thrifty fruits still" (338–39). But, as befits someone who was beginning to understand how closely his own sense of generativity and integrity was and would be bound to his achievements in art and the art of living, Thoreau stresses the virtues of artists and "great men" in "Friday." One crucial concern of middle age and beyond is to leave behind a legacy by which to be remembered, thereby gaining a measure of immortality. "The great poem," he says, "will have to speak to posterity" (377), and "great men," though they may be relatively unknown to their own generation, join the company of the immortals and gain fame "from their high estimate beyond the stars" (340). The poet writes not primarily for his own contemporaries but for "the time when a vision as broad shall overlook the same field as freely" (341). Psychoanalyst Elliot Jaques notes the attraction of "sculpted creativity" for middle-aged artists.[65] Thoreau, expressing his anxiety in "The Poet's Delay" that he will "leave no curious nest behind, / No woods echoing [his] lay" (343), is reassured by Ossian, in whose monumental work, like Homer's, "the phenomena of life acquire almost an unreal and gigantic size." The lives of such artists, and of the heroes they sculpt, have an enduring and monumental quality; they "lead such a simple, dry, and everlasting life, as hardly needs depart with the flesh, but is transmitted entire from age to age" (344).

Although immersion in, and association with, nature—and the expansive, cosmic, even mystical feelings accompanying it—still probably represented to him his primary access to immortality, he was gradually coming to see his art as a means not just to keep his brother alive but to assure for himself some transnatural mode of overcoming death. The desire both to accept and to transcend death—and his acceptance of physical death, his ability to conquer his legitimate fear of death rather than simply deny it, would depend in part on his capacity to convince himself that he would live on in significant ways after he died—would take many forms, sometimes seemingly contradictory but ultimately complementary, and would proceed on many fronts in subsequent years, especially as the youthful "all-feelings" waned and his view of nature became more differentiated and less romanticized.[66] At the same time, and in spite of his extraordinary zest for life, there would also be forces at work which (as had, for instance, been evinced in his own flirtation with death after his brother's) would make death easier to accept, would in fact often make it seem inviting and, finally, appropriate.

If Thoreau finds in the lives and works of artists inspiring examples of those virtues associated with life's later phases and opportunities for symbolic immortality,[67] he eventually and fittingly returns in "Friday" to nature and organic imagery for reassurances of the potential for generativity, integrity, and eternal life in the face of stagnation, despair, and oncoming winter. Lamenting the loss of "many odiferous native plants" (355), and confronted by life's inevitable—but hard to accept—decay and losses (especially, in his case, John's death), Thoreau, reveling in a joyful new life at Walden, finds comfort and inspiration in the lessons of nature's ongoing process of death and rebirth, disintegration and reintegration: "The constant abrasion and decay of our lives makes the soil of our future growth. The wood which we now mature, when it becomes virgin mould, determines the character of our second growth, whether that be oaks or pines" (352). Using imagery that would take on added authority and personal meaning for him in the post-Walden years, Thoreau suggests that we are never too old for growth. The soil of our loss and even of our despair may be the fertile crucible for regeneration and renewal; endings are also beginnings. To be sure, Thoreau here speaks, whether or not he was fully aware of it, primarily to the possibilities of rebirth *within* the parameters of a finite life and tends to downplay, or even deny, the sense in which the cycle of human life, unlike that of nature, has one definitive winter with which to contend. He does, however, show himself elsewhere to be in the early stages of evolving a more "naturalistic" version of immortality. Referring to Elisha, a "friendly Indian" who was buried in Tyngsboro near an apple tree which bore his name, he observes that "no one knew exactly where" he had been buried, "but in the flood of 1785, so great a weight of water standing over the grave, caused the earth to settle where it had once been disturbed, and when the flood went down, a sunken spot, exactly of the form and size of the grave, revealed its locality; but this was now lost again, and no future flood can detect it; yet, no doubt, Nature will know how to point it out in due time, if it be necessary, by methods yet more searching and unexpected" (356–57). But the more dominant theme of a triumphant ripeness and immortality promised by nature to the man of faith who participates in and binds himself to "her" is struck when he observes the late-blooming autumnal flowers:

> Asters and goldenrods reign along the way, and the life-ever-lasting withers not. The fields are reaped and shorn of their pride, but an inward verdure still crowns them. The thistle scatters its down on the pool, and yellow leaves clothe the vine, and naught disturbs the serious life of men. But behind the sheaves, and under the sod, there lurks a ripe fruit, which the reapers have not gathered, the true harvest of the year, which it bears forever, annually watering and maturing it, and man never severs the stalk which bears this palatable fruit. (378–79)

Although, as Thoreau well knew, there is reason to grieve the shadows cast by "not [the] body only, but [the] imperfectly mingled spirit," even the "darkest grief" may, he contends, be "dissipated, like the dark, if you let in a stronger light upon it" (352).

Before reaching the Concord River, Thoreau reflects on the necessity of venturing forth before one can truly come home. "When we have travelled a few miles," he says, "we do not recognize the profiles even of the hills which overlook our native village, and perhaps no man is quite familiar with the horizon as seen from a hill nearest to his house, and can recall its outline distinctly when in the valley." This experience is "as if our birth had at first sundered things, and we had been thrust up into nature like a wedge, and not till the wound heals and the scar disappears, do we begin to discover where we are and that nature is one and continuous every where" (349). Only with maturity, this passage suggests, can we gain fresh and integrated perspectives, become more authentically in touch with our place and meaning in the scheme of things, and recognize completely the continuity of nature and of our lives; only then can the "wound of birth" —not only the "wound" of the mother but the scars of separation and loss we carry with us from birth—be fully healed. By the time Thoreau returns to the placid Concord River, in the mellow, autumnal warmth of the afternoon conducive to a ripe, "contemplative mood," he appears to have made progress toward learning the lessons that make a serene homecoming possible, toward making the transition "from a comparatively narrow and partial . . . view of things, to an infinitely expanded and liberating one" which "implies a sense which is not common, but rare in the wisest man's experience" (386). Blessed with an autumnal wisdom[68] that would often be so elusive after he left the pond, Thoreau is "sensible that behind the rustling leaves, and the stacks of grain, and the bare clusters of the grape, there is the field of a wholly new life" (377).

Though attuned to the "rustling of the withered leaf" that is the "constant music" of the autumnal sun's "grief" and of his own, Thoreau is able to affirm his faith in the continuity of life and of his enduring, everlasting bond with the mother who is nature. "Sometimes," he writes, "a mortal feels in himself Nature, not his Father but his Mother stirs within him, and he becomes immortal with her immortality" (378). But coming home also represents a reconciliation with the father—and, we may conclude, with his brother and other significant male figures. While "the common man with reverence speaks of 'the Heavens,'" the "seer," the wise man of uncommon sense, "will in the same sense speak of 'the Earths,' and his Father who is in them" (382). Having articulated this vision of concord and continuity, one that he would have to struggle to keep in sight as the Walden experience receded, Thoreau expresses his contentedness with the silence that is the "indispensable sequel" (392–93) to any book, as death is the indispensable sequel to life. For Thoreau, "the rest is silence,"[69] and at least through and in his art, he has made a truce, if not a lasting peace, with its profundity and mystery and put temporarily to rest much of his guilt and anxiety. Silence is finally a way to recovered innocence and peace.

Having anticipated his own "autumnal work" (388)—which might be *A Week* itself, other works such as *Walden,* or the developmental "work" in which all people in middle age and beyond must engage—Thoreau draws "nearer to the fields where our lives had passed" (389) as the sun sets, and by late evening he returns to his Concord home. His odyssey has brought him full circle, though with riper vision, back to his "native" and "natal" port and the nurturing Concord mud, reunited with mother-nature and father-earth and, of course, still accompanied by the brother he has managed to keep alive. In many ways that mattered, life was a round trip. Finally, the brothers fasten their boat with umbilical ties to the wild apple tree, at once a symbol of home—even Paradise—regained and, as Thoreau would further develop in later writings,[70] a symbol of high and persistent aspiration, fruitfulness, integrity—a life well lived.

2 *Spring Growth*

*T*HOREAU moved into the Walden hut, the only abode he would ever own or inhabit alone, a week before his twenty-eighth birthday. The hearth had not been built, and the walls were far from airtight,[1] but, anxious to dramatize the urgency of the event, he chose to make his move on July 4, 1845. On that Independence Day, while many Concordians were no doubt proclaiming their support for the Mexican War and Texans were voting in convention to accept terms of annexation to the United States,[2] Thoreau was intent on making his own public statement—registering a firm dissent against the war and pointedly refusing the terms of annexation proffered by his country and community.

The decision to go to Walden was, as has already been suggested, the product of a complex mix of motives and opportunity; one of the most crucial and explicit reasons, as indicated by the July 4 moving date, was Thoreau's need to demonstrate, to declare defiantly and decisively, his independence of, and separation from, a society that could countenance, even celebrate, militarism and imperialism; that tolerated forms of slavery and oppression not only in the South but also in the North; that was growing ever more smugly conventional, "respectable," commercial, competitive, capitalistic, materialistic; that was generally unsupportive of—even hostile to—the heroic ideals and spiritual aspirations of creative young people like him; that seemed to be gradually betraying and abandoning the values and dreams of its promising youth. That he had been branded a "woodsburner" by many Concordians for starting, carelessly allowing to spread, and arrogantly refusing to help extinguish a fire that had consumed at least 300 acres of forest and even threatened the town in April 1844[3] had further fanned the flames of his already burning desire to distance himself from, even wage a self-protective war against, the town. Going to Walden, whatever else it was, was clearly a statement—which the upstanding citizens of Concord only two miles away could not help hearing—of what he would absolutely not consent to become committed to; it was a steadfast declaration of moratorium in the face of perceived pressures to accept prevailing definitions of personal, social, and national identity.

At the same time, however, the passage to Walden was also Thoreau's way of getting on with the largely unfinished business of early adulthood. One of the critical tasks of this developmental era, according to Daniel Levinson, is "to explore, to expand one's horizons and put off making firmer commitments until the options are clear." This task is characterized by a "sense of adventure and wonder";[4] it was just such a sense of adventure, not unmixed with apprehension, that Thoreau exhibited in a journal entry two days after moving to Walden: "Life! who knows what it is— what it does? If I am not quite right here I am less wrong than before—and now let us see what they [the gods] will have" (PJ, 2:156). Certainly, he had devoted much of his energy in the pre-Walden years to exploration and deferring commitments; indeed, between 1837 and 1845 he had still been struggling with issues of identity and separation from family that are most frequently associated with late adolescence and the transition to early adulthood. But there is another task central to early young adulthood on which Thoreau had made considerably less progress: "to create an initial life structure, to have roots, stability and continuity."[5] His postgraduate life, with the partial exception of two years of schoolteaching with his brother, had consisted largely of floundering, halting, abortive, ultimately unsuccessful attempts to establish a stable initial life structure he could call his own. Now, in setting up housekeeping at the pond, Thoreau was seizing what he may have sensed was his last chance, at least in early young adulthood, to put a more solid foundation under his youthful dreams and concentrate, albeit belatedly, on those developmentally imperative tasks already undertaken by his contemporaries, most of whom presumably had managed to separate from their families, at least to the overt extent that they had established their own occupations, families, and domiciles, had entered into "real life" as it was culturally defined. There were undoubtedly times when Thoreau feared life was passing him by. He had rebelled so strongly against his neighbors' expectations about adulthood partly because he felt their influence so powerfully; and, even if he often denied it, he cared about, and took to heart, what they thought of him. While he wanted his neighbors to hear what he had to say, he was, for all his protests, also listening to and watching them, comparing—both positively and negatively—his own life situation with theirs. Even his eccentric friend Ellery Channing, who had urged him in March 1845 to "build yourself a hut & there begin the grand process of devouring yourself alive" (C, 161), had himself recently married, become a father, and bought a house. There was cause to eat his heart out, to feel envy, to wish to emulate in some way. With a few exceptions, such as college and the disastrous 1843 stay on Staten Island during which a homesick Thoreau sought halfheartedly to promote his literary career, he had lived primarily under the parental roof; though he had a mentor and a dream[6]—key components in the formation of identity in early young adulthood—he had not been able to establish a home, career, and family of his own. He was still in some respects a "parcel of vain strivings" (CP, 81–82), as he had described himself in 1837; he needed to make a whole life out of disparate parts. Living at Walden was a balancing act. Thoreau wished to have it both ways: to affirm his commitment to constructive noncommitment and exploration *and* to define the nature and parameters of the commitments he *was,* as a young adult, prepared to make. Under the rubric of experimentation and revolt, the Walden sojourn also had all the earmarks of a young man's needing and seeking to *settle,* however provisionally, on a life he could truly say was his.

The "life structure," Levinson says, is the "basic pattern or design of a person's life at a given time." Its components consist of the most significant choices made by adults—"work, family, friendships and love relationships of various kinds, where to live, leisure, involvement in religious, political and community life, immediate and long-term goals."[7] In his life and work at Walden, Thoreau labored hard at the business of establishing an early adult life structure that would be, however, an alternative to that available to other "young men, my townsmen," whose "misfortune" it was, he wrote in the first version of *Walden,* "to have inherited farms, houses, barns, cattle and farming tools" (106).[8] He opposed his "settling" project to those of his conventional contemporaries: "In accumulating property for ourselves, or our posterity, in founding a family, or a state, or acquiring fame, we are mortal, but in dealing with truth we are immortal, and need fear no change nor accident" (146). Nevertheless, he wryly conceded that he was involved at Walden in paralleling—but not replicating—the niche-carving "business" activities of his Concord counterparts: "I went for a long time," he says, "I may say it without boasting, faithfully minding my business, till it became more and more evident that my townsmen would not after all admit me into the list, nor make my place a sinecure, with a moderate allowance." "So," he continues, "I turned my face more exclusively than ever to the woods where I was better known; —I determined to go into business at once, without waiting to acquire capital. . . .

I have thought that Walden Pond would be a good place for business, not solely on account of the railroad and the ice-trade. It offers advantages which it may not be good policy to divulge. It is a good port and a good foundation" (114–15). An enterprising young man in his own right, he had gone into "business" by himself and was determined to build his life from the ground up. While "the whole ground of human life seems to some to have been gone over before us by our predecessors, both the heights & the valleys" (109), he proposed to break new ground, start from scratch. As he had suggested in *A Week,* a foundation of trust and faith in continuity was essential to getting off to an auspicious start in the developmental adventure; the river had provided one such "grounding" for future growth. Trust was also a key to success at Walden; he indicated in the first draft of *Walden,* "I think we may safely *trust* a good deal more than we do," and he lamented that those persons suffering from "incessant anxiety & strain" were "determined not to live by faith" (109–10).

At Walden and in his writings at Walden, there was a dual foundation for trust. First, there was the pond itself—and the nature of which it was emblem and embodiment—which was "a good port and a good foundation" (115). Thoreau recalled being brought to Walden when he was a young boy (his family was then living in Boston and had gone to Concord for a visit with his grandmother);[9] it was "one of the most ancient scenes stamped on the tablets of my memory" (177). The pond, then, was a motherly presence associated with fondest childhood memories, nurturing breast and womb, and continuity with the "golden age" that preceded the driving of Adam and Eve out of Eden (188). But the other part of the ground plan, the blueprint for growth, involved—as befitted one going into "business" for himself—"economy," a searching reconsideration of what was truly necessary and what could be trusted as one laid the groundwork for a new life structure. Trustful attachment to nature thus was not the only precondition for healthy development; the other prerequisite was to meet the "vital facts" (PJ, 2:156) head on, determine what must be kept and what discarded, what was arbitrary and what not, thereby setting the stage securely for the growth and change that was sure to follow. It is "by an internal industry and expansion" that "the snake casts its slough—and the caterpillar its wormy coat" (117). Without a fundamental, thoroughgoing reexamination of "economy," people were, he believed, doomed to base their lives on a flimsy and factitious foundation: "By closing the eyes and slumbering and consenting to be deceived by shows men establish and confirm their daily life of routine and habit everywhere which still is built on purely imaginary foundations" (154).

One "necessity" to which he devoted much attention in his Walden journal and *Walden*'s first draft was, not coincidently, housing, which supplied one apt metaphor for breaking new ground and building a new life structure. Other young men inhabited houses (and bought farms) by which they became imprisoned, mortgaging their energies and very lives (120–21). As he bluntly put it, "the cost of a thing . . . is the amount of life it requires to be exchanged for—immediately or in the long run" (120). These men, he commented, "do not know what a house is—and the mass are actually poor all their days because they think they must have such an one as their neighbors" (PJ, 2:182). They did not have their inner houses in order, their priorities straight: "before we can adorn our houses with beautiful objects—the walls must be stript—and our lives must be stript—and beautiful housekeeping and beautiful living be laid for a foundation" (122). Thoreau, on the other hand, sought to construct a house—an integral part of a larger framework for life—that would provide a foundation for authentic growth, where he could "root" himself "firmly in the earth," so that he might eventually "rise in the same proportion into the heavens above," like the "nobler plants" that "bear their fruit at last in the air and light" (112). "When I first went to the pond," he recollects, "my house being unfinished for winter . . . was itself an inspiring object, which reacted on me the builder. From our village houses to this lodge on the shore of a beautiful lake . . . was a transition as from a dungeon to an open cage at least in a pleasant grove" (137). In his first journal entry at Walden, on July 5, 1845, he compares his hut to "some mountain houses I have seen, which seemed to me to have a fresher auroral atmosphere about them as I fancy of the halls of Olympus. . . . It was the very light & atmosphere in which the works of Grecian art were composed, and in which they rest" (PJ, 2:154–55).

Living in such a setting, settled in such a trustworthy, inspiring structure, Thoreau could forge a sense of identity—and identifications—conducive to the pursuit of a crucial segment of his own business—art and the art of living. There he was capable of convincing himself that he was the member of another, more heroic family. Sitting by his door on July 7, he remembers that "I too am at least a remote descendant of that heroic race of men of whom there is tradition. I too sit here on the shore of my Ithaca, a fellow wanderer and survivor of Ulysses" (PJ, 2:156). Never having left Concord for any appreciable time, he was nonetheless linked to, even transported to, Ithaca and another golden age, that of the Greeks;[10] he was able to feel fraternal bonds with the archetypal "wanderer" he had "survived" and whose odyssey he had taken up. He inquires, "And now where is the generation of heroes whose lives are to pass amid these our northern pines? Whose exploits shall appear to posterity pictured amid these strong and shaggy forms?" (PJ, 2:156–57). It is evident that Thoreau was, as he arrived at Walden, in the process of convincing himself that he could be counted as kin to that "generation of heroes." Not only did the structure at the pond encourage him to conceive of himself as hero and artist, it also helped fortify the sense of purity for which he yearned. "Verily a good house is a temple," he writes on July 7, "A clean house—pure and undefiled as the saying is" (PJ, 2:157). Elsewhere he indicates that he "imagined" his house "had its site actually in such a withdrawn, but forever new and unprophaned part of the universe. If it were worth the while to settle in those parts of the system near to the Pleiades or the Hyades, or Orion or Aldeboran, then I was really there, or at an equal remoteness from the life I had left behind. . . . Such was that part of creation where I had squatted" (139). The details of how he converted James Collins's shanty into his own house, how he financed its construction, and how the house finally appeared—all so lovingly and minutely dwelled on in his writings of the Walden period—served further to underline his ingenuity and self-sufficiency, qualities that he so needed to ascribe to himself. The Walden hut and its setting, then, became part and parcel of the life structure and identity he was building; indeed, the focus on residence—"where I lived"—was finally inseparable from, and a prerequisite for, the consideration of "what I lived for." "With this more substantial shelter about me," he observes, "I had made some progress toward settling in the world" (W, 85).

If one element of "settling in the world," of building a stable life structure, was to move into his own house, another critical task of settling was to have a family, and occasions for intimacy, separate from his family of origin, which evoked many threatening feelings and on which he was far more dependent that he could usually afford to admit. While other young men his age had traditional families—more or less intimate relationships with wives, children of their own, other kinfolk, friends of their own choosing in the community—Thoreau worked on weaning himself to alternative and compensatory modes of intimacy, family, and community. Already alluded to was his attempt to see himself as part of the family of "heroes." On July 14, 1845, he waxed lyrical about another, and even more central, familial and kindred relationship—with nature: "What sweet and tender, the most innocent and divinely encouraging society there is in every natural object. . . . There can be no really *black* melancholy to him who lives in the midst of nature, and has still his senses. . . . While I enjoy the sweet friendship of the seasons I trust that nothing can make life a burden to me" (PJ, 2:159). Before going to Mount Katahdin, he spoke on April 18, 1846, of his awareness of "my *kindred,* even in scenes which we are accustomed to call wild . . . the nearest of blood to me & hu-

manest was not a person nor a villager" (PJ, 2:236). In the first draft of
Walden, nature is usually a member of the family, a "ruddy and lusty old
dame who delights in all weathers and seasons—and is likely to outlive all
her children yet" (168). Subsequently, in a passage drawn from his pre-
Katahdin journal, he becomes even more specific as he extols

> the indescribable innocence & beneficence of nature—of sun and wind & rain
> —of summer & winter—such health—such cheer, they afford forever, and
> such sympathy have they ever with our race—that all nature would be affected
> —and the sun's brightness fade—and the winds would sigh humanely—and
> the clouds weep rain—and the woods shed their leaves and put on mourning
> in mid-summer if any man should ever for a just cause grieve. —Shall I not
> have intelligence with the earth? Am I not partly leaves and vegetable mould
> myself? God is my father & my friend—men are my brothers—but nature is
> my mother & my sister. (168–69)

If nature was a friend, mother, and sister (or, as one neighbor suggested
sarcastically, a "mother-in-law")[11] who yet encouraged his autonomy, it
was also, on occasion at least, an ersatz wife and lover. There was certainly, for example, something erotic in his description of nature's response to
a brief bout of loneliness, a "slight insanity" of mood, he experienced a few
weeks after coming to Walden: "Every little pine needle expanded and
swelled with sympathy" (165). Of course, Walden Pond itself took on
qualities of both mother and lover. While it was associated with purity, a
motherly security, it also was libidinized. In penetrating its crystalline waters and plumbing its depths; in cutting through its ice and sounding its
bottom; in gazing affectionately and longingly on its fair surface, Thoreau
was, in his own sublimated way, being an ardent lover and husband. And
absence would make his heart grow fonder; in his post-Walden life and in
subsequent drafts of *Walden*, it is clear that his need to maintain, expand,
and expound upon his bond with the pond and all it signified became increasingly urgent.

For many men of his generation, children were an integral part of the
familial and larger life structure. Although nature could provide Thoreau
with many familial relationships, it could only partially fill the vacuum left
by his childlessness and offer alternative forms of fatherhood. Apart from
entertaining children at Walden, his caring for and about, being "friend
and defender" of, the animals and plants with which he was surrounded
did represent a limited kind of fathering (191); this mode of "fathering"
would grow in importance over the years and would evolve eventually
into, among other things, a profound concern for conservation. Moreover,
he became a husbandman and developed a proprietary, paternal attitude

toward the beans he raised: "I came to love my rows—my beans—so many more than I want. Why should I raise them? . . . what shall I learn of beans or beans of me? I cherish them I hoe them early & late I have an eye to them" (177). But it was first and foremost in his writing, in the fertile generation of words, that he could satisfy his parenting needs at Walden. As he admitted, it was not beans he was most intent on raising; rather, he wanted, "as some must work in fields if only for the sake of tropes & expressions—to serve a parable-maker—one day" (181). Thoreau, himself engaged in the writing of a book at Walden that he hoped would become a classic, realized that books themselves were generative, "the treasured wealth of the world, and the fit inheritance of generations & of nations. . . . How many a man has dated a new era in his life, a second birth as it were from the reading of a book?" (149–50). A man who had been, in some sense, reborn through the reading of such works as *Nature* and "The American Scholar" and who was in the process of giving birth to himself in the writing of books, he recognized his potential, as an author, to be a "father" to others, who would themselves become more worthy and enlightened "founder[s] of a family" (w, 103).

Though Thoreau had to concede and confide—to himself and his readers, if not always to his Concord neighbors—that he loved "society as much as most" (165), he nevertheless was bent on setting up a community in sharp contrast to the one he had left behind.[12] When he went into Concord village, it was, he claimed, like "running the gauntlet" (185–86)—with its post office, barroom, grocery, bank; its coarse gossip; its proliferating shops with signs "hung out on all sides to allure the traveller" (185). *His* chosen community, on the other hand, was populated not only by his "brute neighbors" (191) but also by "simple and natural men" like Alek Therien, the woodchopper, and other "healthy and sturdy working men, descended from sound bodies of men, and still transmitting arms & legs & bowels from remote generations to posterity" (173). More generally, he felt more comfortable and less defensive about his interactions with others on his own trustworthy turf at Walden: 'I have had more of [men's] society since I lived in the woods than at any other period of my life. I met many men there under more favorable circumstances than I could anywhere else" (169). At his house, where he "had 3 chairs—1 for solitude— 2 for friendship 3—for society," he was more in control of the situation and visitors did not seem so obtrusive, though there were times when he wished for more room in order to maintain "a sufficient distance from my guest when we began to utter the big thoughts in big words" (174). In his ideal community, good fences made good neighbors, and there was a need for demilitarized zones: "We need a considerable neutral ground—though it be disputed territory, for individuals like nations must have suitable broad and natural boundaries" (175). Mindful of being a survivor, Thoreau also incorporated into his community the memory of those "former inhabitants" who once dwelled in the neighborhood and who had left behind traces, "dent[s] in the earth" (197). Paying his respects and pondering why "this small village" revealed by these traces did not thrive, he could only hope that "Again, perhaps, Nature will try, with me for a first settler" (198).

"Determined to go into business at once," Thoreau went to Walden in part to settle more fully issues of occupation and vocation central to early young adulthood. It was critical that he—unlike most of his contemporaries who "come home at night only from the next field or street" (PJ, 2:177), who lead "mean and sneaking lives . . . trying to get into business and . . . out of debt . . . seeking to curry favor" (108)—be "well-employed." In the first version of *Walden*, he recounts some of the vocational false starts of the pre-Walden period:

> I have thoroughly tried school keeping and have found that my expenses were increased in a greater proportion than my salary and I lost my time into the bargain. As I did not teach for the good of my fellow men, but simply for a livelihood, this was a failure—I have tried trade, but I found that it would take 10 years to get under way in that, and that then you would probably be on the way to the devil.

"Doing good," he had learned, did "not agree with my constitution," and he had resolved not to "deliberately forsake my particular calling to do the good which society demands of me" (132, 134). Wary of becoming overcommitted to dutiful involvement in his father's pencil-making business, he was forcibly struck with the "wisdom" of the "greek fable" in which "The God Apollo (Wisdom—Wit Poetry) [was] condemned to serve—keep the sheep of *King* Admetus" (PJ, 2:184). At the same time, it was important that he renounce any intention to surpass his father—though he had, in fact, been primarily responsible for the invention of an improved pencil.[13] In his sojourn at the pond, he sought to extricate himself from these failures and binds of the past. As one who valued "broad margins" and "could fare hard and succeed well," he discovered at Walden that "the occupation of a day laborer is the most independent of any"; there he could claim, "I maintain myself solely by the labor of my hands, and I find that by working about six weeks in a year I can meet all the expenses of living" (132). The laborer, as opposed to an employer, is "free to devote himself to his chosen pursuit, independent of his labor" (133). Accordingly, among the jobs he took on while living at Walden, especially in the winter months, were painting, building fences, carpentry, gardening, and surveying.[14] One job, "steady and self respecting labor" (177), that this self-proclaimed jack-of-all-trades undertook was cultivating beans. "Determined to know beans," he took the job both seriously and playfully and managed to make agricultural work an important part of his private, seemingly self-sufficient economy. Yet, unlike most men, who were too "busy about their beans," raising the crop ultimately was a means to an end; he acknowledged that he worked in the fields "for the sake of tropes & expressions" (181); to the scholar, agricultural labor "yields a classic result—to the literary it is literary" (178). Having spent many an hour his first summer on literal cultivation, he finally determined, "I will not plant beans and corn with so much industry another summer, but such seeds, perhaps, if the seed is not lost, as sincerity—truth—simplicity—faith—innocence—and see if they will not grow in this soil even with less soil & manurance and sustain me" (182). Though, strangely enough, writing is one activity he does not stress having worked on in his journal and *Walden*'s first draft (perhaps revealing a wish not to face the fact that in his writing he was creating a fictive identity), it is clear that he was preoccupied, sitting at the desk in his hut, with "nursing other crops" which would yield an abundant harvest by the time he left the pond.

By the end of his first year at Walden, Thoreau had finally succeeded in settling on and building a solid early adult life structure—including his own house, family, children, community, and vocation—a framework he could trust, in which he could be comfortable, productive, and true to his dreams. He had, in fact, lived out a dream and had met "with a success unexpected in common hours"; he had "put the foundations under" his "castles in the air" (W, 323–24). With such foundations he was able to achieve a satisfying sense of identity—committed not only to constructive noncommitment, to the provisional and experimental, but also to his writing and to forging an identity compatible with his ego ideal: pure, autonomous, heroic. The sense of identity that emerged from, and was crystallized by, his alternative life structure helped unleash the latent creative energies and gifts of this late-blooming young man and gave them direction. In his major literary endeavors of this period of artistic expansion—one can picture his often writing at a white heat as well as craftily revising—he was able to fashion versions of a persona that embodied the ego ideal he wished and needed to believe in and to work on issues that had disturbed him and blocked or retarded his development in previous years. Without the re-creation and assurance of identity nurtured and buttressed by the Walden experience, it is questionable whether Thoreau would have had the psychic impetus—not to mention the relatively uninterrupted time

—to write as he did. His artistic development might well have been permanently crippled or arrested by all the ills that had plagued him before 1845. In turn, the continuing daily absorption in creating, speaking through, and identifying with his literary persona helped animate, replenish, and solidify his sense of self. Thus at Walden life and art inspired, complemented, and reinforced one another. Everything seemed to have come together—for a time. After that life structure broke up, there would be an increasingly insistent, compelling need to hold on to—and reconstitute through selective memory, art, and imagination—the Walden experience and identity. Walden would assume a central place in his life myth. And in what would become the fortuitously drawn-out process of revising *Walden,* he would give himself the opportunity to keep alive—as well as to modify, elaborate, and expand upon in light of his post-Walden life—a myth of personality and experience that helped sustain him.

Thoreau thrived at Walden as he never had before. It was a time of spring growth and morning hope, as the imagery of *Walden*'s first draft indicates. A road of unlimited possibilities still stretched before him. It was a time when, despite having witnessed his brother's tragic death, he could experience intimations of perennial youth and immortality, even believe (as many young people still do, on an emotional level) that he would live forever, could stop time in its tracks.[15] Like many in early adulthood, he not only felt safe, he also felt saved; he had gained an assurance (precarious though it was) of grace. There were no doubt many moments of ecstasy, "peak experience," transcendence, epiphany, mystical feelings of oneness with the universe. One such revelatory moment is recorded in connection with the "memorable crisis" of winter's transition to spring. The change

> is instantaneous—at last. Suddenly an influx of light fills the house—though the clouds of winter still hang over it *and the leaves are dripping with sleety rain.* I look out on the pond which was cold grey ice but yesterday—and already the signs of fair weather were there and it was become a calm & smooth lake, full of promise as a summer evening—seeming to have some intelligence with distant horizons. . . . I heard a robin in the distance the first I had heard for many a thousand years, methinks, whose sound has the same meaning it was wont to have. . . . The pitch pines about my house, which had so long drooped —suddenly looked brighter, more green & more alive and erect, as if entirely cleansed by the rain—and fitted once more to express immortal beauty. . . . I knew that it would not rain anymore. (205)

There was joy and spontaneity in both the writing and the life. And, at least in the first year by the pond, he perhaps did not have to rely so heavily on the words because the experience itself was so authentically rich and exhilarating. Though he developed the coming of the spring in a far more rudimentary fashion (after a much shorter and less symbolic winter) in *Walden*'s first draft than in later versions, he clearly viewed the coming of spring metaphorically as well as literally: at Walden he had thawed out after a long period of "winter discontent" (123), budded and blossomed in the bright sunshine (208), and finally come into his own. The first draft ends, "Thus was my first year's life in the woods completed" (208), and (though he used the device of condensing two years into one) it may be suggested that much of his triumphantly revitalizing experience and artistic accomplishment occurred even before the arrival of the second spring he spent at the pond. Thoreau apparently started work on *Walden*'s first version in late 1846 or early 1847 and had completed a substantial part of it before the spring of 1847.[16] By the time he finished the book in 1854, the spring and the preceding winter would take on personal dimensions and symbolic meanings he would have had difficulty foreseeing in 1845–47. The years intervening between Walden and *Walden* would exert an incalculable impact on the book's development and final significance.

Just as going to Walden had been the result of complicated motivations and circumstances, so was leaving it. Given its advantages and successes, there is much reason for asking (as he had frequent cause to ask himself in subsequent years) why Thoreau began to contemplate the vacating of his premises at the pond and returning to "civilized life." In the final version of *Walden* he would write,

> I left the woods for as good a reason as I went there. Perhaps it seemed to me that I had several more lives to live, and could not spare any more time for that one. It is remarkable how easily we fall into a particular route, and make a beaten track for ourselves. I had not lived there a week before my feet wore a path from my door to the pond-side; and though it is five or six years since I trod it, it is still quite distinct. It is true, I fear that others may have fallen into it, and so helped to keep it open. The surface of the earth is soft and impressible by the feet of men; and so with the paths which the mind travels. How worn and dusty, then, must be the highways of the world, how deep the ruts of tradition and conformity! I do not wish to take a cabin passage, but rather to go before the mast and on the deck of the world, for there I could best see the moonlight amid the mountains. I do not wish to go below now. (w, 323)

In a considerably less self-assured, more vexed journal entry of January 1852, he would inquire,

> But why I changed? why I left the woods? I do not think that I can tell. I have
> often wished myself back. I do not know any better how I ever came to go
> there. . . . Perhaps I wanted a change. There was a little stagnation, it may be.
> About 2 o'clock in the afternoon the world's axle creaked as if it needed greas-
> ing. . . . Perhaps if I lived there much longer, I might live there forever. One
> would think twice before he accepted heaven on such terms. (J, III:214–15)

We lead many lives within our life, pass through numerous, often unre-
corded eras. Thoreau was no exception. If it had been a developmental necessity to live away by the pond to establish a new life structure, his leaving
the pond was also developmentally imperative and inevitable. Levinson
has observed that the "primary task of each stable period is to build a life
structure," but the "primary tasks of each transitional period are to question and reappraise the existing structure, to explore various possibilities
for change in self and world and to move toward commitment to crucial
choices that form the basis of a new life structure in the ensuing stable period. . . . No matter how satisfactory a structure is, in time its utility declines
and its flaws generate conflict that leads to modification or transformation
of the structure."[17] Although some people, especially young people, are
not prepared or quick to accept it, life is a series of settlings and unsettlings.
Every life structure, even Walden, carries within it the seeds of its own de-
stabilization and dissolution and at some point calls for restructuring, of a
subtle or dramatic nature. The move to Walden had ushered in a brief but
relatively stable—and scintillating—period in Thoreau's life and encouraged the more or less successful completion, after long delay, of the there-
tofore unfinished tasks of early adulthood. Walden constituted a round of
life in which he was more than grateful to settle for a time, in which he had
seemingly managed to resolve many problems and conflicts. He had gone
there with something to prove, and he had largely proved it to his satisfaction. Yet, as he himself grew aware, this structure finally bred a sense of
"stagnation" and staleness, had become a well-worn path. Even off the
beaten track, the track could get beaten. Walden, he had to remind himself
sometimes, was an "experiment," and this man who was wary of commitment in any case began to see that his life at the pond could become a tender trap, an obstacle to growth. Further progress was contingent on the
gradual realization that he had "several more lives to live, and could not
spare any more time for that one."

Thus, almost no sooner than Thoreau had constructed, later than
most and at virtually his final opportunity, a satisfying early young adult
life structure, it was necessary to consider modifications. The creaking axle
"needed greasing." It is likely that, not long after the first anniversary of

the passage to Walden and his twenty-ninth birthday, Thoreau started to feel somewhat restless, experiencing stirrings in some ways akin to what Levinson refers to as the "Age Thirty Transition," during which "the provisional, exploratory quality of the twenties is ending and a man has a sense of greater urgency. Life is becoming more serious, more restrictive, more 'for real.'"[18] Thoreau had by degrees recognized that he could not live at Walden forever—not without foreclosing other developmental opportunities. He would eventually have to move on, reenter society, and again "go before the mast and on the deck of the world."

As already indicated, Thoreau ended his first draft of *Walden* by referring to the conclusion of his first year at the pond. It was probably quite significant that two of the most provocative experiences of the 1845–47 period occurred soon after the beginning of his second year at Walden: the night, July 23 or 24, he spent in jail for refusing to pay his poll tax as a protest against the recently declared Mexican War, and his late summer trip to the Maine woods. Both these episodes were associated with a desire to ward off an incipient sense of stagnation, to remain in touch with "wildness," to shore up some of the tiny cracks appearing in the Walden life structure and identity. To be sure, he did not choose the exact timing of his arrest by Sam Staples—Thoreau had a history of poll tax resistance—but the jailing nevertheless gave him a providential opportunity to reassert his distance from the townspeople. Soon after this incident, he discussed tax resistance in his journal, accused society of moral turpitude ("Countless reforms are called for because society is not animated enough or instinct enough with life. . . . Better are the physically dead for they more lively rot" [PJ, 2:262–64]), and observed, "Even virtue is no longer such if it stagnate."[19] One may justly conclude that he was as concerned about his own potential for "stagnation" at Walden as he was about the undeniable moral lethargy and corruption his country was demonstrating in the Mexican War. But while his act of civil disobedience may have provided a temporary pick-me-up, it also served to highlight a flaw in the life at Walden. By the evening of his arrest, someone—most likely his proper Aunt Maria—had paid his tax for him, and it was only because Staples wouldn't take the trouble to put his boots back on and inform him that he spent the rest of the night in jail. Staples said that Thoreau was "as mad as the devil" that the tax had been paid for him, and understandably so. It was no doubt deeply embarrassing for him, the supposedly heroic and self-sufficient rebel and sojourner at Walden, to have underscored for all the community and himself to see the extent to which he remained linked to, and indebted to, his family (particularly the women) and civilized society. One at least has to wonder whether he anticipated that he would eventually be bailed out. Indeed, Aunt Maria or other family members would continue for years to pay the poll tax for him.[20] Thus, the night in jail, though it would ultimately be transmuted into a remarkable and enormously influential political document, left Thoreau with mixed feelings. The act of passive resistance to civil government was intended to be subversive, but it was itself subverted. As much as it represented an act of courage and conviction, it also left him with questions about the authenticity and viability of the life he was then leading.[21] And the trip to Maine the next month, which may well have been perceived as offering a means to reassert aliveness and wildness in response to the discomfiting aspects of the civil disobedience episode, would itself be disconcerting and chastening, as will soon be discussed; it dramatized to him just how much a member of human society he really was, led him further to ponder the viability of his Walden life, and forced him to face the fact that the next developmental phase had to be lived out in civilized society.

During the second year, "Walden became . . . less of a home and more of a headquarters. He spent more time back in Concord than he had spent the season before."[22] Perhaps it was primarily because his first year at Walden had been such a success, and because he now had his writing and a persona to cling to and believe in, that he had the relative ego strength and confidence to accept the extent to which he was a "civilized" man who needed to be part of society. As early as late spring of 1846 he disclosed, "When my friends reprove me for not devoting myself to some trade or profession, and acquiring property I feel not the reproach— I am guiltless & safe comparatively on that score— But when they remind me of the advantages of society of worthy and earnest helpful relations to people I am convicted" (PJ, 2:248–49). One of the flaws of the life structure at Walden, one that Thoreau may have been able to acknowledge at least subliminally —only after he had achieved a solid foundation of identity—was the manner in which his life *had* been "social" even at the pond, how dependent he *had* been on civilized society. All his talk of heroism and independence aside, he had hardly made a clean break with his community or family. And despite his disclaimers about loneliness, it is likely that he would have felt severely lonely had he really lived an appreciable distance from other people. He remained within walking distance of Concord; visited the town frequently; ate often at his mother's, the Emersons', and the houses of other friends; relished his mother's cooking and was visited almost every Saturday at the pond by his mother and sisters, who brought with them some culinary delight.[23] Some townspeople contended that "he would have starved, if it had not been that his sisters and mother cooked up pies and doughnuts and sent them to him in a basket." An apocryphal but revealing piece of gossip had Thoreau, upon hearing Mrs. Emerson's dinner bell, "bounding through the woods and over the fences to be first in line at the Emerson dinner table."[24] As has already been argued, his stay at Walden was a psychologically strategic removal, a way to remain dependent on home, mother, and familial associations while simultaneously convincing himself—partly in response to the fact that he *was* so dependent—that he was *more* independent and self-sufficient than other men. The Walden experience, and his writing there, *had* fortified this sense of autonomy he so desperately needed, and it was thus less important always to be so extremely on the defensive.[25] At some point during the second year, the basic facts of his reliance on family and friends while at the pond may have come to be recognized and perceived as something of a burden. The disjunctions between real and ideal were somewhat clearer: in a way he was leading a double life at Walden and was still linked in countless ways to the family and friends he had ostensibly left behind. Some Concordians doubtlessly branded him a hypocrite, even if his own self-estimate was not so severe. In a relatively undefensive moment, in the spring of 1846, he wrote, for instance, "For the most part I know not how the hours go. Certainly I am not living that heroic life I had dreamed of" (PJ, 2:242). However reluctant he may have been usually to own up to it (and writing the first draft of *Walden* helped protect him from too much threat), it must have been a relief to him in some respects to contemplate returning to the town, where he would no longer have to maintain a dual existence, where he could bring into harmonious conjunction all components of his life and self. Having built a life structure, identity, and persona on what he thought were firm foundations, he no longer felt quite as imperiled by family and community; he was more readily prepared to consolidate the "civil" with other parts of his identity.

Previously referred to was the Maine woods trip, which had a powerful impact on Thoreau and further inclined him to consider a return to civilized life. Undertaken in part to reaffirm his wildness and get even more closely in touch with the wildness of nature, the excursion wound up seriously calling into question some of the assumptions and emotions associated with "life in the woods" at Walden. In the spring of 1846, he had written in his journal of being "aware of the presence of my *kindred,* even in scenes which we are accustomed to call wild" (PJ, 2:235–36). Thoreau had adopted nature, and (he thought) vice versa, as an alternative family at Walden. While nature was a mother, sister, wife, and even lover for him, there was yet another family figure with whom nature offered the promise and perception of intimacy: his elder brother. In the aftermath of John's death, Thoreau—as a means of keeping his brother alive, reaffirming closeness to him, and thereby assuaging grief and guilt—had sought in nature the spirit or presence of John, who had himself been on close terms with nature.[26] In one poem (probably from 1842) lamenting the loss of his "great friend," he resolved, "I still must seek the friend/Who does with nature blend,/Who is the person in her mask,/He is the man I ask" (CP, 144). In the 1843 poem, "Brother Where Dost Thou Dwell," he asked imploringly, "Where chiefly shall I look/To feel thy presence near?/Along the neighboring brook/May I thy voice still hear. . . . Dost thou still haunt the brink/Of yonder river's tide?/And may I ever think/That thou art at my side. . . . What bird wilt thou employ/To bring me wind of thee?" The final stanza, deleted from the published version, was an anxious prayer and plea for benediction: "May thy influence prevail/O'er this dull scenery,/To lift the heavy veil/Tween me and thee?" (CP, 151–52, 314–15). One "bird" allied to John, an amateur ornithologist, in a closely associated poem was the marsh hawk: "In each heaving of thy wing/Thou dost health and leisure bring,/Thou dost waive disease & pain/And resume new life again" (CP, 143). Withdrawing to the monastic life at Walden, Thoreau felt that he had done penance for his imagined sins against John; he had waived "disease & pain" and resumed "new life again." Living close to a beneficent nature at the pond, he was able to "lift the heavy veil" between himself and his brother and reassure himself that he had gained absolution. In his trip to the Maine wilderness, Thoreau endeavored to approach even closer the essence of his brother's spirit as well as to sup again of life's "uncontaminated sources," which, as the Amonoosuck River suggested, never became stagnant (PJ, 2:268). Encounters with the Indians of Maine also would, he hoped, re-create and strengthen his sense of intimacy with John. That the trip to Maine and Katahdin was in some ways connected with his brother is confirmed in part by his journal entries. A short time before embarking for Maine, for instance, he reminisced about previous experiences climbing mountains, including, revealingly, the White Mountains portion of the Concord-Merrimack trip (PJ, 2:265–69). Soon thereafter, on August 31, 1846, at the invitation of his cousin George Thatcher of Bangor, he started for the Maine woods—seven years to the day since he had begun the Concord-Merrimack excursion with John.

If he was seeking John's spirit, or other kindred spirits, in Maine, however, and if he tended to romanticize wildness and Indians in the pastoral settings of Concord and Walden, he must have been deeply troubled by his wilderness experience. Early in his journal recounting of the trip, written after returning to Concord, he describes the wilderness as "vast and grim and drear" (PJ, 2:277). Descending from Katahdin, he says, was when "I first most fully realized that that *[sic]* this was unhanselled and ancient Demonic Nature" (PJ, 2:278). Passing over "burnt lands" (which may well have aroused uneasy memories of his own woodsburning mishap),[27] he "reflected what a man—what brother or sister or kindred of our race farmed it. . . . and I expected the proprietor to dispute my passage" (PJ, 2:278). Nature here was frequently not a welcoming brother or other kin but rather a disapproving "proprietor" who was inimical to Thoreau's desire for intimacy, even threatening to punish him for his transgressions.

Soon before a highly suggestive description of a logging mill, Thoreau characterizes the experience of traveling as often having an eerie, dreamlike quality:

> There are singular reminiscences in the life of every man—of seasons when he was leading a wholly unsubstantial and as it were impossible life—in circumstances so strange—in company so unfit and almost this time the creature of Chance. As the hours spent in travelling by steam boat night or day— It is a transient and dream-like experience—for which I have no other place in any memory but such as I assign to dreams. In a longer voyage no doubt the circumstances and scenery would become familiar and we might realize how we too could be sailors—and so lead our lives. (PJ, 2:279)

Certainly his journal portrayal of the Maine trip (and, to a lesser degree, the final version of "Katahdin") often has a dream- or trancelike quality, which hints at Thoreau's prevailing state of mind as he both experienced and re-created the journey. In dreams we are more in touch with, and susceptible to, the unconscious substratum; in a trance, we are less in control, more impressionable and open to suggestion. Similarly, in the Maine woods—and in his writing about it—Thoreau was peculiarly liable to "doze off" fitfully and "dream," unusually subject to the dark spell cast by the wilderness, a "strange" environment where he felt off-balance, out of his element, not in control. Later in his journal, still in the midst of recalling his excursion, he speaks almost phenomenologically of the experience of having fallen asleep "in my chair Betwixt day-light and dark" and of having been jarred "back to life" by "some trivial sound." Reflecting on this disorienting nodding off (and sleep in general), he asks, "And this is half our life? Who'd undertake the enterprize if it were all? . . . Bribed with a little sunlight and a few prismatic tints—we bless the maker—and deprecate his wrath with hymns" (PJ, 2:324). Traveling in the Maine woods was in some ways like being in such a "twilight zone," weaving drowsily in and out of sleep, falling in and out of a hypnotic state. It was difficult there entirely to "deprecate" (or "stave off," as he put it in one version)[28] the "wrath" of the "maker"; Maine aroused, and lowered his resistance to, those deep-seated fears and anxieties that dreams bring so disconcertingly close to the surface.

As his description of the logging mill reveals, the anxieties evoked by the Maine trip had some sexual underpinnings. While, to be sure, human inventions and intervention are the primary villains here, the account does suggest the generalized, free-floating state of apprehension engendered by the wilderness. In his susceptible condition Thoreau finds himself identifying with the logs he observes. "Here," he says, "is a close jam a hard rub all seasons," and "the sorely driven logs are at last driven through the narrowest gut of all and most finely slitted" (PJ, 2:281). The sexual connotations are inescapable: each log, after a "close jam a hard rub," enters "the narrowest gut"—suggesting phallic penetration—and then is "finely slitted"—implying a fear of the consequences of sex associated both with *vagina dentata* (an "emasculating" mother and other women) and the oedipally linked punishment of castration. While each log in the logjam "expects" peaceful communion with his already "wounded" "brothers," this is not to be: "The log which has shot so many falls only with injury to its sap wood—and bears the scars of its adventures—may think here to lie quietly embraced by its boom with its companion's as in a fold—but not so. for here comes the closest rub of all—one inch—two 3 inches at a time —with your sap pared off—and then you may go" (PJ, 2:281–82). In drafting this description, he at one point interpolated the "unkindest cut of all" as a complementary image for "the closest rub of all."[29] This passage —which is significantly altered and less intense in "Katahdin" (thereby revealing perhaps its disturbing, even prurient, implications for Thoreau)— implies severed ties between companions, the loss of potency (he would later associate sap with sexual vigor), and, of course, the connections between the "closest rub" and the "unkindest cut of all." If Thoreau in any way identified, moreover, with those men or machines doing the cutting— he was, after all, a representative of the cutting edge of civilization in the wilderness—then he may also have been led to see himself guiltily as the agent that has slit and dismembered his "brother" logs. The use of "you" lends further personal overtones to the passage. On his 1853 trip to Maine, he would repeatedly and explicitly identify with the pine; here he also identifies and empathizes with the white pine—"loped—scarified— soaked bleached—shaved—& slit" (PJ, 2:282). Instead of finding a benevolent mother or having a blissful reunion with his brother in the wilds of Maine, he discovered forces, both feminine and masculine, that activated guilt and anxiety, threatened to cut off integrity and vitality, sap initiative. Such forces could create an emotional logjam that would jeopardize all enterprise. In "Katahdin," he would brood about the possibility of becoming a piece of driftwood in just such a logjam: "Methinks that must be where all my property lies, cast up on the rocks on some distant and unexplored stream, and waiting for an unheard-of freshet to fetch it down. O make haste, ye gods, with your winds and rains, and start the jam before it rots!" (MW, 52–53.)[30] Clearly, the logging mill sequence, as well as other facets of the trip, had nightmarish resonances for Thoreau.

If Thoreau had hoped to replicate in the wilderness his "Indian brave" relationship with his brother, he was sorely disappointed. Wishing to engage Indians as guides for his trip, he speaks with one Indian, seemingly "half mullattoe," who "told us in his sluggish way that there *were* Indians going 'up river' he and one other" (PJ, 2:287). In one version, he describes this "half mullattoe" as a "stalwart but greasy-looking fellow" who answered his question "as if it were the only serious business he had had that day."[31] The "other" Indian was Louis Neptune, a "small wirey man with a puckered and wrinkled face" (PJ, 2:287), who yet "seemed the *chiefer* man of the two." These men offer to guide Thoreau and Thatcher, who thought themselves "lucky to have secured such guides and companions" (PJ, 2:288). However, the Indians "fail" them (PJ, 2:302) by never appearing, and, after recounting the Katahdin climb, Thoreau comments that they were "lucky to have exchanged our Indians" for two white men "who were at once guides and companions. . . . the Ind. is not so skilful in the management of a batteau" (PJ, 2:308). Finally, they come across Neptune and his friend again, "on their way up to Chesuncook after Moose," but

> they were so disguised that we hardly knew them— At a little distance they might have been taken for Quakers—seeking a settlement in Pennsylvania—with broad brimmed hats & cast off coats They looked like London dandies the morning after a spree—
>
> Neptune at first was only anxious to know "what we kill"—seeing some partridges in our hands—but we had assumed too much anger to permit of a reply— We thought Ind. had some honor before— But me been sick— O me unwell now— You make bargain then me go.
>
> —He was still plainly under the influence of the disease that had attacked him, his bottle— (PJ, 2:348)

These remarks indicate just how disenchanted Thoreau was with the Indians he met; the anger was that of one whose youthful romantic illusions had been all but dashed. If he had counted on coming closer to the Indians and, in the process, to his brother, he probably came away from the wilds of Maine feeling a sense of alienation that may have been quite threatening.

By contrast, he was impressed and relieved by the civilized qualities and comforts of the white men's households. A savory dinner at one such house delighted him (PJ, 2:299), perhaps reminding him of his mother's home cooking. He responds approvingly of efforts to educate—and thus "civilize"—backwoods children: "Here one of my companions commenced distributing a small store of little books among the children to learn them to read as well as old newspapers among the parents. There was a book for Helen and a book for John—grinning flaxen headed children—who were true enough not to say thank you sir because they were told to" (PJ, 2:295). Perhaps only in these safer circumstances were brother and sister, "John" and "Helen," accessible. In the wild, even wild apples needed cultivation, "comparatively worthless for want of a grafter" (PJ, 2:286). The comforts and advantages he found in civilization and civilized sensibilities amidst wildness undoubtedly inclined him to question his appetite for genuine wilderness, his preference for the wild over the civil and domestic. As would usually be the case, he was less on the defensive about being "civilized," less resentful of society, more heartily social when traveling in the wilderness than when he was back in Concord.

Thoreau did have his ephemeral moments of intuited communion with nature and wildness, as when his party came upon North Twin Lake —"the first time I had realized my conception of a secluded Lake of the Woods.— The impression was, and I presume it agreed with the fact, as if we were upon a high table land between the states and Canada" (PJ, 2:311). However, in such untrammeled "New Country," where "the evergreen woods had decidedly a sweet fragrance which was racy and invigorating like root beer" and where "we walked on boyantly and full of expectation," "one could no longer accuse institutions—and society but must front the true source of evil" (PJ, 2:294). And the deeper he delved into the heart of the wilderness, the more difficult it became to domesticate or feel some kinship with nature, and the more disoriented and troubled he became.

Approaching Mount Katahdin, as close to the "true source" as he would come, the scenery is "drear and grim" (PJ, 2:336); "it is," he comments, "the most treacherous and porous country I ever travelled" (PJ, 2:337). The night before the ascent of Katahdin, one of Thoreau's companions is "startled in his dreams by one of these sudden upblazings of a fallen fir whose green boughs were suddenly lighted by the wind sprang up with a cry from his spruce leaf couch—thinking the world afire and drew the whole camp after him" (PJ, 2:338). Thoreau, who had an all-too-real conversance with the ravages of a forest fire, may have had his anxieties intensified by his friend's dream of a "world afire." When he had awakened from a dream of trout fishing on an earlier night, there had "stood Katah-din" (PJ, 2:331), almost as if it were a continuation of the dream. And his description of the climbing of that imposing mountain itself has a mes-meric, dreamlike, sometimes nightmarish character. He ascends by him-self, his companions "lost" to his view, and after clambering up the for-midable and dangerous rockslide, he reaches the steppelike tableland, a stark and strange terrain, where he "entered within the skirts of the cloud which seemed forever drifting over the summit" (PJ, 2:339). Occasional-ly, there are some clearings in the clouds, but then all is enveloped in clouds once again. Seeking to penetrate the wilderness, he feels himself to be not only violator but violated. Here, beholding when he can the "vast titanic" scenery, he senses that "even some vital part [of the beholder] seems to es-cape through the loose grating of the ribs" and there is "less of fair calcula-tion & intellectual fullness than in the plains where men inhabit" (PJ, 2:339). In this foreboding, intimidating landscape, he no longer can feel any soothing kinship with wild nature: "Vast Titanic inhuman nature has got him at disadvantage caught him alone—& pilfers him" (PJ, 2:339). Even in characterizing the alienation of self from nature, however, Tho-reau "humanizes" nature, first as a feminine entity:

> She does not smile on him as in the plains— She seems to say sternly why came Ye here before your time— This ground is not prepared for. Is it not enough that I smile in the vallies I have never made this soil for thy feet, this air for thy breathing—these rocks for thy neighbors. I cannot pity thee then nor fondle thee here—but relentlessly drive thee where I am kind. Why seek me where I have not called you and then complain that I am not your genial mother. (PJ, 2:339–40)

Surely, it was frightening and chastening to realize that nature might not always be the nurturing mother. Significantly, the angry female entity also becomes a hostile male spirit. The tops of the mountains, which in the past were usually scenes of constructive challenge, expansion, and liberation for Thoreau, here become inhospitable, even vengeful; he wonders if it is "some slight insult to the Gods to climb and pry into their secrets" and then observes,

> Pomola whom the Penobscot consider as the evil genius of the mt—or God in his angry mood is ever angry with him who climbs here.
> For what canst thou pray here—but to be delivered from here.— And should thou freeze or starve—or shudder thy life away—here is no shrine nor altar—nor access to my ear. (PJ, 2:340)

Neither the Indian gods nor "God" offer blessings to Thoreau on the tableland below the Baxter summit of Katahdin. Any hopes of finding intimacy with his brother, or an alternative mother and father, have been crushed and replaced by an anxious sense of the disapproval, even wrath, of male and female figures. From an oedipal standpoint, it is particularly understandable why he did not try to climb all the way to the Baxter summit (he gave his companions' desire to return and the thick clouds as the overt reasons): to do so would be to pierce the veil and "enter within the skirts" of clouds, surmount male figures, and invite guilt and punishment.

This experience at Katahdin so alarmed and unhinged him that in "Katahdin" he appears to be momentarily unbalanced and uncharacteristically out of control; there is an "insanity of mood" less "slight" than that he was subject to when he felt lonely a few weeks after arriving at Walden. He speaks first of the "Earth . . . made out of Chaos and Old Night," of "Matter, vast terrific . . . the home this of Necessity and Fate," of "the presence of a force not bound to be kind to man. . . . to be inhabited by men nearer of kin to the rocks and to wild animals than we" (MW, 70–71). Then, in unusually disjointed and cryptic language, he continues,

> I stand in awe of my body, this matter to which I am bound has become so strange to me. I fear not spirits, ghosts, of which I am one —*that* my body might, —but I fear bodies, I tremble to meet them. What is this Titan that has possession of me? Talk of mysteries! —Think of our life in nature, —daily to be shown matter, to come in contact with it, —rocks, trees, wind on our cheeks! the *solid* earth! the *actual* world! the *common sense! Contact! Contact! Who* are we? *where* are we?" (MW, 70–71)

Here, Thoreau is not only alienated from nature but is also beside himself; the Katahdin episode clearly terrified and disoriented him, calling into question as it did the validity and solidity of the identity established at Walden and the legitimacy of his transcendental beliefs. The Maine woods, the *real* woods as opposed to Walden's, were intractable to human molding, imaginatively unmalleable and impenetrable. It was, in some sense, untouched and untouchable by human hands and minds.

Upon returning to the pastoral and human confines of Walden and Concord, Thoreau could not avoid modifying his perspectives. He was somewhat more willing to own up to the fact that he was more at home with the pastoral and civil than with the untamed and untamable wilderness. He still needed to know that the wilderness was "out there" and, furthermore, that he could, if he wished, return to it occasionally as an antidote to stagnation and smugness. But now he was more predisposed to admit—though this insight hardly remained a constant in subsequent years, as his memory of the nightmarish aspects of the Maine trip faded—

that it was the "tonic" of "wildness" that he craved. Not only could he turn to the actual wilderness for inspiration (even if that wilderness sometimes inspired trepidation), he could also try to redefine and relocate "wildness" as a quality of mind to which even outwardly civilized men might have access. In the first draft of *Walden,* he would write, "Our village life would stagnate, I think, if it were not for the unexplored forests and meadows which surround it. We need the tonic of wildness. . . . We need to witness our own limits transgressed, and some life pasturing freely where we never wander" (207). To be sure, he often diluted and backtracked from this realization—one which caused some bewilderment and anxiety for a man who relied so heavily on his intimacy with, and trust in, literal nature. Even in the "tonic" passage, he makes the sweeping and (in light of Katahdin) sentimentalized contention that "We can never have enough of nature" (207). The inconsistencies would remain and coexist; different versions of nature and wildness would gain the upper hand at certain times and under certain external and psychological circumstances.[32] While he would entertain various attitudes and stances toward nature and wildness, and while he was finally able to recover a sense of being "at home" in nature and with the wild, the search for "wildness" would in many ways be a frustrating one. The closer he approached wildness, the more elusive it was in some respects, because he always brought with him the sensibilities of a civilized man. The putting of pencil and pen to paper was, after all, an eminently civilized act, and wildness would remain in this regard something elusive and ineffable.[33]

In any event, it is evident that his view of wildness as "tonic," which he developed in the wake of Katahdin (though it did not then sink in completely or become a monolithic viewpoint), made it easier for him to contemplate leaving Walden; he could bring this tonic with him when he went back to the town. His 1847 correspondence with Louis Agassiz, the noted Swiss naturalist, and James Eliot Cabot reveals a man who has more of a proclivity to perceive nature through a distinctively human and collegial prism. Thus was Thoreau able to incorporate, however shakily and subtly, into his identity an acknowledgment of his civilized side that made the leaving of Walden emotionally feasible. Indeed, the Maine woods journey made salient another flaw in the Walden life structure: he could no longer boast so confidently to others—or claim to himself—that he was living in the wilderness at Walden. In Maine he had seen the actual "life in the woods"; it would be a relief not to have to maintain, in his daily life at least, that he was living in the wilderness while at the pond.

Furthermore, the attempted penetration of, and confrontation with, elemental wilderness had stirred up many disturbing emotions associated with his brother and other family members. If he had sought his brother's spirit in the nature and Indians of Maine, or expected nature to be a "genial mother," he had been severely shaken by what he had found. If anything, the Maine excursion had reactivated some of the anxieties that the stay at Walden had managed to allay. It was almost as if his own family had rejected him. Viewed in this light, returning to Concord, even further removed from the wilderness than Walden, was a way to make himself even less vulnerable to the psychic threats posed by an untamed, seemingly hostile nature.

The Maine woods trip, then, played a significant role in destabilizing the Walden life structure and identity. It is likely, however, that the impetus to leave Walden was, as has already been suggested, provided most emphatically by the successes of the Walden experiment. Levinson observes, "A [developmental] period begins when its major tasks become predominant in a man's life" and ends "when its tasks lose their primacy and new tasks emerge to initiate a new period."[34] Whatever flaws or threats started to become apparent after the first year or so at Walden, the fact remained that Thoreau had constructed a new life and sense of self that he hoped and expected would serve as the basis for further growth and achievement after he left the pond. He had managed to create an early adult life structure he could believe was his own and had been built on his own terms; now it was time to move on to other tasks and challenges of early adulthood.

Perhaps most crucially, Thoreau was now as emotionally and pragmatically prepared and positioned as he would ever be to pursue a writing career, one presumably modeled to some degree on Emerson's career. One of the early emotional blocks to aggressive pursuit of such a career had been his deep-seated reluctance to gain success and thereby supersede both brother and father. At Walden he had managed, to an unprecedented degree, to purge himself of the guilt and anxiety associated with his brother's death. Writing two drafts of *A Week* (the first in 1845 and the second in early 1847)[35] had been especially therapeutic in this regard. Of course, as the Maine trip demonstrated, the menacing emotions were still there, in a state of semiremission but capable of flaring up under certain circumstances. The conflict between initiative and guilt still lurked in the psyche and was still potentially the source of profound ambivalence, but at some point between 1845 and 1847 the scales were tipped in the direction of initiative and ambition. With the grief and guilt so far subsided, if not absolutely dormant, he was no longer so emotionally held back from his ambitions to make it in the literary world, to become the recognized "great man" he had always, on some level, yearned to be.

The Walden period had given him confidence in his writing abilities;

there he had miraculously expanded as a writer and experienced an enormous burst of productivity; he completed most of *A Week*, the first draft of *Walden*, essays on Carlyle and Katahdin (published with Greeley's help), and he kept religiously at work on his journal, the source book for so much of his formal writing. In his final year at the pond, he was growing more anxious, beginning to strain at the bit, to build another less provisional and more permanent life structure, to "settle down" more decisively than he had at Walden. This project involved such tasks as "establishing a niche in society" and "planning, striving to succeed, moving onward and upward, progressing along a timetable." One important but often unacknowledged component of his dream, one piece of unfinished business— that of vocational consolidation and advancement—had yet to be played or lived out, and he was hungry for the experience. "A man has devoted himself until the early thirties," Levinson says, "to creating a foundation on which the [career] ladder can be built."[36] He allowed himself to hope that the Walden period had provided such a foundation, on which he could build and climb a ladder to the stars. He had paid his dues.

Of course, Thoreau remained resistant to the image of himself as a "man on the make" and was critical of shallow gestures or lockstep measures to secure rank. As he writes in December 1846, "As the youth studied minutely the order and the degrees in the imperial procession and suffered none of its effect to be lost on him—so the man at last secured a rank in society which satisfied his notion of fitness & respectability." In the process, he "was defrauded of so much which the savage boy enjoys" (PJ, 2:356). But shortly thereafter he seems to be preparing the ground for what he sees as his own peculiar and authentic form of advancement: "Let the youth seize upon the finest and most memorable experience in his life—that which most reconciled him to his unknown destiny—and seek to discover in it his future path. Let him be sure that that way is his only true and worthy career" (PJ, 2:357). Walden, it may be concluded, was the "finest and most memorable experience" in *his* life, one that helped immensely with the work of reconciliation, and he had used that "experiment" to "discover his future path." The path around Walden was becoming worn; with the assurance that he had found "his only true and worthy career" and an identity that would sustain and promote his literary craft, he was more than ever ready to settle down to the writing career he had dreamed of. It was a career that would fulfill his sense of destiny.

Thoreau's 1847 correspondence reveals a young man who was now more and more preoccupied with "business" matters, more determined than previously to gain a foothold in the literary world. A letter of January 14, apparently to Evert Duyckinck of Wiley and Putnam, indicates that he had already sent out one draft of *A Week* and wanted it returned for some revisions (C, 173). Horace Greeley, editor of the *New York Tribune*, who made something of a career of judiciously helping aspiring writers and who would become a key career coach and sponsor for Thoreau in the post-Walden period,[37] wrote him in February that his essay on Carlyle would be *"the leading article"* in a soon-to-appear issue of *Graham's Magazine* (C, 173–74). Perhaps responding to what he perceived to be Thoreau's anxiety to get his article published as soon as possible, or apologizing for the tardiness of the placement, he advised him that the delay was worth it: "It is immensely more important to you that the article should appear thus (that is, if you have any literary aspirations) than it is that you should make a few dollars by issuing it in some other way." Clearly, Greeley saw this promising young man, a protégé of the renowned Emerson, as one with serious "literary aspirations" and welcomed the opportunity to show him the ropes of publishing and alert him as to how he could maximize his chances of getting published. Probably answering an inquiry from the eager-to-learn Thoreau, he says, "As to lecturing, you have been at perfect liberty to deliver it ["Carlyle"] as a lecture a hundred times if you had chosen—the more the better" (C, 174). He also offered money for articles on Emerson and Hawthorne. Harding and Bode speculate that he probably did not write these articles "because he did not wish to profit by his friendship for them" (C, 175); in a more general sense, it may be surmised that the prospect of writing an article evaluating such a "significant other" and career sponsor as Emerson was far too uncomfortable, even intimidating. A March 1 letter from Henry Williams, the secretary of his Harvard class of 1837, which asked Thoreau to fill out a questionnaire regarding marriage, profession, residence, and the other trappings of established young adulthood, may well have been threatening and may have further impelled him to get on with the tasks of establishing himself in society. He would not answer the letter until after he left Walden.

In a March 12 letter to Duyckinck, Emerson extolled the virtues of *A Week*:

> The book has many merits. It will be as attractive to *lovers of nature*, in every sense, that is, to naturalists, and to poets, as Isaak Walton. It will be attractive to scholars for its excellent literature, & to all thoughtful persons for its originality & profoundness. The narrative of the little voyage, though faithful, is a very slender thread for such big beads & ingots as are strung on it. It is really a book of the results of studies of years. (L, III:384)

While Thoreau, if he had known the contents of this letter, might have been uncomfortable with the equivocation in Emerson's analysis, he was no doubt grateful that such a figure was throwing his considerable weight behind the book. Duyckinck agreed to consider the manuscript. Seeking to polish the book—perhaps reluctant to let it go and wanting to remain in control—Thoreau did not send it to Duyckinck until May 28, but at that point he was hoping for prompt action from Wiley and Putnam. Time and timing were becoming more pressing issues. "I will remind you," he writes to Duyckinck, "to save time, that I wish to be informed for what term the book is to be the property of the publishers, and on what terms I can have 30 copies cheaply bound in boards without immediate expense. —If you take it—It will be a great convenience to me to get through with the printing as soon as possible, as I wish to take a journey of considerable length and should not be willing that any other than myself should correct the proofs" (c, 181). Harding tells us that Emerson, "learning of Thoreau's restlessness" while at the pond, tried to arrange with Charles T. Jackson, his brother-in-law, that Thoreau be allowed to accompany and assist his government-sponsored survey of Michigan's mineral lands.[38] Even though he was beginning to chafe at the bit to find an acceptable way to leave Walden, and even though this Michigan expedition would have given him a gracious exit and frontiersman credentials, it may be questioned how enthusiastic he was about the prospect of leaving Concord at this time. After all, he had a history of homesickness and disorientation when away from Concord, he had frequently denigrated geographical traveling, and his disquieting experience in the wilds of Maine was still relatively fresh in his mind. Probably even more important, he was eager to concentrate on consolidating his writing career, instead of removing himself even farther from the circles of influence and opportunities to refine his craft. It would, then, probably be most accurate to conclude that he was ambivalent about going off to Michigan. Perhaps the acceptance of *A Week*, proof that his career was well underway, would have made it easier to consider a hiatus. In any event, the job did not materialize, possibly because of a lack of political connections,[39] or because Thoreau simply was not enthusiastic about pursuing it.

Meanwhile, his publishing fortunes had not improved. After even more revisions and Duyckinck's recommendation that *A Week* be published, Wiley and Putnam first stalled and then eventually offered to print it, but only—as Thoreau would report in a November 14 letter to Emerson in Europe—at the author's own risk (c, 191). An obviously impatient and exasperated Thoreau wrote to Duyckinck on July 27, "If Messrs. Wiley & Putnam are not prepared to give their answer now, will you please inform me what further delay, if any, is unavoidable, that I may determine whether I had not better carry it elsewhere—for time is of great consequence to

me" (c, 184). His concern about time may still have been related to the
Michigan trip, but it is more likely that his rush to publish was associated
with his desire to follow an internal timetable; it was important that the
book be accepted, if at all possible, before he left the pond, so that he could
return to Concord in some triumph, having secured tangible evidence of
the success of his stay there and his right to be respected by the community
as a productive adult. Both Alcott and Emerson encouraged him to believe
that his timetable could be met, that the book would be welcomed by other
publishers. Trying to beat the clock before he sailed to England, Emerson
wrote on August 6 to William Henry Furness of Philadelphia, hoping his
friend might pull some strings with publishers in that area. He made the
book sound like an expanded travel essay;[40] perhaps this was in part a ploy
to make *A Week* appear more marketable, though it also seems to have reflected his shifting estimation of the book. Nothing came of Furness's efforts. On August 28, still clinging to the dream of making a grand reen-
trance into Concord, Thoreau, who by this time had submitted his manuscript to James Munroe and Co. and received an offer comparable to Wiley
and Putnam's, suggested that he would pay Munroe back half of the costs
outstanding *"at the end of six months after the day of publication"* (c,
185). He was not above slipping a comparison with Emerson into the letter
("The book is about the size of one vol of Emerson's essays").[41] But this
proposal, too, bore no fruit. Still, there were other irons in the fire—Cros-
by and Nichols and Harpers' at least—when Thoreau left the pond.[42]
Emerson wrote Margaret Fuller on August 29 that Thoreau was "on the
point of concluding the contract for *A Week*" (L, III:413). While the book
had not yet been published or even accepted on satisfactory terms, there is
no question but that Thoreau anticipated the inevitable positive response
from a publisher that would finally insure his position on the ladder of a
bona fide literary career.

With the matter of *A Week*'s publication still up in the air but apparently
near resolution, Thoreau left Walden Pond on September 6, 1847. Emerson, planning to sail for Liverpool in early October, wrote to his brother
William on August 30, "Lidian has invited Henry Thoreau to spend the
winter here" (L, III:415). It must have been perceived as a stroke of good
luck and synchronicity when Lidian requested he stay with her and the
children while her husband went off to Europe for an extended period.
Thoreau was ready for a change, perhaps especially before the onset of another winter. Indeed, he may have responded to Lidian's invitation with
some measure of relief and gratitude; it gave him "permission" to leave,

a socially legitimate and even face-saving pretext for a move he had no doubt been contemplating for some time before the invitation. The imminent conclusion of the Mexican War also may have made the return more feasible and palatable. He had seized the opportunity provided by his mentor Emerson's purchase of land by Walden Pond in the autumn of 1844 to move away—but not too far away—from Concord, and just in the nick of time too with respect to his developmental needs. Just as, back in 1841, Emerson's stately white house on Lexington Road had served as a sort of halfway house, a means by which he could slowly disengage from reliance on family and eventually "go . . . and live away by the pond" (PJ, 1:347),[43] so now was it fitting that the Emersons had offered him a way station, a sort of decompression chamber, allowing for a gradual return to civilized life and his family. The invitation thus preempted any whispered or imagined accusations from skeptical townspeople and avoided any lurking self-accusations that the Walden experiment had only been a histrionic gesture, or that he was going directly from his cocky but questionable independence at Walden to the safe nest of home and mother. At the Emersons', living in the small room at the top of the stairs, he would be the "man of the house." It was a role he felt unusually prepared to assume, having affirmed his "manhood" at Walden and now intent on settling down even more solidly. Before long, however, "settling down" would become deeply unsettling.

3 A Sojourner in Civilized Life Again

HE transition from sojourner at Walden to "sojourner in civilized life again," as he referred to himself in an 1849 version of *Walden*,[1] was not as smooth or uncomplicated as Thoreau had hoped. Ensconced at the Emersons', with Waldo sailing for England within a week, he found himself tempted to hang on to the Walden identity and persona when he finally got around to answering Henry Williams's questionnaire—the only time he ever did respond to any invitations from the class of 1837.[2] Of his occupation he writes, "I dont know whether mine is a profession, or a trade, or what not. It is not yet learned and in every instance has been practised before being studied. . . . It is not one but legion. I will give you some of the monster's heads. I am a Schoolmaster—a Private Tutor, a Surveyor —a Gardener, a Farmer—a Painter, a Carpenter, a Mason, a Day-Laborer, a Pencil-Maker, a Glass-paper Maker, a Writer, and sometimes a Poetaster." He goes on to claim, "I have found out a way to live without what is commonly called employment or industry attractive or otherwise. Indeed my steadiest employment, if such it can be called, is to keep myself at the top of my condition, and ready for whatever may turn up in heaven or on earth. For the last two or three years I have lived in Concord woods alone, something more than a mile from any neighbor, in a house built entirely by myself" (c, 185–86). He does not mention that he is living at the Emersons' and therefore not as self-sufficient and self-employed as he suggests. It is revealing that he waffles about the length of time he spent at Walden, perhaps wishfully and wistfully stretching two years and two months to as much as three years. In making his claims he follows a characteristic pattern: when most obviously back in "civilized life," he tended to be more rebellious, more on the defensive, more sensitive to the anticipated or imagined criticisms of his neighbors and contemporaries. Moreover, he does not indicate the extent to which he *was* deeply involved in cultivating his career. Possibly he was uneasy because he could still not, on September 30, 1847, point victoriously to conspicuous success in getting *A Week* published. Already he may have been beginning to develop cold feet about investing so much of himself in the risky project of advancing his literary career. And there must have been occasions when, out of his Walden element, he felt like a fish out of the water. Thus the letter to Williams was, in part, a means of protecting his emotional flanks. He may well have started to ask himself how he could have felt the way he had just a short month ago, when the decision to leave the pond had seemed so right.

Thoreau was clearly not prepared for the setbacks to, and disappointments of, his writing career in the first months of his stay at the Emersons'. Nor was he quite ready for the progressively more uneasy sentiments associated with Emerson,[3] Waldo's long absence, and his assumption of the position of "man of the house." Reporting on October 24 to his sister Sophia, then visiting in Maine, on Emerson's departure for England, he implies some criticism of his mentor's actions: "instead of a walk in Walden woods he will take a promenade on deck where the few trees, you know, are stripped of their bark" (c, 187). Aside from possible veiled self-criticism—he himself had, after all, left Walden woods to "go before the mast and on the deck of the world"—the suggestion is that Emerson is not being entirely true to his own precepts, that he is forgoing absolutes for superficialities. When he instructs Sophia to tell "the whole Penobscot tribe" that "I trust we are good brothers still, and endeavor to keep the chain of friendship bright, though I do dig up a hatchet now and then" (c, 188), one wonders if, in the absence of real Indians, he is drawn to them again, wishes to reassert a fraternal intimacy, but also cannot avoid digging up the hatchet with respect to his friendship with Emerson and his brother-Indian, John Jr. Certainly the 1847–49 period would mark a serious crossroads in his relationship with Waldo and would reawaken buried anxieties connected to his brother.

It is not farfetched to suggest that Thoreau was counting heavily on Emerson to sponsor his career. After all, Waldo was a highly influential American writer, and his successful career as a man of letters (though also subsidized and supplemented by the inheritance from his first wife, Ellen Tucker Emerson) helped Thoreau to feel that such a vocation might be within his reach. While he may have been thankful that Emerson had encouraged him, affirmed the importance of "patiencehood,"[4] provided him with the land to squat on at Walden, wrote letters on his behalf to further his career, and—by going to Europe—offered him a chance to return with dignity to Concord, the fact was that Emerson, for all his perceived power and connections, had not been able to help him get the book upon which he had staked his career published. Indeed, just when Thoreau may well have felt he needed Emerson the most to promote his interests, Waldo had (as he saw it) deserted him for Europe. Before leaving he had written one last letter to his brother William, hoping he would investigate New York publishers for *A Week,* but this attempt too had come to naught. No doubt Emerson was at least embarrassed by his failure to aid Thoreau decisively; he was probably uncomfortable in Thoreau's company under these circumstances. To leave such a problem behind was in some way to have a weight taken off his shoulders. If Thoreau had once regarded Emerson with awe and gratitude, he was now vulnerable to feelings of disillusionment, resentment, disappointment—emotions that are very frequently inevitable in some degree for both participants in a mentor relationship[5] and that would gather momentum in the coming months and years. He could not resist harboring secret feelings of outrage at Emerson's seeming laxness or impotence at this critical juncture, and he was subject to competitive sentiments. There was Emerson, popular, even world-renowned, invited to England to give a series of lectures. While he was over in Europe, enhancing his reputation and advancing his already substantial career, Thoreau was back in Concord, his dream of a writing career, and a life structure based on it, jeopardized. "News of Emerson's reception," indicates Gay Wilson Allen, "led Henry Thoreau to suppose he was triumphant wherever he went."[6] In the meantime, Thoreau was becoming increasingly sensitive to whisperings that he was but a second-rate imitator, a satellite, of Emerson. One woman who met him at an Alcott Conversation in Boston on January 15, 1848, recorded her impressions: "Thorault [sic] amused me. . . . He is all overlaid by an imitation of Emerson; talks like him, puts out his arm like him, brushes his hair in the same way, and is even getting up a caricature nose like Emerson's."[7] Such invidious comparisons, if and when they reached his ears, must have cut to the quick and increased his resentment. Not only was Emerson not providing the proper nurturance, he was casting his shadow over him. Compounding his disenchantment was Waldo's apparent willingness, even eagerness, to leave behind not only him but his sickly wife and the children who needed him to go gallivanting on the Continent.

It would probably have offered the uneasy Thoreau little solace to know that his previous idol was himself feeling "bored and dissatisfied with his life in the spring of 1847"[8] and that his trip to England was a means of mitigating restlessness, seeking renewal in the face of creative and personal stagnation, and, in general, experiencing some form of midlife crisis. The timing was just not right: Emerson did not have the emotional resources or inclination to be a strong mentor for Thoreau at this point. He was, among other things, probably tired of the pressures of responsible mentorship. Indeed, Waldo was hoping to reestablish contact with one of *his* heroes and mentors, Carlyle, but was disappointed with what he found. Carlyle "talks like a very unhappy man," he wrote to Lidian.[9] It is also not wholly fanciful to speculate that Emerson was threatened by his protégé's relative youth, promise, and apparent commitment to practice what he preached—a commitment that Emerson, now increasingly linked to the Establishment he had once excoriated, may have felt defensive about, unable to live up to. In the summer of 1847, he had revealed a cooler attitude toward Thoreau in his journal, in part associated with the latter's combativeness and inability to lift his subdued spirits: "T sometimes appears only as a gen d'arme[,] good to knock down a cockney with, but without that power to cheer & establish which makes the value of a friend" (JMN, X:106–7). What had once appeared to Waldo as virtues—Thoreau's refusal to compromise, to countenance lapses in concentration and commitment—were now coming to be seen as liabilities and limitations. His barbed wit and his refusal to give quarter to laxness, qualities Waldo had once admired, were now less appreciated. Thoreau was overzealous, intolerant, as in his criticisms of novels: "You do us great wrong, Henry T[horeau][,] in railing at the novel reading. The novel is that allowance & frolic their imagination gets. Everything else pins it down" (JMN, X:48). His younger counterpart, in general terms, was showing unwelcome signs of independence; he did not seem to want unhesitatingly to heed his advice. Emerson could not help questioning whether Thoreau would ever live up to his dreams for him; and the judgments of publishers concerning *A Week* seemed to be confirming these evolving suspicions.

It is altogether likely that Thoreau was deeply ambivalent about Emerson, and vice versa, by the time he sailed for England, and this ambivalence can be detected in the correspondence. Thoreau's letters combined an overtly friendly bantering and joshing with some underlying anxiety and anger, even depression. Humor sometimes allowed the freedom of expressing bottled-up negative emotions that serious language would not permit. Certainly there *was* a serious undertone to the correspondence; more was going on than a cursory glance would indicate. The extent to which Thoreau, at this point, was consciously able to own up to his ambivalence is an open question; to be sure, he may have had some difficulty facing the threatening emotions and no doubt sought to repress or suppress them. In any event, the ambivalence, the psychological dynamics of his feelings about Emerson and his relation to him, did begin to seep through in the letters. It would at least gradually dawn on him, over the ensuing months, how very mixed his feelings for Waldo were.

In his remarkable first letter, of November 14, to Emerson in England, he begins by lamenting the intractability of the civilized society to which he had returned, a society to which, one may infer, Emerson's absence and lack of support made it even more difficult to adjust. "The world," he says, "is a cow that is hard to milk, —life does not come so easy, —and oh, how thinly it is watered ere we get it! But the young hunting calf, he will get it! . . . There is no way so direct. This is to earn one's living by the sweat of his brow. It is a little like joining a community, this life, to such a hermit as I am; and I don't keep the accounts, I don't know whether the experiment will succeed or fail finally" (c, 188–89). Clearly, the "experiment" of living at the Emersons' and returning to civilized life was more in doubt without Emerson's presence and active support. Thoreau then turns his attention to the family, commenting that "Lidian and I make very good housekeepers. She is a very dear sister to me." In part, this seems to be a backhand way of saying that the house is functioning well without Emerson. But Thoreau's reference to his brother-sister relationship with Lidian may have been a way to deny to Emerson—and to himself—that she was anything *more* than a sister to him. After all, only four years earlier, he had expressed an ardor bordering on love for Emerson's wife, and only Lidian's discouragement of his fervent confessions of affection had overtly dampened a fire that may have had an element of latent romance in it.[10] The lukewarm, comparatively unpassionate nature of Lidian's marriage to Waldo may, in 1847, have aroused Thoreau's sense that in some way Lidian continued to be "available" or at least attracted to him.[11] Waldo was not, it seemed, meeting her needs. In fact, Emerson implies in a Christmas Day letter from Manchester that Lidian was dissatisfied with her husband's lack of intimacy in his letters. Pleading busyness, he writes, "I fear that I shall not be able at this time to write you yet, those full and 'private' letters, which you so rightfully demand" (L, III:454). Obviously, the situation Thoreau was in—a substitute husband and father for a man who was already a father figure[12]—may have troubled him by activating the oedipal anxieties he experienced in his own household, with his attractive and assertive mother and his relatively passive, even "psychologically absent" father, and with his rivalry with John Jr. for Ellen Sewall. That he was engaged in a submerged but very real competition with Emerson for literary status and recognition could only serve to exacerbate severely the oedipal tensions engendered by his present living arrangement. He was still a "junior" to Emerson's "senior," an apprentice to the master, but he had designs on eventually becoming an acknowledged senior and master himself. Thus, while he did derive enjoyment from being head of the Emerson household (and took particular delight in being "father" to Waldo's children), during this period he was also susceptible to feelings that he was challenging a father figure on his own professional turf, that he wished to compete with and defeat this father, that—especially in his father's absence—he was succeeding in winning the mother. A gradually developing hostility to Emerson increased exponentially the guilt and anxiety generated by his living situation. That Thoreau was to some degree conscious of the implications of living with Lidian and the children is evident in his report on his relationship with young Edward Emerson, who "very seriously asked me, the other day, 'Mr. Thoreau, will you be my father?' I am occasionally Mr. Rough-and-tumble with him that I may not miss *him,* and lest he should not miss *you* too much. So you must come back soon, or you will be superseded" (C, 189). While articulated in the lightest and most genteel modulations, it is evident that Thoreau is castigating, taunting Waldo for abandoning his responsibilities as a father (not only to Edward but to himself) and putting himself in the position of superseding the father, a role he liked in many ways but which also spurred anxieties. That he comments in this November 14 letter on the proposal of marriage he received from Sophia Ford also suggests subterranean misgivings. He writes, "How could I deliberate upon it? I sent back as distinct a *no* as I have learned to pronounce after considerable practice, and I trust that this *no* has succeeded. Indeed, I wished that it might burst, like hollow shot, after it had struck and buried itself and made itself felt there. *There was no other way.* I really had anticipated no such foe as this in my career" (C, 190–91). Perhaps it was important for him to get permission not to marry from his mentor and remind him that his first priority was his literary career. Or perhaps this is Thoreau's attempt to defuse an emotionally explosive situation, to assure Waldo and himself that he was not attracted to women, sexuality, and marriage and therefore was no threat to take over for his father figure as husband and father. Certainly, there is some overkill in his wish that his refusal "might burst, like hollow shot, after it had struck." Another possible, though unintended, inference was that he preferred the housekeeping arrangement with Lidian over marriage to other women. One unrecognized irony was that he could not have anticipated that Emerson himself would be such a "foe" in his career—or in his desire for intimacy with a woman.

Having left the Walden hut in the late summer of 1847, Thoreau may have been at least secretly dismayed by the task of helping Bronson Alcott build a summer house for Emerson. "I feel a little oppressed when I come near it," he says. Alcott was one of the few older men with whom he felt comfortable, yet in the letter of November 14 Thoreau suggests that even

Alcott does not fully understand him: "He forgets that I am neither old nor young, nor anything in particular, and behaves as if I still had some of the animal heat in me" (C, 189). In a covert way, he may also have been displacing feelings that Emerson misunderstood him onto Alcott. His mention of Hugh Whelan, who was considering purchasing—and would soon do so—the hut at Walden (which Emerson had bought from Thoreau),[13] taken together with the erecting of Waldo's summer house, points to what may have been Thoreau's incipient regrets about leaving the pond. His own hut about to be sold for the second time, a house going up for Emerson, his halfway-house existence at Emerson's home: these facts may have highlighted for him the autonomy he had given up in returning to Concord —and in response to Waldo's vacating the premises at that! Indeed, Thoreau hints, perhaps with a tinge of accusation, that he is drifting or creatively stagnating: "I do not know what to say of myself. I sit before my green desk, in the chamber at the head of the stairs, and attend to my thinking, sometimes more, sometimes less distinctly. I am not unwilling to think great thoughts, if there are any in the wind, but what they are I am not sure. They suffice to keep me awake while my day lasts, at any rate. Perhaps they will redeem some portion of the night erelong" (C, 191). The foundation he had built at Walden now, like the Walden hut itself, seemed to have a precarious future.

A most telltale sign in the November 14 letter of Thoreau's state of mind is his mention of his publishing efforts. About the book he has nothing new or "worthwhile" to say. Several publishers, he notes, have "declined printing it with the least risk to themselves; but Wiley & Putnam will print it in their series, and any of them, anywhere, at *my* risk. If I liked the book well enough, I should not delay; but for the present I am indifferent. I believe this is, after all, the course you advised, —to let it lie"(C, 191). Toward the end of this first transatlantic letter, he discusses politics, observing that "some men have signed a long pledge, swearing that they will 'treat all mankind as brothers henceforth.' I think that I shall wait and see how they treat me first. I think that nature meant kindly when she made our brothers few" (C, 192). While he speaks overtly in jest, it is clear enough that Thoreau was exceedingly sensitive to how he was being treated by society and how he was regarded by his "brothers," including Emerson.

One can imagine Thoreau's consternation when he received a reply in Emerson's December 2, 1847, letter. If he thought he was following his mentor's advice in "letting it lie," he had badly misunderstood him, or been badly misled, for Waldo writes, "I am not of opinion that your book should be delayed a month. I should print it at once, nor do I think that you would incur any risk in doing so that you cannot well afford. It is very certain to have readers & debtors here as well as there. The Dial is absurdly well known here" (C, 195). It is hard to avoid the conclusion that Thoreau must have felt like a fool, telling his mentor he was heeding his counsel and then learning that Emerson supposedly had advised nothing of the sort, or was contradicting earlier advice he could not recall having given. At the very least he must have been confused, and at the most quite angry; obviously, they had missed signals, and Thoreau could not avoid apportioning some or all of the blame for the misunderstanding to Emerson. It is, in any event, difficult to accept at face value Thoreau's characterization of "indifference" regarding the publication of *A Week*. On the contrary, he wanted above almost anything else to further his career with the book, and perhaps he claimed indifference as a defense, in part a reversion to the Walden identity, against overeagerness, ambition, and disappointment. And he *thought* Emerson had given him permission to be indifferent for a time. Now he felt both internal and external pressure to keep pushing *A Week*. It is not entirely surprising, therefore, that Thoreau rebelled against Emerson's most recent advice, sought refuge from further immediate rejections and blows to the ego, and recognized belatedly his desire to "improve" the book by proclaiming a moratorium on efforts to publish *A Week*. By the end of 1847, he informed James Munroe and Co., "I do not intend to print *my book* anywhere immediately" (C, 198). Of course, the hurtful rejections by publishers—which he no doubt took to heart without much other support—forced him to reevaluate his work and consider how he might polish it. But also, with his nostalgia for the relative insulation and exhilaration of the Walden experience growing more insistent, he may have wished, as he would with *Walden,* to hold on indefinitely to the book and the identity and vision it embodied. Letting go of *A Week* might have meant letting go of the strength and solace provided by both pond and book. Moreover, there were insidious stirrings of guilt associated with competition with Emerson for literary recognition, the slow ebbing away of the sense of purity he had regained at the pond, and the aggressive pursuit of tangible literary success.

Other aspects of Emerson's early December letter may also have agitated Thoreau. Waldo's infatuation and intoxication with London and England upset and disillusioned Thoreau, who had usually been a critic of cities, machines, industrialization, and standardization. Waldo writes,

Everything centralizes, in this magnificent machine which England is. Manufacturer for the world she is become or becoming one complete tool or engine in herself. —Yesterday the *time* all over the kingdom was reduced to Green-

wich time. At Liverpool, where I was, the clocks were put forward 12 minutes.
This had become quite necessary on account of the railroads which bind the
whole country into swiftest connexion, and require so much accurate interlocking, intersection, & simultaneous arrival, that the difference of time produced confusion. Every man in England carries a little book in his pocket
called "Bradshaws Guide," which contains time tables of arrival & departure
at every station on all railroads of the kingdom. (C, 194)

The revolution Emerson *now* seemed taken by was the Industrial Revolution. Not only would such a celebration of these aspects of England have
irritated the self-proclaimed, defensively sedentary "traveller in Concord"
and enemy of the artificial and socially reified, but it also might have cast
serious doubt on whether Emerson remained truly supportive of his vision
and values. Since Emerson's letters to Lidian were not "private" (though
she obviously wished some of them had been) but were intended to be
shared, Thoreau indubitably had access to the many long, newsy, breathlessly detailed, and fascinated letters Waldo wrote about his sojourn in a
highly civilized, refined, cultivated England.[14] If Thoreau had thought he
could somehow fit into civilized society again when he left Walden, his distaste for the civil may have been reawakened by Emerson's infatuation
with it. In this context, it is likely he lost some respect for the man who had
inspired him with *Nature,* "The American Scholar," and "Self-Reliance":
Emerson was selling out to the very Establishment he had once attacked so
vigorously. Possibly the most stunning blow was Emerson's reference to
the "Pleasaunce at Walden" in the context of Hugh Whelan's remodeling
problems with the hut. (In a January 12, 1848, letter to Waldo, he reports
that Whelan was drinking, unhappy with his wife, and had left Concord
with the Walden remodeling incomplete [C, 203].) Such diction, even if
partly in jest, could have suggested to Thoreau that his friend simply had
not understood, or was devaluing the importance—beyond pleasure or
leisure—of the Walden experience. These must have been times that accentuated the loss of Walden and when Thoreau may even have fantasized
buying back the hut and returning to the pond.

   To be sure, there is considerable charm, wit, and apparent good will
in his letters to Emerson. On December 29, two days after withdrawing his
book from publication consideration (and therefore not following Emerson's counsel), he writes, "I . . . shall not trouble you with my complaints
because I do not fill my place better. I have had many good hours in the
chamber at the head of the stairs—a solid time, it seems to me." Rather
than directly "complaining" or confronting him, Thoreau simply informs
him of his latest professional activity—the lecture he will be giving to the

Lyceum on his "expedition to Maine." There is, in addition, an affectionate discussion of his relationship with Ellen, Edith, and Eddie, though the account could not avoid reminding Emerson that he was neglecting his parental duties.

Toward the end of this last letter of 1847, Thoreau includes a poem, "The Good how can we trust?" (C, 199–200), which he incorporated into the lecture he was then, significantly, working on. Then, in his first correspondence of 1848, on January 12 (the day after the sixth anniversary of his brother's death), he reports to Waldo in his "historical fairyland," "I have also written what will do for a lecture on Friendship" (C, 204). It is impossible to ignore that at the time he was in the process of beginning to reevaluate Emerson and his friendship with him. In fact, his renewed interest in the subject can probably be precisely linked to his conflicting feelings about his mentor. The "Wednesday" chapter of *A Week* had been devoted largely to an exposition on friendship and intimacy, and the "Friendship" lecture—which he would incorporate into the final version of the book— was an expansion and revision of that original discussion. The "Friendship" segment of *A Week* had initially constituted, among other things, an attempt to perform grief work with respect to John, and Thoreau's burgeoning ambivalence toward Emerson reawakened some of the guilt and anxiety that had haunted him regarding his brother. If John had been a major "Friend," so was Waldo. Such comments as "What avails it that another loves you, if he does not understand you?" and "I have a Friend who wishes me to see that to be right which I know to be wrong" (*Week*, 278, 282) may very well have been aimed at Emerson. Thus, when he worked on expanding the "Friendship" essay, he was vulnerable to the threatening and complicated emotions he had sought to lay permanently to rest at Walden. That the lecture was probably never delivered (C, 205) suggests that its content may have been too intimate and intimidating for a public presentation to his townspeople. Among the observations not in *A Week*'s first draft[15] but appearing in the book's final version is one concerning the "sternest tragedy in the relation of two who are more than usually innocent and true to their highest instincts" (*Week*, 276). At another point he writes, "Faults are not the less faults because they are invariably balanced by corresponding virtues, and for a fault there is no excuse" (*Week*, 282). "The only danger in Friendship," he remarks elsewhere, "is that it will end. It is a delicate plant though a native. The least unworthiness, even if it be unknown to one's self, vitiates it" (*Week*, 277). Perhaps the most dramatic statement (though originating in the early 1840s) is a poem, "Let such pure hate underprop/Our love," the last stanza of which says, "Implacable is Love,—/Foes may be bought or teazed/From their hostile in-

tent,/But he goes unappeased,/Who is on kindness bent" (*Week*, 289).
Surely such characterizations of friendship drew on, or applied to, not only
earlier experiences with friends (especially John) but also, quite heavily,
his recent experience with Emerson and his current jaundiced view of civilized society. No matter how he tried through convoluted logic and paradox to resolve his ambivalence in a positive manner, he was subject to
unsettling anxieties as his relationship to Emerson changed; his communi-
cations with Waldo, however loving, were "underpropped" by hate.

While Thoreau might have hoped his return to Concord would calm
the disquieting whispers of anxiety and guilt he had heard in the wilds of
Maine, and while he presumed he had done sufficient penance at Walden,
he was on some level becoming cognizant that his sojourn in civilized life
was insidiously contributing to the loss of serenity. "Civil Disobedience,"
or, as it was first entitled, "Resistance to Civil Government," was very
much of a piece with the concerns of this period, when Thoreau was again
feeling defensive, experiencing blocks to his career, questioning his return
to civilized society, and—whether or not he could fully face it on a conscious level—growing ever more disenchanted with Emerson. He first delivered the lecture, which had been incubating since his one-night stay in
jail eighteen months earlier, in public on January 26, 1848, in the same
month he completed his troubled essay on friendship. A few weeks later he
presented it again at the Lyceum, probably adding another installment or
revision.[16] At the time of his arrest in July 1846, Emerson, according to
Bronson Alcott's journal, commented that Thoreau's action was "mean
and skulking, and in bad taste."[17] Paul Hourihan speculates that "Thoreau would inevitably have received Emerson's precise response, since he
and Alcott were in frequent touch during this period and, moreover, Alcott
the social crusader not only *disagreed* with Emerson's views on this vis-
ceral subject but three years earlier, though escaping a jail-stay, had refused to pay the poll tax himself."[18] Whether or not Alcott passed on
Emerson's biting comment is a matter of conjecture (though the Concord
rumor mill was always churning). It is interesting in this light that, in his
January 12 letter to Emerson, Thoreau—perhaps making an implied comparison with Waldo—praises Alcott as "certainly the youngest man of his
age we have seen" (C, 204). Emerson's journal entries in July of 1846 reveal him to be more ambivalent and—patronizingly—tolerant of his fiery
friend's behavior. While he advises, "Don't run amuck against the world.
. . . It is the part of a fanatic to fight out a revolution on the shape of a hat or
surplice," he also states, "The abolitionists ought to resist & go to prison
in multitudes on their known & described disagreements from the state."
His mixed attitude is further revealed in his image that the "State is a poor

good beast who means the best: it means friendly. . . . You who are a man walking cleanly on two feet will not pick a quarrel with a poor cow. . . . But if you go to hook me when I walk in the fields, then, poor cow, I will cut your throat." It seems that he disapproves less of the dissident's motives and more of the efficacy of such protest: "In the particular it is worth considering that refusing payment of the state tax does not reach the evil so nearly as many other methods within your reach. The state tax does not pay the Mexican War. Your coat, your sugar, your Latin & French & German book, your watch does. . . . The prison is one step to suicide" (JMN, IX:446, 447). Thus, although Emerson was clearly uncomfortable with Thoreau's behavior (partly, no doubt, as it reflected on his own relative inaction), his response may have been more muted and paternalistic—at least to Thoreau's face. At this time, with Emerson still something of a hero and certainly a mentor, Thoreau may have been more willing to accept Waldo's opinion, even if he disagreed with it. Of course, had the "mean and skulking" remark somehow reached his ears, he might have been badly shaken. In any event, to a greater or lesser extent, Emerson's less than wholehearted support of the night in jail helped plant the seeds of future hurt and outrage, especially after Emerson's image of omnipotence and heroism had tarnished.[19] If Thoreau had in any way been wounded by Waldo in the summer of 1846, the wound had begun to open again by January 1848.

It is difficult to understand fully the intensity and anger of "Civil Disobedience" without reference to the issues Thoreau was confronting, and the emotions he was drawing on, in the months after leaving Walden. The lecture could perhaps only have been hatched after the return to Concord, when he felt more vulnerable to family, friends, and the demands, expectations, and corruptions of civilized life. In some ways, the lecture was another defiant declaration of independence, as going to Walden had been in part. Once again, he separates himself from his community and society and insists on his heroism, autonomy, and purity. Re-creating the night in jail was a means of removing himself imaginatively to the Walden hut. Once more he was walled in, insulated from townspeople, inhabiting pure and pristine territory, cleansing himself in Walden's purgative waters. "It is not a man's duty, as a matter of course," he claims in the lecture, "to devote himself to the eradication of any, even the most enormous wrong; but it is his duty, at least, to wash his hands of it." In his prison cell, he "saw that, if there was a wall of stone between me and my townsmen, there was a still more difficult one to climb or break through, before they could get to be as free as I was. I did not for a moment feel confined, and the walls seemed a great waste of stone and mortar. I felt as if I alone of all my

townsmen had paid my tax" (RP, 71, 80). Rejecting genteel proprieties, he
is the one genuine citizen of the country he inhabits. Thoreau, a "human
plant" who in a March 8, 1848, letter to Cabot would express his "sympathy" with the barberry bush (C, 210) and who has come to wonder
whether he should have transplanted himself in civil society again, intro-
duces his account of the jail experience with the observation that "If a
plant cannot live according to its nature, it dies; and so a man." The jail
cell, like the Walden cabin, is portrayed as a clean and pure setting; it "was
the whitest, most simply furnished, and probably the neatest apartment in
the town." His fellow prisoner, whom he "presumed to be an honest man"
and who—in jail—"got his board for nothing," claimed that he had been
falsely accused of burning a barn; Thoreau, who had been convicted without a trial as a "woodsburner" by many townspeople and who had gone
into self-enforced exile at Walden partly in response to the judgment, speculates mildly that "he had probably gone to bed in a barn when drunk, and
smoked his pipe there; and so a barn was burnt." (At the time of his arrest,
Thoreau may have imagined on some level that the jailing was a way for
Concordians to get even with him for burning the woods.) Also like Walden, the cell is a place of creative, even poetic, productivity. As Thoreau
observes, "Probably this is the only house in the town where verses are
composed, which are afterward printed in a circular form, but not published. I was shown quite a long list of verses which were composed by
some young men who had been detected in an attempt to escape, who
avenged themselves by singing them" (RP, 81, 82). Perhaps "Civil Disobedience" was itself a form of vengeance written by a young man who felt unjustly imprisoned in civilized society and wanted to escape. In the second
and third versions of *Walden,* worked on in 1849, Thoreau would speak of
the necessity for the writer to present a "simple and sincere account of his
own life . . . some such account as he would send to his kindred from a distant land; for if he has lived sincerely, it must have been in a distant land to
me" (W, 3–4).[20] If at Walden he sensed that he had inhabited a "distant
land," so being in jail for the night and, though he does not say so, writing
about it was "like travelling into a far country, such as I had never expected to behold." He resurrects, too, the Walden-related lessons of economy: "It will not be worth the while to accumulate property; that would
be sure to go again. You must hire or squat somewhere, and raise but a
small crop, and eat that soon. You must live within yourself, and depend
upon yourself, always tucked up and ready for a start, and not have many
affairs" (RP, 82, 78).

When he recounts his experience of being released from prison, he
also appears to be reviewing some of his responses upon reentering civil-

ized life after leaving the pond. He "came out of prison" because "some one interfered, and paid the tax"; somewhat similarly, he had said farewell to Walden because Emerson had "interfered" by deciding to go to England. Lidian's invitation had bailed him out of his Walden hut. Of course, there were many underlying reasons for his bailing out of his life at the pond, and the "interference" was almost surely viewed by him as a blessing at the time. Now, with the passage of several months, there was a temptation to reinterpret the past and view the "interference" as a curse. Since he had changed so much at Walden, he had perhaps expected that Concord, or his feelings about it, would also have changed; but upon taking up residence at the Emersons', he discovered his old hostile feelings reemerging. In like manner, he found upon his release from prison "that I did not perceive that great changes had taken place on the common." Yet his own shift in perspective led him to perceive a change "over the scene, —the town, and State, and country, —greater than any that mere time could effect." He saw his neighbors as being even more morally bankrupt than he had previously suspected. Probably the most revealing indictment is his realization of the extent to which "the people among whom I lived could be trusted as good neighbors and friends; that their friendship was for summer weather only" (RP, 83). It is likely that Emerson was among the most prominent of these "fair-weather friends." If Emerson had been unexpectedly critical of his night in jail, after he came back from the pond Waldo had not provided the support, encouragement, or "presentness" Thoreau had needed. His jail sojourn had not met with general community approval, and, if he had hoped for some sort of welcome or renewed appreciation from his neighbors when he returned to Concord, his hopes had not been realized. "My neighbors did not thus salute me," he remarks in "Civil Disobedience," "but first looked at me, and then at one another, as if I had returned from a long journey" (RP, 83). After his release from jail, he picked up the shoe he had left to be mended at the shoemaker's. After leaving Walden, it was imperative that he not lose his soul. His final act in the jailing episode was to join a huckleberry party, where the "State was nowhere to be seen" (RP, 83–84). His recollection, fictionalized or not, about having joined a huckleberry party mirrors, to some degree, his decision to withdraw *A Week* from publication consideration and "sympathize . . . with the barberry bush, whose business it is solely to *ripen* its fruit (though that may be not to sweeten it)"—he was adding, among other things, some sour reflections on friendship to *A Week*—"and to protect it with thorns, so that it holds on all winter, even, unless some hungry crows come to pluck it" (C, 210). At this point, he suggested, the absent Emerson or his influence was, like the state, "nowhere to be seen."

Early on in the lecture, he contends that "action from principle" is "essentially revolutionary" and that it "not only divides states and churches, it divides families; aye, it divides the *individual,* separating the diabolical in him from the divine" (RP, 72). Certainly, Thoreau appears to be drawing on powerful "family feelings" in "Civil Disobedience." As Raymond Gozzi has argued, the state was, in a crucial sense, the "parental state" for Thoreau.[21] The rebelliousness evident in the lecture is, whatever its undeniable merits and legitimacy as a response to injustice and oppression, on some level against parents and quasi parents, people he has looked to and looked up to in the past. In one variant of "Civil Disobedience," he included a segment from a poem by George Peele, which begins, "We must affect our country as our parents."[22] Often he uses feminine pronouns in reference to the state (as, in *A Week,* he employed feminine pronouns and imagery with respect to orthodox religion). Clearly, his mother—whose expectations he frequently experienced, at least unconsciously, as "impositions" (RP, 64), whose forceful style threatened his sense of autonomy, but whose love and approval he relied upon so heavily—may be regarded as one parent he is bent on resisting. "I was not born to be forced" (RP, 80–81), he writes, and he may have been more fearful of coming under her sway now that he was back in Concord. At another juncture he connects his own father directly with his revolt against church and state, though his mother was generally more involved with the church:

> Some years ago, the State met me in behalf of the church, and commanded me to pay a certain sum toward the support of a clergyman whose preaching my father attended, but never I myself. "Pay it," it said, "or be locked up in the jail." I declined to pay. But, unfortunately, another man saw fit to pay it. . . . at the request of the selectmen, I condescended to make some such statement as this in writing:—"Know all men by these presents, that I, Henry Thoreau, do not wish to be regarded as a member of any incorporated society which I have not joined." (RP, 79)

If, however, his father had been an Admetus whom he had served as an Apollo, if he had not been the dynamic male identity model his son had wished him to be, if he evoked unresolved oedipal anxieties and guilt, there was another "father" who was, perhaps more than any other family figure, the object of wrath and disappointment in the lecture: Emerson. "Civil Disobedience" is not only an attack on the state itself (which is described in one passage as "pitiable," "foolish," "blundering," "half-witted," and "timid" [RP, 80]) but is also, even more harshly, an assault on the men who do not go to jail to resist it and who condemn or belittle those who do. There is a strong undercurrent of being let down by authorities and neighbors. "Oh for a man," he laments, "who is a *man,* and, as my neighbor says, has a bone in his back which you cannot pass your hand through!" (RP, 70). If Emerson was indeed critical or condescending with regard to his act of civil disobedience and he knew it, then Thoreau could no longer respect or venerate him as he once had. Waldo's refusal to be one of those "honest men" who withdrew from the state and went to jail constituted moral cowardice for Thoreau. For all his brave talk, Emerson had been but a patron of, and patronizing about, protest. Thoreau comments, "There are nine hundred and ninety-nine patrons of virtue to one virtuous man" (RP, 69). Waldo's mettle was tarnished; he was no longer the "great man" who had been such a radical in the 1830s and early 1840s. "A very few," Thoreau says, "as heroes, patriots, martyrs, reformers in the great sense, and *men,* serve the State with their consciences also, and so necessarily resist it for the most part; and they are commonly treated by it as enemies" (RP, 66). One story, apocryphal perhaps but nonetheless suggestive, had Thoreau, upon his release from jail, responding to Emerson's inquiries about why he had gone to prison with the rejoinder, "Why did you not?"[23] In "Civil Disobedience," maybe with Emerson in mind, he restates this point: "Under a government which imprisons any unjustly, the true place for a just man is also a prison" (RP, 76). Whether or not the two men had had a direct confrontation in 1846, the fact remains that the lecture reflects Thoreau's state of mind in 1848, when his esteem for Emerson was on the wane. It is indicative, moreover, that at the time Waldo was enraptured with England's manufacturing prowess, Thoreau chose to make prominent in the lecture the image of the unheroic individual and the state as machine: "The mass of men serve the State thus, not as men mainly, but as machines, with their bodies." Elsewhere he observes that "all machines have their friction; and possibly this does enough good to counterbalance the evil. At any rate, it is a great evil to make a stir about it. But when the friction comes to have its machine, and oppression and robbery are organized, I say, let us not have such a machine any longer" (RP, 66, 67). In a justly famous metaphor, he adds later, "Let your life be a counter friction to stop the machine" (RP, 73–74). That Emerson was praising civil society in his letters may have spurred Thoreau to be even more contemptuous of it. "Civil Disobedience," then, represented an indirect way of differentiating himself starkly from and rejecting the mentor he had once idolized. It has the tone of a former worshiper disabused of his illusions.

The pent-up aggressive emotions released by, and unleashed in, the lecture, while undeniably cathartic for Thoreau, were also threatening. In challenging the state's authority, and in excoriating the men who refused to take or even countenance bold actions, Thoreau was challenging signifi-

cant figures—particularly male—in his life. It is wholly in character that
he would have hit upon a mode of protest that would combine passiveness
and withdrawal with aggressiveness, nonviolence with militant resistance.
Elsewhere I have made the argument that not only did Thoreau and Gandhi espouse very similar public strategies but also that their strategies had
comparable private roots.[24] Both had been "cursed" by a guilt-provoking
death, in Gandhi's case the circumstances surrounding the death of his
father and in Thoreau's the untimely death of his elder brother. Each developed a style or strategy that permitted him to challenge authority, try to
defeat a "superior adversary,"[25] but also deny the wish to supersede, hurt,
or destroy them. In this way each could shield himself from the guilt and
anxiety aroused by hostile feelings toward, and confrontations with, authority. Even before the disenchantment with Emerson became pressing,
then, Thoreau was oriented to an aggressive-passive, militantly nonviolent
pattern; indeed, his dramatic act of civil resistance had occurred when Emerson was still perceived as something of an ally and model, even if he already felt stirrings toward a break and even though the ally's reaction to
his behavior had apparently been one of the wedges that would drive them
apart. The strategy of militant nonviolence, firmly embodied in the act itself, was even more crucial when he delivered the text of "Resistance to
Civil Government," for he now had to deal with the residual and rising
guilt regarding his brother and with the inevitable discomfort involved in
his shifting emotions toward Emerson. That he was responding to affect
associated with his brother *and* Emerson (the two "friends" who loomed
largest in the "Friendship" essay he was working on at the same time)
made the passive-aggressive stance of "Civil Disobedience" all the more
imperative. For all the rage and defiance evinced in the lecture, toward its
end Thoreau seeks to pull back from, even forswear, any monomaniacal
destructiveness or murderous intentions. It is not simply rhetorical concession when he remarks, "I do not wish to quarrel with any man or nation. I
do not wish to split hairs, to make fine distinctions, or set myself up as better than my neighbors. I seek rather, I may say, even an excuse for conforming to the laws of the land. I am but too ready to conform to them."
And the final lines of the lecture express not outrage but rather the concil-
iatory vision of a state that will be a "good father," generative, ripely wise,
tolerant, and just:

> There will never be a really free and enlightened State, until the State comes to
> recognize the individual as a higher and independent power, from which all its
> own power and authority are derived, and treats him accordingly. I please my-
> self with imagining a State at last which can afford to be just to all men, and to

treat the individual with respect as a neighbor; which even would not think it inconsistent with its own repose, if a few were to live aloof from it, not meddling with it, nor embraced by it, who fulfilled all the duties of neighbors and fellow-men. A State which bore this kind of fruit, and suffered it to drop off as fast as it ripened, would prepare the way for a still more perfect and glorious State, which also I have imagined, but not yet anywhere seen. (RP, 89–90)

If "Resistance to Civil Government" served critical psychological functions for Thoreau—revivifying his early Walden identity, expressing his evolving hostility toward Emerson and "civilized life" in the framework of a relatively nonthreatening verbal mixture of passiveness and aggression—in real life he was not so close to resolving his ambivalence and subduing his anxieties. A letter of January 28 from Waldo suggests how oblivious the continental traveler was to any distress his friend may have been feeling. Addressing Thoreau in a somewhat unctuous, condescendingly flattering manner, he expresses gratitude for his friend's recent letter, "which was a true refreshment. Let who or what pass, there stands the dear Henry, —if indeed any body had a right to call him so, —erect, serene, & undeceivable. So let it ever be! I should quite subside into idolatry of some of my friends, if I were not every now & then apprised that the world is wiser than any one of its boys" (C, 205). But if other evidence of the period is any indication, Thoreau was far from "serene & undeceivable"; indeed, his serenity had been disturbed partly by his sense of having been deceived or misled by Waldo. For all the patronizing encouragement in his letter, Emerson was not "hearing" Thoreau on some important level, not picking up the subtle distress signals he was sending out.

One notable reverberation of the subterranean rumblings that were no doubt occurring is registered in Thoreau's February 23 letter to England, in which he addresses Emerson for the first time in writing as "Waldo" and makes much of it: "For I think I have heard that that is your name. . . . Whatever I may *call* you, I know you better than I know your name, and what becomes of the fittest name—if in any sense you are here with him who *calls,* and not there simply to be called" (C, 207). Naming had symbolic significance for Thoreau: after all, he had changed his own name from David Henry to Henry David soon after graduating from Harvard (and resigning from his first teaching job) as a dramatic assertion of autonomy.[26] Now, in the context of an epoch when doubts about Emerson's stewardship were accumulating and he was no longer the demigod he had once been—Emerson, whether sincerely or not, had recently spoken of his temptation to idolize *him*—Thoreau was addressing his erstwhile mentor as an equal, and in some respects he felt he was his superior.[27] There is, to be sure, a tone of authentic gratitude in his subsequent remarks: "I believe I never thanked you for your lectures—one and all—which I heard formerly read in Concord— I *know* I never have— There was some excellent reason each time why I did not—but it will never be too late. I have had that advantage at least, over you in my education" (c, 207). But this is the statement of one who is in the process of breaking away from his mentor;[28] it is as if Thoreau, in thanking Emerson, is trying to take leave of him—as one would try to thank a parent one knows will not be around much longer or as one would eulogize a person or relationship already dead. There is, however, another probable dimension to this passage. Addressing Emerson as "Waldo" was threatening, as were all the increasingly negative emotions associated with him, and in this context the expression of appreciation may represent a drawing back from the precipice of hostility and alienation. The passage may, in this regard, be a kind of reaction formation, in which he expresses the sentiment diametrically opposed to the predominant feeling as a defense against frightening or forbidding emotions. There could also be a tinge of remorse here, particularly in light of Emerson's flattering letter of January 28. In any case, the words of gratitude represent more than meets the eye. That immediately following the thankful paragraph is a graphic account of Lidian's suffering, which was chronic anyway but more acute at this time ("the most trying illness of her life"),[29] suggests another pendulum swing, a rising toward the surface again after brief submersion of troubled feelings. He writes,

> Lidian is too unwell to write to you and so I must tell you what I can about the children, and herself. I am afraid she has not told you how unwell she is, today perhaps we may say—has been. She has been confined to her chamber four or five weeks, and three or four weeks, at least to her bed—with the jaundice, accompanied with *constant* nausea, which makes life intolerable to her. This added to her general ill health has made her *very* sick. She is as yellow as saffron. (c, 207)

Implicit, it appears, in this description is an accusation that Emerson is not where he should be—at his wife's side. The portrayal of Lidian's "intolerable" condition could easily have provoked guilt in Emerson. Waldo's letter to Lidian of March 8 and 10 shows how successful Thoreau was in making his friend feel compunction and shame: "I am surprised & grieved to hear of your repeated illness & of the illness of the children. Instead of the perfect tranquillity which I thought secured to you by my absence, you have had no rest. . . . I can hardly regret my journey, on the whole, & yet it seems in every way to have cost too much" (L, IV:32). The further implication of Thoreau's letter is that he has had to take over the duties of husband and father abandoned by Waldo when his family most needs him and, moreover, that Lidian and her husband do not communicate too well. Again, he seems to have struck a raw nerve, for Emerson writes to his wife, "Ah you still ask me for that unwritten letter always due, it seems, always unwritten, from year to year, by me to you, dear Lidian" (L, IV:33). Thus, in a letter that contains lavish gratitude, Thoreau also reminds Emerson of his points of vulnerability and limitation.

While his comments on Alcott in this same letter are gentle, his characterization of Ellery Channing is surprisingly negative, particularly in light of his having recently shown his laudatory poem, "Walden Hermitage," to Thoreau. Perhaps the fact that Emerson had taken to writing to Channing directly rather than to Thoreau (who could show him Waldo's letters [L, IV:35]) colored his attitude. Of the capricious Channing, he writes, "Sometimes he *will* ride a broom stick still—though there is nothing to keep him or it up—but a certain centrifugal force of whim which is soon spent—and there lies your stick—not worth picking up to sweep an oven with now. His accustomed path is strewn with them" (C, 208). The phallic nature of the broomstick image is unmistakable. Maybe Thoreau is being hard on Channing in his own right and writing; perhaps he was distressed by Channing's impotence to be a strong and solid brother figure. Maybe, too, the imagery of impotence (or premature ejaculation) he attributes to Channing represents in part a rechanneling of his dammed-up feelings toward Waldo. And, if Channing is undependable and lacks the will for sustained productivity, Thoreau needs to prove that *he* is generative. Among the lectures that "begin to multiply on my desk" is one on friendship and another on "The Rights & Duties of the Individual in relation to Government." The reading of the latter was "much to Mr. Alcott's satisfaction" (C, 208): we may suppose that Thoreau is hinting that Waldo would not be satisfied or approving of it. And, indeed, Emerson never did mention "Civil Disobedience" in the *Journal* or *Letters*.[30]

His "barberry bush" letter to Cabot (an editor of *Dial*) on March 8 shows Thoreau fluctuating between patience and impatience, between a sense of frustrated ambition and a willingness to defer, if not entirely renounce, ambition. He explains—after informing Cabot of Emerson's itinerary—"My book, fortunately, did not find a publisher ready to undertake it," and he adds in what must surely be understatement, "you can imagine the effect of delay on an author's estimate of his own work. However, I like it well enough to mend it, and shall look at it again directly when I have dispatched some other things." Anxious, it seems, to protect himself with "thorns" from disappointment and failure and betraying a reemergent ambivalence about literary ambition, he continues, "I have been writing lectures for our own Lyceum this winter, mainly for my own pleasure and advantage. I esteem it a rare happiness to be able to *write* anything, but there (if I ever get there) my concern for it is apt to end. Time & Co. are, after all, the only quite honest and trustworthy publishers that we know." Then comes his expression, already quoted, of "sympathy" with the barberry bush. All this is a strange way, an apologia, to introduce an inquiry about whether *Dial* would be willing to pay him for any articles he might submit: "I see I must get a few dollars together presently to manure my roots. Is your journal able to pay anything, provided it likes an article well enough?" Then he shrinks again from any acknowledgment of ambition, almost inviting a negative response: "I do not promise one. At any rate, I mean always to spend only words enough to purchase silence with; and I have found that this, which is so valuable, though so many writers do not prize it, does cost much, after all." As his own agent or promoter, Thoreau was on shaky ground. His capacity to support himself as a writer or bolster his literary career coming increasingly into question, he could not avoid daydreaming sometimes of getting back to the life at Walden. But he sensed that he had reached the point of no return: he informs Cabot that "my house was removed immediately after I saw you, and I have been living in the village since" (c, 210).

Thoreau's next letter to Emerson, postmarked March 24, is yet another laying on of guilt regarding Waldo's absence from home: he should be with his family instead of enhancing his reputation and having a fling across the Atlantic. Eddie, he notes, "says he cannot sing 'not till his mother is agoing to be well.' We shall hear his voice very soon in that case I trust." Thoreau then addresses the issue of what will happen when Emerson does come back and the extent to which he has adequately replaced him: "Ellen is already thinking what will be done when you come home, but then she thinks it will be some loss that I shall go away. Edith says that I shall come and see them, and always at teatime so that I can play with her. Ellen thinks she likes father best because he jumps her sometimes" (c, 211). Emerson's note of March 25, which may have crossed Thoreau's in the mail, reveals a continuing crossing of signals between the two, an inability of the elder to appreciate or take seriously enough the idealism and spirituality of the younger: "It is pity . . . that you should not see this England, with its indiscribable material superiorities of every kind; the just confidence which immense successes of all pasts have generated in this Englishman that he can do everything" (c, 212). This letter, which may well have deepened Thoreau's disillusion with Emerson, was, curiously, the last extant letter he addressed while overseas to Thoreau, even though he did not reach New England soil again until July 1848. One may legitimately wonder if Emerson was gradually beginning to read the subtle, between-the-lines messages in Thoreau's correspondence and became uncomfortable about the prospect of writing to him, suspecting that, whatever he said, it would not be enough, would be misinterpreted, or would not meet with his friend's approval. Walking on eggshells was not a task he relished. Thoreau was clearly taken aback by Waldo's not writing him. In an April 20, 1848, letter to Lidian, Emerson says, rather defensively, "He [Thoreau] says, I do not write to him, or you say it, but I have, almost sheet for sheet, as I believe" (L, IV:58).

At this critical crossroads, when Thoreau was growing more disenchanted with his mentor and was in the preliminary and painful phase of breaking away from him, he received his first letter from Harrison Gray Otis Blake, who, along with Daniel Ricketson, would become his most loyal disciple. Blake had been born, the youngest of ten children, in Worcester, Massachusetts, on April 10, 1816, a bit more than a year before Thoreau, and he had been a graduate of the Harvard class of 1835. His father had been a highly esteemed lawyer, but he died only ten months after Harrison was born. Surely, being deprived of his father before he even knew him helped make Blake a man who would be in search of, in desperate need of, a father or father figure. His own father, Francis, had been an impressive man with experience as an editor, a bank director, and an orator who even had some of his addresses and lectures published by Isaiah Thomas. His eloquence, erudition, passion, wit, charm, dignity, and hatred of dishonesty and injustice were testified to by many who knew him.[31] It is not surprising that Harrison Blake, bereft so young of his father, began to cast about for his father's qualities and similar attainments in other men and that he developed a special affinity for the Transcendentalists, first the great orator Emerson and then Thoreau.

The formation of Blake's identity was probably made more problematic both by his father's formidability and by his early death. In some ways, of course, he clearly wished to identify with him; and we may surmise that his mother, "a woman of force and character," encouraged him to walk in Francis's footsteps. Having survived his father at such an early age (and, on an oedipal level, perhaps suspecting that he had wished to defeat and kill him, and had succeeded) and sensing pressure from his mother to measure up to, if not surpass, his father—he was sent to Harvard at the age of fifteen—his initiative may have been severely checked by guilt.[32] That he had so many older siblings may, on the one hand, have diminished the intensity of the oedipal bond with his mother, but on the other hand it may have increased sibling competition for the mother's affections, generating hostility and, thus, guilt. In any case, he was subject to identity confusion and needed an extended moratorium; he followed a pattern of avoiding or rejecting success in young adulthood not unlike that of Emerson, whose father had died when he was only eight,[33] and Thoreau, whose father had in significant ways been psychologically absent or in the background. Indeed, after studying in divinity school while still at Harvard and becoming minister of a Unitarian church in Milford, New Hampshire, he was apparently deeply influenced by fellow-minister Emerson's refusal to administer the sacraments, wrote the young Boston clergyman that he was supportive of his stand, and developed more serious doubts about his own career. Within a year, he, like Emerson, left the ministry, "a profession which might consider his views too radical." Having rejected this vocation, and wanting no part of his father's profession or of medicine, the "only logical occupation left him"—as it had been for Thoreau—was teaching. He first taught in Boston, at a school in the old Park Church. His mother died in 1839, leaving him without "a Worcester residence he could call his own"; and it may be that her death hastened his attempts to establish a home and settle down. On June 25, 1840, he married Sarah Chandler Ward, who also resided in Boston.[34] That his mother was deceased and that Sarah's mother was his mother's first cousin may have led to some moral queasiness.

Not long before his first letter to Thoreau, Blake experienced a double tragedy, which depressed him and may have activated guilt, underlined his mortality, and made him, in general, hungrier for guidance. His wife died unexpectedly, after giving birth to his second child and first son, Harry, on May 11 or 12, 1846; four days later, Harry died. The grief and guilt accompanying these enormous losses must have been overwhelming for Blake. The need to find some meaning, to feel pure, to find an approving male figure to absolve him of guilt and provide some direction was no doubt intense.

Testimony abounds that Blake was a man of seemingly compulsive honesty and scrupulosity; he had a very demanding, probably quite punitive, conscience. Emerson would later characterize him as a "terribly conscientious man, a man who would even return a borrowed umbrella." One story tells of Blake's ringing the doorbell of his sister's house late one evening: "Apologizing to her husband for arousing him, Blake explained that he could not sleep until he corrected an inaccuracy of statement of which he had been guilty. He had told his sister that 'he was going to Boston tomorrow,' when he should have said he *expected* to go to Boston." In another example of his overscrupulosity, "after one of his two trips abroad, he met a friend and absently told him, 'I'm very glad to see you.' They parted and walked in opposite directions when suddenly Harry Blake stopped and ran back. 'I wish to tell you,' he said, 'that I am not very glad to see you, I am only glad to see you.'" E. Harlow Russell of Worcester said that he was "such a man as reduced an oath in a court of justice as superfluosity."[35] This testimony serves to illustrate how vulnerable to guilt he was and how urgently he quested after a therapeutic purity that would be provided by a father figure who would give him his blessings and a formula for the recovery of innocence.

This quest had special immediacy around the time he first wrote to Thoreau, whom he must have been acquainted with "at least by sight in college"[36] and through his Concord connection with Emerson. Having recently read Thoreau's article on Aulus Persius Flaccus "revived" in Blake a "haunting impression" of him, "which I carried away from some spoken words of yours." When Blake had last been in Concord, Thoreau had spoken—possibly before going to Walden—"of retiring farther from our civilization" and, when asked if he would miss his friends, Thoreau's reply had been, "in substance, 'No, I am nothing,'" a reply that was "memorable" to Blake. The man from Worcester latched onto this remark as suggesting those qualities that he needed to foster in himself: "It indicated a depth of resources, a completeness of renunciation, a poise and repose in the universe, which to me is almost inconceivable; which in you seemed domesticated, and to which I look up in veneration" (c, 213). "Veneration": this is the word that best characterizes the tone of the only surviving letter he wrote to Thoreau. In some respects, the man who says "I am nothing" becomes All, becomes associated with an almost godlike entity. "I would know of that soul," he says, "which can say 'I am nothing.' I would be roused by its words to a truer and purer life. Upon me seems to be dawning with new significance the idea that God is here; that we have but to bow before Him in profound submission at every moment and he will fill our souls with his presence" (c, 213). Infused with wishful thinking, Blake's sense of who Thoreau was had much in common with the young writer's ego ideal. Interpreting his would-be idol's character, Blake writes, "You would sunder yourself from society, from the spell of institutions, customs, conventionalities, that you may lead a fresh, simple life with God. Instead of breathing a new life into the old forms, you would have a new life without and within. There is something sublime to me in this attitude, —far as I may be from it myself" (c, 213). Blake seems to be yearning for a conversion experience, a great awakening, a rebirth, and, "shivering on the brink," he beseeches Thoreau to show him the way to the light and a "new life."

Coming as it does during a period when issues of his mentor-disciple relationship with Emerson were paramount, and when he was growing increasingly uneasy with the turn events were taking, Thoreau's response to Blake's letter is fascinating and instructive. He reveals himself divided: leery of being an authority figure, wary of being built up by Blake as he had himself blindly venerated Emerson. There is ample evidence he was losing his blinders regarding Waldo. On the other hand, in the very course of discouraging Blake from considering him—or anyone—a perfect mentor, he seems bent on preaching his own gospel, anxious to influence Blake and to justify to himself that he was becoming his own man, a man worthy of being a mentor in his own right. He begins, "I am glad to hear that any words of mine, though spoken so long ago that I can hardly claim identity with their author, have reached you"(c, 214). While he is being conventionally humble, there is more than a grain of truth in his acknowledgment that he does not perceive that his current sense of self is not wholly in conjunction with previous self-images or his ego ideal. At the same time, the letter from Blake does give him a tangible ego boost, suggesting that he is not as far from his ego ideal as he had recently been inclined to believe, that the gap between real and ideal can be narrowed or closed. Blake's letter of adulation, moreover, gives him the hope that he may have an audience for his writing; he feels "pleasure," he says, "because I have therefore reason to suppose that I have uttered what concerns men, and that it is not in vain that man speaks to man"(c, 214). Disappointed that *A Week* has yet to have an impact on a wide public audience and that his attempts at close communication with Emerson have been in vain, he is clearly encouraged by Blake's receptiveness, though he is also uneasy with his passionate intensity and neediness.

Thoreau then proceeds to affirm his own beliefs, employing imagery of "distant country" used in "Civil Disobedience" and soon to be incorporated into the next draft of *Walden:* "To set about living a true life is to go a journey to a distant country, gradually to find ourselves surrounded by new scenes and men; and as long as the old are around me, I know that I am not in any true sense living a new or a better life" (c, 214). Even if he presently feels he has not completed his journey to this "distant country," there is the indication that he is doing a more authentic form of traveling than such "elders" as Emerson. At Walden he had built the edifice for the new life he had dreamed of, but since returning to civilized life he has learned how problematic it is to transplant or graft the foundation onto the ground of the society to which he has returned: "We are apt to speak vaguely sometimes, as if a divine life were to be grafted on to or built over this present as a suitable foundation. This might do if we could so build over our old life as to exclude from it all the warmth of our affection, and addle it, as the thrush builds over the cuckoo's egg, and lays her own atop, and hatches that only; but the fact is, we—so there is the partition—hatch them both, and the cuckoo's always by a day first, and that young bird crowds the young thrushes out of the nest. No. Destroy the cuckoo's egg, or build a new nest" (c, 214–15). It may be suggested that Thoreau at this time was particularly averse to remaining in Emerson's nest—putting all his eggs in that basket, so to speak—and was growing more anxious to fashion or refashion a new one all his own. Surely this was far less threatening than destroying his competitor's nest or egg. Thoreau's subsequent indictments of other men, who "very pathetically inform the old, accept and wear it," and who think they "must attend to [many trivial affairs] in a day," may be influenced by his feelings about Emerson. It is difficult to avoid the conclusion that he is thinking of Emerson, who had been trumpeting the virtues of Englishmen, when he observes, "This, our respectable daily life, in which the man of common sense, the Englishman of the world, stands so squarely, and on which our institutions are founded, is in fact the veriest illusion, and will vanish like the baseless fabric of a vision" (c, 215). Claiming that he has no illusions about the value or help of intermediaries, sponsors, or mentors, he proclaims himself an antinomian: "Let nothing come between you and the light. Respect men as brothers only. When you travel to the celestial city, carry no letter of introduction. When you knock ask to see God—none of the servants." "In what concerns you much," he continues, not without a trace of bitterness, "do not think that you have companions—know that you are alone in the world" (c, 216). If, on the one hand, he is advising Blake not to look to him for answers (though even his advice is part of the answer!), he is, on the other hand counseling himself that he can no longer depend on Emerson. For all his self-doubts, he does claim in upbeat fashion toward the end of the letter, "I am simply what I am, or I begin to be that" (c, 216). While he may have once thought that the Walden sojourn was the culmination of his efforts to become his own person, he was now coming to understand that he still had a long way to go and that leaving Emerson's nest was imperative for future growth.

Whatever his admonitions about not relying on anyone's help, Thoreau—possibly more emboldened by Blake's worshipful tribute than he let on—stuck his neck out again and wrote to Greeley about the long-standing matter of his not having been paid yet by *Graham's Magazine* for his "Carlyle" essay and about the possibilities of publishing his "Katahdin" essay.[37] Depressed about his prospects for a full-fledged literary career, fearing further doors slamming in his face, and especially circumspect about asking for help in light of Emerson's failures, he had not written Greeley for a long time. With his literary fortunes seemingly at low ebb, Thoreau may have felt Greeley's response had come just in the nick of

time. There is an impression of deep concern and even urgency in the celebrated editor's reply of April 3: "I have but this moment received yours of
31st ult. and was greatly relieved by the breaking of your long silence. Yet
it saddens and surprises me to know that your article was not paid for by
Graham; and, since my honor is involved in the matter, I will see that you
are paid, and that at no distant day." Not only did Greeley offer to redress
grievances, he also showed a genuine readiness to promote Thoreau's career by trying to place "Katahdin and the Maine Woods," which, he says,
he will "take" and send him payment "if I cannot dispose of it more to
your advantage within the weeks ensuing." "I hope I can," he adds (c,
217). Eventually he succeeded: "Katahdin" was finally accepted by *Union
Magazine* and published in five installments from July to November 1848.

   This letter, Thoreau may have perceived, represented a turning point
in his career and state of mind. Just when his hopes for acceptance into the
literary world had dimmed to a flicker, just when he had soured on the
prospect of receiving any meaningful, quickly dispatched aid from a career
sponsor, Greeley had stepped in. Indeed, in his next letter of April 17, he
sent Thoreau twenty-five dollars for the "Katahdin" piece, even though—
following the principle of stroking authors so well cultivated by literary
editors and agents—he knows "it is worth more." The essay is "rather
long for my columns and too fine for the million; but I consider it a cheap
bargain, and shall print it myself if I do not dispose of it to better advantage." While generous and discerning in his praise, he does not seek to be
pushy or overpossessive with regard to his author: "You will not of course
consider yourself under any sort of obligation to me, for my offer was in
the way of business and I have got more than the worth of my money."
Furthermore, he is apologetic about—"a little ashamed of"—"Graham's
tardiness," and, though he has "not yet settled" the affair, he has begun to
intercede personally with Graham (c, 218). Here was a man of considerable power in publishing circles praising him lavishly, offering respectful
apologies, sympathizing with the struggles of a young writer, tangibly going to bat for him—putting his money where his mouth was. Once again,
Thoreau's dream of consolidating his writing career, getting on with business, was returning to life and credibility; the New York editor had thrown
him a lifeline. Greeley's generative commitment to provide succor served
to highlight his sense that Emerson had let him down badly. Surely, the
comparison between the two could not be avoided, especially when a quiz-
zical Greeley himself, in the context of inquiring about *A Week*, asks, "Is
any thing going on about it now? Why did not Emerson try it in England?
I think the Howitts could get it favorably before the British public. If you
can suggest any way wherein I can put it forward, do not hesitate, but com-

mand me" (C, 218–19). Not having much, if any, evidence to the contrary, Thoreau believed that Emerson had not gone out of his way to "put forward" his work, and Greeley's questions must have stirred up indignation and resentment. Emerson had, in fact, told his English friends and audiences about him and *A Week*,[38] but Thoreau might be forgiven for his likely conclusion that Waldo had tried only halfheartedly and that, in any case, he had nothing to show for any efforts he had made. Greeley, in whom he did not have such a heavy and threatening emotional and historical investment, who was less of an imposing father figure than Emerson, seemed a candidate to replace Emerson as sponsor, agent, and coach.

It is understandable that Thoreau, who had just received his first payment for literary work accomplished at Walden, would address the issue of earning a living in his letter to Blake of May 2. "How shall we earn our bread is a grave question," he states, "yet it is a sweet and inviting question. Let us not shirk it, as is usually done. It is the most important and practical question which is put to man. Let us not answer it hastily. Let us not be content to get our bread in some gross, careless, and hasty manner" (C, 220). It is most likely that he felt more comfortable and confident giving this advice when the possibility of earning his bread (at least to some extent) through writing glimmered. Perhaps seeking to come to terms with the doubts, delays, obstacles, and fluctuation of moods that had characterized recent months, he writes,

> If one hesitates in his path, let him not proceed. Let him respect his doubts, for doubts, too, may have some divinity in them. That we have but little faith is not sad, but that we have but little faithfulness. By faithfulness faith is earned. When, in the progress of a life, a man swerves, though only by an angle infinitely small, from his proper and allotted path (and this is never done quite unconsciously even at first; in fact that was his broad and scarlet sin, —ah, he knew of it more than he can tell), then the drama of his life turns to tragedy, and makes haste to its fifth act. When once we thus fall behind ourselves, there is no accounting for the obstacles which rise up in our path, and no one is so wise as to advise, and no one is so powerful as to aid us while we abide on that ground. (C, 221)

Thoreau had been in danger of losing his way; now he dared have faith again that he was on the right track. One can only agree with him when he confides to Blake, "You will perceive that I am as often talking to myself, perhaps, as speaking to you" (C, 222). His preaching is often a way of rallying himself.

Thoreau's trust in Greeley's kind offices was confirmed by the latter's next letter, of May 17, in which he carried through on a promise, sending

him fifty dollars for the "Carlyle" piece and explaining that he has for-
warded this amount (rather than the seventy-five dollars he had procured
from Graham) because, "having got so much for Carlyle, I am ashamed
to take your 'Maine Woods' for $25." Greeley speaks of having "expec-
tations of procuring it ["Katahdin"] a place in a new magazine of high
character that will pay. I don't expect to get as much for it as for Carlyle,
but I hope to get $50. If you are satisfied to take the $25 for your 'Maine
Woods,' say so." He concludes, as would many a good agent, by soliciting
"one or two" shorter articles that he can "sell . . . readily and advanta-
geously." "The length of your papers," he manages to slip in gently, "is
their only impediment to their appreciation by the magazines" (c,
222–23).

In his reply of May 19, Thoreau practically (for him) gushes with gratitude: "My Friend Greeley, I know not how to thank you for your kindness—to thank you is not the way— I can only assure you that I see and
appreciate it. —To think that while I have been sitting comparatively idle
here, you have been so active in my behalf!" (c, 224). Clearly Greeley was,
to his way of thinking, the relatively frank and solicitous "angel," willing
to get down to the nuts and bolts of the business, that Emerson had at least
recently not been.

Even here, to be sure, Thoreau is not entirely sanguine or unambivalent about the arrangement—since Greeley does not make anything for
himself through his efforts on behalf of him; to be disproportionately in
debt, financially or psychologically, to anyone was an uneasy situation for
one for whom indebtedness connoted a vulnerable dependence. In part, he
seems inclined in this May 19 letter to forswear *his* interest in the money
he has received, saying that it "comes as a free and even unexpected gift to
me" (c, 224) and explaining in detail—though bending the truth by not
mentioning his frequent dependence on the village for food, housing, and
other favors—how he has managed to fend for himself, supporting himself
"solely by the labors of my hands" and not receiving "one cent from any
other source" during the past five years. He even gives the impression, intentionally or not, that he is still residing at Walden Pond where "all my
expenses have amounted to but 27 cents a week" (c, 223–24). Ostensibly
on the verge of gaining some measure of literary success, perhaps he feels
the need to insist, as he had written to Blake, that he is keeping his "true
path" in sight, that he is not about to surrender what is pure and pristine
for material gain or "success without identity." Whenever he got too close
to success, he was not only exhilarated but scared. Thus, on the one hand,
the invocation of the Walden identity may have been a means to remain
pure and impervious to indebtedness. On the other hand, it may have been

a way to test Greeley's loyalty and even a calculated attempt to introduce the editor to the *other* book he wished to have published. Whatever his reservations, Thoreau does seem anxious here to make an impression on Greeley; he cares very much what Greeley thinks of him. The postscript to the letter is anything but incidental: "P.S. My book is swelling again under my hands, but as soon as I have leisure I shall see to those shorter articles" (C, 225). There appears to be a more ambitious, go-getter Thoreau in evidence here, one who, though still hedging his bets, unwittingly uses patently autoerotic imagery to describe the expansion of *A Week;* who feels willing and able to follow Greeley's directions and produce what he wants; who says to the world, "Look out; here I come!"

It is likely that Greeley's replacement, for all intents and purposes, of Emerson as a career sponsor (at the very least the editor was now Thoreau's ace in the hole), the acquisition, in Blake, of *his* first disciple, and his bolstered sense that he was at last about to gain his own niche in the literary world and settle in to a new creative era made him feel even freer to assert more directly his independence from, and disagreements with, Emerson. In his final letter to Waldo in England, written on May 21, he takes special pains to separate himself from his erstwhile mentor. Once more, he addresses Emerson as "Dear Friend" rather than as "Waldo," as if the issues he was preoccupied with in his previous letter are no longer so pressing, the investment no longer so deep. Of Waldo's concern about the establishment of literary journals and the survival of the *Massachusetts Quarterly Journal,* which "will fail, unless Henry Thoreau & Alcott & Channing & Charles Newcomb . . . fly to the rescue" (L, IV:56), Thoreau says, in what amounts to a repudiation of Emerson's plea *and* priorities, "I am more interested in the private journal than the public one, and it would be better news to me to hear that there were two or three valuable papers being written in England & America—that might be printed sometime— than that there were 30,000 dollars to defray expenses—& forty thousand men standing *ready to write* merely, but no certainty of anything valuable being written" (C, 226). Elsewhere he shows the gumption again to talk back to Emerson, commenting that the *Review* "should have been suppressed for nobody was starving for *that*" (C, 227). Reacting even more strongly to Waldo's support of Chapman's project to "establish a journal common to Old & New England" (L, IV:56), he asks, "Who has any desire to split himself any further up, by straddling the Atlantic? We are extremities enough already. There is danger of one's straddling so far that he can never recover an upright position. There are certain men in Old & New England who aspire to the renown of the Colossus of Rhodes, and to have ships sail under them" (C, 227). This withering observation clearly seems aimed not only at the journal project but at Emerson himself, whom the "traveller in Concord" saw as "straddling the Atlantic," seeking to spread his fame, and dissipating his genius in the process. The same man who had expressed gratitude for Emerson's lectures in his preceding letter here says, "I am glad to hear that you are writing so much. Lecturing is of little consequence" (C, 227). Yet what else is Thoreau himself doing here than lecturing to, preaching to, the person he had once looked up to? Surely Emerson could not by this time avoid picking up on the shift in Thoreau's attitude toward him. He could not, at least, have been completely insensitive to the acerbic, almost supercilious tone of parts of Thoreau's correspondence. In a June 8 letter to Lidian he would write, "Thank Henry for his letter. He is always *absolutely* right, and *particularly* perverse" (L, IV:81).[39] While one could argue that this is an instance of good-natured banter, it is difficult to believe Emerson's barb did not have a sharp point.

Almost as an afterthought (but maybe with a trace of implied rebuke or vindication), Thoreau mentions in his May 21 letter to Emerson that "Greeley has sent me $100 dollars and wants more manuscript" (C, 227). He seems to be signalling Waldo that he has been getting along well without him, who seemed more concerned that Thoreau plant his garden and tend his orchard than he was with cultivating the young man's career. His confidence in Greeley as an alternative cultivator was further bolstered when, in his note of May 25, the editor told him he had published "a part of your last private letter [of May 19] in this morning's paper." That "part" had concerned how Thoreau had earned his living at Walden Pond; Greeley apparently bought his version entirely: "I am so importuned by young loafers who want to be hired in some intellectual capacity so as to develope their minds—that is, get a broadcloth living, without doing any vulgar labor—that I could not refrain from using against them the magnificent weapon you so unconsciously furnished me" (C, 228). Living in a town where some people persisted in considering him a "loafer," he must have been delighted by this validation that he was who he wished himself to be and that he was keeping alive his Walden identity. In the course of promulgating this identity, he could maximize his literary reputation, rejecting careerism and at the same time enhancing his career. He could entertain visions of fame if not fortune. Apparently Greeley was willing to go all out in puffing him; he asks Thoreau for "one shorter article from your pen that will be quoted" in order to "let the public know something of your way of thinking and seeing. It will do good" (C, 229). He suggests that he write an essay on "The Literary Life"; Thoreau may well have taken this as a sign that he *was* leading a "literary life," that he was finally to be admitted into that select company of people who could justifiably call writing their profession.

The ensuing months, however, would once more seriously call into question whether Thoreau had any future as a writer of broad acceptance and reputation. It would be a time when he would again have to hedge his bets, painfully reevaluate his life and aspirations, and hope for the best. Even though he may not have been continually aware of it, the storm clouds were already beginning to regather when he wrote his final letter to Emerson in England. On May 21 he had written:

> The Steam mill was burnt last night—it was a fine sight lighting up the rivers and meadows. The owners who bought it the other day for seven thousand dollars, though it was indeed insured for six, I hear since will be gainers rathers that *[sic]* losers—but some individuals who hired of them have lost—my Father probably more than any—from four to five hundred dollars, not being insured. Some think that it was set on fire. I have no doubt that the wise fates did set it on fire. I quite agree with them that that disgrace to Concord enterprise & skill needed to be burnt away. It was a real purification as far as it went, and evidence of it was come to every man's door. (c, 225–26)

It is understandable that one who was sensitive to the issue of a destructive fire set by someone would observe it in the best possible light, as something ordained by the "wise fates" to purify wicked Concord commercialism. But the devastation of part of the mill that made the wooden part of his father's pencils would have onerous consequences for Thoreau. This "severe financial blow" would put unavoidable pressure on him to help his father "recoup his loss."[40] Again he would be compelled to become an Apollo to King Admetus, just when things were beginning to break his way with respect to his writing career, just when he might even have been entertaining fantasies of setting the world on fire.

Moreover, Emerson's return from Europe on July 27, 1848, precipitated an emotional crisis for which, for all his rehearsals of and overtures to emancipation, he was not fully prepared. That there was a palpable tension in their relationship is apparent in Emerson's journal entries soon after he came home. "I spoke of friendship," he says, "but my friends & I are fishes in their habit. ⟨I⟩ As for taking T.'s arm, I should as soon take the arm of an elm tree." Soon thereafter he writes, "Henry Thoreau is like the woodgod who solicits the wandering poet & draws him into antres vast & desarts idle, & bereaves him of his ⟨wits⟩ memory, & leaves him naked, plaiting vines & with twigs in his hand. Very seductive are the first steps from the town to the woods, but the End is ⟨indigence⟩ ↑want↓ & madness" (JMN, X:343, 344). The stridency of these remarks, however much he may have kept them to himself, can hardly be exaggerated. In any case, upon returning home Emerson was in no mood or condition to help Thoreau appreciably, even if he had wanted to. He realized that financial problems would necessitate a whirlwind lecture tour and more time away from home. Lidian remained in poor health; Edward got a fever; his mother's health worsened; Bulkeley, his mentally retarded brother, had to be placed elsewhere after the farm where he had been boarding had been sold. Irritated by economic and family demands that threatened to frustrate his literary projects, he also sought to extricate himself from any responsibility for the survival of the *Massachusetts Quarterly Review*.[41] Thus, in the months immediately after coming back to Concord, he had little time, energy, or inclination to advance Thoreau's prospects. His letters reveal little action on his friend's behalf. Perhaps Thoreau found it easier and less disconcerting to throw barbs at Emerson from afar, to distance himself emotionally when Waldo was actually distant. But it is likely that the cooling of their relationship, Emerson's lukewarm support, and quite possibly his thinly veiled disapproval were considerably more painful and intimidating now that this most significant mentor was again living in close proximity to him.

Furthermore, Emerson's reappearance dramatized forcibly the comparison and competition between them: Emerson, the already established celebrity, and Thoreau, the promising writer still struggling to gain a secure foothold in the literary world. Such competitive sentiments could only have reaggravated anxiety and guilt. That Thoreau found Emerson wanting as both husband and father—and wished on some level to supplant him—added to the hostility and guilt. In his journal he compared "real" marriages, including that of the Emersons, which he had seen at such close hand, to his ideal and found them sadly lacking (PJ, 3). Waldo's return, moreover, usurped him of the chance for daily intimacy with Lidian and his larger role as ersatz head of the household. He felt that loss keenly, as is suggested by 1849 journal entries (which may also have been linked to the anticipated death of his sister Helen). One may conclude that it is Lidian he has in mind when he says plaintively, "I still think of you as my sister. I presume to know you. Others are of my kindred by blood or of my acquaintance but you are part of me. . . . I cannot tell where I leave off and you begin. . . . My sister, whom I love I almost have no more to do with. . . . It is those whom I do not love who concern me—and make affairs for me" (PJ, 3). There is some confusion as to whether this person is mother or sister—and there is a denial of any sexual motives—but clearly

Thoreau was injured and angry at being deprived by Emerson of close contact with "the feminine of me" (PJ, 3).

If he had tried to coax Emerson home in his letters, now he realized that Waldo's homecoming created a host of problems for him, not the least of which involved where to live. There probably was very little choice but to return to the Texas Street house to live with his parents, as he did on July 30, 1848.[42] After all, his father needed him to help get the pencil business back on its feet. But moving back with his parents put into relief the question of how much real growth had occurred since he had gone to Walden Pond. He had moved from the Texas house to the pond; now he was back where he had started, perhaps in many ways feeling like a child again (as it is often difficult *not* to feel when one lives as an adult with one's parents) and subject to suspicions that he was not an autonomous adult. The closer he approached to the old living situation and dependencies, the more eager he was to prove to himself and others that he was his own person. To go home again was undoubtedly perceived on some level as backsliding, which threatened the ego ideal he had so nearly approximated at Walden, a self-image that had helped to generate some of his best writing. The pressures to be a family breadwinner and chore runner also increased once he returned to the Texas house. Little wonder, then, with all the demands and anxieties of civilized life closing in on him, that his appetite for "the wild" was whetted again. Though the wilderness may have temporarily lost its appeal to him, by August 24 he was writing to cousin Thatcher in Maine that he was "tempted" to visit him again, "but then, as usual, I have so much idle business that cannot be postponed" (C, 230). In that same letter, which included the third part of his "everlasting mountain story," he reveals his ambivalence about Emerson and civilized society: "I think that he [Emerson] has seen English men, such as are worth seeing, more thoroughly than any traveller. . . . He had access to circles which are inaccessible to most travellers, but which are none the better for that" (C, 229–30). In late summer, probably feeling the urge to get away *somewhere,* he took a four-day walking trip in southern New Hampshire with Channing.[43] Probably not coincidentally, he embarked on this tour around the same time as he and John had nine years earlier; he climbed Uncannunuc Mountain, with Channing on this occasion having to do for a brother substitute. One can imagine him reliving the 1839 expedition and seeking to recapture the innocence, wildness, closeness, and certainty of fraternal good will that seemed to be slipping away with the lapse of years.

The trip was but a temporary respite from the obligations and expectations of civil society. The stifling atmosphere to which he returned is suggested by Aunt Maria's comment on his New Hampshire interlude: "I wish [Henry] could find something better to do than walking off every now and then."[44] In his revisions of *A Week* during this period, he added much of his "Sunday" attack on orthodox religion (including one story, based on the trip he had just completed, about a "clergyman who accused him of breaking the sabbath laws").[45] It is more than likely that the stridency of his denunciations was heightened by his need to assert autonomy and give vent to anger in response to what must have been experienced in some way as the smothering domesticity and orthodoxy of the Texas house environment. If he wished on any level to scandalize family members, *A Week*'s assaults on the church had a certain shock value. In late 1848 the temptation to embrace any form of wildness with an uncritical bear hug was marked: "How much of nature & vigor of true action and eloquence must there be in the speech of every wild man. . . . Our public speaking is comparatively tame" (PJ, 3).

Save for the revisions of *A Week,* the summer and early fall of 1848 was an epoch of comparative outward silence for Thoreau;[46] there were few letters, relatively sparse journal entries, and little indication of work on other writing projects. The shifts in his life structure—adjustments related to living under the parental roof again, renewed family responsibilities, preoccupation with finely honing *A Week*—absorbed much of his time and energy. Reminders of Emerson, whose return home had forced him to trade in one problematic living situation for another, also were distracting, even bruising. In early October, Waldo was working to get published the prose translation by Carlyle's brother of Dante's *Inferno,* though ultimately all he could arrange was publication without royalties (L, IV:115).[47] But his actions on Thoreau's behalf were limited to an ineffectual effort to get James Freeman Clarke to accept him for a lecture in Boston; however, Clarke was interested only in the real article, Emerson himself.[48] Though Waldo praised "Katahdin" in October,[49] he apparently could find little time in his busy schedule of late 1848 and early 1849 to help a friend hungry even for small victories.[50] Nathaniel Hawthorne, who had known and appreciated Thoreau since he and his wife had moved into the Old Manse in 1842 (they had since moved to Salem) and who would be a staunch supporter, did intervene in late October, inviting him to lecture before the Salem Lyceum for twenty dollars. There Thoreau gave the lecture, "Student Life in New England, Its Economy," on November 22 and repeated it in Gloucester on December 20, where the local newspaper reported, "The lecturer gave a very strange account of the state of affairs at Concord. In the shops and offices were large numbers of human beings suffering tortures."[51] If, in this version of *Walden*'s "Economy" chapter, the townspeople were "suffering tortures," so had Thoreau been put on the rack by James Russell Lowell in his devastatingly satiric portrait of him (and perhaps Channing) as imitator of Emerson in *A Fable for Critics,* published on October 31, 1848:

> There comes ———, for instance; to see him's rare sport,
> Tread in Emerson's tracks with legs painfully short;
> How he jumps, how he strains, and gets red in the face,
> To keep step with the mystagogue's natural pace!
> He follows as close as a stick to a rocket,
> His fingers exploring the prophet's each pocket.
> Fie, for shame, brother bard; with good fruit of your own,
> Can't you let Emerson's orchards alone?
> Besides, 'tis no use, you'll not find e'en a core, —
> ——— has picked up all the windfalls before.[52]

Lowell's caricature, though it suggested he might have potential, could not have failed to increase the tension between Thoreau and Emerson. Certainly Thoreau, so thin-skinned at this time, was at the least embarrassed and even more anxious to take up the challenge of going his own way. The clock was ticking loudly.

Thoreau had probably not heard from Greeley for months (probably since the spring), a circumstance that may well have renewed misgivings about his newfound sponsor and his literary prospects. His heart set on getting his two books, *A Week* and *Walden,* into print, he had been unable or unwilling to produce the shorter articles Greeley had called for; perhaps the editor, like Emerson, was cooling to or even giving up on him. When Greeley finally does write him on October 28, he speaks of "break[ing] a silence of some duration to inform you that I hope on Monday to receive payment for your glorious account" of the Maine trip (c, 231). He has been offered seventy-five dollars for the essay and encloses twenty-five dollars in the letter. But, seemingly struck by Thoreau's inattention to his earlier request for shorter articles, he firmly counsels, "You must write to the magazines in order to let the public know who and what you are. Ten years hence will do for publishing books" (c, 232). Surely Greeley's comment about "ten years hence" must have disturbed an increasingly impatient Thoreau, not disposed to churn out short pieces and willing to stake his career on the longer works in which he had invested so much. It may be that his growing distrust of Emerson overflowed onto Greeley; whatever the case, the editor was pushing him in directions he was not eager to take. Although Greeley published extracts from "Katahdin" in the November 17, 1848, *Tribune,*[53] his letter of November 19 could hardly have been perceived as fully heartening: "I think you will do well to send me some passages from one or both of your new works, to dispose of to the magazines. This will be the best kind of advertisement whether for a publisher or for readers." In what amounts to an admonition of Thoreau's intention to publish the books in toto, he adds, "You may write with an angel's pen, yet your writings have no mercantile, money value till you are known and talked of as an author. Mr. Emerson would have been twice as much known and read if he had written for the magazines a little, just to let the common people know of his existence." He concludes with a sigh, unenthusiastically and resignedly, "However, do as you please. If you choose to send me one of your MSS. I will get it publisher [*sic*], but I cannot promise you any considerable recompense; and, indeed, if Monroe will do it, that will be better" (C, 232–33). Thoreau, at this moment almost tasting publication of one or both of his volumes, was apparently in no mood to compromise or go along with Greeley, however well-intentioned or influential he was. He rejected the editor's advice about how to make it. While he still held onto the dream, not without ambivalence, to pursue a literary vocation, he stubbornly refused—more so than earlier in the year—to make it on anything but his own terms. He put himself in the position of rising and falling on the basis of his two books. Some might be inclined to label this self-defeating behavior or to suggest that, as ambivalent as he was, he in some ways wished to court failure. Though he had, in this period, generally been more willing to heed the rules for advancement laid down by Greeley and publishers, when the final reckoning came he could certainly not be accused of being overly prudent or of being a sycophantic careerist. He believed in his work, and, almost in spite of himself, he would find things going his way in subsequent months.

The first half of 1849 was a mercurial period, with an ebbing and flowing of ambition and a mixture of excitement and elation, anxiety and apprehension, for Thoreau. His attempts to publish *A Week* and *Walden* probably represented to him a final bid to build, and settle into, a life structure based primarily on some measure of literary success. If his two books could not serve as vehicles for consolidating his career as a man of letters, then serious reappraisals would be in order. It would be a make-or-break year according to his internal timetable. On February 8 he received word from Ticknor and Co., one of the publishing houses he had contacted, that they might assent to print *Walden* but not *A Week*, "the style of printing & binding to be like Emerson's Essays" (C, 236). For Thoreau, to whom *A Week* meant so much and which was at least psychologically scheduled to come out first, this proposal was unacceptable, and he so informed them. Their reply on February 16 agreed to publish *A Week* first, but only if he would provide $450 in advance for publishing costs. In no position to shoulder such costs, Thoreau offered his books to James Munroe and Co. and got his big break: they agreed to publish *A Week,* to be followed later by *Walden,* allowing him to "pay the costs out of sales," provided that he would assume ultimate responsibility to cover costs if sales did not.[54]

Not only had he made the crucial, if risky, publishing arrangements, but he also was unusually busy with speaking engagements—delivering lectures in Concord on January 3, Salem on February 19 and 28 (by Hawthorne's invitation), and Portland, Maine, on March 21. On April 2, the persistent Greeley publicized Thoreau's Walden experiment in a *Tribune* editorial, apparently still under the false impression—encouraged by Thoreau himself—that he was still living in the woods.[55] Even the *Yeoman's Gazette* of Concord, referring to the *Tribune* piece, praised their native son, though they were careful to point out that Thoreau no longer resided at Walden. Although a letter to the *Tribune* criticized humorously Greeley's "commendation" of "the Concord hermit," the editor vigorously defended him as one who "has set all his brother aspirants to self-culture, a very wholesome example." The controversy and hype would, a calculating Greeley surely figured, generate considerable public interest in Thoreau and his work, even if he hadn't published as widely in the magazines as Greeley had suggested.[56] Probably basking in the glow of this unanticipated publicity, Thoreau gave three April lectures in Worcester at Blake's invitation.[57] His letters to Thatcher show him busily playing the part of the aspiring and in-demand man of letters, intent on striking while the iron was hot. On March 16, announcing that he will be lecturing in Portland, he says, "It happens, as I feared it would, that I am now receiving the proof sheets of my book from the printers, so that without great inconvenience I can not make you a visit at present" (C, 240). The man who had been tempted the previous August to recapture wildness in Maine was so wrapped up now in his career that he could not find the time to visit relatives. On March 22 he further informs Thatcher, "I am just in the midst of printing my book, which is likely to turn out larger than I expected. I shall advertise another, 'Walden, or Life in the Woods,' in the first" (C, 241). Early in April, in a letter to Elizabeth Peabody, who had requested permission to publish "Resistance to Civil Government," he again seeks to impress with how busy and in demand he is: "I have so much writing to do at present, with the printers in the rear of me, that I have almost no time left, but for bodily exercise" (C, 242). He does, however, agree to send her "the article in question" soon. His run of good career luck continued with the prompt publication of the "Resistance" essay in Peabody's *Aesthetic Papers* in May 1849. In his promotion of Thoreau, Greeley portrayed him as offering an alternative to young men going west for the Gold Rush and to the injunction with which he would become identified, "Go West, young man."[58] As Thoreau wrote to Thatcher on February 9, several young people from Concord and Boston had gone to California, but for his part, he would have preferred to go before the gold was discovered.[59] He may well have fancied himself as poised to provide, as Greeley had suggested, an eminently popular and provocative prototype of a young man who could fulfill his ambitions without leaving native ground. Perhaps one of his claims to fame would be as one who said, "Stay in the East, young man." His name might even become part of the public debate on this issue. His own "gold rush" to literary recognition was unquestionably on.

This was, to be a sure, a heady and promising time for Thoreau, but it was not without its stresses and an uneasiness that often tempered ambition. A rambling, disjointed letter of February 28, 1849 (the day he went to Salem to lecture), from Aunt Maria to Prudence Ward paints a vivid picture of his strained living situation:

> Henry . . . is preparing his Book for the press, and the title is to be Waldien (I dont know how to spell it) or life in the Woods. I think the title will take if the Book don't. I was quite amused with what Sophia told me her mother said about it the other day, she poor girl was lying in bed with a sick head ache when she heard Cynthia (who has grown rather nervous of late) telling over her troubles to Mrs. Dunbar, after speaking of her own and Helen's sickness, she says, and there's Sophia she's the greatest trial I've got, for she has complaints she *never will* get rid of, and Henry is putting things into his Book that never ought to be there, and Mr. Thoreau has faint turns and I don't know what ails him, and so she went on from one thing to another hardly knew where to stop, and tho it is pretty much so, I could not help smiling at Sophia's description of it.

"As for Henry's book," she adds—and it is not entirely clear here whether she is referring to *Walden* or *A Week*[60]—"you know I have said, there were parts of it that sounded to me very much like blasphemy, and I do not believe they would publish it, on reading it to Helen the other day Sophia told me, she made the same remark, and coming from her, Henry was much surprised, and said she did not understand it, but still I fear they will not persuade him to leave it out."[61] At the same time that Thoreau was laboring to make his mark finally as a man of letters, there were family dynamics that may well have been a drag on his confidence and ambition. It is hard to imagine Cynthia—usually so strong-minded and sure of herself— "nervous," but it is not difficult to envisage that any aura of anxiety would have been picked up by, and rubbed off on, her only son. All members of his immediate family had physical complaints or ailments, reason enough to be edgy. His successful career initiatives contrasted sharply with the family's current frailty and discomfort. Helen's illness—the family curse of tuberculosis, it seems, though she had not been well for some years— was a serious blot on his plans and ambitions. Still awaiting a reply from Ticknor and Co., he informs Thatcher on February 9 that Helen's health remains approximately what it has been for some time, though she may be, as she believes, a bit more feeble. He adds, with what may be a tinge of irritation or frustration, that if Helen were not ill, his mother and Sophia quite possibly would be.[62] On February 16 he updates Thatcher: "We fear that she may be very gradually fading, but it may not be so. She is not very uncomfortable and still seems to enjoy the day." It is suggestive indeed that he links his "condition" with Helen's: "I do not wish to foresee what change may take place in her condition or in my own" (C, 237). In some respect he could not extricate himself from the suspicion that his fate was tied to Helen's, as it had been to his brother's. When he says in conclusion, "The rest of us are as well off as we deserve to be," one wonders if Thoreau divined that he did not deserve to be well physically or well-off in his career. It was surely a burden for him to pursue literary glory as his sister verged on death and, with this reminder of his own mortality, success could well have taken on a more ephemeral value. His father's undiagnosed "faint turns" undoubtedly were alarming as well, invoking not only understandable apprehensions about the frailty of a parent's life but also stirring up oedipal guilt and painful memories of the other John's demise. That *A Week*, originally a pure and loving memorial to his brother, was to be his vehicle for recognition, may well have troubled him. Under such circumstances, the prospect of literary fame and (though much less likely) fortune would not have been experienced as an unmixed blessing. The imperious demands of conscience might require that he relinquish any grand career designs.

The adverse reactions of his mother, Sophia, Aunt Maria, and a dying Helen to certain passages in his work must also have caused consternation; that such steadfast supporters would express reservations about, and even try to convince him to delete, some of his most audacious pronouncements on religion and economy would have been particularly upsetting. Of course, he had written provocatively and rebelliously partly *because* of his fear that, living at home, he might be—or might be considered to be—too domesticated and tame. By embracing wildness and unconventionality, he could defend himself against the outer and inner charges that he was overdependent and unadventurous. To the extent that he felt pressed by the women in his family to smooth out the rough edges and be more orthodox, he was inclined to distance himself from the same civilized society from which he was seeking validation. As Canby says, at this point "Henry must often have wished himself back in the woods or at Emerson's."[63] He writes in his 1849 journal, "We pine & starve and lose spirit on the thin gruel of society" (PJ, 3). Not surprisingly, he was absorbed at this time in revising *Walden* and, in some sense, in living there again.

Yet, no matter how torn he was about the outlook for success, the publication of *A Week* on May 30, 1849, albeit with paltry publicity,[64] was a day for which he had waited for many years. He had put many eggs into this one basket; from his vantage point, the book must have seemed a pearl, a polished accretion of ten years of living, thought, and devotion to his craft. If anything, this book—to be followed by the less well-developed but certainly captivating *Walden*—would be his claim to the recognized status of a professional writer whose star was still on the rise. The life structure he had dreamed of establishing would firm up or crumble on the basis of the book's reception by critics and the public. He waited with bated breath, hoping that he was not casting pearls before swine.

Even before the early reviews, however, an ominous cloud settled overhead. Sister Helen died on June 14, only two weeks after *A Week*'s publication. At the funeral on the eighteenth, "Thoreau sat seemingly unmoved with his family through the service, but as the pall-bearers prepared to remove the bier, he arose and, taking a music box from the table, wound it and set it to playing a melody in a minor key that seemed to the listeners 'like no earthly tune.' . . . She was buried in the burying ground next to her brother John."[65] Three days before his brother had succumbed to lockjaw, Thoreau had written in his journal of listening to a music box: "Am I so like thee my brother that the cadence of two notes affects us alike?"(PJ, 1:362). Now, the music box reappeared in connection with Helen's death, and, especially considering her burial site next to John's, it is impossible not to conclude that Helen's death was linked with his brother's. Her death could not have failed to rekindle many of the agonizing emotions associated with John. Coming as it did, when he was seemingly on the brink of a literary triumph, Thoreau may have felt with renewed intensity that he deserved to be thwarted or even punished for his pursuit of success, or at least that any vaulting ambitions were unworthy, sinful, vain, and insignificant. Whatever his deep yearnings for recognition and adulation, they were tainted.

While the negative and mixed reviews probably served to confirm his sense of unworthiness, the undeniably proud and ambitious side of him was nevertheless deeply hurt and angered. The first review, on June 12, probably written by Greeley himself, was long, prominently displayed on the *Tribune*'s front page, and had many laudable things to say. But it condemned Thoreau's "Pantheistic egotism vaguely characterized as Transcendental" as "second-hand, imitative, often exaggerated—a bad specimen of a dubious and dangerous school. . . . We would have preferred to pass the theme in silence, but our admiration of his book and our reprehension of its Pantheism forbade that course. May we not hope that he will reconsider his too rapidly expressed notions on this head?"[66] The charge that he was "imitative"—no doubt of Emerson—must have rankled, and the attacks on his "Pantheism" left him open to recriminations and "I-told-you-so's" from the Thoreau women. Indeed, Greeley's criticisms showed him to be in some ways yet another ally of those domesticating forces that threatened to rob him of his autonomy. It is likely that he felt some sense of betrayal in response to the *Tribune* editor's reservations. In the summer there were some favorable reviews, *Holden's Dollar Magazine* declaring that "Mr. Thoreau may be safely judged, in reference to his own merits, without comparing his name to Emerson's," and the *New Hampshire Patriot* contending that it was "a remarkable volume and its author a remarkable man."[67] But the unfriendly or lukewarm reviews—which tended to be written by the more prominent figures—were probably taken more to heart by the sensitive Thoreau, as they are by many artists. The Duyckinck brothers in *Literary World* on September 22 had some kind words but could not refrain from noting, snidely, "We are not so rash or uninformed in the ways of the world as to presume to give counsel to a transcendentalist, so we offer no advice; but we may remark as a curious matter of speculation to be solved in the future—the probability or improbability of Mr. Thoreau's ever approaching nearer to the common sense or common wisdom of mankind."[68]

The "failure" of *A Week,* when all the returns were in, did not simply provoke a crisis in the Emerson-Thoreau relationship; rather, as should now be evident, it precipitated an intensification of a crisis that had already existed for some time—at the least since Thoreau had returned from Walden. A storm had been brewing for years, but now it would be impossible for either man to ignore, deny, or only hint at its existence. On virtually the eve of *A Week*'s appearance, May 22, 1849, Emerson had written to Ellen Rendall in England,

> There is nothing very good to tell you of the people here, no books, no poets, no artists; nothing but their incessant activity as pioneers & geographers. . . . In so great a population as ours, —all readers & writers—we must now

& then be entitled to a good & happy soul. The possibility of a great one in-
creases every hour. I ought to say, however, that my friend Thoreau is shortly
to print a book . . . which, I think will win the best readers abroad & at home.
(L, IV: 145)

Emerson's estimation of Thoreau and his book is made clearer by what
precedes it.[69] The implication is that Thoreau is neither the "good & happy soul" nor the "great one" he had once hoped and expected him to be.
While the book has value, it is not, he implies, a work of greatness. He may
also have been put off by what he took to be indirect rebukes of him in his
friend's book. To the extent that Thoreau was aware of Emerson's relatively tepid appraisals of him and his work (and there is considerable evidence that he was), he was privy to feelings of bitterness. Soon after *A
Week*'s publication, Emerson proved once again that he was not to be
completely trusted. He refused to do a review for the new *Massachusetts
Quarterly Review,* claiming with some justification that he was of Thoreau's "same clan & parish" (L, IV: 151) but probably also hesitant to commit to writing a less-than-rave review that would reflect well on neither his
friend nor his tutelage of him. But Emerson's passing up of the chance to
support his friend at this crucial hour set in motion an unfortunate chain of
events that further sabotaged the book's prospects. Theodore Parker, the
Review's editor, who found fault with the "sauciness" and "affectation"
in the volume, "the latter from his trying to be R. W. Emerson, & not being
contented with his own mother's son," put the book's fate at the mercy, or
mercilessness, of none other than James Russell Lowell, who had skewered
Thoreau so eagerly in *A Fable for Critics.* Lowell's review, though not
without some positive comment, was—not at all surprisingly—sharp and
satiric, ending with the statement, " 'Give me a sentence,' prays Mr. Thoreau bravely, 'which no intelligence can understand!'—and we think that
the kind gods have nodded."[70] When Emerson, to his credit, and others
sought to push the book by sending copies overseas, few Europeans responded with ardor. An anonymous reviewer for the *London Athenaeum*
in Emerson's beloved England hastily dismissed Thoreau: "The manner is
that of the worst offshoots of Carlyle and Emerson: all Mr. Thoreau's best
things are spoiled in the utterance. If he would trust in his own genius, he
has that to say which might command a larger audience. But imitations of
an imitation! The world is too old and the prophets are too many for such
things to have a chance of a public hearing in these days."[71]

Without question, Thoreau's perception that he had been let down
and undermined by Emerson in his moment of greatest professional need,
combined with the invidious comparisons made between him and his for-

mer mentor, brought to a boil already simmering, disquieting emotions. His resentment was no doubt heightened by a feeling of injustice. After all, hadn't Emerson gotten away with—indeed, partly established his reputation and notoriety on the basis of—his attacks on Establishment religion and society? He could not help but think that a double standard was being applied to him. Moreover, he had during this epoch played more than was his wont by the rules of civility and career advancement; had he received what he deserved? Often those imbued with the most acute sense of social injustice, the most idealistic, tend to be the most horrified and disillusioned when they experience the world, and the people they have looked to, dealing *them* a raw or calloused hand. Thoreau, the man who had been called "the judge" as a boy, who had cherished the idealistic conviction that justice and merit are destined to triumph and that laws of compensation informed the universe, could no longer ignore the amplified voice of experience: life was not always fair to those with merit, and worthy dreams can be dashed on the rocks of a not fully controllable reality. Even the most deserving people can be ground down.

In the immediate aftershock of *A Week*'s reception, Thoreau seems to have martialed his defenses against feelings of shame, self-doubt, failure, regret, and "what might have been," though there were no doubt moments when he was privy to such emotions. Although it must have been painful to face up to it squarely at this time, there would be occasions, especially later and in less defensive moments, to consider whether there was any validity to some of the criticisms, whether he had overestimated *A Week* as a virtuoso work of art, and whether he had deceived himself into misjudging the book's potential appeal to a reasonably wide audience.

In the short run, the sense of bitterness and injustice seems to have prevailed by and large, even if there is also a suggestion that the book could have been better if he had received honest feedback before its publication. The direct, conscious acknowledgment of the breakdown of the friendship with Emerson is poignantly documented in Thoreau's 1849 journal. The most pointed reference to Emerson is also clearly a reference to *A Week*: "I had a friend, I wrote a book, I asked my friend's criticism, I never got but praise for what was good in it—my friend became estranged from me and then I got blame for all that was bad, —& so I got at last the criticism which I wanted." "While my friend was my friend," he continues, "he flattered me, and I never heard the truth from him, but when he became my enemy he shot it to me on a poisoned arrow" (PJ, 3). It certainly appears from this comment that Thoreau had sensed for some time the strains in their relationship. In his view Emerson had encouraged him to publish *A Week*, had led him down this primrose path with flattery and praise, and then—when he most needed his friend's further support, understanding, and frank evaluation—Waldo had abandoned him to the wolves, found wanting the book he had previously lauded, and left him twisting in the wind. Moreover, the very qualities of cranky independence Emerson had once celebrated in his protégé he now condemned. To be sure, Thoreau was an often difficult, headstrong, prickly man who claimed cockily to know his own mind; Emerson was understandably hesitant to be perceived as an overbearing judge of his friend's work. Perhaps too, Emerson, aware of Thoreau's sensitive and proud side, his emotional investment in the book, and his sense of self-importance and specialness, could not bring himself to be completely candid and thereby hurt the younger man's feelings. However charitably his motives could be viewed, however—and one cannot discount less benign motives, at least on an unconscious level—the fact remained that Emerson stood convicted by Thoreau of being at best negligent and at worst disloyal and dishonest. Referring, no doubt, to himself in 1849, Thoreau writes, "Hence probably a man is said to be gulled when he is taken in" (PJ, 3). A friend, clearly Waldo, whom he swears he loved "heartily" has "indirectly accused" him of "coldness and disingenuousness" (PJ, 3). "We never have the benefit of our friend's criticism, and none is so severe & searching—until he is estranged from us," he says a bit later; Thoreau has not learned the "fatal truth which it concerns me most to know until he is estranged from [sic]—& then the harmless truth will be shot with a poisoned arrow will have a poisoned barb" (PJ, 3). The vehemence of these remarks indicates how deeply poisoned the relationship had become.

One could argue that, had both been able to "tell their wrath" at some earlier point, the tree might not have borne such poisoned fruit; but both men tended to hold in their negative emotions, letting them fester or expressing them only indirectly or privately. However, as has already been suggested, what had happened cannot be understood only within the framework of their particular personalities, but must also be considered within the framework of developmental imperatives. During this period, as he gradually came to realize and as the serious rift with Emerson over *A Week* brought into the open and accelerated, Thoreau was at least in the early throes of confronting a primary task of later young adulthood, what Levinson calls "becoming one's own man." An essential part of this stage, in which one aspires "to be more independent and self-sufficient, and less subject to the control of others," is, as one would expect, the severing of ties with significant mentors. In this phase, "Mentor relationships are likely to be especially stormy and vulnerable," and breaking the bonds is a "mutually painful, tortuous process."[72] Though there is the possibility for good mentoring relationships (especially among those mentors who recognize the importance of these relationships and are willing to work on them and give generously of themselves), even these good mentoring relationships may not escape entirely the uneasy emotions bred by this bond.[73] The protégé is in some respect a "son" who wants a "good father" to guide his efforts, provide him with trustworthy ground rules, and "magically" help him win a place for himself in the world. But this "son" also is likely to project his anxieties about the "bad father" onto the mentor, who therefore may be regarded as a tyrannical, uncharitable, manipulating, condescending, and competitively advantaged authority figure.[74] On his side, the mentor is subject to the wish to have a "good son" in his protégé and is therefore susceptible to feelings that his son is "bad" and has "failed" him in one way or another. He is also vulnerable to feelings of competitiveness, jealousy, envy, and resentment with respect to a "son" who is on the rise as he is, or is soon to be, on the decline. On both sides, the bond can evolve into a double bind and form of bondage. Certainly these dynamics strongly applied to the Emerson-Thoreau relationship. That Emerson was a full fourteen years older than Thoreau, and that the younger had been a "junior" to Emerson's "senior" for over ten years, only heightened the father-son transferences.[75] Though oedipal issues[76] and Thoreau's association of his mentor with his elder brother clearly were crucial factors complicating and intensifying the relationship, it is apparent that Thoreau's challenging and eventual rejection of his mentor were part of a "developmental process" by which he would ultimately become more "adult" and autonomous.[77] However necessary this breaking away from the mentor is, it can nevertheless be wrenching for both, the relationship frequently ending with

> strong conflicts and bad feelings on both sides. The young man may have powerful feelings of bitterness, rancor, grief, abandonment, liberation and rejuvenation. The sense of resonance is lost. The mentor he formerly loved and admired is now experienced as destructively critical and demanding, or as seeking to make one over in his own image rather than fostering one's individuality and independence. The mentor who only yesterday was regarded as an enabling teacher and friend has become a tyrannical father or smothering mother. The mentor, for his part, finds the young man inexplicably touchy, unreceptive to even the best counsel, irrationally rebellious, and ungrateful. By the time they are through, there is generally some validity in each one's criticism of the other.[78]

Thoreau's farewell would be a drawn-out and painful affair, and there would be flare-ups both of yearning and of rage in the future, most notably but not exclusively in 1851–52. But the long good-bye had gathered irreversible momentum by 1849.

By the late summer or early fall of 1849, it was all too clear that *A Week* would bring Thoreau neither renown nor appreciable income; it would not simply languish on the shelves but would be consigned to the basement. "Booksellers," says Harding, "returned their stocks to the publisher and the publisher relegated his stock to the cellar."[79] In the wake of *A Week*'s fate, Munroe and Co. reneged on their plans to publish *Walden*. It would be a blessing in disguise.[80] An era was coming to an end. But another life within his life was about to begin.

4 Seedtime

*T*HE abysmal public failure, and the relative critical failure, of *A Week* represented a crucial turning point, or, in Levinson's words, "marker event,"[1] in Thoreau's life. Blocked decisively in his bid for a life structure founded on some measure of economic support and social acclaim provided by a literary career, the thirty-two-year-old Thoreau gradually disengaged himself from investment in that particular dream and sought some other, more solid foundation for satisfactorily and definitively settling down.

Part of the readjustment, of course, was necessitated by financial exigency. In considerable debt, he explored ways to keep his head above water. "He thought briefly," Harding informs us, "of speculating in the cranberry market, buying wholesale in Boston and selling retail in New York City, only to discover to his dismay that the New York retail price was lower than the Boston wholesale."[2] Reluctantly, he returned to the family pencil factory and helped make "a thousand dollars' worth of pencils," but unfortunately the would-be entrepreneur wound up selling them at a loss in New York. Confronted by dire need (and, no doubt, by his desire to move emphatically outside the orbit of his father's business), he began to settle on surveying as a way to make the minimal income required to support the new life edifice he was intent on building. While he did pay room and board to his parents, it certainly did not hurt economically that he lived at home. By November 1849 he was "doing enough surveying to justify purchasing a notebook to keep his records straight."[3] Surveying was an especially congenial means to earn a meager living, providing as it did some remuneration to a man eager to reestablish his identity as a "traveller in Concord," to stake out and define the parameters of a new life, to survey the possibilities. He was a man who now insisted, with renewed fervor, that he was marginal to the town and all it stood for and that he was capable of retaining "broad margins"; surveying was an occupation that underlined this insistence. Yet even this livelihood, for all the free-lance independence and opportunities for excursions to the woods and margins of the town it offered, could be perceived as an impediment to the more liberated existence for which he yearned. On September 20, 1851, he would report that he had been "perambulating the bounds of the town all the week, and dealing with the most commonplace and worldly-minded men, and emphatically *trivial* things." He feels as if he "had committed suicide in a sense. I am again forcibly struck with the truth of the fable of Apollo serving King Admetus. . . . A fatal coarseness is the result of mixing in the trivial affairs of men." When forced to deal, while surveying, with "mean and narrow-minded men," he complains that he labors "under a curse" and walks "not with God but with the devil" (J, III:5, 23–24). Establishing a novel and inviolate life would not be easy.

In a November 20, 1849, letter to Blake, Thoreau portrays himself as in the process of laying the groundwork for a set routine that would serve as the basis for the new life he was contemplating: "Within a year my walks have extended themselves, and almost every afternoon, (I read, or write, or make pencils, in the forenoon, and by the last means get a living for my body) . . . I am astonished at the wonderful retirement through which I move, rarely meeting a man in these excursions" (C, 250–51). On the verge of extricating himself from the harried and often harrowing focus on "making it," he says, "I cannot help feeling that of all the human inhabitants of nature hereabouts, only we two have leisure to admire and enjoy our inheritance" (C, 251). By 1850, with pencil making becoming less prominent and surveying more so, Thoreau—working to refine and revise his life in a manner that would allow him more genuinely to settle down—had, according to Harding and Bode, "become as much of a settled man as he was ever to be" (C, 253). In 1850 he writes, "Commonly I am not at home in the world" (J, II:76), and one fundamental project of this period was to make again for himself—as he had done at Walden, building from the ground up—a home in the world. Morning writing, afternoon walking, some surveying: these were essential cornerstones for the new framework that was emerging.

The *Journal*, which started to expand enormously in 1850, with many long, dated entries, was the heart and hearth of the "home" he was constructing.[4] It represented, along with his walks, not just a part of life but, in essence, life itself during this transitional period. Whatever took him away from journalizing for any appreciable time, as surveying occasionally did

(his surveying expeditions frequently coincided with sparse journal entries), could cause considerable irritability and anxiety. The *Journal* was,
of course, his primary source book and workbook for more formal writings; he had not, after all, scrapped the idea of a literary career but rather
shifted gears to a concept far less dependent on quick acceptance or acclaim by the public or fickle critics.[5] But it would not be an exaggeration to
say that the *Journal* was itself becoming a kind of Walden, a moratorium
and settling down insulated from threat,[6] where he could safely experiment with new and more suitable versions of identity; establish and maintain assurance of continuities with his past—both holding onto and subtly
modifying the Walden ego ideal; reconstruct and revise his life and vision
in a selective and satisfying way; rediscover his own voice—distinguishing
between "mine" and mime; be intimate with (even make love to) himself
and idealized readers, feel generative, and ward off stagnation; determine
without outside interference the directions in which he wanted to move
and grow. It was a way of daily *composing* himself and his self, of retaining
sanity, of regaining a sanatory composure and control over his life.[7] The
Journal was, in its sheer physicality as well as in its ideas and images, an
embodiment of Thoreau, a reification of himself, an alter ego that grew
with him. There he daily stayed in touch with himself, took his pulse, read
his barometer, and learned afresh how vital he was. The *Journal*, then, had
many and shifting meanings for Thoreau; its centrality to his post-1849
life in particular is indisputable. And over the years new meanings and dimensions would evolve—his journal would be "field notes" (J, V:32),
book of Concord,[8] "meteorological journal of the mind," Kalendar of
both the natural and human seasons. Though always remaining a writer's
"workshop," where he could hone his craft, generate ideas and images,
and glean essays, more and more—especially after *Walden*—it would
stand on its own as the record and testament, the surviving remnant, of
Thoreau's life; it would more and more become, in his eyes, its own reason
for being, the book of Thoreau.

In November 1850, he connects the *Journal* with his cravings for further growth and his sense of the phase of life he has entered:

> My Journal should be the record of my love. I would write in it only of the
> things I love. . . . I have no more distinctness or pointedness in my yearnings
> than an expanding bud, which does indeed point to flower and fruit, to sum-
> mer and autumn, but is aware of the warm sun and spring influence only. I feel
> ripe for something, yet do nothing, can't discover what that thing is. I feel fer-
> tile merely. It is seedtime with me. I have lain fallow long enough. (J, II:101)

Even earlier in his 1850 journal he had recorded his intimation that he was on the brink of another seminal period, as Walden had been. "Seeds," he says, are "beginning to expand in me, which propitious circumstance may bring to the light & to perfection" (PJ, 3). It was a time combining qualities of a winterlike moratorium—a period of testing and being tested, of hibernation and the sounding of inner resources—and of early spring when the seeds have sent fragile roots downward and have extended buds and early shoots skyward, still quite vulnerable to wintry blasts but already avatars of the secure rootedness, blossoming, and fruition to follow.[9] During this time of reorientation and renewal, of reactivated identity crisis and gradual identity consolidation, Thoreau was ready to be a "forest dweller" once again.[10]

Before the seeds can be safely planted, the soil must be given a rest, cleared, and prepared. For Thoreau, part of this process of paving the way for future expansion involved the acknowledgment that he was not as self-directed as he had often claimed and believed himself to be. As Levinson observes, a person moving into later young adulthood "who has prided himself on his ability to act autonomously realizes now that he is not as independent as he had thought."[11] Looking back on his 1847–49 sojourn in civilized life, he was coming to realize, when he could afford to let down his guard and be honest with himself, that he had oriented himself too much to others' expectations and demands—his family's, Emerson's, his townspeople's, the literary establishment's. Further jarring him from any temptation to give in to civil society's demands was the state of the Union. While Congress was passing compromises and making ignoble concessions to slave states (including the Fugitive Slave Law), Thoreau was resolved to be on the lookout for any signs of compromise, concession, or moral stagnation in himself that would jeopardize self-emancipation; the only strategy he could see himself following was to withdraw from a society that was making laws that compromised it.

An April 30, 1850, letter to Blake shows Thoreau adding a chapter to his personal mythology, articulating a new version of his young adulthood, revised in the light of what he has now learned about even his susceptibility to social influence. After commenting that he does not fear exaggerating "the value and significance of life" but rather that he will "not be up to the occasion which it is," he says of the past several years, "I shall be sorry to remember that I was there, but noticed nothing remarkable . . . lived in the golden age a hired man; visited Olympus even, but fell asleep after dinner, and did not hear the conversation of the gods" (C, 257–58). For an extended period, in what should have been the "golden age" of early young adulthood, he had been but a novice and apprentice, an Apollo to many an Admetus. Then he had "visited Olympus," presumably moved to

Walden Pond and lived in a rarefied and clarified Olympian atmosphere
that inspired his art and fortified his sense of self. However, he had fallen
"asleep after dinner": in the process of seeking the affirmation and rewards conferred by civilized society, he had forsaken the lean but often
ambrosial staples of his spiritual diet for the coarse, overly rich feast and
desserts offered by society and had grown sluggish, no longer sufficiently
vigilant or alert to the "conversation of the gods." Unable to hear or feel
assured of the grace of the gods, out of touch with the mountain's uncontaminated sources, he had come perilously close to losing his bearings and
forfeiting even that measure of personal authenticity and grace previously
granted him. Only now, after *A Week*'s publication—compelled to face
the fact that he would probably never make it as a popular, universally esteemed writer in his lifetime and that he could not rely on Emerson or anyone else to show him the way—could he let go of the ladder, relinquish preoccupation with a dream of success that had in retrospect become a kind of
tyranny (though the dream, as will be seen, did not flicker out entirely),
renounce competitive strivings, and truly become his own person. Only
through a new resolve could he avoid the fate of the horse he described in
a parable in June 1850, "who persisted in wintering out," whose master
finally gave up trying to catch, but who eventually "had had enough of free
life and pined for his stable, and so suffered himself to be caught" (J,
II:37–38). He would have to resist the urge to come in from the snow. He
would have to look more to himself, less to others. For all his proclama-
tions that he had been marching to a different drummer, he had not been as
inner-directed as he had boasted after college, in his earlier writings, even
at Walden, and—most obviously to him at this point—in the 1847–49
period. The flaws and dangers of the post-Walden versions of his life structure were now apparent. In the April 30 letter to Blake he remarks,
"There is none who does not lie hourly in the respect he pays to false appearance. . . . We wonder that the sinner does not confess his sin. . . . when
we are weary with the burden of life, why do we not lay down this load of
falsehoods which we have volunteered to sustain, and be refreshed as
never mortal was?" (C, 256–57). He had realized some of his "sins"; now
he could repent.

No longer so entirely under the sway of the illusion that he had fully
become his own man, even *at* Walden, Thoreau anticipated with some
exhilaration embarking even more adventurously on his own path. "I delight," he says in the spring of 1850, "to come to my bearing—not walk in
procession with pomp & parade—but to walk with the builder of the universe." The image of regaining the high ground of the "upland farmer" (C,
260)—invoked in a May 28 letter to Blake—spoke to his desire for an

Olympian retirement. On November 25, 1850, he expresses the wish to "forget all my morning's occupations, my obligations to society" in the walks that were emerging as so indispensable to his ritualized disengagement from society. He longs for "one of those old, meandering, dry, uninhabited roads, which lead away from towns, which lead us away from temptation . . . on which you can go off at half-cock and wave adieu to the village." He was inclined to see society, which had seemed so real to him only recently, as an arbitrary and artificial entity; he saw "nothing permanent" in the society "around" him and was "not quite committed to any of its ways." His "freedom" he was more than "usually jealous of," and his "connections with and obligations to society" he experienced as "at present very slight and transient" (J, II:110, 322, 47, 141).

The theme of the need for more authentic self-liberation is often repeated in 1850–51. As he knew firsthand, "Men are generally very spoiled by being so civil and well-disposed" (J, II:328–29). He recognized what he had sacrificed by trying, however inconsistently and ambivalently, to be (as he perceived it) a "good boy" who follows the arbitrary rules in an effort to reap society's dubious approval and rewards. And, in any case, there was no ironclad guarantee that hard work, merit, and justice *would* prevail, even in supposedly genteel and "civilized" circles. "If I repent of anything," he writes on January 5, 1851, "it is of my good behavior. What demon possessed me that I behaved so well?" (J, II:137). It thus had taken Thoreau more years to learn than he was usually wont to admit—he didn't learn it (and then only incompletely) until *after* the Walden experience and after years of seeking to establish himself in the literary profession—that it is not easy to find your own way. It is one thing to *say* (and even convince yourself for a time) that you are fully grown, but it is altogether another truly to become your own person. As Thoreau can finally bring himself to say in July 1851, "O my dear friends, I have not forgotten you. I will know you to-morrow. . . . I had ceased to have faith in myself. I thought I was grown up and become what I was intended to be, but it is earliest spring with me." Soon thereafter he refers to "some sad experience in conforming to the wishes of friends" (J, II:315, 319). Just as it was "earliest spring" when he had first started to prepare for the move to Walden, so now it was in some way "earliest spring" again—another chance—as he began to reconstruct life and identity in later young adulthood with middle age looming. But it was also deepest winter; breaking away was an even more difficult and fateful crisis than he could have imagined, made even more so because time was no longer so much on his side and harder, less tentative choices had to be made.

Already alluded to is the extent to which breaking away from Emerson was a crucial—and often threatening—part of the process of coming into his own. Before his seeds could thrive, Thoreau needed to push on with the unfinished business of laying to rest his reliance on, and attachment to, the man who had exerted such an immense influence on him. Imagery of death, loss, and mourning abound in his early 1850 reflections on friendship, and it is highly likely that Emerson is still preeminently the "friend" from whose orbit he needed to separate himself. "W[e] lose our friends," he remarks, "when we cease to be friends not when they die—then they depart—then we are sad & go into mourning for them. Death is no separation compared with that which takes place when we cease to have confidence in one with whom we have walked in confidence. . . . How completely he is departed! . . . No things can be further asunder than friends estranged." Only by acknowledging the death of the friendship and walking away from the grave—for "Friends estranged are buried alive"—can he get on, unburdened, with other developmental tasks. Yet burying the friendship is not easy: he alternates between rage and conciliation, between a recognition of "lingering sympathy" and a wish to sever all ties. If Thoreau has difficulty forgetting that "my so called friend comes near to being my greatest enemy—for when he deceives me, he deceives me more than any— He betrays as an enemy has no opportunity to," he also seeks to put the injury and fury in the past: "My friend died long ago—why follow a body to the grave yard?"(PJ, 3). In one of his more placid moments, he imagines himself standing at a crossroads where he must reluctantly bid a protracted but definitive farewell:

> Friends meet & part as when two pilgrims who have walked together many days . . . reach a point where their courses diverge and linger there awhile and then bidding each other fare one takes goes this road & the other that & as they . . . mutu[a]lly turn to wave a last fare well & watch each other's retreating figure—until at last they are concealed from one another by a bend in the road behind a rock and the sun goes down behind the mountains. leaving each alone.

The friends are "sorry to part but their duty calls them different ways" (PJ, 3). Elsewhere he comments, "I should consider this friend of mine is a *Great* fellow. . . . I do not despair of knowing him better" (PJ, 3). But if Thoreau was under the temporary impression that he had fully made his peace with Emerson, he would discover by late 1851 that coming tranquilly to terms with the death of a significant friendship and mentor relationship was easier said than done. The break was even harder to make because the two men continued to see each other, and Thoreau was still called on by Waldo to perform pragmatic tasks for him.[12]

It would be misleading to suggest that Thoreau's urge at this time to disengage himself from civilized society had its source entirely in growthful, progressive, self-actualizing motivations. The resurgence of his craving for wildness—"How near to good is what is wild," he writes in 1849 (PJ, 3)—and his galvanized desire to distance himself from the town represented in part a return to the old need to defend and insulate himself from vulnerability to others. Just as the embarrassment of the woodsburning episode in 1844 had propelled him in the direction of the pond, so did the community's response (and his *imagining* of their response) to *A Week*'s failure humiliate him, leave him exposed, and act as a catalyst that drove him again toward the woods. It is little wonder that at the end of 1849 he was musing again about a forest retreat and refuge: "I longed then to go there & live & never come back to Concord streets" (PJ, 3). James Kendall Hosmer remembers meeting Thoreau sometime after *A Week*'s dismal popular reception:

> This strange man [Thoreau], rumor said, had written a book no copy of which had ever been sold. . . . The edition fell dead from the press, and all the books, one thousand or more, he had collected in his mother's house, a queer library of unsold books which he used to exhibit to visitors laughing grimly over his unfortunate venture into the field of letters. My aunt sent me one day to carry a message to Mrs. Thoreau and my rap on her door was answered by no other man than this odd son who, on the threshold received my message. . . . Thinking of the forest fire I fancied he smelled of smoke and peered curiously up the staircase behind him hoping I might catch a glimpse of that queer library all of one book duplicated many times.[13]

This anecdote may be taken as suggestive or symptomatic of the attitude of some townspeople, their skepticism about Thoreau seemingly vindicated, eager to pounce on his literary disgrace and not to let him forget it. Certainly Thoreau must have suspected or imagined that this was a common attitude. After all, some owners of the forest he had burned, he writes, "declared behind my back that I was a 'damned rascal:' and a flibbertigibbet or two, who crowed like the old cock, shouted some reminiscences of 'burnt woods' from safe recesses for some years after" (J, 11:25). If they still mumbled behind his back about his being a "woodsburner" (even Hosmer refers to the "forest fire" and the lingering smell of smoke), they now had the ammunition further to scorn him, to brand him an arrogant pretender, an artistic lightweight, a lazy hypocrite. Certainly any fantasies about being the local boy who makes good had been dashed, and he had been forced to eat crow and hear the "crowing" of others. Thoreau would write in the fall of 1850, "If I could wholly cease to be ashamed of myself, I think that all my days would be fair" (J, II:77). The self-protective, retractive reflex set off by the perception of being stigmatized was rather similar to that of the turtle: "We have repeatedly to withdraw ourselves into our shells of thought like the tortoise, somewhat helplessly" (J, II:46). Like the apple tree, he needed thorns to ward off his foes (J, III:75).

That he was living with his parents, who on September 29, 1849, had, largely due to growing business prosperity, purchased a house (the "Yellow House") on Main Street, near the town center, and were planning to move from the modest Texas Street house he had helped to build to this more prestigious (and pretentious) address, made Thoreau even more defensive.[14] It was all the more necessary to assert his wildness fiercely and thereby fend off any charges that he was an eminently tame and civilized "mother's son." Clearly he was not comfortable with this move, as his Aunt Maria reported, though ultimately he managed to transform his attic room into a congenial environment, a sort of Walden hut combined with a museum of natural history and Indian relics.[15] The compulsion to re-create, and restore himself to, some version of Walden was intensifying. He was a prophet without honor in Concord; the "fathers and the mothers of the town," he remarks acidly in 1851, "don't want to have any prophets born into their families, —damn them!" (J, III:119).

The context of this period thus helps explain why, six years after the event, Thoreau was impelled to discuss the 1844 woodsburning in his May–June 1850 journal.[16] The reaction of his neighbors to *A Week*'s failure was, in his mind, roughly analogous to their responses to his actions with regard to the 1844 fire, and it reactivated memories of this earlier misadventure. Thoreau, whose "edition fell dead from the press," still "smelled of smoke." The startlingly quick demise of *A Week* rekindled and added fuel to the fire of the community's disapproval. The would-be nature lover and woodsman had "carelessly" started a fire and then perched atop Fair Haven Hill, refusing to help his fellow Concordians extinguish it; the would-be author had written a book that fell flat on its face. Thoreau was feeling the heat—and the flush of shame—from his neighbors, and in his journal of 1850 he tried to start a backfire. His preoccupation in 1850 with the fire suggests, moreover, his fixation on the event; though years had passed, it yet remained a touchy issue. To be sure, he was in part prompted to think about fire because of "burnings" at this season; in early June he was "tending a burning" and gave advice in his journal on how to control fires (J, II:27–30). A business letter of March 11, 1850, from Emerson quite possibly led him to think, with some discomfort, about the fire and *A Week*'s flop: "Will you also, if you have opportunity, warn Mr Bartlett, on my part, against burning his woodlot, without having there present a sufficient number of hands, to prevent the fire from spreading into my wood, —which, I think, will be greatly endangered, unless much care is used" (C, 256). That Emerson would allude to careless fire setting betrays at best a poor memory or insensitivity to an issue about which Thoreau was highly sensitive; indeed, he may have detected some hint of accusation, or of rubbing salt into the wound, in Emerson's reminder about the dangers of unsupervised fires—this from the same man who had, from his point of view, behaved rather negligently with respect to his book and literary career—and thereby felt compelled to offer a defense of himself, both past and present.

His discussion of the fire surely insinuates at least as much about his present state of mind as it does about 1844. The journal passages in question constitute an elaborate self-defense and rationalization. In denying any culpability or persistent discomfort regarding the woodsburning episode, Thoreau is also proclaiming that he is not going to be distressed or discouraged by the townspeople's current opinions of him. While he had "hitherto . . . felt like a guilty person, —nothing but shame and regret," he had finally reached the conclusion that "I have set fire to the forest, but I have done no wrong therein, and now it is as if the lightning had done it. These flames are but consuming their natural food." Parenthetically—but revealingly—he adds, "(It has never troubled me from that day to this more than if the lightning had done it. The trivial fishing [which he had been doing with Hoar and which had led to their attempts to cook the fish over a fire set in a tree stump] was all that disturbed me and disturbs me still)" (J, II:23). In questioning his townspeople's judgment of his 1844 behavior, he is also distancing himself from their current evaluations and thus shielding himself from shame and guilt. Triviality, in fishing or any other pursuit, disturbs him more, and he seeks here to dissociate himself from the trivialities of Concord. That the locomotive engine "has since burned over nearly all the same ground and more" further exonerates him. Having reached this verdict, "I at once ceased to regard the owners and my own fault, —if fault there was any in the matter, —and attended to the phenomenon before me [the fire], determined to make the most of it." Similarly, he seems by 1850 to be reconciling himself to the "phenomenon" of being burned by *A Week*'s failure and is prepared to "make the most of it," learn from it, and strike out in new and more rewarding directions.

The fire had ushered in a period of both moratorium and accomplishment, and now *A Week*'s going up in flames promised to do the same. "To be sure," Thoreau writes of 1844, "I felt a little ashamed when I reflected on what a trivial occasion this had happened, that at the time I was no better employed than my townsmen." Soon after, he had found "better employment" at Walden; in like manner, he implies, he is once again, after the futile struggle to make it, in a position to be better employed than his townsmen. In September 1851 he would ask, "How happens it that there are few men so well employed [as he] . . . but that a little money or fame would buy them off from their present pursuits?" (J, II:473). For all their mocking and disparagement of his offbeat endeavors, he was at least beginning again to feel superior to them, special, and impervious to their criticisms.

As if to strike a more positive note and underscore the necessity of a "trial by fire" if one is definitively to clear one's ground and grow again, he turns on June 25, 1850, to considering the virtues of fire:

> It is without doubt an advantage on the whole. It sweeps and ventilates the forest floor, and makes it clear and clean. It is nature's broom. By destroying the punier underwood it gives prominence to the larger and sturdier trees, and makes a wood in which you can go and come. I have often remarked with how much more comfort and pleasure I could walk in woods through which a fire had run the previous year. It will clean the forest floor like a broom perfectly smooth and clear, —no twigs left to crackle underfoot, the dead and rotten wood removed, —and thus in the course of two or three years new huckleberry fields are created for the town, —for birds and men.

He continues, clearly referring to the 1844 fire but also perhaps to the conflagration of his dreams of becoming a successful man of letters, "When the lightning burns the forest its Director makes no apology to man, and I was but His agent. Perhaps we owe to this accident partly some of the noblest natural parks. It is inspiriting to walk amid the fresh green sprouts of grass and shrubbery pushing upward through the charred surface with more vigorous growth." The fire is both purifying and generative; it ultimately leads to the "noblest parks," "fresh green sprouts," and "more vigorous growth." By the same token, *A Week*'s failure was prompting a clean break, he thought, with his desires for social validation; it had "cleared and cleaned" the ground for a period of "more vigorous growth" on his part. It promised to wipe clean the slate of his own life. Suggestively, immediately after this entry on the regenerative qualities of fire, Thoreau makes the statement, reiterated in the "Village" chapter of *Walden*, "Wherever a man goes men will pursue and paw him with their dirty institutions." In coming to terms, however defensively, with the 1844 fire, he is surely engaged in the process of clearing away the "punier underwood" that his attachment to civil society's "dirty institutions" at least in part represents. After the sentence on dirty institutions, he observes, "Sometimes an arrowhead is found with the mouldering shaft still attached" (J, II:39–

40). It was Thoreau's hope that his "trial by fire" would reveal new arrowheads and that he, like the arrowhead, would rise phoenixlike from the ashes.

Like the fire, which permits a fresh start, *A Week*'s failure, he wished to convince himself, was ultimately purifying. The woodsburning incident had insured a moratorium; and so had his book's going up in smoke. For all his visions and fantasies of literary acclaim, Thoreau may well have been aware of a feeling of relief as the chances for unambiguous success receded. As he could perhaps more readily if intermittently concede now, the obstacles to such success had not been entirely external. His forays into the "civilized" realm of career consolidation had, among other things, reaggravated guilt and anxiety and necessitated another period of withdrawal, during which worldly ambition would again be safely submerged. He had written to Blake on August 10, 1849—when *A Week*'s fate was still up in the air—"Be not anxious to avoid poverty. In this way the wealth of the universe may be securely invested" (C, 247). And the day after the anniversary of his brother's birth, July 6, 1851, he says, "There is some advantage in being the humblest, cheapest, least dignified man in the village, so that the very stable boys shall damn you. Methinks I enjoy that advantage to an unusual extent" (J, II:285). His trips to Cape Cod in 1849–51 were in part attempts to recapture a sense of wildness and put distance between himself and the pollution of civilization; the ocean was a vaster (though less benign) version of the pond. In *Cape Cod* he would associate wildness with another kind of purifying fire: "My spirits rose in proportion to the outward dreariness. The towns need to be ventilated. The gods would be pleased to see some pure flames from their altars. They are not to be appeased with cigar-smoke" (CC, 51).

Perhaps most disturbing in its implications had been the unfolding conflict with, and estrangement from, Emerson. If at Walden Thoreau had been able to convince himself of his purity, that conviction had been sullied as he strove for success. To have had such a serious falling-out with a man he had worshiped was threatening enough; but the emotions evoked also had a markedly oedipal component and summoned again the demons associated with John and his death. If the friend with whom he had once had "differences" in the late 1830s and early 1840s had been his brother, that friend had now also become Waldo: "In a difference with a friend I have felt that our intercour[s]e was prophaned when that friend made haste come to speech about it." He was "grieved" and "wounded" by his friend's actions, and such a wound "cannot be permanently healed" (PJ, 3). Thoreau had lost Emerson (funereal imagery permeates his references to Waldo), and he had lost his brother, under equivocal and nettlesome circumstances; the wounds, more grave because inflicted in connection with his two most significant friends, would never completely heal. The Walden experience had only anesthetized and stitched up loosely the deep incisions of grief and guilt related to his brother; and under certain conditions—the conflict with Emerson, the spiking of ambition, such reminders as significant anniversaries associated with John, for instance—the anodyne could wear off and the stitches fall out. Vulnerable with respect to Emerson as he was regarding John, Thoreau observes, "My friend can wound me / For to him I bear my breast" (PJ, 3). The imagery of "wounding" and of phallic "poisoned arrows" (PJ, 3) is quite fitting for one with unshakable oedipal anxieties; it is not surprising that in such a frame of mind some form of self-inflicted mutilation is acceptable, even welcome: "His [the Western man's] cowardly *legs* run away with him—but the Hindoo [with whom Thoreau identifies] bravely cuts off his legs in the first place" (PJ, 3). He observes later, in a similar vein, "The inquiry in Hindoo philosophy is how to commit suicide in an effectual and worthy manner" (PJ, 3). The victims of love's wounds can accept their maiming or invalidism with relative equanimity: "Love's invalides [*sic*] are not like those of common wars / More than its scars—/ They are not disabled for a higher love / But taught to look above" (PJ, 3). Guilt could also be kept at bay by forswearing any negative feelings or destructive intentions; Thoreau claims on occasion that he loves his friend "heartily" and would "always treat" him "tenderly" (PJ, 3). But that he could not always repress or suppress anger only served to aggravate the guilt: "I had tenderly cherished the flower of our friendship till one day my friend treated it as a weed. It (did not survive the shock but) drooped & withered from that hour" (PJ, 3). If there remains any doubt that his brother and, probably, his sister Helen were also on his mind as he brooded about Emerson, it is dispelled when, in the context of his lamentations about the alienation from Waldo, he says, "To have a brother or a sister—to have a gold mine on your farm—to find diamonds in the gravel heaps before your door—how rare these things are," and then, even more to the point, "What a difference whether you have a brother on earth or not. Whether in all your walks you meet only strangers or in one house is one who knows you. & whom you know" (PJ, 3).

The "tragedy of more than 5 acts" (PJ, 3) of his ruptured friendship with Emerson reawakened the "curse" connected with his brother and precipitated—as his journal entries of 1849–52 indicate—another intense period of grief work. As I have argued elsewhere,[17] Thoreau's account of his October 1849 journey with Channing to Cape Cod—including his visit in Cohasset with Ellen Sewall Osgood and his witnessing with her husband of the wreckage of the *St. John*—reveals just how central the mourning process was to him at this time. Still transfixed by the tragedy of John's death, he remarks, for instance, "A man can attend but one funeral in the course of his life, can behold but one corpse" (CC, 20–21). The sight of battered corpses could not have failed to arouse memories of his brother's broken and wasted body, and his graphic descriptions of these ravaged remains no doubt drew on and further evoked those memories. In June 1850 he traveled to the Cape once again, and in July 1851, close to the eleventh anniversary of John's trip to Scituate to court Ellen Sewall, he returned to Cohasset, where he continued to search for remnants of the *St. John* and, quite possibly, mourn his own losses once more. Though he went to the Cape in pursuit of wildness and purity, he also came to associate it with a coming to terms with death. The estrangement from Emerson, by reopening older wounds, undoubtedly compounded his need to work through grief and guilt.

Thus, however previously and characteristically inclined Thoreau had been to deny or avoid the blunt fact of death, it was difficult to do so entirely during a period when he was confronted with the death of a career dream, of a family member, and of the bond with Emerson. He had witnessed many wrecks even before going to Cape Cod; and *Cape Cod* (parts of which were given as lectures as early as January 1850) is strewn with wrecks and Thoreau's responses to them.[18] In a sense, his own life had been on the rocks. In his ruminations on wrecks, he struggles toward a more general acceptance of death. On the one hand, the death of certain dreams and the accompanying end of an era in his life also offered the promise of a new life, a rebirth. The sea's power, like the fire's, expedited new beginnings. He observes,

> Vessels, with seeds in their cargoes, destined for particular ports, where perhaps they were not needed, have been cast away on desolate islands, and though their crews perished, some of their seeds have been preserved. . . . It is an ill wind that blows nobody any good, and for the time lamentable shipwrecks may thus contribute a new vegetable to a continent's stock, and prove on the whole a lasting blessing to its inhabitants. (CC, 165)

And so Thoreau hoped it would be for him: out of the wreckage there was emerging a regenerative "seedtime," which would ultimately lead to blossom and fruit.

On the other hand, death also signified a finality that was grimmer, more disconcerting, but which had to be acknowledged. The drowning of Margaret Fuller, along with her husband and child, in a shipwreck on Fire Island, New York, on July 19, 1850, functioned as a forceful reminder that death was a fact that could not be easily shunted aside or sentimentalized.

At Emerson's request (as if Waldo could not bring himself to do it and had to call on Thoreau to do his dirty work for him), he set out for Fire Island on July 24 in an effort to retrieve whatever he could of Fuller's manuscripts and belongings.[19] Less than a year before, he had hunted for relics of the *St. John* and had been compelled to take notice of nature's seeming indifference and human life's fragility; at Fire Island, these lessons were driven home again. Unable to find any of Fuller's remains or possessions, he was nevertheless faced with ample evidence of the wreckage, including "the relics of a human body" (later described in *Cape Cod* [CC, 108]) "mangled by sharks," which he thought might be the body of abolitionist Charles Sumner's brother (C, 263–64). It is likely that the image of his own brother's body took possession of him, either consciously or unconsciously, as he contemplated the bones "with a little flesh adhering to them": "As I stood there they grew more and more imposing. They were alone with the beach and the sea, whose hollow roar seemed addressed to them, and I was impressed as if there was an understanding between them and the ocean. . . . That dead body had taken possession of the shore, and reigned over it as no living one could" (CC, 108–9).

The drowning of the remarkable woman who had played such a role in his career and encouraged his work on the "good week"[20] prompted Thoreau to concede, however grudgingly and equivocally, the truth he had so often preferred to ignore or deny as a younger man: his own perishability. Although he claims bravely, early in an August 9, 1850, letter to Blake, which reports on Fuller's death, that "all that we commonly call life and death . . . affects me less than my dreams," he goes on to betray a sense of immediacy pricked by his realization that time is limited: "I say to myself, Do a little more of that work which you have confessed to be good. You are neither satisfied nor dissatisfied with yourself, without reason. Have you not a thinking faculty of inestimable value? If there is an experiment which you would like to try, try it" (C, 265). In a summer journal entry in which he apparently rehearsed much of what he would write to Blake, an intensified, even reckless, urgency is even more pronounced: "Do what you reprove yourself for not doing. . . . Let me say to you and to myself in one breath, Cultivate the tree which you have found to bear fruit in your soil. . . . If you know of any risk to run, run it. . . . Who knows but you are dead already? Do not stop to be scared yet; there are more terrible things to come, and ever to come" (J, II:44–45). Try as he might to be undaunted by the fear of death and time (as he had been to such a degree at Walden), he often gave the impression now that he was whistling in the dark past the graveyard. "Improve every opportunity to express yourself in writing," he says in late 1851, "as if it were your last" (J, III:140).

If the death of others starkly reminded him of "more terrible things to come," so the first telltale signs of his own physical deterioration—he acquired false teeth in May 1851—spurred some rather melancholy thoughts about aging and added to the urgency of his quest for renewal. Though he joked about the experience of being unconscious and under ether—"You expand like a seed in the ground"—the loss of his teeth impressed upon him his mortality and dramatized the extent to which his "seeds" were still dormant and how much yet remained to be done as middle age relentlessly approached. On July 19, 1851, a week after his thirty-fourth birthday, he takes stock of where he is and how far, in a relatively short time, he still has to go: "Here I am thirty-four years old, and yet my life is almost wholly unexpanded. How much is in the germ! There is such an interval between my ideal and the actual in many instances that I may say I am unborn" (J, II:316). To be sure, Thoreau fluctuated during this period, as he had during the identity crisis of his pre-Walden years, [21] between patience and impatience. In the same passage in which he bemoans the discrepancy between the "ideal and the actual," he tries to soothe himself with the reflection that his "seasons revolve more slowly than those of nature; I am differently timed. I am contented. The rapid revolution of nature, even of nature in me, why should it hurry me? Let a man step to the music which he hears, however measured. Is it important that I should mature as soon as an apple-tree? aye; as soon as an oak?" (J, II:316). The dialectic between the desire to establish his own pace and rhythms and the need to get on with the pressing task of expansion was a persistent and often painful one. In order to clear a space for growth, Thoreau yearned to reclaim the posture of patiencehood he had come close to losing in the 1847–49 era, but he knew he was not getting any younger and age had a way of ossifying mind and spirit as well as bones. "The man who does not grow rigid with years and experience! Where is he?" he asks after returning from Cohasset in 1851. "What avails it to grow hard merely? The harder you are, the more brittle really, like the bones of the old. How much rarer and better to grow mellow!" (J, II:361–62).

While steeling himself for the long haul and refusing (as he indicates, soon before going to Cohasset to search for further remnants of shipwrecks) "to be shipwrecked on a vain reality" (J, II:317), he was nevertheless beset with the anxiety that his growth was all in the past, that he had already lost his youthful elasticity and facility for expansion:

> Methinks my present experience is nothing; my past experience is all in all. I think that no experience which I have to-day comes up to, or is comparable with, the experiences of my boyhood. . . . Formerly, methought, nature devel-

oped as I developed, and grew up with me. My life was ecstasy. In youth, before I lost any of my senses, I can remember that I was all alive, and inhabited my body with inexpressible satisfaction. . . . I wondered if a mortal had ever known what I know. I looked in books for some recognition of a kindred experience, but, strange to say, I found none. Indeed, I was slow to discover that other men had had this experience. . . . The maker of me was improving me. When I detected this interference I was profoundly moved. For years I marched as to a music in comparison with which the military music of the streets is noise and discord. I was daily intoxicated, and yet no man could call me intemperate. With all your science can you tell me how it is, and whence it is, that light comes into the soul? (J, II:306–7)

As if both to warm himself to and to warn himself about the pressing work of the present, he invokes Ecclesiastes' admonition to "Remember thy Creator in the days of thy youth; i.e., lay up a store of natural influences. Sing while you may, before the evil days come" (J, II:330).

The nostalgic tug of the past and fantasies of turning back the clock continued to exert a powerful influence on Thoreau, even as he grappled with the problem of how to stay "young," elastic, and expanding as he aged physically. In the fateful struggle to solve what is a central human problem, he oscillated between the polarities of age and youth, between thinking of himself as young, still capable of renewal, and old, dried up, his best days behind him. There were occasions when Thoreau felt unbearably old, weary, constricted, and despairing, but probably the dominant chord struck in the early 1850s was allied to a more youthful, invigorated sense of self. In the same journal entry in which he confesses that he only thought he "was grown up and become what [he] was intended to be, but it is earliest spring with me," he shows himself to be in an upbeat mood, defining himself as childlike, forward-looking, and full of yet untapped potential. It is almost as if he is taking a vow; certainly he is giving himself a pep talk:

What more glorious condition of being can we imagine than from impure to be becoming pure? It is almost desirable to be impure that we may be the subject of this improvement. . . . May I treat myself tenderly as I would treat the most innocent child whom I love; may I treat children and my friends as my newly discovered self. Let me forever go in search of myself; be as a stranger to myself, never a familiar, seeking acquaintance still. . . . The possibility of my own improvement, that is to be cherished. (J, II:314–15)

The child was still in the adult man, and it was important to keep this in mind. In February 1851 he asks, "Why should we not still continue to live with the intensity and rapidity of infants?" (J, II:162), and in December of the same year he offers a variation on this theme: "An innocent child is a man who has repented once for all, and is born again" (J, III:150). Even as an older person it was at least possible to "remember thy Creator" and "justify His ways to man" (J, III:157).

Thoreau thus was a man drawn powerfully to the past but also intent on growth and self-improvement, a man very much still "in search of" himself. During this "seedtime" of the early 1850s, he explored various versions and nuances of identity that would be especially suitable and rejuvenating, that could close the gap between the real self and the ego ideal. He was, as he had put it, "yet unborn" to his new life; and the felt imperative was to give birth to a more "grown-up" and yet essentially youthful, innocent self, to "build" himself "up to the height of [his] conceptions," as he described his task in December 1851. As befits someone who was both backward- and forward-looking, at once regressive and progressive (and beyond some point in the life cycle certain forms of getting back to one's sources and "home" may be viewed as a kind of forward movement), the identity Thoreau sought to forge combined progressive and regressive elements and relied heavily on continuities with the youthful past and, conversely, on making a clean break with whatever was impure, unworthy, or incongruous in the past. At the same time that he was striking out for new territory, he was also feeling the stirrings of a desire to recover the home from which he had seemed to stray so far in recent years. If long-ago youth was part of what he needed to recapture, so was the benchmark Walden experience. In the early 1850s, then, Thoreau was deeply involved in the work of creation and re-creation of the self; his writings were the cocoon in which much of the metamorphosis would take place. Of Linnaeus's father, who had changed the family name, Thoreau says, "it is refreshing to get to a man whom you will not be satisfied to call John's son or Johnson's son, but a new name applicable to himself alone, he being the first of his kind" (J, III:117). The power of naming, of language, in the project of self-creation, of becoming one's own father, was readily apparent to one who had designated himself "Henry David" rather than his given "David Henry" and who wished to insure, once and for all, that he was not merely or primarily "John's son."

One self-representation that became crucial for Thoreau during this phase was that of the afternoon walker, the saunterer, the bold and free crusader and observer of the "other" Concord. This self-concept was embodied in his lecture on "The Wild" (later to become part of an expanded essay which would eventually be entitled "Walking"), which he first delivered at the Concord Lyceum in April 1851. The lecture, significantly, drew on journal entries dating back to late 1849, when *A Week* had fizzled and he had turned to surveying. "Sauntering" was a kind of daily moratorium ritual, a way to create and maintain a time, space, and place for expansion; in this sense, it was another form of returning to Walden, although in this instance he was not tied to any parcel of land. In his lecture, he defined his own turf—on the margins—as he had done while living at the pond. "For my part," he says, "I feel that with regard to Nature I live a sort of border life, on the confines of a world into which I make occasional and transient forays only, and my patriotism and allegiance to the State into whose territories I seem to retreat are those of a moss-trooper" (E, 207). In locating himself in this middle ground, this "neutral zone"[22] distant from other men (while continuing to *live* on Main Street), Thoreau endeavored to re-affirm a Walden-like separation from other men without the necessity of actually residing there: "The walker in the familiar fields which stretch around my native town sometimes finds himself in another land than is described in their owners' deeds, as it were in some far-away field on the confines of the actual Concord, where her jurisdiction ceases, and the idea which the word Concord suggests ceases to be suggested" (E, 207). The lecture asserted his need for a time as well as a space he could call his own: "I think that I cannot preserve my health and spirits, unless I spend four hours a day at least, —and it is commonly more than that, —sauntering through the woods and over the hills and fields, absolutely free from all worldly engagements." The afternoon walk was literally an act of self-preservation, with a tinge of desperation. The "mechanics and shopkeepers" who "stay in their shops not only all the forenoon, but all the afternoon too" merit "some credit for not having all committed suicide long ago" (E, 164–65); and Thoreau knows, "If I should sell both my forenoons and afternoons to society, neglecting my peculiar calling, there would be nothing left worth living for" (J, II:141). In his 1851 journal he echoes earlier aspirations to be a "traveller in Concord," asking "Why should not [a man] begin his travels at home" and claiming that it "takes a man of genius to travel in his own country, in his native village" (J, II:376). Early in 1851 he speaks of the "art of taking walks," which only "one or two persons" he has met can understand.[23] Such persons alone who have "a genius, so to speak, for sauntering"—a word he apparently began using in 1850–51—are able to "exercise both body and spirit" in their walks and "succeed to the highest and worthiest ends by the abandonment of all specific ends" (J, II:140–41). The word "saunterer," he believed, derived from "La Sainte Terre," the Holy Land, and those unlike himself who "never go to the Holy Land in their walks, as they pretend, are indeed mere idlers and vagabonds" (J, II:141). At Walden he had felt special and holy; now, as a saunterer, he could again gain access to that hallowed ground.

An integral component of the "saunterer" self-image was that he was a man in pursuit of the "wild." Yet, as has already been suggested, the "wild" had shifting and often contradictory meanings for him, depending upon outer circumstances, inner needs, rhetorical considerations, and his inclination or ability at any given time to recall just what his actual wilderness experience had been like.[24] At its most extreme (and at the beginning of "Walking" he would concede it *is* extreme, so that he can make his point more emphatically), wildness is associated with untamed and untamable literal nature, "as contrasted with a freedom and culture merely civil" (E, 161). It is revealing that Thoreau, living in the Yellow House on Main Street and anxious to prove that he was not the domesticated, dependent mother's son he could easily have been taken to be, portrays wild nature here as a "howling mother," both antecedent and alternative to the human mother. He bemoans the early weaning from nature's breast to society, "to that culture which is exclusively an interaction of man on man" (E, 201); presumably human mothers play a fundamental role in weaning children from the wild to the tame. In his early 1851 journal he observes, "In society, in the best institutions of men, I remark a certain precocity. When we should be growing children, we are already little men. Infants as we are, we make haste to be weaned from our great mother's breast, and cultivate our parts by intercourse with another" (J, II:159). The quest for wildness, then, is in part an attempt to regress to, regain access to, and claim identity and continuity with a primal self that predates and precedes the weaning from the "great," "howling" mother by his own "civilizing" mother who, as society's agent, sought to instill those instincts "bred in the house."[25] Socialization (as he had earlier suggested in his poem, "Conscience") represented an unnatural "breeding in and in" (E, 201). Thus, this version of the wildness toward which he yearns is at once feminine and feral, at once nurturing and affording an "absolute freedom" (E, 161).

Clearly, the wildness that he appears to embrace in parts of "Walking" deemphasizes the less kindred and more forbidding, foreboding nature he had been exposed to in Maine and at Cape Cod. Disregarding his responses to the Indians he had met in Maine, he states, "Give me for my friends and neighbors wild men, not tame ones" (E, 197). At another point he remarks that, though he might be regarded as "perverse," he would prefer "to dwell in the neighborhood of" a "Dismal Swamp" rather than in "the most beautiful garden that ever human art contrived." As if he has never climbed Katahdin or witnessed the destructive indifference of the ocean, he says, "My spirits infallibly rise in proportion to the outward dreariness. Give me the ocean, the desert or the wilderness!" (E, 189–90).

In the context of such extravagant praise for literal wilderness, and of his own need to see himself as wild and inviolate in 1850–51, it may be more evident why *A Yankee in Canada,* based on an excursion to Quebec in the autumn of 1850, was one of his most lackluster performances, as even Blake had the gumption to tell him (C, 299). He had seen little more than the "urbanized" portion of the country when he probably should have explored "the great Canadian wilderness."[26] In "Walking" he would equate wildness with health (E, 190). Not surprisingly, his health was threatened on his Canadian expedition, leading him to comment in his journal, "What I *got* by going to Canada was a cold, and not till I get a fever, which I never had, shall I know how to appreciate it" (J, 11:418). While the trip to Canada disappointed him, it also helped crystallize further the parameters of his identity; if he was to travel, it would be primarily in New England. He was, after all, a *Yankee* in Canada, even if "his" New England was not that of his neighbors.

In the more private, less rhetorical and embattled confines of his journal, which served as such a key source for the lecture on "The Wild," and the essay on "Walking," there were signs that Thoreau's attitudes toward wildness were gradually becoming more differentiated, reflecting in part his periodic willingness to rehearse and entertain modified versions of self. "For my afternoon walks," he writes in June 1850, "I have a garden, larger than any artificial garden that I have read of and far more attractive"; the vision that enraptures him here is of a woodsy garden but of a garden, a pastoral setting, nevertheless. "Far over the hills on that fair hillside," he continues, "I look into the pastoral age" (J, 11:38–39). He confesses in his journal what he was reluctant to say in his lecture, "Though the city is no more attractive to me than ever, yet I see less difference between a city and some dismallest swamp than formerly. It is a swamp too dismal and dreary, however, for me. . . . I prefer even a more cultivated place, free from miasma and crocodiles, and will take my choice" (J, 11:47). He obviously chooses *not* to live in the Dismal Swamp or some "dreary" wilderness. Viewed in this light, it is, as he had briefly acknowledged in *Walden*'s first draft, primarily the "tonic" of wildness that he seeks. "I, too, love Concord best," he admits, "but I am glad when I discover, in ocean and wildernesses far away, the materials out of which a million Concords can be made" (J, 11:46). In May 1851 he compares himself to the wild apples "who belong not to the aboriginal race here, but have strayed into the woods from the cultivated stock" (J, 11:212). In spite of his propensities to recoil from the civil at this time, he did not *have* to throw out the baby of his humanity and humanism with the bathwater of "civilized life." Even in this phase of retreat from society, Thoreau could at times afford to see himself as a man and artist "from the cultivated stock" who brought his humanity, humanism, and imagination with him when he "strayed" into the woods.

"Wildness" became in this sense more a quality of mind and symbol of a pristine, vital, creative energy than the literal wilderness or the feral self he was most inclined to claim connection and identity with when he felt besieged by society or when he needed to deny as militantly as possible his dependence upon civilization, town, and mother. When the knight could lay down his shield or shed his armor, or generally when he was confronted directly with raw wilderness or with his uneasiness about the body, sexuality, and his most savage and impure impulses—the nature in him—he was more likely to see himself as the humanist and artist bent in some respects on "overcoming" literal nature.[27] Though he would remain subject to profound yearnings for connection with literal nature and wilderness, the desire to "overcome" nature would become more pronounced and insistent in subsequent years. In "Walking" he would associate the wild with the West, but the West is ultimately more a state of mind and spirit than a geographical direction (E, 275). And even in his 1850 journal the more symbolic connotation of "west" is evident: "Every sunset inspires me with the desire to go to a *West* as distant and as far as that into which the sun goes down" (J, II:108). "Westward is heaven," he adds later, "or rather heavenward is the West" (J, II:170).

If the afternoon saunterer had become a central facet of Thoreau's emerging self-concept, it was complemented by another, even more novel, version of self: that of the wanderer by night. By the summer of 1850 he began—not coincidentally—taking his nocturnal walks, and reporting on them in the *Journal*. The "traveller in Concord" was now a night traveler too:[28] "A traveller! I love his title. A traveller is to be reverenced as such. His profession is the best symbol of our life. Going from—toward—; it is the history of every one of us. I am interested in those that travel in the night" (J, II:281). To define himself as a man of the night was to distinguish himself even more radically from his neighbors and to move even more decisively in the direction of the wild. "Many men walk by day," he notes, while "few walk by night. It is a very different season." At night one gains a privileged perspective not available to "day men"; the "potatoes stand up straight, the corn grows, the bushes loom, and, in a moonlight night, the shadows of rocks and trees and bushes are more conspicuous than the objects themselves" (J, II:41). Bent on leaving behind the town and the bustling nineteenth century, he discovers that "the day is more trivial than the night" (J, II:265). The walks increased in frequency in the summer and early fall of 1851. Evidently, Thoreau sometimes even gave up a good night's sleep in order to imbibe his own brand of moonshine; in

September 1851 he remarks, "After I have spent the greater part of a night abroad in the moonlight, I am obliged to sleep enough more the next night to make up for it" (J, II:495). The image of a bleary-eyed Thoreau (who tended to be a morning person and one who kept away from stimulants) yawning through the day for lack of sleep suggests how precious and meaningful his nocturnal forays had become; he was not one of those ordinarily willing to sacrifice being truly awake during the day so that he could stay up late the night before. It seems that his moonlighting was considered eccentric even by his friends, who "wonder that I love to walk alone in solitary fields and woods by night" (J, II:62). Yet, if some of his friends and neighbors thought of him as being on the lunatic fringe, he was willing to accept it. Clearly these "nocturnes"[29] were restorative and reflective occasions, yet another form of moratorium and preparatory experience. "After a hard day's work without a thought," he explains, "turning my very brain into a mere tool, only in the quiet of evening do I so far recover my senses, as to hear the cricket, which in fact has been chirping all day. In my better hours I am conscious of the influx of a serene and unquestionable wisdom which partly unfits, and if I yielded to it more rememberingly would wholly unfit me for what is called the active business of life" (J, II:268).

Yielding to the influence of the night, the mist, the shadows, and the moonlight, moreover, was a means to regain access to the youthful inspiration and vitality he had lost; indeed, submitting to the night, permitting himself to be passive, represented a crucial opportunity for regression, not only to the cosmic feelings of youth but to the mothering breast and nurturing womb. Of one moonlight jaunt he writes, "There is something creative and primal in the cool mist. This dewy mist does not fail to suggest music to me, unaccountably; fertility, the origin of things" (J, II:237). Returning another evening from a walk, he observes the "mist on the river"; the river, he adds, "is taken into the womb of nature again" (J, II:260), and the same may be said of this scene's observer. On his birthday in 1851, he suggests that he "goes forth" by moonlight in order "to be reminded of a previous state of existence, if perchance any momento of it is to be met with hereabouts" (J, II:302–3). The moonlight itself "suggests a long past season of which I dream" (J, II:284). Like Walden Pond, the moist moonlit air had a uterine quality; both were associated with a wish to return to a "calm," "serene" past and place, a wish intensified by his perception that, as he grew older, his connection to that elemental, placental source was faltering. As important as it was for him to grow by extending himself forward and upward, there was a part of him that cried to reestablish continuity with, become more solidly rooted in, a dark, fecund, womblike humus. In the spring of 1851, as he considers the mind's development, he writes that "the most clear and ethereal ideas . . . readily ally themselves to the earth, to the primal womb of things. . . . The thought that comes to light . . . is wombed and rooted in darkness. . . . The mind flashes not so far on one side but its rootlets, its spongelets, find their way instantly on the other side into a moist darkness, uterine" (J, II:204–5).

Traveling by moonlight also afforded Thoreau an almost mystical, magical sense that he was blessed, initiated into the mysteries, singled out to see and hear what other men could not. A moonlight walk of June 22, 1851, provokes a feeling of religious ecstasy: "All the world goes by us and is reflected in our deeps. Such clarity! obtained by such pure means! by simple living, by honesty and purpose. We live and rejoice. . . . I feel my Maker blessing me" (J, II:268–69). At night he is privy to sounds not detected by "day men": "I rarely walk by moonlight without hearing—the sound of a flute, or a horn, or a human voice. It is a performer I never see by day; should not recognize him if pointed out." Deeply dissatisfied with how he spends his day, "this lone musician"—and Thoreau, himself a flute player, identifies with him—plays a strain that "remind[s] him of his heavenly descent. It is all that saves him—his one redeeming trait. It is a reminiscence; he loves to remember his youth." Like Thoreau, this man "cherishes hopes" encouraged by the night; by contrast, he never sees "the man by day who plays that clarionet" (J, II:373–74). Approaching the Mecca of Walden Pond by night—and returning to Walden, as he did so often during this period, was itself an attempt to save himself by renewing his links with the receding Walden experience, all it was coming to mean to him, and the even more distant past—Thoreau notices a phenomenon that he first thought was "some unusual phosphorescence" but was in fact a remarkably beautiful reflection of light off the pond. Ascending the hill toward his now-defunct bean field, he was able to hear (as he often could not during the day) "the ancient, familiar, immortal, dear cricket sound under all others." When that sound ceased, he became tuned in to "the general earth-song" and "wondered if behind or beneath this was not some other chant yet more universal" (J, II:253, 254). Moving away from the pond, he finds that "the walk is comparatively barren," as if Walden itself was the source of his inspiration. At night there was at least the expectation that he might come upon some rare, strange phosphorescence; even if he did not discover phosphorescent stumps or glowworms (J, III:47, 110), the moon was sufficient to cast an enchanting luminosity over the scene. Although the shining stumps and glowworms eluded him, he could at least believe in his *potential* to find such sources of illumination, and the expectation of such wonders was, for the time being, exhilarating enough.[30]

On September 1, 1850, Emerson commented in his journal on the divergent orientations of Channing and Thoreau toward nature and people. While Ellery thought nature "less interesting," Thoreau had told Emerson the day before that "it was more so, and persons less" (JMN, XI:265). Clearly, in the aftermath of his failed bid for social recognition, as he searched for exits from reality as defined by civil society, nature assumed added meanings and functions for Thoreau. This reordering of priorities, partly manifested in his reintensified craving for the wild, evinced itself in other, absolutely critical ways. Although he had, of course, claimed a close familiarity and even kinship with nature in the past, now—in 1850–51— he was prepared to become a more serious, disciplined, original student of nature. "As we grow old we live more coarsely, we relax a little in our disciplines," he writes in September 1851 (J, II:463). Having previously bemoaned the dearth of adult education in Concord, Thoreau took responsibility for arranging his own adult education, with the woods and his Main Street attic quarters as classrooms and laboratories, and with an ample library of natural history texts to complement his hands-on experience.[31] With such a distinguished naturalist as Louis Agassiz of Harvard as one model and such books as Gray's *Botany* as further guides, Thoreau embarked, at first only tentatively, on a course of more careful investigations of flora, fauna, and seasonal phenomena. While still highly skeptical of science per se—in January 1851 he comments, "Science does not embody all that men know" (J, II:138)—he began to make sporadic use of botanical nomenclature, charts, and other forms of classification. In one respect, this hesitant embrace of science may have represented a move toward establishing another "professional" identity, a way to become a more "senior," expert adult. After all, there was a burgeoning interest in science in nineteenth-century America, and in 1850 Emerson himself trumpeted the need for a new profession, "Practical Naturalist" (JMN, XI:277–78). Perhaps still clinging to the wish that his former protégé would yet make something substantial of himself, he identifies Thoreau as one who could well be employed in such a capacity—though in doing so he betrays a tendency to pigeonhole the younger man as a naturalist rather than a writer. Thoreau may have sensed in some way that his nature studies would appease Waldo and even gain him a certain status in the community. And, even though he would never become a professional naturalist, he did become, for all practical purposes, Concord's resident naturalist, sought out by those who needed their questions answered or curiosity sated. In another respect, the desire to become more conversant with natural facts may also have represented a way to show up Emerson, the writer of *Nature* who remained inexcusably weak in his concrete knowledge of nature.

Thoreau's gradual immersion in natural observation[32] had more far-reaching significance, however. In November 1851 he writes, "See not with the eye of science, which is barren, nor of youthful poetry, which is impotent. But taste the world and digest it" (J, III:85). He perceived nature study as a means to an end; it was his hope, in the era that was dawning for him, to ingest (though at first rather indiscriminately) the natural world and then incorporate what he was learning into a more inclusive personal and artistic vision. Ironically, though he was motivated to turn to nature partly as an alternative to social reality, it was his evolving intention (as it had always been, whether or not he could admit it) to see nature with the eye of a humanist and artist, to discern in nature those moral and spiritual facts that would illuminate people's lives. Emerson might not appreciate it, but he was resolved to carry on the project Waldo had called for in *Nature*. Whatever his scientific leanings, he was determined to perceive nature ultimately through a transcendental prism. As he explains in June 1851, after several rather technical journal entries, "My practicalness is not to be trusted to the last. To be sure, I go upon my legs for the most part, being hard-pushed and dogged by a superficial common sense which is bound to near objects by beaten paths, I am off the handle, as the phrase is, —I begin to be transcendental and show where my heart is" (J, II:228). While noting the correspondence between nature and the human condition had been a deeply ingrained habit of mind and fundamental to his vision in the past, and while nature had always been a preeminent font of metaphor, his understanding and use of nature remained incomplete and somewhat derivative. Up to this point, he was still too bookish, too reliant on second-hand information, stock or orthodox metaphors, highly impressionistic and informal observation. In this seedtime Thoreau finally determined that he could no longer take for granted or on faith his understanding of the natural world; he would have to start from scratch, study nature more deliberately, sensitively, and at first hand if he was to glean the lessons to be learned. Essential to his becoming more authentically his own man, forging his own unique vision, was reliance on a fully earned mastery of natural fact.

At the same time, he realized that his understanding of the human life cycle—including his own—was inadequate. He not only needed to remind himself, and to relearn more conclusively, the lessons of human life embedded in *A Week,* but he also had to revise, refine, and elaborate on those lessons in the light of what he had learned, and was learning, since its completion. Clearly, he knew now, *A Week* was not his last word. If natural processes could be understood more fully, he would also grasp more completely the intricacies and mysteries of human existence. A more thorough-going and sophisticated knowledge of nature—its textures, rhythms, patterns, sequences—would lead to a more profound vision of human life. And, most assuredly, he delved into nature study with the passionate expectation that he would thereby be able to make more sense of, and poetry of, his own experience. Nature would provide him with a language, private and yet rooted in external reality, for discussing and imaging his life. He would so absorb, and be absorbed by, nature that he would often not even have to make the analogies explicit. Moreover, he would use analogies and correspondences to confirm or validate what he suspected were the truths embodied in the life he had led and would lead. In the sequences and patterns of nature, he would not only discover but also justify the shapes taken by his life. Conversely, he would sometimes be led to believe that self-knowledge was a necessary preparation for nature study, that only by bringing to his observations an awareness and vision of the transitions he had undergone and was undergoing would he be truly in a position to *see* natural phenomena. For instance, after noting the loss of blossoms on the Norway cinquefoil, he observes that "I can be said to note the flower's fall only when I see in it the symbol of my own change. When I experience this, then the flower appears to me" (J, II:431).

Pondering a book by Wilkinson, which to an extent "realizes" what he has "dreamed of"—"a return to the primitive *analogical* and derivative senses of words"—Thoreau concludes, "The man of science discovers no world for the mind of man with all its faculties to inhabit. Wilkinson finds a *home* for the imagination, and it is no longer outcast and homeless. All perception of truth is the detection of an analogy; we reason from our hands to our head" (J, II:462–63). Discovering afresh the primacy, power, and potential of analogical perception, Thoreau saw another way to secure a home, and be at home, in the world. Analogy provided a bridge of continuity between nature and man, enabling him to be at home in both realms. Into nature he imported the mind of man; and the human mind itself was permeable to, and permeated by, nature. The harshest lessons of Katahdin and Cape Cod, however, had sometimes to be tucked away in some shadowy compartment of the mind in order to maintain the complete integrity of this particular version of home.

The 1850–51 journal—especially in the late summer and fall of 1851 —documents Thoreau's accelerating excitement as he became more and more inured to analogical thinking in the context of his more disciplined scrutiny of nature. At one point he tells himself,

> Improve the opportunity to draw analogies. . . . Improve the suggestion of each
> object however humble, however slight and transient the provocation. . . . Be

avaricious of these impulses. You must try a thousand themes before you find
the right one, as nature makes a thousand acorns to get one oak. He is a wise
man and experienced who has taken many views; to whom stones and plants
and animals and a myriad objects have each suggested something, contributed
something. (J, II:457)

There appears in the *Journal* a developing resolve to chart the phenomena
of the human life and mind in a manner similar to that employed by nat-
uralists to describe nature. In one of his first references to the analogy
process, he writes, "There is, no doubt, a perfect analogy between the life
of the human being and that of the vegetable, both of the body and the
mind." Like the plants described in Gray's *Botany*, human beings follow
a discernible sequence of development: "I am concerned first to come to
my *Growth*, intellectually and morally . . . and then to bear my *Fruit*, do
my *Work*, *propagate* my kind, not only physically but *morally*, not only in
body but in mind" (J, II:201, 202). Scientific analysis, then, could provide
a model for the Herculean task he envisioned. "How copious and precise
the botanical language to describe the leaves as well as the other parts of a
plant!" he writes enthusiastically.

> Botany is worth studying if only for the precision of its terms, —to learn the
> value of words and of system. It is wonderful how much pains has been taken
> to describe a flower's leaf, compared for instance with the care that is taken in
> describing a psychological fact. Suppose as much ingenuity (perhaps it would
> be needless) in making a language to express the sentiments! We are armed
> with language adequate to describe each leaf in the field; or at least to distin-
> guish it from each other, but not to describe a human character. . . . The preci-
> sion and copiousness of botanical language applied to the description of moral
> qualities! (J, II:409)

In August 1851 he speaks of the need for a "meteorological journal of the
mind." While some travel around the world and observe "natural objects
and phenomena" alone, the traveler in Concord stays home and reports
with fidelity "the phenomena of his own life" (J, II:403). Without a
doubt, he came to see his own journal as just such a "meteorological journal of the mind," tied closely to his increasingly detailed investigations of
natural phenomena. His selective observations of nature would also be a
shorthand way to reflect and characterize his own emotional state. He was
contemplating a project he claimed no one else had completed. And he
would document not only the seasons but the seasons *within* seasons. In
mid-1850 he remarks that the "year has many seasons more than are recognized in the almanac," and the following June he reiterated the earlier

impression: "No one, to my knowledge, has observed the minute differences in the seasons. Hardly two nights are alike. . . . A book of the seasons, each page of which should be written in its own season and out-of-doors, or in its own locality wherever it may be" (J, II:239). However, his journal (and perhaps a more polished work eventually to be culled from it)[33] would be an almanac or calendar of the as yet inadequately charted human seasons as well as of nature's seasons. The connections between the two were clear and fascinating to him, as is obvious in October 1851: "There is a great difference between this season and a month ago . . . as between one period in your life and another" (J, III:55). Thus it was evidently Thoreau's budding hope to be able to map out this multiplicity of periods in human life. This enterprise, as he must have realized, was of truly epic proportions, a project of such incredible magnitude that only an ongoing, open-ended journal could, at least for the time being, begin to encompass it. Thoreau could hardly have been entirely unaware of the potential for cliché in his treatment of the human seasons, yet this concept, like the natural seasons themselves, was very real and vital to him. Insofar as he believed that there were correspondences between nature and man, or in any case that organic metaphor and imagery could illuminate the phases and moods of human life, the human seasons constituted an integral part of Thoreau's truth and vision.

Soon after turning to his journal in earnest in 1850, Thoreau began exploring the implications of seasonal imagery and analogy for his own life. In June of that year he asked what would be a key question of that period, "Shall not a man have his spring as well as the plants?" (J, II:34). There were, to be sure, occasions when he sensed that there was an unbridgeable gulf between himself and nature, that his life did not follow nature's pace and pattern. "Methinks my seasons revolve more slowly than those of nature," he writes. "I am differently timed" (J, II:316). At times this disjunction was seen as a sign of his potential superiority: the human spirit was capable of freeing itself from the bonds of naturalistic necessity. Once, for instance, he complains that when he is "constantly merged with nature," he has "less memorable seasons" (J, III:66). At other times the dichotomy signified a kind of inferiority or inadequacy. In August 1851 he finds himself wishing "that I could match nature always with my moods! that in each season when some part of nature especially flourishes, then a corresponding part of me may not fail to flourish" (J, II:391).

For the most part, however, he preferred to overlook or ignore these doubts and discrepancies, seeking in natural observation and analogy reassuring, energizing correspondences with his own life that allowed him to externalize, dramatize, and finally even mythicize his experience. It was

especially pressing to see himself as having the capacity to enter upon another "spring" in his life, another era of expansion as Walden had been.
Oak leaves cling to the trees during the winter and then fall off, just as the
next spring arrives. The same might be said, he reflected, "of a very old and
withered man or woman that they hung on like a shrub oak leaf, almost to
a second spring" (J, II:139). Thoreau endeavored to believe that *he* would
hang on until that second spring arrived. It was another seedtime in his life;
it was, as he was anxious to affirm, "earliest spring with me." Having "lost
faith" in himself since the largely idyllic period at the pond, he eagerly em-
braces the proposition that even the oldest man has the potential for renewal: "In relation to virtue and innocence the oldest man is in the beginning and vernal season of life. It is the love of virtue makes us young ever"
(J, II:315). In the summer and autumn of 1851, his botanical investigations yielded the reassuring conclusion he was seeking. In August 1851 he
witnessed the *Viola pedata* and the houstonia blooming once more:
"What is the peculiarity of these flowers that *they* blossom so early in the
spring, and now are ready for a new spring?" (J, II:431). "Plants commonly soon cease to grow for the year," he observes in September, "unless
they may have a fall growth, which is a kind of second spring" (J, II:481).
Having already passed through the summer, "a season of small fruits and
trivial experiences" (conforming in important respects to his 1847–49 period), "there is an aftermath in early autumn, and some spring flowers
bloom again, followed by an Indian summer of finer atmosphere and of a
pensive beauty." Sensible that his young adulthood is nearing an end,
gradually beginning to fade, he utters a prayer that his life not be "destitute
of its Indian summer, a season of fine and clear mild weather in which I
may prolong my hunting before the winter comes, when I may once more
lie on the ground with faith, as in spring, and even with more serene confidence" (J, II:481–82). On October 10, 1851, he experiences with exultation a further confirmation of his faith: "The air this morning is full of
bluebirds, and again it is spring. There are many things to indicate the renewing of spring at this season. The blossoming of spring flowers, —not to
mention the witch-hazel, —the notes of spring birds, the springing of grain
and grass and other plants" (J, III:61). The witch hazel, one of those plants
that began to play a continuing role as he studied them carefully, is "October and November's child," which yet reminds one of "the very earliest
spring" and suggests, "amid all these signs of autumn, falling leaves
and frost, that the life of Nature by which she eternally flourishes, is untouched. . . . While its leaves fall, its blossoms spring. The autumn, then, is
indeed a spring. All the year is a spring" (J, III:59–60).

While rejoicing over the October spring Thoreau is not entirely content; he needs more incontrovertible proof that "all year is a spring," that there may be even more than two periods of blossoming in the human year. In November 1851 he says, "The *fall* of the year is over, and now let us see if we shall have any Indian summer" (J, III:106). He awaits further evidence with a mixture of tension, resignation, and resolve—as if whatever he discovers will also be reflected in his own life. November is a time to "eat your heart out," but "is not this a glorious time for your deep inward fires?" Disappointed that there has not been any Indian summer in November—"I see but few traces of the perennial spring"—there is nevertheless consolation in the "brave thoughts within you that shall remain to rustle the winter through like white oak leaves upon your boughs." In this climate, "man is very near being made a dormant creature" (J, III:111, 112). November 22 prompts Thoreau to remark "a sort of Indian summer in the day, which thus far has been denied to the year," and on December 13 there is "one hour of almost Indian summer weather" (J, III:129, 136). But as the year draws to a close, his vigilance is even more amply rewarded, his belief in many springs and Indian summers—natural and human—vindicated: "It is warm as an April morning. . . . It is like the first of April. . . . It feels as warm as in summer; you sit on any fencerail and vegetate in the sun, and realize that the earth may produce peas again" (J, III:160–61). To bear witness to such miraculous rebirths was to gain assurance of grace: the potential to be born again is always there, however much we may eat our hearts out over bleak prospects.

As a man without offspring and probably without any interpersonal sexual experience, Thoreau began turning to organic facts and analogies in an ongoing but ever more urgent effort to test out and reimage just what claims he might stake to alternative forms of generativity. As he writes in April 1851, "I am sure that the design of my maker when he has brought me nearest to woman was not the propagation, but rather the maturation, of the species" (J, II:185). Having not taken the road of sexual expression and physical reproduction of the species, he was increasingly drawn to perceiving himself as involved in another kind of reproduction, for which nature offered the analogy:

> In the psychological world there are phenomena analogous to what zoölogists call *alternate reproduction,* in which it requires several generations unlike each other to evolve the perfect animal. Some men's lives are but an aspiration, a yearning toward a higher state, and they are wholly misapprehended, until they are referred to, or traced through, all their metamorphoses. We cannot

pronounce upon a man's intellectual and moral state until we foresee what metamorphosis it is preparing for him. (J, III:71)

Had he been aware of it, or chosen to, Thoreau might also have alluded to the phenomenon of alternation of generations in plants, whereby the gametophyte reproduces gametes sexually and the sporophyte reproduces spores asexually. In this regard Thoreau might well have considered himself a sporophyte. Although "working bees . . . are barren females," they nevertheless have "solicitude for the welfare of the new generation"; in parallel fashion, "maiden aunts and bachelor uncles" (common in the Thoreau family) "perform a similar function" in the human species (J, III:71). Though he himself would never even be a "bachelor uncle"—since none of his siblings had married or had children—he nonetheless could see himself as one concerned, however unconventionally, for the "welfare of the new generation." Like the Norway cinquefoil, he is a "humble weed," and "Not even when I have blossomed, and have lost my painted petals and am preparing to die down to my root, do I forget to fall with my arms around my babe, faithful to the last" (J, II:430). One may conclude that the protected "babe" is, first and foremost at this time, the *Journal* itself which, growing daily, was increasingly acquiring a life of its own; it was one "babe" for whose creation and welfare he was solely and continuously responsible.

Nature was becoming a sort of fertility goddess for Thoreau; he prayed at her altar with the fervent wish that her fertility would rub off on him. By familiarizing, allying himself, and even identifying with nature's pervasive sexuality, its dependable cycles of reproduction and quickening, he gained more confidence in his own fertility and ultimate ripening. The imagery of expanding seeds was an appropriate characterization for this era, when it was so essential to fend off fears of premature stagnation and barrenness that could easily have overwhelmed him after *A Week*'s failure and discouraged further creative efforts. Thoreau often imagines a seed that expands "more surely" in his attic room, "as far as expression goes," but "stores up influences" outdoors. At other times he takes communion with seeds and also becomes the medium in which they grow. "While I am abroad," he says, "the ovipositors plant their seeds in me; I am fly-blown with thought and go home to hatch and brood over them" (J, II:338–39). He seems literally to have ingested seeds and eggs in his desire to participate in, submerge his libido in, nature's bounteous reproductivity. In a fascinating passage of August 1851 he inquires, "How many ova have I swallowed? Who knows what will be hatched within me? There were some seeds of thought, methinks, floating in that water, which are expanding in me" (J, II:393). He goes on to ask when he had "swallowed a snake" and concludes that "I drank of stagnant waters once." Presumably one is susceptible to swallowing a snake—with all its phallic connotations and its associations with guilt and impurity—when one is in a stagnant condition. Thoreau subsequently asks how one can rid oneself of the snake, "which you have swallowed when young, when thoughtless you stooped and drank at stagnant waters, which has worried you in your waking hours and in your sleep ever since." The answer he settles on is that the snake will "ascend to your mouth" and "be gotten rid of" at the "sound of the running water." Drinking of "the running streams, the living waters," will insure the ingestion of "expanding seeds" and prevent snake swallowing.

Thoreau was beginning to take more careful note of the ingenious ways in which seeds were dispersed and propagation guaranteed. "How tenacious," he exclaims, is the seed of "its purpose to spread and plant its race! By all methods nature secures this end, whether by the balloon, or parachute, or hook, or barbed spear like this, or mere lightness which the winds can waft" (J, III:65). In like manner, his seeds would in one way or another find ways to disperse themselves, reproduce, and take root. Even on burnt lands seeds would eventually prosper, as Thoreau discovered to his satisfaction by September 1851. In what may be taken not only as another vindication of his woodsburning mishap but also as an expression of faith in the durability and viability of his own seeds, he says, "In the spring I burned over a hundred acres till the earth was sere and black, and by midsummer this space was clad in a fresher and more luxuriant green than the surrounding even. Shall man then despair? Is he not a sprout-land too, after never so many searings and witherings? If you witness growth and luxuriance, it is all the same as if you grew luxuriantly" (J, II:488–89). One can imagine Thoreau releasing the winged seeds of the milkweed in the fall of 1851 (J, III:17–18) and thereby identifying their prolific numbers and reproductive powers with his own seeds. For him, words *were* seeds and sentences plants, "like so many little resiliencies from the spring floor of our life, —a distinct fruit and kernel itself" (J, III:107). He contrasts himself, the maker of metaphors, with the "prosaic man," who is a "barren and stamiferous flower"; the poet, however, "is a fertile and perfect flower" (J, II:413–14). Unlike the farmer who "is concerned about the crops which his fields bear," he resolves to concern himself with "the fertility of my human farm. I will watch the winds and the rains as they affect the crop of thought, —the crop of crops, ripe thoughts, which glow and rustle and fill the air with fragrance for centuries" (J, II:442). Clearly, he was intent on tilling his seeds in the mind's soil until they yielded a bumper crop. The growth of his seeds, he wished to believe, mirrored that of the organic world; the certainty of nature's expansion portended well for his own.

Even as he anticipated the sprouting of his seeds and the extension of his sprouts, he was coming to feel more rooted than ever in his native New England. "The mind," he had observed in May 1851, "develops from the first in two opposite directions: upwards to expand in the light and air; and downwards avoiding the light to form the root" (J, II:203). He was, as he would reiterate often (J, IV:16, 54), a genuine "radicle," a man who "sends down a tap-root to the centre of things" (J, II:203). In the autumn, by the sandy shores of Long Pond (now Cochichuate) with Channing, he was prompted to designate New England soil not just his home but his final resting place: "Dear to me to lie in, this sand. . . . and I am a New-Englander. Of thee, O earth, are my bone and sinew made; to thee, O sun, am I brother. To this dust my body will gladly return as to its origin. Here have I my habitat. I am of thee" (J, III:95). In one sense, this "tap-root man" who contemplates reclaiming his earthy home, seems prepared here to embrace death; the pond's association with Indians and the imagery of sun as brother suggest that the prospect of joining his brother was not altogether unappealing at this time, especially given the conflicts with Emerson that appear to have been powerfully reactivated in late 1851. In another sense, however, Thoreau does not seem ready to relax his grasp on life and growth. While his bones will gladly lie in Long Pond's clean sand, he yet believes that "these are my sands not yet run out." The imagery of himself as rooted *and* sprouting plant is conjured:

> I shall be ready to bloom again here in my Indian summer days. Here ever springing, never dying, with perennial root I stand; for the winter of the land is warm to me. While the flowers bloom again as in the spring, shall I pine? When I see her sands exposed, thrown up from beneath the surface, it reminds me of my origin; for I am such a plant, so native to New England, as springs from the sand cast up from below. (J, III:97)

Strive as he might to see his life as an organic process of putting down deeper roots and growing toward the light, he was unable to rid himself of those insidious forces that threatened to wither the emerging plant, to cut off the circulation in both stem and root. Through much of 1851, as the work of becoming his own person proceeded, Thoreau appears to have by and large successfully suppressed or repressed the negative emotions associated with the estrangement from Emerson and the perceived loss of Lidian. To be sure, he had written in February, after criticizing the tameness of the English literature Emerson praised, "Fatal is the discovery that our friend is fallible, that he has prejudices," and "now that my friend rashly, thoughtlessly, profanely speaks, *recognizing* the distance between us, that distance seems infinitely increased" (J, II:161). Struggling to make his peace with Waldo, he had sought in a July nocturne to see himself as "moon" to Emerson's "sun": " 'T is true she was eclipsed by the sun, but now she acquires an almost equal respect and worship by reflecting and representing him, with some new quality, perchance, added to his light, showing how original the disciple may be who still in midday is seen" (J, II:299). For the most part the bitterness and lamentations had gone into a sort of remission, with Thoreau preoccupied by the overriding task of establishing a more authentic autonomy and identity. But if he thought it would be easy to banish the ghosts, never look back, he learned by autumn that breaking away from past intense attachments was far more problematic and anguishing than he could have imagined.

Although it is not evident what particular incident, if any, set him off, by October Thoreau was brooding again about friendship and love in his journal. Almost certainly it is Waldo who provokes his agonized ruminations. Amidst images of Indian summer rebirth, he grieves, "Ah, I yearn toward thee, my friend, but I have not confidence in thee. We do not believe in the same God. I am not thou; thou art not I. We trust each other to-day, but we distrust to-morrow. Even when I meet thee unexpectedly, I part from thee with disappointment" (J, III:61). One reason, it seems, why Thoreau continued to be so bereaved by the demise of the friendship was that it erected an even more formidable barrier between him and Lidian, foreclosed any fantasized deeper intimacy with her.[34] He was still, emotionally, part of an oedipal triangle that opened up a Pandora's box of uneasy feelings.

An extraordinary dream reported on October 26 suggests how vexing were the apprehensions aroused by sexuality and oedipal rivalry, at the same that Thoreau was seeking to assume the role of asexual propagator. The dream, from which he awoke with "infinite regret," begins with Thoreau riding on horses that "bit each other and occasioned needless trouble and anxiety." The image may well have reference to the oedipal rivalries Thoreau had experienced vis-à-vis Lidian and Emerson, Ellen Sewall and John, his mother and father. Wishing to deny or squelch the anxiety-provoking rivalry, he tries to hold the horses' heads apart. Then, in what may be an image of intrusive sexuality, he finds himself sailing "in a small vessel" over "the shallows about the sources of rivers" toward a "deeper *channel* of a stream which emptied in to the Gulf beyond"; he is in a small "pleasure-boat," "learning to sail on the sea, and I raised my sail before my anchor, which I dragged far into the sea." Raising the sail, it may be inferred, is phallic and thus guilt-provoking; thus he is dragged down, slowed, by the anchor of guilt. He sees "buttons" from the coats of drowned men; we may conclude that Emerson, his brother, and even his father are all presumed drowned—as on some level he imagined he wished them to be. Another intrusive symbol comes to the fore when Thoreau discovers he is walking in a dry meadow "where the dry seasons permitted me to walk further than usual. There he meets Alcott, who may be taken as a relatively nonthreatening father surrogate (he would later describe him as "broad and genial" and "the sanest man I know" [J, v:130]), and they "fell to quoting and referring to grand and pleasing couplets and single lines"; Thoreau recalls quoting lines that "expressed regret"—perhaps in connection with phallic initiatives. What follows suggests that the dream had direct sexual content, was even, quite possibly, a wet dream. "And then again the instant I awoke," he says, "methought I was a musical instrument from which I heard a strain die out"—as if the "flute" had released semen and was now spent—"a bugle, a clarionet, or a flute. My body was the organ and channel of melody, as a flute is of the music that is breathed through it. My flesh sounded and vibrated still to the strain, and my nerves were the chords of the lyre. I awoke, therefore, to an infinite regret, —to find myself not the thoroughfare of glorious and world-stirring inspirations, but a scuttle full of dirt." In contemplating the dream afterward, Thoreau says sadly, "my regret arose from the consciousness how little like a musical instrument my body was now" (J, III:80–82).[35] The connections among oedipal rivalry, phallic anxieties, discomfort and even disgust with sexual impulses are quite in evidence here. That the musical vibrations follow his meeting with Alcott suggests a possible homoerotic component as well. Mixed with the guilt and anxiety is a continued yearning for sexuality, a "regret" that he does not have access to, or is inadequate regarding, joyful and unambivalent sexual expression. As much as he wanted to, he could not entirely reconcile himself to roads not taken with respect to intimacy. The entry immediately after the dream serves to emphasize that a woman, most likely Lidian, was a primary focus of his sense of loss. As if anchored by his inability to surrender fully the dream of intimacy, he writes, "The obstacles which the heart meets with are like granite blocks which one alone cannot move." Almost certainly referring to Lidian, he continues, "She who was as the morning light to me is now neither the morning star nor the evening star. We meet but to find each other further asunder." And it is likely Emerson is the "friend" who "will be bold to conjecture; he will guess bravely at the significance of my words" (J, III:82, 83). Alienation from Emerson had insured his alienation from Lidian, and this made the loss of his former mentor more complicated and harder to bear.

There was one other friend who occupied Thoreau's thoughts as 1851 neared an end: Channing, one of the very few men with whom he felt comfortable enough to allow him to accompany him on some of his walks. While there may have been a mild, generally unspoken literary rivalry, Channing did not come across as a formidable opponent or encourage traumatic transferences. He was himself an eccentric, with his marriage now on the rocks and with streaks of capriciousness and unambitiousness that could not have impressed Emerson. Unlike the often sober Emerson, Channing had a sharp sense of humor and was not above needling—and nettling—Thoreau. Accompanying his friend to Long Pond, Channing "kept up an incessant strain of wit, banter, about my legs, which were so springy and unweariable, declared that I had got my double legs on, that they were not cork but steel" (J, III:96). There was often a brotherly good-naturedness between the two, and a sense of shared values, which may in some small way have served as a substitute for the camaraderie he once had had with his brother. Yet even in the context of this relatively unthreatening relationship, Thoreau was not above finding fault with, and expressing disappointment with, Channing. While walking, he tried to take notes as Thoreau did, but "all in vain": "He soon puts it up again, or contents himself with scrawling some sketch of the landscape. Observing me still scribbling, he will say that he confines himself to the ideal, purely ideal remarks; he leaves the facts to me." Of his emotional makeup Thoreau concludes that he "is the moodiest person, perhaps, that I ever saw. As naturally whimsical as a cow is brindled, both in his tenderness and his roughness he belies himself." He notes Channing's contradictions with a combination of admiration and opprobrium: "He can be incredibly selfish and unexpectedly generous. He is conceited, and yet there is in him far more than usual to ground conceit upon" (J, III:98–99). It appears that he is able to recognize something of himself in his friend, while at the same time he can point to Channing's deficiencies as compared to *his* strengths. In a somewhat harsher, if still compassionate, tone, he suggests that Ellery is not willing to "pay the price" to accomplish something worthwhile and "will only learn slowly by failure" (J, III:108). Thoreau further indicates that his friend is not disciplined enough; he writes poetry in a "sublimo-slipshod style" and should take up Latin, "for then he would be compelled to say something always" (J, III:118). At a time when Emerson insisted on condemning him for his unambitiousness and lack of drive, it was perhaps comforting for Thoreau both to have someone who offered relief from Waldo's brand of put-down and to have one even *he* could criticize for lacking certain qualities of commitment and determination. Thus Channing served as a useful foil for Thoreau. It is possible that he was more inclined to be querulous about Channing at a juncture when his sense of estrangement and rage regarding Emerson was at flood stage and subject to overflowing onto others. To some degree it appears that the breakdown of *that* friendship cast doubt on the dependability of all friendships.

There can be little doubt that by the end of 1851 Thoreau was again deeply hurt and resentful toward Emerson. On December 12, with his fire blazing, he read through one of Emerson's books, which, he says, "it happens that I rarely look at, to try what a chance sentence out of that could do for me." He refers to an argument he had had with Waldo concerning his former mentor's finding fault with Margaret Fuller's "whims and superstitions." Coming upon a quote which is probably from "The American Scholar," the essay that had so inspired him and been a clarion call to greatness, he reveals how unimpressed he now is with Emerson. He points to the "obviousness of the moral" in the quote, "so that I had, perhaps, *thought* the same thing myself twenty times during the day, and yet had not been *contented* with that account of it" (J, III:134–35). As he moved deeper into December, the scars once again became open wounds. From contacts with "certain acquaintances" (among whom Emerson was unquestionably the most prominent), he acknowledged that he came away "wounded"; "only they," he adds, "can wound me seriously, and that perhaps without their knowing it." He then speaks of being criticized by "one of the best men I know": "O would you but be simple and downright! Would you but cease your palaver! It is the misfortune of being a gentleman and famous" (J, III:139, 141). Thoreau yearns to inform his friend that he is "under an awful necessity" (J, III:146) to be what he is; but some of his acquaintances (presumably including the "famous gentleman" Emerson who had made the charge before) persist in implying that he is "too cold." Defending himself from these accusations, he argues, "It is not that I am too cold, but that our warmth and coldness are not of the same nature; hence when I am absolutely warmest, I may be coldest to you." "You," he continues, addressing, it would seem, the man whose *Nature* had been such a revelation to him, "who complain that I am cold find Nature cold. To me she is warm." Resorting at last to the natural imagery that preserved him, he contends that his warmth is "a less transient glow, a steadier and more equable heat, like that of the earth in spring in which the flowers spring and expand" (J, III:147, 148).

On December 17, Thoreau responds characteristically to the resurgent crisis with Emerson by affirming the compensatory function of nature: "I do not know but a pine wood is as substantial and memorable a fact as a friend. I am more sure to come away from it cheered, than from those who come nearest to being my friends" (J, III:140). Such one-way passions for nature did indeed sustain him. But he goes beyond simply turning away from man to nature; rather, this man who identified with the witch hazel and Norway cinquefoil (and who heartily approved of Linnaeus being "Linden-tree-man") was prompted also to identify with the white pine. "The trees," he says, "indeed have hearts. . . . The pines impress me as human." He clearly has a heartfelt "sympathy" with the pine, and, when near the Deep Cut at Walden, he witnesses the cutting down of a pine, he is contemplating his own demise. There is much imagery with sexual undertones in his description; he alludes to the "mast-like stem" and observes that the pine provides an "inaccessible crotch for the squirrel's nest." The felling of the tree is compared to a crime: he writes that the woodchoppers, their job done, "dropped the guilty saw and axe" (J, III:162–63). In one respect, this scene may represent an accusation of Emerson, whose cutting remarks and disapproval had chipped away at his self-esteem and who threatened to keep chopping away at his lofty aspirations. Even the community has not displayed any comprehension of the resource they are squandering. With the pine dead on the ground, "Why does not the village bell sound a knell? I see no procession of mourners in the streets, or the woodland aisles" (J, III:164). In yet another respect, though, the cutting down of the pine seems to bring a sense of relief, as if Thoreau—responding in part to the guilt and anxiety provoked by the renewed hostilities with Emerson—welcomes this "unkindest cut of all" as a way to atone and gain a lasting serenity: "And now it [the pine tree] fans the hillside with its fall, and it lies down to its bed in the valley, from which it is never to rise, as softly as a feather, folding its green mantle about it like a warrior, as if, tired of standing, it embraced the earth with silent joy, returning its elements to the dust again" (J, III:163). On the last day of 1851, Thoreau indicates with some remorse, "Last night I treated my dearest friend ill" (J, III:167). This confession of transgression is followed by a description of the large dead pine with "tears"—of regret and loss—"streaming from the sap-wood." The final image is of isolation and desolation, "denuded pines" standing in the "clearings" with "no old cloak to wrap about them, only the apexes of their cones entire, telling a pathetic story of the companions that clothed them." Thoreau then makes explicit the analogy to his own condition: "So stands a man. It is clearing around him. He has no companions on the hills. The lonely traveller, looking up, wonders why he was left when his companions were taken" (J, III:169–70). Here he is both denuded pine and lonely traveler, burdened by survivorship (and all the guilt it can entail) as well as by feelings of abandonment. The breech with Emerson, and the emotions it stirred up, did indeed threaten to sap Thoreau's energy and initiative—just as some of his seeds were germinating and some sprouts were first seeing the light of day.

Nevertheless, on the last, foggy, springlike day of December he sought to see in the sand foliage of the Deep Cut evidence of the inevitability of growth and progress unchecked by the past: "I seem to see some of the life that is in the spring bud and blossom more intimately, nearer its fountain-head, the fancy sketches and designs of the artist." His spirits are lifted by what he perceives as "this fundamental fertility near to the principle of growth." The mud forms are, of course, "somewhat foecal"; he concludes that "the poet's creative moment is when the frost is coming out in the spring," but for "some too easy poets, if the weather is too warm and rainy or long continued it becomes mere diarrhoea, mud and clay relaxed" (J, III:164–65). Thoreau would not be such an "easy poet." Out of the Deep Cut, out of the wounds he had suffered and endured, was emerging, however haltingly, his "creative moment." Poised between the old life he had sought to discard and the new life being born, between winter and spring, Thoreau struggled to assure himself that his seeds were safe and viable and that a second spring was at hand.

5 *Second Spring*

*O*N the last day of April 1852, during a period of fickle early spring weather, Thoreau remarked that "the season advances by fits and starts" (J, III:483). And so did his progress toward a second spring. The ground had been by and large prepared, many of the seeds had been planted, and some had begun to germinate. One seed, or cluster of seeds, with which he would become more and more preoccupied, had passed through a time of dormancy and incubation since late 1849: *Walden* and Thoreau's developing conception of its potential. After two years of seed-time, it began to take root and sprout; in January 1852 or thereabouts, Thoreau embarked on a fourth revision of *Walden*,[1] keenly aware that in the transitional era of early spring his precious seeds and young shoots remained vulnerable. But he was resolved to tend to them solicitously. On March 31, 1852, he exclaims, "Woe be to us when we cease to form new resolutions on the opening of a new year!" (J, III:366). And earlier, on January 11, the tenth anniversary of his brother's death—understandably mindful of life's unpredictability and the possibilities of growth being cut short—he betrays a paradoxical urgency in his determination not to bring along his still fragile seeds too quickly: "Let me not live as if time was short. Catch the pace of the seasons; have leisure to attend to every phenomenon of nature, and to entertain every thought that comes to you. Let your life be a leisurely progress through the realms of nature." The next day he further girds himself with the advice, "Go not so far out of your way for a truer life; keep strictly onward in that path alone which your genius points out" (J, III:182, 184).

The distressing rupture with Emerson and the broader crisis of friendship, Thoreau was coming to realize, were both an impediment and a spur to the advance of his own second spring, of which *Walden's* new growth was emerging as such an integral part. On January 13 he writes that "We must withdraw from our flatterers, even from our friends. They drag us down." Reminding himself of the lessons he thought he had learned as he labored to become more fully his own man, he continues, "To please our friends and relatives we turn out our silver ore in cartloads, while we neglect to work our mines of gold known only to ourselves" (J, III:187–88). The dead stems of the Saint-John's-wort and other plants suggest to him how difficult it is to break away from the haunting ghosts and burdens of the past; "why should the dead corn-stalks," he asks, "occupy the field longer than the green and living did?" (J, III:188). The draining interpersonal tensions and pressures and the continuing impression that he had been branded a loafer by townspeople (J, III:193) propelled him forcefully in the direction of Walden and *Walden*. On January 13, he discussed some details of his moving into the Walden hut, surely an indication that he was turning his attention again to the experience and the book.[2] He does not feel "so vitally related" to his "fellow-men"; as they had been when he was living at the pond, his "countrymen" are still to him "foreigners" (J, III:194).

Still seeking the surcease from guilt he had found only temporarily at Walden, he attempted to put his truncated relationship with male figures, especially his brother and Emerson, in the best possible light. After describing the ant battle he was to incorporate into *Walden*—the civil or "internecine war" that evokes such respect for the brave but doomed participants, one dead and the other maimed—he goes on to knock both Higginson and Emerson but then claims, as if to play down any guilt, that he is "peacefully parting company with the best friend I ever had, by each pursuing his proper path" (J, III:212–14). The battle with Emerson and the rivalry with his brother may have left him wounded, but he strives to unburden himself of guilt and grudges, clear the battleground, by giving his rivals their due. As before, however, serenity is not easily come by. On February 1, hurt and anger again rear their heads, once more, it appears, in connection with Waldo: "When I hear that a friend on whom I relied has spoken of me, not with cold words perhaps, but even with a cold and indifferent tone, to another, ah! what treachery I feel it to be! —the sum of all crimes against humanity." Later in the same passage he agonizes, "My friends! my friends! it does not cheer me to see them. They but express their want of faith in me or in mankind; their coldest, cruelest thought comes clothed in polite and easy-spoken words at last" (J, III:262, 265). Perhaps Thoreau's compassion toward Johnny Riordan on February 8— bringing him a new coat to keep him warm—was partly a response to his friend's coldness, and an attempt to prove to himself that *he,* at least, was not cold and clothed in hypocrisy, not deserving of guilt. After all, as he says, "One is not cold among his brothers and sisters." While, he writes immediately after, the French "respected the Indians as a separate and independent people," the English—with whom he now often tended to link Emerson—"have never done" so (J, III:289). Later in February, still reacting against Emerson, he vents his spleen against seniors and mentors in a passage to be used in *Walden:* "I have lived some thirty-odd years on this planet, and I have yet to hear the first syllable of valuable or even earnest advice from my seniors. . . . If I have any valuable experience, I am sure to reflect that this my mentors said nothing about" (J, III:294–95). It is little wonder that Thoreau began taking nocturnal walks again during this period. If his friendships were unraveling, deteriorating, so too was America a country that was slowly going to seed: "the young man pines to get nearer the post office and the Lyceum, is restless and resolves to go to California, because the depot is a mile off. . . . I cannot realize that this is that hopeful young America which is famous throughout the world for its activity and enterprise" (J, III:237–38). His mounting distress with both a fallen Emerson and a declining America dramatized the imperative to immerse himself in trustworthy, uncontaminated waters. "Of all the characters I have known," he wrote into the fourth version of *Walden,*[3] "perhaps Walden wears best, and best preserves its purity" (W, 192).

In this context of crisis, Thoreau's commitment to the growth of *Walden* became firmer, if not yet as single-minded and all-consuming as it would become. According to Shanley, for the fourth version he "added material by simply inserting it in the manuscript at hand by interlining or on separate leaves."[4] The day after his comment about "peacefully parting company" with his "best friend," he ponders why he left Walden; in that passage, which has already been quoted in full,[5] he admits, "I have often wished myself back" (J, III:214). Revising *Walden* was a way not only of wishing himself back but also, in some important sense, of *being* back. But while these revisions provided a retreat from his current malaise, a means by which to recover innocence, a way to affirm continuity with what he valued in the past (including his cherished ego ideal), a means to reconstruct that past and recoup losses that now went even beyond the "hound —and a turtle dove and a bay horse" of the first draft, he appears to reject *actually* returning, announcing his intention to "go before the mast and on the deck of the world" (J, III:215). The past would have to be integrated with whatever he had become and learned—how he had grown—since he had left the pond. Thus, returning to Walden through *Walden* was a golden opportunity for coalescing regressive and progressive tendencies.

Not only would he live in and through the ego ideal already present in earlier drafts, but he would build on and modify that persona in light of his present state of development.

Of course, he also began to spend much more time at the pond itself, reenacting and renewing his ties to it; re-visioning it; animating it; ascribing human qualities to it and even identifying with it; witnessing again the birth of spring in the Deep Cut. Indeed, he began to associate the risings and fallings of his own moods with those of the pond he was now visiting often; in Walden's character were many qualities he wished to claim as his own, or at least those to which he aspired. On January 24 he comments on the amount of wood that has been cut around the pond: "These woods! Why do I not feel their being cut more sorely? Does it not affect me nearly? The axe can deprive me of much. Concord is sheared of its pride. I am certainly the less attached to my native town in consequence. One, and a main, link is broken. I shall go to Walden less frequently" (J, III:224). Again on March 10 he is bereaved by the demise of the familiar woods in which he walked as a youth and asks, "Is it not time that I ceased to sing? My groves are invaded" (J, III:345–46). Yet, if his journal is to be believed, he went to Walden *more* frequently and did not "cease to sing"; if the forests were being cut down and he cut off from the woods that reminded him of "the dewy and ambrosial vigor and of man's prime," the pond itself remained, an impervious and ultimate symbol, in the wake of all his losses, of continuity with his own dreams and with a primal force that was both a mother and a lover. For the fourth version of *Walden*,[6] he would first comment on how, when fish leap or insects fall on the pond, they are "reported in circling dimples, in lines of beauty, as it were the constant welling up of its fountain, the gentle pulsing of its life, the heaving of its breast. The thrills of joy and the thrills of pain are undistinguishable" (W, 188). Elliot Jaques says, and it clearly applies to Thoreau's relation to Walden and *Walden,* "Under constructive circumstances, the created object in mid-life is experienced unconsciously in terms of the 'good breast' which would moderate fear of death."[7]

Notwithstanding the friendship crisis that seemed a constant threat to distract him or drag him down, there is a growing, if fitful, excitement, a deepening sense of possibility, in the early months of 1852, much of it presumably revolving around his gradually unfolding conception of what the *Journal* and *Walden* might become and how his ever-enlarging comprehension of the seasons might contribute to his spiritual and artistic renaissance. He was clearly contemplating a book, for on January 17 he ponders a "chapter" called "Chickweed" or "Plantain"; quite possibly the book was *Walden,* but it is also conceivable that, as Shanley suggests, he was thinking here of the "book on the seasons which he never had time to write."[8] In any case, he did recognize that his journal was a spacious "barnyard" (J, III:207) and each thought a "nest egg"; feeling the pangs of his alienation from friends, he could proclaim at this point, "My thoughts are my company" (J, III:217). He began to see with more clarity how, by juxtaposing in mosaic fashion separate journal entries,[9] a new gestalt could be revealed: "Thoughts accidently thrown together become a frame in which more may be developed and exhibited. . . . Having by chance recorded a few disconnected thoughts and then brought them into juxtaposition, they suggest a whole new field in which it was possible to labor and to think" (J, III:217). Occasionally, though, he would find to his dismay that "Thoughts of different dates will not cohere" (J, III:288).

The urge to get on, in this "early spring" period, with the revisions of *Walden,* to strike while the iron is hot, is evinced in his January journal. Preaching mostly to himself, he intones the writer to "write as if thy time were short, for it is indeed short at the longest. Improve each occasion when thy soul is reached. Drain the cup of inspiration to its last dregs. . . . The spring will not last forever. These fertile and expanding seasons of thy life, when the rain reaches thy root, when thy vigor shoots, when thy flower is budding, shall be fewer and farther between. Again I say, Remember thy Creator in the days of thy youth" (J, III:221–22). The imagery of spring is associated with both his life and his writing at this time of literary expansion. "My life," he says—and, we may surmise, particularly his life in language—"as essentially belongs to the present as that of a willow tree in the spring. Now, now its catkins expand, its yellow bark shines, its sap flows; now or never must you make whistles of it" (J, III:232). *Walden* (and the journal from which it grew), like the catkins, was beginning to expand, and now, he thought, was the time to "whistle" through, speak through, this medium. Invigorated by his vision of *Walden,* however limited it still remained, Thoreau was apparently preparing to give top priority to it. "Let all things give way," he declares, "to the impulse of expression. It is the bud unfolding, the perennial spring. As well stay the spring. Who shall resist the thaw?" (J, III:232). Thoreau's sense of "thawing out"—and much of the natural and seasonal imagery in the *Journal*— would quite frequently coincide with and reflect his emotions concerning the progress, or lack of progress, he was making in creative endeavors; and, as *Walden* began to assume and consume more and more of his creative life—as it in many ways *became* his life—it became the chief criterion and focus of growth and expansion. So much of his life and self-concept eventually was wrapped up in the book that it became a sort of alter ego. Thus, the *Journal* may often be read partly as a fairly accurate barometer of how the work on *Walden* was proceeding and how Thoreau felt about and evaluated himself in connection with that work. Just as spring was a "natural resurrection," and just as the rivers "come out of their icy prison," so too was Thoreau, as he made headway in revising the book, striving to "resume [his] spring life with joy and hope" (J, III:322–23). "When the frost comes out of the ground, there is a corresponding thawing of the man" (J, III:341), and to the extent that he felt able to insure his second spring through his writing, he was indeed thawing. By March 15 he seemed certain that he had made a new, auspicious beginning; his life, he says, "partakes of infinity," and he goes forth to "make new demands on life," hoping to "begin this summer well; to do something in it worthy of it and me . . . to have my immortality now" (J, III:350–51). His spring resolution, inspired by what he had already accomplished in the months immediately preceding, is to "dare" as he has never done, to "persevere" as he has never done, and to "purify [himself] anew as with fire and water, soul and body" (J, III:351).

Only a week after this resolution, however, he complains that "the winter has not broken up with me. It is a backward season with me. Perhaps we grow older and older till we no longer sympathize with the revolution of the seasons, and our winters never break up" (J, III:363). Spring was slow and unsteady in its coming this year; and Thoreau, whose own moods were so attuned to seasonal and meteorological phenomena, writes on April 11, "My spring is even more backward than nature's" (J, III: 398). Given the importance he was beginning to ascribe to *Walden*'s progress, it may be speculated that he was running into roadblocks, internal resistances and external distractions, once again, or perhaps that he was becoming dissatisfied with interlining and inserts as his modes of revision. Earlier he marveled at the four seasons, "each incredible to the other" (J, III:233), and the reality of innumerable seasons within seasons (J, III: 302). The same applied to his own life, his own moods. If one week, or even day, he felt strong, confident, assured that he was on the brink of a second spring, another week he would wonder how he could ever have thought so. His own seasons, like nature's, and sometimes in response to nature's, advanced only by fits and starts, and there was always the possibility of setbacks, of another frost—even a hard freeze—in this chancy, capricious period when growth could be nipped in the bud.

What might well have precipitated this uncertain season within a season were a letter from Horace Greeley on April 11 and the circumstances surrounding it. Flushed by the prospect of a richer journal and an expanding *Walden*—and in apparent financial straits (J, III:282)—Thoreau took the step of inquiring in February whether he might be invited to lecture at the People's Course in New York.[10] This was a big step, considering how, in the previous two years, he had sought to avoid being burned again by involvement in the literary business. Whatever the risk of sticking his neck out, he seemed prepared to lay aside any qualms he may have had about Greeley from past dealings. Perhaps his conviction that he was now reasonably settled and moving forward again on his own path, and that lecturing might be a way to crystallize and disseminate his ideas, as well as make some money, spurred his request to Greeley. The New York editor's response must have aroused mixed feelings. On the one hand, Greeley wrote back on February 24 that he was not well known enough to command sufficient audiences, and in any event the docket was already full. On the other hand, he tactfully says that Thoreau is "a better speaker than many, but a far better writer still" and suggests that he send some of his "wood-notes wild" or other, shorter, articles for which Greeley would try to procure publication and payment (C, 276–77). On March 5 Thoreau replied, offering Greeley some articles and his excursion to Canada; Greeley promised to get money for the articles but suggested that the "canadian tour" appeared "unmanageable" in its present form, ought to be broken up, and in any case Thoreau was more "at home" describing nature than cities (C, 277). Finally, he did manage to get the articles accepted by Sartain "for a low price" and again advised breaking up the "excursion to Canada" so that it might be accepted (C, 278). At the beginning of April, Thoreau did take up an offer by T. W. Higginson to lecture—cautioning him that he had little to "*entertain* a large audience" (C, 278–79)—and offered to read something from "Walden, or Life in the Woods." He was at least beginning to believe that speaking and writing on his own terms, no longer in Emerson's shadow, might even yield a very modest income.

The shock came, however, in Greeley's letter of April 3. He proposed that Thoreau write an article of "one hundred pages, or so" on "Ralph Waldo Emerson, his Works and Ways." The article would "take the form of a review of his writings" and would "give some idea of the Poet, the Genius, the Man. . . . Your 'Carlyle' article is my model, but you can give us Emerson better than you did Carlyle" (C, 279). He expressed his intention to have the article published in the *Westminster Review*—if that was agreeable—and to pay Thoreau fifty dollars after or prior to publication. One can imagine the inner turbulence and ruefulness provoked by this letter. On April 4, probably before he had even received Greeley's proposal, he had written despondently in his journal of having reached "that pass with my friend that our words do not pass with each other for what they are worth." "He"—almost certainly Emerson—"finds fault with me that I walk alone, when I pine for want of a companion, that I commit my thoughts to a diary even on my walks, instead of seeking to share them generously with a friend; curses my practice even." This "curse" he takes very much to heart: "Awful as it is to contemplate, I pray that, if I am the cold intellectual skeptic whom he rebukes, his curse may take effect, and wither and dry up those sources of my life, and my journal no longer yield me pleasure nor life" (J, III:389–90). On April 7 there was no journal entry and only short ones on the sixth and eighth, suggesting either that Thoreau was too distraught or distracted or that, indeed, he was questioning whether his journal would yield him more pleasure or life. The "curse" of such a significant figure clearly shook him. And, as he quite possibly saw, Greeley's request that he do a "just summing up" of Emerson was at best an example of exquisitely bad timing and at worst an indication of insensitivity. He may well have felt that Greeley (who had made a somewhat similar request several years ago) should have been aware of his wish no longer to be so closely identified or compared with his former mentor; and, after all, the editor had recently said that his strength lay primarily in portrayals of nature and man in nature. Certainly Greeley could not expect him to write, as he put it, "calmly" about Emerson. Any calm he might have been achieving had been undermined by his friend's "curse," not to mention the lingering crisis in their friendship over the previous months and years.

The Greeley letter, then, momentarily upset the delicate equilibrium Thoreau had been cultivating as he started to rework *Walden* and to "thaw" in the warmth of this budding new spring in his life. After commenting on the "backwardness" of his spring on April 11, he intimates, "For a month past life has been a thing incredible to me. None but the kind Gods can make me sane. If only they will let their south winds blow on me! I ask to be melted" (J, III:398). The evidence suggests that the events relating to Greeley and Emerson had played a large part in bringing him to this state. Indeed, on that same day he refers again to Emerson's accusation, turns to nature for solace, and invokes his own law of compensation: "If I am too cold for human friendship, I trust that I shall not soon be too cold for natural influences. It appears to be a law that you cannot have a deep sympathy with both man and nature" (J, III:400). Almost immediately thereafter, in what may be a reference to the complications of seeking help or money from Greeley, he writes, "It is hard for a man to take money from his friends, or any service" (J, III:401). That night, trying to relieve the tension, he took another nocturnal stroll. On April 16, just before refusing the Greeley proposal that he write about Emerson, he notes with disdain, "How many there are who advise you to print! How few who advise you to lead a more interior life! In the one case there is all the world to advise you, in the other there is none to advise you but yourself. Nobody ever advised me not to print but myself. . . . Only he can be trusted with gifts who can present a face of bronze to expectations" (J, III:420). It is unlikely that Thoreau seriously considered Greeley's proposal; and the editor's response on the twentieth seems somewhat chastened, more remote and curt than usual. Addressing Thoreau as "Dear Sir," he indicates that he is "rather sorry" that he will not do the Emerson piece but "glad" that he will be "able to employ [his] time to better purpose." Concerning the "Quebeck notes," Greeley expresses relative apathy (C, 281).

The "better purpose" was, quite probably, preeminently though not yet so exclusively the work on *Walden*. Thoreau needed to protect and nourish its newly formed roots and tender seedlings during the vagaries of his early spring emotional climate. In one respect, the Emerson-Greeley fiasco sent him back to nature with even greater zeal. On April 24 he speaks of the existence of two species of men, those of society who have "many letters to write" (an activity that had dropped off sharply for him since 1849), for whom success is "wealth and the approbation of men," and those who are not "of" society. Thoreau obviously located himself firmly in the latter camp. The same day that he wrote his negative reply to Greeley, his journal entries were quite nature-oriented, and he devoted more energy than ever to clinical investigations of organic processes. He asked more questions about natural facts of which he was not sure; and he began, by April 28, making more extensive use of lists and botanical nomenclature (J, III:473). He did not at this point perceive his scientific bent as a threat to artistic vision. He was still, as it were, learning the ropes, and his scrutiny of nature was starting to yield insights and analogies critical to *Walden*'s further development.

On April 18 he sets down an insight that some critics have regarded as a breakthrough:[11] "For the first time I perceive this spring that the year is a circle" (J, III:438). While this remark may be read as indicating that Thoreau had not seen the year as a circle before, it is difficult to accept this interpretation, given Thoreau's experience as poet and nature watcher. More likely, he was indicating that this was the first time *this spring* that he had seen the year as a circle. It can, however, be granted that this vision of year as circle became even more vivid to him as he observed nature more minutely and as he pondered the applications to his own life: however delayed (and the delay could be unexpectedly long), spring was finally coming around again and his own springlike expansion with it. His perception of how long the winter could hang on, in nature and in human life, may well have led him to consider eventually expanding the winter sections of *Walden* to reflect how much spring had to be prepared for and earned. The image of "buffeting the winter through" (W, 81) was added in the fourth version.[12] While Thoreau would oscillate among different conceptions of life—as an unbroken and returning circle, as a line of forward progress but with a finite conclusion, and as a transnatural tangent or parabola[13]— clearly the image of the circular seasons would be the dominant ordering principle of *Walden,* though he did not begin to make full use of this principle until he embarked on the fifth version of the book in late 1852.[14] In any event, this newly reinforced revelation of the year as circle gave him forward momentum and the intuition at least that *Walden* could be more than he had previously dreamed. Immersion in the revolving seasons, then, renewed faith in the inevitability of his own second spring and suggested how the book could tell the story of his seasons, only incompletely rendered in earlier versions. On the same day he notes the year's circularity, he exclaims with reawakened excitement and determination,

> I would fain explore the mysterious relation between myself and these things [nature's sights and sounds]. I would at least know what these things unavoidably are, make a chart of our life, know how its shores trend, that butterflies reappear and when, know why just this circle of creatures completes the world. Can I not by expectation affect the revolutions of nature, make a day to bring forth something new? (J, III:438)

Although it is not clear whether the "chart" was to be incorporated into *Walden,* the *Journal,* or an entirely separate work, it is apparent that Thoreau felt he was growing again, the caterpillar metamorphosing into a butterfly. The observation that the river "hasn't risen this high for a long time" served as both a reflection of his rising spirits and a harbinger of things to come. On April's final day he further describes the state of his mind and work in characterizing the era of the year. "Now is the time," he says, "to set trees and consider what things you will plant in your garden" (J, III:482).

While the outlook was more promising, Thoreau was becoming increasingly sensitive to the fitful, fragile, inconsistent, sometimes imperceptible character of nature's development and of his own. To be sure, spring did bring growth, but there could always be relapses to winter, unpleasant if reversible checks on growth. To accept that no season brought with it completely uninterrupted, consistent patterns of forward development and that there were an almost infinite variety of subtle natural and human seasons within the seasons was crucial. It was difficult indeed to capture and embrace the texture of our experience, how much things could change, how many epochs there could be, within a relatively short time span. In early May Thoreau comments on the impossibility of remembering even the previous week. There was a "river of Lethe [which] flows with many windings the year through, separating one season from another." By the same token, "our moods vary week to week, with the winds and the temperature and the revolution of the seasons" (J, IV:41, 44). Walden Pond's relatively equable temperature was a notable and appealing exception in this regard, suggesting a resistance to the otherwise prevalent vagaries of life and nature. What Thoreau now generally perceived in nature, he was also coming to see, and be more understanding of, in himself: "What subtle differences between one season and another. . . . The seasons admit of infinite degrees in their revolutions" (J, IV:117). Even the poet—perhaps especially the poet—has his "spring-tides and neap-tides" (J, III:8). Just as there could be temporary setbacks to growth within a given season, there could also be an almost imperceptible but nonetheless real forward movement, like the growth of a plant or the moving hands of a clock. Thus, even if in his work and life it might not always *appear* to the untutored and impatient eye that he was growing, he *was* nevertheless. Patience and persistence would ultimately be rewarded.

Thoreau needed to remind himself of these lessons as he moved into late spring and summer 1852. He pronounces May 17 the apex of the season of hope (J, IV:61). As the year inclined toward summer, he monitored his moods in connection with the "revolution of the seasons" and began to notice some signs of incipient stagnation that threatened to retard if not block his progress. On May 19 he says that for the past five days, "both from poor health and multiplicity of objects," he has not watched the "progress of the season" as closely and has "noted only what falls under my observation" (J, IV:65). Whether the poor health may in this case be interpreted as a cause or as a symptom of stagnation, there *was* less philosophizing, more arid observation and use of scientific terminology during this period, which appears to have aroused some anxiety. The overabundance and heat were, in their own way, as much of a trial as the winter, perhaps even more so. Already, by June 9, the grass was not as green as it had been, and on the twenty-first he revealed what must have been a scary experience for him: "Nature has looked uncommonly bare and dry to me for a day or two. With our senses applied to the surrounding world we are reading our own physical and corresponding moral revolutions. Nature was so shallow all at once I did not know what had attracted me all my life" (J, IV:126). While encouraged by his appreciation of an apple tree's beauty, he was also struck by the perception that the buds were more lovely and hopeful than the already expanded flowers (J, IV:142). Perhaps it was around this time that Thoreau was coming to feel that he had gone as far as he could go with a fourth version of *Walden;* the flower he had already produced was unsatisfactory compared to the promise of a budding fifth draft. Absorbed in the abundance, or overabundance, of natural details that the summer presented, he characterized the era as "my year of observation" and, it may be speculated, accepted reluctantly the deferral of hopes for *Walden*'s further growth until a more propitious season, when the details could be imaginatively assimilated and "associated with humane affections" (J, IV: 163).

Also contributing to his frame of mind was apparent financial exigency. Still worried (as he was on July 1) that he was considered a loafer by many Concordians—a concern intensified by his own imaginative sluggishness—he nevertheless found himself in the uneasy position of needing a loan. A proud man, Thoreau must have been somewhat chagrined and upset about asking Greeley, who had seemed so to misread him earlier in the year, for a seventy-five-dollar loan. But he could at least justify his request on a business basis; he would look on the loan as an advance against future payments for his work. Soothing to him in this time when, as he put it in a letter to Sophia on July 13, he was "sadly scientific" (C, 283) and, as he described it in a letter to Blake on the twenty-first, when his life was "almost altogether outward" (C, 284) was the image of water lilies which, though subject to rotting by insects (J, IV: 179), finally came out of the stagnant mud and blossomed.

Whatever his anxieties, he had enough self-understanding to assume that this season too would pass and that it might even be necessary to his eventual flowering and fruiting. After all, he had made it through crises before, including the most recent crisis with Emerson, even if the pain had not entirely subsided. *Walden* had undergone revisions, grown, during this same period; indeed, working on the book, which may in part have been prompted by the turbulence, had helped him extricate himself from the doldrums and had helped reassure him that all his growth was not in the past. *Walden,* and the daily revelations in his journal, both recorded and embodied the progress he had made. That he had come through so many straits gave greater character and value to what he had achieved thus far; he and his work had been tested and tempered by suffering. If he had once been inclined to give the impression that things came easily, that facile optimism now had to be dropped. In January 1852 he had written, "The rainbow is the symbol of the triumph which succeeds to a grief that has tried us to our advantage, so that at last we can smile through our tears" (J, III: 201). And in February, with the wounds of his latest rupture with Emerson still fresh, he saw himself as the toughened survivor, the man who has ridden out the storm:

> To get the value of the storm we must be out a long time and travel far in it, so that it may fairly penetrate our skin, and we be as it were turned inside out to it, and there be no part in us but is wet or weather-beaten, —so that we become storm men instead of fair-weather men. Some men speak of having been wetted to the skin once as a memorable event in their lives, which, not withstanding the croakers, they survived. (J, III:323)

On the last day of March he repeated and amplified on this theme, pointing out the value of suffering and the possibilities it afforded for renewal: "Our spirits revive like lichens in the storm. There is something worth living for when we are resisted, threatened. . . . What would the days, what would our life, be worth, if some nights were not as dark as pitch, —of darkness tangible or that you cut with a knife?" (J, III:367). Less willing than previously to subscribe to a simply sunny optimism, to deny the existence of dark nights that had to be suffered through and survived, he was more prepared to stress crisis as a sine qua non for authentic growth. To be sure, this shift was more a matter of emphasis and tone than of complete reversal; many of his earlier writings, including *A Week* and *Walden*'s early drafts, had shown some awareness of "tough problems" and crises, however understated, underestimated, or deemphasized. Even if he still shied away from it sometimes, his sense of himself as "storm man" now enriched and deepened his vision, fostered a desire to "share every creature's suffering" (J, III:367). It was a "good experience" to "have gone through" a winter of "intense cold, deep and lasting snows, and clear, tense winter sky" (J, III:376–77). When the storm caused by Greeley's proposal to write about Emerson was still subsiding, on April 21, he heard a robin's song in the midst of a dreary rain, and he identified with that song: "It sings with power, like a bird of great faith that sees the bright future through the dark present, to reassure the race of man. . . . They are sounds to make a dying man live. They sing not their despair" (J, III:450). *Walden* would be the work of a man who saw himself as thoroughly seasoned. It is revealing in this context to note that the parable of the "artist in the city of Kouroo," who survives against all odds and in spite of his being "deserted" by "his friends" to create his "perfect work" (W, 326–27), first found its way into *Walden* in the fourth version.[15]

These variations on the more prevalent theme of weathering, and being seasoned by, crisis prepared the way for a closely related theme and insight, recorded on July 14, when the torpid and creatively sparse summer was at its zenith and about to descend to autumn:

> Trees have commonly two growths in the year, a spring and a fall growth, the latter sometimes equalling the former, and you can see where the first was

checked whether by cold or drouth, and wonder what there was in the summer to produce this check, this blight. So is it with man; most have a spring growth only, and never get over this first check to their youthful hopes; but plants of hardier constitution, or perchance planted in a more genial soil, speedily recover themselves, and, though they bear the scar or knot in remembrance of their disappointment, they push forward again and have a vigorous fall growth which is equivalent to a new spring. These two growths are now visible on the oak sprouts, the second already nearly equalling the first. (J, IV:227–28)

The imagery of "fall growth" and "new spring," while hardly novel at this point to Thoreau, is more richly developed and intensely felt, supplemented as it had been by firsthand experience and fresh observations of nature. Clearly, the analogies applied not only to human life in general but to his life in particular; they were central to his continually evolving life myth. A late bloomer, he had nonetheless had his spring growth, most decisively and memorably at Walden, but his growth had subsequently been checked by many winter snows, early spring frosts, and summer droughts: his failed attempts to "make it" as a man of letters in the post-Walden period; the battering and buffeting he had taken from a society "civil" in name only; the frigid reception extended to *A Week;* the submersion in business details that had distracted him from creative work; the excruciatingly prolonged falling-out with Emerson and the accompanying feelings of bitterness, betrayal, desertion, and grief; the Greeley incident in April; and, most immediately, the languor and immersion in nature's difficult-to-assimilate details that plagued him during the summer. Thus the period since Walden had been in many respects a series of checks to be overcome and challenges to meet; struggle now seemed more the rule than the exception, and it had not been easy to keep up his spirits and chart his own course. In 1852 the scars and knots remained, to be sure, but he sensed that he was once more expanding, though still gradually, and the growth of *Walden,* however incomplete and vulnerable to further checks, was both a sign and a source of that expansion. As summer gave way to fall, the conviction was strengthening that he too would have "a vigorous fall growth," a "new spring" that would be more seasoned than, qualitatively different from, his spring growth. *Walden* was the avatar of that conviction; already, like the oak, it showed new sprouts. By this time, as Shanley indicates, Thoreau had "accumulated such quantities of new material that in the fifth version (1852–53) he had to make fresh copy of most of the second half of *Walden*."[16] That fifth version was probably begun in late 1852.[17]

The reflections on suffering, crisis, and fall growth were of a piece with the developmental epoch in which the thirty-five-year-old Thoreau now found himself. There is evidence aplenty to suggest that he perceived himself to be on the cusp between late young adulthood and middle age. It is probable that, with the shorter life expectancy in nineteenth-century America, middle age was seen as coming somewhat earlier than it is today. And for Thoreau, the middle and later stages of the life cycle would be compressed and telescoped. Certainly, in some respects the 1850–52 period had represented a more satisfactory version of what Levinson has called "late settling down" (occurring in late early adulthood)[18] after his earlier attempts at "settling" had failed or been blocked. He had managed, by and large, to settle on, into, and for a life structure that provided for both pragmatic exigencies and opportunities to become more fully his own man. He had put down deeper roots and was extending his shoots. If he had not established himself as a "senior" member of the literary profession, he was at least relatively confident in his own mind that the *Journal* and *Walden* would put him on an equal or superior footing with mentors and elders. Though still bearing scars and knots, and though there was yet much unfinished emotional business, he had made substantial progress toward self-emancipation and self-definition. At this point, having come so far but also knowing he had far to go, Thoreau perhaps saw himself as being in some ways in the July or August of his life, awaiting the first stirrings of fall and encroaching middle age. In his July 21 letter to Blake he had described himself as "stupidly well" (C, 284); but if this summer was a period of comparative stupor or stasis, he knew it was but the prelude to another, more dynamic, season.

Not that he approached middle age with absolute equanimity. There was, to be sure, a tendency—one that would remain in evidence for many years—to want to hold onto spring and summer and put off the fall, to prolong young adulthood indefinitely, as he had prolonged adolescence. As the *Journal* shows, he alternated between a desire for "perennial youth" and a yearning for maturity. Sometimes middle age could be associated primarily with loss—of youth, vitality, inspiration, imagination. Earlier in 1852 he had commented that "men may be born to a condition of mind at which others arrive in middle age by the decay of their poetic faculties" (J, III:311–12). A little later he had written, "Perchance as we grow old we cease to spring with the spring, and we are indifferent to the succession of years, and they go by without epoch as months" (J, III:366). And there is a cluster of reflections in July and August that further reveal his ambivalence about middle age and aging at this time. Immediately preceding the passage on spring and fall growth he makes the wry observation that the "youth gets together his materials to build a bridge to the moon, or perchance a palace or temple on the earth and at length the middle-aged man concludes to build a wood-shed with them" (J, IV:227). Although forced by mundane realities and exigencies to build many a "wood-shed," it was Thoreau's wish not to lose his essential relation to youth and the moon (and all, on his moonlight walks, it connoted). In recent years, at the same time that he was building woodsheds, he had nevertheless persisted to work assiduously to construct the foundations for his "bridge to the moon." He could only trust that the foundations would not crumble as he grew older, though sometimes his faith would falter.

Anxieties and reservations notwithstanding, Thoreau, still languishing in the heat and haze of summer, began to anticipate the fall with the relish and vigor he had once reserved for anticipating spring. "Do not all flowers that blossom after mid-July remind us of the fall?" he asks on July 30. "After midsummer, we have a belated feeling as if we had been idlers, and are forward to see in each sight and hear in each sound some presage of the fall, just as in middle age man anticipates the end of life" (J, IV:267). He watched attentively for the signs of a reinvigorating autumn in his own life just as he did in the natural world: the "absence of flowers, the shadows, the wind, the green cranberries," the rising of the water, the "new depths" of the cricket's chirps (J, IV:269, 278). By as early as August 6, still in the midst of the drowsy dog-day weather that so often put a damper on his spirits, he pronounces the year already somewhat stale: "Has not the year grown old? Methinks we do ourselves, at any rate, somewhat tire of the season and observe less attentively and with less interest the opening of new flowers and the song of the birds. It is the signs of the fall that affect us most. It is hard to live in the summer content with it" (J, IV:282).

Life cannot stay contentedly settled for too long; within each stage and season are the seeds of its dissolution. Stability must ultimately give way to transition and further growth. And each transitional season presents a necessary crisis, "as if a man were himself and could work well only at a certain rare crisis" (J, IV:300). Already, with autumn approaching, the "small fruits of most plants are now generally ripe or ripening"; his seeds having taken root and sprouted in the past year, Thoreau could feel the fruits of his own life beginning to ripen, and "By their fruits ye shall know them" (J, IV:303, 306). The autumn promised an even richer harvest, as the changing hues of the leaves suggested:

> This coloring and reddening of the leaves toward fall is interesting; as if the sun had so prevailed that even the leaves, better late than never, were turning to flowers, —so filled with mature juices, the whole plant turns at length to one flower, and all its leaves are petals around its fruit or dry seed. A second flower-

ing to celebrate the maturity of the fruit. The first to celebrate the age of puberty, the marriageable age; the second, the maturity of the parent, the age of wisdom, the fullness of years. (J, IV:308)

In much the same way, Thoreau had blossomed first in the "marriageable" years (at the pond), and though his leaves (*Walden,* the *Journal,* other creative efforts) were just beginning to show tinges of mature color, he hoped he was in the process of moving toward that autumn which would be a "second flowering." On August 27 he observes that Walden, the objective correlative of *Walden* in some respects, "has risen steadily for a year past, apparently unaffected by drouth or rain, and now, in the summer of '52, is as high as it was twenty years ago" (J, IV:321). Walden Pond, as *Walden* promises to do, had risen to great heights, and with it Thoreau's spirits rose. He would visit the pond often in the next several months.

By September 28, with flowers blooming again and birds singing, he declares, "This is the commencement, then, of the second spring" (J, IV: 367). Now, however, he was more mindful than before that the "second spring" was also, at least in part, fall growth, and this second growth had a maturity the first growth did not have. On the first day of December he observes "the form of the buds which are prepared for spring" and characterizes the first week in December as "true Indian summer" (J, IV:419, 425–26). Only on December 12 does winter begin in earnest (J, IV:427). By this time, Thoreau had put aside the fourth version of *Walden* and was at least about to embark on the fifth—and much more extensive—revision, requiring the rewriting of the book's entire second half.[19] It would have been fitting (but it has not been established) if he had begun this crucial redrafting at a time coinciding with his observations of nature's second spring.

Accompanying Thoreau's gradual passage from later young adulthood to middle age, a passage Levinson refers to as the "Mid-Life Transition,"[20] was—as is true for many people—a somewhat increased sensitivity to the dark, tragic, demonic, ornery, ambiguous, contradictory, limited side to life, to nature, and to himself.[21] Times of transition and expansion also tend to be times when one is more open to previously unacknowledged (or dimly acknowledged) inner and outer realities; in order to expand, a certain psychological flexibility and elasticity are required. At this juncture when Thoreau was feeling so alive, so engaged in the resurrection of *Walden,* he was also unusually subject to glimpsing the dark side of the moon, to peering at those irreducible facts he saw "as through a glass darkly" (J, IX:407). Some of these glimpses found their way into the book and modified it; on the other hand, working on *Walden* also helped to stave off or exorcise some demons. Certainly this move from innocence to experi-

ence had been an ongoing, incremental process, and particular events—
the death of his brother, the failure of *A Week,* and the estrangement from
Emerson, to cite some major examples—had stirred up a hornets' nest of
uncomfortable questions. Now this process, partly in the context of this
phase's developmental necessities, was accelerated and exacerbated.
However haltingly and reluctantly, he was forced to slough off another
layer of innocence and naiveté. To be sure, Thoreau's self-knowledge
would remain partial and selective.[22] His tendencies to deny the negative
and accentuate the positive; to defend militantly his ego ideal (now partly
protected by immersion in *Walden* and the Walden persona); to seek absolution and purification rather than accept or embrace desire, guilt, imper-
fection, orneriness, evil as ineradicable marks of humanity and of his own
humanity: these tendencies were too fundamental to his personality, to his
very psychic survival, for him to let go of them. Yet, though he remained a
person whose ego was vigilantly on the defensive (and often took the offensive), the gates of these defenses were lowered to some degree during
this period, and he was more given to perceiving the entrenched, sometimes sinister paradoxes and dualities of life, nature, and the self. These
moments of insight and reduced illusions[23] were more likely to appear in
the privacy of his journal, before the ego defenses and the conscious artist
had the chance to excise them and build new and therapeutic illusions.[24]
Nevertheless, the increased, if still circumscribed, openness to looking
through the glass darkly, to four-o'clock-in-the-morning thoughts, would
enrich (and sometimes complicate) his vision, would be woven into the
texture of *Walden,* and would help the book seem—more than it had previously—to be a hard-won victory over, not simply an evasion of, the perverse and the problematic.

Already alluded to was Thoreau's heightened emphasis in 1852 on
the inevitability and worth of suffering. There was some penchant, if not
eagerness, to peer over the precipice and into the abyss. Closely allied to
that emphasis was a more clearly realized tragic sense of life. Even the
word "tragedy" finds its way more frequently into the *Journal,* as in his remarks—which would be worked into *Walden*—revealing deeper insight
into the splitting of consciousness; he speaks of "the doubleness by which I
stand as remote from myself as from another" and includes a remark on
"the play—it may be the tragedy of life" (J, IV:291). Having taken a brief
river trip on August 31, 1852—the anniversary of his Concord-Merrimack voyage with John—and planning to climb another New Hampshire
mountain (Monadnock) on September 6, Thoreau was understandably
prompted to reflect on the necessity of incorporating the tragic into any
holistic view of life. On September 1 he writes, "Some tragedy, at least

some dwelling on, or even exaggeration of, the tragic side of life is necessary for contrast or relief to the picture" (J, IV:335).[25] Given his previous elaborate attempts to deny or downplay the tragedy of his brother's death (sometimes claiming that, even in this case, the laws of compensation and transcendence entirely prevailed), his acknowledgment of the need for a balancing sense of tragedy must be taken as a sign of progress.

Levinson argues that a genuinely tragic sense of life "derives from the realization that great misfortunes or failures are not merely imposed upon us from without, but are largely the result of our own tragic flaws."[26] Thoreau had once, perhaps taking the image lightly or superficially, described his relationship with Emerson as a "tragedy of more than 5 acts"; in the context of the latest crisis with Emerson, he seems more amenable than he usually had been to exploring not only the flaws in others but those in himself which have resulted in a staggering personal loss. No longer is rage or bitterness (or the repression or denial of these feelings) sufficient. There is, for instance, the remarkably insightful entry of August 24 about friendship, in which he speaks of "one who almost wholly misunderstands me and whom I too probably misunderstand, toward whom, nevertheless, I am distinctly drawn" (J, IV:313). Though the passage contains ample indictment of the friend who "has complained, cursed me even," it is not without reflections about the extent to which he is remorsefully implicated in the failure of friendship. "Is it all my fault?" he asks (though his answer is clearly "no"), and later he comments, "Like cuttlefish we conceal ourselves, we darken the atmosphere in which we move; we are not transparent. . . . Our sin and shame prevent our expressing even the innocent thoughts we have. I know of no one to whom I can be transparent instinctively" (J, IV:314–15). Earlier referred to was an entry of April 4 in which Thoreau "prayed" that "if I am the cold intellectual skeptic whom he [presumably Emerson] rebukes, his curse may take effect, and wither and dry up those sources of my life" (J, III:389–90). For one to whom such "curses" could be terribly threatening, it is a mark of some strength that Thoreau could entertain the possibility that his defects and limitations, his resistance to being "transparent," contributed heavily to his problems with intimacy.[27] As if aware of his own self-defeating and even self-destructive behavior, he further writes in October 1852, "It is suicide to become abetters in misapprehending ourselves. Suspicion creates the stranger and substitutes him for the friend. I cannot abet any man in misapprehending myself" (J, IV:397). That he could not blame entirely the other, that he himself abetted the misunderstandings, was a revelation he was primarily privy to when he let his defenses down—not something he found it easy to do. In November 1853 he would further admit his fallibility: "If there is any one with whom we have a quarrel, it is most likely that that one makes some just demand on us which we disappoint" (J, v:515). His self-knowledge was enhanced when he could confront his need and unrealistic expectations for—along with his frustrating ambivalence about—people, as he would in April 1853: "No fields are so barren to me as the men of whom I expect everything but get nothing. In their neighborhood I experience a painful yearning for society, which cannot be satisfied, for the hate is greater than the love" (J, v:87). Like the blackbirds he observes the next day, he gets "uneasy and anxious" in proximity to people (J, v:91).

One of the most startlingly honest self-appraisals Thoreau ever made appeared in his February 1852 journal, surrounded by broodings about Emerson and denigrations of the advice of seniors and mentors. While he funneled much psychic energy into dodging or submerging guilt and self-loathing, here the guilt has surfaced and is confessed:

> Now if there are any who think that I am vainglorious, that I set myself up above others and crow over their low estate, let me tell them that I could tell a pitiful story respecting myself as well as them, if my spirits held out to do it; I could encourage them with a sufficient list of failures, and could flow as humbly as the very gutters themselves, I could enumerate a list of as rank offenses as ever reached the nostrils of heaven; that I think worse of myself than they can possibly think of me, being better acquainted with the man. I put the best face on the matter. I will tell them this secret, if they will not tell it to anybody else. (J, III:293)

Significantly, Thoreau considered using this passage as an epigraph to *Walden* but later dropped the idea. It was apparently a secret he needed to keep in the recesses, for it grated too harshly against the ego ideal that was so necessary to self-preservation; his "spirits" would not easily have "held out" to tell the whole sorry tale of his "rank offenses." With this epigraph, *Walden* might have had another explicit dimension; still, he does plant some clues regarding this "story" in the book. In the seventh draft of *Walden*,[28] for instance, he would confide, "I have never dreamed of any enormity greater than I have committed. I never knew, and never shall know, a worse man than myself" (w, 78). In any event, this more candid Thoreau displayed at least some readiness to admit the darkness within. If he put the "best face on the matter" in his public writings, it was not an entirely unconscious process, and *Walden*, though written in a largely affirmative mode, would give more of an impression than previously that positive virtue was attainable, not through the absence of vice, but by a triumph *over* vice.

Though Thoreau was intermittently able to shoulder some of the responsibility for failed intimacy, an intimacy he sometimes pined for, his revulsion toward humanity nevertheless seemed to become especially acute in early 1853. Perhaps partly provoked by a letter from Greeley he received in early January, which advised him to eliminate his "flagrant heresies" and "defiant Pantheism" (C, 293) from his writing, and in any case down on humankind, he writes, "I love Nature partly *because* she is not man, but a retreat from him. None of his institutions control or pervade her. . . . How infinite and pure the least pleasure of which Nature is basis, compared with the congratulation of mankind" (J, IV:445). While this statement is a somewhat blunter acknowledgment than he had made previously of one motivation for turning to nature, what follows, a short couplet equating the human with the demonic, is even more revealing: "Man, man is the devil,/The source of all evil." In the same dualistic vein, he continues, "Nature is a prairie for outlaws. There are two worlds, the post office and nature" (J, IV:445, 446). Later in the month, reflecting on a dream, he speaks sourly of the "rottenness of human relations," which "appeared full of death and decay, and offended the nostrils." The full morbidity of his state of mind is reflected in his dream image of having "delv[ed] amid the graves of the dead and soiled my fingers with their rank mould." The dream was, he concludes, "*sanitarily, morally,* and *physically* true" (J, IV:472).

Quite probably the dream's grotesque imagery owed much to a disaster that befell Concord in early January, the explosion of a powder mill that killed several men. He had been attracted by the sound and had witnessed the grisly aftermath of the explosion, in much the same way that he had formerly observed shipwrecks. Indeed, in June of 1853, he would make an explicit connection between the two kinds of wrecks, speculating on how the human debris of the powder-mill blast was carried from the Merrimack River to the ocean and then cast up like driftwood on the shores of distant lands, "still bearing some traces of burnt powder." He was led to ponder again the brittleness and sheerly physical basis of human existence: "To see a man lying all bare, lank, and tender on the rocks, like a skinned frog or lizard! We did not suspect that he was made of such cold, tender, clammy substance before" (J, V:211–12). Clearly, this calamity had resonance for him months after the event. And at the time of the explosion, on January 7, he describes the human carnage in similar stark, naturalistic language, almost as if it were another instance of seed dispersal: "The kernel-house was swept away, and fragments, mostly but a foot or two in length, were strewn over the hills and meadows, as if sown, for thirty rods, and the slight snow then on the ground was for the most part melted around" (J, IV:454). However, his response two days later is not so matter-of-fact; nature is here neither wholly benevolent nor indifferent. Brooding over the possibilities of being struck by lightning in June of the previous year, Thoreau had observed, "There is no lightning-rod by which the sinner can finally avert the avenging Nemesis. Though I should put up a rod if its utility were satisfactorily demonstrated to me, yet, so mixed are we, I should feel myself safe or in danger quite independently of the senseless rod" (J, IV:157). Now, in January 1853, lightning *has*, in a sense, struck humankind, and Thoreau again invokes the image of an avenging nature. Looking at "the mangled and blackened bodies of men which had been blown up by powder," he feels "that the lives of men were not innocent, and that there [is] an avenging power in nature" (J, IV:459). In a way, a temporarily misanthropic Thoreau appears to welcome the catastrophe as a confirmation of his judgment that men are evil and rotten; they deserve to be punished for their transgressions.

That the explosion, and Thoreau's explosion of emotions, occurred around the eleventh anniversary of his brother's death suggests a suspicion of his own sinful complicity, however. Not surprisingly, he searches for signs of life in the John's-wort (and thus reassurance that John still lives and forgives him) and praises the "unambitiousness" of the patient crowfoot buds (J, IV:460–61). "May I lead my life the following year as innocently as they," he implores, obviously aware of his own impurities. It was important, in this context, to allay his own guilt by forswearing competitiveness and rivalry, especially as associated with his brother (and, perhaps, Emerson). Noting that Trench says the word "rivals" derives from "those who dwell on the banks of the same stream" but, "since the use of water rights is a fruitful source of contention," the word has taken on "this secondary sense," Thoreau finds it necessary to insist that his "friends" are his "rivals" only in the more "primitive sense of the word." "There is no strife," he adds, "between us respecting the use of the stream" (J, IV:467–68).

It is his relation to nature, he strongly and frequently implies, that enables him, unlike most men, to do penance and gain salvation. Woven into the passage on the "avenging power in nature" is the comment that the telegraph harp is his "redeemer" and "always brings a special and general message to me from the Highest." On this day he attends to "this immortal melody, while the west wind is blowing balmily on [his] cheek" and prepares for a "roseate sunset." "Are there not two powers?" he concludes (J, IV:459). It is not entirely clear what the "two powers" are; he may be perceiving nature as both avenging and uplifting, or he may be contrasting the sinfulness and evil of man with the virtuousness of nature. In any event, the presence of this homage to natural powers in the midst of an account of the powder-mill explosion points to one of the vexing dualities, contradictions, that Thoreau could not completely avoid being sensitive to during this period. Nature was at least a double-edged sword. In its circularity it promised or supplied intimations and images of immortality; in its separation from the human it offered purity and inspiration. But nature could also, as an indifferent or even avenging force, dash men against the rocks, strike them with lightning or fire, hurl them into trees, dismember them with impunity, as Thoreau was forcefully reminded by the human ruins of the powder-mill calamity:

> Some of the clothes of the men were in the tops of trees, where undoubtedly their bodies had been and left them. The bodies were naked and black, some limbs and bowels here and there, and a head at a distance from its trunk. The feet were bare; the hair singed to a crisp. I smelt the powder half a mile before I got there.

By way of recommendation he adds, "Put the different buildings thirty rods apart, and then but one will blow up at a time" (J, IV:454–55).

Whatever man's contribution to the holocaust, the laws of nature still determined and presided over the outcome. The powder-mill explosion could not have failed further to impress on Thoreau more divided, less benign versions of nature. Certainly the more naturalistic view contained facets that disturbed him: the dreaded prospects of life's finite linearity and uncontrollability and of personal annihilation. To be sure, even a naturalistic vision offered the circularity of returning to one's "home" in one's native soil, to be reincarnated in and with the elements. But this vision sometimes wavered, often not gaining the upper hand, and when Thoreau was prone to see what were for him the alarming facets of naturalism—or was under the sway of a view that ascribed or projected onto nature disapproving or avenging qualities—he was far from sanguine or enthusiastic about approaching middle age. On the same day as the "avenging power in nature" passage, he reflects on the possibility that middle age is part of an inevitable linear decline leading eventually to a dead end, a time when reaching back into the lost past is the only consolation: "How much—how, perhaps, all—that is best in our experience in middle life may be resolved into the memory of our youth" (J, IV:460). "Oppressed and saddened" on January 21 by "the sameness and apparent poverty of the heavens" (J, IV: 469), left with the sour residue of his dream on the "rottenness of human relations," and still haunted by the images of blunt mortality burnt into his retina and memory by the powder-mill explosion, he mournfully says, "Death is with me, and life far away. If the elements are not human, if the winds do not sing or sigh, as the stars twinkle, my life runs shallow" (J, IV: 472). Death was in him: nature was in some respects his redeemer, but it was also his jailer. Death was at least a part of nature, and as he aged it was ticking away in him like a time bomb, as volatile as the powder at the mill. Upon making a "roaring fire" in a meadow on January 26, he "burnt off [his] eyelashes when the fire suddenly blazed up with the wind" (J, IV:479). Clearly such incidents as the powder-mill blast and the eyelash singeing, especially in the context of this midlife transition, prodded him to brood about human vulnerability and mortality and in the process challenged him not simply to accept but also to devote all the more energy to ways in which human frailty and impermanence could be circumvented or overcome.

He was forced to concede, then, that death was in him, and so was nature; man was—however threatening the idea—part animal, still partaking of the carnal, the savage, and the limitations imposed by a finite, earthbound existence. The natural—the darker and limiting aspects of the animal—inside had always been an explosive issue for a man bent on purification and transcendence; it had frequently been safer to sit on that powder keg rather than expose it to the flammable light and air of consciousness. But, during this period when so many of his demons had been dredged near or to the surface, Thoreau showed a greater willingness to acknowledge the existential dilemma of the divided nature of man—the mind-body, animal-spirit duality—as well as the darker side of nature itself.[29] This willingness would lead to, among other things, the complexities and contradictions of *Walden*'s "Higher Laws" chapter. In August 1851 he had spoken disparagingly of having "swallowed a snake" and thus presumably partaken of the animal, and in September of that year he had observed, "Life is a warfare, a struggle, and the diseases of the body answer to the troubles and defeats of the spirit. Man begins by quarrelling with the animal in him, and the result is immediate disease" (J, II:393, 449–50). Aside from its important implications about the relation between health and the flesh-spirit struggle, this passage suggests the long psychic quarrel Thoreau had with the animal in him, his inclination even to deny whatever was threatening with regard to that animal. Now it was sinking in (more completely and decisively than, for instance, after the Katahdin experience) that there *was* a quarrel, that nature could be antagonistic to spirit, that the "wild" was not necessarily the "good."

Prompted by Blake's remarriage (one can almost imagine Blake seeking some kind of absolution from his father figure) but also by his need to bring to the fore and work through more thoroughly some unfinished emotional business, Thoreau in September 1852 wrote letters to Blake—

actually short essays drawing in part on earlier writings—that purported to address male-female intimacy and sexuality more frankly and forth-rightly than in the past.[30] To be sure, he remains reticent, inhibited, and preachy in his discussion, and his ambivalence concerning these matters is still very much in evidence. Earlier in the year he had been taken aback by the "coarseness and vulgarity" of Channing, who could only "jest" about sex and was "not capable of serious conversation" on the topic (J, III: 335, 406). He could only approach the "sexual relation" as one would approach an altar, with a mixture of utter gravity, reverence, diffidence, and awe. In the Blake letters, he still does not display deep insight into the underlying reasons, psychological and cultural, for his uneasiness about the body and sexuality. But he does seem more aware of his ambivalence and, as his introduction to the essays "Love" and "Chastity and Sensual-ity" suggest, he was somewhat more willing to own up to his hesitancies and limitations, his lack of credentials to speak on these, to him, delicate matters: "I send you the thoughts on chastity & sensuality with diffidence and shame, not knowing how far I speak to the condition of men generally, or how far I betray my peculiar defects. Pray enlighten me on this point if you can" (C, 288).

To his credit, Thoreau at least broaches the subject of his "peculiar defects," even if his understanding of the *sources* of the "defects" was very incomplete. It is virtually certain that one main "defect," or at least defi-ciency, was his lack of any firsthand heterosexual (or homosexual) experi-ence. Any direct experience he had had was apparently limited to dreams and autoerotic episodes (which probably left a residue of uneasiness and perhaps even the anxiety that the townspeople, knowing of his confirmed celibacy, might imagine him indulging in such activities).[31] What the sources, no doubt multiple, were of his "peculiar defects" is, of course, open to question. Apart from his repressive, moralistic, Calvinistic heri-tage and the family tradition of bachelorhood, it is likely that he was un-able to dissociate sex—and women in general—from mother and oedipal issues, and thus sex remained threatening, even forbidden, to him. In 1850 he had inadvertently revealed this association: "The tenderness & affec-tion of woman—her mild prophetic eye—her finer instincts exert an influ-ence on men from which he is never wearied— So that in this sense the um-bilical cord is never cut—though the apron string may be" (PJ, 3). In a similar vein, based on his perception of his parents (and on the fact that his sister Helen had been born only five months after his father and mother had been married), he may have come to see women and sexuality as en-trapping, potentially emasculating forces, to be avoided at almost any cost. More generally, he had a strong need for control, which may have led him to be apprehensive about the loss of control, or of vital energy, with which he connected sexuality. And, insofar as it stresses the bodily and animal nature of the self, sex may have been linked to fears of death. Though, to my mind, it is probably a less salient factor, there is also room to speculate that, stemming in part from inborn predisposition or oedipal anxieties, Thoreau had a stronger than "normal" "unconscious homoerotic orientation,"[32] never directly acted upon but coloring his relationships with, and attitudes toward, women, men, and heterosexuality. A much more remote possibility in my view is that there was some physical or psychosomatic difficulty in sexual function.[33] One certainly cannot discount the fact that, though largely due to his own self-limiting behavior, he had few opportunities for sexual expression in the restricted and provincial confines of the native town he could not leave. Even his courtship of Ellen Sewall, sincere as it was, was ambivalent.[34] Another plausible partial explanation is that Thoreau simply was blessed—or cursed—with an unusually low level of sexual desire, that he was relatively asexual. While he may well have experienced himself in this way, it is quite probable in my view, however, that his comparative lack of interest in sex was in part the result, not primarily of a deficit of libido (Thoreau was, after all, a very intense and passionate man), but of his ability and proclivity to displace and sublimate his libidinal energies onto and in nature and his art. Indeed, he was becoming more aware of how this process operated in himself.

Even though Thoreau had by and large accommodated himself to his "peculiar defects," Blake's remarriage may have pricked his sense of loss, underlining as it did a road not taken, a realm of experience and relatedness he would never personally enter. There is real poignancy in his comment in "Chastity and Sensuality" that "the intercourse of the sexes, I have dreamed, is incredibly beautiful, too fair to be remembered. I have had thoughts about it, but they are among the most fleeting and irrecoverable in my experience" (EEM, 277). The essays maintain a characteristically idealistic stance toward love and marriage, but they do recognize at least the existence of desire, even if Thoreau wishes to minimize or underestimate it. "Men commonly couple," he explains, "with their idea of marriage a slight degree at least of sensuality" (EEM, 274). It is, of course, revealing that in seeking to treat a subject that "sooner or later . . . occupies the thoughts of all," about which there is a sort of conspiracy of silence and avoidance, Thoreau is himself quickly tempted to move from discussing sex to considering how it ought to be transcended. Sexuality is soon equated with the "lusts or base pleasures" that "must give place to loftier delights" (EEM, 275). To be sure, there is a place in marriage for "copulation," but it must be engaged in with such a purity of spirit that it begins to bear little resemblance to the physical act at all. Indeed, if "it is the result of a pure love, there can be nothing sensual in marriage. Chastity is something positive, not negative" (EEM, 274). Like nature's flowers, which "are intended for a symbol of the open and unsuspected beauty of all true marriage," virginity also "is a budding flower, and by an impure marriage the virgin is deflowered. Whoever loves flowers, loves virgins and chastity. Love and lust are as far asunder as a flower garden is from a brothel" (EEM, 276). By splitting off lust from love, Thoreau hopes to turn sex into another form of chastity; in the process, it becomes almost indistinguishable from chastity, and his discussion devolves into a justification for celibacy. Only, in the end, by transforming sexuality into something spiritual does he seem able to handle it, and then only gingerly. The "intercourse" Thoreau dreams of, as he notes on September 26, 1852, is preeminently with with purity: "Dreamed of purity last night. The thoughts seemed not to originate with me, but I was invested, my thought was tinged, by another's thought. It was not I that originated, but I that *entertained* the thought" (J, IV:363). Thus does Thoreau betray, partly inadvertently, his own "peculiar defects," but as curious, idiosyncratic, and perfectionistic as his discussion becomes, it does show him conceding that there *is* such a thing as "lust" and that it must be faced before it can be overcome.

In the context of grappling with sexuality, Thoreau was again forced to reconsider his attitudes toward nature and wildness. To the extent that sexuality was a form of wildness—and in "Walking" he would write that "the wildness of the savage is but a faint symbol of the awful ferity with which good men and lovers meet" (E, 197)[35]—he was not comfortable with it and sought at almost every turn to purge himself of the lustful animal that still lurked within. It is little wonder that, in January 1853, he was drawn to a redefinition of wildness suggested by Trench, who "says a wild man is a *willed* man. . . . The perseverance of the saints is positive willedness" (J, IV:482). Around the time of, or not long after, sending off the "Chastity and Sensuality" essay, he apparently began working on the fifth draft of *Walden,* in which he added much on "Higher Laws."[36] His greater readiness to own up to his ambivalent feelings about nature and wildness, partly crystallized by his considerations of sexuality, led to a chapter with seemingly irreconcilable differences, beginning with an expression of an urge to "seize and devour" a woodchuck "raw" (W, 210) but ending with a prescription for purification from the animal that is nature in man:

We are conscious of an animal in us, which awakens in proportion as our higher nature slumbers. It is reptile and sensual, and perhaps cannot be wholly expelled; like the worms which, even in life and health, occupy our bodies. Possibly we may withdraw from it, but never change its nature. I fear that it may enjoy a certain health of its own; that we may be well, yet not pure. . . . Yet the spirit can for the time pervade and control every member and function of the body, and transmute what in form is the grossest sensuality into purity and devotion. The generative energy, which when we are loose, dissipates and makes us unclean, when we are continent invigorates and inspires us. Chastity is the flowering of man; and what are called Genius, Heroism, Holiness, and the like are but various fruits which succeed it. Man flows at once to God when the channel of purity is open. By turns our purity inspires and our impurity casts us down. He is blessed who is assured that the animal is dying out in him day by day, and the divine being established. (w, 219–20)

No longer was he so prone to delude himself into thinking that the wild and the good were simply and inextricably one. The man who, in *Walden*'s first draft, had said, "We can never have enough of nature" (207), by the fifth version was prompted to say, "Nature is hard to be overcome, but she must be overcome" (w, 221).

It is indicative that, around the same time he sent off his essays to Blake, he was writing of Walden "heaving its breast," of "touch-me-not seed vessels" that "go off like pistols, —shoot their seeds off like bullets," and "explode" in his hat (J, IV:358, 365). The previous spring he had taken more careful notice of frogs coupling and of male and female blossoms (J, III:486, 483). More and more, his own libidinal, "generative" energy was becoming submerged in, and expressed in his observations of, the sexuality in nature—and, as he was increasingly aware, in his writing. Surely the process he described—of transforming sex to chastity—was a crucial form of sublimation. He ends his "Chastity and Sensuality" essay with a distinction between reproduction for "improvement" and simply for "repetition": "Beasts merely propagate their kind, but the offspring of noble men & women will be superior to themselves, as their aspirations are. By their fruits ye shall know them" (EEM, 278). Back in February, he had argued that the most "superior" offspring was the "genius" who bore another—even more original and precious—kind of fruit, which did not depend upon ordinary sexual propagation. Speaking of budding and grafting practices, he says, "The genius is a seedling, often precocious or made to bear fruit early. . . . The common man is the Baldwin, propagated by mere offshoots or repetitions of the parent stock. At least, if all men are to be regarded as seedlings, the greater part are exceedingly like the parent stock" (J, III:316–17). While Thoreau, if pushed, might have conceded that comparing the reproductive achievements of common folk to the loftier generativity of the genius or artist would be akin to comparing apples and oranges (that is, both are invaluable), he was without question working through the issue of his own childlessness and eager to accept artistic sublimation as a worthy alternative. That he was, in 1852–54, in the midst of a particularly fecund creative period helped to bolster his confidence in and to gain perspective on sublimation as a healthy, constructive process, a transmutation of animal energy into pure art.[37] His "peculiar defects" could be converted into virtues and strengths. He may be referring unwittingly to the growth of *Walden* when he writes, at the end of his essay on love, "The object of love expands and grows before us to eternity, until it includes all that is lovely, and we become all that can love" (EEM, 273). In the summer of 1852, the "flower" to which he alluded may, above all, have been *Walden:* "Each human being has his flower, which expresses his character. In them nothing is concealed, but everything published" (J, IV: 150). In January 1852 he dealt even more forthrightly and consciously with the question of sublimation, indicating, "I do not know but the poet is he who generates poems. By continence he rises to creation on a higher level" (J, III:191). Later in the month he added, "There must be the copulating and generating force of love behind every effort destined to be successful. . . . The poet's relation to his theme is the relation of lovers" (J, III: 253). There was, as became increasingly clear to him, a limited amount of "generative energy," which had to be conserved and channeled into pure and creative endeavors. In October 1853 he would remark, "When, after feeling dissatisfied with my life, I aspire to something better, am more scrupulous, more reserved and continent . . . suddenly I find myself full of life. . . . So I dam up my stream, and my waters gather to a head" (J, V:456). This vision of continence leading to a more noble and vital form of creativity, a supranatural generativity, would be incorporated into "Higher Laws." Though he could not prove his potency and fertility, like most men, by pointing to actual children he had sired, he nonetheless could count himself as one who had the "seeds of life" in him (J, IV:478).

Also leaving its mark on "Higher Laws" was Thoreau's trip to the Maine woods beginning September 13, 1853, the anniversary of the day he had returned from the Concord-Merrimack excursion with John; this was a trip that further exposed him to, and reminded him of, the dark, savage side of human nature and the literal wilderness he had so often been predisposed to see as an alternative to humanity. On June 26 he had observed tolerantly (as he would in "Higher Laws") that all men pass through a hunter stage of development, "until at last the naturalist or poet distinguishes that which attracted him and leaves the gun and fishing-rod behind" (J, V:304). He was prepared to concede, it appears, that Indians, who hunted for survival, were justified in their killing of moose. But he was not entirely prepared for the gritty and grim reality of hunting, participated in by grown men, in the Maine woods.

As it turned out, it was his cousin George Thatcher, a rank amateur, who shot a cow-moose, which Thoreau and Joe Aitteon, his Indian guide, retrieved. His account of Aitteon's skinning of the moose is both sickening and sickened: "a tragical business it was; to see that still warm and palpitating body pierced with a knife, to see the warm milk stream from the rent udder, and the ghastly naked carcass appearing from within its seemly robe, which was made to *hide* it." He was truly jolted and chastened by the experience:

> on more accounts than one I had had enough of moose-hunting. I had not come to the woods for this purpose, nor had I foreseen it, though I had been willing to learn how the Indian manoeuvred; but one moose killed was as good, if not as bad, as a dozen. The afternoon's tragedy, and my share in it, as it affected the innocence, destroyed the pleasure of my adventure. (MW, 115–16, 118–19)

Although he admits that he might "spend a year in the woods fishing and hunting just enough to sustain myself, with satisfaction," he is revolted by the "hunting of the moose merely for the satisfaction of killing him." Given his reactions, however, we may suspect he would have been revulsed had he seen moose, "God's own horses," killed by Indians (MW, 119). And, in fact, when he later comes to an Indian encampment where many moosehides were "stretched and curing on poles like ours," he describes it as "about as savage a sight as was ever witnessed":

> There was the whole heart, black as a thirty-two pound ball, hanging at one corner. . . . Refuse pieces lay about on the ground in different stages of decay, and some pieces also in the fire, half-buried and sizzling in the ashes, as black and dirty as an old shoe. . . . Also a tremendous rib-piece was roasting before the fire, being impaled on an upright stake forced in and out between the ribs. (MW, 134–35)

The moose killing further raised Thoreau's consciousness regarding human savagery:

> This afternoon's experience suggested to me how base or coarse are the motives which commonly carry men into the wilderness. The explorers, and lumberers generally, are all hirelings, paid so much a day for their labor, and as such, they have no more love for wild nature, than wood-sawyers have for forests. Other white men and Indians who come here are for the most part

hunters, whose object is to slay as many moose and other wild animals as possible. But, pray, could not one spend some weeks or years in the solitude of this vast wilderness with other employments than these—employments perfectly sweet and innocent and ennobling? For one that comes here with a pencil to sketch or sing, a thousand come with an axe or rifle. What a coarse and imperfect use Indians and hunters make of nature! No wonder that their race is so soon exterminated. I already and for weeks afterward felt my nature the coarser for this part of my woodland experience, and was reminded that our own life should be lived as tenderly and daintily as one would pluck a flower. (MW, 119–20)

"Base" and "coarse": these words begin to suggest Thoreau's intense and horrified response to actual savagery and primitiveness. He may once have been able to convince himself that he wished to live like a healthy animal or "noble savage," but the moose-hunting sequence made it clear to him that he would not make a "good" savage or animal, or especially a good predator.

Man was, then, the guilty animal, and Thoreau felt he was implicated in the guilt by being party to the moose hunt. He recalls wondering, on that same night, "if any bear or moose was watching the light of my fire, for nature looked sternly upon me on account of the murder of the moose" (MW, 120–21). Of course, he overlooks here the fact that it was nature—the carnal and carnivorous inside the human being—that was asserting itself in the "tragedy" of the moose. Most important, though, is the observation that, however much he indicted others, he himself stood convicted of a crime and deserving even of some punishment from a "stern" entity. It was distasteful enough to realize how "coarse" and animalistic humankind could be, but it may be speculated that Thoreau's own sense of guilt was governed and compounded by more personal factors. In some respects, the "murder"—not simply "killing"—of the moose (coming at a time when he was beginning to envision the completion and possible success of *Walden*) may have unleashed, or threatened to unleash, the still deep-seated guilt related to his brother's death and the imagined wish to vanquish or do away with other significant figures. The wilderness remained populated with hard-to-appease spirits. At the Indian encampment, he is prompted to associate the smoking of moose meat on crates with a 1592 representation depicting the natives of Brazil smoking human flesh on similar crates (MW, 134). The moose, then, is linked to the human, and the hunters become in some sense connected to cannibals. It is also suggestive that Thoreau uses the masculine pronoun—"merely for the sake of killing him—not even for the sake of his hide"—though his own most immediate experience had

been with the skinning of a cow-moose. One reason why he continued
to be drawn to the Maine woods was his frustrated but still unquenched
thirst to come closer to the Indian, which in part represented on a deeper
level his insistent wish to reach some sort of definitive rapprochement with
his brother, to recapture the essence of fraternal camaraderie. In this regard, Joe Aitteon was somewhat less disappointing than those Indians he
had met on his 1846 expedition to Maine,[38] perhaps partly because his expectations had been moderated by that earlier trip. Certainly, he found
them "more in the open air" and "much more agreeable, and even refined
company, than the lumberers" (MW, 133). And Aitteon displayed many
Indian skills, even though he was far from the quintessentially "wild" Indian about whom Thoreau continued to fantasize. With respect to their
moose hunting, however, Aitteon and the others were *too* "wild"—too
coarse and savage—for Thoreau. It is clear that, though he was repulsed
by Thatcher's sportive hunting, he also felt some unease and hostility
toward Aitteon, "to whom the shooting is a common and necessary human practice."[39] His hostility is evinced in his agitated comment about the
"coarse and imperfect use Indians and hunters make of nature" and in his
startling exclamation, "No wonder that their race is so soon exterminated" (MW, 120). Thus the "murder" of the moose (as well as such "savage sights" as the moosehides "stretched and curing on poles") aroused an
anger in Thoreau toward the Indians leading to an expression that almost
seems to wish destruction on them. In turn, such hostile, even murderous,
feelings may well have stirred up the festering guilt he harbored concerning
the brother-Indian comrade whose death on some level he suspected he
had wished and been responsible for. His conscience continued to look
"sternly" on him for that imagined transgression; now it reasserted itself
with respect to the murder of the moose and his response to the Indians.

The moose-hunting episode had, to a considerable degree, "destroyed
the pleasure" of his "adventure." What had begun with a longing for
"wildness" and a desire to learn more about the woods and Indians had
become another descent into the heart of darkness; though still not willing
to give up entirely on either the wilderness or the Indians, he was nonetheless repelled and taken aback by what was "coarse" and "savage" about
them—and about himself. What immediately follows the account of the
moose murder is an attempt to transcend it through the invocation of
"higher laws"—another prelude to *Walden*'s "Higher Laws" chapter,
which must have been both an influence on and further influenced by the
1853 trip. He would work on the "Chesuncook" essay at the same time
he was working on *Walden*. If the pine had been a symbol in "Katahdin,"

it became here a more critical one. In a way, Thoreau wishes in "Chesun-cook" to see himself as the protector and defender of pines—forswearing any design to cut them down and, it is likely, seeking to deny that he has ever wished to "cut down" significant male figures such as his brother. In another way, he identifies with the tree, links his fate to its, thereby evading guilt and allying himself to a spirituality that overcomes coarseness and death. Pine-moose-man: they are all connected in Thoreau's mind. "The pine," he explains

> is no more lumber than man is, and to be made into boards and houses is no more its true and highest use than the truest use of a man is to be cut down and made into manure. There is a higher law affecting our relation to pines as well as to men. A pine cut down, a dead pine, is no more a pine than a dead human carcass is a man. . . . Every creature is better alive than dead, men and moose and pine-trees. (MW, 121)

It is neither the lumberman nor the tanner who is the "friend and lover" of the pine, whom "posterity will fable was changed into a pine at last," but rather the poet—Thoreau himself—who makes the "truest use" of the pine. He does not come brandishing a starkly phallic axe or rifle; he brings instead the less imposing—yet creatively potent—"pencil to sketch or sing." It is the poet "who loves them"—the moose and such men as his brother as well as pines—"as his own shadow in the air, and lets them stand." The lumberyard, the carpenter's shop, the tannery, the lampblack factory, the turpentine clearing: these do not put the pine to its highest use. "It is not their bones or hide or tallow that I love most," he says. "It is the living spirit of the tree, not its spirit of turpentine, with which I sympathize, and which heals my cuts. It is as immortal as I am, and perchance will go to as high a heaven, there to tower above me still" (MW, 120–22). By tenderly respecting and keeping alive the tree's spirit, Thoreau gains a triumph over the corporeal and mortal; by extension, not just the tree but the moose, his brother, and he himself are assured a place together in "heaven," a disembodied immortality. Only such assurance can salve the guilt and anxiety and thereby "heal" the deep psychic "cuts." As if further to fend off any anxieties, he readily grants his elder brother–tree a more lofty position in heaven, where he-it "will tower above me still."

The 1853 Maine woods journey, even as it stirred up some demons, seems to have represented yet another turn of the screw, making it more difficult for Thoreau to romanticize literal wilderness. It was even more problematic to maintain the illusion that he was entirely at home in the forest primeval. Nor was he as likely to idealize simplistically either nature or human nature. The conclusion of "Chesuncook" is instructive in this regard. While lamenting the cutting down of trees and expressing the concern that "Maine, perhaps, will soon be where Massachusetts is," he is able to admit that "it was a relief to get back to our smooth, but still varied landscape." "For a permanent residence"—and here he seeks to define where he is most at home—"it seemed to me that there could be no comparison between this and the wilderness, necessary as the latter is for a resource and a background, the raw material of all our civilization." He continues,

> The wilderness is simple, almost to barrenness. The partially cultivated country it is which chiefly has inspired, and will continue to inspire, the strains of poets. . . . Our woods are sylvan, and their inhabitants woodmen and rustics. . . . A civilized man, using the word in the ordinary sense, with his ideas and associations, must at length pine there, like a cultivated plant, which clasps its fibres about a crude and undissolved mass of peat.

Although "the poet must, from time to time, travel the logger's path and the Indian's trail, to drink at some new and more bracing fountain of the Muses, far in the recesses of the wilderness," Thoreau now perceived himself more clearly as a "cultivated plant" who "pined" in the wilderness (MW, 153, 155, 156). There yet remained the frequent temptation to ignore, or lay aside, the lessons he learned in Maine, but the insights gained in 1853 sunk in relatively deeply. It is possible that this trip helped swing his pendulum back a bit toward greater involvement with civilized life, as the 1846 trip had done.

At the same time that Thoreau was more open to de-illusionment and darkness,[40] which helped make *Walden* a more richly textured and tough-minded work, he was protected, it must be stressed, from being overwhelmed by his very work on the book. The fact that he was in a period of midlife transition and crisis made the focus on building and inhabiting the imaginative world and self of *Walden* all the more imperative. Thus it is not difficult to understand how a Thoreau safely immersed in the book could afford sometimes to lift the veil and peek over the abyss; and, in turn, we can more easily comprehend why, even in the midst of hesitant descents into the maelstrom, he was by and large able to persevere. Darkness and dawn could, at this time when he was going so often to Walden and *Walden,* relatively safely coexist. As an artist, he could yet aspire to immortality, perfection, purity; if the world did not live up to his ideals or conform to his illusions, if *he* could not live up to his ego ideal, he was nevertheless provided with opportunities to transform, transcend, and triumph over these realities.[41]

Perhaps, in the early months of 1853, his progress on *Walden* had been slowed, and that was one reason why this winter had been an unusually trying time for him. Certainly there were many specific factors, other than those already alluded to, that contributed to his often glum mood: financial concerns (he paid back much of his loan to Greeley in February [C, 294]); surveying, which distracted him and made his February journalizing comparatively sparse; the request by *A Week*'s publisher that he unburden them of their numerous unsold copies; anxieties about the criticisms and quality of the "Canada" manuscript and about the possible loss of some of that manuscript by the printers (C, 293, 299, 301). It may have been an honor to be nominated in March for membership in the Association for the Advancement of Science, but Thoreau was quick to eschew any suggestion that he was a scientist, particularly at a time when he feared he was being too scientific. On March 23 he writes, "I feel that I am dissipated by so many observations. . . . I have almost a slight, dry headache as the result of all this observing" (J, V:45). The branch of science that merited his attention, he claims in response to the association, "deals with the higher law." He is "essentially a mystic, a transcendentalist, and a natural philosopher to boot." Confronted by the many challenges to his transcendentalism in recent months, he found it even more a question of self-preservation to affirm his devotion to these "higher laws" and absorb himself in the world and work of *Walden*. On February 27 he reminds Blake and himself, "you have to put on the pack of the Upland Farmer in good earnest the coming spring" (C, 298).

With the first signs of spring in early March, the "very beautiful and exhilarating sights, a sort of diet drink to heal our winter discontent" (J, V: 13–14), he was on the alert for signs of the imminent arrival in full bloom of his second spring. Presumably still seeking to break the spell of winter discontent, he begins his March 13 journal entry with the observation that the sap is not yet flowing from a hole he made in a maple tree and then comments, "All enterprises must be self-supporting, must pay for themselves. . . . a poet must sustain his body with his poetry. . . . You must get your living by loving" (J, V:19). He had noted the previous March that the spring advances by "fits and starts" and had in the process characterized his own sense of progress. He supplemented this observation in March 1853 with the image and concept of "false spring" or "Indian spring":

Now, then, spring is beginning again in earnest after this short check. Is it not always thus? Is there not always an early promise of spring, sometimes answering to the Indian summer, which succeeds the summer, so an Indian or false spring preceding the true spring, —first false promise which merely excites our expectations to disappoint them, followed by a short return of winter? Yet all things appear to have made progress, even during these wintry days, for I cannot believe that they have thus instantaneously taken a start. (J, V:22–23)

Just as there had been authentic springs in his life—most notably the Walden experience—there had also been many false springs. And, it can be surmised, he may in retrospect even have regarded late 1852, when he had apparently begun to take up the fifth draft of *Walden,* as something of a false spring in that the period of expansion had to some degree been "checked" by his unanticipated "winter discontent." But now he was at least not starting from scratch, and, whether or not it had yet been translated into his art, some growth had occurred "even during these wintry days"; those wintry days would lend added depth, conviction, and authenticity to the *Walden* that was beginning to take shape. Having suffered and survived the recent "short return of winter," he is even more grateful for the sun "promising to shine out" through the rain, "lighting up transiently with a whiter light the dark day and my dark chamber," which "affects" him as he has "not been affected for a long time." The concluding "I must go forth" (J, V:22) may be taken partly as a resolution to go forward full-steam-ahead with *Walden.* That he had probably received Greeley's March 16 letter, which indicated that he considered himself "paid in full" and which expressed his friendly "desire to serve you, however unsuccessfully," may have been a sign to Thoreau that the slate was now clear, the debts paid, and that he was ready for a fresh start. On March 23 he proclaims that "all nature"—and, we must believe, he too—was "thus forward to move with the revolution of the seasons" (J, V:23).

The steady melting of Walden (J, V:28) was a particularly moving event and symbol for Thoreau at this juncture. Like the pond, he has passed through the region of ice and is now in the process of coming alive again. He revels in the "resurrection of the year," intuiting that he too is being resurrected, has undergone a metamorphosis like the large butterfly he sees which has burst from its chrysalis. Cutting a maple for a bridge, he "rejoices" while observing "the sap falling in large, clear drops from the wound"; wounded though he may be, he is now feeling his own creative juices beginning to flow. On the first day of spring, as he continues to monitor the "breaking up" of Walden, he characterizes his own corresponding breaking up:

> We become, as it were, pliant and ductile again to strange but memorable influences; we are led a little way by our genius. We are affected like the earth, and yield to the elemental tenderness; winter breaks up within us; the frost is

coming out of me, and I am heaved like the road; accumulated masses of ice
and snow dissolve, and thoughts like a freshet pour down unwonted channels.
(J, v:29, 31, 32, 34)

It is altogether likely that (in spite of his complaints on March 23 about
being "dissipated by so many observations") this "thaw" was a decisive
one so far as his new spring, and *Walden*'s, was concerned. He seems, on
March 22, to be reasonably confident that he has put his "false springs"
behind him: "I am sure to be an early riser. I am waked by my genius. I
wake to inaudible melodies and am surprised to find myself expecting the
dawn in so serene and joyful and expectant a mood. I have an appointment
with spring" (J, v:36).

He kept the appointment. The subsequent months of 1853 and early
1854 represented an epoch of virtually unchecked creative expansion and
ripening unlike anything he had experienced since the Walden period. The
fragments of the *Journal,* often inspired in themselves, came together and
coalesced in a miraculous artistic chemistry; he also added much material
not in his journal, which suggests how creatively fluent and prolific he was
at this point. He was now genuinely re-visioning *Walden,* coming to see it
as a transformed whole. During this second spring he would devote little
time to letter writing; it is safe to say that his life and inner life were largely
consumed with, and defined by, his art. The fifth, sixth, and seventh drafts
of *Walden* would be completed within a year.[42] In the fifth version, he
apparently marked off chapters and definitely adopted chapter titles;[43] the
cycle of the seasons became the dominant structural principle.[44] He also
added to his earlier descriptions of Walden Pond and discussions of "higher laws." And it was particularly in the sixth and seventh drafts that such
chapters as the autumnal "House-Warming," "The Pond in Winter,"
"Spring," and "Conclusion" were developed.[45]

On March 21 Thoreau broaches again a theme that appears to have
been a catalyst to *Walden*'s wondrous growth and one key to what he perceived as the book's new depths and dimensions. Having experienced,
since leaving Walden, a series of crises endemic to both later young adulthood and the transition to middle age, he could speak with considerably
more authority, maturity, and intensity about just what it took and meant
to make it to a second, even more authentic and appreciated, spring. In
A Week he had, both wittingly and unwittingly, displayed some prescience
about such crises and opportunities, but it was one thing to contemplate or
hint at them and another actually to live them. Only by passing through
prolonged winters of discontent, through darkness and dark thoughts,
through fallow and false springs, through stagnant summers, through

suffering and even despair—through a multitude of trials to tax faith and spirit—could one reach the promised land: "Is then the road so rough that it should be neglected? Not only narrow but rough is the way that leadeth to life everlasting. Our experience does not wear upon us" (J, V:35). He was now (though not without lingering guilt) willing to wear the mantle of a survivor who has truly *suffered* a sea change and is therefore stronger, more courageous, and more sensitive. Approaching middle age, he has genuinely become a seasoned veteran who has shown his mettle. "Whatever your sex or position," he proclaims, "life is a battle in which you are to show your pluck, and woe be to the coward. Whether passed on a bed of sickness or a tented field, it is ever the same fair play and admits no foolish distinction" (J, V:36). The "tenacity of life" of the leek buds was one of many convenient symbols (J, V:127). Another was the night hawk, which "sits motionless on its eggs," enduring tempests, "with its eyes shut and its wings unfolded, and after the two days' storm, when you think it has become a fit symbol of the rheumatism, it suddenly rises into the air a bird, one of the most aerial, supple, and graceful of creatures, without stiffness in its wings or joints!" (J, V:230–31).

Another revealing and related analogy was provided by the galls he observed June 1 on young white oaks. He is struck by the notion that "a disease, an excrescence, should prove perchance, the greatest beauty, —as the tear of the pearl. Beautiful scarlet sins they may be. Through our temptations, —aye, and our falls, —our virtues appear" (J, V:210). One clear implication is that genuine beauty and virtue do not emerge from untested innocence. But the metaphor is carried further:

> As in many a character, —many a poet, —we see that beauty exhibited in a gall, which was meant to have bloomed in a flower, unchecked. Such, however, is the accomplishment of the world. The poet cherishes his chagrins and sets his sighs to music. This gall is the tree's "Ode to Dejection." (J, V:210)

If Thoreau appears to be identifying himself as that "poet" who "cherishes his chagrins" and writes an "Ode to Dejection," however, the continuation of the passage suggests that he perceives himself as having gone a significant step beyond this poet or the common man:

> How oft it chances that the apparent fruit of a shrub, its apple, is merely a gall or blight! How many men meet with some blast in the moist growing days of their youth, and what should have been a sweet and palatable fruit in them becomes a mere puff and excrescence, ripening no kernel, and they say that they have experienced religion! For the hardening of the seed is the crisis. Their fruit is a gall, a puff, an excrescence, for want of moderation and continence. So many plants never ripen their fruit. (J, V:210)

Thoreau saw himself as having endured many "blasts." Indeed, also on June 1, he contemplates again the January blast at the powder mill and compares the human debris to that scattered by a sea wreck, going eventually "to swell the pile of driftwood collected by some native" (J, V:212). There were many occasions, he no doubt pondered, when he could have been permanently "blasted" or become "galled": his brother's death, *A Week*'s bombing and all the crippling regrets and "might-have-beens" to which it could have given rise; the difficult period of readjustment following it; the bitter deterioration of the relationship with Emerson, about which he had written only a week earlier ("Talked, or tried to talk, with R. W. E. Lost my time—nay, almost my identity. He, assuming a false opposition where there was no difference of opinion, talked to the wind— told me what I knew—and I lost my time trying to imagine myself somebody else to oppose him" [J, V:188]). He still had his moments of doubt, and there was still an occasional sense of identity confusion, of drifting, that he would have found more ominous had he not been so attached to the world and persona of *Walden;* in an April letter to Blake, he compares himself to "dandelion down that never alights" (C, 303). There remained, too, family strains, as is suggested in his March 28 journal entry: "My Aunt Maria asked me to read the life of Dr. Chalmers, which however I did not promise to do. Yesterday, Sunday, she was heard through the partition shouting to my Aunt Jane, who is deaf, 'Think of it! He stood half an hour to-day to hear the frogs croak, and he would n't read the life of Chalmers'" (J, V:58).

All these blasts, checks, and potential blights notwithstanding, his capacity to produce a "sweet and palatable fruit" had survived and was now asserting itself. Although he can now appreciate the beauty exhibited in the gall, the poet's "Ode to Dejection"—could even have written such an ode himself—he is determined not to give in to dejection. To be sure, even in early drafts of *Walden*,[46] he had touched on this issue, stating that "We should impart our courage, and not our despair, our health and ease, and not our disease" (W, 77). But now, so strongly reinforced and deepened by the often harrowing crises he had experienced since leaving the pond, this perspective was given added weight, authority, and dimension. On June 2, 1853, he testifies to his resolve "to crow like chanticleer in the morning, with all the lustiness that the new day imparts, without thinking of the evening, when I and all of us shall go to roost, —with all the humility of the cock, that takes his perch upon the highest rail and wakes the country with his clarion" (J, V:215–16). This statement of intention mirrors the epigraph to *Walden*, repeated also in the text,[47] "I do not propose to write an ode to dejection, but to brag as lustily as chanticleer in the morning, stand-

ing on his roost, if only to wake my neighbors up" (w, 84). If Thoreau had
a deeply rooted penchant for denying underlying despair and dejection,
this passage, particularly taken in the context of this period's themes and
concerns, reveals some consciousness of his potential for writing an ode to
dejection. Certainly loss, sorrow, tragedy could not be glossed over entirely; he had experienced his share, and much since he had left Walden. But he
was resolved, through choice as well as by dint of personality and unconscious need, to accentuate the positive. Such affirmation in the face of dejection and despair represented to him an uncommon courage and self-
discipline. Unlike those "plants" that "never ripen their fruit," his fruits,
as palpably embodied in *Walden, were* ripening rapidly in 1853. That he
could write, in fact, was primarily what prevented him from falling prey to
"gall," "disease," dejection; his art helped keep doubt, confusion, and distress at bay.

   In the critical entry of March 21, Thoreau had characterized the road
that "leadeth to life everlasting" as "rough" and "narrow"; but "our experience does not wear upon us" because it "is seen to be fabulous or symbolical, and the future is worth expecting. Encouraged, I set out once more
to climb the mountain of the earth, for my steps are symbolical steps, and
in all my walking I have not reached the top of the earth yet" (J, v:34).
"Fabulous" and "symbolical": these words indicate the direction in which
he realized *Walden* was now more decisively and surefootedly going.[48]
The nature that had so absorbed his attention provided him with the "raw
material of tropes and symbols" with which to describe his life:

> If these gates of golden willows affect me, they correspond to the beauty and
> promise of some experience on which I am entering. If I am overflowing with
> life, am rich in experience for which I lack expression, then nature will be my
> language full of poetry, —all nature will *fable* and every natural phenomenon
> be a myth. (J, v:135)

Of course, he had been using nature for "tropes and symbols," a private
language, for some time, but now he was more prepared to see *Walden* as
the place where this language would find its archetypal, definitive expression. As an artist, he could portray his life in nature's "tropes and symbols"; in this respect, personal reference was often gratuitous.[49] Although
his faith in the *complete* correspondence of himself with nature had been
shaken in recent years, he nevertheless continued to find it a rich fount of
analogy, symbol, and myth that could communicate his own unfolding life
myth, one that had kept evolving in the years after Walden. "Some incidents in my life," he writes on May 31, "have seemed far more allegorical
than actual; they were so significant that they plainly served no other use.

That is, I have been more impressed by their allegorical significance and fitness; they have been like myths or passages in a myth, rather than mere incidents or history which have to wait to become significant" (J, v:203). In the following months there would be a veritable explosion of natural imagery of death and resurrection; of autumn, winter, and the coming of spring; of the thawing clay of the Deep Cut and the rebirth of the pond; of the "lumpish grub in the earth" metamorphosed into the "airy and fluttering butterfly" (w, 306); of the "strong and beautiful bug" emerging at last from the apple-tree table (w, 333). Such natural imagery would be tropes, symbols, and parables of his life and self as he wanted and needed to see them.

In *A Week* he had associated the climbing of mountains with those challenging passages by which more authentic identity, autonomy, and individuation is attained. Understandably, then, his March 31, 1853, entry finds him contemplating the New Hampshire mountain range. "It is affecting," he says,

> to see a distant mountain-top, like the summits of Uncannunuc . . . whereon you camped for a night in your youth, which you have never revisited, still as blue and ethereal to your eyes as is your memory of it. It lies like an isle in the far heavens, a part of earth unprofaned, which does not bear a price in the market, is not advertised by the real estate broker. (J, v:77)

In this period of rejuvenation he has set out once again to "climb the mountain of the earth"; he feels himself journeying again to "Unappropriated Land." It is a land that not only revives youthful dreams but also prompts him to look forward with serenity. Gazing at the mountains from the cliffs on May 10, he reflects that "they are stepping-stones to heaven . . . by which to mount when we would commence our pilgrimage to heaven; by which we gradually take our departure from earth, from the time when our youthful eyes first rested on them —from this actual bare earth, which has so little hue of heaven. They make it easier to die and easier to live" (J, v:141). In *Walden,* the pond itself would be a sort of inverted mountain or well, the "summit" of which was its bottom. Sounding its depths was another form, perhaps a more profound form, of scaling the mountain. Getting to the bottom of things was also a way of getting on top of them. It was not by accident that the pond reminded him of "a tarn high up on the side of a mountain" (w, 86) or that, in general, there is so much mountain imagery associated with the Walden experience. And while one aspect of *Walden*'s structure, with "The Ponds" and Walden at its center, was in some sense concave, it also constituted a mirror image of upward ascent. Thus, as he immersed himself imaginatively in Walden and *Walden* in

1853–54, he also found himself mounting closer to a "heaven" in which the best of youth and early maturity were mingled. The spring aromas he detected with his keen sense of smell were, in 1853, reminiscent of the ineffably sweet "air of Elysium," a region Thoreau had earlier equated with living at the pond; now, living in and through *Walden,* the Elysian fields were again accessible to him. Ripe berries evoked an image of Mount Olympus, the mountain most intimately linked with the Walden experience: these fruits are "fit to grow on Olympus, the ambrosia of the gods. . . . It does not occur to me at first that where such a thought is suggested is Mt. Olympus and that I who taste these berries am a god" (J, V:360–61). While working on *Walden,* Thoreau was undergoing another peak experience.

On May 12 he portrays himself as an intrepid explorer who has "passed the Rubicon"; it was "too late to retreat from the summer adventure" (J, V:146–47), at least part of which involved the creation of a "perfect summer life" (W, 333) of *Walden.* He had, he believed, crossed the Rubicon in his own life now; as his thirty-sixth birthday loomed, he was embarking on the second half of life. The adventure he had begun involved, as it had in *A Week,* a venturing forth that would lead eventually to a more profound version of homecoming. Later in May he writes,

> I have passed the Rubicon of staying out. I have said to myself, that way is not homeward; I will wander further from what I called my home—to the home which is forever inviting me. In such an hour the freedom of the woods is offered me, and the birds sing my dispensation. In dreams the links of life are united: we forget that our friends are dead; we know them as of old. (J, V:187)

At the same time that he was crossing the Rubicon, it was important not to burn his most valued bridges behind him. Apparently with the birds'—and his ornithologist brother's—blessing, he was lighting out for new territory, yet bent on maintaining or reestablishing continuity with the past. And *Walden* in particular afforded him at this time a "home" where the "links of life" could be "united."

It was not simply because the year was turning toward summer and fall that Thoreau turned to images and issues of ripeness. Nature was providing him with a language to ponder and express his own sense of, and concerns about, ripening. Even in May it was not too early to hear the cricket's chirp, which "foretells autumn" and which sets him "thinking, philosophizing, moralizing at once. It is not so wildly melodious, but it is wiser and more mature than that of the wood thrush" (J, V:158). The modulated voice of the cricket was also a voice to which Thoreau was beginning to aspire in his life and *Walden.* Perhaps he conceived of his maturity and the book's as similar to that of young twigs that "do most of their growing for a year in a week or two" in spring (as he had to some extent done at Walden), and then, "the rest of the year they harden and mature, and perhaps have a second spring in the latter part of summer or in the fall" (J, v:189), as seemed to be happening to him in this late summer or still-early autumn of his life. Even if in some ways anxious for ripeness, he still was concerned about claiming any final ripeness for himself. It was, after all, felicitous that he had not begun ripening too early or hastily, as the "monstrous precocity" of the huckleberry-apple in June suggested: "What should have waited to become fruit is a merely bloated or puffed-up flower." Conversely, however, he was reminded by the parched ground of early summer that such "sweet" and "palatable" fruits as the huckleberry, which is "not matured before July," incur "the risk of drying up . . . in droughts and never attaining [their] proper size" (J, v:269). Thus, there were dangers not only in premature ripening but also in postponing it for too long. By August 9, exactly one year before *Walden*'s publication, Thoreau remarked on how "fatally the season is advanced toward the fall"; in this "season of small fruits," it was important to believe that he was also "maturing some small fruit as palatable in these months" (J, v:364). The imagery of "small fruits" suggests that *Walden* had still not matured to his complete satisfaction or that, on the brink of completing it, he was inclined in some respects to shrink from considering it the ripest work of which he was capable—or from considering *himself* fully ripe. The closer he sensed himself coming to his own autumn, the more ambivalent he would become.[50]

One strategy for holding on to hope and inspiration even in an arid season—one that would be evident in *Walden*—was to view each day as having its "seasons," as the "epitome" of the year. On August 24, Thoreau reflects, "I am again struck by the perfect correspondence of a day,—say an August day,—and the year. I think that a perfect parallel may be drawn between the seasons of the day and of the year. Perhaps after middle age man ceases to be interested in the morning and in the spring" (J, v:393). But if morning and spring begin to lose their fascination for the middle-aged man, late afternoon and evening provided their own unique opportunities. "What shall we name this season?" he asks,

> this very late afternoon or very early evening, this severe and placid season of the day, most favorable for reflection, after the insufferable heats and the bustle of the day are over and before the dampness and twilight of evening. . . . The pensive season. It is earlier than the "chaste eve" of the poet. . . . It is the turning-point between afternoon and evening. . . . It is a season somewhat earlier

than is celebrated by the poets. There is not such a sense of lateness and approaching night as they describe. . . . The poet arouses himself and collects his thoughts. He postpones tea indefinitely. (J, V:370–71)

Thoreau appears to see himself as nearing, or as having reached, this "turning-point between afternoon and evening," between late summer and fall. It was a time when he had to collect his thoughts and get on with his work, before evening shadows and winter drifts closed in.[51] But a man such as he at this "turning-point" was not immune to intimations of wasted time, irretrievable loss, steadily diminishing powers, and mortality, as is evident on August 16:

> What means this sense of lateness that so comes over one now, —as if the rest of the year were down-hill? . . . The season of flowers or of promise may be said to be over, and now is the season of fruits; but where is our fruit? The night of the year is approaching. What have we done with our talent? All nature prompts and reproves us. How early in the year it begins to be late! The sound of the crickets, even in the spring, makes our hearts beat with its awful reproof, while it encourages with its seasonable warning. It matters not by how little we have fallen behind; it seems irretrievably late. The year is full of warnings of its shortness, as is life. (J, V:378–79)

The significance of the cricket's chirp was in the ear of the hearer: sometimes it suggested ripeness, sometimes uneasy lateness and urgency. Although, in the main, Thoreau was wont to stress the positive and productive during this period, it is clear from this passage that there were some faint rumblings of anxiety about the implications of autumn and ripening.

Leaving aside for further scrutiny these still rather vague anxieties, one cannot fail to notice the signs of Thoreau's burgeoning excitement in the months when *Walden* was itself maturing and relatively near to completion. On September 1 he observes that, just as July "has its spring side," so does August have "its autumnal side" (J, V:407). And, indeed, there is evidence of an exhilarated autumnal mellowness in his late August journal and thereafter. Pondering the ripe poke stems on August 23, he exclaims,

> What a success is its! What maturity it arrives [at], ripening from leaf to root! May I mature as perfectly, root and branch, as the poke! Its stems are more beautiful than most flowers. It is the emblem of a successful life, a not premature death, —whose death is an ornament to nature.

On the same day he says, "Live in each season as it passes; breathe the air, drink the drink, taste the fruit, and resign yourself to the influences of each.

... Some men think that they are not well in spring, or summer, or autumn, or winter; it is only because they are not *well in* them" (J, V:393, 394–95). To a man who can accept all the seasons and let them wash over him (and Thoreau was further than he thought from such acceptance), even death may be contemplated with relative equanimity. The cycles of nature and the seasons suggested a generativity and immortality to which such art as *Walden* could also aspire. The fallen October leaves would ultimately "afford nourishment to new generations of their kind," would provide "myriad wrappers for germinating seeds," and by a "subtle chemistry" would "mount up again, climbing by the sap in the trees" (J, V:441–43). The leaves of *Walden* were ripening on his desk and would soon fall into other hands; they too might "afford nourishment" to "new generations."

In such a comparatively equable state of mind, even the return by Munroe of 706 unsold copies of *A Week* could not upset him unduly; on October 28 he finds himself "sitting beside the inert mass of my works," and yet he celebrates his ability to "take up my pen to-night to record what thought or experience I may have had, with as much satisfaction as ever" (J, V:460). After all, as the "gossamer webs" of spiders—which can be seen only in a certain slant of light—prove, "No industry is vain" (J, V:469). In fact, this final disposition of his first book helped clear the decks for the second. His debts were paid off (he settled with Munroe on November 28); the whole sorry affair was now behind him. As he notes with some wit in contemplating these new additions to his library:

> They are something more substantial than fame, as my back knows, which has borne them up two flights of stairs to a place similar to that to which they trace their origin. . . . I have now a library of nearly nine hundred volumes, over seven hundred of which I wrote myself. Is it not well that the author should behold the fruits of his labor? (J, V:459)

With the perspective of time and greater maturity, and most especially because he was wrapped up in a current project of inestimable significance, he was not at this point inclined to brood about, or rage over, the past. *A Week* was a worthwhile fruit, even if, in comparison to *Walden,* it had fallen earlier from the tree. Imbued with the sense that he is destined for a more mature harvest, he observes, "October answers to that period in the life of man when he is no longer dependent on his transient moods, when all his experience ripens into wisdom, but every root, branch, leaf of him glows with maturity. What he has been and done in his spring and summer appears. He bears his fruit" (J, V: 502). *Walden* was the culminating event of his spring and summer being and doing; it was also at least the vanguard of autumnal wisdom. As if anxious, as *Walden* came closer to completion, to see it as a "second spring" of the "latter part of the summer" or of earliest fall rather than of October or later, in November he was already playing with the idea for another book, to "be entitled October Hues or Autumnal Tints" (J, V:516), which presumably would embody an even riper, more fully autumnal, vision. But that project would have to be deferred at least until *Walden* was done, and he would have to feel that he was truly in correspondence with October before he could write it. Amidst observations of the "third frost flowering" of the cistus plant, the "springlike vigor of many plants," and the second-growth white pines (J, V:476, 530), Thoreau worked diligently at putting the finishing touches on his finely sculpted masterwork, not unlike the Assyrian king who made a record of his deeds in stone at Nineveh and therefore insured his immortality (J, VI:11).

Thoreau completed the sixth version of *Walden* by early 1854. Late in the winter of 1854 he added a seventh set of revisions to the manuscript, and it was this draft that he submitted to Ticknor and Fields in late February or early March.[52] A letter from Greeley indicates that the book was accepted by the publisher sometime in March (C, 324). Yet another set of revisions appeared in the copy to the printer; there are passages in *Walden* drawing from journal entries as late as April 27, 1854.[53] In that entry, Thoreau implicitly identifies the pond with the book and with himself, noting that it "attains its maximum [water level] slowly and surely, though unsteadily" (J, VI:227).

Certainly, this was a period of much anticipation, although, as will soon be argued, it was not without signs of a gathering storm. As a thirty-six-year-old man, Thoreau saw himself as in some sense having followed Cato's advice: "In earliest manhood the master of a family must study to plant his ground; as for building he must think a long time about it. . . . he must not think about planting, but do it. When he gets to be thirty-six years old, then let him build, if he has his ground planted" (J, VI:69). Thoreau had, after "planting his ground" during his "seedtimes," constructed a magnificent edifice—*Walden*—and much of that building had taken place in his thirty-sixth year. He had made it from his period of "spring growth" at Walden to the second spring of *Walden*. His reflections on April 8, 1854, surely refer at least in part to himself and his book:

Some poets mature early and die young. Their fruits have a delicious flavor like strawberries, but do not keep till fall or winter. Others are slower in coming to their growth. Their fruits may be less delicious, but are a more lasting food and are so hardened by the sun of summer and the coolness of autumn that they keep sound over winter. (J, VI: 190)

On August 9, 1854, with the elderberries ripe and "waxwork yellow-ing" (J, VI:429), *Walden* was published.

6 But a Morning Star

*E*VEN before *Walden*'s publication, there were warning signs of an impending crisis. In the years following *A Week*'s flop, Thoreau had exerted enormous energy to reorient his life away from literary ambition and civil society. To a great extent, he had accomplished this task, and, relatively unimpeded by the guilt and vexation accompanying conventional ambition and his dependence on social recognition, he had rebuilt his life and liberated himself in such a way that he was able to flourish creatively, as was testified to by the *Journal* and the miraculous expansion of *Walden*. However, if he believed that he had gotten out of his system all ambition or desire for social recognition, it soon became apparent, as *Walden* neared completion, that his desire for a "greatness" and "specialness" validated by society was gradually, insidiously reemerging. Amidst all the scorn for trade evident in his journal of late 1853, there began to be hints that Thoreau was impatient with the obscurity and humble pursuits he had once so eagerly embraced. To be sure, on the last day of 1853, he asks (partly, no doubt, responding to Munroe's return of the remainders of *A Week*), "How can a poet afford to keep an account with a bookseller?" (J, VI:40). Yet, however contemptuous of the literary establishment he may have convinced himself he was (and the contempt was itself not without a trace of defensiveness), there remained a part of him—however much it had been submerged—that craved a wide and appreciative audience. For instance, on December 22, reacting to his surveying experience, he bemoans the manner in which he has been underemployed:

> I have offered myself much more earnestly as a lecturer than a surveyor. Yet I
> do not get any employment as a lecturer; was not invited to lecture once last

winter, and only once (without pay) this winter. . . . Woe be to the generation that lets any higher faculty in its midst go unemployed! (J, VI:21)

Whatever his stated misgivings about booksellers, when he finished *Walden* to his satisfaction, he wasted little time in submitting the manuscript to Ticknor and Fields, the publishers whose offer to print it in 1849 Thoreau had resisted in his anxiousness to publish *A Week* first. When the book was quickly accepted—largely because of Fields's enthusiasm for it—he must have felt vindicated and, understandably, encouraged to dream ambitious dreams again. Ticknor and Fields's agreement to pay him 15 percent royalties—rather than the 10 percent figure offered to most authors[1]—undoubtedly gave a further boost to his dreams of prominence. Greeley's promise to "announce" the book's publication, and Charles Scribner's decision to include him in his *Encyclopedia of American Literature,* also gave him reason to contemplate some measure of renown.

To the extent to which ambition had once again resurfaced, it was accompanied even in the prepublication months by psychic risks and dangers, including reawakened guilt. Never able fully to dissociate the pursuit of conventional success and competitive striving from the oedipal project, the surpassing of his father, and his survival of his brother, Thoreau was wont to remind himself, around the time of his brother's birthday, "We survive, in one sense, in our posterity and in the continuance of our race, but when a race of men, of Indians for instance, becomes extinct, is not that the end of the world for them?" (J, VI:30). Viewed in such a light, his own bid for fame and glory was tainted by the remembrance of those who were "extinct." Particularly sensitive to gaining success over his brother's dead body,[2] he asks, as he would in *Walden* (W, 264), to be delivered "from a city built on the site of a more ancient city. . . . There the dwellings of the living are in the cemeteries of the dead, and the soil is blanched and accursed" (J, VI:15). Only a short time before submitting his manuscript to Ticknor and Fields, he expresses "sympathy" for the suffering muskrat who is also a "brother": "Shall we not have sympathy with the muskrat which gnaws its third leg off, not as pitying its sufferings, but through our kindred mortality, appreciating its majestic pains and its heroic virtue. Are we not made its brothers by fate?" (J, VI:98–99). Ambition meant aggressiveness, and it was therefore crucial to reassert that he wished to be a hunter only "in pursuit of nobler game" (J, VI:44). He had to insist that he did not intend to forget, indeed wished to keep alive, the "Indian" who had been his brother. In late April, around the same time that he was putting the finishing touches on *Walden,* he sought to deny any coarse, worldly ambition in a passage soon to be incorporated in a lecture he appropriately titled "What Shall It Profit?": "How can a man be a wise man, if he does n't know any better how to live than other men? —if he is only more cunning and intellectually subtle? Does Wisdom work in a treadmill?" (J, VI: 208–9). Clearly, Thoreau was concerned lest he gain the world through his literary "cunning" and intellectual subtlety but lose his soul, forfeit his innocence, in the process. It is little wonder that a Thoreau seemingly on the verge of some acclaim would write, on June 4, 1854, that "Fame is not just" (J, VI:328). And on June 9 he would identify with the "queenly orchis," which he associates with the "Indian" he is so anxious not to betray: "How little anxious to display its attractions. . . . I am inclined to think of it as a relic of the past as much as the arrowhead, or the tomahawk I found on the 7th" (J, VI:338). Just two days before *Walden*'s appearance, an event occurred that may well have had ominous implications: Thoreau was stung by a bee on the forefinger of his left hand. "I could not," he comments, "completely close the finger, and the next finger sympathized so much with it that at first there was a *little* doubt which was stung" (J, VI:428). John's fatal cut had been on the ring finger of his left hand,[3] and Thoreau could hardly have failed to remember it. The talk of one finger "sympathizing" with another further suggests that Thoreau, who had "sympathized" with his brother's lockjaw, was especially susceptible, as *Walden* went public, to intimations of punishment, judgment, of being "stung" at the very moment he was about to enter the limelight and bask in it. Even a sense of ripeness—as connected with success, seniority, and even mere survival—could set off pangs of guilt.

Preparations for *Walden*'s publication, moreover, upset the delicately balanced routines and priorities that had been the foundation for the life of integrity, autonomy, and creativity he had built in the post-1849 period. Just as the Walden cabin had inevitably been dismantled, so now did the life structure that had led to the expanded *Walden* begin to show signs of crumbling. He was, for instance, so impatient to get the book printed, and so busy correcting proofs, making revisions, making arrangements, that "for the first time in years he missed the breaking up of the ice on Walden Pond."[4] Missing a momentous natural event was symptomatic of Thoreau's developing concern that he was frittering away his time, losing some control, in danger of sacrificing the inviolate core of his identity, as the contacts with civil society increased and the demands of interacting with it intensified. On the day before *Walden* came out, he confessed to Blake, "Methinks I have spent a rather unprofitable summer thus far. I have been too much with the world, as the poet might say" (C, 330). He felt himself more susceptible to the influence of others, as is revealed in his remark (probably referring to Channing), "My companion tempts me to certain licenses of speech, i.e. to reckless and sweeping expressions" (J, VI:165). Having worked so hard in the preceding years to distance himself from the opinions and expectations of his townsmen, he now found himself again more vulnerable and defensive, less serene. He was, after all, putting himself, his life, on the line again as *Walden* went public. On the one hand, he yearned for adulation; on the other, he was again—as when *A Week* was published—the potential object of public criticism and scorn. All his denials to the contrary, he was not immune to being stung by the opprobrium of townspeople, many of whom, he realized, would be offended and outraged by the barbs and swagger of *Walden*. He had addressed the book ostensibly to his neighbors; now he had to anticipate his neighbors' responses. Thus it is evident that it is not only his neighbor but himself who is "thin skinned" in his remarks: "Farewell! I will wait till you get your manners off. Why make politeness of so much consequence, when you are ready to assassinate with a word? I do not like any better to be assassinated with a rapier than to be knocked down with a bludgeon." "Why will men," he asks, "so try to impose on one another? . . . O such thin skins, such crockery, as I have to deal with!" (J, VI:199–200). In short, then, Thoreau's sense of self was less certain and solid as the day of *Walden*'s publication approached; the shored-up identity so essential to both his creativity and his serenity were in jeopardy.

An integral part of his identity related to his artistic productivity and fecundity, and 1853 had been a year when that sense of creative aliveness and generativity had flourished as *Walden* had blossomed and ripened. Yet, even before the book was in print, there were signs that Thoreau was beginning to feel and fear stagnation. These anxieties, which seem so incongruous during a period when the publication of his richest work was pending, were linked partly to factors already touched upon: the manner in which his reemergence into civil society, with all its distractions, obligations, and expectations, and the resurfacing of literary ambitions, with its attendant guilt and anxiety, threatened to compromise and complicate the life that served as a basis for his creative achievements. However, the most prominent threat to generativity was, paradoxically, the very completion and publication of *Walden*, for so long the primary and preoccupying focus and embodiment of generativity and now to be abandoned. The first twinges of concern may be seen in late January 1854 when he was working on a late draft of *Walden*. After commenting on January 27 that "we begin to die, not in our senses or extremities, but in our divine faculties," he remarks on the thirtieth, "Let not the year be disappointed of its crop," suggesting that there was some question in his mind about the continued viability of his "crop." The next day he laments that, despite the probability of January thaws, "I do not melt; there is no thaw in me; I am bound out still" (J, VI:80, 85–86, 87). While this sort of "thaw" imagery was by now characteristic enough, the inability to "thaw"—however short-lived— must have been especially disquieting at a time when he perceived he would soon no longer be carried along by the ongoing current of *Walden*. After the book's acceptance, the lapses in creative flow became even more serious matters. Looking at the pond, he broods, "This great expanse of deep-blue water, deeper than the sky, why does it not blue my soul as of yore? It is hard to soften me now" (J, VI:165). Though, as always, there *were* thaws and softenings during the prepublication period, the times of artistic incrustation were increasingly foreboding. In March and April, when his journal entries were rather bland and matter-of-fact, when he bought a telescope, perhaps as a way to compensate for the lack of more creative vision, and when he was working over the first proofs of *Walden*, he betrayed irritation with the way in which, even on an "elysian day," he seemed "always to be keeping the flocks of Admetus" (J, VI:185). On April 27, the last day on which he added a passage from his journal to *Walden*, he appears intent on keeping at bay the stagnation that seemed to be creeping into his life, a staleness that could easily become a disease: "A little relaxation in your exertion, a little idleness, will let in sickness and death into your own body. . . . Every human being is the artificer of his own fate in these respects. The well have no time to be sick" (J, VI:226). Whether these words were uttered in a self-vindicating or self-doubting way (or both), they would be prophetic of his own bout with an illness born partially out of stagnation.

However minor and sporadic these expressions of anxiety were—it must be stressed that the predominant mood was positive and expectant— they were the first trickle of what later would become streams and torrents. Part of Thoreau's evolving concern centered around attitudes toward science and nature. In May he began devoting more energy to his journal again, but much of his writing consisted of relatively scientific observations and lists. On May 6, as if to remind himself of his priorities, he writes,

> There is no such thing as pure *objective* observation. Your observation, to be interesting, i.e., to be significant, must be *subjective*. The sum of what the writer of whatever class has to report is simply some human experience. . . . No mere willful activity whatever, whether in writing verses or collecting statistics, will produce true poetry or science.If you are really a sick man, it is indeed to be regretted, for you cannot accomplish so much as if you were well. All that

a man has to say or do that can possibly concern mankind, is in some shape or other to tell the story of his love, —to sing; and, if he is fortunate and keeps alive, he will be forever in love. This alone is to be alive to the extremities. (J, VI:236–37)

Yet Thoreau himself had reason to question whether his own scientific observation would, without sufficient inspiration and perspective, lead him into a dead end or trap. In some way, the turning to science may have seemed a new departure, a way ultimately to chart minutely the human as well as the natural seasons. But to the extent that he was turning to science in the absence of any clearer direction or inspiration, the "aliveness" of his own "extremities" was threatened. A narrow scientific focus could be murderous to both the scientist and his subject. On May 28, after musing that the "least conscious and needless injury inflicted on any creature is to its extent a suicide. What peace—or life—can a murderer have?" he remarks, "The inhumanity of science concerns me, as when I am tempted to kill a rare snake that I may ascertain its species. I feel that this is not the means of acquiring true knowledge" (J, VI:311).

And, as if the concern about science's "inhumanity" was not perplexing enough to one who was becoming more scientific, even nature itself, the mother lode of his inspiration and insight and the object of so many of his current observations, could ultimately let one down. "We soon get through with Nature," he writes on May 23. "She excites an expectation which she cannot satisfy. The merest child which has rambled into a copsewood dreams of a wildness so wild and strange and inexhaustible as Nature can never show him" (J, VI:293). The man who had written in *Walden*'s first draft, "We can never have enough of Nature," now entertained a vision in the book's "Conclusion" that might prove antithetical: "Start now on that farthest western way, which . . . leads on direct a tangent to this sphere, summer and winter, day and night, sun down, moon down, and at last earth down too" (W, 322). While this view of a supranatural tangent, neither circle nor straight line,[5] suggested new opportunities for a humanistic, symbolic transcendence and immortality, it did call into question the sufficiency of the nature with which Thoreau had so often and willingly cast his lot. And in any event he was beginning to feel a dearth of inspiration as provided both by nature and by his own inner resources. In the same May 23 entry he adds, "There was a time when the beauty and the music were all within, and I sat and listened to my thoughts, and there was a song in them. . . . When you walked with a joy which knew not its own origin. . . . When your cords were tense" (J, VI:294). Here, Thoreau is feeling age and loss; with his cords "relaxed," his sense of aliveness, wonder, and mystery are in mortal danger. The tightly coiled vision of *Walden* was already becoming past tense. Furthermore, if the very nature he had relied upon could no longer yield him the metaphors and analogies, the tropes and symbols, that defined his creative vision (and *Walden*'s), then it was difficult to know where to turn. It was an unanswered question whether he could milk nature for copious metaphors *beyond* "second spring." The theme of disappointed expectations in the May 23 entry also may be related to *Walden*'s publication; with the book about to come out, he was beginning to sense that, far from conclusively resolving his problems and bestowing upon him a permanent state of grace, *Walden*'s imminent publication served to highlight the difficulties and deficiencies of life after *Walden*, after second spring.

A similar chord is struck in a June 17 entry. With summer—for some time now a season in which for him stagnation was evident—coming, and with *Walden*'s publication impending,

> It is dry, hazy June weather. We are more of the earth, farther from heaven, these days. We live in a grosser element. We [are] getting deeper into the mists of earth. Even the birds sing with less vigor and vivacity. The season of hope and promise is past; already the season of small fruits has arrived. The Indian marked the midsummer as the season when berries were ripe. We are a little saddened, because we begin to see the interval between our hopes and their fulfillment. The prospect of the heavens is taken away, and we are presented only with a few small berries. (J, VI:363–64)

"Is that all there is?" This seems to be one of the moods evoked by this season of the year and of his life. He had built his castles in the air and put the foundations under them. But now the realization of his dreams, as embodied in *Walden*, did not seem enough to sustain or satisfy him. In one sense, of course, *Walden* was all he could ever have hoped for. But it was, after all, a work of art and imagination, a book, and there must have begun to develop an awareness of an unbridgeable "interval" between the "prospect of the heavens" it offered and the hard, imaginatively unmalleable realities of the gross, mundane world. In another sense, it was to some degree frightening to consider *Walden* itself as the ripest fruit he could bear; if so, then what more could be anticipated, hoped for? Thus Thoreau, although frequently inclined to perceive *Walden* as his most mature fruit, was also anxious at times to put his *real* ripening at some indeterminate point in the future. Also, to accept that he was fully ripe was to accept that he was already in the autumn of life, and this was a threatening prospect. Just as he once was tempted, ambivalently, to put off adulthood, remain adolescent or perennially young, now he was tempted to put off middle age.[6] Ripening, moreover, carried connotations of being a "father" and "senior," which prompted oedipal anxieties, guilt, and fears of imminent death. It was often more inspiriting to see *Walden* as embodying the "second spring" of late summer and very early fall rather than the "spring" and "Indian summer" that occur when autumn is completely entrenched and inclined toward winter. He was growing increasingly wary, now that *Walden* was almost in the past, of putting all his eggs—or berries—in the one basket of the book. Thoreau's ambivalence, his desire to see himself as ripe but also to see *Walden* as only the "small fruit" of spring and summer rather than the even more mature fruit of a later ripening, is revealed in his journal entry of August 7:

> Do you not feel the fruit of your spring and summer beginning to ripen, to harden its seed within you? Do not your thoughts begin to acquire consistency as well as flavor and ripeness? How can we expect a harvest of thought who have not had a seed-time of character? Already some of my small thoughts— fruit of my spring life—are ripe, like the berries which feed the first broods of birds. (J, VI:426)

If *Walden* was primarily the "fruit" of spring and summer, then, he sought to reassure himself with only intermittent success, he might still anticipate an even more bountiful and mellow harvest in the autumn. By such devices, by deferring complete ripeness to the future, did he attempt to forestall his own autumn, cling to spring and summer, and head off disappointment and anxieties about stagnation and death.

All his excitement about *Walden*'s publication notwithstanding, Thoreau often felt melancholy in the summer days preceding August 9. In July he was forced to spend more of his time downstairs with his family because the intense heat prevented him from staying in his attic room (J, VI:415). Without his private space, he may well have felt uneasy, not only because of the temporary displacement but also because it symbolized his concerns about more permanent changes in his life and intrusions into his time and creativity. The oppressive heat itself depressed him, as it both caused and mirrored his own lethargy. There was a "broad invisible lethean gulf" (J, VI:382) between this season of the year—and of his life—and spring. It was a period as "trivial as noon" and had a "sultry, debauched" appearance (J, VI:401), which Thoreau regarded as signaling a "crisis," not unlike the one he was verging on. By July 28 it was the "afternoon of the year," and the year's "indefinite promise" was gone, requiring the "postponement" of "the fulfillment of many of our hopes for this year" (J, VI: 413). On August 2, with a specimen copy of *Walden* in hand, "thought" was again possible, and he proceeded to brood on the shallowness of his life: "I feel the necessity of deepening the stream of my life; I must cultivate privacy. It is very dissipating to be with people too much. As C. says, it takes the edge off a man's thoughts to have been much in society" (J, VI: 415). His letter of August 8 to Blake, moreover, reflects clearly the extent to which, on the brink of his greatest triumph, he was preoccupied with issues of stagnation:

> I find it, as ever, very unprofitable to have much to do with men. It is sowing the wind, but not reaping even the whirlwind; only reaping an unprofitable calm and stagnation. Our conversation is a smooth, and civil, and never-ending speculation merely. I take up the thread of it again in the morning, with very much such courage as the invalid takes his prescribed Seidlitz powders. (C, 330)

Bordering on a spiritual invalidism that preceded any physical symptoms, he asks Blake questions he was more and more apt to ask himself in the months that followed:

> What is the state of your crops? Will your harvest answer well to the seed-time. . . . Is there any blight on your fields, any murrain in your herds? Have you tried the size and quality of your potatoes? It does one good to see their balls dangling in the lowlands. . . . Are you killing weeds nowadays? . . . Did you plant any Giant Regrets last spring, such as I saw advertised? . . . Is there likely to be a sufficiency of fall feed in your neighborhood? What is the state of your springs? . . . Be careful not to drink too much sweetened water, while at your hoeing, this hot weather. You can bear the heat much better for it. (C, 331)

Despite evidence of his potency, his "balls dangling" in *Walden,* Thoreau was himself worried about the future state of his crops and the "sufficiency of fall feed"; he wondered if he or his crops would be "spoiled" by the "sweetened water," the blandishments of civil society.

Beginning in late May, Thoreau had started to make journal entries regarding the Anthony Burns case. Burns was a fugitive slave who had been arrested in Boston and was, the efforts of abolitionists notwithstanding, sent back to slavery, only finally to have his freedom purchased by northern philanthropists.[7] Thoreau was justifiably distracted, upset, and enraged by the situation, writing in his journal on June 16, "Who can be serene in a country where both rulers and ruled are without principle? The remembrance of the baseness of politicians spoils my walks. My thoughts are murder to the State; I endeavor in vain to observe nature; my thoughts go involuntarily plotting against the State" (J, VI:358). Clearly, his response was dictated by long-held principles; nevertheless, in speaking out

on the Burns affair he was also contending with other, more personal issues, which plagued him as he awaited *Walden*'s publication. On some
level, the distraction may have represented a welcome deflection from direct consideration of his own gathering problems, even a way to excuse
himself for his inability to be a creative and inspired observer of nature at
this time. It certainly was not just the Burns affair that kept him from feeling serene. He delivered his address, "Slavery in Massachusetts," appropriately enough, on Independence Day, and the speech reflected his need at
the time to reestablish the sense of autonomy he felt slipping away, to return again to a kind of Walden. As he had in "Civil Disobedience," he declares his separation from other Concordians who "are not prepared to
stand by one of their own bridges, but talk only of taking up a position on
the highlands beyond the Yellowstone river." Wary of how he had been,
and might be, compromised by his own renewed contacts with civil society, he insists that he, like nature, will not be a "partner" to "the Missouri
Compromise"—or any compromise. Indeed, his own "murderous" rage
at the state may have emanated in part from his need to defend himself militantly against perceived threats to his authenticity and freedom. "We have
used up all our inherited freedom," he says. "If we would save our lives, we
must fight for them" (RP, 91, 108, 107–8).

If identity was at issue, so was generativity, and his speech was also an
effort to ward off any current or impending stagnation. The very fact that
he was willing to enter the public, political fray suggests that he was anxious to prove to himself that he could have some sort of tangible impact on
a collectivity and, in the process, show how much he cared for oppressed
people. Thoreau frequently uses the language and imagery of decay, decline, and stagnation to characterize slavery and those, including his
townspeople, who appear to countenance it. "Our Buttricks, and Davises,
and Hosmers," he says, "are retreating hither [beyond the Yellowstone
river], and I fear that they will have no Lexington Common between them
and the enemy." In obsequious newspapers he hears the "gurgling of the
sewer." At the end of the piece he portrays "slavery and servility" as
"merely a decaying and a death, offensive to all healthy nostrils," and advises, "Let the living bury them; even they are good for manure" (RP, 91,
101, 109). By way of contrast, he invokes the water lily as "an emblem of
purity" that "bursts up so pure and fair to the eye, and so sweet to the
scent, as if to show what purity and sweetness reside in, and can be ex-
tracted from, the slime and muck of earth." However mired in stagnation
he may personally have felt, he surely identifies with the water lily's ability
to grow out of the stagnant water and emit a sweet, fresh fragrance. "The
foul slime," he adds, "stands for the sloth and vice of man, the decay of hu-

manity; the fragrant flower that springs from it, for the purity and courage which are immortal" (RP, 108, 109). To attack the "decay of humanity" was also to take up arms against the incipient sense of decay in his own life. At the same time, to display intense concern for the downtrodden was not only to seek escape from lethargy and stagnation but also to seek some surcease from the guilt that began gnawing at him as he contemplated *Walden*'s possible success. While his "murderous" hostility to the state may very well have intensified the guilt, his defense of his "brothers and sisters" helped to mitigate it:

> The majority of the men of the North, and of the South, and East, and West, are not men of principle. If they vote, they do not send men to Congress on errands of humanity; but while their brothers and sisters are being scourged and hung for loving liberty, while—I might insert here all that slavery implies and is, —it is the mismanagement of wood and iron and stone and gold which concerns them.

Refusing to wait patiently and peacefully "until perchance, one day when I have put on mourning for them dead, I shall have persuaded you to relent" (the "attitude" he ascribes to Massachusetts), Thoreau would "side with the light, and let the dark earth roll from under me, calling my mother and my brother to follow" (RP, 102). As the genuine nurturer and mourner of his "family," he could disavow any desires to surpass, hurt, or betray them. It was also necessary, in light of his guilty ambitions for some measure of celebrity and his fears about whether he would be spoiled by whatever success might be forthcoming, to forswear any desire for prominence. "The events of the past month," he says, "teach me to distrust Fame. I see that she does not finely discriminate, but coarsely hurrahs" (RP, 104–5).

The sense of loss that Thoreau articulates with respect to the Burns episode is very definitely of a piece with a more pervasive and personal feeling of loss characteristic of this era just before *Walden*'s publication. "I have lived for the last month," he notes, "with the sense of having suffered a vast and indefinite loss. I did not know at first what ailed me. At last it occurred to me that what I had lost was a country" (RP, 106). But the sense of "vast and indefinite" loss that had "ailed" him was not limited to the recognition that he, the disillusioned radical, was now in some respect a man without a country, the nation having shown signs of thickening and settling into a corpulent, compromised middle age wholly at odds with the earlier, idealistic hopes he had had when both he and the country had been younger. He was not only losing a country that had seemingly failed to live up to its promise; he was also growing older and in the process of losing a book. This loss would be devastating and frightening. "For my part," he writes,

> my old and worthiest pursuits have lost I cannot say how much of their attraction, and I feel that my investment in life here is worth many per cent. less since Massachusetts deliberately sent back an innocent man, Anthony Burns, to slavery. I dwelt before, perhaps, in the illusion that my life passed somewhere only *between* heaven and hell, but now I cannot persuade myself that I do not dwell *wholly within* hell. (RP, 106)

That *Walden* was passing out of his hands clearly informed this state of mind. Much of his own "investment in life" was in the book, and now that his emotional life could no longer be organized around it, life itself may not have appeared as attractive as before. In *Walden* he had gone a long way toward creating an uplifting and sustaining "illusion" of "heaven." Itself in some respects a version of a "middle landscape"[8]—with Walden Pond at its center, mediating between sky and earth, heights and depths—a time and space of hallowed in-betweenness in which, unlike the real world, everything still remained possible and potential was inexhaustible, the book at least allowed him to occupy a middle ground between art and life, which helped insulate him from the hells of temporal reality. Now, about to be deprived of this "heavenly" dwelling, he could not entirely persuade himself that he would not "dwell *wholly within* hell." He could not rid himself of the fear that he was about to spend a season in hell.

Just two days before *Walden* came out, Thoreau saw signs of the declining power of the sun and the passing of the summer and commented, "I realize what a friend I am losing" (J, VI:427). But the summer sun (which had, in truth, often been an enemy of thought and clarity) was not the most significant "friend" he was losing. If the prepublication period had involved some anticipatory mourning, the publication of *Walden* ushered in an even more intense period of grief and apprehension, though diluted in its preliminary stages by the excitement of his apparent publishing triumph and the brief renown that accompanied it. As anxious as he had been to complete *Walden* and get it into print, he was not prepared to reach closure with it, to separate from it and all that it meant for him.

Rather than "Life in the Woods," a more apt and accurate subtitle for *Walden*, by the time it was completed, would have been "Life in the Words." Even the first draft of *Walden* had been more artful and crafty than a "simple and sincere" account of Thoreau's life in the woods, ostensibly written primarily to answer the "very particular inquiries" made by townspeople; he had managed artfully to dodge, play down, or transform some of the realities of his historical life and identity in the Walden years to satisfy a multitude of needs and wishes. By the time it was published, eight years after he left the pond, *Walden* was a far more fully realized, far-reaching, and radical transformation and reification of historical realities, notwithstanding the truths it conveyed regarding the crises, challenges, and victories Thoreau had experienced. In its final form, *Walden* was a multilayered woods of words, a world in words. It was a rich, magical, densely thicketed and wooded forest of first and second, of spring and second spring, growth. In part, the forest consisted of evergreens and deciduous trees left standing from the first draft. In turn, the needles and leaves of these trees, fallen to the forest floor, had helped fertilize the soil and generate *Walden*'s new growth. And the words themselves had taken on a life, inertia, and momentum of their own, providing an organic crucible, a breeding ground, for the book's expansion. But it was also, fatefully so, the experience and increasingly urgent needs of the writer in the years between Walden and *Walden* that had provided the impetus and direction for the forest's further development. Thoreau had written prophetically in *A Week* that "the constant abrasion and decay of our lives makes the soil of our future growth." The abrasion and decomposition of his life in the 1847–54 period had impelled him to new composition, to a *Walden* of expanded proportions and dimensions.

To be sure, this woods of words was not without the texture, complexity, and apparent internal contradictions that would make walking through it a more difficult task. In a sense, this literary forest partakes of a certain reality because of its epigenetic, organic, cumulative mode of composition, in which later passages and perceptions coexist with—rather than supplant—earlier ones. *Walden*, then, is partly an accumulation of, and response to, life at many stages, rife with the unresolved conflicts and ambivalence to which we are all heir. Moreover, in choosing (as in "Higher Laws") not to exclude *all* the inconsistencies, Thoreau not only revealed more faithfully, beyond logic, some of his conflicts but also suggested that, during a life, one may explore a range of possibilities and alternatives, some of which indeed may be antithetical but some of which may in the end prove to be complementary or supplementary rather than contradictory.

Another reality that the book embodied, though usually covertly or implicitly, was the extent to which it testified not only to the Walden experience itself but also to the years between Walden and *Walden*.[9] "For the sake of convenience" Thoreau condensed two years into one. But even in the first draft there was reference to two winters, and two springs. When he first wrote of a "winter of discontent" (alluded to in "Economy") and the spring that followed it, he was presumably referring to the 1837–45 period (or parts of it) and the spring he went to Walden. Both this winter and this spring were given short shrift, compared to the descriptions of the following winter and the concluding spring, which, even in the first draft, was something of a metaphor for the spring growth and reawakening he had experienced while at the pond. But by the time the book was completed, even the winter and spring, real and symbolic, of the Walden experience were to some degree telescoped. For the final draft, the concluding spring of Walden was further developed and expanded, as was the treatment of the intervening winter (and, to some extent, autumn, to complete the seasonal cycle and provide images of his own greater maturity).[10] That winter probably now represented, even more than those he had spent at Walden, the "winter" of the post-Walden period, a season both of storms that had to be weathered and of dormancy, sounding one's depths, preparation, and anticipation—the early part of seedtime. And the spring in the penultimate chapter was now not simply the real or symbolic one of the Walden experience (though recovery and selective re-creation of *that* experience, and of an even more distant "golden age," were also important) but the "second spring" of growth and expansion of which the book itself was the most conclusive proof. By the final version, then, Thoreau had drawn on his later young adult experience and his transition to middle age to tell the tale not just of the two years at Walden but, perhaps even more primarily, of the protracted period of discontent, crisis, and seedtime since Walden and of his eventual metamorphosis, blossoming forth, and even more heroically earned triumph as embodied by *Walden*. The book takes on much of its authority and passion from the crisis and perceived growth of the post-Walden years.

In this regard, *Walden* was another version and vision of human life and the human seasons with much truth in it—building on what the author had now learned more definitively from firsthand experience about human development and growth, partly as it corresponded with the seasons he had studied more originally and closely since *A Week* and Walden. That *Walden* was written in response to the crises of later young adulthood and midlife transition as well as the earlier crises of youth and earlier young adulthood helps to account for why it is so powerful and influential a work for people at various stages of the life cycle. It speaks not only to the youthful "student" but to the older seeker and student of human life, the person bent on continuing adult education. It encourages each person, not only in youth or early adulthood but at more chronologically advanced phases of the life cycle to seek and savor a more authentic, awake life. Such a quest demands a moratorium—subtle or dramatic—from entanglements and expectations, a transitional season of trial, taking stock, experimentation, and preparation, a seedtime that will eventually bloom into a spring of greater authenticity and expansion. Whatever one's age (and it must be pointed out that Thoreau does not take fully enough into account such harsh limitations as those imposed by social class, race, or gender, by political and economic oppression), the opportunities for moratoria, for seedtimes, are there, and one is never too old for new growth, for springs of authentic rebirth and rededication. *Walden*, then, provides a blueprint, archetype, and affirmation of the moratorium and seedtime that will eventually lead to a new, expanded life. And the memorable images and symbols, largely grounded in organic natural and seasonal cycles, of heroic transcendence, rebirth, transformation, and immortality have been stirring, moving, and therapeutic for countless readers.

Thoreau had ended *Walden* on what he intended to be a note of affirmation: "There is more day to dawn. The sun is but a morning star" (w, 333). But there is another side to this message of hope and anticipation. If the sun was "but a morning star" and if *Walden* was but the dawn of day, what would the rest of the day be like—especially considering how much he had invested in the book and how great a work of art it was? Thoreau was inevitably forced to ask challenging and disturbing questions: Was there life after *Walden*, and, if so, what would it be like? The answers would not be easily forthcoming.

In spite of the many truths it embodied about human life and about the joy and solace to be found in alert appreciation of the beauties of this world; in spite of its eloquent and often still relevant social criticism; in spite of its rich philosophical insights; in spite of its occasional acknowledgments of the author's limitations and liabilities; in spite of the vivid details; in spite of brief references that suggest the extent to which Thoreau was writing of more than the two years he spent at the pond—in spite of all these things, *Walden* was preeminently the work of a consummate artist who reshaped his life in the woods into an artful world of words quite distinct from historical reality. "Life in the Words" suggests much of the genuine significance of the book to Thoreau: it was life and self re-created and revised in words, and he lived in the words he had created. Living at Walden Pond, he had been better able to believe himself the man of independence, heroism, and purity he so much wished to be. The writing and the protracted period of revision had offered him a way to cling to, and maintain continuity with, his Walden identity, his ego ideal of young manhood; moreover, with the idealized experience and self providing a relatively secure foundation, he was able to build on and revise the earlier self-concept and incorporate into the book a more seasoned ego ideal. In working on *Walden,* he had created a myth of personality and experience, a persona who was in fact purer, more heroic, autonomous, mature, and serene, than the real man who had lived by the pond and who in the past several years had lived away from the pond. To be sure, Thoreau *had* grown in the preceding years, but there remained a considerable gap between the persona and the historical man, a chasm that the book's publication served to dramatize. Indeed, much of the force of the book and the power of the persona had come from his need to deny, compensate for, and transcend the deficits and deficiencies of his real life and self. Though he had not forgotten that he was once a caterpillar, it was difficult to face the fact that in many respects he still was one, that the butterfly was to a great extent pressed between the pages of his book.

While he worked on the book, held onto it, was absorbed by and in it, it was easier to remain a believer in the myth. What *Walden* dealt with directly only infrequently was that the writer of the book *was* a writer, an artist. Perhaps the most notable acknowledgment of this fact was in the parable, in "Conclusion," of the "artist in the city of Kouroo": "When the finishing stroke was put to his work, it suddenly expanded before the eyes of the astonished artist into the fairest of all the creations of Brahma. He had made a new system in making a staff, a world with full and fair proportions. . . . The material was pure, and his art was pure; how could the result be other than wonderful?" (w, 327). Literary artists not only have the resources of imagination and language to create an illusive, symbolic world (as elusive in the real world as the loon of *Walden*) but also often seek or wish to inhabit the "system" or "world with full and fair proportions" they have created. Either wittingly or unwittingly, consciously or unconsciously, they have the potential to be taken in by the myths they have forged. As Ernest Becker puts it, "This is the problem of the artist generally: that he creates his own new meanings and must, in turn, be sustained by them. The dialogue is too inverted to be secure."[11] *Walden* was a persuasive fiction (as is confirmed by all those readers who have believed it and taken it literally), and Thoreau, however much self-knowledge he had achieved, had a large capacity for self-deception. When the need to believe in some things and deny others is great, as it was in this case, there is all the more chance that the writer will identify with the created ideal. Perhaps, had he dealt more directly and forthrightly throughout *Walden* with the reality that he was, first and foremost, a writer, that the experience and the persona in the book were constructs, not simple autobiographical realities, he might have been more prepared for the inevitable letdown, the realization of the disjunction between real and ideal, between historical fact and myth; he might conceivably have been able to head off the crisis precipitated by separation from the world and words of the book. As it was, however, the final publication of *Walden* led to a severe reaggravation of Thoreau's identity crisis, which the experience and the book had partially and temporarily helped to resolve. He found himself on the verge of having to let go of the self-concept that, particularly through the writing of *Walden,* he had struggled so hard to gain. Around the time of the book's publication, then, he was quite probably mourning the loss of the Walden identity so integral to his well-being. Not only did *Walden*'s publication threaten to destabilize his life structure in a manner inimical to his ideal identity, but it was in the book that his ego ideal was most thoroughly realized.

Walden and its symbols had been a buffer and fortress against unpleasant historical realities and against mortality. Now Thoreau was faced with the threat of desymbolization,[12] and he was no longer so immune from those inner and outer realities he feared, despised, found distressing, and wished to deny. Immersed in the writing, and awash in *Walden*'s symbols, he still had access to those oceanic, cosmic feelings that provide intimations of an imperviousness to time. While he had evolved to a certain extent the notion of more symbolic kinds of immortality, he had not fully accepted, on an emotional level, his finiteness or given up entirely on the wish to be exempted from literal death and the sense that somehow he could be. Cut adrift from the book, he was washed up more emphatically on the shores of time. Although *Walden*'s later drafts had in part developed in the crucible of, and drawn on, his recent experience in the early phases of midlife transition, his absorption in the book had also helped protect him from a more pervasive, profound, and menacing form of midlife crisis.[13] Without the book he was all too vulnerable to such a crisis.

In crucial ways *Walden* was the culmination of the strivings of young adulthood and early maturity, and it was the pinnacle of his writing career; after the milestones or "marker events" of its completion and publication, Thoreau must have wondered, as do so many writers, whether he would or could produce anything more of value. He had given his all and put the best of himself into the book. If the "fruit" had ripened so fully in *Walden,* withering and death could follow. The intermittently employed strategy of claiming that only the "small fruits" of his "spring life" had thus far ripened (or, for that matter, that there was "more day to dawn" and that the "sun" of *Walden* was "but a morning star") did not significantly reduce the anxiety. The fear of forfeiting his Walden identity could itself have been a prominent threat to his sense of generativity, since the Walden self-concept had helped set free and channel his creative energies. The writing of *Walden* had in part been a way to reinforce and build on that sense of self which had been such a critical catalyst to his creativity. No longer firmly buttressed by his Walden identity, or reassured by his ongoing work on the book, Thoreau could not avoid the suspicion that his creative river would dry up. And the flowing of this river was essential to his adaptation to life.[14] Signs of stagnation that he could shrug or stave off while *Walden* was still expanding could now, without the generative prop of the book to fall back on, take on ominous meanings. He had reached an unexpected impasse, a creative cul-de-sac. That he had devoted himself so fully to *Walden,* put so much of himself into it, had left him drained; he was understandably subject to at least temporary "burnout,"[15] and this could only have intensified his anxieties about stagnation.

Walden was, to this childless man entering middle age, a most cherished offspring, a testimony to his fruitfulness. What followed the book's appearance might also be considered a form of the postpartum depression (and perhaps empty-nest syndrome) many writers experience in varying degrees. However much Thoreau might try to insist that it was the ripe fruit of but his "spring life," it was evident that he could not avoid perceiving the book as the masterpiece of his "summer" prime—a "perfect summer life" as opposed to the imperfections of the actual natural and human summers. And in many respects it must have seemed to him his last word. With the book, his best work, behind him, everything else could have seemed anticlimactic, and he may well have doubted whether he would or could give birth to any more such children. And, indeed, from his standpoint (as well as from the modern perspective that has judged the book an American classic), *Walden* was a hard, if not impossible, act to follow. In *Walden*'s "Conclusion" he had said, "There is a solid bottom every where" (w, 330). But if in the book Thoreau had sounded the depths to discover the bottom, with the conclusion of *Walden* he learned that it was possible to hit another kind of rock bottom. *Walden* was a chapter in his life he could close only with the deepest reluctance, difficulty, and grief.

The days immediately following *Walden*'s publication were a mixture of anticipation and apprehension for Thoreau. There are observations of "ripened seeds," "ripened grains," and ripe "dangle-berries" on August 10, and Thoreau, perhaps holding his breath and hoping he could somehow avoid them in his own life, notes that there had been "hardly any dog-days yet" (J, VI:430–31). But the "first *marked* dog-day" on the thirteenth seems to have prompted him, acutely sensitive to what outer

phenomena might imply or portend about his inner state, to reflect ruefully
on the languor that had stolen into his life:

> I remember only with a pang the past spring and summer thus far. I have not
> been an early riser. Society seems to have invaded and overrun me. I have
> drank tea and coffee and made myself cheap and vulgar. My days have all been
> noontides, without sacred mornings and evenings. (J, VI:436)

The crickets' creak suggests an "unprofanedness" that he knew had been
compromised: "It is with infinite yearning and aspiration that I seek solitude, more and more resolved and strong; but with a certain genial weakness that I seek society ever" (J, VI:439). Letters of praise from potential
disciple Daniel Ricketson of New Bedford and from Higginson, as well as
early favorable reviews, undoubtedly gave him a lift, confirming his generativity even if they also confirmed his "weakness," his desire for approval,
and made salient his misgivings, in the light of his own experience, about
being a mentor. And a letter from Catherine V. Devero, soliciting a contribution from Thoreau, who was already mourning his losses, to a book for
mourners, divided into sections dealing, in somewhat maudlin fashion,
with death as it occurs in different seasons of life,[16] may well have been received by him with very mixed feelings in that it suggested that he was far
from alone in his use of human seasons and that such usages could deteri-
orate into cloying conventions.

It was a year of great drought in Concord, and Thoreau unquestionably was led to consider whether he too was experiencing, or would experience, a creative drought. On August 18 he notes that there was "little
fruit formed, and that small and dying ripe"; the next day he witnessed the
effects of drought on trees, including the red maples, "whose leaves are
very generally wilted and curled, showing the under sides. Perhaps not
only because they require so much moisture, but because they are more
nearly ripe, and there is less life and vigor in them" (J, VI:450, 454). Feeling
himself ripe or "nearly" so, he must have wondered whether there was less
"life and vigor" in him as a result. Walden Pond, he was reassured to see on
more than one occasion, was not afflicted by drought (J, VI:456, 491), and
he could only hope he would be as drought-resistant as the pond. But his
own journal and activities were suggesting otherwise. Not only was the capacity to integrate entries into a coherent and well-sculpted whole apparently weakened, but even the parts, the spontaneous short passages, were
not strong. Not just putting thoughts together but *having* thoughts was a
problem. There were many scientific, matter-of-fact entries around this
time, and on August 15–18 he was visited by John Russell, a distinguished
amateur botanist from Salem with whom in years to come he would occa-

sionally engage in primarily scientific activities.[17] On the evening of the fifteenth, Russell "showed his microscope at Miss Mackay's" and "examined a section of pontedaria leaf" (J, VI:446). The subsequent entries, which describe the two going to such places as climbing fern and Fair Haven, are devoted almost entirely to minute scientific observation and classification. Russell seems to have brought out the scientist in him and reinforced his wavering belief in the value of science, at least as a means of acquiring a deeper knowledge of natural processes and therefore, eventually, of gleaning more profound "moral facts" and correspondences.

In this sense, the scientific, or quasiscientific, study of nature, though a far cry from natural history, was a continuation of his search for a more complete understanding of the human—and his own—life cycle. And science too, as part of a long and continuing chain of human inquiry, could provide some manner of immortality for those engaged in it.[18] But to the extent that scientific scrutiny and writing were stripped of the vision of correspondence for Thoreau, or lacked an accompanying artistic inspiration, it could become very sterile indeed. Science could represent a form of "psychic numbing,"[19] a terrifying form of desymbolization, and he needed symbols desperately to sustain him. *Walden,* and his more unpleasant wilderness experiences, had even occasionally called into question whether nature, or by implication the study of nature, was sufficient, and now Thoreau found himself depending more heavily on a minute and even technical nature study. Perhaps, he may have started to suspect, reliance on nature might prove to be too limiting if one were to get at human truths.

On the evening of the eighteenth, with Russell not mentioned and presumably not there, Thoreau has second thoughts in the aftermath of "killing the cistudo" (a small turtle) "for the sake of science":

> I cannot excuse myself for this murder, and see that such actions are inconsistent with the poetic perception, however they may serve science, and will affect the quality of my observations. I pray that I may walk more innocently and serenely through nature. No reasoning whatever reconciles me to this act. It affects my day injuriously. I have lost some self-respect. I have a murderer's experience in a degree. (J, VI:452)

This passage, coming as it does on the heels of his wanderings with Russell, the publication of *Walden,* and his own scientific writing, reveals eloquently Thoreau's fears that he might sacrifice his poetic sensibilities as he became more involved in science, a pursuit that he nevertheless seemed more and more tempted to take up, partly to fill at least temporarily the vacuum created by the loss of *Walden* and the dearth of other promising directions, inspiration, and imaginative energy. He was more vulnerable to the loss of "self-respect" with the loss of *Walden*'s sustaining ego ideal. He was more concerned than before about whether his best creative days were behind him, whether his emerging scientific orientation signified, or was symptomatic of, the stagnation of his artistic powers, a "great drought" of "poetic perception." Additionally, the guilty response to the killing of the cistudo (which clearly had some resonance with his complicity in the "murder" of the moose in Maine) may, as will be seen, have been conditioned by the guilt surrounding his book's publication and his own flirtation with fame. He was indeed subject to the loss of innocence as he ventured again into the public, literary arena; on an oedipal level and with respect to his brother's death, his wish for success in this case, as in previous cases, left him with "a murderer's experience in a degree."

Emerson, in a letter of August 28, presented a remarkable, if somewhat distorted, portrait of his former protégé in what appeared to Waldo to be the heady first days after *Walden*'s publication:

> All American kind are delighted with "Walden" as far as they have dared to say, The little pond sinks in these very days as tremulous at its human fame. I do not know if the book has come to you [George Bradford in London] yet; —but it is cheerful, sparkling, readable, with all kinds of merit, & rising sometimes to very great heights. We account Henry the undoubted King of all American lions. He is walking up & down Concord, firm-looking, but in a tremble of great expectation. (L, IV:459–60)

The references to Thoreau, only part of a paragraph in a long letter, suggest Emerson's own ambivalence. While there is high praise for Thoreau and *Walden,* there is also something of an exaggerated, satiric, and ultimately belittling modulation. Though, for instance, the first reviews were generally positive (with the exception of a scathing piece just coming out in the *Boston Atlas*),[20] it could hardly be said, as fact or prophecy, that "all American kind" were likely to respond favorably to the book. There is a hint that Thoreau, the "King of all American lions" and "in a tremble of great expectation," was a man on the make, a bit conceited and puffed up by the success and fame he was anticipating. Emerson gives his evaluation of *Walden* in one sentence, displaying only limited sensitivity to what the book meant to Thoreau; there is so much more he could have said about the book—not only about its "heights" but about its depths. If to some degree he wanted to make amends for letting his friend down with respect to *A Week,* he perhaps also felt some resentment or envy toward the younger author, whose masterpiece was coming out when his own creative powers seemed on the wane. Possibly he could afford to give the book, whatever its virtues, only a somewhat grudging admiration. Or perhaps, as with *A*

Week, he had reservations about *Walden* (as he clearly had about its author), reservations he was this time reluctant to express even after the book had come out. In his funeral oration for Thoreau, *Walden* would be mentioned only in passing. In any case, the depiction of Thoreau is colored by his own ambivalence. It is revealing that his erstwhile "American Scholar" had not relied on his help, either to make suggestions for revision or to aid in getting the book published or publicized.[21] He could no longer trust Emerson entirely. Had he read the letter to Bradford, he may well have been taken aback.

Of course, Thoreau *was* in a "tremble of great expectation," but he was also trembling *because* of his lofty aspirations for fame. For all the pride and even hubris he, as an "American lion," may have been experiencing, he was subject, like the pond, to sinking, tremulous as he was at the prospect of renown. Emerson's image of him as "King of all American lions" suggests a kind of potency and dominance, which, to the extent he entertained these emotions, would inevitably exacerbate oedipally related guilt.[22] Moreover, with fame came possible notoriety and public criticism. Although he could, in the flush of triumph, shake his fist arrogantly at those in Concord who had demeaned or undervalued him, he remained vulnerable to the attacks on his character and on the book that the risks of publication made unavoidable. As tough as he thought himself to be, he did not have the "insensitivity and toughness" of the snapping turtle, "born with a shell," who "makes our life, with its diseases and low spirits, ridiculous" (J, VII:9–10). A fire, started in the "dry and withered grass" by a locomotive in late August, "ran over forty or fifty rods" (J, VI:485) and may have sparked unpleasant thoughts of the "woodsburner" label he had never fully been able to shrug off. Writers frequently take more to heart the negative reviews than the positive ones, and the *Boston Atlas* review, for example, could have shaken him badly, particularly since so much of himself was wrapped up in his book: "Pithy sarcasm, stern judgment, cold condemnation—all these abound in the pages of this volume. . . . There is not a page, a paragraph giving one sign of liberality, charitableness, kind feeling, generosity, in a word—heart."[23] To be sure, the several positive reviews,[24] such as that in the *National Anti-Slavery Standard* of December 16, perhaps written by Blake himself, could be highly gratifying, flattering, and comforting: "The striking peculiarity of Mr. Thoreau's attitude is that, while he is no religionist, and while he is eminently practical in regard to the material economies of life, he yet manifestly feels, through and through, that the loftiest dreams of the imagination are the solidest realities, and so the only foundation for us to build upon."[25] This review portrayed Thoreau largely as he would have liked to see himself. Fan mail from such people as Richard Fuller also encouraged him.[26] But such praise could also heighten the sense of disparity between his real and ideal selves, a sense particularly strong as the foundation of imagination established by *Walden* crumbled under his feet. To the extent that he knew he was not identical to the book's persona, he may well have felt an almost paralyzing pressure to live up to the image, both publicly and privately, and this could have been stressful and exhausting indeed. And the very fact that he was seeking recognition, paying the day-to-day price of distraction and compromise for it, further put in jeopardy his sense that he was living up to his ideal identity.

On the very day that Emerson wrote the letter referring to him as an "American lion," Thoreau was writing about depression and remorse: "In my experience, at least *of late years,* all that depresses a man's spirits is the sense of remissness, —duties neglected, unfaithfulness, —or shamming, impurity, falsehood, selfishness, inhumanity, and the like" (J, vi:483). That "sense of remissness," of having lost his bearings, was, it can be surmised, especially intense as he trembled on the brink of a success that, on some level, he feared would be soul-destroying. The next passage steers the meditation in another direction: "From the experience of late years I should say that a man's seed was the direct tax of his race. It stands for my sympathy with my race. When the brain chiefly is nourished and not the affections, the seed becomes merely excremental" (J, vi:483). Perhaps reacting in part to a recent loss of his own "seed" (either in a nocturnal emission or through masturbation),[27] he betrays his concern about the connection between sexuality, the releasing of seed, and pollution (excrement). For him, initiative—including at its root sexual, oedipal initiative—had always been accompanied by some degree of guilt; coming as it did at a time when he was ambivalently courting success, the association between seed and excrement, or soiling, was even more evident. His "sympathy" with his "race" and, more to the point, with his brother was being put into question by the temptation of ambition; to the extent that he was following a calculated course in realizing his ambition, his "seed" would not be in "sympathy" with his brother (or other significant male figures) and would thus be distasteful, a waste product rather than a worthy offering. Although he seems here to be referring to "seed" in its primary, sexual sense, the passage may inadvertently reveal (especially in connection with the immediately preceding entry) Thoreau's concern that his artistic seeds may be transformed into something excremental, unworthy. Having, to put it delicately, spent himself in *Walden,* and thus paid the "direct tax" to his "race," he was now worried lest he be unable to find again that truly generative combination of head and heart in his future writings. His scientific proclivities, in which "the brain chiefly is nourished," could not have seemed encouraging in this context. Even *Walden* itself, where the excremental had been transformed into the generative, the fecal clay into new organic forms, could take on a taint as it became linked with impure initiatives. Thoreau had earlier prided himself on his having produced fruit rather than gall in his art. Now generativity was linked to gall; on September 4 he inquires, "Is not Art itself a gall? Nature is stung by God and the seed of man planted in her. The artist changes the direction of Nature and makes her grow according to his idea. . . . Genius stings Nature, and she grows according to its idea" (J, VII:10). God stings nature, and Genius stings nature: the sexual implications are clear enough. Whatever the positive connotations of this passage, the conclusion is inescapable that Thoreau, galled by what was happening in the wake of *Walden*, was in some way uneasy even about the state of his art, regarding it as possibly gall or excrement.

On August 29, with a break in the hazy, searing weather, Thoreau experienced a brief surge of resolve; he now felt more "continent" in his thought as he was at a more "respectful distance" from his "mistress," the sun. On that day he made some relatively hopeful comments associating generativity with seeds, grain, and the lecturing he projected for the autumn and winter:

> If the drought has destroyed the corn, let not all harvests fail. Have you commenced to thresh your grain? The lecturer must commence his threshing as early as August, that his fine flour may be ready for his winter customers. The fall rains will make full springs and raise his streams sufficiently to grind his grist. We shall hear the sound of his flail all the fall, early and late. It is made of tougher material than hickory, and tied together with resolution stronger than an eel-skin. (J, VI:486–87)

He had complained less than a year earlier, when he had felt the renewed stirrings of a desire for social recognition, that he had not been given sufficient opportunities to lecture. Now, in Harding's words, Thoreau "decided to capitalize on the fame of *Walden*: he decided to offer himself as a lecturer on a nationwide scale and try to arrange a tour through the Midwest where Emerson was regularly so successful."[28] Samuel Worcester Rowse's crayon portrait of late summer 1854 shows Thoreau in a very refined light.[29] But despite his excitement at the coming of fall—on September 8 he speaks of his "autumnal madness" while gathering grapes, his anticipation of the "ripening year," and on the eleventh he dares to speculate that he is beginning to "throw off" his "summer idleness" (J, VII:27, 34) —the prospect of lecturing, particularly as a way to cash in on *Walden*'s relative success, provoked ambivalence and doubt. On September 19, the same day he accepted an invitation to lecture, he writes,

> Thinking this afternoon of the prospect of my writing lectures and going abroad to read them the next winter, I realized how incomparably great the advantages of obscurity and poverty which I have enjoyed so long (and may still perhaps enjoy). I thought with what more than princely, with what poetical, leisure I had spent my years hitherto, without care or engagement, fancy-free. I have given myself up to nature; I have lived so many springs and summers and autumns and winters as if I had nothing else to do but *live* them, and imbibe whatever nutriment they had for me. . . . I could have afforded to spend a whole fall observing the changing tints of the foliage. Ah, how I have thriven on solitude and poverty! I cannot overstate this advantage. I do not see how I could have enjoyed it, if the public had been expecting as much of me as there is danger now that they will. If I go abroad lecturing, how shall I ever recover the lost winter?

He then adds, "It has been my vacation, my season of growth and expansion, a prolonged youth" (J, VII:46). Lecturing, then, posed a threat, a "danger," to the very life structure and sense of identity that had been instrumental to his "season of growth and expansion" in the preceding years; stepping back from the perception that he is fully ripe—for if he was already ripe, what was there to look forward to?—he preferred now to see the pre-*Walden* period as one of "prolonged youth" and anticipated in his own life "the Indian summer that is to come" (J, VII:47). In lecturing, in seeking to meet the public's expectations, he feared that he might lose his chances for a creative, autonomous, and pure autumn.

Two days after articulating these reservations about lecturing, he confides in his journal:

> I sometimes seem to myself to owe all my little success, all for which men commend me, to my vices. I am perhaps more willful than others and make enormous sacrifices, even of others' happiness, it may be, to gain my ends. It would seem even as if nothing good could be accomplished without some vice to aid in it. (J, VII:48)

The connections between lecturing, success, and vice were strong and disquieting for him. That he pondered following a lecture circuit similar to Emerson's—thus putting himself again in indirect competition with a former mentor and father figure, as the publication of *Walden* had already done—may well have intensified a guilt and anxiety already insistent at the time. In a letter written the same day, in which he informs Blake of his intention to "go a-lecturing to Plymouth . . . and to Philadelphia in November, and thereafter to the West, *if they shall want me*," he voices his regret that he did not take the opportunity to go on an excursion with Blake and Theo Brown (a Worcester tailor, friend of Blake, and another Thoreau devotee), "for in that case I should have been able to enter into it with that infinite margin to my views, —spotless of all engagements—which I think so necessary" (C, 339). Clearly, he was feeling anything but "spotless" these days, and his next letter to Blake in early October, in which he notes the visit of "a young English author"—Thomas Cholmondeley (who had come to Concord to see Emerson but who "immediately took to Thoreau and lost all interest in Emerson")[30]—"who asks me to teach him *botany*," is written "in haste"; presumably he is harried by the new demands made by celebrity. On October 8 he would give a lecture entitled "Night and Moonlight" in Plymouth, possibly with the intention of recapturing the "night wanderer" self-image that had been so important to him in the early 1850s. It is only by moonlight, he remarks on September 22, that "all is simple" and that "we are enabled to erect ourselves. . . . We are no longer distracted" (J, VII: 51). But that self-image remained only fleetingly accessible. On November 20 he went to Philadelphia to lecture, and in a letter of the same day he announced his plans to lecture in Hamilton, Canada, and his intention to lecture in Akron, Ohio, as part of his Midwest itinerary (C, 352). Only later, in the absence of solid invitations, would the plan for a Midwest journey be scrapped[31]—at least partially to his relief, no doubt, as it would have dramatized how far he had come, or how much he had strayed, from being primarily a "traveller in Concord." Thoreau met with varying degrees of success in his lecturing,[32] probably in some respects not *wanting* to be well received and even inviting tepid or negative responses. The following February he would note,

> Many will complain of my lectures that they are transcendental. "Can't understand them." "Would you have us return to the savage state?" etc., etc. . . . But the fact is, the earnest lecturer can speak only to his like, and the adapting of himself to his audience is a mere compliment which he pays them. If you wish to know how I think, you must endeavor to put yourself in my place. If you wish me to speak as if I were you, that is another affair. (J, VII: 197)

Certainly his style of delivering lectures was usually less than riveting.[33] But invitations continued to be extended to him throughout the fall and early winter, when he lectured in Providence, New Bedford (where he first met Ricketson), Nantucket, and Worcester.[34] Though he could not have foreseen it in the breathlessly busy days of the previous autumn, his final lecture of 1855 would be delivered in Concord on February 14.

The lecture Thoreau gave at Providence on December 6, "What Shall

It Profit?" (which he would retitle "Higher Laws" soon before his death and which would posthumously be called "Life without Principle"),[35] served several important, if only transiently effective, psychic functions for Thoreau. Apart from the evidence it offered that he could still "produce" something relatively new, it furnished him some reconnection with the Walden persona and enabled him to condemn—and thus dissociate himself from—those very tendencies that seemed to be gaining the upper hand in his life. He attacks the meretriciousness, pretentiousness, pettiness, and triviality of his society, its business, its "infinite bustle," its gold digging, its post offices, its newspapers. In a sense, all of America was to him one big Gold Rush. Partly these were counterattacks, a means of circling the wagons and bringing reinforcements against the onslaughts of those, in Concord and out, who would vilify his presentation of them in *Walden*. They were also a ringing defense against those same townspeople who were wont to accuse him of being a loafer for sauntering "in the woods for love of them half of each day"; if, he comments acidly, a man were to devote himself daily to speculation, "shearing off those woods and making earth bald before her time," that man would be "esteemed an industrious and enterprising citizen" (RP, 157). By defining success in other than conventional, competitive terms, he was seeking to disavow any desire for it and thus reduce guilt. "You must get your living by loving," he says. And as was so often the case in his lectures, this one tried to establish a Walden-like distance from the crassness and corruption of his town and modern life: "Wherever a man separates from the multitude, and goes his own way . . . there indeed is a fork in the road. . . . His solitary path across lots will turn out the *higher way* of the two" (RP, 160, 164). However, viewed in the context of this relatively busy, ambitious, and "civil" post-*Walden* period, one must question the extent to which Thoreau felt he was going his own way; in some respects he was still at the crossroads. "What Shall It Profit [a Man if He Gain the Whole World But Lose His Own Soul]?" was an urgent question for him at this time. "It is remarkable," he says, "that there are few men so well employed, so much to their minds, but that a little money or fame would commonly buy them off from their present pursuit" (RP, 159). That he was himself ambivalently drawn to the prospect of "a little money or fame" and that this prospect had distracted him from his former pursuits must have given him pause. If the "community has no bribe to tempt a wise man," then Thoreau must have wondered about the depth of his own wisdom. Indeed, notwithstanding its predominantly superior tone, there are hints of his dilemma in the lecture. "Not without a slight shudder at the danger," he confesses, "I often perceive how near I had come to admitting into my mind the details of some trivial affair, —the news of the street. . . . Shall the mind be a public arena, where the affairs of the street and the gossip of the tea-table are discussed?" (RP, 171). Attuned at this point to the news and gossip about how *Walden* was doing and how he was doing as a lecturer, he had every reason to "shudder at the danger."

The effects of the drought on autumnal vegetation provoked anxious thoughts in a Thoreau who was in the early stages of a creative drought and who feared that his own future and more decisive ripening might be thwarted. On September 25, 1854, he expresses his suspicion that "the brilliancy of the autumnal tints" depends on "the greater or less drought of the summer. If the drought has been uncommonly severe, as this year, I should think that it would so far destroy the vitality of the leaf that it would attain only to a dull, dead color in autumn, that to produce a brilliant autumn the plant should be full of sap and vigor to the last" (J, VII: 56). His "sap and vigor" in great doubt, he cannot help wondering if his "leaves" are doomed to be a "dull, dead color." On September 29 he notes the impact of the drought on oak leaves, which "have only begun to be sprinkled with bloody spots and stains" and which are "hastening to a premature decay" (J, VII:60). Even whatever brightness there was reminded him of blood, of "premature decay" before ripeness was attained, of death. In the same vein, the "clear bright-scarlet leaves of the smooth sumach" he observed on the thirtieth were "curled and drooping, hanging straight down, so as to make a funereal impression," reminding him of a "red sash and a soldier's funeral." He concludes that they "impress" him "quite as black crepe similarly arranged, the bloody plants" (J, VII:61–62). To Thoreau, who felt his own life's blood slowly dripping from him, images of impending mortality, or at least of the loss of what was most dear to him, were unavoidable, even if nature seemed in November "prepared for an infinity of springs yet" (J, VII:71). That "the river is not nearly so high as last year" (when *he* had been so "high" working on *Walden*), that "Walden went down quite rapidly about the middle of November" and was frozen over by December 21 (J, VII:78, 88), may have been taken as portentous signs by Thoreau, who was seeking to divine his own fate by observing nature.

The same day that he lectured in Providence his feelings of loss and impurity regarding his post-*Walden* life were too overwhelming to be ignored:

> After lecturing twice this winter I feel that I am in danger of cheapening myself by trying to become a successful lecturer, i.e., to interest my audiences. I am

disappointed to find that most that I am and value myself for is lost, or worse than lost, on my audience. . . . I would rather that my audience came to me than that I should go to them, and so they be sifted; i.e., I would rather write books than lectures. That is fine, this coarse. (J, VII:79)

Reading to a "promiscuous audience" (J, VII:80), he himself felt promiscuous. But the prospects for writing a book were bleak, partly because he did not have the creative reservoir he had drawn on so deeply for *Walden*, partly because he did not have the time. He had been so preoccupied preparing for lectures that the winter had come "unnoticed" to him. A recuperative walk to an ice-encrusted Walden could go only so far in restoring his ties to *Walden*; he was now, as he admits on December 8, leading "the life most lead in respect to Nature. How different from my habitual one! It is hasty, coarse, and trivial, as if you were a spindle in a factory. The other is leisurely, fine, and glorious, like a flower. In the first case you are merely getting your living; in the second you live as you go along" (J, VII:80).

The shortness of the very cold early winter days reminded Thoreau that "you must make haste to do the work of the day before it is dark" (J, VII:82), and he was increasingly feeling a sense of impatience and frustration about his inability to get on to more meaningful work with the dawn so far behind him. In a December 19 letter to Blake, in which he admits that he has been a "very bad correspondent," he struggles mightily to see the silver lining in the cloud that was hanging low over him. He concedes, "I have not yet learned to live, that I can see, and I fear that I shall not very soon," although, he claims, the "day is never so dark, nor the night even, but that the laws at least of light still prevail." Beset with an emotionally unbalancing crisis in the afternoon of his life, he speaks from experience when he says that "there is considerable danger that a man will be crazy between dinner and supper" but suggests that a man can choose to step back from the precipice: "it [being crazy] will not directly answer any good purpose that I know of, and it is just as easy to be sane." In his exhortations to Blake (who had no doubt on more than one occasion implored Thoreau to provide him with a prescription for depression), he hearkens back to the necessity and imagery of coming through the storm: "We have got to know what both life and death are, before we can begin to live after our own fashion. Let us be learning our a-b-c's as soon as possible. I never yet knew the sun to be knocked down and rolled through a mud-puddle; he comes out honor-bright from behind every storm" (C, 354). Certainly the severe storm that seemed now to be overtaking him was largely unexpected. What he found "truly monstrous"—in others and in himself—was "our cowardice and sloth" (C, 355); in this regard the Indian could provide a model of courage and grace under fire: "when an Indian is burned, his body may be broiled, it may be no more than a beefsteak. What of that? They may broil his *heart*, but they do not therefore broil his *courage*, —his principles. Be of good courage! That is the main thing" (C, 354). However, the message of stoicism and willed good cheer failed to drive away the clouds permanently; the intimation, uttered at Ricketson's, that "winter is breaking up in me" (J, VII:90) would be intermittent and short-lived. In late December he saw too much of himself in the "last Indian" of Nantucket whose picture he saw "with a basket of huckleberries in his hand" (J, VII:96); at the same time, he was prompted to consider "the sin which God would punish by the Indian war," an Indian named John Gibbs who had been pursued by Philip, and his own guilty complicity in the "Indian war" he had ambivalently waged with another John (J, VII:97). He had wished Blake—and himself—a "really *new* year" (C, 356), but for him the new year would be in many respects an increasingly disappointing and disturbing extension of the old.

On January 7, 1855, there was a thaw, and the "soft, spring-suggesting air" prompted Thoreau to remark, "Life becomes again credible to me. A certain dormant life awakes in me, and I begin to love nature again" (J, VII: 104). Perhaps it was gradually dawning on Thoreau, as the lecturing tapered off, that he would not be embarking on an extended lecture tour to the Midwest and, more fundamentally, that he was not going to be as successful—at least as a lecturer and promoter of *Walden*—as he both wished and dreaded to be. Finding a "crop of arrowheads" in the "bare sand" (J, VII:105) as the anniversary of his brother's death approached was quite possibly regarded as a promising sign of forgiveness and redemption. Observing the lichen, he is led to exclaim, "How full of life and of eyes is the damp bark! It would not be worth the while to die and leave all this life behind one" (J, VII:105). The implication is that Thoreau had more than once considered, in the wake of *Walden*, whether he was on the verge of death and even whether it might be preferable to die. But now, checking his own vital signs as he noted the "evergreen radical shoots of the St. John's-wort" (J, VII:107), he intuited that he was destined to, and preferred to, live. It once more seemed at least possible that he could backtrack to that fork in the road where he sensed he had begun to lose his way; on January 9 he comments, "Sometimes a lost man will be so beside himself that he will not have enough sense to trace back his own tracks in the snow" (J, VII:109). Part of tracing back his own tracks and getting back "home" was to recover his sense of connectedness to nature and wildness, as he had done after *A Week*'s publication. On January 12, upon hearing the "caw-ing of crows" from "their blessed eternal vacation," a Thoreau yearning to be born again into a purifying and regenerative wildness writes, "bless the Lord, O my soul! bless him for wildness, for crows that will not alight within gunshot!" (J, VII: 112–13).

The search for a renewed and renewing relation to wildness coincided with a temporary period of longer journal entries, suggesting an associa-tion between wildness and generativity. The new snow on January 20 was "like the beginning of the world" (J, VII: 123), and Thoreau had hopes that he was on the brink of another beginning. There are many references at that time to an "Indian book"; indeed, he had completed one Indian notebook and started another this very month. There is a possibility that Thoreau, so desperate for new directions after *Walden*, had hit upon an "Indian book" for his next major project,[36] a book that would reestablish his links to, and identification with, wildness and would also be another guilt-allaying, redemptive memorial to his brother, the student of Indian lore and, on some profound psychic level, the Indian comrade he wished to keep alive. Having left behind the woods of *Walden*, he could now bring to life again the more primitive woods and the "wild" men who inhabited them. Reading Wood's *New England Prospect*, he reflects, "We can per-haps imagine how the primitive wood looked from the sample still left in Maine. . . . One would judge from accounts that the woods were clearer than the primitive wood that is left, on account of Indian fires" (J, VII: 133). It was reassuring to see that the Indians had made the woods "clearer" by setting fires (given his own woodsburning experience), and the prospect of returning in spirit to that cleansed forest set fire to his imag-ination. A letter from Cholmondeley (who was entering the navy) decried the imperialism, industrialization, and decay in England (C, 364–66). Thoreau saw similar signs of decline in America: the loss of and disrespect for the wild, the moral stagnation. "The State of Maryland," he comments on January 27, "is a moral fungus. Her offense is rank; it smells to heaven" (J, VII: 151). And New England was implicated in the decay. In turning his back on America's decay (in *Cape Cod* he would speak of putting "all America behind him" [CC, 238]) and in retreating imaginatively to wild-ness, Thoreau sensed he could extricate himself from the quicksand in which he had been bogged down in previous months. As he says on Febru-ary 3, this was his "winter of skating" (J, VII: 164), an apt metaphor for one who was anxious to avoid sinking. He reports that, skating on January 31, he was "able to *connect* one part (one shore) with another in my mind, and realize what was going on upon it from end to end, —to know the whole as I ordinarily knew a few miles of it only" (J, VII: 167–68). Skating with the legs, then, corresponded to his seemingly slowly regenerating ability to glide imaginatively, to make connections and see continuity, to perceive and make things whole again. As he skates, his blue shadow on the ice suggests "that there may be something divine, something celestial, in me" (J, VII:178).

Thoreau's February reply to Cholmondeley confirms one primary reason, already suggested, why he seemed poised for recovery:

> I am from time to time congratulating myself on my *general* want of success as a lecturer—*apparent* want of success, but is it not a real triumph? I do my work clean as I go along, and they will not be likely to want me anywhere again. So there is no danger of my repeating myself and getting to a barrel of sermons which you must upset & begin again with. (C, 372)

Apparently relieved by his general lack of success as a lecturer—which enabled him to feel "clean" about his work and himself—he could yet claim "triumph" in a noncompetitive, unconventional sphere. While he could avoid competition with male figures such as Emerson, who was "off westward, enlightening the Hamiltonians & others, mingling his thunder with that of Niagara," Thoreau would pursue his "dream of a glorious *private life*" (C, 371). What he could not afford to acknowledge was that his denial of ambition and of the need for public approbation could also be stressful in that they *were* part of him; lecturing, moreover, was very visible, tangible evidence of generativity, and without it he would be forced to rely almost exclusively on questionable inner resources for that sense of fruitfulness.

Winter was often associated with purity, dormancy, and gestation. As he wanted to perceive it, this winter was another brief moratorium (for which skating itself provided something of an analogy), part of another seedtime in which he could regain control of his life, sound himself, and begin to chart a new creative course, which yet maintained continuity with the past and his ego ideal. As early as February 18, he thought he saw some of his seeds about to sprout as he anticipated spring: "We now begin to look decidedly forward and put the winter behind us. We begin to form definite plans for the approaching spring and summer" (J, VII:193). But Thoreau's seeds were unusually sparse and fragile, perhaps even defective, as this spring approached, and those few that germinated would by and large perish in the cold ground or be nipped in the bud. On February 21 he asks, "What is the peculiarity in the air that both the invalid in the chamber and the traveller on the highway say these are perfect March days?" and then he notes that the warmth is "very cheering to invalids who have weak lungs, who think they may weather it to summer now" (J, VII:203–4).

These remarks hint that, even before the spring of 1855, Thoreau may have had intimations of potential invalidism. If he thought that he was now casting off any such predisposition and would "weather it to summer," he was mistaken. In this particular instance, the pattern in which a period of involvement in civil society precipitates and is succeeded by a period of withdrawal and a burst of creative productivity would not be followed. This seedtime would be abortive. Before the spring was over, he would be stricken with an illness that would for a time make him a partial invalid.

The seasonal phenomena Thoreau selected to see and discuss frequently reflected, intentionally and unintentionally, his state of mind, and he often employed them to draw analogies with his emotional life. Moreover, these phenomena could themselves exert an influence on this man so "allied to the elements" (J, VII:186), so preternaturally in touch with the seasonal and meteorological. Not only, for instance, were languid weather and drought metaphors for creative languishing and drought, but they could also directly affect his state of mind and creativity. Thus, the weather —and its effects on nature—could influence his affect and could even be taken by him as signs or portents of, and sometimes as contrasts with, his own inner climate. The natural phenomena accompanying the long, cold winter and the late, fitful spring contributed to, as well as reflected and informed, Thoreau's emotional dis-ease in 1855. After his first mention of invalids on February 21, he says, "Now look for an early crop of arrowheads, for they will shine" (J, VII:203). Although he managed to find "half a dozen arrowheads" on March 2, by March 6 he says that the "sands are too dry and light-colored to show arrowheads so well now" (J, VII:226, 232). Neither had he been able to find new direction, inspiration, or renewed intimacy with his brother in spite of his hopes and efforts. He is "surprised," after an early spring frost, to "see that the radical johnswort leaves, which have been green all winter, are now wilted or blackened by it, and where a wood was cut off this winter on a hillside, all the rattlesnake-plantain has suffered in like manner" (J, VII:228). In early March he could not yet hear the bluebird; on the nineteenth he hears the bluebird, but sight of it still eludes him (J, VII:230, 257). Bluebird, John's-wort, arrowhead: these were a constellation of signs of reawakened generativity and connectedness to John, ornithologist and builder of bluebird boxes,[37] Indian comrade, sainted in death. And Thoreau felt deprived of them this spring. On March 8 he observes the "young trees and bushes . . . broken down by the ice after the last freshet"; on the tenth he remains unaware of "growth in any plant yet" (J, VII:234, 238), including himself, the "human plant." The river was very low for the season. The *Journal* tended to emphasize that winter was hanging on, as it was in his own life. The ice played "havoc" with the trees, making the alder limbs droop and "bending down," "holding in," the limbs of the willow catkins (J, VII:259). Such observations, along with those related to the cutting down of woods during the winter, were common at this time, suggesting some form of death-castration anxiety and foreshadowing the illness that would attack *his* lower limbs this spring. As March neared its end, Thoreau could not help reflecting that "these cold and blustering days" were "the worst to bear in the year, —partly because they disappoint expectation." He looked

> almost in vain for some kind of life stirring. The warmest springs hardly allow me the glimpse of a frog's heel . . . and I think I am lucky if I see one winter-defying hawk or a hardy duck. . . . As for the singing of birds, —the few that have come to us, —it is too cold for them to sing and for me to hear. The bluebird's warble comes feeble and frozen to my ear. (J, VII:274)

There is a subtly ominous tone, a sense of impending danger, in many of the entries of this period, and it is likely that Thoreau was very much "sympathizing" with weather and nature. His own expectations for a creative surge were disappointed, he looked in vain for life stirring within him, and the little "singing" that he did was "feeble and frozen." Desperate to reestablish some connection with his ideal, most creative self (though perhaps also inadvertently expressing suicidal inclinations), he feels an "impulse" on March 29 to "jump into the half-melted" Walden Pond (J, VII: 275). Betraying his own anxieties about whether he remained vital, he comments on March 30 that a man "must have a great deal of life in him to draw upon, who can pick up a subsistence in November and March" (J, VII:276). In past crises he had frequently been able to draw on a "superfluity of life"; now he had reason to wonder whether there was anything substantial left.

One further foreshadowing of his imminent illness may be found in a journal entry of March 10:

> Miss Minott says that Dr. Spring told her that when the sap began to come up into the trees, i.e. about the middle of February (she says), then the diseases of the human body come out. The idea is that man's body sympathizes with the rest of nature, and his pent-up humors burst forth like the sap from wounded trees. This with the mass may be that languor or other weakness commonly called spring feelings. (J, VII:239)

In one sense, the imagery of "pent-up humors" bursting forth (which calls to mind Whitman's "From Pent-up Aching Rivers" in "Children of Adam") suggests a link between sap and semen; that is, sap is viewed by

Thoreau as a sticky, precious fluid associated with productivity, a vital force that cannot be squandered or lost without an accompanying "languor," "weakness," or sense of stagnation. Himself a "wounded tree" who feared he was losing or wasting whatever "sap" he had, he was a prime candidate for "languor or other weakness." In another sense, the sap may be taken in this passage as the "diseases of the body" (and sexuality was itself in some respect a disease, or source of dis-ease, for Thoreau) which, when released, leave the person weak, if ultimately purged. In either sense, the passage conveys Thoreau's own concern about the depletion of sap, consequent exhaustion, and vulnerability to "spring feelings."

Indeed, coinciding with spring's arrival, Thoreau succumbed to a mysterious, lingering illness that drained and sapped his strength and energy, most particularly and suggestively in his legs. On June 27 he writes to Blake:

> I have been sick and good for nothing but to lie on my back and wait for something to turn up, for two or three months. This has *compelled* me to postpone several things. . . . I should feel a little less ashamed if I could give any name to my disorder, but I cannot, and our doctor cannot help me to it, and I will not take the name of any disease in vain. However, there is one consolation in being sick, and that is the possibility that you may recover to a higher state than you were ever in before. I expected in the winter to be deep in the woods of Maine in my canoe long before this, but I am so far from that that I can only take a languid walk in Concord streets. (C, 376)

The vagueness of the time of onset, as reported by Thoreau, suggests that the illness came upon him gradually in the period between late March and late April.

It is probable that the disease had some organic component—perhaps, for instance, some indeterminate and stubborn virus or even, as Howarth speculates, a "mild form of tuberculosis."[38] That the weather was especially capricious and extreme in April—with frosts, cold snow, sudden oppressive warmth, and then snow again as late as April 29—and that Thoreau was putting on and taking off his gloves and greatcoat throughout the month suggest circumstances likely to put stressful adaptive demands on the body and its immune system, thus making it less resistant to illness or triggering a latent condition. And, of course, whatever the nature of his malady, the infirmity could not have failed to arouse and compound psychological dis-ease. It must have been uncomfortable, to say the least, to have such a nonspecific, undiagnosed ailment. The man who so prided himself on his stoicism may have been embarrassed, imagining himself open to suspicions that he was a hypochondriac. The man who claimed he was so independent was now put in the awkward position of being partially dependent on the care of others. The illness threatened his sense of identity, his way of life, and his energy. Moreover, not knowing exactly what was plaguing him, he may, understandably, have been scared. His body was a stranger to him, out of his control. Perhaps, he may have thought, the illness was potentially life-threatening, or at least the harbinger of a fatal disorder. In any case, it cast doubt on his longevity and heightened his sense of mortality.

Whatever the organic component, it is highly likely that this strange, undiagnosed malady had a significant psychosomatic component. There can be little doubt that Thoreau was, for various reasons, under stress and distressed; that his psychological state played an important role in making him more susceptible to, predisposing him to, and quite possibly inducing illness and bodily symptoms; that the illness was itself in some ways symptomatic of, and a manifestation of, his deep malaise and sense of *dis*order at this time, in large part bred by a particularly virulent strain of midlife crisis for which the work on *Walden* had to some degree inoculated him but from which he had lost his immunity after the book was completed and published; that the physical and emotional had a synergistic relationship and that physical recovery was linked to emotional recovery.

Thoreau could hardly have been blind to the possible link between mind and body in matters of illness. After all, he had come close to dying of "sympathetic" lockjaw after his brother's death, and numerous journal entries suggest an inextricable connection between mind and body.[39] It will be recalled, for example, that he had written in 1851 that "Life is a warfare, a struggle, and the diseases of the body answer to the troubles and defeats of the spirit. Man begins by quarrelling with the animal in him, and the result is immediate disease" (J, II:449–50). "What is called genius," he had observed in 1852, "is the abundance of life or health" (J, IV:218). In 1853 he had noted that, "as is the sun to the vegetable, so is virtue to the bodily health" (J, V:19). He had reported having a "slight, dry headache" as a result of too much scientific observation in 1853 (J, V:45). Particularly striking and prophetic had been his comment that "Miasma and infection are from within, not without. The invalid . . . does not love Nature or his life, and so sickens and dies, and no doctor can cure him. . . . Some men think that they are not well in spring, or summer, or autumn, or winter; it is only because they are not *well in* them" (J, V:394–95). In the April before *Walden*'s publication he had written, "A little relaxation in your exertion, a little idleness, will let in sickness and death into your own body. . . . The well have no time to be sick. Events, circumstances, etc., have their origin in ourselves" (J, VI:226). "Health is a sound relation to nature," he proposed a few months later. And, of course, there had been the discussion of "spring feelings" soon before he fell victim to illness. While he could not have been fully conscious of all the psychological and "spiritual" factors contributing to his ill health, it is clear that he had identified previously many of the emotional-spiritual conditions that contributed to his own physical breakdown in 1855: the quarrel between the animal and spiritual; the sense of being abandoned by genius and creative energy; the inability to live fully and productively in the present; the sense of compromised virtue; the drift toward science and the relative loss of "sympathy" with nature; the feeling and fear of being mired in stagnation.

Also revealing are some comments he made about legs, that part of the body most severely affected by the malady. In May of 1854 he wrote: "All that a man has to say or do that can possibly concern mankind, is in some shape or other to tell the story of his love, —to sing; and, if he is fortunate and keeps alive, he will be forever in love. This alone is to be alive to the extremities" (J, VI:237). The passage suggests that, unable by 1855 adequately to "tell the story of his love," his own sense of aliveness, as experienced especially in his lower extremities, was severely threatened. In late 1856, struggling to overcome his illness, he would seek to perceive his legs as fertilizing, a sign that the rest of him was also coming back to life: "We push through the light dust, throwing it before our legs as a husband man grain which he is sowing" (J, IX:196). Certainly, his legs—with which he had sauntered around Concord and defined himself as a "traveller in Concord" (and other variations such as "night-wanderer")—were an important part of, and symbol of, his ego ideal. It is thus more understandable why his anxieties about identity and generativity would be expressed by a loss of energy in, and full control over, his legs. And it must be noted that another "extremity," his writing hand, had, as the primary medium through which to express his creative aliveness, already shown unmistakable signs of languor prior to the lethargy in his legs.

The enigmatic malady of uncertain diagnosis and prognosis that plagued Thoreau for over two years may be seen as the culminating manifestation of all those anxieties, guilt feelings, and concerns that increasingly beset him in the wake of *Walden*'s completion and publication. Even if, for instance, it now appeared that he would not be a widely renowned and prosperous lecturer, he had certainly *tried* to strike while the iron of *Walden* was hot, and in any case *Walden* itself was a relative success, having sold by this time a large proportion of its first-print run of 2,000. In September 1855 there would be less than 260 unsold copies, a far cry from *A Week*'s disastrous commercial history.[40] Indeed, on the basis of *Walden*'s decent sales, he proposed on April 30, 1855, to Ticknor and Fields that *A Week* be republished (C, 375), and he was negotiating for the publication of parts of *Cape Cod*.[41] However modest in absolute terms *Walden*'s success was, it aroused guilt feelings, partly oedipally rooted, associated not only with surpassing his father but also with surviving his brother, and such intense feelings can lead to physical breakdown, whether as a form of self-punishment or as a way to deny, "avoid," or "negate" success.[42] It is crucial to point out that, the question of objective or perceived success aside, Thoreau had at least felt, during this period, a flaring-up of ambition and conventional competitive initiative that would have been sufficient in itself to activate severe guilt. His aspirations and achievements served to highlight the degree to which he wanted, or had wanted, to surpass or defeat both brother and father—and to which he was competing with such father surrogates as Emerson. Insofar as *Walden* was an assertion of maturity and ripening, a bid for "seniority," it may also have exacerbated oedipal fears. If one of his contemplated projects had been a book on the Indians (which would have been another indirect tribute and memorial to his brother, in part an attempt to reestablish solidarity and intimacy with him, but which could also be seen as an exploitation of John), and if he had hoped to be "deep in the woods of Maine" in the summer of 1855, Thoreau discovered—and his illness told him—that he was too conflicted and guilt-ridden to throw himself into an ambitious "Indian book" at this time; it would have provoked painful, ambivalent feelings.

But Thoreau was caught in a bind, for—however much he may not have wanted to admit it—he did have ambitions, the desire to be "great" and to be considered so. He had to hide from himself the pent-up anger of having his ambitions foiled. Thus, to the considerable degree that he was under the necessity to deny or repress any vaulting ambition, any visions of worldly glory, he was trapped in an even more stressful and untenable psychological bind, which made him even more susceptible to a lingering illness. On the one hand, being sick protected him from his ambitions; on the other hand, it made him even more distressed and angry because he could not make substantial progress toward realizing ambition or pursuing those ambitious projects he had contemplated. In more general terms, suppressed or repressed rage and fear, and feelings of "entrapment" and "immobilization," can lead to and exacerbate sickness or somatic symptoms.[43] Thoreau was one who tended to keep such feelings bottled up. Certainly there had been hints that he had felt somewhat trapped in the post-Walden period, and he was close to at least partial creative immobilization even before his symptoms hampered his mobility.

With *Walden*'s completion and publication, moreover, Thoreau had gone into a kind of mourning. After losing his close experiential and written connections with the Walden experience and *Walden,* after having to let go of the book that had so eloquently incorporated his ego ideal and most inclusive vision, Thoreau feared that he had lost a treasured part of himself and that he and his life would never be the same. The loss of vitality in his legs, which had been such a cherished and integral part of his "saunterer" identity—they had once been described as "springy and unweariable" (J, III:96)—may be perceived as a bodily expression and symbolization of his grief, of the death of a crucial part of himself and his life, of his loss of control. The times seemed out of joint, and his knees were now failing him. With the abrupt break in continuity precipitated and signified by the loss of the book,[44] Thoreau was plunged again into identity crisis; the illness may have been one way of coping with the confusion, of shielding himself from having to make difficult identity decisions, and of manifesting a profound bereavement at the apparent death of his pure, free, brave, and youthful ideal self, who represented the most satisfying, productive parts of his life.[45]

If the illness was in part related to his reactivated identity crisis, it was also very much associated with the generativity crisis so evident as he left *Walden* behind. Beyond depriving Thoreau of the firm grasp on the Walden experience and identity that had been such a catalyst—even precondition—to his creativity, the loss of *Walden* provoked very real fears of stagnation, fears that had been in evidence in the months before illness struck. After having put so much of himself into *Walden,* was there any more left? Did he have anything more of comparable or superior value to say? Could anything else ever measure up to *Walden?* Where—creatively—could he go from here? Were his plans for future projects so hopelessly ambitious and monumental that he could not even get started on them? Were the scope and scale of contemplated tasks such that he was left with little short-term direction? Thoreau had no doubt posed some of these questions in 1854 and early 1855, and he had found no definitive or comforting answers. He had labored with enormous energy and given birth to a very special "baby" in *Walden,* and it was proof of his fertility. But in the aftermath of the book, he had experienced a kind of postpartum depression (and depression itself can lead to illness) and anxieties about whether his fertility could be sustained. Thoreau's writing had always served to give him *some* measure of generative fulfillment; it enabled him to feel that he was a "maker," a "begetter" of words, images, and ideas. But in order to sustain this fragile and compensatory generativity, in the absense of actual children and other conventional assurances of generativity, Thoreau had to keep producing, keep writing. And his standards of productivity and artistry were very high. Thus, with the empty-nest syndrome that accompanied *Walden*'s departure, with little assurance of the ability to set out single-mindedly in other creative directions, with some sense of weariness after the monumental effort necessitated by *Walden*, he was persistently haunted by the dread of barrenness, sterility, stagnation. Possibly his letter to Ticknor and Fields of April 30 inquiring whether it might be time to republish *A Week* (C, 375) reveals in part Thoreau's need for a revalidation of his generativity at this time, even as it also gives evidence that some residue of ambition remained. According to Erikson, individuals who have not been able to sustain a consistent sense of generativity, who feel stagnant, "often begin to indulge themselves as if they were their own—or one another's—one and only child, and where conditions favor it, early invalidism, physical and psychological, becomes the vehicle of self-concern."[46] Thus the psychosomatic component of his post-*Walden* infirmity may be construed partially as an acute manifestation of his sense of stagnation and of a neediness to which he could not readily own up. It may also be hypothesized that the illness represented a way to protect himself from feelings of stagnation, giving him a legitimate reason for not being productive and preventing him from learning how unproductive he might be if he were well.

The possibility cannot be discounted that, on some level, the illness was an expression of a wish to die, thus not only appeasing guilt but also preempting the possibility of a life of quiet desperation and sterility and relieving himself permanently of the seemingly relentless, merciless pressures to be generative, to prove himself over and over again. Elliot Jaques, in "Death and the Mid-Life Crisis," discussed the lives of artists and noted how many of them seem to have been plagued by an unanticipated "crisis in their creative work in their middle and late thirties."[47] In one form of this crisis, the "artist may burn out creatively or literally die." Quite suggestively, "the age of 37 kept coming up as a prominent death line among artistic and highly industrious people";[48] Thoreau was precisely thirty-seven in the year of *Walden*'s publication, the crisis precipitated by it, and the onset of his illness. There appears at least to have been the possibility that he might not have survived, either creatively or literally. It is testimony to Thoreau's strengths, however, that he did hang on, that he dug down deep to tap inner resources, and that he and his art did survive this crisis (even if there are varying critical judgments as to how well, especially compared to *Walden*, his art survived).[49] He and his creativity would be both further weathered and further seasoned by this tempest; he would not pass through it unchanged. The ailment, which in some sense threatened and symbolized death and which may have been a precursor of the severe

health problems and fatal illness that would later beset him, also eventually forced him to make subtle shifts in, and further elaborations on, his
adaptive styles; to modify his perspectives on life and death; and to consider anew what was "home" for him and proceed with the homeward
odyssey that becomes increasingly urgent in middle adulthood.[50] His
body's messages must have been frightening to him, but—if he listened
carefully enough—the body was also telling him something constructive.

His growing involvement in relatively objective, scientific observation
was probably especially troubling to him at this time. On April 6, 1855, he
reports having skinned and stuffed a duck (J, VII:291), and he later took
the brain out of the duck and studied it. Such activities suggest a certain
cold-blooded, clinical attitude that had formerly been uncharacteristic of,
and uncomfortable to, Thoreau. Although he may have seen his scientific
investigations as something of a new departure or at least a change of pace,
he was, as has previously been indicated, anxious about them. Aside from
the questions they provoked regarding whether he had been deserted by
the Muse and whether nature could provide him with sufficiently energizing and legitimate tropes and insights into the human condition, there was
another factor. As has been briefly touched upon, to the extent that he was
studying nature in order to find correspondences with and ultimately chart
the human seasons, he was taking on a project of such immense magnitude
and scope as to be frustrating and intimidating. Certainly in the short run it
would be difficult, in seeking to assimilate the multitude of natural facts,[51]
to see the forest for the trees; and there was hardly a guarantee that in the
long run he would be able successfully to complete the task. In some respects Thoreau may be said to have suffered from what may be called a
tour de force syndrome. *A Week* and then *Walden* were tours de force that
it was not easy to conceive of topping, yet he was apparently bent on contemplating such projects as a book on Indians, a book of Concord, or a
Kalendar that would also have to be tours de force, requiring incredible
devotion to a long-range perspective that defers many quick rewards.
Though such grandiose projects may be admirable, they may also lead to
serious creative blockages. Thoreau's penchant for the monumental (partially symptomatic of the intensity of the generative urge)[52] was usually
leavened by the short-term satisfactions provided by the *Journal,* from
which he could build shorter essays and lectures that might even become
part of larger, more magnificent structures. But even these short-run rewards were not often forthcoming during this period, in part quite possibly *because* he saw himself as having undertaken such a gargantuan project in assimilating nature that it was problematic and overwhelming even
to embark on it with any confidence and fluidity. And even when the *Jour-*

nal did show some spontaneity and inspiration (a rare occurrence these days), there was still perceived to be a yawning chasm between these fragments and their incorporation into a grand design. Thus, to the degree that Thoreau came to scientific study preoccupied with intimidating long-term intentions, he got caught up in a self-defeating, self-blocking process from which, for a time, it was difficult to extricate himself.

On April 12, 1855, Thoreau looked over Walden Pond with his spyglass, but could "see no living thing," presumably either without or within. There was "generally" no "*obvious* greening as yet." The sight of a hunter firing into the bushes (which strikes one as reminiscent of a scene from *The Heart of Darkness*) was another foreboding sign (J, VII:302, 303). Observing that the hazel catkins "know when to trust themselves to the weather" (J, VII:305), he implies that perhaps he has relied too heavily on good weather to raise his spirits. Certainly his own trust in the weather had been weakened this season, not only because it was so variable, harsh, and health-endangering but also because, to the extent there *was* recognizable progress toward spring, he could not see corresponding growth in himself. Thus sudden warm days on April 16 and 17 evoke an ambivalent response; such a day "takes off some birds and adds others. It is a crisis in their career. . . . So the pleasanter weather seems not an unmixed benefit" (J, VII:319). In one sense, these remarks suggest that the "warmth" provided by *Walden* had led not only to gains but also to unforeseeable losses, leading to an acute crisis in *his* career. In another sense, the warm days served to highlight Thoreau's own lack of warmth, his inability to thaw. He was out of sync with the season, and the more consistently warm and vibrant the season became, the more dramatic would be the contrast between himself and the spring, a lush, green epoch that reminded one of nature's immortality and recuperative powers and that usually could be counted on to inspire and energize him. Spring was blooming and blossoming, born again, but he was not. Indeed, it is possible that the coming of the spring, as it contrasted with his own depressed state, was itself one reason Thoreau fell ill at this particular time. He sensed that he could no longer participate in the circularity or immortality of nature; his life, it often seemed to him, was lamentably linear and ebbing, on a downward slope toward attrition, extinction, annihilation. Viewed in this light, it is no accident that suicides are so common in the spring.

For the next four months, from May through August, a physically weak and frequently downcast Thoreau made only relatively sparse, short entries in his journal. Sometimes, as in early May, he did not even write full sentences. The robin, he reflects on May 4, was "better acquainted with the springs of the day" than he was (J, VII:354). He did begin to show an increased interest in birds' nests and eggs, although his entries on these subjects were mostly matter-of-fact. Even in his darkest hours, Thoreau had some instinct for self-preservation drawing him to those phenomena that could ally him at least indirectly with generativity. Birds he associated in part with his brother; nests were a form of nurturance; eggs were an obvious symbol of fertility and new life. By studying them, he could seek to reassert closeness to his brother and throw out a lifeline connecting him to the generativity of birds and nature. By caring for and protecting birds, nests, and eggs, he could begin to believe, however skeptically, that he was a nurturer. But any such reassurances were fleeting. He would, however, sometimes go to great, even dangerous lengths: in May, he

> found a screech owl sitting on its eggs and reached in and stroked it repeatedly, the owl showing no resistance. When he returned for later visits, the owl flew off at the sound of his approach, which gave him the opportunity to examine the eggs and young. The babies soon became so tame that he could handle them without their protesting. Although his friend Minott warned him that he knew of a man losing his eyes from an owl's attack, Thoreau was not in the least deterred.[53]

In early June, it was "very dry indeed, and the grass is suffering. Some springs commonly full at this season are dried up" (J, VII:401). The same, he realized, could be said of his own dehydrated creative spring. One especially poignant incident, on June 2, involved a cecropia moth he observed coming out of its cocoon, "revealing some new beauty every fifteen minutes" (J, VII:402). Acting as the scientist but with, it appears, an ulterior motive, he gave the moth ether and "so saved it in a perfect state" (J, VII: 402). If one of *Walden*'s great symbols had been that of metamorphosis, of a "strong and beautiful bug" enjoying its "perfect summer life at last," Thoreau felt impelled to kill and preserve that metamorphosed moth in a "perfect state" (suspended in time like Keats's Grecian urn) as a means of recapitulating and encapsulating *Walden*'s myth, thus achieving a symbolic if only momentary stay against the myth-dispelling imperfections of the post-*Walden* experience. The strong winds of June 10 seemed to dramatize for him the fragility, uncontrollability, and unpredictability of life and generativity: "I do not remember such violent and incessant gusts at this season. Many eggs, if not young, must have shaken out of birds' nests, for I hear of some fallen. It is almost impossible to hear birds—or to keep your hat on" (J, VII:413). During June, he spent much time traveling with Channing, who was perhaps welcome as one who could watch out for him and his health. But at this nadir of his life, he was feeling a piercing loneliness for which even nature could not compensate. On June 11 he laments, "What if we feel a yearning to which no breast answers? I walk alone. My heart is full. Feelings impede the current of my thoughts. I knock on the earth for my friend. I expect to meet him at every turn; but no friend appears, and perhaps none is dreaming of me. . . . I depart with my secret untold" (J, VII:416–17). With imagination having failed him, with only a flimsy relation to nature, with a suspicion that time was running out on him, Thoreau was unusually susceptible to depression about lack of close friends. That this period was a very low point is suggested by an insertion he makes just after mourning his unfound friend: "Now (September 16, '55), after four or five months of invalidity and worthlessness, I begin to feel some stirrings of life in me" (J, VII:417). The implication is that he found the "friend" passage particularly morose (and perhaps excessively confessional) and felt compelled to assert that his "invalidity and worthlessness" were temporary conditions. In any event, his observation of birds on June 12 appears also to have been a reflection on his own "feeble" and "anxious" self: "Young red-wings now begin to fly feebly amid the button-bushes, and the old ones chatter their anxiety" (J, VII:418).

On June 27 he reported to Blake that he had been "sick and good for nothing but to lie on my back and wait for something to turn up, for two or three months" and announced that he had been "peripathetic" but intended to go to Cape Cod "simply for the medicine of it" (C, 376). Thoreau had often used trips to cure himself of stagnation, and this one was no exception. He planned on an Independence Day departure—possibly wishing to make a connection between this journey in search of restoration and the tenth anniversary of his move to Walden Pond. Perhaps this helps explain why he was so upset when he learned that the boat for Provincetown would not leave until the next day (J, VII:431–32). Indeed, he does refer to Walden at Cape Cod, remarking at one point that the "sea, like Walden, is greenish within half a mile of shore, then blue" (J, VII:438). In a July 14 letter to Blake he remarks, "Methinks I am beginning to be better" (C, 378). But the weak recovery he was making (based on the stimulant of the trip and his writing associated with it) was only an interlude. One passage from "The Beach Again," part of which he submitted for publication in August 1855 (C, 379) and which contains more ruminations on wreckage wrought by the sea, appears to embody his lingering state of mind. Upon finding a bottle of wet sand, still containing some red ale, he pours out its contents:

> as I poured it slowly out on to the sand, it seemed to me that man himself was like a half-emptied bottle of pale ale, which Time had drunk so far, yet stop-

pled tight for a while, and drifting about in the ocean of circumstances, but destined erelong to mingle with the surrounding waves, or be spilled amid the sands of a distant shore. (CC, 117)

Thoreau was inclined to see himself, and the hourglass of his life, as half empty rather than half full; he was drifting, out of control, toward death or the loss of whatever vitality he still harbored within. Alcott, who had seen him on July 4, just before he had embarked for the Cape, had observed in his journal that his friend acted "shiftless."[54] If Thoreau knew of Emerson's letter of July 21, 1855, to Whitman, "greeting" him at the "beginning of a great career," he might well have felt even more anxiety and anger about Emerson's desertion of him and his own lack of productivity. His failure to be Emerson's "American Scholar" was again underscored. Toward the end of July, throughout August, and into September, his journal entries dwindled even further. The first frost of the year came early, appropriately and ominously on August 31, the sixteenth anniversary of the beginning of the river trip with his brother.

In mid-September, after scaring off a hen hawk and noting he has not yet seen a fringed gentian, Thoreau says, "It costs so much to publish, would it not be better for the author to put his manuscripts in a safe?" (J, VII:455). While the economic costs may have been foremost in his mind here, he clearly had reason to ruminate over the other costs. The publication of *Walden* had taken quite a toll on him. Though on the twenty-sixth he began to "feel the stirrings of life" in him, only ten days later he writes to Blake, "I do not see how strength is to be got into my legs again. These months of feebleness have yielded few, if any, thoughts. . . . I hope that the harvest is to come" (C, 383). While he claims that he has passed these months not "without serenity, such as our sluggish Musketaquid suggests" (C, 383), there is every reason to believe that here Thoreau's deeply rooted stoicism and propensity for denying or minimizing distress were asserting themselves. Perhaps, too, the remark reflects a somewhat more hopeful attitude toward the future, even if it distorts or glosses over the recent past. On that same day, he went up the Assabet to collect fuel, often a therapeutic activity for him this fall, and observed in his journal,

> It grieves me to see how rapidly some great trees which have fallen or been felled waste away when left on the ground. There was the large oak by the Assabet, which I remember to have been struck by lightning, and afterward blown over, being dead. It used to lie with its top down-hill and partly in the water and its butt far up. Now there is no trace of its limbs, and the very core of its trunk is the only solid part. (J, VII:462)

Thoreau's "grief" about the loss of strength in his limbs and a more general sense of bereavement are probably reflected here as well, although there is some indication of hope in the survival of the trunk's core.

By the autumn and winter of 1855–56 Thoreau did seem to be recuperating, both physically and spiritually. To be sure, the recovery was halting and limited; there were lapses and relapses. The first really encouraging signs can be detected around the time of his trip to New Bedford to visit Ricketson in late September. On September 27 he wrote to Ricketson, "Methinks I am regaining my health, but I would like to know first what it was that ailed me" (C, 385). Ordinarily, Thoreau could be expected to be put off by someone like Ricketson who was so preoccupied by his ill health or imagined ill health. While, according to Harding, youthful accidents had left Ricketson with "weakened eyesight, an injured hip, and frequent headaches," by the time he developed a relationship with Thoreau he was a "confirmed hypochondriac."[55] Four years older than Thoreau and with a substantial private income, he "adored his children and spent much time with them," but "his marriage was not a particularly happy one and he preferred his shanty to his house."[56] In his September 23 letter to Thoreau, after a visit to Concord, he discloses much about himself:

> I regret exceedingly that I was so interrupted in my enjoyment while at Concord by my "aches and pains." My head troubled me until I had got within about 20 miles of home, when the pain passed off and my spirits began to revive. I hope that your walks, &c, with me will not harm you and that you will soon regain your usual health and strength, which I trust the cooler weather will favor; would advise you not to doctor, but just use your own good sense. I should have insisted more on your coming on with me had I not felt so ill and in actual pain the day I left—but I want you to come before the weather gets uncomfortably cool. I feel much your debtor, for through you and your Walden I have found my hopes and strength in those matters which I had before found none to sympathize with. (C, 382)

Thoreau would not always be patient with the earnest, admiring, and obviously needy Ricketson, but at this particular time they seemed to need each other. They were, for one thing, a community of sufferers; Ricketson was not ashamed to discuss his ills, and Thoreau too was quite preoccupied with his ailments, even if he did not dwell on them as Ricketson did. It was at this point comforting for Thoreau to have someone as a friend who could express sympathy with his poor health and even provide nurturing and supportive suggestions for recovery without putting him on the defensive or questioning his ego ideal. Surely Ricketson would not be one to accuse him, or suspect him, of being a hypochondriac. At the same time, seeing how dragged down Ricketson was by his almost constant health complaints, he was probably spurred to differentiate himself from his friend: *he* would not become the chronic complainer and partial invalid that Ricketson was. In a letter of December 4 Ricketson would fret about his various infirmities. He also expressed his wish that Thoreau's condition was getting better.[57] *He* would not be broken down, hobbled, brought to his knees, as the man from New Bedford was. Ricketson's persistent ailments, then, helped put his own health problems into some perspective and encouraged him to believe he was not, compared to Ricketson, as bad off as he thought himself to be. Moreover, Ricketson furnished him with confirmation of his own generativity. This man, who was himself a writer of poetry and local history, a friend of other writers, and a builder of a "shanty" in the mid-1840s not unlike Thoreau's,[58] indicated that he needed and venerated him. Indeed, in a letter of October 18, supplicant Ricketson professes his need for the sickly Thoreau to doctor him: "But I must appeal to you as a brother man, a philanthropist too. I am in need of help. I want a physician, and I send for you as the one I have the most confidence in. . . . I am in need of a physician—so Dr. Thoreau, come to my relief" (C, 394). The support of such disciples and "brother men" as Ricketson and Blake was required by Thoreau more than usually during this period, as the volume and tone of his correspondence suggests. That his friend Channing was to leave Concord in October 1855 to return to his wife and children in Dorchester probably intensified his need for companionship; as it turned out, Channing would live away from Concord until early 1858.[59] One of the few notes of irritation in his fall 1855 correspondence with Ricketson was provoked when his new disciple expressed a reluctance to come to Concord when he learned that Channing would be absent (C, 392–93).

When Thoreau returned from New Bedford on October 6, his journal entries began to get longer again, an indication that spirits and body were temporarily on the mend. On October 16 he explains to Ricketson that he will not soon be rejoining him in New Bedford because he is "planning to get seriously to work after these long months of inefficiency and idleness. I do not know whether you are haunted by any such demon which puts you on the alert to pluck the fruit of each day as it passes, and store it safely in your bin." In the same letter he pronounces himself on the road to recovery: "Methinks I am getting a little more strength into those knees of mine; and, for my part, I believe that God *does* delight in the strength of a man's legs" (C, 393). Ricketson justly concluded on December 22 that Thoreau was urgently fixed upon his work.[60] On October 16, reflecting on his "own unsatisfactory life," Thoreau speaks of his new determination, in contrast to avaricious gold diggers, to "sink a shaft down to the gold within me and work that mine"; he again aspires to be that man who "separates from the multitude and goes his own way," who takes a "fork in the road" other travelers cannot see (J, VII:491–92). The gold mining he has in mind is noncompetitive and therefore evades anxiety and guilt:

> if a digger steal away prospecting for this true gold into the unexplored solitudes, there is no danger, alas, that any will dog his steps and endeavor to supplant him. He may claim and undermine the whole valley, even the cultivated and uninhabited portions, his whole life long in peace, and no one will ever dispute his claim. (J, VII:496)

Clearly, Thoreau's chances for recovery hinged largely on his capacity to move into such a "golden age," a time of "autumnal work" as golden as the October leaves. Just as he tried to "restore to their places" the fragments of a tortoise shell (J, VII:493), so did he need to work on putting together again the pieces of his life, reconstructing—with the modifications of a fuller, more decidedly autumnal maturity—that sense of life and self which had been such a catalyst to creativity. But rebuilding his life and self, finding the right chemistry, and making a conclusive passage into autumn would be problematic. There still would be many setbacks.

7 Sugar Maple Man

*A*UTUMN 1855 brought mixed feelings for a Thoreau in precarious shape. Although the "woods about the pond" were "now a perfect October picture," there had been "no very bright tints this fall"; the young oak leaves had "withered before the frosts came, perhaps by the late drought after the wet spring" (J, VII:498). Resolved as he was, he could yet see few "bright tints" in himself. The smells of fall were "the scent of the year, passing away like a decaying fungus" (J, VII:501), a year that had seen his own powers in decay. Indeed, much of the evidence of ripeness he does see in nature is this year disquieting, sometimes even repugnant to him, contrasting as it does with his own relative lack of further ripening or fruitfulness. "I have never liked," he says on October 21,

> to have many rich fruits ripening at the same season. When Porter apples, for instance, are ripe, there are also other early apples and pears and plums and melons, etc. Nature by her bounteousness thus disgusts us with a sense of repletion—and uncleanness even. Perhaps any one of these fruits would answer as well as all together. She offers us too many good things at once. (J, VII:504)

The abundance of October could be as heartbreaking and threatening as the blossomings of April and May. Yet this autumn also presented him with new interests, images, and opportunities. His discussions with his father concerning the history of houses on Concord's Main Street suggest that Thoreau may have been considering the idea of an all-encompassing book of Concord—which the *Journal* in some sense already was.[1] On October 22, he discovers an "inward sunniness" on a cloudy day (J, VII:508). The same day it is a "new spring," and he is delighted to find that "many small shrubs which have been protected by the forest are remarkably fair and bright. They, perhaps, have not felt the drought nor been defaced by insects" (J, VII:511). If there was hope for some leaves, there was hope for him. Perhaps beginning again to see the possibility of a ripeness still to come, he comments that "there are two seasons when the leaves are in their glory, their green and perfect youth in June and this their ripe old age" (J, VII: 512).

Thoreau had, of course, identified before with trees (and other plants), had projected onto and ascribed to them human qualities (sometimes even linking them to other particularly significant figures as well as to himself), and had seen them as providing tropes for human life. These processes, not always conscious, had been important adaptive, coping modes for him in the past and were beginning to emerge as even more central and urgent during this period. For a while he had sensed that his capacity for such processes was slipping—and he would again for a time. He returned now to trees with a new passion, an even deeper need to find human and personal meaning in them. On October 23 Thoreau records his remorse at throwing stones to shake down chestnuts:

> I sympathize with the tree, yet I heaved a big stone against the trunks like a robber, —not too good to commit murder. I trust that I shall never do it again. . . . It is worse than boorish, it is criminal, to inflict an unnecessary injury on the tree that feeds or shadows us. Old trees are our parents, and our parents' parents, perchance. (J, VII:514)

Suggesting the presence of a lingering guilt with respect to his parents and father figures (a guilt that would be exacerbated as his parents aged and became ill), the passage also reveals Thoreau's desire to cast himself in the role of caretaker of trees. To the extent that he, as an older man further weathered by his illness, identifies with the tree, he seeks to proclaim his own worth and to fend off mutilation and death. In any case, it is clear that he is here "sympathizing" with nature and using it to work through his concerns.

On October 26 his desire to withdraw again to the purifying, revivifying "wild," both to restore and to grow beyond his Walden identity, is evident: "I sometimes think that I must go off to some wilderness where I can have a better opportunity to play life, —can find more suitable materials to build my house with, and enjoy the pleasure of collecting my fuel in the forest" (J, VII:519). However, he was also in the process of discovering, or rediscovering, in what he hoped was another seedtime, that the materials for rebuilding his life and feeling at home could be found without going off to live in the wilderness. The wild apple tree and its fruit became one of many symbols to him of the mature, post-*Walden* identity—at once wild and mellow—he was struggling to forge, an identity that would restore health and vitality. "To appreciate the flavor of those wild apples," he writes on October 27, "requires vigorous and healthy senses," and two days later he continues, "This natural raciness . . . which the diseased palate refuses, are the true casters and condiments. What is sour in the house a bracing walk makes sweet. Let your condiments be in the condition of your senses. Apples which the farmer neglects and leaves out as unsalable, and unpalatable to those who frequent the markets, are choicest fruit to the walker" (J, VII:521, 526–27). Such imagery of the mature but wild fruit, unappreciated by the market, could apply, he realized, to himself. In describing nature he would seek to define and reinforce a modified ego ideal appropriate to the latter phases of the life cycle, with death in mind. It is not surprising that he follows his celebration of the wild apple with what appears to be a calm reflection on the end of life:

> When the leaves fall, the whole earth is a cemetery pleasant to walk in. I love to wander and muse over them in their graves, returning to dust again. Here are no lying nor vain epitaphs. The scent of their decay is pleasant to me. I buy no lot in the cemetery which my townspeople have just *consecrated* with a poem and an auction, paying so much for a choice. *Here* is room enough for me. (J, VII:527)

Such a passage shows Thoreau trying to write out of a decidedly middle-aged emotional recognition that youthful intimations of literal immortality had to be put aside or exchanged in favor of more symbolic (though nonetheless quite "real" in their own ways) forms of immortality. But it would take some time and struggle before he could write consistently and comfortably out of such an autumnal mode and identity.

An Indian summer day on November 1 seemed further to encourage and reflect belief in an imminent recovery. "This too," he says, "is the *recovery* of the year, —as if the year, having nearly or quite accomplished its work, and abandoned all design, were in a more favorable and poetic mood, and thought rushed in to fill the vacuum" (J, VIII:3). The implication is that by acknowledging that he *has* (perhaps especially in *Walden*) completed substantial work and "by abandoning all design"—by not putting pressure on himself to produce comparable or even more formidable work, by relinquishing any schemes about how to profit from his accomplishments—he will be able to attain that relaxed, receptive frame of mind so conducive to fresh thought and creativity. Freed from stress, he could regenerate imaginatively and physically. Part of the stress had come from trying to win the approval and adulation of civilized society. The wild apple reminded him that health and serenity could be regained when he rejected even more firmly society's definitions of taste and worth:

> From my experience with wild apples I can understand that there may be a reason for a savage preferring many kinds of food which the civilized man rejects. . . . It takes a savage or wild taste to appreciate a wild apple. I remember two old maids to whose house I enjoyed carrying a purchaser to talk about buying their farm in the winter, because they offered us wild apples, though with an unnecessary apology for their wildness. (J, VIII:7)

He need make no apologies for himself, either to himself or to those who would not or could not appreciate him. He "relished" the thought of "getting [his] living" "in a simple, primitive fashion"; he realized all over again that "the fellow-man to whom you are yoked is a steer that is ever bolting right the other way" (J, VIII:7–8). On November 7, a misty day, he reports the hopeful sign that his "power of observation and contemplation is much increased," his "attention does not wander," his "world" and "life" are "simplified" (J, VIII:14). Warmed by the activity of gathering wood, and by Cholmondeley's lavish gift of forty-four Indian and other oriental books (J, VIII:29, 36)—"I send you information of this," Thoreau writes to Ricketson, "as I might of the birth of a child" (C, 403)—he believed that he had sufficient fuel for the winter, a superfluity of warmth. On December 11 he is "struck by the perfect confidence and success of nature"; the birds in winter are like flowers "created now to be in bloom," and in the snowy winter scene he sees a "crystalline, jewel-like health and soundness" (J, VIII:42–43). His "body is all sentient"; if he no longer feels exempt from death and human infirmities, he yet is able to associate himself with nature: "If any part of nature excites our pity, it is for ourselves we grieve, for there is eternal health and beauty" (J, VIII:44). Gifted, for the time being, with the ability to focus again on the health and generativity of nature, he reports to Ricketson on December 25, "My legs have grown considerably stronger, and that is all that ails me" (C, 403).

"It is one of those mornings of *creation*" (J, VIII:74), Thoreau exults on the last day of 1855, and on the first day of the new year he made one of his pilgrimages to Walden, the site and symbol of his own creative morning. But morning was never far from mourning during this period. Tracks in the snow, suggesting the fox chasing after the rabbit, prompt him to remark, "We unwittingly traverse the scenery of what tragedies! Every square rod, perchance, was the scene of a life or death struggle last night." Imagining the feelings of the rabbit and fox, one's "own feelings are fluttered proportionately" (J, VIII:79). Thoreau was engaged in his own "life or death struggle"; his feelings "fluttered" and oscillated. Recovery was persistently threatened by, and competed with, lapse and relapse. A year later, he would recall a recurring dream of youth, which, he says, "might have been named Rough and Smooth":

> All existence, all satisfaction and dissatisfaction, all event was symbolized in this way. Now I seemed to be lying and tossing, perchance, on a horrible, a fatal rough surface, which must soon, indeed, put an end to my existence, though even in the dream I knew it to be the symbol merely of my misery; and then again, suddenly, I was lying on a delicious smooth surface, as of a summer sea, as of gossamer or down or softest plush, and life was such a luxury to live. My waking experience *always* has been and is such an alternate Rough and Smooth. (J, IX:210–11)

Whatever else this dream suggests (and the sexual and oedipal connotations, the cycle of pleasure and fatal punishment, are clear enough), Thoreau's own interpretation of its application to his "waking" hours is highly instructive. This man, who was so intense of affect yet who so often prided himself on his stoicism and outward equanimity, admits here to frequent swings of mood and perception. While he had aspired to serenity and sanguinity—and while his public and literary persona frequently gave the impression that he had attained them, save for his outrage regarding the pretense and oppressiveness of his society—he was privy to much emotional fluctuation and could sometimes privately concede it. Indeed, his previous journals had been "meteorological journals of the mind," and, as he matured, he had become increasingly sensible of, and occasionally accepting of, the rising and falling of his barometer, of the seasons within seasons within seasons, emotionally speaking. As he would put it on June 6, 1857, "A year is made up of a certain series and number of sensations and thoughts which have their language in nature. Now I am ice, now I am sorrel" (J, IX:407). But Thoreau certainly was not prepared for the unusually intense emotional variability and lability, the swings between roughness and smoothness, the waxing and waning of health, the crises of identity and generativity, that plagued him after *Walden*'s completion and publication. Eighteen fifty-six would be a year of considerable emotional buffeting, in which the forces of recovery and relapse, generativity and sterility, uneasily coexisted and sometimes struggled fiercely with one another.

On January 4 Thoreau revived a "superficially frozen" pickerel at Walden, obviously hopeful that he too was only superficially frozen and was on the verge of thawing. A letter to Calvin Greene of Michigan, responding to Greene's interest in *Walden*, also reflected that hope: "As for the 'more' that is to come, I cannot speak definitely at present, but I trust that the mine—be it silver or lead—is not yet exhausted. At any rate, I shall be encouraged by the fact that you are interested in its yield" (c, 406–7). However, on January 20 he was once again in a black, self-rebuking mood:

> In my experience I have found nothing so truly impoverishing as what is called wealth, i.e. the command of greater means than you had before possessed, though comparatively few and slight still, for you thus inevitably acquire a more expensive habit of living, and even the very same necessaries and comforts cost you more than once they did. Instead of gaining, you have lost some independence, and if your income should be suddenly lessened, you would find yourself poor, though possessed of the same means which once made you rich. Within the last five years I have had the command of a little more money than in the previous five years, for I have sold some books and some lectures; yet I have not been a whit better fed or clothed or warmed or sheltered, not a whit richer, except that I have been less concerned about my living, but perhaps my life has been the less serious for it, and, to balance it, I feel now that there is a possibility of failure. Who knows but I *may* come upon the town if, as is likely, the public want no more of my book or lectures (which last is already the case)? Before, I was much likelier to take the town upon my shoulders. That is, I have lost some of my independence on them, when they would say that I have gained an independence. (J, VIII:120–21)

In this candid self-appraisal, Thoreau acknowledges his dependence upon the town, questioning whether he has squandered his riches, and concedes the possibility of failure. His somber mood may have been in part a delayed response to the stories of his childhood told to him on January 7 by his parents. Most potentially disturbing was the story, told by his mother, of an early confrontation with his brother. Each child had a garden plot, and young Henry had just discovered a potato sprouting in his. But then,

> John came in with a potato which he had found and had it planted in his garden, —"Oh mother, I have found a potato all sprouted. I mean to put it in my garden." . . . But next I came crying that somebody had got my potato, etc., etc., but it was restored to me as the youngest and original discoverer, if not inventor, of the potato, and it grew in *my* garden, and finally its crop was dug by myself and yielded a dinner for the family. (J, VIII:94)

This recollection of sibling rivalry with his brother, the anniversary of whose death was but four days later, and his seeming triumph over him may well have led to a flare-up of guilt that cast a pall over all his hopes for emotional and physical recovery and caused him to reflect on the "possibility"—and even the justice—of "failure." That his father and mother related, in the same breath as the garden story, the details of such childhood accidents or traumas as falling on a stairway and fainting, cutting his toe, and being "knocked over by a hen with chickens" (J, VIII:93–94) suggests a possible further connection between the sibling rivalry and the reactivation of oedipal, castration, and other anxieties rooted in early childhood.[2]

At a time when he was having trouble with his limbs and was haunted by sibling and oedipally related guilt and anxieties, as well as by fears of failure and sterility, his description of the cutting down of an old elm tree on January 21 takes on a powerful significance. Use of words like "stump" and "crotch" begins to suggest the human dimensions of the incident for Thoreau (J, VIII:125–26). These dimensions become explicit on January 22, when he gravely characterizes the felling of the venerable elm as a "funeral" and himself as "the chief if not the only mourner there" (J, VIII: 130). In eulogizing the tree, he is able to mourn redemptively for the brother he has survived and to grieve for himself:

> How the mighty have fallen! Its history extends back over more than half the whole history of the town. Since its kindred could not conveniently attend, I attended. Methinks its fall marks an epoch in the history of the town. . . . Its virtue was that it steadily grew and expanded from year to year to the very last. How much of old Concord falls with it! The town clerk will not chronicle its fall. I will, for it is of greater moment to the town than that of many a human inhabitant would be. Instead of erecting a monument to it, we take all possible pains to obliterate its stump. . . . Another link that bound us to the past is broken. (J, VIII:131)

The passage is at once a generative, caretaking plea for conservation (and thus a way of assuring himself he was not barren and was protector and nurturer of valuable resources and people—including his brother) and a poignant expression of concern about whether his days were numbered, whether his continuity with a vital and generative past had been forever broken, whether he and his work were to be forgotten and unappreciated, prematurely and irrevocably lost to subsequent generations.

His observations of stately elms two days later allow him a further opportunity to assert his identification and identity, though this time in a more positive and defiant vein:

> See what scars they bear, what limbs they lost before we were born. . . . They attend no caucus, they make no compromise, they use no policy. Their one principle is growth. They combine a true radicalism with a true conservativism. . . . They do not, like men, from radicals turn conservative. Their conservative part dies out first; their radical and growing part survives. (J, VIII: 140–41)

The more affirmative tone is again evident that same day in his reflection that a "journal is a record of experiences and growth" (J, VIII:134). Two days later, he records his displeasure with the townspeople who speculate on the age of the great elm when he has identified the age of the tree by counting its rings: "Truly they love darkness rather than light. . . . Truly all men are not men of science" (J, VIII:145–46). But to the extent that he experienced a brief spurt of confidence in his generativity and radicalness (in contrast to other Concordians, including, it would seem, Emerson whom he perceived as having from radical turned conservative) in observing the elms closely and counting rings—in being a "man of science"—Thoreau was putting himself into a bind. His journal, that record of growth, began once more in late January to be increasingly scientific and matter-of-fact, and by the spring, at the latest, when the tendency was most pronounced, he would be distressed at the relative barrenness of his writing.

Ruminating on the ruins of old sawmills, he was led to lament the loss of wildness, not only in Concord but also undoubtedly in himself: "It is observable that not only the moose and the wolf disappear before the civilized man, but even many species of insects, such as the black fly, and the almost microscopic 'no-see-em'" (J, VIII:149–50). He would reiterate this theme more emphatically in March: "I cannot but feel as if I lived in a tamed, and, as it were, emasculated country. . . . Is it not a maimed and imperfect nature that I am conversant with?" (J, VIII:220–21). With his illness, he was more needy, more dependent on parents (and quite possibly on some level he *wanted* to be solicitously cared for), and less robustly mobile; it is likely that these factors contributed to a sense of claustrophobic, domesticated confinement and "emasculation," which spiked his yearnings for the absolutely untamed. It was not just nature that was "maimed and imperfect" but the man who was "conversant" with it.

The sense of impaired or lost capacity and tenuous identity is again evinced in a letter to Greene of February 10:

> You may rely on it that you have the best of me in my books, and that I am not worth seeing personally—the stuttering, blundering, clodhopper that I am. Even poetry, you know, is in one sense an infinite brag & exaggeration. Not that I do not stand on all that I have written—but what am I to the truth I feebly utter! (C, 407)

The feebleness of his utterances was undeniable in his generally matter-of-fact February journal, and "feeble" was a word he would often use to characterize himself and his activities in the months to come. Perhaps contributing to his feebleness was the prospect of a "war between England and America. Neither side sees how its country can avoid a long and fratricidal war without sacrificing its honor" (J, VIII:189). The possibility of a war with "fratricidal" overtones (especially compounded with the chances for an even more "fratricidal" Civil War) was profoundly threatening to Thoreau's emotional and physical health, evoking as it did the specter of his own rivalry with, and the death of, his brother.[3] In such frightening political and psychological circumstances, all he could do was hang on, try to keep a grip on life and hope. Amidst the observations of nature in February, there is one poignant passage in which Thoreau seeks to identify with the willow tree:

> May I ever be in as good spirits as a willow! How tenacious of life! How withy! How soon it gets over its hurts! They never despair. Is there no moisture longer in nature which they can transmute into sap? They are emblems of youth, joy, and everlasting life. Scarcely is their growth restrained by winter. (J, VIII: 181–82)

On June 8 he would return to the willow for reassurance:

> So vivacious is the willow, availing itself of every accident to spread along the river's bank. The ice that strips it only disperses it the more widely. It never says die. May I be as vivacious as the willow. Some species are so brittle at the base of the twigs that they break on the least touch, but they are as tough above as tender at the base, and these twigs are only thus shed like seeds which float away and plant themselves in the first bank on which they lodge. (J, VIII: 369–70)

Clearly, it was therapeutic for Thoreau to identify with the willows; at the same time, he could not have been unaware of the extent to which he diverged from the ideal they represented. He was feeling unusually brittle and vulnerable, and he was not all that sure that he could get over his hurt, fend off despair, and disperse his seeds.

Replying to a February 26 letter from Ricketson, who indicated a desire not to be "prodigal of time" and to meet occasionally with him "ere the evil days" (C, 409), preferably in April, Thoreau writes of his reluctance to venture forth from Concord: "I dare not engage myself, nor allow you to expect me. The truth is, I have my enterprises now as ever, at which I tug with ridiculous feebleness, but admirable perseverance—and cannot say when I shall be sufficiently fancy-free for such an excursion" (C, 413–14). A letter from Horace Greeley, however, proposing that he leave Concord to tutor his children at his "farm" in Chappaqua, New York—which Thoreau apparently received soon after replying to Ricketson—seems to have provoked serious, if deeply ambivalent, consideration (C, 411). The effect of this proposal on Thoreau should not be underestimated; and since the matter was not resolved before May, the issue of whether or not to leave Concord must have weighed heavily on his mind for some time. Greeley's offer no doubt held some attraction for him. Getting away from Concord had often been a means of combating stagnation; moving to New York would be a strikingly new departure for one who desperately needed one, a refreshing change of pace for a man who feared he was going stale. Moreover, tutoring—teaching—would provide new avenues for generativity and make it harder for him to dwell on, or indulge himself in, his imaginative and physical "feebleness." Indeed, new surroundings might furnish him with new inspiration. It had been flattering to receive such an invitation from Greeley, and perhaps he found himself in some way yearning for the nurturance, fathering, friendship, and sponsorship Greeley might provide if he accepted the offer. After all, he had written mournfully in his March 4 journal of "two friends" he had once had—he emphasized the past tense; one was almost certainly Emerson, who "would not meet [him] on equal terms, but only be to some extent [his] patron," and the other was probably the now-absent Channing, whose "slight obtuseness" had spoiled "the dignity of friendship" (J, VIII:199). With the field of friendship so relatively barren in Concord, and with his wariness of unappreciative townspeople, Greeley's solicitude was particularly appealing. Leaving Concord would also answer those, including himself, who suspected that he was overly dependent on his family.

For all these attractions, however, Thoreau did not commit himself when he wrote back to Greeley on March 10, although the editor was left with the impression that the arrangement, in terms of both pay and length of service, could be worked out. On March 12 Greeley advises, "I concur entirely in your suggestion that both parties be left at liberty to terminate the engagement when either shall see fit. But I trust no such termination will be deemed advisable, for a year or two at least. . . . I expect to have you join us, if you will, in early summer" (C, 419).

It is difficult to believe that, in spite of its promise, the offer by Greeley did not also come as something of a shock and threat to Thoreau, another call of the sirens luring him from home, and he may have been bewildered as to why he was even tempted to ponder it. Possibly he did not refuse Greeley immediately partly out of some sense of courtesy. Certainly, going to Chappaqua would represent a major change in his life, would cast doubt on at least some of the "enterprises" he was considering, put into even more serious question his already fragile sense of identity, which had for so long been wrapped up in his concept of himself as traveler and saunterer in Concord. It would be a decisive break of the umbilical cord linking him to home, family, Walden, and the past. His previous experience no doubt also suggested the dangers of such a move. When, for instance, he had gone to Staten Island in 1843 to tutor William Emerson's children, he had been grievously homesick, disoriented, and generally unhappy. Indeed, he had long ago abandoned formal teaching as a satisfying vocation for him. Furthermore, it was still difficult for him to trust any would-be patron, particularly given his experience with Emerson and even, to a lesser extent, with Greeley himself. He would be making himself vulnerable to the editor by putting so much of his life into his hands. And the move to Chappaqua could also have been associated with another move back to smothering, suffocating involvement in civil society, meeting social obligations and expectations, seeking social recognition, and advancing ambitions; he would be serving, and gaining the favor of, a very influential man. His journal entries of March 11 appear to touch on many of these concerns. Ostensibly addressing the issue of traveling abroad, he is clearly dealing with the more pressing issue of going to Chappaqua:

> When it was proposed to me to go abroad, rub off some rust and *better my condition* in a worldly sense, I fear lest my life will lose some of its homeliness. If these fields and streams and woods, the phenomena of nature here, and the simple occupations of the inhabitants should cease to interest and inspire me, no culture or wealth would atone for the loss. I fear the dissipation that travelling, going into society, even the best, the enjoyment of intellectual luxuries, imply. If Paris is much in your mind, if it is more and more to you, Concord is less and less, and yet it would be a wretched bargain to accept the proudest Paris in exchange for my native village. (J, VIII:204)

It is evident that Thoreau is here evaluating what he would lose were he to leave Concord for any appreciable time. To the extent that, for him, Emerson had been the archetypal traveler abroad, the passage also indicates his suspicions of Waldo and, perhaps, other mentors, including Greeley. That moving to Chappaqua was in some way connected with an ambitiousness that would widen the breach with, even betray, his brother and compromise his values is suggested in his remark that the "sight of a marsh hawk" —which had been one significant symbol of his brother in the poem "To a Marsh Hawk in Spring" (CP, 143)—"in Concord meadows is worth more to me than the entry of the allies into Paris. In this sense I am not ambitious. I do not wish my native soil to become exhausted and run out through neglect. Only that travelling is good which reveals to me the values of home and enables me to enjoy it better. That man is the richest whose pleasures are the cheapest." He concludes with a reference to teaching and, implicitly, to the prospect of tutoring: "It is strange that men are in such haste to get fame as teachers rather than knowledge as learners" (J, VIII:204–5). The marsh hawk is again invoked on April 8, in an entry almost surely relating to the decision about Chappaqua: "If he [the marsh hawk] returns from so far to these meadows, shall the sons of Concord be leaving them at this season for slight cause?" (J, VIII:262).

Whatever his reservations, Thoreau was apparently ambivalent enough to defer a decision until early May; that he did continue to consider Chappaqua for so long, in spite of the risks and losses involved, suggests how at sea he was at this time, how much he longed for a transforming change in his life. On April 30 Greeley writes with delicacy to an obviously hedging Thoreau:

> Please write me with your ideas with regard to the whole matter, including the amount of compensation that you consider fair and just. I prefer that you should come to us feeling at perfect liberty to leave at any time when you think best to do so; but I hope you will be reconciled to stay with us for one year at least. Of course, this does not preclude your going away to lecture or visit when you should see fit. (C, 422–23)

Even at this point, it seems that Thoreau was ambivalent enough not to turn down Greeley flatly but rather to name a price he probably knew the editor would think was too high to pay. He heard the *"don't, don't"* of the bullfrog on May 7 (J, VIII:324). In a respectful, sensitive reply to Thoreau's May 5 letter, Greeley expresses his belief that they would not be able to reach agreement about the teaching arrangement and indicates that Thoreau had asked a price higher than he anticipated paying. He says that he will consult Mrs. Greeley, but, picking up on the signals Thoreau was sending, adds that he will not request Thoreau to defer any other plans he may have contemplated since it seemed probable that they would not be able to negotiate an agreement satisfying to both of them.[4] The Chappaqua affair seems to have ended with this letter. But months later, in September, responding to a Ricketson invitation to lecture or "teach," he makes a comment that also can be construed as a retrospective judgment on the Greeley proposal: "It would require such a revolution of all my habits, I think, as would sap the very foundation of me. I am engaged to Concord & my very private pursuits by 10,000 ties, & it would be suicide to cut them" (C, 432–33). Thoreau had by that time finally realized and accepted, once and for all, that uprooting himself, breaking the ties of continuity with Concord and "home," would be a form of "suicide." He would never again entertain the idea of living anywhere but his native home.

"Sap the very foundation of me": Thoreau indeed felt sapped, or in danger of being sapped, quite intensely in March and April 1856. He remained physically weak—and perhaps he had especially to hold onto his illness as a means of preventing himself from leaving Concord for Chappaqua. In general, the emotional turmoil of this period drained his energies and tested his resilience.

The death of his eccentric uncle, Charles Dunbar, on March 27—"unquestionably Thoreau's favorite relative" in Harding's view[5]—further unnerved him and impressed upon him again the inevitability of loss and death. On the previous day he had brooded, "If so many purposes are thus necessarily left unaccomplished, perhaps unthought of, we are reminded of the transient interest we have in *this life*" (J, VIII:229), and the day on which Charles was buried he would write a moving "farewell" to friends, perhaps partly in anticipation of leaving Concord for Chappaqua but also in a broader framework of grieving. "The meadows are like barren ground," his "path grows narrower and steeper," the "night is approaching." His "former friends . . . belong to an era . . . long past"; he "recognize[s] still your fair proportions, notwithstanding the convulsions which we have felt, and the weeds and jackals that have sprung up around. . . . We are no longer the representatives of our former selves" (J, VIII:230–31).

It was particularly fitting that, within this context of sapping crisis, Thoreau turned to the sugar maple tree and its sap in an attempt, partly conscious, partly unconscious, to secure his identity foundations, to ward off his sense of barrenness and stagnation, to reassure himself that he remained inwardly rich, fertile, vital, to see himself as caring in a "fatherly" way for coming generations and as capable of leaving behind a valuable legacy. Thoreau began his remarkable letter to Blake on March 13 with a comment that he is "fast growing rich" due to the dearth of lecturing invitations but that he has not "recovered strength enough for such a walk" as Blake proposed, "though pretty well again for circumscribed rambles & chamber work." Then, partly questioning, partly answering, he writes, "Shall then the maple yield sugar, & not man? . . . While he [the farmer] works in his sugar camp, let me work in mine—for sweetness is in me, & to sugar it shall come; —it shall not all go to leaves & wood. Am I not a *sugar maple* man then?" Thoreau proceeds to counsel Blake—and to rally himself—to "Boil down the sweet sap which the spring causes to flow within you— Stop not at syrup; go on to sugar, —though you present the world with but a single crystal—a crystal not made from trees in your yard, but from the new life that stirs in your pores." He suggests to Blake, moreover, that the sap he has tapped and crystallized into sugar will be a sweet and enduring legacy to posterity—and it was to posterity that Thoreau was beginning to turn more decisively for a sense of vindication and immortality:

> Then will the callers ask— Where is Blake? — He is in his sugar-camp on the Mt. side. — Let the world await him.
>
> Then will the little boys bless you, & the great boys too, —for such sugar is the origin of many condiments—Blakeians, in the shops of Worcester, of new forms, with their mottos wrapped up in them.
>
> Shall men taste only the sweetness of the maple & the cane, the coming year? (C, 421–22)

It is clear that Thoreau is seeking here to reassure himself as well as Blake that he still has the capacity to be fruitful, that his own sap and seasonings would produce new "condiments" and perhaps even converts—"Blakeians in the shops of Worcester," Thoreauvians in the fields and woods of Concord, and, he hoped, far beyond. The images and conception of a generative legacy would grow on and with Thoreau, as would be evident, for instance, when he turned again to the maples in October 1857.[6]

Only a week after Thoreau sought to represent himself as a "sugar maple man," the tapping of sap, a preoccupation of this month, was once again the focus of his deep concerns about generativity. He reports on March 21 that he has been at his "red maple sugar camp" and remarks that the "sap is an agreeable drink, like iced water (by chance), with a pleasant but slight sweetish taste" (J, VIII:216). It is quite revealing that Thoreau mentions here that he had a "dispute with Father about the *use* of my making this sugar when I knew it could be done and might have bought sugar cheaper at Holden's" (J, VIII:217). Gozzi proposes that Thoreau's father "may have had some uneasy sense that the experiment had some strange emotional meaning for Henry."[7] And, indeed, it is likely that Thoreau, by gathering his own sap and turning it into sugar, was struggling to prove something to himself—that *he* still had "sap," and that with his own sap, his generative powers, he could still be a self-sufficient "begetter" of "sugar." The drinking of the sap was a sensual experience with sexual undercurrents—as if by drinking it he could restore and reclaim his creative potency. His description of the flowing of sap also intimates—even imitates—a sexual experience, with sap as a form of semen: "It dropped from each tube about as fast as my pulse beat, and as there were three tubes directed to each vessel, it flowed at the rate of about one hundred and eighty drops in a minute into it" (J, VIII:217). That he had made "holes as large as a pencil" (suggesting the connection between sexuality and his writing) and that he had provided spouts, the "organ" through which the sap-semen passed, added to the sexual overtones of the activity. To have mastery over such a creative process, to participate in and identify with it, constituted an attempt to dispel fears and feelings of stagnation, to insist—in the face of all the evidence to the contrary at this time—that he was as fertile as the maples he had tapped.

The association of sap with generativity is apparent throughout this maple sugar season. On March 10 he was collecting sap in a pail when he slipped on the ice—perhaps an accident related to the weakness in his legs —and spilled all but one pint. While the loss of sap could be a threatening omen, here he is led to muse that when "the river breaks up, it will go down the Concord into the Merrimack, and down the Merrimack into the sea, and there get salted as well as diluted. . . . It suggests, at any rate, what various liquors, beside those containing salt, find their way to the sea, —the sap of how many kinds of trees!" (J, VIII:209). His sap too, he fancied, would be disseminated, find outlet to the sea. The "pith" of the smooth sumac was a form of semen, a "white sticky juice [that] oozes out of the bark where cut," as was the sap, "sweet and thick as molasses" (J, VIII:215, 220), oozing from red maple twigs. The color of this sap was "black as blacking or ink," hinting again at the link between sap and writing, the most crucial kind of generativity for Thoreau. On March 24 he made a hole with his knife in a maple and witnessed the sapwood beginning to "glisten with moisture, and anon a clear crystalline tear drop flows out." "This is the sap," he continues, "of which the far-famed maple-sugar is made"; it is the "sweet liquor which the Indians boiled a thousand years ago" (J, VIII:225). Tapping sap, then, was also a way of linking himself to the wildness and vigor of Indians, and perhaps a means of communion with his brother. In early April he tasted canoe-birch sap and compared it to wild apples that "must be tasted in the fields" to be savored (J, VIII:274). Some yellow birch sap tasted "slightly medicinal" to him (J, VIII:272), and indeed there was a sense in which it was medicine for him; the next April he would associate the drinking of yellow birch sap with the restoration of "sappy vigor" "in our limbs" (J, IX:341). Recovery was integrally bound to renewed generativity, and sap was itself symbol and embodiment of the fecundity for which he yearned.

Thoreau hoped that the "copious" flowing of birch sap in April before "there is any other sign of life in the tree" (J, VIII:266) might also have implications for his prognosis—that there was some sap flowing in him, even if there were yet few visible signs of new life. In answer to Hosmer's "despairing" question about "what life is for," he says, "be brave and hopeful with nature. Human life may be transitory and full of trouble, but the perennial mind . . . is superior to change. I will identify myself with that which did not die with Columella and will not die with Hosmer" (J, VIII: 245). But the hopefulness, the ability to identify consistently with the immortal and perennial in nature, was as fleeting as the maple sugar season. Indeed, if the flowing of sap was in some respects connected with the recovery of health and life, it was also a time of heightened vulnerability to disease and death, as Thoreau well knew from his own experience. It could be a seedtime, but it could also be a time when one discovers the seeds are *not* viable. The previous year he had spoken of "spring feelings," languor and weakness, as linked to sap coming up into trees and the bursting forth of pent-up humors; this April he notes (prompted no doubt in part by Uncle Charles's death)

> how many old people died off on the approach of the present spring. It is said that when the sap begins to flow in the trees our diseases become more violent. It is now advancing toward summer apace, but to perform what great deeds? Do we detect the reason why we also did not die on the approach of spring? (J, VIII:269)

"To perform what great deeds?" This was Thoreau's quandary. The coming of spring highlighted, as it had the previous year, his own failure to find direction or to resurrect fully his creative powers. April was the cruelest month. His health continued to suffer along with his creativity. On April 10 he was so "feeble" that he had to give up sailing in a strong wind (J, VIII: 271). Collecting sap was the most physically demanding activity in which he could engage. In such a state, nature's renewed activity and productivity not only rebuked him but was distasteful to him. May was "Nature's rutting season. . . . All the pregnant earth is bursting into life like a mildew, accompanied with noise and fire and tumult" (J, VIII:349).

Toward the end of April, Thoreau's journal entries became more consistently clinical and scientific than they had ever been; this was to be one of his most scientific—and artistically barren—phases. His sense of analogy was at low ebb and would continue to be so through the rest of the spring and most of the summer. A May 31 letter from Thoreau to John Russell,[8] in which he notes various spring flowers and uses much botanical nomenclature, is typical and suggestive of the period, clearly of a piece with the *Journal*, which was replete with painstaking scientific observation and classification and almost entirely devoid of philosophizing and flights of imagination. Entries of May, June, and early July reveal Thoreau, perhaps partly in preparation for Russell's July visit alluded to in the May 31 letter, identifying many flowers, including several of the Ranunculus variety mentioned on May 31. And when Russell actually did arrive in Concord on or before July 23 (after writing a letter about seeing *Magnolia glauca* on the eighteenth, which Thoreau received on July 21), Thoreau made good on his promise to show Russell Nuphar kalmiana, Hydropeltis, and Ranunculus (J, VIII:421–25), and Russell helped him identify Concord plants about which he had been curious. Evidently the two men learned much from each other, though Russell seems more the mentor, Thoreau the student. By July 24 the visit arranged in the May 31 letter appears to have ended; yet even after Russell's visit, the *Journal* maintains its scientific tone and substance.

On May 31 Thoreau indicated to Russell that his sister Sophia, then in Worcester, was in "such feeble health" that she would be unable to press any plants or flowers. (Ironically, she would outlive her brother by several years.) Yet, quite revealingly, in a letter written to Calvin Greene on that same day he characterizes *himself* as in some respect feeble: "As for my pen, I can say that it is not altogether idle, though I have finished nothing new in book form. I am drawing a rather long bow, though it may be a feeble one, but I pray that the archer may receive new strength before the arrow is shot" (C, 426). It is not completely clear here whether Thoreau's feebleness is primarily physical or artistic; almost certainly it is both. During this phase, health suffered, in part due to the enervating sense of creative decline and stagnation, and art was enfeebled, partly due to continued precarious health. They were inextricably intertwined threads. Although Thoreau mentioned to Russell on May 31 that certain "engagements" prevented him from committing himself to pressing flowers, one wonders to what engagements he was referring. The earlier plan for a western lecture tour had been canceled (C, 422), and by the end of May the matter of his going to Chappaqua in July was closed; he informed Russell that he planned to be home in July. To be sure, he did join Sophia in June for a week-long (his longest) Worcester visit with Blake and Brown.[9] It was here that the Maxham daguerreotypes were taken,[10] showing a man with a beard now and with unforgettable eyes: large, liquid, probing, shrewd, profound, but also, to this observer at least, sad and tired. Harding says, "They show a sober-faced individual with turbulent hair and the Galway whiskers he had grown under his chin during his illness of the year before, hoping to prevent further throat colds."[11] The beard may also have reflected Thoreau's sense of himself as a man no longer young. When he returned from Worcester, Ricketson was waiting for him; to have the admiration of disciples was probably especially important at this time as a confirmation of generativity. But his agenda for late spring and summer does not seem to have been particularly full. It is possible that Thoreau's reluctance to take on the task of pressing flowers for Russell represents further evidence of his lethargy.

It is quite apparent that Thoreau perceived his generativity as being relatively "feeble" at this point and that he saw an intimate link between his scientific orientation and the at least short-run attrition of his creativity. Just ten days before writing to Russell in May, he writes to Blake (responding to an invitation to lecture in Worcester), "In fine, what I have is either too scattered or loosely arranged, or too light, or else is too scientific and matter of fact (I run a good deal into that of late) for so hungry a company." In the same letter he voices the hope that meticulous scientific investigation will eventually allow him to "speak with more precision & authority," but he portrays himself as "still a learner, not a teacher, feeding somewhat omnivorously, browsing both stalk & leaves," and confesses his anxiety to Blake about the prospect of "philosophy & sentiment" being "buried under a multitude of details" (C, 423–24). Scientific observation could in some sense serve as a lifeline for Thoreau, giving him something to focus on when other modes of perception, sensibility, and inspiration were inaccessible. And clearly the "omnivorous" absorption and consolidation of natural facts was central to any grand or grandiose long-range plans he may have had for writing a Kalendar (or book of Concord), which would rely on inclusive mastery and transmutation of natural facts. But an already physically and creatively exhausted Thoreau had cause for deep concern about whether he could bring off such a feat. As has already been suggested, the very ambitiousness and magnitude of his long-term projects could be self-defeating and frustrating, leading him to contemplate whether he had bit off more than he could chew, whether it was even worthwhile to carry on at all. To devote so much energy to details might be to "fritter away" his life with them; it was a gamble. Certainly the short-term returns were meager and fragmented, serving only to fuel anxieties about generativity. By drawing such a "long bow," Thoreau was subject to doubt about whether the arrow would ever be shot or, if it were, whether it would be as "feeble"—as lacking in inspiration and coherence—as the archer seemed to be. Even after his last journal references to Russell in September 1858—when he visited the Essex Institute and went to Marblehead, Gloucester, and Rockport with his companion (J, XI:170–80)—he was not through wrestling with conflicting feelings about his submersion in scientific detail and its implications for his art. In his final years he would gain greater confidence in the significance, artistic and personal, of his scientific studies, but there is no question that in 1856 he was swimming in facts and had to struggle to keep his creative vision above water.

The chirp of the alder cricket in August signified a "turning point" in the year (J, VIII:444), and Thoreau, reminded of "past autumns and the lapse of time," was prompted to assess the interval between his expectations and his own recent achievements: "Such preparation, such an outfit has our life, and so little brought to pass!" (J, IX:8). On what would turn out to be the last dog day of August, the twenty-sixth, he observes the hatching of a tortoise and seeks to glean a reassuring lesson from its gradualness:

> June, July, and August, —the livelong summer, —what are they with their heats and fevers but sufficient to hatch a tortoise in. Be not in haste; mind your private affairs. Consider the turtle. A whole summer—June, July, and August —is not too good nor too much to hatch a turtle in. Perchance you have worried yourself, despaired of the world, meditated the end of life, and all things seemed rushing to destruction; but nature has steadily and serenely advanced with a turtle's pace. (J, IX:32–33)

Worry, despair, concern about death and destruction: no doubt Thoreau was subject to these emotions as his legs and art went along at a turtle's pace throughout the summer. Try as he might, it was difficult to accept equably the languor with which his life had proceeded.

With the approach of autumn Thoreau hoped that he was nearing a period of reinvigoration. His experience of August 30, at a time when his journal entries were again growing longer and more reflective, gave some credence to these hopes. It was apparently one of those subtle turning points, one of those "important events" in life that are often overlooked; as he had said toward the end of 1855, "In a true history or biography, of how little consequence those events of which so much is commonly made!" (J, VIII:64). He planned on August 30 to go cranberrying, though —appropriate for one with weak limbs—he "kept foreseeing a lame conclusion" (J, IX:35). But the fact that he had "expected little of this walk" helped it turn out serendipitously, prompting an extraordinarily long, exhilarated, and philosophical entry. Although he had observed eggs and other forms of natural reproduction throughout the summer, he wrote dryly and could not seem to ally himself with nature's sexuality and fertility. Here though, far from being bogged down in the cranberry swamp, Thoreau not only describes the berries in sexualized terms—with their "stiff erect" vines and fruit reminding him "forcibly of eggs"—but also feels an intense, libidinally charged bond with the swamp itself: "I enjoyed this cranberrying very much . . . and the swamp seemed to be yielding its crop to me alone, for there are none else to pluck it or to value it" (J, IX: 39–40). It is as if he were coming home to a nurturing wife or mother with whom, in the past, he has enjoyed an exclusive relationship. In the process of trustingly yielding to nature and being yielded to in return, he experiences an almost orgastic, renewed intimacy with his own "genius": "I got

further and further away from the town every moment, and my good genius seemed [to] have smiled on me, leading me hither, and then the sun
suddenly came out clear and bright" (J, IX:40). Such words as "agreeable
shudder," "shock," "thrill," "agreeable surprise," "rush," and "unexpected harvest" (J, IX:42–43) are used to characterize his emotions as he
encounters the "wildness and novelty" of this "new world" in which he is
so at home. The epiphany is partly a rediscovery of that essential "wildness" accessible—even sexually so—to him in his native Middlesex
County: "I believe almost in the personality of such planetary matter, feel
something akin to reverence for it. . . . We are so different we admire each
other, we healthily attract one another. I love it as a maiden. . . . It would
imply the regeneration of mankind, if they were to become elevated
enough to truly worship stocks and stones" (J, IX:44–45). Certainly his
own health and regeneration depended in part on a sense of renewed intimacy with a maidenly and motherly nature, virginal and yet eroticized. At
the end of May 1857, when his health was considerably improved, he
would describe another swamp in both motherly and erotic terms: "That
central meadow and pool in Gowing's swamp is its very navel . . . where
the umbilical cord was cut that bound it to creation's womb. Methinks every swamp tends to have or suggests an interior tender spot" (J, IX:394).
Nature here seems both mother's womb and lover's vagina.[12] It was crucial for Thoreau to restore his trusting attachment to nature, to be able to
surrender to a nature that would then yield its richness and inspiration to
him. To a certain extent, such a sense of renewed connectedness could be
regained only by laying to one side, at least on an emotional level, the darker, more disturbing views of nature he had had to ponder in the past several
years. By permitting himself some measure of regression to intimacy and
reunion with a nurturing, inviting nature, to a feeling of "reverence" rather than threat and alienation with regard to "planetary matter" (no longer,
in the cranberry swamp, the forbidding "vast, Titanic, Inhuman Nature"
of Katahdin),[13] to a sense of "wildness" unsullied by the coarseness and
savagery dramatized by such incidents as the "murder" of the moose, Thoreau could make progress toward healing body and spirit. The epiphany in
the cranberry swamp involved an intimation that he could recover the inner home and a relation to wildness he feared he had lost:

> I have got in my huckleberries. I shall be ready for Thanksgiving. It is in vain to
> dream of a wildness distant from ourselves. There is none such. It is the bog in
> our brain and bowels, the primitive vigor of Nature in us, that inspires that
> dream. I shall never find in the wilds of Labrador any greater wildness than in
> some recess in Concord, i.e. than I import into it. A little manhood or virtue

will make the surface of the globe anywhere thrillingly novel and wild. That alone will provide and pay the fiddler; it will convert the district road into an untrodden cranberry bog, for it restores all things to their original primitive flourishing and promising state. (J, IX:43)

The man who had wandered from his nourishing roots and lost his way now had an inkling of how he could find his way home.

On September 1 Thoreau accepted an invitation, extended much earlier, to visit Alcott in Walpole, New Hampshire (C, 429–30); he intended also to spend some time in Brattleboro, Vermont. In the letter he expressed his wish to

> get some hints from September on the Connecticut to help me understand that season on the Concord; —to snuff the musty fragrance of the decaying year in the primitive woods. There is considerable cellar room in my nature for such stores, a whole row of bins waiting to be filled before I can celebrate my Thanksgiving. Mould is the richest of soils, yet *I* am not mould. (C, 430)

That Thoreau was prepared to undertake a trip suggests that his health was improving along with his state of mind. The next day he speaks of the "thrilled and expectant mood" in which he has made his most "interesting botanical discoveries" and asserts how, in studying certain wild plants, he has "communicated" with, and reestablished continuity with, Indians (J, IX:54, 56). The trip north appears to have given him a chance to test his health; indeed, in Bellows Falls he climbed Fall Mountain "with a heavy valise on my back, against the advice of the toll-man. But when I got up so soon and easily I was amused to remember his anxiety" (J, IX:75). Upon his return from the trip, he was further encouraged by the superior "fertility" of the Concord River as compared with the Connecticut and by the asters, flowering late when "you thought that Nature had about wound up her affairs" (J, IX:80–81, 82). By the time he wrote to Ricketson on the twenty-third, he had come fully to the realization that, travel as he might, his life was inextricably bound to Concord:

> You propose to me teaching the following winter. I find that I cannot entertain the idea. It would require such a revolution of all my habits, I think, as would sap the very foundation of me. I am engaged to Concord & my very private pursuits by 10,000 ties, & it would be suicide to cut them. If I were weaker, & not somewhat stronger physically, I should be more tempted. (C, 432–33)

Earlier in the year Thoreau had had to grapple with Greeley's invitation, and perhaps that incident, which helped clarify for him just how important "home" was, is (as has already been suggested) especially what he is thinking of here. In any case, it is evident that Thoreau now saw a link between rootedness in Concord, his generativity, and his health. He would have to resist being "tempted" by the sirens that would keep him from home. Concord was his home, and he embraced it, cherished his umbilical ties with it. He was "engaged" to Concord. In fact, in a certain sense even death, being buried in his native soil, would not tear them asunder but would rather bring them closer together, merge them, reconnect the umbilical cord once and for all.

Although the sugar maples of October 1856 did not prompt any extended analogies or philosophical discussion, Thoreau clearly was feeling rejuvenated, if not altogether recovered. He noticed the "thick prickly burr" of the chestnuts, which kept them "safe until they are quite mature" (J, IX:120), and saw his own "prickliness" as a similar safeguard for eventual maturity. His life, he said, was "very homely," and he felt more at home with it, less seduced by ambition and society's definitions of success than he had at any time since *Walden* had approached publication:

> Joy and sorrow, success and failure, grandeur and meanness, and indeed most words in the English language do not mean for me what they do for my neighbors. I see that my neighbors look with compassion on me, that they think it is a mean and unfortunate destiny which makes me to walk in these fields and woods so much and sail on this river alone. But so long as I find here the only real elysium, I cannot hesitate in my choice. My work is writing, and I do not hesitate, though I know that no subject is too trivial for me, tried by ordinary standards. . . . Give me simple, cheap, and homely themes. (J, IX:121)

Just before setting out to do some surveying at Eagleswood, New Jersey (an experimental cooperative community), on October 24,[14] a month-long trip in the course of which he would meet another writer, Walt Whitman, he wrote a letter to Cholmondeley, thanking him again for the oriental books and explaining that though he was still "run-down," his "spirits . . . are as indifferently tough, as sluggishly resilient, as a dried fungus. . . . I dwell as much aloof from society as ever: finding it just as impossible to agree in opinion with the most intelligent of my neighbors" (C, 436). Though this letter, characteristically, glosses over his recent crisis, it does provide further evidence of Thoreau's more positive frame of mind.

In his funeral oration, Emerson would refer to a "person not known to this audience" who had an important impact on Thoreau; later, Emerson would tell Sanborn, who had become friendly with Thoreau by the summer of 1856, that the man he had referred to was Walt Whitman.[15] Accompanied by Alcott, Thoreau visited Whitman at his house on Myrtle Avenue, just outside Brooklyn.[16] The contrasts, and even tension, between the two men were no doubt hard for them to ignore. Indeed, Whitman felt it necessary to apologize for the use of Emerson's celebrated "I greet you at the beginning of a great career" letter at the front of the 1856 edition of *Leaves of Grass*. Probably Whitman was aware of the former master-student relationship between Thoreau and Emerson and was sensitive about seeming to have supplanted and superseded Thoreau as a candidate for "American Scholar" and Poet in Emerson's eyes; certainly there was a great deal of hubris and self-promotion evident in his exploitation of Emerson's praise. Overtones of sibling rivalry for the favor of a father were undoubtedly present. There may well have been some envy or resentment on Thoreau's part, even if it was also a relief for him to be a comparative failure by societal standards. The two men, moreover, were startlingly different in personal style; Whitman was naturally expansive, easygoing, warm, colorful, affectionate, while Thoreau was considerably more reserved, cool, introverted. Their opinions on the common man were divided, with Whitman speaking with reverence of America and the masses and with Thoreau displaying a haughty contempt for the nation and most of its inhabitants.[17] And, of course, Whitman celebrated the body and sexuality in what was ostensibly a most unrepressed, revolutionary way, while Thoreau tended to be unusually reticent and inhibited with regard to the pleasures of the flesh.

Despite the dramatic contrasts and tension, Thoreau did come to feel a bond with Whitman. They were both, after all, rebels and radicals who had challenged the smugness, pettiness, hypocrisy, and conventionality of modern society, and both had been lambasted by critics. Thus Thoreau, although admitting that he felt uncomfortable with some of Whitman's opinions and poetry, was supportive of Whitman's boldness and called his critics "reprobates." When Whitman questioned his use of the word, he took his remark one step further: "Do you regard that as a severe word? reprobates? what they really deserve is something infinitely stronger, more caustic: I thought I was letting them off easy." Although Whitman was put off by Thoreau's apparent "supercilious" attitude toward the masses, he seems to have showed respect for his fellow artist, stating that he "was a man you would have to like—an interesting man, simple, conclusive." And, although Thoreau had reason to be threatened and intimidated by Whitman, he came away conceding to Alcott, "That is a great man."[18]

It is probable that Whitman grew on Thoreau in the days after the meeting, as he reflected on him and was no longer confronted with Whitman's imposing physical presence. In a November 19 letter to Blake he writes,

He is apparently the greatest democrat the world has seen. . . . A remarkably strong though coarse nature, of a sweet disposition, and much prized by his friends. Though peculiar and rough in his exterior . . . he is essentially a gentleman. I am still somewhat in a quandary about him, —feel that he is essentially strange to me, at any rate; but I am surprised by the sight of him. . . . He said that I misapprehended him. I am not quite sure that I do. (C, 441)

Whitman continued to be on his mind in the following weeks. On December 7 he informs Blake that Whitman

is the most interesting fact to me at present. I have just read his 2nd edition . . . and it has done me more good than any reading for a long time. Perhaps I remember best the poem of Walt Whitman an American & the Sun Down Poem. There are 2 or 3 pieces in the book which are disagreeable to say the least, simply sensual. He does not celebrate love at all. It is as if the beasts spoke. . . . But even on this side, he has spoken more truth than any American or modern that I know. I have found his poem exhilarating encouraging. As for its sensuality, —& it may turn out to be less sensual than it appeared—I do not so much wish that these parts were not written, as that men & women were so pure that they could read them without harm, that is, without understanding him. . . .

On the whole, it sounds to me very brave & American after whatever deductions. . . .

We ought to rejoice greatly in him. He occasionally suggests something a little more than human. You cant confound him with the other inhabitants of Brooklyn or New York. How they must shudder when they read him! He is awfully good.

To be sure I sometimes feel a little imposed on. By his heartiness & broad generalities he puts me in a liberal frame of mind prepared to see wonders. . . .

Since I have seen him I find that I am not disturbed by any brag or egoism in his book. He may turn out to be the least braggart of all, having a better right to be confident. (C, 444–45)

Quite revealing is Thoreau's claim that he is "not quite sure" he "misapprehended" Whitman and that the bard's poetry may "turn out to be less sensual than it appeared." It seems likely that Thoreau, for all his uneasiness about sexuality (on October 16, upon seeing a phalluslike fungus, he calls it "disgusting" and adds that nature "almost puts herself on a level with those who draw in privies" [J, IX:116–17]), detected the "secret" meaning behind much of Whitman's celebration of sexuality; in many of the poems, sexuality is a metaphor for the creation of poems, art—for generativity.[19] Thoreau, who was frequently aware of the connections he made between sexuality and artistic generativity, of the libidinal roots of creativity, of the centrality of sublimation, took heart from Whitman's own celebration of the creative process, even if it was often hidden by the more overt "programme" of reverence for the body and procreation. Whitman's responses to nature, as to art, were libidinized, as Thoreau was sometimes wont to admit they were for himself. Furthermore, in such poems as "Song of Myself" and the "Sun Down Poem," art is portrayed, along with connectedness to nature, as a means of transcending time and providing a kind of symbolic immortality; indeed, art is the enduring legacy and embodiment of the artist, his "leavings." Through his poems Whitman, himself childless, sought to be a self-sufficient "begetter," a father and even a mother to future generations; and the poems themselves became children in which he had a "libidinal investment" and which would provide him with assurances of generativity and immortality. It can be surmised that Thoreau recognized the extent to which Whitman had articulated, in a profound and eloquent way, what art was also coming to mean more decisively for him. Beneath the surface of "programme" and persona, he shared a common ground with the bard.

That he was not "disturbed by any brag or egoism" in Whitman was, of course, also a reflection on himself, whose announced intention in *Walden* had been to "brag as lustily as chanticleer in the morning." Whitman's "egoism" was leavened by a deep and heartfelt appreciation for the common man and, all his objections to the contrary, the New York bard's vision of the common man's dignity and of human solidarity, fraternal camaraderie, and fellowship did have an impact on Thoreau, who was, in any case, more critical of the "masses" and of his relatively well-to-do townsmen than he usually was of simple, humble men of the earth.

Whitman, he said, put him in a "liberal frame of mind": upon his return home, it appears that, in his responses to nature and to the common man, the Whitmanesque spirit had rubbed off on him, at least for a time. On December 1, back in Concord, Thoreau writes appreciatively of a farmer, Cyrus Hubbard, "a man of a certain New England probity and worth, immortal and natural, like a natural product, like the sweetness of a nut, like the toughness of hickory! He, too, is a redeemer for me" (J, IX: 144). There *was* something redemptive about this newly affirmed sense of the common man. The next day it was Melvin, the muskrat hunter, who was the object of his enthusiasm:

> He follows hunting, praise be to him, as regularly in our tame fields as the farmers follow farming. Persistent Genius! How I respect him and thank him for him! . . . I trust the Lord will provide us with another Melvin when he is

> gone. . . . I think of him with gratitude when I am going to sleep, grateful that
> he exists, —that Melvin who is such a trial to his mother. . . . Awkward,
> gawky, loose-hung, dragging his legs after him. He is my contemporary and
> neighbor. He is one tribe, I am another, and we are not at war. (J, IX:148)

The exclamatory, almost breathless, tone, the serialized description, and the sentiments probably owe something to Whitman; indeed, immediately following this passage in the *Journal* is a discussion of Whitman. There was, it seems, something therapeutic for Thoreau in these Whitmanesque celebrations of his fellowman. For one so often subject to guilt over the imagined betrayal or supersession of male figures, most particularly his brother, the ability to express openly and profusely his affection for and gratitude to his "brothers" was immensely heartening. Such a sense of camaraderie helped give him the feeling that he was not "at war" with any "brothers." On December 3, soon after comparing himself to a moose not unlike the one whose "murder" he had participated in while in Maine, he describes the last words of a man who had been killed by a train at the Lincoln Bridge: "The only words he uttered while he lingered in his delirium were 'All right,' probably the last which he had uttered before he was struck—brave, prophetic words to go out of the world with!" (J, IX:151). Thoreau's own last words would suggest a guilt-allaying solidarity with the moose and Indian who have already disappeared from the scene; always concerned about the significance of last words and the manner of one's death, he is here enabled to express solidarity with another fallen "brother" whose last words, "All right," may be interpreted partly as a redemptive absolution from any wrongs the still living brother may suspect he has committed. Of course, these words also suggest an acceptance of life and death akin to Hamlet's "let be." Just after his discussion of the man's last words, he launches into another valedictory of the common men he knows:

> How I love the simple, reserved countrymen, my neighbors, who mind their
> own business and let me alone. . . . For nearly twoscore years I have known, at
> a distance, these long-suffering men, whom I never spoke to, who never spoke
> to me, and now feel a certain tenderness for them, as if this long probation
> were but the prelude to an eternal friendship. What a long trial we have with-
> stood, and how much more admirable we are to each other, perchance, than if
> we had been bedfellows! I am not only grateful because Veias, and Homer,
> and Christ, and Shakespeare have lived, but I am grateful for Minott, and Rice,
> and Melvin, and Goodwin, and Puffer even. (J, IX:151)

His wish for "eternal friendship" with these men reflects, too, his long pin-

ing for a sense of eternal friendship with his brother. Allying himself to the
common man, and forswearing any ambitions to be anything but poor and
homely, allowed him to feel closer to John. Inspired by Whitman but also
responding to a deeply held (though sometimes denied) need for closeness
to others, he says on December 5,

> My themes shall not be far-fetched. I will tell of homely every-day phenomena
> and adventures. Friends! Society! It seems to me that I have an abundance of it,
> there is so much that I rejoice and sympathize with, and men, too, that I never
> speak to but only know and think of. . . . It is the greatest of all advantages to
> enjoy no advantage at all. I find it invariably true, the poorer I am, the richer I
> am. (J, IX:160)

No longer perceiving himself as endangered by conventional success,
"sympathizing" with the humble common man (though not with his more
affluent and "civilized" townsmen), identifying his true home as with the
"homely," Thoreau was beginning to feel inwardly rich again, and this
feeling of renewed potential aided him in his physical recovery. On December 30 he remarks on how Indians, for all their wars, have shown great capacity to "enter into the most formal compact or treaty of peace, burying
the hatchet" (J, IX:202). The "homing process" had, of course, been in evidence before his meeting with Whitman, and part of it involved a leveling,
humbling sense of "sympathy" and identification with the "homely." Further encouraged and set free by Whitman to recognize and articulate solidarity with "brothers," and more assured (partly by comparison with
Whitman) that he would not enjoy worldly, pompous celebrity, he could
be more convinced that the hatchet was buried. He writes to Blake on the
last day of 1856, "O solitude! obscurity! meanness! I never triumph so as
when I have the least success in my neighbor's eyes" (C, 461).

Some trace of Whitman's influence may also be seen in Thoreau's love
affair with a shrub oak during December. To be sure, he had often been
given to identifying with, and professing his affection for, trees and other
forms of vegetation. And his electric experience in the cranberry bog in late
August had been an important stepping-stone on the way to recapturing a
sense of intimacy with, and being at home in, nature. But the effusiveness
and unashamedness with which he asserts his bond with the shrub oak, the
extent to which he equates it with a woman to be loved, most likely owes
something to his encounter with Whitman and his poetry. He begins on
December 1 by describing the "dear wholesome color of shrub oak leaves,
so clean and firm, not decaying, but which have put on a kind of immortality" (J, IX:145). Whitman's "leaves" aspired to immortality, and so

did Thoreau's. Next comes perhaps his most graphic and Whitmanesque statement:

> I love and could embrace the shrub oak with its scanty garment of leaves rising above the snow, lowly whispering to me, akin to winter thoughts, and sunsets, and to all virtue. . . . Rigid as iron, clean as the atmosphere, hardy as virtue, innocent and sweet as the maiden is the shrub oak. In proportion as I know and love it, I am natural and sound as a partridge. I felt a positive yearning toward one bush this afternoon. There was a match found for me at last. I fell in love with a shrub oak. . . . Low, robust, hardy, indigenous. . . . I love to go through a patch of shrub oak in a bee-line, where you tear your clothes and put your eyes out. (J, IX:146–48)

Clearly, the shrub oak, which Thoreau would like to embrace in its "scanty garments" and by which he would have his clothes torn, represents the feminine principle in nature, the alternative mother, wife, and lover—at once pure and libidinized—which he can trust, with which he needs to reconnect himself and thus regain a "soundness" he was prone to losing when he viewed nature as barren scientific object or as threatening force. To be "married" to an oak was a "match" unto, and even beyond, death. It is also evident that Thoreau wishes to see himself—his recovered self—in the pure, "Low, robust, hardy, indigenous" plant. On December 17, this wish is even more obvious:

> But these [shrub oak] leaves still have a kind of life in them. They are exceedingly beautiful in their withered state. If they hang on, it is like the perseverance of the saints. . . . How poetically, how like saints or innocent and beneficent beings, they give up the ghost! How spiritual! Though they have lost their sap, they have not given up the ghost. Rarely touched by worm or insect, they are as fair as ever. (J, IX:185–86)

Like the shrub oak, he has persevered; he has lost much "sap," but he has refused to "give up the ghost."

A long December 16 letter from Cholmondeley, responding in part to Thoreau's characterization of himself as "run down," had included the admission that "I have had it [being run down] so badly as to have meditated suicide more than once. But it goes away with the merest trifle, and leaves you stronger than ever" (C, 453). By the time he received it, Thoreau could not have failed to recognize how it applied to him: he had come perilously close to wanting to "give up the ghost," but the crisis seemed to be passing—slowly—and he was coming to feel somewhat stronger, both physically and emotionally. As he walks through a light snow on December 24, he compares himself to a "husband-man" sowing grain (J, IX:196). On December 29 he sets forth a portion of the prescription that seemed to be working for him:

> We must go out and re-ally ourselves to Nature every day. We must make root, send out some little fibre at least, even every winter day. I am sensible that I am imbibing health when I open my mouth to the wind. Staying in the house breeds a sort of insanity always. Every house is in this sense a hospital. . . . I am aware that I recover some sanity which I had lost almost the instant that I come abroad. (J, IX:200)

Out of the house, Thoreau was seeking to rediscover home, and thus recover sanity and health.

While doing some surveying in the first days of 1857, Thoreau was led to observe, "It does look sometimes as if the world were on its last legs. How many there are whose principal employment it is nowadays to eat their meals and go to the post-office!" (J, IX:205). Although he had, in the immediate past, suspected that he, too, had been on *his* "last legs"—and had connected his condition to how he had "employed" himself—he was now more confident that he had the remedy, one particularly necessary after a stint of surveying:

> After spending four or five days surveying and drawing a plan incessantly, I especially feel the necessity of putting myself in communication with nature again, to recover my tone, to withdraw out of the wearying and unprofitable world of affairs. The things I have been doing have but a fleeting and accidental importance, however much men are immersed in them, and yield very little valuable fruit. I would fain have been wading through the woods and fields and conversing with the sane snow. . . . when my task is done, with never-failing confidence I devote myself to the infinite again. (J, IX:205)

The imagery of recovery, sanity, and health is common in the January journal; though he is aware of the alternating "smoothness" and "roughness" of his experience (J, IX:210–11), the prevailing mood is upbeat. He speaks like a man who has discovered the formula for happiness, who is finally coming home to himself. "In the street and in society," he says, "I am almost invariably cheap and dissipated," but "alone in the distant woods or fields . . . I come to myself, I once more feel myself grandly related. . . . I come to my solitary woodland walk as the homesick go home. . . . I wish to get the Concord, the Massachusetts, the America, out of my head and be sane a part of every day" (J, IX:208). He adds that it "is as if I always met in those places some grand, serene, immortal, infinitely encouraging, though invisible, companion, and walked with him" (J, IX:209). It is quite likely that one "invisible companion" with whom he could now walk, as he severed his ties with society and allied himself with the "homely," was his brother. In fact, on January 11, the fifteenth anniversary of John's death, a Thoreau at home with obscurity notes with satisfaction:

> For some years past I have partially offered myself as a lecturer; have been advertised as such several years. Yet I have had but two or three invitations to lecture in a year, and some years none at all. I congratulate myself on having been permitted to stay at home thus, I am so much richer for it. I do not see what I should have got of much value, but money, by going about, but I do see what I should have lost. It seems to me that I have a longer and more liberal lease on life thus. (J, IX:214)

His "success" in the woodlands is that he has a "kindred" experience; there he is "cleansed of all impurities," and "*there* is nothing petty or impertinent, none to say, 'See what a great man I am!' " (J, IX:215–16). To be a "great man" in a conventional sense was to defy and betray his "kin"; he was therefore anxious to deny any ambitions to be great by mundane standards. On January 15 he suggests that he has, like others, known despair but has been saved by his responsiveness to the beautiful:

> We are all ordinarily in a state of desperation; such is our life; ofttimes it drives us to suicide. To how many, perhaps to most, life is barely tolerable, and if it were not for the fear of death or of dying, what a multitude would immediately commit suicide! But let us hear a strain of music, we are at once advertised of a life which no man had told us of, which no preacher preaches. (J, IX:222)

On January 16 he observed that the holes he had bored in the maples the previous spring were "nearly grown over last summer" (J, IX:224), and he believed that his wounds, too, were healing. At a time when he was trying to get back on his feet, when his legs were getting strong enough to propel him in the direction of a "sanative" wildness, he agreed to read a modified version of "The Wild" or "Walking" in Worcester in February (C, 465).

Approaching his fortieth birthday, Thoreau quotes on February 6 a passage from Winckelmann's "History of Ancient Art": "I am now past forty, and therefore at an age when one can no longer sport freely with life. I perceive, also, that a certain delicate spirit begins to evaporate, with which I raised myself, by powerful soarings, to the contemplation of the beautiful" (J, IX:243). As he reflected on that passage in the context of his own life and considered how his own delicacy of spirit was threatened by social encounters and obligations, including lecturing, he again resolved to avoid being compromised by such entanglements: "By poverty, i.e. simplicity of life and fewness of incidents, I am solidified and crystallized. . . . It is a singular concentration of strength and energy and flavor." Having established a cocoonlike life structure, he could count on yet another metamorphosis: "in my solitude I have woven for myself a silken web or *chrysalis*, and, nymph-like, shall ere long burst forth a more perfect creature" (J, IX:246).

As he recognized with anguish, however, on February 8, and later on the twenty-third and twenty-fourth, he was not invulnerable to loneliness and loss, even if he sought solitude. "And now another friendship is ended," he laments. There are differing views on which friendship is referred to in the long, mournful passage that follows.[20] It was either Waldo, who was away lecturing at the time, or Lidian, who was at this time an invalid. Whichever it was—and I am inclined to believe it was Lidian, given her proximity, the references to pain, and the extent to which he had already written off Waldo as a close friend[21]—both figures were emotionally intertwined for Thoreau, and the realization of another loss was acutely felt. It represented an additional (and to some degree, it seems, unanticipated) hurdle to recovery. The emphasis on a "grand physical pain, such as gods may feel, about my head and breast, a certain ache and fullness" (J, IX:249), suggests that he saw this "eternal separation" as having a negative impact on his physical as well as emotional health. A bit later in the passage he says, "I am perfectly sad at parting from you. I could better have the earth taken away from under my feet, than the thought of you from my mind" (J, IX:250). With the "earth taken away" from under his feet, there might be even more difficulty walking. And on February 23, still brooding over his loss, he would add, "Morning, noon, and night, I suffer a physical pain, an aching of the breast which unfits me for my tasks" (J, IX:276). In a broader sense, the perceived loss of this friendship (under what circumstances we cannot be sure) seems to have spurred a more profound grief related to midlife, when "never" takes on a "grand significance," when one must accept, however reluctantly, "that there may be incessant tragedies, that one may treat his fellow as a god but receive somewhat less regard from him. I now almost for the first time *fear* this" (J, IX:249, 250). The "tragedy" of this "ending" also may have briefly shaken his confidence that he had reconciled with his brother and evoked oedipal anxieties associated with both Waldo and Lidian. If "friends are our kindred" (J, IX:279) with whom we feel sympathy, Thoreau feared that he could be dragged down by them: "Must friends then expect the fate of those Oriental twins, —that one shall at last bear about the corpse of the other, by that same ligature that bound him to a living companion?" (J, IX:278).

Thoreau appears to have been momentarily knocked off his improving stride by the ending of this friendship and the emotions it engendered.

His journal entries are rather short and less philosophical through much of March, and a premature, or "Indian," spring was followed by a late frost that mowed down "many a first faint crop mantling the pools" (J, IX: 293), perhaps giving rise to some anxieties about whether his recovery, this most recent seedtime, would also, again, be aborted. On March 5 he includes in his journal another quote from Winckelmann on Beauty: "I have meditated long upon it, but my meditations commenced too late, and in the brightest glow of mature life its essential has remained dark to me; I can speak of it, therefore, only feebly and spiritlessly" (J, IX:288). Feebleness and dispiritedness had been familiar conditions for Thoreau; he almost certainly quoted Winckelmann as a reminder of what he had been fighting against, and wished to avoid, in his own "mature life." Even in the depths of February, however, he had brief glimpses of a "seed-time whose harvest cannot fail, an irresistible expedition of the mind, at length to be victorious" (J, IX:275), and toward the end of March he was once more exuding optimism about the fate of seeds:

> When I witness the first plowing and planting, I acquire a long-lost confidence in the earth, —that it will nourish the seed that is committed to its bosom. I am surprised to be reminded that there is warmth in it. We have not only warmer skies, then, but a warmer earth. The frost is out of it, and we may safely commit these seeds to it in some places." (J, IX:310)

That he follows this observation with a discussion of his writing (J, IX: 311) further suggests the close connection for Thoreau between seeds and words.

By the end of March he perceived himself as hardy enough to undertake an expedition to New Bedford, and he wrote to Ricketson to invite himself for a visit. After Ricketson accepted, he wrote another note, which clarifies the extent to which he saw himself as on the mend:

> I wish that there were a few more signs of spring in myself—however, I take it that there *are* as many within us as we think we hear *without* us. I am decent for steady pace but not yet for a race. I have a little cold at present, & you speak of rheumatism about the head & shoulders. . . . In a concert, you know, we must sing our parts feebly sometimes that we may not injure the general effect. I shouldn't wonder if my two-year old invalidity had been a positively charming feature to some amateurs favorably located. Why not a blasted man, as well as a blasted tree, on your lawn? (C, 472–73)

Although he still wishes for a "few more signs of spring" in himself, he appears to have regained some measure of trust that he does have the inner resources for another creative spring (which in this case would also be an

Indian summer) and that his legs, while not yet ready "for a race," are nevertheless more "springy" than they have been for quite some time. The impression, then, is of progress—perhaps too gradual to please him entirely, but progress nonetheless. His reference to his "two-year old invalidity" indicates that he remembered very vividly that he had been stricken with the approach and arrival of spring, that April (he wrote this letter to Ricketson on April 1) was an exceedingly vulnerable month. But he does not, in spite of "a little cold" and his still limited strength and creative output, seem to be anticipating another attack of "spring feelings" this year. He had had much occasion and reason to feel that he was a "blasted man"—who had, indeed, sometimes equated his condition with that of a "blasted tree." At this point, however, he believes that he has withstood the blasts and can even joke about them, though not without a trace, perhaps, of black humor. Joined by Alcott and Channing, Thoreau spent a relatively active two weeks in New Bedford, doing considerable walking; investigating frog spawn, which was a new sort of generative sap or condiment, suggesting "the addition of cream and sugar, for the table" (J, IX:318); visiting the shanty Ricketson had built around the same time he had put up his Walden cabin; exploring the woods and the Middleboro Ponds; even dancing to Mrs. Ricketson's piano accompaniment.[22]

One person he met at Ricketson's was twenty-year-old Kate Brady, who expressed a "strong love for outward nature" and who wished to "live free" by herself in a deserted house (J, IX:335). Thoreau was impressed with her as he had been with few other women and spoke glowingly of her in his journal: "she has a strong head and a love for good reading, which may carry her through. I would by no means discourage, nor yet particularly encourage her, for I would have her so strong as to succeed in spite of all ordinary discouragements." These "discouragements" included "jeering" by "tamely bred" women for her "entertaining such an idea" (J, IX:335–36). For all his misogyny, a significant blind spot for one who was so sensitive to forms of oppression other than sexism, Thoreau was unquestionably attracted to this woman who reminded him so much of himself. However, it was to another "woman," nature, that he was more profoundly drawn and to whom he declared primary attachment. In the same breath with which he discusses Brady, he professes, "How rarely a man's love for nature becomes a ruling principle with him, like a youth's affection for a maiden, but more enduring! All nature is my bride" (J, IX:337). Earlier in the same passage, he identifies nature as "home," a crucial theme of this period when he was seeking to clear the trail by which he could come home:

Such seem to have a true home in nature, a hearth in the fields and woods, whatever tenement may be burned. The soil and climate is warm to them. They alone are naturalized . . . fairly rooted in the soil, and are the noblest plant it bears, more hardy and natural than sorrel. The dead earth seems animated at the prospect of their coming, as if proud to be trodden on by them. It recognizes its lord. Children of the Golden Age. (J, IX:336)

To unite or, rather, reunite with nature was to repossess in part the "Golden Age"—a trusting, womblike, preoedipal, prerivalry era—from which he so often feared he had been forever evicted. Responding on April 26 to B. B. Wiley's inquiry about the "hound, bay horse, and turtle-dove" passage in *Walden,* Thoreau writes,

If others have their losses, which they are busy repairing, so have I *mine,* & their hound & horse may *perhaps* be the symbols of some of them. But also I have lost, or am in danger of losing, a far finer & more ethereal treasure, which commonly no loss of which they are conscious will symbolize. . . .

Methinks a certain polygamy with its troubles is the fate of almost all men. They are married to two wives—their genius (a celestial muse) and also to some fair daughter of the earth. Unless these two were fast friends before marriage, and so are afterward, there will be but little peace in the house. (C, 478).

At the same time that he was willing to admit, though still in somewhat cryptic fashion, his losses and his apprehensions about losing something even more precious, he was also seeking to recuperate by recouping, in some measure at least, his loss of the golden age. By wedding his muse not with a "fair daughter of the earth" but with earth-nature itself, he anticipated that he could reconstitute a "peaceful house" for himself. With nature as his marriage partner, his muse itself, "that amount of thought we have had," will, as he writes on May 1, become his *real* "real estate," and the "ground we have thus created is forever pasturage for our thoughts." Working with "imagination and fancy and reason" results in "a new creation . . . a possession forever. . . . You have to that extent cleared the wilderness" (J, IX:350).

Although he had not been as preoccupied with sap this year as the previous one, he did this April associate the drinking of yellow birch sap with "vigor in our limbs" (J, IX:341–42). As a letter to Ricketson reveals, he was by May 13 feeling substantially more "vigorous" and healthy: "Since I left NB I have made several voyages equal to the circumnavigation of the Middleboro Ponds, and have done much work beside with my hands

— In short, I am suddenly become much stouter than for the past 2 years" (c, 480). It was probably not coincidental that Thoreau acknowledges the "receit of 'Tom Bowling'" in the letter, just after the description of his improved health. The song had long been associated with his brother,[23] and his recuperation depended in part on renewing a sense of closeness to, and blessing from, John. The day after the letter he saw two marsh hawks "hovering very near" him, and the day before the letter he had heard a "bay-wing," which he described as a "brother poet" (J, IX:367, 363–64). As previously suggested, birds—and the marsh hawk, in particular—were linked to John, the amateur ornithologist, and it may be surmised that these two experiences with birds reaffirmed or highlighted the sense of at least partial recovery of intimacy with John. Soon after he sang "Tom Bowling" during a thunderstorm on May 30 (he had been protected from the rain by a rock and was prompted to exclaim "how fit that Nature would thus shelter her own children!" [J, IX:398]), Thoreau saw a "slight rainbow" on his way home, as if, by remembering John with affection, he had to some degree been able to regain his brother's blessing. That he had managed to renounce worldly ambition, and be at home with homeliness, no doubt contributed to his growing sense of reconciliation.

The marked, if still not complete, return of physical and of emotional health coincided with each other, and improvement in one unquestionably influenced improvement in the other. Unlike the previous two springs, the coming of which had served as painful and threatening contrasts with his weakened bodily and creative condition, this spring Thoreau was inclined to identify with, and wax lyrical about, positive signs of life and rebirth. He witnesses and describes graphically the copulation of frogs, and hearing the ring of a single frog sets off sympathetic vibrations in himself that replicate a sexual experience: "One that rings within a foot of me seems to make the earth vibrate, and I feel it and am thrilled to my very spine. . . . It takes complete possession of you, for you vibrate to it, and can hear nothing else" (J, IX:354–55). The "fertile flowers of many plants," it was reassuring to see, "are more late than the barren ones" (J, IX:361). He was also glad to see that, unlike last year, "Everything in the shape of a peach tree blossoms this season," even a "mutilated shrub on the railroad causeway, sprung from a stone which some passenger cast out." Wounded as he had been, his limbs the focus of fears of stagnation, he had made it through the winter, like the peach tree's "lowest limbs, which were covered by drifts" and which "have blossomed much the earliest and fullest" (J, IX:372). Counseling one who "dwelt on the sufferings of life" on May 24, he indicates the need to "go about one's business, suggesting that no ecstasy was ever interrupted, nor its fruit blasted. As for completeness and roundness, to be sure, we are each like one of the laciniae of a lichen, a torn fragment, but not the less cheerfully we expand in a moist day and assume unexpected colors" (J, IX:377–78). *His* "fruit," he now had some faith, was not blasted, or at least not permanently so; "torn fragment" though he was, he was again expanding. Bathing in the river, "we are baptized into nature," and he was feeling that he was, again, in the process of being born.

In his "stouter" condition, it was more difficult to sympathize with those preoccupied with somatic complaints; this man, whose own symptoms had never been medically substantiated or diagnosed, sought—partly defensively—to make a break with his own invalidity and patienthood and to put as much distance as possible between himself and "notional nervous invalids." Ricketson was in Concord in late May and was even contemplating a move to this Mecca of transcendentalism. In late April Thoreau had spoken of Ricketson's "singular" "fear of death" (J, IX: 345), obviously implying that it was not a healthy state of mind. It appears that Ricketson's complaints were getting on his nerves; perhaps, too, he was edgy about the prospect of having someone so emotionally open, worshipful, illness-oriented, and death-fearing living in such close proximity to him, someone who continually reminded him of his own recent bout with an illness of uncertain etiology and his own death anxieties. In any case, he portrays these "notional nervous invalids"—clearly as opposed to himself—in very unflattering, disdainful terms. They "report to the community the exact condition of their heads and stomachs every morning, as if they alone were blessed and cursed with these parts"; they "go more than half-way to meet any invalidity, and go to bed to be sick on the slightest occasion, in the middle of the brightest forenoon, —improve the least opportunity to be sick." With the vehemence of one reacting against a part of himself he needed to deny or exorcise, Thoreau concludes that such people are "self-indulgent persons, without any regular and absorbing employment" (J, IX:379). Now that *he* was "absorbed" in generative activities again, he no longer had such a proclivity to focus on bodily symptoms as a "vehicle of self-concern"[24] or as a metaphoric expression of emotional angst and struggle.

In spite of his improved health and his intimations of restored generativity, the coming of June and summer offered a new test. Whatever evidence of generativity his richer journal entries and thoughts provided, vigor and fecundity had to be reclaimed, proved again, every day and every season, or they could once more come into question; he did not have such stable generative props as children. Spring was already in the past, and summer would be a decisive test of his recovery. Thoreau could not fail to forget that the previous summer had been one of his most barren—and that summer in general, with its wilting humidity, heat, haze, and sometimes perplexing profusion of natural details, was a season that threatened stagnation. Thus on June 6, along with the aspens which were "trembling again," he was quaking a bit as he contemplated what the "new summer" offered to him:

> I feel a little fluttered in my thoughts, as if I might be too late. Each season is but an infinitesimal point. It no sooner comes than it is gone. It has no duration. It simply gives a tone and hue to my thought. Each annual phenomenon is a reminiscence and prompting. Our thoughts and sentiments answer to the revolutions of the seasons, as two cog-wheels fit into each other. . . . A year is made up of a certain series and number of sensations and thoughts which have their language in nature. . . . Each experience reduces itself to a mood of the mind. (J, IX:406–7)

The facts that could *not* be reduced to a "mood of the mind" he saw "as through a glass darkly" (J, IX:407), and he had cause to worry whether, despite his rejuvenated vision of the connection between the natural and human seasons, he might be incapable of grasping the opportunities of this season, might be unable to assimilate summer's facts without deteriorating into sterile, uninspired, scientific observation. Indeed, his entries of June 6 and 7 do become somewhat botanical and matter-of-fact.

But, as he had said on May 3, "All well men and women . . . come abroad this morning by land and water, and such as have boats launch them and put forth in search of adventure" (J, IX:352). He was determined to prove that he was "well" again—physically, emotionally, and creatively—and he made plans to go abroad this summer on several major excursions. Before the summer was over, he would make his final journeys to Cape Cod and the Maine woods. On June 3 he complains of having

> several friends and acquaintances who are very good companions in the house or for an afternoon walk, but whom I cannot make up my mind to make a longer excursion with. . . . You should travel as a common man. . . . Every one would see that he was trying an experiment, as plainly as they see that a lame man is lame by his limping. (J, IX:400–401)

His trips would be experiments, putting him to the test, and he hoped that he would not betray any "lameness." Perhaps to his secret relief, Channing, his prospective companion for the Cape Cod excursion, withdrew at the last moment,[25] and Thoreau went to the Cape alone. He set out by himself on June 12 and returned on June 22. This trip was only a partial success. Still in search of an Indian who could inspire him, and reaffirm his connectedness to wildness and to his brother, he was somewhat disappointed by those he met. The Indians in a small cluster of "one-storied cottages" were *"just beginning to build a meeting-house today!"* One Indian, "a respectable-looking young man not darker than a sunburnt white man," replied, when Thoreau "observed to him that he was one of the aboriginal stock," " 'I suppose so' " (CC, 249). The sight of a wreck, which "looked very small and insignificant," may have revived guilt with respect to his surviving his brother, that young "Tom Bowling" who had been drowned by the elements. When he went to renew his acquaintance with the crusty Wellfleet Oysterman, he discovered that Newcomb was dead.[26] The time spent in Cape villages was unsatisfying. The inhabitants "take it for granted that my way is a direct one from village to village," and he was often depressed by signs of settlement: "I go along a settled road, where the houses are interspersed with woods, in an unaccountably desponding mood" (J, IX:431). Only when he was rambling by himself, away from civilization, was he at home: "when I come out upon a bare and solitary heath [I] am at once exhilarated." "This," he says, "is a common experience in my travelling. I plod along, thinking what a miserable world this is and what miserable fellows we that inhabit it . . . but anon I leave the towns behind and am lost in some boundless heath, and life becomes gradually more tolerable, if not even glorious" (J, IX:431–32). Solitude is described by Thoreau as "the medicine for which I had pined," and it was while alone that he was able to find the Indian relics that suggested continuity with wildness and with his brother's spirit. Clearly, Thoreau monitored his health and strength as the trip proceeded and noted that his legs were in better condition when he was "home" again in wildness and solitude. "When I go through a village," he observes, "my legs ache at the prospect of the hard gravelled walk. I go by the tavern with its porch full of gazers, and meet a miss taking a walk or the doctor in his sulky, and for half an hour I feel as strange as if I were in a town in China; but soon I am at home in the wide world again, and my feet rebound from the yielding turf" (CC, 251). Upon returning to Concord, he immediately invited Blake for a visit, and they boated together up the Assabet.

While the Cape Cod journey had had its rewards, it did not provide all that Thoreau was seeking this summer. His journal account of the trip had been detailed and even lively, but it hardly gave conclusive evidence of an inspired generativity or vision. Answering an inquiry by Calvin Greene, he writes on July 8, "Though my pen is not idle, I have not published anything for a couple years at least. I like a private life, & cannot bear to have the public in my mind" (C, 485). Though his pen was not idle, and though publishing seems not to have been his top priority at this time, he was anxious to have more substantial creative "fruit"—beyond the *Journal*—to show for his recent comeback.

In a letter to George Thatcher of July 11, in which he announces his intention to travel to Maine and suggests that Thatcher's son be part of the party, he declares that he is "somewhat stronger than for 2 or 3 years past" and is ready for a "leisurely & economical excursion" (c, 485–86). In another July 11 letter to Eben Loomis, a young Cambridge mathematician he had met in 1853 whom he wanted to invite to accompany him on his Maine excursion,[27] he reveals that, even physically, he still considers himself somewhat impaired. Alluding to the projected Maine expedition, he says that he does not plan on anything perilous for he yet remains something of an "invalid." But, he adds, since he has been in Maine twice in September, he would like to go there earlier in unhurried fashion.[28] Obviously, Thoreau wished to allow more time for this journey—and not only because of his health. It was important that he glean something worthwhile and energizing from Maine. Considering his previous experiences in the Maine woods, going there would be a risk and a test of his responses to genuine wilderness. In his two letters of July 11, he mentions the possibility of engaging an Indian as a guide or traveling companion. Given his disappointments with Indians on previous forays to Maine, Thoreau was understandably wary about staking too much on further encounters with Indians. On the other hand, the dream of finding an Indian whom he could respect, admire, and befriend—and thus more decisively recapturing the sense of relation to his "Indian" brother and to wildness—was a potent one. Perhaps it was under the spell of this dream that he wrote in his July 13 journal,

> I sometimes awake in the night and think of friendship and its possibilities, a new life and revelation to me, which perhaps I had not experienced for many months. . . . I suddenly erect myself in my thoughts, or find myself erected, infinite degrees above the possibility of ordinary endeavors, and see for what grand stakes the game of life may be played. . . . I catch an echo of the great strain of Friendship played somewhere, and feel compensated for months and years of commonplace.
>
> Friendship is the fruit which the year should bear; it lends its fragrance to the flowers, and it is in vain if we get only a large crop of apples without it. (J, IX:479–81)

Though he could only have been engaging here in a reverie, it was a remarkably prophetic one: on the trip to Maine, with the stakes so high, he would meet and develop a bond with an Indian that would be a "revelation" to him and encourage further revelations; basking in the light of this

Indian friendship, he would be "erect" and fruitful again.

Thoreau set out for the Maine woods on July 20 with Edward Hoar, the judge's son who had been involved with him in the woodsburning episode of 1844; both Loomis and Charles Thatcher were unable to accompany him.[29] Upon arriving in Maine, he was advised by George Thatcher that a certain Joe Polis would make an excellent Indian guide. Perhaps hesitant to be too direct, Thoreau asked Polis if he knew "any good Indian" (MW, 158) who could serve as a guide for the projected Allegash–East Branch journey, and Polis offered himself. After some negotiations about pay, the pact was made. Thoreau's journal explanation of what he was looking for is illuminating:

> We wanted to get one [an Indian guide] who was temperate and reliable, an older man than we had before, well skilled in Indian lore. I was warned not to employ an Indian on account of their obstinacy and the difficulty of understanding one another, and on account of their dirty habits in cooking, etc., but it was partly the Indian, such as he was, that I had come to see. The difficulty is to find one who will not get drunk and detain you whenever liquor is to be had. . . . But I was bent on having an Indian at any rate. (J, IX:486)

He had come to see "the Indian," and he was "bent" on having one as his guide; to find the "right" Indian, to reach some sort of accommodation with, and understanding of, the Indian was crucial to the success of the trip —and to his own peace of mind. Among other things, on the trail of the "good Indian" he was seeking the spirit of his elder brother. It is thus not a complete coincidence that the Indian traits he sought were also characteristics of his brother, who was "temperate and reliable," older than he, and a dedicated student of Indian lore. Polis, who was eight years older than Thoreau, with a reputation for steadiness, reliability, and intimate knowledge of Indian ways, seemed to fit the bill of an elder-brother surrogate extraordinarily well. He was a promising blend of the wild and civilized, the red and the white.[30] Thoreau's fascination with, feelings about, and attachment to Polis—and the Indian's deep influence on him—owed much to transference between Polis and John.

To be sure, at the beginning of the journey Polis remains elusive, "saying nothing to anybody, with a stolid expression of face, as if barely awake to what was going on," and when he is addressed in the stage, or at the taverns, Thoreau is "struck by the peculiar vagueness of his replies" and observes that Polis "was merely stirred up, like a wild beast, and passively muttered some insignificant response" (MW, 162). While Thoreau seeks to see his behavior in a positive light, as contrasted with the "conventional palaver and smartness of the white man" (MW, 162), he is obviously discomfited by the dearth of communication and seeming lack of rapport. Was he to be disappointed again? But the situation improves as they move farther away from civilization. There is a growing sense of regression to a more peaceful world, a world of infinite promise, not unlike that experienced on the Concord-Merrimack trip. Upon reaching a lake the first evening, Thoreau writes, "it was still steadily raining, and harder than before; and, in that fresh, cool atmosphere, the hylodes were peeping and the toads ringing about the lake universally, as in the spring with us. It was as if the seasons had revolved backward two or three months, or I had arrived at the abode of perpetual spring" (MW, 163). In some respects, this water excursion did represent for Thoreau a reexperiencing of the Concord-Merrimack voyage with his elder brother. The language sometimes evokes and echoes that of the earlier trip: "It was inspiriting to hear the regular dip of the paddles, as if they were fins or flippers, and to realize that we were at length fairly embarked. We who had felt strangely as stage-passengers and tavern-lodgers were suddenly naturalized there and presented with the freedom of the lakes and the woods" (MW, 165). A bit later, Thoreau asks the Indian the meaning of the word "Musketicook"—though he already knows the meaning; the question itself suggests that he was to some degree recollecting the trip with his brother. Now that they are "fairly embarked" and "naturalized," Polis becomes less "strange," more relaxed and conversational. One of his first "friendly" and reassuring acts (one that recalls John's ornithological interests) is to identify birds with their Indian names.

In paternal or elder-brother fashion, Polis builds a fire and explains that hemlock is better than white pine bark (MW, 166). Thoreau speaks of young ducks floating on the "bosom" of Moosehead Lake and remarks that he "felt as if they were under its protection" (MW, 166). He, too, feels under the protection not only of his "mother" in nature but also of the "brother" who guides him, who seems to know by some instinct his way through the woods, who is at home with the wilderness, who is a skilled woodsman. Thoreau and Hoar's overeager embrace of the wild leads to "a series of blunders and misadventures, but in each case Polis rescues them."[31] For instance, Hoar "trailed for trout" as they "paddled along," but when the Indian warned him that "a big fish might upset us, for there are some very large ones there, he agreed to pass the line quickly to him in the stern if he had a bite" (MW, 172). In Polis's company, under his wing, the wilderness may still have its dangers, but it does not seem to be as threatening, horrifying, or impure as on his last two Maine trips. Even Polis's killing and skinning of a moose does not seem to leave Thoreau unduly troubled. He observes that he would "like to go to school" to Polis "to learn his language" (MW, 168), Polis agrees, and they reach a mutual agreement to share all they know with each other. For all his vigor and know-how, though, Polis, like John, is not without a certain frailty, as is evinced in his inability to climb Mount Kineo and his sickness after eating moose meat; moreover, he had come close to starving when he was a young boy. It is possible that these instances of vulnerability, particularly as they were linked emotionally to his elder brother's frail health and death, may have caused Thoreau some anxiety.

By the time they make camp, the two have established a special relationship, not unlike that which Thoreau fantasized having had with his brother. With Polis, as with John, he could feel "wild" and yet dependent. In the Indian's presence, he could believe that John's spirit was alive and that he had his blessings. In short, the friendship with Polis re-created, in some significant way, the ideal fellowship he imagined he had once enjoyed with his brother, and that re-creation was therapeutic and inspirational for Thoreau. Music had always soothed and lulled him, and Polis's singing at the campsite is particularly soothing, encouraging as it does regression to a more tranquil, trusting state, a preoedipal, prerivalry "golden age":

> His singing carried me back to the period of the discovery of America, to San Salvador and the Incas, when Europeans first encountered the simple faith of the Indian. There was, indeed, a beautiful simplicity about it; nothing of the dark and savage, only the mild and infantile. (MW, 179)

In such a guiltless, trusting, relaxed, almost reverent state, Thoreau was prepared for revelation. He had never before seen phosphorescent wood, but now, awaking in the night to the wild sound of an owl or loon, he caught sight of a "perfectly regular, elliptical ring of light," which was

> fully as bright as the fire, but not reddish or scarlet like a coal, but a white and slumbering light, like the glowworm's. I could tell it from the fire only by its whiteness. I saw at once that it must be phosphorescent wood, which I had so often heard of, but never chanced to see. Putting my finger on it, with a little hesitation, I found that it was a piece of dead moose-wood . . . which the Indian had cut off in a slanting direction the evening before. Using my knife, I discovered that the light proceeded from that portion of the sap-wood immediately under the bark . . . and when I pared off the bark and cut into the sap, it was all aglow along the log.

When he "cut out some little triangular chips" and placed them in his hand, the inside of his hand was illuminated. He also noted that "part of a decayed stump . . . shone with equal brightness" (MW, 179–80). Harding comments, "How he had missed it [the phosphorescent wood] in all his years of walks in the Concord woods after dark is hard to explain, for it is a phenomenon familiar to the most amateur of woodsmen."[32] But from a psychological point of view, his sighting the wood under these circumstances is not entirely incomprehensible. As Thoreau may have sensed on some deep level, only in the glow of Polis-John's presence and blessings was he permitted to be sufficiently receptive to see the light. Thoreau himself says,

> I little thought there was such a light shining in the darkness of the wilderness for me. . . . I did not regret my not having seen this before, since I now saw it under circumstances so favorable. I was in just the frame of mind to see something wonderful, and this was a phenomenon adequate to my circumstances and expectation, and it put me on the alert to see more like it." (MW, 180–81)

Even though the incident occurred early in the trip, Thoreau's discussion of its significance, written largely, no doubt, after he had returned to Concord, portrays it as in some ways the culminating event of his Maine woods expedition. As he puts it, "I was exceedingly interested by this phenomenon, and already felt paid for my journey." He adds, "It could hardly have thrilled me more if it had taken the form of letters, or of the human face" (MW, 180). The next day Polis gave him the Indian name of this phenomenon, and he is prompted to conclude that Indians are privy to a "thousand revelations" of nature "which are still secrets to us" (MW, 180–81). But, having come so close to Polis, he has been able to share those secrets. The full impact and meaning of this episode (and, to an extent, of the entire trip) is suggested in the long passage with which Thoreau concludes his account of his responses:

> I exulted like "a pagan suckled in a creed" that had never been worn at all, but was bran new, and adequate to the occasion. I let science slide, and rejoiced in that light as if it had been a fellow-creature. . . . A scientific *explanation*, as it is called, would have been altogether out of place there. That is for pale daylight. Science with its *retorts* would have put me to sleep; it was the opportunity to be ignorant that I improved. It suggested to me that there was something to be seen if one had eyes. It made a believer of me more than before. I believed that the woods were not tenantless, but choke-full of honest spirits as good as myself any day, —not an empty chamber, in which chemistry was left to work alone, but an inhabited house, —and for a few moments I enjoyed fellowship with them. Your so-called wise man goes trying to persuade himself that there is no entity there but himself and his traps, but it is a great deal easier to believe the truth. It suggested, too, that the same experience always gives birth to the

same sort of belief or religion. One revelation has been made to the Indian, another to the white man. I have much to learn of the Indian, nothing of the missionary. I am not sure but all that would tempt me to teach the Indian my religion would be his promise to teach me *his*. (MW, 181–82)

The communion with phosphorescent wood is clearly a religious or quasi-religious experience, another epiphany. It represents, in part, a return to a trusting "suckling" mode, a reaffirmation of faith in, and kinship with, the mystery, primitive vigor, and fertility of the mother who is in nature. Having reestablished a reverent intimacy with nature and with the Indian who worshiped at nature's shrine, Thoreau was allowed access to a "bran new" vision and gained assurance that he would not be confined, in his writing, to the stagnant scientific outlook of "pale daylight" and of the paleface. This, of course, had been a critical part of the assurance he had sought in coming to the Maine woods, and writing about it was itself inspiriting. But this renewed faith, this reveling in his generativity, in his capacity for new forms of ripeness, also rested on another, perhaps even deeper, conviction. It was not only that he had reconnected with the nurturing and life-giving mother's breast or with the Indian who also "suckled" there but also that, in the process of this realliance epitomized so powerfully in the friendship with Polis and the subsequent revelation of the glowing wood, he had re-communed and reunited with his brother. More than before, he could now believe that the "woods were not tenantless, but choke-full of honest spirits," and at least for "a few moments" he had "enjoyed fellowship with them." His experience in the Maine woods confided to him, on some level, that John's spirit was still animate in nature and that they were close. With Polis as a brotherly companion incarnate, the sense of comradeship with John had been reconstituted, and he had been in "just the frame of mind" to see the phosphorescent wood whose radiance was a sign to him that he had achieved, for a time at least, a state of grace, redemption, reconciliation. He now had his brother's blessings. Liberated by a sense of continuity, connectedness, fraternal camaraderie, and dispensation, Thoreau seemed on the verge of making a complete physical, emotional, and creative recovery.

While the anxieties and dangers of this trip should not be minimized,[33] Thoreau returned to Concord with a glow he sought and expected to keep alive. Indeed, his journal entry on August 18 concerns some glowworms that Marston Watson had sent him from Plymouth; it is "a greenish light, growing more green as the worm is brought into more light. A slumbering, glowing, *inward* light, as if shining for itself. . . . they look like some kind of rare and precious gem" (J, X:3–4). In the next breath, he mentions a talk he has had with Dr. Reynolds "about the phosphorescence which I saw in Maine" (J, X:5). Obviously, he was concerned about keeping the revelations and the spirit of the Maine excursion alive, a spirit that would inspire and sustain his creativity; and he was thus delighted to find, in the glowworm, propitious evidence of a continuity of glow from Maine to his native town. As he writes back to Watson, "It was a singular coincidence that I should find these worms awaiting me, for my mind was full of a phosphorescence which I had seen in the woods." In the same letter, he speaks of "one Joseph Polis, the chief man of the Penobscot tribe of Indians," from whom he has "learned a great deal" (C, 487, 488). Clearly, Polis and the glow were connected in his mind. On August 10 he reflects that we "escape fate continually by the skin of our teeth" and asks, "What kind of gift is life unless we have spirits to enjoy it and taste its true flavor?" (J, X:6). In his own subsequent meditations on health, he reveals the extent to which he has "escaped fate" by the "skin of [his] teeth" and is all the more ready, with restored spirits and vigor, to appreciate the flavor of life's gift:

> We should first of all be full of vigor like a strong horse, and beside have the free and adventurous spirit of his driver; i.e., we should have such a reserve of elasticity and strength that we may at any time be able to put ourselves at the top of our speed and go beyond ordinary limits, just as the invalid hires a horse. . . . The poor and sick man keeps a horse . . . but the well man is a horse to himself; is horsed on himself; he feels his own oats. . . . First a sound and healthy life, and then spirits to live it with. (J, X:6–7)

A refreshed, reenergized, renewed Thoreau wrote these words; he was feeling his oats upon the return of his physical and spiritual health. The way he had endured, and in many ways thrived, during the undeniable physical ordeal of the Maine journey had tested and proved his revived vigor. But he had also drawn strength from his bond with Polis, his luminous vision in the forest, and his ability to front the facts of wilderness predominantly with exhilaration rather than with horror and anxiety. For the most part, he was feeling strong as a horse now, with all the physical and creative potency suggested by a horse. He had passed the risky, rigorous test that he had set for himself in going to Maine, and he had come through, he felt, with flying colors. It is indicative that, though he would have other transient health complaints before his final illness, he would rarely if ever again mention the mysterious leg malady that had hampered him physically and had been so closely tied to his generative feebleness. Even if his August 11–24 journal entries were relatively short and matter-of-fact, he was convinced that he now had a "reserve of elasticity and strength." And his rich work on "The Allegash and East Branch" would be one of the most auspicious fruits of his renewal. In the glow of the Maine experience, his writing promised to be much less lackluster.

Thoreau's August 18 letter to Blake suggests how much he continued to live off and under the influence of the Maine excursion after he came back to Concord:

> Having returned, I flatter myself that the world appears in some respects a little larger, and not, as usual, smaller and shallower, for having extended my range. I have made a short excursion into the new world which the Indian dwells in, or is. He begins where we leave off. It is worth the while to detect new faculties in man, —he is so much the more divine; and anything that fairly excites our admiration expands us. The Indian, who can find his way so wonderfully in the woods, possesses so much intelligence which the white man does not, —and it increases my own capacity, as well as faith, to observe it. I rejoice to find that intelligence flows in other channels than I knew. It redeems for me portions of what seemed brutish before. (C, 491)

Emerson, in his funeral oration, would characterize Polis as another of the three men (along with Whitman and John Brown) who had the most significant impact on Thoreau in his later years, and that impact is very much in evidence here. In the wake of his bond with Polis—and of his sense of re-communion with his brother—his "capacity, as well as faith," had been regenerated. Polis's meaning for him was genuinely redemptive. That he was able to keep brother-Polis alive in his writing was also redeeming to a degree. The Maine woods trip, moreover, restored his sense of continuity in his life, reaffirmed some of his most profound promptings, and renewed more fully his intimate, trusting, fertile ties with nature and wildness. He continues to Blake,

> It is a great satisfaction to find that your oldest convictions are permanent. With regard to essentials, I have never had occasion to change my mind. The aspect of the world varies from year to year, as the landscape is differently clothed, but I find that the *truth* is still *true*, and I never regret any emphasis which it may have inspired. Ktaadn is there still, but much more surely my old conviction is there, resting with more than mountain breadth and weight on the world, the source still of fertilizing streams, and affording glorious views from its summit, if I can get up to it again. As the mountains still stand on the plain, and far more unchangeable and permanent, —stand still grouped around, farther or nearer to my maturer eye, the ideas which I have entertained, —the everlasting teats from which we draw our nourishment. (C, 491–92)

Shunted aside was the nightmarish terror and disequilibrium Katahdin had once evoked and the haunting memory of the "murder" of the moose. The Maine woods trip not only left Thoreau feeling more "wild"—and less defensive—but also left him feeling once more firmly attached to, and drawing nurturing sustenance and inspiration from, the "everlasting teats" of nature. He felt more at home with and in nature again. And he could believe that not all his "peak" experiences were in the past.

On the occasion of the first fall rain on September 20, Thoreau comments that "there has been no drought the past summer. Vegetation is unusually fresh. Methinks the grass in some shorn meadows is even greener than in the spring" (J, x:36). No, there had been no drought—literally or figuratively—this past summer, as Thoreau had feared there might be when it had begun. He felt, moreover, resuscitated and fresher as fall approached, and capable of further growth. The lack of drought, he expected, would lead to well-matured fall leaves and bounteous fruits. He was now, at the age of forty, more fully prepared for an autumnal ripening.

8 Ripe for the Fall

*O*N October 26, 1857, Thoreau made it clear that he was coming around again to, and homing in on, a strong sense of the correspondence between the natural and human seasons:

> These regular phenomena of the seasons get at last to be—they were *at first*, of course—simply and plainly phenomena or phases of my life. The seasons and all their changes are in me. I see not a dead eel or floating snake, or a gull, but it rounds my life and is like a line or accent in its poem. Almost I believe the Concord would not rise and overflow its banks again, were I not here. After a while I learn what my moods and seasons are. I would have nothing subtracted. I can imagine nothing added. My moods are thus periodical, not two days in my year alike. The perfect correspondence of Nature to man, so that he is at home in her! (J, X:127)

It is understandable why Thoreau felt this sense of correspondence most keenly in the autumn. This was the crisp and brisk season that now most invigorated and inspired him, and it was the one with which he was most in harmony. No longer was he wont to resist the fact that he was middle-aged; he had had to accept this fact more fully before he could feel genuinely synchronized with the autumn and entirely receptive to the whole new creative field of imagery and vision that this season opened up for him. It is, as in *A Week*, as if he had awakened to find it autumn, and he was now truly ready to take on "autumnal work." Even before this fall, he had made incremental gains in his perception of being once more "at home" in nature; his ability to see—"at last" as he had "*at first*"—the connections between seasonal phenomena and his current phase of life helped him feel even more intensely that he was closing in on "home" at last, that his life was ripening and rounding itself out. It was a Thoreau ostensibly more in season than he had been for some time who appears in the *Journal* of early and mid-fall 1857. Indeed, much of his most moving and inspiring writing in the time left to him—autumn would be a very condensed season for him —would be in an autumnal mode.[1]

On October 5 he contrasts summer and fall in a manner that also suggests a comparison between young manhood and middle and old age: "There is not that profusion and consequent confusion of events which belongs to a summer's walk. There are few flowers, birds, insects, or fruits now, and hence what does occur affects us as more simple and significant" (J, x:64). With the clutter, distractions, complexities, and heat of summer at least to a certain extent behind him, the autumnal man can see things more clearly and equably, can discern what is most important and what can be discarded.

Thoreau's prose in the autumnal mode would frequently take on a kind of finely sculpted spareness; natural observation would often stand on its own, without involved or bookish philosophizing, because the correspondences, to Thoreau, were so clear as to be self-evident. The universal and specific, the general and personal, would often implicitly and peacefully coexist. Natural facts would "stand for," and be emblematic of, human and moral facts without much need for overt analogy. While there would be times when he would use explicit analogy, he was more trustful than ever that the language of nature was an eloquent medium for communicating his vision of human life and his own life. "I have been forty years learning the language of these fields," he observes on November 20, "that I may the better express myself" (J, x:191). The "Autumnal Tints" and "Wild Apples" essays he would, for instance, harvest largely from his autumn journals would rarely need the intermediary injection of an aggressive ego to articulate, in mellow and elegiac tones, the human as well as natural truths to which Thoreau subscribed. However, the writings on John Brown would be most dramatic, and in their own way quite revealing, exceptions to these tendencies, and equanimity would by no means always be easily come by.

On September 27 Thoreau, who had—in a markedly more uncertain time—posed the question, "Am I not a *sugar maple* man, then?" sets forth a newly revised version of his ego ideal, building on Walden and *Walden* but also going beyond them, based on implicit analogy and identification with the maple:

> A small red maple has grown, perchance, far away on some moist hillside, a
> mile from any road, unobserved. It has faithfully discharged the duties of ma-

ple there, all winter and summer, neglected none of its economies, added to its stature in the virtue which belongs to a maple, by a steady growth all summer, and is nearer heaven than in the spring, never having gone gadding abroad; and now, in this month of September, when men are turned travellers, hastening to the seaside, or the mountains, or the lakes, —in this month of travelling, —this modest maple, having ripened its seeds, still without budging an inch, travels on its reputation, runs up its scarlet flag on that hillside, to show that it has finished its summer work before all other trees, and withdraws from the contest. Thus that modest worth which no scrutiny could have detected when it was most industrious, is, by the very tint of its maturity, by its very blushes, revealed at last to the most careless and distant observer. It rejoices in its existence; its reflections are unalloyed. It is the day of thanksgiving with it. At last, its labors for the year being consummated and every leaf ripened to its full, it flashes out conspicuous to the eye of the most casual observer, with all the virtue and beauty of a maple. . . . In its hue is no regret nor pining. Its leaves have been asking their parent from time to time in a whisper, "When shall we redden?" It has faithfully husbanded its sap, and builded without babbling nearer and nearer to heaven. Long since it committed its seeds to the winds and has the satisfaction of knowing perhaps that a thousand little well-behaved and promising maples of its stock are already established in business somewhere. It deserves well of Mapledom. It has afforded a shelter to the wandering bird. Its autumnal tint shows how it has spent its summer; it is the hue of its virtue. (J, x:46–48)

Although Thoreau had, of course, traveled this past summer (and had "grown steadily" during this period, especially in Maine), his travel had been a means of finding his way back home to his brother, nature, and wildness. And in September he was back in Concord and more firmly rooted there than ever. On September 9 he writes to Ricketson that he cannot accept his invitation to visit: "I have an immense appetite for solitude, like an infant for sleep, and if I don't get enough of it this year, I shall cry all the next" (C, 493). In a larger sense, he had for the most part spent his summer life without "having gone gadding abroad" (though he had been tempted by societal inducements and had lost his bearings for a time), and he was now inclined to believe and accept that his spring and "summer work"—including *Walden*—was in the past and that he had more emphatically "withdrawn from the contest," discarded any notion that he would be, wanted to be, or needed to be a conventionally successful author in his own lifetime. Moreover, as a provider of shelter to "wandering birds" (an image associated partly with his brother), he was a nurturer rather than competitor; and as a conservator of trees, he could see himself as a gentle and generative caretaker, a "father" protecting his "children." He would, on September 28, indict those "vandalic proprietors" who should be "prosecuted for maltreating the face of nature committed to their care" just as "some are prosecuted for abusing children" (J, x:50–51). In his emerging concept of self, concern for the public domain would assume increasing significance and centrality.

Although he had to a great extent given up on his dream of being a legend in his own time, he struggled to believe that, like the maple, he had "faithfully husbanded" his supply of "sap." Already many of his "seeds," his words and deeds, had been committed to the "winds" of the future, and, he hoped, they would establish "promising maples of its stock." But he was also putting much stock in the new, even riper generative era on which he seemed to be embarking, an era in which he needed to insure that he would leave behind a worthy legacy. After all, he was working on the "Allegash and East Branch" essay, and his fall journal entries—fragments, to be sure, but many as brilliant as the ripening leaves—held out considerable creative promise. Although the strength of his generative needs was great, and although he had not given up on his more monumental projects, he seemed, in September and October, less fixated on tours de force, more willing to accept the *Journal* as a primary work in and of itself: "Is not the poet bound to write his own biography? Is there any other work for him but a good journal? We do not wish to know his imaginary hero, but how he, the actual hero, lived from day to day" (J, x:115). He was, in these months, somewhat more prepared to accept his limitations and the limitations of time; he was less tempted to make Faustian bargains. But no mistake should be made about it: generativity assumes paramount importance in middle age, and Thoreau had to lean heavily on alternative forms. Continuing generativity and ripening were thus profoundly urgent concerns in this season of his life. As hopeful as he was in the early and mid-autumn of 1857, the crisis of generativity was by no means behind him; the quest and struggle for assurance of generativity, often beset with anxiety and guilt, would be absolutely pivotal in the months and years to come. His relation to the Muse would wax and wane. As far as his literary ripening is concerned, it turned out that much of his most artistically successful, most completely realized work was already in the past, and his final era of ripeness would, in strictly artistic terms, be a modest, if still quite meaningful, one—striking on some newer autumnal themes and issues, revealing Thoreau's own greater personal maturity, and highly flavorful and rewarding in its own unique ways. Passing through the storms of life, his creativity appears to have become not just seasoned and weathered but, to some extent, weather-beaten; while he maintained the ability to write wonderful fragments and even coalesce them into some memorable and often moving essays, the mysterious gift of rendering fragments into magnificent, coherent, and towering wholes he had displayed in *Walden* appears to have diminished. Whether this gift was slipping away, or simply relatively dormant, we can never know for sure: time and circumstance would not be on his side. The troubling events from late 1857 on would spur but also threaten generativity and ripening, and Thoreau's season of ripening would be cut short.

The prospects looked bright, however, in the peak-foliage season of 1857. Just as, in October, the "year is ripened like a fruit by frost, and puts on brilliant tints of maturity but not yet of decay" (J, x:85), so had Thoreau been ripened by the "frosts" in his life. Having had so many brushes with physical and spiritual exhaustion (from which he had not emerged unscathed), having lived several lives and died many little deaths, he had reason, like the maple, to "rejoice" in his existence. The "serious sound of the funeral bell" was "more in harmony with" the autumnal scene "than any ordinary bustle could be"; it reminded him that "a man must die to his present life before he can appreciate his opportunities and the beauty of the abode that is appointed him" (J, x:74). Endings had to be accepted, and often seen as necessities, in order to make new beginnings. Thoreau himself had had to die to the bustle and compromise of his post-*Walden* life (a process that had led to physical, emotional, and creative impairment, signified a kind of death, and threatened to sap and strip away his life) before he could most fully "appreciate" and take entire advantage of the "abode . . . appointed" him. Now that he had made his acquaintance with death and now that, in autumn, the toll of the funeral bell could not go unacknowledged, life was even less likely to be taken for granted. It was all the more precious, to be relished, for "only through the gate of death would man come to appreciate . . . the beauty of the world he has abused" (J, x:76), a beauty at once breathtaking and heartbreaking in this autumnal phase. There were fates worse than death: dissipation, spiritual and creative deterioration, enervation, death in life. Firsthand experiencing of the "early maturing frosts" and foreknowledge of the more severe and killing frosts to come were prerequisites for fall ripening. He now had a new lease on life, but it was a lease with a fixed term—and shorter than he expected.

The more mature, autumnal Thoreau, then, was no longer as inclined to deny or seek literal escape from the reality of death as the youth and young man had been. To be sure, this reality could still be unsettling, as when he came upon the remains of a rabbit in an old trap on October 8. While it "was wholly unoffensive, as so much vegetable mould," he could not avoid reflecting on the starkness of the "tragedy," particularly the manner of death: "After days and nights of struggle, heard for a few rods through the swamp, increasing weakness and emaciation and delirium, the rabbit breathes its last" (J, X:77–78). But if death was an undeniable fact that had to be broached—emotionally as well as intellectually—Thoreau was, aided by nature's example and natural imagery, increasingly looking to other forms of immortality that would stand him in good stead. Contemplating the death of pine needles on October 16, he exclaims, "How beautifully they die, making cheerfully their annual contribution to the soil! They fall to rise again, as if they knew it was not one annual deposit alone that made this rich mould in which the pine trees grew. They live in the soil whose fertility and bulk they increase, and in the forests that spring from it" (J, X:101). In the naturalistic sense, as Whitman had stressed in *Leaves of Grass*, the human being lived on in the elements of which he was composed, and his "mould" would increase the "fertility and bulk" of the soil, even ultimately springing forth itself, reincarnated in new forms of life like the grass. Similarly, the "greenness of ferns" in autumn was an "argument for immortality," as were the skunk-cabbage buds, which already were "advanced toward a new year" and thus were destined to complete the "circle of life." Although Thoreau would sometimes see "mortal human creatures" as a linear contrast to nature's circularity, he felt (owing, of course, not just to a naturalistic perspective but also to his pantheistic impulses and his deep yearnings to be at one with the mother and brother-father in nature) so absorbed in, allied to, the elements that death was less to be feared. Though his spirits might "flag a little" (J, X:150) as he pondered death, he could still frequently conceive of his life in the circular terms suggested by nature. In death, he would but be making it all the way home, returning from whence he came, and eventually shooting up again through the soil. Even in the respect that he—the unique individual, Thoreau—would not literally evade death, it was reassuring to know that the nature he so loved and identified with would live on after he was gone. In another sense, he, as a symbol-making human creature, was the creator of words that would continue to fertilize the readers of the future; in them he would be remembered and brought back continually to life. If he had been tempted in the past to live in the world created by his words, he was now somewhat less reliant on living in that world and unquestionably more concerned that his words, his deeds, and his deeds in words would *survive him*, providing another, exceedingly meaningful, kind of permanence and reducing the fear of death. In one way this brand of immortality was similar to nature's and could be articulated through natural imagery: through art he would return, in circular fashion, to earth again, be resurrected. In *Walden* (and as he had implied in *A Week*), he had said, "Our voyaging is only great-circle sailing" (w, 320). Yet he had also spoken in the "Conclusion" of starting on that "farthest western way, which . . . leads on direct a tangent to this sphere" (w, 322). Though symbolic immortality through art was in some ways circular, and could be imaged in natural terms, it could also be construed as a tangent—in this case a particularly human trajectory—that transcends nature and time. Both circle and tangent (as well as the parabola, the nonreturning curve referred to in "Walking")[2] would be ways, ultimately complementary, to image and conceive of the life that survives even after we, as "mortal human creatures," come to the end of the line.[3]

Even if the awareness of death was becoming an integral part of his unfolding maturity, he was, in October 1857, by no means ready to die. To be sure, his brother's and sister's early deaths, his attack of sympathetic lockjaw, the family history of tuberculosis, and his own recent illness had made him sensitive to the possibility that he could die young. But he still had much unfinished creative business; there was still so much to accomplish, to harvest, before the end of the season. Thoreau was feeling ripe but not yet ripe enough for a fall from life's tree; ripeness was not yet so inexorably close to death. Images of his own ripeness for further accomplishment appear often in his October journal. On the sixth, in one of his lyrical, almost Keatsian, odes to autumn, he writes, "Everything—all fruits and leaves, the reddish-silvery feathery grass in clumps, even the surfaces of stone and stubble—are all ripe in this air. Yes, the hue of maturity has come even to that fine silver-topped feathery grass . . . in clumps on dry places. I am riper for thought, too" (j, x:67). On October 14 he provides a variation on this theme: "I take all these walks to every point on the compass, and it is always harvest-time with me. I am always gathering my crop from these woods and fields and waters, and no man is in my way or interferes with me. My crop is not their crop. . . . There are other crops than these, whose seed is not distributed by the Patent Office" (j, x:93–94). Yet, even amidst all this reveling in his regained sense of generativity, there remained a part of him that desired to put an even more profound ripening at some point in the indefinite future; on the same day that he claims "it is always harvest-time with me," he writes, after describing the "particolored pines," "So it should be with our own maturity, not yellow to the very extremity of our shoots, but youthful and untried green ever putting forth afresh at the extremities, foretelling a maturity as yet unknown" (j, x:95).

As he had with the maple, so did Thoreau return to the wild apple, an image and symbol he had drawn on in earlier years, to embody and elaborate on his revised sense of who he was in this season of maturity:

> Suppose I see a single green apple, brought to perfection on some thorny shrub, far in a wild pasture where no cow has plucked it. It is an agreeable surprise. What chemistry has been at work there? It affects me somewhat like a work of art. I see some shrubs which cattle have browsed for twenty years, keeping them down and compelling them to spread, until at last they are so broad they become their own fence and some interior shoot darts upward and bears its fruit!

Here he cannot resist the temptation to make explicit the connection between tree and man:

> What a lesson to man! So are human beings, referred to the highest standard, the celestial fruit which they suggest and aspire to bear, browsed on by fate, and only the most persistent and strongest genius prevails, defends itself, sends a tender scion upward at last, and drops its perfect fruit on the ungrateful earth; and that fruit, though somewhat smaller, perchance, is essentially the same in flavor and quality as if it had grown in a garden. That fruit seems all the sweeter and more palatable even for the very difficulties it has contended with. . . . the apple emulates man's independence and enterprise. Like him to some extent, it has migrated to this new world and is ever here and there making its way amid the aboriginal trees. (J, X:137–38)

Persistent; successfully defending his own genius; moving on an upward course; fruitful; unappreciated by the "ungrateful" and overcivilized yet tangy and palatable to those who are appreciative of the "wild"; flavorful despite—and partly because of—the "many difficulties" contended with; independent and enterprising: these were qualities Thoreau wished to ascribe to himself. The following year he would amplify even further on his identification with the wild apple tree and fruit as well as with the maple.

"My moods are thus periodical, not two days in my year alike," Thoreau had recognized on October 26, but he was undoubtedly not fully prepared for the shift in emotional climate that November would bring. By early November, his father, already suffering from a cold of some duration (which may have unsettled him even earlier in the year), developed more alarming symptoms. As he reports to Thatcher on November 12,

> Father has received your letter of Nov. 10, but is at present unable to reply. He is quite sick with the jaundice, having been under the doctor's care for a week; this, added to his long standing cold, has reduced him very much. He has no

appetite, but little strength and gets very little sleep. We have written to Aunts Maria & Jane to come up & see him. (C, 495)

It was one thing to ponder death intellectually and even make emotional progress toward coming to terms with one's own death; it was another to be so harshly confronted with conclusive proof that one's parent was in decline and could die at any time. That the aunts had been called in indeed suggests the seriousness of John Sr.'s affliction. For Thoreau, his father's deteriorating health was all the more disconcerting; it reawakened anxieties related to surpassing, superseding, and surviving not only his father but also his brother—anxieties that had so recently been mollified. The prospect of replacing his weakened father as head of the household and family business was unsettling; aside from the oedipal issues, these added responsibilities would force another modification in his newly refurbished life structure. No sooner, it seemed, had he gotten his own house in order than a portentous crack appeared in the foundation. The imminent death of a parent, moreover, calls into question one's own hold on life; one feels one's mortality in a most powerful way, is led to wonder how much more time for oneself is allotted, and considers with some urgency how one is to spend that time. The lingering illness that would afflict his father for over a year would, on the one hand, increase Thoreau's sense of urgency about his own generativity and give him opportunities to be "generative" in the sense of taking on more family responsibilities; on the other hand, it cast a pall over his aspirations for ripeness—How much ripeness would be permitted to him, and was he permitted to be ripe?—and made demands on his energies that made it difficult for him to be consistently ripe. It would become more and more difficult for him to separate ripeness from a death that follows closely and inexorably on its heels. His father's life-threatening illness set in motion a process leading to a gradual, subtle loosening of his own grip on life. The intimations of ripeness Thoreau had felt in September and October became more problematic.

On November 14 the weather was "considerably colder," and Thoreau notices that his "hands suddenly fail to fulfill their office, as it were begin to die." "What a story to tell an inhabitant of the tropics," he says, "perchance that you went to walk, after many months of warmth, when suddenly the air became so cold and hostile to your nature, that it benumbed you so that you lost the use of some of your limbs" (J, X: 177–78). After "many months of warmth," in which Thoreau had finally and fully regained the use of his limbs, he may well have sensed that his limbs—and his physical, emotional, and creative health—were again threatened with relapse, even "begin[ning] to die." It must have seemed ironic to him that, so soon after his recovery from feebleness, his father had become decisively enfeebled. And now he, once more, was troubled with health problems that threatened his ripeness, his sustaining sense of relation to nature. On November 18 he writes that in a "healthy" state "I find myself in perfect connection with nature. . . . But in sickness all is deranged. I had yesterday a kink in my back and a general cold, and as usual it amounted to a cessation of life. I lost for the time my *rapport* or relation to nature. Sympathy with nature is an evidence of perfect health" (J, x:188). One wonders if his illness and backache were not in some way a "sympathetic" response to his father's condition. Two days after this confession of at least temporary loss of "rapport" with nature, he reiterates just how crucial to him is the feeling of being at home:

> A man is worth most to himself and to others, whether as an observer, or poet, or neighbor, or friend, where he is most himself, most contented and at home. There his life is the most intense and loses the fewest moments. Familiar and surrounding objects are the best symbols and illustrations of his life. . . . The poet has made the best roots in his native soil of any man, and is the hardest to transplant. . . . If a man were rich and strong anywhere, it must be on his native soil. (J, x:190–91)

But in the latter days of November Thoreau found nature generally to be inscrutable, impenetrable, inhospitable:

> Not only the fingers cease to do their office, but there is often a benumbing of the faculties generally. . . . Nature has herself become like the few fruits which she still affords, a very thick-shelled nut with a shrunken meat within. . . . The prospect looks so barren . . . not a companion abroad in all these fields for me. I am slow to go forth. I seem to anticipate a fruitless walk. (J, x:203–4)

In this "November Eat-heart" season he was especially prone to eating his heart out; his relations to people as well as to nature seemed even more barren than usual:

> I do not know if I am singular when I say that I believe there is no man with whom I can associate who will not, comparatively speaking, spoil my afternoon. That society or encounter may at last yield a fruit which I am not aware of, but I cannot help suspecting that I should have spent those hours more profitably alone. (J, x:204)

But circumstances did not militate toward his being "profitably alone" these days. There was his father to care for, and the relatives in attendance as well. Moreover, there were, and would be, more financial pressures and responsibilities in the coming months. For one thing, there were hard times abroad in the land, the devastating Panic of 1857. While Thoreau was better prepared than most to deal with economic calamity—in October he had compared the "solvency" of sandbanks and nature with the country's financial panic and insolvency (J, X:93), and on November 16 he wrote to Blake, "Hard times, I say, have this value, among others, that they show us what such promises are worth, —where the *sure* banks are" (C, 496)—he now, in the wake of his father's debilitation, as well as the economic uncertainties, had to think of contributing more extensively to his family's support. It was incumbent on him to do a considerable amount of surveying, an activity he characterizes on December 7 as "barren work," even if there is occasionally a "cheering and compensating discovery" (J, X:221). In comparison with the autumn months, the December journal would be quite sparse, no doubt partly due to his surveying responsibilities. In the coming year, Thoreau became increasingly involved with the details of the family pencil business. In May 1858 he would even go to New York in order to improve the Thoreau share of the pencil market, which had been seriously jeopardized by the price-cutting actions of a competitor; in order to keep the business afloat, he acquired an agent in New York and was forced to cut in half the price of the Thoreaus' black lead.[4] Furthermore, he "did what overseeing was necessary at the mill, brought the lead back to the house on Main Street, and did the heavier work of boxing and packing."[5] While these activities, which put him in the role of responsible provider for his family, certainly helped give Thoreau some sense of generativity, they also gave rise to anxieties and guilt. In taking over so many financial duties, he was taking over the role of father, a role that stirred up oedipal anxiety and guilt. Furthermore, the embroilment in economic and competitive activities distracted him from creative work, coarsened his sensibilities, and threatened the sense of identity he had been in the process of reconstructing.

In November 1857 he contrasted untested youth invidiously with age: "In youth, when we are more elastic and there is a spring to us, we merely receive an impulse in the proper direction. To suppose that this is equivalent to having travelled the road, or obeyed the impulse fruitfully throughout a lifetime, is absurd" (J, X:202). Thoreau believed that he had "travelled the road" and that he had sought to remain faithful to his grandest impulses. But he suspected, too, that he had still to travel farther on the road and that it might be a struggle to maintain that faith. In the very act of affirming his faith, he suggests on December 13, again connecting a sickness he may still have had with stagnation, that he had been subject to feeling "mean and barren": "In sickness and barrenness it is encouraging to believe that our life is dammed and is coming to a head, so that there seems to be no loss, for what is lost in time is gained in power. All at once, unaccountably, as we are walking in the woods or sitting in our chamber, after a worthless fortnight, we cease to feel mean and barren" (J, x:222). There can be little doubt that the "worthless fortnight" to which he refers was at least partially his own. With the first winter snow, and with Walden "almost entirely skimmed over," Thoreau continued to reflect, with a mixture of moroseness and determination, on life's trials:

> One while we do not wonder that so many commit suicide, life is so barren and worthless; we only live on by an effort of the will. Suddenly our condition is ameliorated, and even the barking of a dog is a pleasure to us. So closely is our happiness bound up with our physical condition, and one reacts on the other. . . .
> Do not despair of life. You have no doubt force enough to overcome your obstacles. (J, x:227–28)

Surely this passage indicates that Thoreau was himself struggling with a resurgent sense of despair, barrenness, and, possibly, unstable health. He seems here to be giving himself something of a pep talk. He would survive, overcome his obstacles, regain soundness and hope, but it could sometimes only be accomplished through "force" of mind, "effort of the will."

On the first day of 1858, Thoreau gives cousin Thatcher an update on his father's condition.

> Father seems to have gotten over the jaundice some weeks since, but to be scarcely the better for all that. The cough he has had for so long is at least as bad as ever, and though much stronger than when I wrote before he is not sensibly recovering his former amount of health. On the contrary we cannot help regarding him more & more as a sick man. I do not think it a transient ail— which he can entirely recover from—nor yet an acute disease, but the form in which the infirmities of age have come upon him. He sleeps much in his chair, & commonly goes out once a day in *pleasant* weather. (C, 502)

Thoreau realized, then, that his father's infirmity was not a temporary condition but one likely to persist as long as he continued to live. He could only hope that he could accommodate to it and that his own situation would soon improve. Brooding the same day over his recent surveying, he expresses the "fear" that "this particular dry knowledge may affect my imagination and fancy, that it will not be easy to see so much wildness and native vigor there than formerly." The Maine woods were "different essentially from ours," he adds (J, x:233), clearly lamenting that there seemed to be such a gulf between the radiant revelations and ripeness inspired by the Maine trip and the opaque and dim character of recent days.

The rejuvenation of the previous summer now seemed far away, and he notes, "How completely a load of hay in the winter revives the memory of past summers!" (J, x:237). Even the "glow" of the Andromeda on January 3 prompts only the remark that "it is long since a human friend has met me with such a glow" (J, x:235). The bloom was off the rose. Feeling "very cheap" on the sixth, only the sight of a snowflake on his sleeve encourages him "a little," for he had begun "to believe that Nature was poor and mean" (J, x:238–39). Along with his father's poor health had come disturbing transferences with his brother's death, associations that could be even more troubling around the time of the anniversary of John's passing. As his experience with Polis (and his writing about it—he had finished it by January)[6] faded into the past, and as his father's health reawakened anxieties about his brother, his attitude toward the Indian became, for the time being, at once more mournful and problematic. The Indians, he writes on the twenty-third, are "inevitably and resignedly passing away"; most startlingly, he adds, "The fact is, the history of the white man is a history of improvement, that of the red man a history of fixed habits of stagnation" (J, x:251–52). To the extent that he, too, identified with Indians, he might have been led to reflect on his own gradual eclipse and "passing away" due to "fixed habits of stagnation." Also on January 23, he wrote a letter to James Russell Lowell, who had earlier proposed that he submit his "Allegash and East Branch" essay for publication. Thoreau offered "Chesuncook" but declined to offer the 1857 excursion because "my Indian guide, whose words & deeds I report very faithfully, —and they are the most interesting part of the story, —knows how to read, and takes a newspaper, so that I could not face him again" (C, 504). He had always been sensitive about using his brother for his own literary gain; now, with renewed sensitivity to exploiting a "brother" who was himself part of a "dying" race, he felt distinctly uneasy about the prospect of gaining recognition by making use of Polis. Thus perhaps the richest and most vivid character portrait in all of Thoreau's writing would not be published until after his death. In some sense, it would have been a betrayal of brother-Polis to go public with the narrative when the author was still alive to benefit from it.

Thoreau was feeling separated from friends, both living and dead, during this period, and he once again turned to nature. Apparently seriously concerned about some sort of physical or spiritual relapse, he observes on the twenty-third,

> To insure health, a man's relation to Nature must come very near to a personal
> one; he must be conscious of a friendliness in her; when human friends fail or

die, she must stand in the gap to him. I cannot conceive of any life which deserves the name, unless there is a certain tender relation to Nature. This it is
which makes winter warm, and supplies society in the desert and wilderness.
Unless Nature sympathizes with and speaks to us, as it were, the most fertile
and blooming regions are barren and dreary.

Later that day he continues,

> I do not see that I can live tolerably without affection for Nature. . . . I do not
> think much of that chemistry that can extract corn and potatoes out of a bar-
> ren [soil], but rather of that chemistry that can extract thoughts and senti-
> ments out of the life of a man on any soil. It is in vain to write on the seasons
> unless you have the seasons in you. (J, x:252, 253)

But for much of 1858—until, significantly, the first signs of autumn—
the "chemistry" rarely worked; the personal and sympathetic relationship
with nature was not the overtly dominant mode. Whatever catalysts were
necessary to set off a chain reaction with "imagination and fancy," they
were in seemingly short supply. One suspects that the distractions and concerns related to his father's illness weighed heavily on him. Certainly, there
was little evidence of soaring, coherent, or sustained creative vision in early and middle 1858. The *Journal* for February is mostly filled with short,
amorphous entries, many somewhat scientific, and in March the natural
observation is detailed, matter-of-fact, with little attendant philosophizing. There is, on March 9, an impassioned plea for the conservation of forests (J, x:297), which prefigures one of his central concerns in subsequent
years. But when he says, on March 20, "All Nature *revives* at this season.
With her it is really a *new* life" (J, x:314), one gets the sense that Thoreau
does not feel entirely in tune with the season. The gathering of data continued in April, with special attention to an investigation of frog spawn (using
Ed Hoar's microscope). The spawn was but another kind of seed, and one
is led to believe again that Thoreau's absorption in nature's reproduction
represented a means to associate and identify with generative forces. Although May was a month of botanical and zoological observation, in
which little thought was apparent, his portrait of the "thinker" on May 6
reveals his underlying aspirations:

> The thinker, he who is serene and self-possessed, is the brave, not the desperate
> soldier. He who can deal with his thoughts as a material, building them into
> poems in which future generations will delight, he is the man of the greatest
> and rarest vigor. . . . Common men . . . can *read* poems perchance, but they
> have not the vigor to beget poems. . . . He is the man truly—courageous, wise,

ingenious—who can use his thoughts and ecstasies as the material of fair and durable creations. (J, x:404)

Clearly, this entry, written soon after a description of spawn, reflects Thoreau's own persistent intention to spawn art; he could only trust that the "materials" with which he was currently working would strengthen, rather than sap, the foundations of the creative edifice he hoped would reach "future generations." Perhaps it was partly his concern for artistic immortality, not to mention his legitimate desire for fair treatment, that led him to write a scathing letter to Lowell on June 22, excoriating him for excising from the "Chesuncook" essay, "in a very mean and cowardly manner," the sentence, "It [the pine tree] is as immortal as I am, and perchance will go to as high a heaven, there to tower above me still" (c, 515–16). If we consider his identification with the pine (and remember that the pine also appears to have been associated with his brother),[7] it is all the more understandable why Thoreau would take the omission personally. In any case, leaving out the reference to immortality was unacceptable to one who was so anxious to assure himself meaningful forms of immortality.

In May natural observation begins to alternate in the *Journal* with reports of trips. Indeed, though none of his excursions yielded any genuinely memorable prose, he did take numerous jaunts in the spring and summer, perhaps seeking once more to prove that he was healthy, possibly needing to extricate himself from the demands of his family responsibilities and his father's incapacity, and probably hoping to battle stagnation and recapture some of the invigoration and inspiration he saw himself as having experienced the previous summer. But none of the trips seemed to fire his imagination in any noteworthy way. Toward the end of May he went to Worcester (where he walked along Quinsigamond Pond with Blake and Brown and did some naturalizing) and then on to New York where, along with conducting pencil business, he visited the aquarium at Barnum's and the Egyptian Museum.[8] Early in June, eventually joined by Blake, he set out for Monadnock. Although he sought to put himself in touch with the enduring and immortal in his confrontation with the mountain, he also came to feel he was in "the presence of some vast, titanic power" (J, x: 473), which may have disturbed him, challenging as it did his recent sense of being at home in and with nature. Also in June, he spent much time in botanical observation and in studying nests and eggs. Collecting eggs had become a "fad" with Concord youth at the time,[9] and Thoreau was often consulted by such children as Edward Emerson, Edward Bartlett, and Storrow Higginson in his capacity as egg expert (J, x:497). Not only did this interest in eggs give him the opportunity to be generative with the children of Concord, but, as has already been argued, the eggs themselves offered him another chance to ally himself with nature's fertility.

His most physically demanding trip, begun in early July, was to the White Mountains, accompanied by Edward Hoar, his Maine woods companion. Upon coming to the Merrimack, he experienced a "relief and expansion" of thought; the current "conducts our thoughts as well as bodies to classic and famous ports, and allies us to all that is fair and great" (J, XI: 4). Quite possibly the sight of the Merrimack gave him a fleeting sense of continuity and alliance with his brother, the person whose memory and spirit was most evoked by the river. But the adventure in the White Mountains was not to be a comforting re-creation of the Concord-Merrimack trip (including the mountain hiking with John) or of those inspiriting parts of the last Maine woods expedition. While they were staying overnight in a shanty on their way up Mount Washington, "the wind, blowing down the funnel [of the chimney], set fire to a pile of dirty bedquilts . . . and came near to burning up the building" (J, XI:16). Starting out for Tuckerman's Ravine, they found the fog "bewildering" (J, XI:21); it would be easy to get lost, or to lose one's footing. In one particularly "hard and dangerous" spot, Thoreau reports, "I tore up my nails in my efforts to save myself from sliding down [the] steep surface" (J, XI:24–25). One of his companions, Wentworth, inadvertently set fire to some fir leaves; the fire spread "with great violence . . . crackling over the mountain, and making us jump for our baggage." They left the "fire raging" (J, XI:27). Considering his prior experience with accidental fires, one may speculate that this incident may have left Thoreau in a somewhat anxious state. After they were joined later that day by Blake and Brown, "wet, ragged, and bloody with black flies," they "slept five in the tent . . . and it rained, putting out the fire we had set" (J, XI:29). The next day, Thoreau sprained his ankle "jumping down the brook" in Tuckerman's Ravine, and the following day he was "prevented" by his "lameness" from "pursuing" and identifying a "peculiar and memorable songster" (J, XI:32, 34). A trip that Thoreau hoped would confirm his physical and, possibly, creative energy thus had a relatively "lame" conclusion. The inability to pursue the elusive songbird has a metaphoric quality, as if he was not only physically but spiritually unable to gain access to the bird's inspiring strain or, perhaps, his own Muse. For the rest of the journey, there is much observation of nature but little inspiration, save for another statement about conservation which contends that more of nature "should belong to mankind inalienably" rather than to private interests (J, XI:55). The summit of a mountain one is ascending, he noted, "is not the easiest thing to find, even in clear weather"; the "surface was so irregular that you would have thought you saw the summit a dozen times before you did, and in one sense the nearer you got to it, the further off it was" (J, XI:52). Similarly, this was a time when Thoreau wondered if the "summit" to which he was aspiring (and which had seemed so close the previous summer and autumn) was not still far off, whether, in fact, he could see it at all. The excursion to the White Mountains underlined the inhospitability of nature in the wilderness and thus called into question again his sympathy for, and attachment to, nature. It at least momentarily brought to the surface the contradictions and anxieties he had in recent years subordinated, or tucked away in a corner, in his search for a home in nature and wildness. He would write to Blake on January 1, 1859, "I confess that the journey did not bear any fruit that I know of" (C, 538).

It was not, appropriately, until the cricket's chirp in August heralded the impending autumn, recalling "the moods of that season" (J, XI:95), that Thoreau again sensed the imminence of another period of resurgent creative inspiration, expansion, and consolidation. It now seemed that it was primarily autumn that spoke most eloquently to his own condition. Though, as he botanized and boated on the Concord, some farmers might think of his ilk as "idlers," "we, too, are harvesting an annual crop with our eyes" (J, XI:77). He was, as he put it on the fourth anniversary of *Walden*'s publication, "chewing the cud" of a "few thoughts" (J, XI:89). It was the "heart of the huckleberry season," and he was reminded not only of the "declining year" but of the decline in the American civilization he once had had such high hopes for; he bemoaned the extent to which huckleberry fields formerly open to the public now had "stakes set up with written notices forbidding any to pick there" (J, XI:78). He was feeling his age, mourning the loss of a world of infinite promise and its supplantation by a far more perturbing and perverse world. "We are not grateful enough," he says, "that we have lived part of our lives before these evil days came" (J, XI:78). More and more, as a man who wanted to bequeath something memorable and substantial to future generations, he was coming to the defense of the common, public welfare as against the interests of private property, which had stripped people of their "natural rights" to the "wild fruits of the earth" (J, XI:78–79) and helped bring on the "evil days." If the pleas for conservation enhanced his sense of generativity and his prospects for symbolic immortality, so did the shift in his journal, as autumn approached, to longer, richer, more reflective entries. On August 26 he finds himself "sympathizing" again with nature, this time with the purple grasses "because they are despised by the farmer and occupy sterile and neglected soil. They also by their rich purple reflections or tinges seem to express the ripeness of the year. It is high-colored, like ripe grapes, and expresses a maturity the spring did not suggest." The scientific orientation was again giving way to the recognition that "each humblest plant . . . stands there to express some thought or mood of ours" (J, XI:125–26). Leaves that have fallen in a heavy rain remind him, on August 28, that he has "crossed the summit ridge of the year and . . . begun to descend the other slope. The prospect is now toward winter." Embarked on the journey toward winter, he could yet anticipate harvests along the way. "Has not the mind, too, its harvest?" he asks on August 29 (J, XI:130).

While in September there remained much botanizing as well as a trip to Cape Ann to meet with John Russell, Thoreau was feeling ripe again, even more so than the previous autumn. If in some sense the fall of 1857 had been his September, the autumn of 1858 would be at least part of his October. Feeling himself the poet once again, he exclaims, "How differently the poet and the naturalist look at objects!" (J, XI:153).The fall answered to where he saw, and needed to see, himself as being in his own life cycle, and contemplating its significance and imagery aided him in coming to terms more fully with a "winter" that was ever closer on the horizon for his father and, he was beginning to suspect on some level, for himself. Perhaps the passage of time had given him the opportunity to accommodate, as much as he could, to his father's condition and gain back some control over his daily life. On January 1, 1859, he would write to Blake, "I have lately got back to that glorious society called Solitude, where we meet our friends continually" (C, 536). Also likely is that he was, partly due to his father's impending death and its reactivation of emotions related to his brother's death, starting to rehearse his own demise, one that would absolve him of oedipal and survivor guilt and reconcile him with both male figures. The closer he was to death, the riper he was permitted to be, and ripeness was never very far from a death that could even seem beckoning in certain respects. One cannot avoid speculating that he has himself and his "Indian" brother in mind, as well as his father, when he describes the "wild-looking" Indian grass on September 6: "It stands like an Indian chief taking a last look at his beloved hunting-grounds. The expression of this grass haunted me for a week after I first passed and noticed it, like the glance of an eye" (J, XI:147). Six days later he voices his resolution to "Die like the leaves, which are most beautiful in their decay. Thus gradually and successively each plant lends its richest color to the general effect, and in the fittest place, and passes away" (J, XI:155). In October, finding a bullet alongside an arrowhead at Walden, he has a vision of reconciliation through death between white man and Indian that may testify to the reconciliation he yearned for with male figures; it is "as if, by some [un]explained sympathy and attraction, the Indian's and the white man's arrowheads sought the same grave at last" (J, XI:212–13). His meeting with

Whitman's brother on October 20 prompts remarks that also suggest the extent to which his idealized elder brother is in his thoughts: "In all cases we esteem rather the suggested ideal than the actual man, and it is remarkable that so many men have an actual brother, an improved edition of themselves, to whom we are introduced at last. Is he his brother, or his other self?" (J, XI:232).

On October 1 Thoreau wonders, upon seeing the "perfectly ripe" elm leaves, "if there is any answering ripeness in the lives of those who live beneath them" (J, XI:191). This is the question that had persistently plagued him. And, as far as he was concerned this autumn, the answer seemed to be in the affirmative. The sighting of phosphorescent wood in Concord on October 4 and the discovery of breams in Walden Pond in late November were in some way signs to him that he would be allowed some further revelations, a period of grace, before his own winter came. Any setbacks he had experienced had been necessary, he concluded, for the full maturing of his vision: "A man runs down, fails, loses self-respect, and goes a-fishing, though he were never seen on the river before. Yet methinks his 'misfortune' is good for him, and he is the more mellow and humane" (J, XI:196). "Mellow and humane" describe well much of the tone of Thoreau's writing this autumn. He was confident that "genius" was "inspired by its own work" and therefore "hermaphroditic" (J, XI:204). The dulling haziness of summer was gone; in its place, during this "season of the fall of the leaf, just before the cool twilight has come," was air of a "finer grain." Correspondingly, "our mental reflections are more distinct at this season of the year" (J, XI:216). One indication that Thoreau had a more clearly distilled sense of direction and was starting, at least in a modest way, to put things together and see them whole was his letter to Ricketson of November 6, reporting that he was at work on "something about the autumnal tints" (C, 525), a subject he was surprised "has left no deeper impression on our literature yet" (J, XI:254). Although there would be no book on October hues, certainly much of his most eloquent and well-developed prose of the fall centered around this subject.

It comes as no surprise that Thoreau reserves some of his most ardent remarks about "autumnal tints" for the sugar maple. As a more mature man, he no longer demands that these trees "yield up sugar in the spring, while they yield us so fair a prospect in the autumn." He is able to express his nurturing, "fatherly" impulses in calling for the protection of such trees. In the village that is a "merely trivial and treeless waste" will be found, he says, "the most desperate and hardest drinkers." And, to the very great extent that he identifies with the sugar maple, he seeks to confirm what in recent years he had had to struggle to believe in: his enduring generativity. He speaks with the air of a man with an eye to posterity, one who has contemplated his death and what he will leave behind. Repeatedly he stresses the lasting contributions the sugar maples will make to children and future generations: "Hundreds of children's eyes are steadily drinking in this color, and by these teachers even the truants are caught and educated the moment they step abroad. . . . Do you not think it will make some odds to these children that they were brought up under the maples?" His words are both poignant and prophetic when we recognize, over a century later, that they are written by one who wanted and needed to consider himself a generative "sugar maple man": "They are cheap preachers, permanently settled, which preach their half-century, and century, aye, and century and a half sermons, with continually increasing influence and unction, ministering to many generations of men" (J, XI:217–22).

Another tree—and its fruit—with which Thoreau had long identified and felt a special, intense kinship was the wild apple. On October 31, his description of the "hour-glass apple shrub" and its fruit was, thus, also a self-representation:

> By the end of some October, when their leaves have fallen, you see them glowing with an abundance of wild fruit, which the cows cannot get at over the bushy and thorny hedge which surrounds them. Such is their pursuit of knowledge through difficulties. Though they may have taken the hour-glass form, think not that their sands are run out. So is it with the rude, neglected genius from amid the country hills; he suffers many a check at first, browsed on by fate, springing in but a rocky pasture, the nursery of other creatures there, and he grows broad and strong, and scraggy and thorny, hopelessly stunted, you would say. . . . But at length, thanks to his rude culture, he attains to his full stature, and every vestige of the thorny hedge which clung to his youth disappears, and he bears golden crops of Porters or Baldwins, whose fame will spread through all orchards for generations to come. (J, XI:269–70)

The "rude, neglected genius" has pursued "knowledge through difficulties," suffered "many a check," endured suspicions that he was "hopelessly stunted," protected himself—from others and from his own self-doubts —with his thorns; but now, in the fullness of years, the thorns recede, even disappear, and he bears a fruit which, if not immediately noticed or prized, will eventually be known and celebrated by "generations to come." Such a vision of himself provided an antidote to the despair that had so often threatened to overcome him.

Clearly, the autumn journal is replete with natural imagery that embodies versions of Thoreau's ego ideal. Even the "humblest plant" finally gets its moment in the sun and achieves an unprecedented individuation and authenticity:[10] "sooner or later" each "plant" acquires "its peculiar autumnal tint or tints, though it may be rare and unobserved, as many a plant is at all seasons." And these brilliant colors of leaves and fruit, Thoreau maintains, "stand for all ripeness and success." In these autumnal hues the "plant" shows its true and bravest colors:

> We have dreamed that the hero should carry his color aloft, as a symbol of the ripeness of his virtue. . . . The warrior's flag is the flower which precedes his fruit. He unfurls his flag to the breeze with such confidence and brag as the flower its petals. Now we shall see what kind of fruit will succeed.

The scarlet oak becomes another justifying emblem and metaphor for the heroic and noble man: "Was not this worth waiting for? Little did you think ten days ago that that cold green tree could assume such color as this. Its leaves still firmly attached while those of other trees are falling around it" (J, XI:240, 243, 244). Thoreau was thus also a "scarlet oak man," "lasting into November," still "full of sap and life," flowing "like a sugar maple in the spring" (J, XI:277–78).

But no matter how "full of sap and life" he felt, he was a man whose ripening seemed ever more insistently accompanied by a sober anticipation of death. On November 1 he writes, "As the afternoons grow shorter, and the early evening drives us home to complete our chores, we are reminded of the shortness of life, and become more pensive, at least in this twilight of the year" (J, XI:273). With night and winter coming on, it is incumbent upon him to complete his "chores"—particularly the creative work that will insure a kind of transcendence—as soon as possible. November's "harvest of thought," he remarks, is "worth more than all the other crops of the year. Men are more serious now" (J, XI:312). As long as he can finish his "chores," reap his "harvest," he need not fear death. There are, after all, as he would say in late December, others forms of death more to be dreaded. "All the community may scream because one man is born who will not do as it does, will not conform because conformity to him is death"; but in the long run, the "man of genius" who rejects the "death" of conformity will be exonerated and will in some sense overcome death: "In the course of generations, however, men will excuse you for not doing as they do, if you will bring enough to pass in your own way" (J, XI:380). If he is able to believe that he has brought, or will bring, enough to pass in his own way before he dies, he can claim, as he does in early November, "The hangman whom I have *seen* cannot hang me. The earth which I have *seen* cannot bury me" (J, XI:273). Thoreau seems to be encouraged by the progress he has made, however interrupted it was, toward ripening from last fall to this one: "the utmost possible novelty would be the difference between me and myself a year ago" (J, XI:274). It is this progress which is his "fuel for the approaching winter." Part of the apparent contentment he feels is also due to the renewed autumnal conviction not only that he is preparing well for the return "home" but that, in a very real sense, he has already accepted, embraced, and reconciled himself to that home. Though Cholmondeley is going off to the West Indies and has invited Thoreau to join him, he writes on November 1,

> Here I am at home. In the bare and bleached crust of the earth I recognize my friend. . . .
>
> Think of the consummate folly of attempting to go away from *here*! When the constant endeavor should be to get nearer and nearer *here*. . . . *Here*, of course, is all that you love, all that you expect, all that you are. Here is your bride elect, as close to you as she can be got. (J, XI:274–75)

He would repeat this theme in a January 1 letter to Blake: "What a fool he must be who thinks that his El Dorado is anywhere but where he lives" (C, 538). Observing the "higher color" that appears in a leaf and proves that it has "arrived at a late and more perfect and final maturity," Thoreau wants to believe that he sees evidence of this "higher color" in himself. And he was at least on the verge of such a "late and more perfect and final maturity." In these "serious" days of November, he could not avoid noting the derivation of the word "ripe" from "reap," "according to which that is ripe which is ready to be reaped" (J, XI:317). The more "perfectly" ripe he would grow with the approach of November twilight, the more "final" this ripeness was, and the more ready he would be to be "reaped."

With the arrival of winter, his father's winter seemed ever closer. The death on December 8, 1858, of Rev. Barzillai Frost, who had presided over his brother's funeral,[11] may have intensified this conviction on Thoreau's part. His portrait of the "sincere life" of the farmer on December 27 included a somber version of what life might be like for him with John Sr.'s passing; he no doubt imagined himself the "middle-aged son" who "sits there in the old unpainted house in a ragged coat and helps his old mother about her work when the field does not demand him" (J, XI:378–79). He spent time these days listening to his father review parts of his life. As with the small fish swimming underneath the ice, who were tragically "liable at any moment to be swallowed by the larger" (J, XI:380), so was Thoreau's father liable to die at any moment. At the same time, Thoreau could perhaps see himself in those small fish who could no longer expect to be protected or cared for by their parents: "Parent fishes, if they care for their off-spring, how can they trust them abroad out of their sight?" Without his father's buffering presence, he would be one less step removed from his own death. But maybe there would still be some valuable time allotted to him, just as—he notes on January 2, 1859—the younger oaks, possibly because they have more "sap and vigor," "retain their leaves while old ones shed them" and maintain "some life at the base" while the older trees "wither through at the base" (J, XI:385). He kept looking for reassuring signs of life and abundance in the goldenrods, asters, and alders (J, XI: 385, 394–95). After January 13, John Sr. was "confined to his bed-room, although he still insisted on sitting in his chair each day."[12] No longer would he see his father except in a sickroom habitat, and it was probably not coincidental that Thoreau remarked on the thirteenth that "the weeping willow seems to weep with more remarkable and regular curve than ever" (J, XI:399). Weeping inwardly, nursing his father, and awaiting the end, he sought to keep his spirits up. The frostwork on the trees, the beautiful mackerel sky: these sights provided some diversion and consolation. He tried also to ward off the gathering grief and despair by looking to the example of the musquash hunter, "not despairing of life, but keeping the same rank and savage hold on it that his predecessors have for so many generations, while so many are sick and despairing" (J, XI:422–23). In a letter begun on the nineteenth, in the course of arranging a visit to Worcester to lecture in the near future, he explains to Blake, "My father is very sick, and has been for a long time, so that there is the more need of me at home." He adds on the twenty-ninth, "I am expecting daily that my father will die, therefore I cannot leave home at present" (C, 540). On the twenty-eighth there is the suggestion in his journal that he has "for several nights" been "deprived" of his "usual quantity of sleep" (J, XI:431).

He did not have to wait much longer. On February 3, 1859 (less than a month after the anniversary of John Jr.'s death), John Thoreau, Sr., died at the age of seventy-one. As it is for many middle-aged persons, the death of his parent was a watershed event for Thoreau. Though he had antici-pated his father's death and had had some time to gird himself for it, it was one thing to expect it but another actually to experience it; it is hard to believe that a parent will die until he or she really does. With the parent's passing, whatever lingering youthful fantasies there may be of invulner-ability and physical immortality usually die a decisive death. The succes-sion of generations becomes a key issue for those in middle age—never more insistently than when a parent dies—and it would be especially so for Thoreau.

Raymond Gozzi has argued, from a Freudian point of view, that Thoreau's father's death provoked deep oedipal guilt and that this guilt led him to wish himself dead.[13] This perspective does have much validity, but it also has its limitations. For one thing, as has already been suggested, the mere fact that John Sr. had been seriously ill for some time before his death, that the son had expected his father's demise, had already begun to loosen his hold on life, though, to be sure, the death itself, with its attendant powerful finality and trauma for which Thoreau could not have been fully prepared emotionally, accelerated and exacerbated this loosening process. Furthermore, the Freudian view tends not to take into account issues and influences rooted in postchildhood phases of the life cycle. The shocking, premature death of Thoreau's brother in 1842, as should be abundantly clear by now, had been a lifelong "curse" on Henry, one he had only periodically been able to keep in some sort of remission. Not only, therefore, was the passing away of his father a painful and guilt-inducing event in itself; it also harshly and forcefully reimposed the curse and reawakened the feelings Thoreau had experienced when his brother died. Indeed, that his father had been "very silent for many months" (J, XI: 435) before his death may have increased Thoreau's anxiety; on an unconscious level at least, his father's silence may have been interpreted as a sign of hostility, disapproval, reluctance to communicate love, alienation, just as he may have picked up hints of accusation and alienation in his brother's deathbed behavior.[14] In any case, his father's relative silence presumably made it difficult for him to make final peace with John Sr. It is clearly no accident that Thoreau—apparently seeking in part to make up for his sense that he had somehow tried to hurt or even do away with his father as he had his brother—nursed John Sr. with the same devotion and gentleness with which he had nursed John Jr. in his agonizing final hours. His mother, for some reason not remembering how solicitously Henry had ministered to his brother, said after her husband's death, "If it hadn't been for my husband's illness, I should never have known what a tender heart Henry had."[15]

As he described it in a letter to Ricketson (drawing to a considerable extent on his February 3 journal account), the calm and courageous manner of his father's death could not have failed to remind him of his brother's valiant and serene demeanor seventeen years earlier:

> thinking that he was dying he took his leave of us several times within a week before his departure. Once or twice he expressed a slight impatience at the delay. He was quite conscious to the last, and his death was so easy, that though we had all been sitting around the bed for an hour or more, expecting that

event, as we had sat before, he was gone at last almost before we were aware of it. (C, 546)

Thoreau's February 3 journal report of his father's deathbed appearance takes on added significance and poignancy when we recognize he is also thinking of his brother—and of himself: "When in sickness the body is emaciated and the expression of the face in various ways is changed, you perceive unexpected resemblances to other members of the same family; as if within the same family there was a greater general similarity in the framework of the face than in its filling up and clothing" (J, XI:435–36). That Thoreau, also on that momentous February 3, immediately follows a brief biography and appreciation of his father—"one of the oldest men in Concord, but the one perhaps best acquainted with the inhabitants, and the local, social, and street history of the middle of the town"[16]—with observations about, and a defense of, the "inexhaustibly interesting Indians" (J, XI:436–38) further confirms that his brother—his fellow Indian brave who had transmitted his interest in Indian lore to Henry—was very much on his mind. As has been stressed throughout, Thoreau's long-standing concern for the Indians had been in part a form of grief work, a manifestation of his desire to keep alive, and assert intimacy with and love of, his fallen comrade. After his father's death, he would frequently write of searching for arrowheads, which were enduring signs, he would say in March, that "the subtle spirits that made them were not far off"; they were "a perpetual reminder to the generations that come after" (J, XII:92). In this context, he would even, in March, mention Tahatawan, the Indian chief whose name he had adopted in a mock Indian letter to his brother in 1837 (C, 16–18). As he wished, in his grief, to believe, a "friend is present when absent" (J, XI:452).

Two days after John Sr.'s death, Thoreau remarks that when "we have experienced many disappointments, such as the loss of friends, the notes of birds cease to affect us as they did" (J, XI:439). This journal entry once again hints at the close emotional connection between the deaths of father and brother. John Jr., as we know, was an avid amateur ornithologist and lover of birds, and it was not uncommon for Thoreau to link John with the birds he observed. If the Indians have largely passed from the scene, yet the birds remain to help convince him that some vestige of his brother (and father) survives: "This bird [the crow] sees the white man come and the Indian withdraw, but it withdraws not. . . . It sees a race pass away, but it passes not away" (J, XII:12).

Right after the passage on the "inexhaustibly interesting Indians" on

February 3, Thoreau returns to a direct consideration of how death affects the survivors:

> I perceive that we partially die ourselves through sympathy at the death of each of our friends or near relatives. Each such experience is an assault on our vital force. It becomes a source of wonder that they who have lost many friends still live. After long watching around the sick-bed of a friend, we, too, partially give up the ghost with him, and are less to be identified with the state of things. (J, XI:438)

When his elder brother and "friend" had died, Thoreau had indeed almost "given up the ghost"—he had suffered a near-fatal attack of sympathetic lockjaw, and he had never entirely recovered from the trauma. If he had almost died from psychosomatic lockjaw in 1842, and had since experienced the deaths of other close relatives (including his sister and Uncle Charles), friends, and friendships (including that with father-mentor Emerson), his inclination toward death was now compounded greatly by his father's passing. He was now—at least—doubly "cursed." When the John Brown affair surfaced in October, Thoreau would exclaim, "How many a man who was lately contemplating suicide has now something to live for" (J, XII:439). One implication is that on some level he had himself wanted, and perhaps even expected, to die. His experiences with death had a cumulative and accumulating impact on him; the "assaults" on his "vital force" were escalating.

Certainly the death of a parent brought home with stunning force death's inevitability to one whose health was already precarious. On February 25 health was again at issue: "Measure your health by your sympathy with morning and spring. If there is no response in you to the awakening of nature, —if the prospect of an early morning walk does not banish sleep, if the warble of the first bluebird does not thrill you, —know that the morning and spring of your life are past. Thus may you feel your pulse" (J, XI:455). Thoreau would take his pulse often this year, and it would not always be steady; he did know that the "morning and spring" of his own life were in the past, and his "sympathy" with the bluebird—a bird associated with his brother—was in question. For one for whom the focus of recent health problems had been his legs, it was perhaps foreboding that it was the unfortunate fate of many maples and alders to die when they dipped their "lower limbs" into a freshet that then froze and that falling ice had "stripped down" the "lower branches" of "young maples" for "a foot or two" (J, XI:441, 455). And for one who wrote and worked with his hands, it may have been portentous that, in April, when he was planting trees around Walden Pond he "pricked" his "fingers smartly against the sharp, stiff points of some sedge coming up" (J, XII: 156). Soon before giving a lecture at Worcester in late February on "Autumnal Tints," he reflected—prophetically—"How much the writer lives and endures in coming before the public so often! A few years or books are with him equal to a long life of experience, suffering, etc. It is well if he does not become hardened. He learns how to bear contempt and to despise himself. He makes, as it were, *post-mortem* examinations of himself before he is dead" (J, XI:452). To go public again was partly to placate his insistent generativity needs, but it also aroused, as it had in the past, anxieties about compromising himself and guilt about any signs of conventional ambition. In any case, the point to be emphasized here is that Thoreau *was* given to making "*post-mortem* examinations*" of himself at this time; he was in some manner anticipating his own death. And, indeed, his health would falter in the months to come.

In the period following the death of his father, Thoreau became the masculine head of the Thoreau family and business.[17] He was, according to the 1860 census, the head of the household; he was in March 1859 the executor of John Sr.'s will. He took over the management of the graphite business and made some successful manufacturing modifications. Aside from such formal duties, he also assumed responsibility for the family garden, for fence building, and even for picking up the family's mail.[18] As he now was—a critical point—the only surviving man in the immediate family, it no doubt hit him full force that there would be no male to carry on the family line or name. There seems to have been an even more pronounced urgency than previously in Thoreau's actions and words of this period—as if he knew that his days were numbered, as if his need for a validated generativity in deeds and words was asserting itself all the more strongly because he sensed how little opportunity remained to leave behind a substantial legacy. In April, after noting that the oak-leaf petioles were breaking off and thus making room for the next generation, he writes, "Nothing must be postponed. Take time by the forelock! . . . Now or never! . . . Fools stand on their island opportunities and look toward another land. There is no other land; there is no other life but this, or the like of this. . . . Take any other course, and life will be a succession of regrets" (J, XII: 158–60). Though in some ways uncomfortable with being a nurturer or "father," Thoreau felt impelled to become more "fatherly." For example, in May of 1859 it was he who handled the arrangements for the funeral of Emerson's mentally incapacitated brother, Bulkeley.[19] Two years earlier, he had indicated to Emerson his dissatisfaction with the "barren sand" around his former cabin site at Walden. In the spring of 1859 he finally planted 400 pines and 100 larches (J, XII: 166). He later expressed a desire to make Walden a park (J, XII: 387), which would, he presumably conceived, in some way serve as a memorial to his life and work. He seemed especially concerned that unoccupied land be given over to huckleberry fields (J, XII:387), and the huckleberry would become one central focus and symbol of his increasing zeal for conservation.[20] The years 1859 and 1860 would be peak ones for his advocacy of conservation; his appeal, for example, in April 1859 to preserve and protect the forests, parks, rivers, ponds, birds, and wildlife, which had become the prey of fur traders (J, XII:120 ff.), was one way to make a durable, tangible contribution to future generations. As 1859 progressed, Thoreau also gave more public lectures than he had in any previous year.[21] In his journal he condemns all those he considers to be "non-producers" (J, XII:330). This was a period, then, in which Thoreau seemed increasingly and urgently concerned about caring for and contributing to society[22]—leaving his mark on the public sphere—even if his former (and still competing) tendency had been to shy away from or wash his hands of the public and celebrate the private.

During this time span, however, reflections on barrenness appeared alongside of, and sometimes competed with, images of generativity and ripeness. The creaking tree boughs reminded him of "departed spirits," as did the rustling of dead, dry oak leaves in the wind (J, XII:127–28, 172). Still haunted by the deaths of his father and brother—not to mention his own experiences teetering over the abyss and wandering through desert places—Thoreau wrestled with the demons of stagnation, despair, and death. "Sometimes in our prosaic moods," he writes less than two weeks after John Sr.'s death,

> life appears to us but a certain number of days like those which we have lived, to be cheered not by more friends and friendship but probably fewer and less. As, perchance, we anticipate the end of this day before it is done, close the shutters, and with a cheerless resignation commence the barren evening whose fruitless end we clearly see, we despondingly think that all of life that is left is only this experience repeated a certain number of times.

Yet in the very next sentence he steps back from the precipice when he observes, "And so it would be, if it were not for the faculty of imagination" (J, XI:445). On the day of his father's death he says, "The writer must to some extent inspire himself. Most of his sentences may at first lie dead in his essay, but when all are arranged, some life and color will be reflected on them from the mature and successful lines" (J, XI:438–39). The tenacity of the desire to sustain creative productivity and resist dejection and barrenness asserts itself here. Indeed, it is possible that artistic generativity was less guilt and anxiety inducing than real-life generativity; it provided, to some extent at least, an alternative to direct competition, comparison, and confrontation with others. However, such activities as taking over almost completely the "fatherly" household and business responsibilities, surveying to pick up the family's financial slack, and lecturing—all of which served in part to satisfy his pressing generative urge—were to some degree at odds with artistic generativity. They unsettled the pure, solitary life structure and sense of identity so crucial to the full employment and deployment of his literary powers. They could sap him of some of his time and energy, distract him, and lead him to wonder if he was falling into the same traps that had earlier ensnared him and threatened his art and spirit. In the process of discharging his family and business duties, he may even have been led to feel a guilt-provoking anger against his father for leaving him in such a quandary. Admetus was still making heavy demands on Apollo. As he writes to Blake of his business preoccupations, "This is the way I am serving King Admetus, confound him! If it were not for my relations, I would let the wolves prey on his flocks to their bellies' content" (C, 557).

It became ever more difficult, in these later years, for Thoreau to avoid associating his own ripeness (in real life *and* in his art) with death. "There is," he proposes in March 1859, "no ripeness which is not, so to speak, something ultimate in itself and not merely a perfected means to a higher end. In order to be ripe it must first serve a transcendent use. The ripeness of a leaf, being perfected, leaves the tree at that point, and never returns to it" (J, XII:24). At the point of perfect ripeness, the leaf—or the apple—must fall. With the sickness and death of his father, the stem holding the leaf or apple to the tree was markedly weakened, atrophied, and the leaf and fruit themselves, Thoreau perceived, were ripening rapidly to a more mature—and fatal—perfection. Though the stem's hold on the tree, and his grip on life, would soon be weakened by further developments—the John Brown controversy and Brown's death, the Civil War, and, of course, the onset of his final illness—the process weaning him from life was already well underway. He had a predilection to death that was gathering momentum.[23] It is likely, then, that Thoreau was having increasing trouble conceiving of ripeness apart from the context of a guilt-arousing supersession and survival of significant male figures. To strive for any form of generative "success," however much he needed it, was now, unavoidably, to compete with, and defeat, his brother and father.[24] Only in the purifying shadow of imminent death was ripeness in some sense permissible. He could not forget, in a very private sense, that, as he says in July 1859, "Past generations have spent their blood and strength for us. . . . In all fields men have laid down their lives for us" (J, XII:242). The maturing of men might, as he notes in August 1859, be comparable to the ripening of fruit, and he could believe that the fruit of *his* summer was "hardening and maturing a little" (J, XII:302). However, he was also mindful of the elderberry's lesson: when the elderberries were green they were "perfectly erect," but when they were "perfectly ripe" they hung "straight down" (J, XII:297). He could identify himself, as he does in August, as an unambitious gatherer of ripe huckleberries—with whose ripening and wildness he could also identify—who has "served my apprenticeship" and has "since done considerable journey-work in the huckleberry field" (J, XII:299), but the era of unrestrained, noncommercialized picking of huckleberries and other wild fruits was passing, and the Indians who had once picked them were almost extinct.[25] In seeking to monitor in late summer when the watermelon and other fruits were fully ripe (J, XII:298 ff.), he was also questioning if he, too, was ripe enough to be reaped.

A primary reason why Thoreau, as part of his progressively more deliberate study of the "dispersion of seeds," was, as will be explored more fully later,[26] so intrigued by the "succession of forest trees" was because it furnished him with the chance to study the mechanisms by which one generation could yield peacefully and productively to the next. Seeds, he noted, could not flourish in the shade of parent trees, just as—he remarks in August—"the boy does not camp in his father's yard" but rather "marches off twenty or thirty miles and there pitches his tent" (J, XII:296). The "offspring" of a tree, then, are unlikely to survive if they are put in a competitive situation with "parents" (J, XIV:333–34). And a man, he stresses, to "save his soul and *live*," "has got to *conquer* a clear field" (J, XII:344). Thoreau, who at some level did not believe that he had "conquered" a "clear field," nevertheless sought to deny that genuine success could be achieved through competition or conscious striving. "What we would do best or most perfectly," he writes in March 1859, "is what we have most thoroughly learned by longest practice, and at length it falls from us without our notice, as a leaf from a tree. It is the *last* time we shall do it, —our unconscious leavings" (J, XII:39). In July of 1859, amidst the investigations he had been hired to conduct regarding the stagnancy of the Concord River,[27] and considering his own potential for stagnation, he reveals in his journal that he was feeling "very heavy-headed these days," and in August, just before stressing that the "boy does not camp in his father's yard," he refers, in a discussion of Jonas Potter, to his "lameness"— either in the present or past tense (J, XII:242, 296). As the autumn of 1859 approached, with an uncommonly early and destructive frost on August 17 (J, XII:291), a Thoreau in apparently uncertain health seemed to anticipate an early killing frost for himself; *his* leaves might bloom and burn brightly one last time—before they fell off to become his "leavings."

A principal reason, it must be emphasized, why Thoreau responded so strongly to the John Brown affair was that he held deep and long-standing convictions about the cause for which Brown fought. His fierce support of a righteous cause (and his other political writings and acts over the years) ought to be respected and ought not to be reduced merely to an expression of his private, psychic agenda. Considering the psychological roots of political positions and actions should not necessarily delegitimize or invalidate them; they need to be evaluated on their own merits, apart from any private motivations their supporters (or detractors) may bring to them.

The intensity, vehemence, and content, however, of Thoreau's response to the Brown episode cannot be easily or fully explained without reference to underlying psychological factors. For one thing, his active participation in the Brown controversy seems to be one of the clearest, most profound manifestations of his generative urge. In mid-October, only a few days before hearing of Brown's raid on Harper's Ferry, he had proposed in his journal that "Each town should have a park, or rather a primitive forest of five hundred or a thousand acres, where a stick should never be cut for fuel, a common possession forever, for instruction and recreation. . . . All Walden Wood might have been preserved for our park forever." He continues, "If any owners of these tracts are about to leave the world without natural heirs who need or deserve to be specially remembered, they will do wisely to abandon their possession to all" (J, XII:387). Previously he had been reluctant to involve himself directly in the public, political sphere. In taking a public stand in defense of Brown, Thoreau, himself "without natural heirs," could see himself as making a contribution to society that would be "specially remembered." If he had been one of those men "lately contemplating suicide," he now had "something to live for," one last shot at having an impact on the body politic. Channing remarked that Thoreau's "pulses thrilled and his hands involuntarily clenched together at the mention of Captain Brown."[28] His "cords" were "tense" again, though only briefly and though stretched almost to the breaking point. The fact that, threatening as it must have been, he felt compelled to endorse force and violence if necessary (though he probably did not yet know the terrible details of Brown's massacre of five unarmed slavery supporters at Pottawatamie Creek, Kansas, in 1856)[29] may be partially attributed to the strength of his need for generativity at this penultimate phase of his life. Sensing now that he had little time left, he may have come to feel that only Brown-like tactics would yield quick and tangible results. Yet Thoreau's advocacy of such tactics—partly given impetus by his urgent generativity needs (involving the need to act out in life as well as in words)—led also to intense guilt and anxiety, for in defying the state that so vociferously condemned Brown he was impelled to unleash the rage he already harbored toward "fathers" and to express violent hostility toward authority and, ultimately, toward significant male figures in his life, including his father.[30] Thus, in many ways, the generative drive came into conflict with, and further exacerbated, the guilt, uneasiness, and fear of retribution (partly oedipal) linked with taking bold initiatives as a "father" and as one who challenged town and societal "fathers."

While his "pulses thrilled" at the mention of Brown, he also, according to Channing, was "driven sick" "at the time of the Brown tragedy."[31] He was at once revived and stricken. What Brown said about himself (as he is quoted at the end of Thoreau's "Plea for Captain John Brown") applied also, Thoreau sensed, to himself: "You may dispose of me easily. I am nearly disposed of now" (RP, 138). When Brown was judged guilty and hanged by the state in December (and was burned in effigy by some Concordians as a protest against the memorial service in which Thoreau participated), it may well be that part of Thoreau's unconscious perceived it as a just judgment on himself for attacking authority.[32] Although, in the wake of his father's death, he was more predisposed to death, "less to be identified with the state of things," the verdict on, and hanging of, Brown was one more significant factor loosening his grip on life, not only because he felt in some way that he deserved to be punished like Brown but also, very important, because he viewed Brown as another father or elder-brother figure he could not survive without guilt *and* because he identified so strongly with him. Identifying so intensely with Brown, he could not, with his death, fail "less to be identified with the state of things."

In putting himself out on a limb, in making his passionate, last-ditch plea for Brown (which, gleaned largely from his journal, he first delivered at the Concord Town Hall on October 30),[33] Thoreau was endeavoring to justify his right to exist, even if he also sensed that he deserved and was destined to die. If, as is likely, he suspected that many of his fellow Concordians would have preferred his death to his father's or his brother's,[34] he would have to fight the threat of violence *with* violence—or at least violent words. Edward Emerson wrote that Thoreau read his paper "as if it burned him."[35] The 1844 fire—particularly his behavior after the fire had raged out of control—had been, among other things, a way of expressing hostility toward those who might have wished him dead instead of his brother and a way to protect himself against, even destroy, those he perceived as deadly enemies. He had reinvoked the fire, and fire imagery, in his 1850 journal, when he had again felt especially threatened by the community. Now, set afire himself by the treatment of Brown and by his own urge to make a difference, with both his brother and father gone, he was kindling yet another fire—albeit a verbal one—in Concord, a blaze that both represented and precipitated the reignition of his long-smoldering life-and-death struggle with the community.

Thoreau's actions after the 1844 fire had also been a means to insure his ego ideal, at a time when he was in danger of being too well accepted as the responsible, hard-working son of John and Cynthia Thoreau in the aftermath of his brother's death, and he had discussed the fire in his journal at a time, in 1850, when he felt anew a threat to his identity and needed to establish a seedtime.[36] Now again, in 1859, he was alarmed that he was, as the responsible male head of his household, in danger of forfeiting his ideal identity as a man of wildness, one who was separated by his purity, autonomy, and heroism from his smug, expedience-oriented neighbors. Though taking over family responsibilities may in some manner have satisfied his generative needs, it also put him in the position of being *too* respectable, too well accepted by the community; his fragile ego ideal might be jeopardized in such a situation. He could not let the opportunity of the Brown controversy pass—an opportunity he had probably unconsciously been looking for—without setting another fire that would separate and differentiate himself from his neighbors, particularly those who were either hostile or apathetic regarding Brown's actions and his cause. To do otherwise, to stand mute while Brown was being vilified or ignored, was unthinkable; it would be a conclusive admission of a servile acquiescence to conventional community standards. Even in the month or so before news of the Harper's Ferry raid reached him, Thoreau had displayed a less than mellow side, expressing, for instance, distaste for domesticity, for houses and the people who inhabited them. Indeed, he connects houses *with* slavery:

> It would be fit that the tobacco plant should spring up on the house-site, aye the grave, of almost every householder of Concord. These vile weeds are sown by vile men. When the house is gone they spring up in the corners of cellars where the cider-casks stood always on top, for murder and all kindred vices will out. And that rank crowd which lines the gutter, where the wash of the dinner dishes flow, are but more distant parasites of the host. What obscene and poisonous weeds, think you, will mark the site of a Slave State? (J, XII:341)

In late September of 1859 he writes, "It is remarkable what a curse seems to attach to any place which has long been inhabited by man" (J, XII:340). He was himself "cursed" for having become the head of a household—not only because of the guilt that accompanied taking over from the father but also because his self-conception was threatened by overassimilation, absorption into the community associated with assuming such responsibilities. In early October he observes, "if I see or know the occupant [of a house], I am affected as by the sight of the almshouse or hospital." Immediately thereafter he says, "Wild apples are perhaps at their height, or perhaps only the earlier ones" (J, XII:368). There can be little doubt that Thoreau preferred to identify at this time with the tart, tangy ripeness of wild apples rather than with the stolid maturity of the household head; to associate with wild apples, which could only be appreciated outside of houses, was at least to downplay his position as household head. In a September letter to Blake he complains, "I am not sure that I am in a fit mood to write to you, for I feel and think rather too much like a business man, having some very irksome affairs to attend to these months and years on account of my family" (C, 557). The Brown controversy was Thoreau's last chance to prove that he was what he in many ways wished himself to be—the fiery, independent man who had forsworn conventionality, no matter what the inducements.

In the very month of his father's death, Thoreau, as already noted, had observed that the writer "makes, as it were, *post-mortem* examinations of himself before he is dead" (J, XI:452). In a very real sense, the public declarations that he culled from his autumn and early winter journal represent a post-mortem examination of himself, a sort of anticipatory self-eulogy. When Brown had visited with F. B. Sanborn in the winter of 1857, Thoreau had met him and had been impressed. He had come to Concord again in May of 1859, and Thoreau had heard him lecture at the town hall; he had come away even more taken with him.[37] Emerson would indicate that Brown was the third in the triumvirate (along with Whitman and Polis) of people who had made the most memorable impression on him in his later years. But it was as a selective mirror image or double of Thoreau himself that he served his most crucial function in 1859 and beyond. Thoreau identified closely with Brown, seeing in him what he most wanted and needed to see in himself, omitting and denying whatever did not square with his own desired self-image and psychological needs.[38] The "Plea for Captain John Brown" is a plea for *Thoreau*'s generativity and integrity; it is an attempt to ward off accusations and chronic self-doubts that his life had not been productive, meaningful, and worthy of remembrance. His characterization of Brown is also a description of a large component of his own ego ideal. He could not easily leave out of his plea that

Brown had once been a surveyor—just as he was and had been. Moreover, Brown is portrayed as a "man of Spartan habits" and as one of the few remaining Puritans (RP, 113–15). Spartan and Puritan: Thoreau was anxious to lay claim to the virtues of such men. He also could not resist describing Brown as "a transcendentalist above all, a man of ideas and principles" (RP, 115). In his 1860 lecture, "The Succession of Forest Trees," Thoreau would label himself a transcendentalist (E, 135), and of course many orthodox townspeople had strongly disapproved of his transcendental ways. After his brother's death, Rev. Barzillai Frost in his eulogy had suggested that John, to his everlasting credit, was not an ardent transcendentalist. It was Henry who was the acknowledged "transcendental brother" and who therefore should be condemned; the implication, to Henry, was that it was he rather than John who should have died.[39] By characterizing Brown as a transcendentalist, Thoreau was in part taking a stand against the community that had judged him harshly for *his* transcendentalism. If Brown's actions had been portrayed by some as "insane" or "misguided," so had many Concordians viewed Henry's behavior as peculiar and irresponsible. Therefore, what he claims in Brown's defense he is also saying in his own: "No man in America has ever stood up so persistently and effectively for the dignity of human nature" (RP, 125). Brown is depicted as an essentially nonviolent man who "resolved that he would never have anything to do with any war, unless it were a war for liberty" (RP, 112). By identifying with a man who in his eyes had not sought to hurt others or outdo them in a conventional sense, whose actions had been on behalf of "oppressed people," Thoreau was trying to perceive himself as fundamentally a tender and loving man, one who has been a caretaker rather than rival of his fellow man, one who has not wished harm to significant male figures in his life. To the extent that he did learn, as is almost certain,[40] of Brown's brutal actions in Kansas through newspapers or word of mouth and could not ignore or deny them, these reports may well have been threatening to him, suggesting as they did a destructiveness and callousness toward life that would have made identification with Brown more problematic.

Just before he learned of Brown's raid on Harper's Ferry, Thoreau had been focusing, as he had the previous two years in particular, on nature's ripening and its correspondence to his own. Part of this ripening was apparently expressing itself in his consideration of his "Kalendar" of "annual phenomena": "Natural objects and phenomena are the original symbols or types which express our thoughts and feelings, and yet American scholars, having little or no root in the soil, commonly strive with all their might to confine themselves to the imported symbols alone." He continues, "They go on publishing the 'chronological cycles' and 'movable festivals of the Church' and the like from mere habit, but how insignificant are these compared with the annual phenomena of your life, which fall within your experience!" (J, XII:389–90). Clearly, his own ripeness at that point involved continued sensitive study of the seasons—and, now especially, of the fall which so intrigued and stimulated him—and their correspondence with the phenomena of human life. But this year, significantly, his studies of "autumnal tints" would be largely supplanted by his preoccupation with Brown. On November 12 he notes that it has been difficult for him to appreciate the beauty of the sunset, when his mind has been so "filled with Captain Brown. So great a wrong as his fate implied overshadowed all beauty in the world." Five days later he adds, "I have been so absorbed of late in Captain Brown's fate as to be surprised whenever I detected the old routine running still" (J, XII:445, 447). For a time, then, the consuming interest in Brown preempted the mellow sense of ripeness that had prevailed the previous two falls as he had made connections between autumnal phenomena and his own life. Ironically, in October 1858 he had contrasted the "autumnal tints" with most political speeches, which "are colorless and lifeless as the herbage in November" (J, XI:254). But now even "political speeches" could be a form of ripeness. The writings on Brown were in themselves a bursting forth of blazing and blood-red—rather than golden—autumnal tints, a sort of spectacular conflagration before the inevitable dying down. Thoreau was sensible of being in a certain kind of peak form, even as he knew what happens after the peak season for fall foliage. He was, moreover, anxious to use imagery of ripeness—in this season when "the year itself begins to be ripe" (J, XII:373)—to describe Brown and himself. What Brown had done was "a deed ripe and with the bloom on it" (J, XIII:17). To be sure, Brown and his men were, as he says on October 22, "ripe for the gallows" (J, XII:420), and so, increasingly, did he feel ripe for a fall to earth. In any event, though, Brown and he could still trust that they would make their mark on posterity, even if they were condemned in and by the present: "Such do not know that like the seed is the fruit, and that, in the moral world, when good seed is planted—good fruit is inevitable, and does not depend on our watering and cultivating; that when you plant, or bury, a hero in his field, a crop of heroes is sure to spring up. This is a seed of such force and vitality, that it does not ask our leave to germinate" (RP, 119).[41] Just as he had once envisioned "Blakeians in the shops of Worcester," so now would there be a "new sect of *Brownites* ... formed in our midst" (J, XIII:6). Brown, like Blake and Thoreau himself, would be a "sugar maple man."

In one of those revealing moments of conjunction between private conflict and historical dilemma, Thoreau could translate and expand his personal struggle against stagnation into a public cause; Brown, like himself, he saw as combating the "stagnation of spirit" (J, XII:408–9) that appeared to have infected and permeated antebellum American society and culture. In his September journal he had inquired, "Of what account are titles and offices and opportunities, if you do no memorable deed?" (J, XII: 339). He stresses in his "Plea" that it is not so much Brown's life as it is his "immortal life" (RP, 137) for which he is pleading. In the *Journal* he says that he finds himself "anticipat[ing] a little . . . most naturally thinking and speaking of him as physically dead" (J, XII:422). He adds a bit later (and would incorporate into the "Plea" [RP, 137]), "I almost fear to hear of his deliverance, doubting if a prolonged life, if any life, can do as much good as his death" (J, XII:429). He compares the persecution of Brown to Christ's crucifixion, a comparison to which, significantly, he would return in December 1860, the same day he developed the cold that marked the beginning of his fatal illness.[42] Brown and Christ, he says, are "two ends of a chain which is not without its links" (RP, 137), and it is clear that he would like to consider himself another link in that chain. He, too, was prepared to be crucified, or burned at the stake as a heretic. In the meantime, maimed though he already was, he affirmed that "Heroes have fought well on their stumps when their legs were shot off" (J, XII:423). In "The Last Days of John Brown" he insists that Brown has *not* died, that he has "earned immortality" and "works in public, and in the clearest light that shines on this land" (RP, 152–53). Even if his time and Brown's—the time of the idealistic radical and revolutionary who had dreamed great dreams for his country—seemed to be passing away, and they with it, they would continue to live. In some sense like Christ, Brown—and he—had been martyred but would be resurrected. Like Christ, they have been "sons" who have done their "father's" bidding and were prepared to die in order to redeem the world and insure eternal life and salvation. John Brown's body, and his, might lie "mouldrin' in the grave," but their souls would go marching on. Thus did Thoreau strive to affirm that *his* "memorable deeds," including his all-out, last-stand defense of Brown, would help earn him immortality and would provide a radiant, redemptive legacy to the future. Perhaps the assertion of Brown's immortality also permitted Thoreau to believe that the other significant Johns in his life had not truly died either, thus purging him to some extent of the burden of guilt he felt as a survivor.

In *Walden* Thoreau had explained that he went to the woods so that, when he died, he would not "discover that [he] had not lived" (W, 90). The prospect of Brown's death, coming on the heels of his transition to middle age, his father's death, and presentiments of his own death, amplified greatly Thoreau's need to confront whether he could say that he *had* lived, that he was the possessor of what Erikson calls integrity.[43] As he writes in his October journal and in the "Plea," Brown's situation "advertised" for Thoreau what is driven home so dramatically to most persons who are middle-aged and have suffered the loss of a parent, sibling, or friend—namely, "that there is such a fact as death—the possibility of a man's dying" (J, XII:437; RP, 134). The "man" that he has in mind is probably as much himself as it is Brown. It comes, then, as no surprise that his "Plea" echoes the celebrated words of *Walden*: "It seems as if no man had ever died in America before, for in order to die you must first have lived" (RP, 134). Thoreau seems to be reaching for a wise serenity, a vision of his life cycle as, to quote Erikson, "something that had to be, and that, by necessity, permitted of no substitutions"[44] when he advises his audience in the "Plea," "Be sure you do die nevertheless. Do your work, and finish it" (RP, 134). He appears intent here on banishing regret, on affirming that he has done *his* work well and is now prepared to die—because he has truly lived. His defense of Brown, in words and deeds, was itself a sort of capstone effort, confirming his accession to a more perfect ripeness that immediately precedes the fall of leaf and fruit. On the last day of 1859, he is surely identifying with the wise person who "speaks with most authority," "is not ignorant of what has been said by his predecessors," and "will take his place in a regular order, and substantially add his own knowledge to the knowledge of previous generations" (J, XIII:68).

With the coming of winter, Thoreau could not help but reflect that such men as Brown "in teaching us how to die have . . . taught us how to live" (RP, 134). His deep concern with what he perceived as the courageous, noble, exemplary manner of Brown's death takes on additional significance when we consider Thoreau's previous experience with the "last days" and hours of men who knew they would die and, as will be seen, his own conduct and consciousness in what he intuited—rightly—were *his* last days. While his brother's excruciating and fatal bout with lockjaw had severely wounded Henry, John Jr.'s valiant behavior in his final, painful hours came to serve as an unforgettable model for him. The peaceful manner of the death of John Sr., who even at one point expressed "a slight impatience at the delay," was also still fresh in his mind. Another inspiration had been Sir Walter Raleigh. On the day of Brown's hanging, December 2, 1859, he read one of Raleigh's poems, "The Soul's Errand," to a Concord gathering,[45] and he mentioned Raleigh in "The Last Days of John Brown." While his brother was dying, he had referred in his journal to Raleigh; and, in a lecture given at the Concord Lyceum quite soon after his brother's death, he had commented on the redemptive nobility of Raleigh's death and his behavior as he faced it and remarked that "the death scenes of great men are agreeable to consider only when they make another and harmonious chapter of their lives" (EEM, 195). Now, John Brown's demeanor at death's door provided another, highly dramatic example, worthy of emulation: "They did not hang his four followers with him; that scene was still postponed; and so his victory was prolonged and completed. No theatrical manager could have arranged things so wisely to give effect to his behavior and words" (RP, 151). It is highly likely that Thoreau, who had divined that his grip on health and life was tenuous even before the Brown affair, resolved that his last days would serve as a crowning achievement, a legacy to the future and a final confirmation that he had measured up to his ego ideal. He would be yet another link in the chain that included John Jr., John Sr., and John Brown.

The weather in November 1859 had been "very pleasant . . . with quite a number of Indian-summer days, —a pleasanter month than October was" (J, XII:458). In some ways, Thoreau was now more prepared to be at home in, more in correspondence with, a later autumnal, even early winter, mode, with the leaves now past their peak, still hanging onto the tree perhaps but brown, the first snow flurries in the air and likely to begin accumulating on the ground at any moment. He had, to be sure, experienced an "Indian summer" of sorts this past autumn; and it *had* been more of a later Indian summer than a Septemberish second spring for him, one of those few precious reprieves before the decisive onslaught of winter. Maybe there would be more such reprieves, but they would be limited. It was perhaps of some consequence to him that the weather had been unusually warm and sultry, with "threatening clouds overhead and an ominous feeling in the air,"[46] on the day of Brown's hanging and that the next day it was "Suddenly quite cold, and freezes in the house" (J, XIII:3).[47] The first snow "of any consequence" was on the ground by December 4. He was no doubt inclined to identify now with the late fall flowers, which "have a sort of life extended into winter" (J, XIII:18). In these newly wintry days, even before winter's official arrival, "there are fewer men in the fields and woods," so you "see the tracks of those who had preceded you, and so are more reminded of them than in summer" (J, XIII:21). Thoreau could not help but remember well who had preceded him into the winter woods, and he had a strong proclivity now to follow in their tracks. He could go to Walden, view the "little white pines" he had planted in the spring, and imagine the time in a few years when "this little forest of goldenrod" would be "giving place to a forest of pines" (J, XIII:30). He wanted to believe that he had planted well, that his deeds and words would endure. Yet on Christmas Day he expressed concern with improper forest management: "Will not the nobler kinds of trees"—and he likely had himself and Brown in mind here, too—"bear comparatively fewer seeds, grow more and more scarce?" (J, XIII:50–51). The concern with conservation and preservation of "nobler kinds of trees" and their "seeds" would become a preoccupation in the time left to him.

At the age of forty-two, he was feeling at once very old and very young. As he sensed the approach of his own winter, Thoreau was finding that he had more in common with a young person, "not an assured inhabitant of the earth," than with the person who has "settled" into a thickened middle-aged mold, "whose thoughts are few and hardened like his bones . . . truly mortal." As one who has escaped or bypassed this condition, who was "less to be identified with the state of things," like the youth "not quite earthy," he was more allied with, in contact with, a "noble race of beings"; a man sensing death's proximity who still has many "thoughts," he was more in touch, like the youth or young man, with "a larger sphere of existence than this world." The youth has just "lately arrived from this sphere"; the man in the shadow of death feels the resonances of that sphere and is soon to return there. They are both "but half here" (J, XIII:35). Though keenly feeling his mortality, Thoreau was inclined not to see himself as a common, "mere mortal," as were those narrow-minded men with thick carapaces (and perhaps a thickening around the middle) who condemned or ignored Brown. He, like Brown, would bathe in "the clearest light that shines on this land," would enjoy a genuine immortality. With his father's death and the Brown episode behind him and inside him, it was a season to begin changing from the "shoes of summer to the boots of winter" (J, XIII:14). "In winter," he would say in February 1860, "we are purified and translated" (J, XIII:142).

9 Tracks in the Snow

*H*OW much the snow reveals!" (J, XIII:77), Thoreau marveled in January 1860. It recorded such tragedies as the killing of a rabbit; it provided vivid evidence, too, of the ongoing life and vitality in nature (J, XIII: 72–77). Not only did the snow remind him that he was following in the tracks of those who had preceded him into winter and that he remained on the trail of the "hound, bay horse, and turtle-dove" he had lost, but it also prompted him to meditate on the manner in which he had been, as he put it on January 5, tracking himself:

> A man receives only what he is ready to receive, whether physically or intellectually or morally, as animals conceive at certain seasons their kind only. We hear and apprehend only what we already half know. If there is something which does not concern me, which is out of my line, which by experience or by genius my attention is not drawn to, however novel and remarkable it may be, if it is spoken, we hear it not, if it is written, we read it not, or if we read it, it does not detain us. Every man thus *tracks himself* through life, in all his hearing and reading and observation and travelling. His observations make a chain. The phenomenon or fact that cannot in any wise be linked with the rest which he has observed, he does not observe. By and by we may be ready to receive what we cannot receive now. (J, XIII:77)

His most dramatic recent experience in self-tracking had been, of course, the response to, and defense of, John Brown.[1] It is, indeed, possible that this insightful passage represents a recognition of his intensely subjective reaction to Brown and of his refusal to allow incompatible facts—such as, perhaps, news of Brown's massacre of five unarmed persons at Pottawatamie in 1856—to vitiate his vision or his identification with Brown.

This passage has much more far-reaching implications and ramifications, however, for one who sensed on some level that he was entering a final phase of the life cycle. He was a man at least on the verge of being "ready to receive"—already "but half here" and "half-knowing"—the most fateful fact of all: that he was soon destined to die. Some people justifiably rage to the very end against the dying of the light. Others accommodate to death by turning to promises of immortality offered by many religions. Still others look primarily to symbolic forms of immortality.[2] Some have the experience of discovering that, when death is or seems near, and sometimes *only* then, they are more readily able to accept it; they reach a state of at least partial acceptance that in many cases they never could have conceived of in some earlier season of their lives. The transition to this state may, as we age, come as gradually, and often as fitfully, as one season gives way to another, though in certain cases it may come more abruptly, forced upon one by acute illness or some other unusually painful or traumatic crisis. No one response—and they are frequently mixed and overlapping rather than mutually exclusive—is the "right" one. All are understandable and legitimate reactions to the human condition; people do what they must, in their own very personal ways, when brought face to face with the facts of mutability and mortality. For Thoreau, a combination and convergence of factors—circumstance, personality, intellectual and emotional seasoning—would be especially kind, and when the season for dying came, however early it was and whatever underlying despair it engendered, he would be unusually "ready to receive" this season too. Subscribing to no orthodox religious formula for eternal life and salvation, with no literal offspring to carry on, with an awareness that he was the last male in an immediate family that would die out without leaving behind children as links of continuity with the future, Thoreau's acceptance of death would hinge to a great extent on his ability to assure himself that he would, as he trudged off into winter, leave behind him enduring tracks in the snow.

Thoreau's final years, both before and after the onset of his fatal illness, would be largely taken up with the project of tracking himself and leaving tracks, thereby gaining conviction and assurance of his generativity, integrity, and immortality. Such self-tracking had, of course, always been crucial to him; in seeking to maintain the continuity and consistency of his ego ideal and vision, in attempting to meet his psychological needs, he had depended heavily on selecting to acknowledge only those facts, observations, and phenomena that would be compatible with his needs, would be consistent with, provide further confirmation of, and expand the desired gestalt. When he was not able to achieve satisfactory alignment, when discordant notes had been struck, he was most vulnerable to a sense of drift, stagnation, dejection, and despair. Now, with death somewhere around the bend, the tracking process, on both conscious and unconscious levels, assumed even greater and more pressing significance. Integrity versus despair, Erikson says, is an inherent conflict in life's final stages; essential to a sense of integrity is the achievement of "integration," which furnishes assurance of the "order and meaning" of life and leads to an "acceptance of one's one and only life cycle . . . as something that had to be and that, by necessity, permitted of no substitutions."[3] Thus, tracking oneself, seeking integration and wholeness, is to some degree the task of each person when the end is in sight, though some may maintain a high tolerance for ambiguity and inconsistency even then. Certainly much of Thoreau's energy and effort would be devoted to the process of integration, to making a chain of observations that would be "linked with the rest which he has observed" and was "ready to receive." In this way he could achieve a sense of internal concord, cement the connections between himself and the world, and ultimately feel at home with both. As he writes to Blake on May 20, 1860, the man who is not finally at home with himself and the world, who is not "well housed" because he cannot "tolerate the planet" on which he puts his house, "despairs of himself" and is "in the condition of a sick man who is disgusted with the fruits of finest flavor" (c, 578–79). To be sure, in the process of tracking himself, Thoreau would have to (as he almost always had to) cover or erase, unconsciously and consciously, some tracks that were out of line, too painful, too threatening, or too revealing. And sometimes, particularly as in his Minnesota journey, he would find himself temporarily off the track. He would, moreover, frequently find it necessary, when he felt lost and loss, to retrace his steps. He had, after all, once written, "Sometimes a lost man will be so beside himself that he will not have sense enough to trace back his own tracks in the snow" (j, vii: 109).

It was especially in the observations he would make concerning wild fruits, the succession of forest trees, the dispersion of seeds, woodlots, conservation, seasonal phenomena, and the remembrances and relics of Indians that Thoreau would enhance his sense of the "order and meaning" of his existence. These observations would be far from random and would be integrated into the wished-for constellation, affording thereby confirmation of the worth and internal congruity of his life and self. In the first several months of 1860, Thoreau studied berries, seeds, pollen dissemination, trees, birds and other animals, and the successive phenomena of March. Although there is much disciplined and ostensibly scientific observation in the *Journal* of this final period, he appears more confident and enthusiastic about the approach he is taking—aware in some respects at least that he is tracking himself, making observations that are links in a chain, seeing mostly what he wants and needs to see and disregarding the rest. While such studies may have occasionally aroused fears of creative sterility (as earlier scientific or quasi-scientific studies often had), the very fact that he was so absorbed in organic processes, identifying and corresponding with them, helped substantially to alleviate such anxieties. On February 15 he reaffirms his creatively and psychologically indispensable ability to see nature as trope:

> As in the expression of moral truths we admire any closeness to the physical fact which in all language is the symbol of the spiritual, so, finally, when natural objects are described, it is an advantage if words derived originally from nature, it is true, but which have been turned (*tropes*) from their primary significance to a moral sense, are used, i.e., if the object is personified. The man who loves and understands a thing the best will incline to use the personal pronouns in speaking of it. To him there is no *neuter* gender. (J, XIII: 145–46)

Though some would see his transcendentalism as "moonshine" (J, XIII: 145), his belief was now all but unshakable that "A fact stated barely is dry. It must be the vehicle of some humanity in order to interest us. . . . Ultimately the moral is all in all" (J, XIII: 160). Though he obviously had respect for the "scientific view" of "steady progress according to existing laws"—which disproved, among other things, the belief in "spontaneous generation" (J, XIV: 311–12)—it was primarily as science provided confirmation of his vision of life and of himself that he chose to receive it. In an entry indicative of many in 1860 and 1861, he remarks, "our science, so called, is always more barren and mixed up with error than our sympathies are" (J, XIII: 169).

In recording his observations for posterity, Thoreau was deeply aware that it was, fundamentally, himself, or at least the best of himself, he was leaving behind. As he would write in the May 20 letter to Blake, "a man never discovers anything, never overtakes anything or leaves anything behind, but himself. Whatever he says or does he merely reports himself" (C, 579). Thus, in the process of self-tracking, he was leaving behind his own unique imprint. Erikson says that, peering over the abyss of death, one experiences "a new edition of an identity crisis which we may state in the words, 'I am what survives of me.'"[4] This man who had prided himself on his independence from others finally staked much of his claim to immortality on how he would be remembered by others. He was anxious that his tracks be noticed and valued by future generations; as he went on his way, he looked over his shoulder, hoping that others were and would be on his trail. Each person, Thoreau notes, has his own "individual gait," and he believed that his own personal style and individuation would, both intentionally and unintentionally, be evinced in the words and observations that would survive him. "It is not," he says, "merely by taking time and by a conscious effort that he betrays himself. A man is revealed, and a man is concealed, in a myriad unexpected ways" (J, XIII:128).

In the end, tracking himself was a means of examining ultimate concerns, of searching, as his winter drew nearer, for the abiding truths of his seasons and of the human seasons in general. He would say of poets and philosophers on November 20, 1860, "There are never any hard times or failures with them, for they deal with permanent values" (J, XIV:284). Thoreau, too, saw himself as on a quest for "permanent values," and his observations of nature were among the means to that end. On October 13, 1860, he says, "all nature is to be regarded as it concerns man; and who knows how near to absolute truth such unconscious affirmations may come?" He then adds, "Which are the truest, the sublime conceptions of Hebrew poets and *seers,* or the guarded statements of modern geologists, which we must modify or unlearn so fast?" (J, XIV:117). Clearly, as a poet and philosopher, and as a *seer* of nature, he was on the track of some "absolute truth" and that ripe, transcendent wisdom, that "detached yet active concern with life bounded by death,"[5] which immediately precedes the fall to earth.

Eighteen-sixty would be a year of many "last times." On February 8 he delivered what would be his final Concord Lyceum lecture. His subject, fittingly, was "Wild Apples," the tree and fruit that so embodied Thoreau's ego ideal of generativity and integrity. His last public lecture, given on December 11 in Waterbury, Connecticut, was, also appropriately, "Autumnal Tints."[6] Eighteen-sixty would be the last time that he would enjoy a period of relatively decent health—though as early as July Thoreau indicated in a letter to Sophia that he had sprained his thumb and "What is worse, I believe that I have sprained my brain too, —i.e. it sympathizes with my thumb" (C, 581). One wonders if, aside from the summer weather and overabundance of detail that often had "sprained" his "brain," his sprains were in any way sympathetically connected with the arrival of John Brown, Jr., in Boston (which he mentioned in the same letter to his sister [(C, 582]) or with his mother's ill health that summer. At a time when he was experiencing such "lasts," Thoreau was unwilling—and perhaps physically unable[7]—to deliver his address, "The Last Days of John Brown," at North Elba in the Adirondacks on July 4; the essay was finally published in the *Liberator* of July 27, 1860. It was no doubt getting more

difficult to separate Brown's last days from what he was increasingly intuiting to be his own. In early August he took his final camping and
mountain-climbing expedition, to Monadnock with Channing; there he
was able briefly to review, re-create, and recapture the spirit of his experiences ascending other mountains, both real and symbolic, in his life. Never
again, after 1860, would he have the physical strength or stamina to climb
mountains or even saunter with ease and regularity in the fields and woods
of Concord. And 1860 would be the last full year for the *Journal*. The last,
briefly sustained burst of richness and suggestiveness in his journal would
begin, as it had for so many recent years, with the approach of fall and end
in the early winter of 1861.

On September 4 Thoreau remarks, "I feel like a melon or other fruit
laid in the sun to ripen. I grow, not gray, but yellow" (J, XIV:73). He was
clearly tracking himself in his study of such wild fruits as blueberries, rasp-
berries, thimbleberries, cherries, strawberries, wild gooseberries, wild apples, and, of course, the huckleberries that were to be the subject of a lecture he never completed but which has since been reconstructed from
"Wild Fruits."[8] In one sense, he identified himself with wild fruits; he, too,
was an unambitious "wild fruit" who wished to see himself as ripening toward gold, not gray, in the autumn sun. And, though the individual fruit
would die, it would lend itself to the fecundity of an ongoing nature, which
would produce new fruits. His relation to these fruits was more complicated than simple identification, however. The consideration of fruits was
an attempt to affirm that the fruits of his life and labors would survive, endure, even if he, as a mortal entity, would not. "The fruit a thinker bears,"
he had written on April 1, 1860, "is *sentences*. . . . I occasionally wake in
the night simply to let fall ripe a statement which I had never consciously
considered before" (J, XIII:238). His eloquent pleas for the conservation
of such fruits as the huckleberry were, then, in part pleas for the enduring
generativity of his works and deeds. The profusion of berries was a trope
for his own fertility; in gathering together material for "Wild Fruits" (and
the essay on huckleberries) he was providing testimony of his own fruitfulness. In "tasting" his fruits, readers to come would receive "health and
happiness and inspiration" (H, 251). "Fruit," he notes, was derived from
the Latin "*fructos*, meaning that which is *used* or *enjoyed*" (J, XIV:273),
and this is what he hoped the destiny of his own fruits would be—to be
"used or enjoyed" by future generations. The value of the experience of
huckleberrying was "the amount of development we get out of it"; the
fruits "educate us, and fit us to live in New England" (J, XIV:274). Similarly, it was Thoreau's wish that his words would provide education, promote growth, and suggest how to live a life. Tropical fruits did not appeal

to him as much as "many an unnoticed wild berry whose beauty annually lends new charm to some wild walk"; fruits of the tropics "are for those who dwell within the tropics; their fairest or sweetest parts cannot be exported nor imported" (J, XIV:261). In like manner, Thoreau's works were fruits of his native New England and derived much of their charm, tangy palatability, and character from the region in which they had grown— "unnoticed" by many but eminently worthy of attention and appreciation. The berries were themselves generative, educating the children, "introducing" them to "the fields and woods" (H, 244), and promoting the public welfare; and in making the case for their safekeeping Thoreau was able to be generative, "fatherly," himself. To the extent that he sought to conserve them, he was bequeathing a legacy of words, deeds, and the fruit itself to the public domain. Indeed, in the context of a January 3, 1861, entry on huckleberries, he is the caring father, seeking to pass along intact to his "children" and the public in general—against the onslaught of profit-oriented, rapacious capitalists—the "precious natural objects" with which he so identifies:

> If inhabitants of a town were wise, they would seek to preserve these things, though at a considerable expense; for such things educate us far more than any hired teachers or preachers, or any at present recognized system of school education. . . . It would be worth the while if in each town there were a committee appointed to see that the beauty of the town received no detriment. If we have the largest boulder in the county, then it should not belong to an individual, nor be made into door-steps.

Too many concern themselves with material things "when the question is whether their children shall be educated. . . . It is safest to invest in knowledge." In a most prophetic statement he adds, "Thank God, men cannot as yet fly, and lay waste the sky as well as the earth! . . . It is for the very reason that some do not care for those things that we need to continue to protect all from the vandalism of a few" (J, XIV:303–7).

If in one sense Thoreau was committed to conserving the wild fruits, he was in another sense convinced that their time was passing away (H, 247–48). The end of his "Wild Apples" essay, for instance, is a prophecy and lament that the "era of the Wild Apple will soon be past" (E, 304–6); here he is a Jeremiah, a prophet without honor, a voice in the wilderness. In this regard he associated berries not only with himself but with the Indians, also aboriginal, whose era too had come and gone, whose wildness had vanished with the encroachments of civilization. In "Huckleberries," the wild berries are referred to as "the most persevering Native Americans" (H, 227). The strawberry, too, he connects with the Indians who picked this fruit.[9] On November 23, 1860, he writes in his journal, "The apple and perhaps all exotic trees and shrubs and a great part of the indigenous ones named above would have disappeared . . . and perchance the red man once more thread his way through the mossy, swamp-like, primitive wood" (J, XIV:263). On January 3, 1861—soon after the anniversary of Brown's execution, approaching the anniversary of his brother's death, and soon after he had developed his severe cold—he indicates that the "[huckle]berries which I celebrate" were "coterminous with what has been called the Algonquin Family of Indians." He can imagine the Indians eating huckleberry cake (J, XIV:303,308–9). With the passing away of these significant people, as well as of the fruits with which he linked them, Thoreau suggests that his era, too, was passing and that, in any case, he would be uncomfortable surviving the demise of berry and Indian—and, we may surmise, of John Sr., John Jr., and John Brown. He is uneasy, in "Huckleberries," to be counted as part of that civilization that "supplanted the Indians" (H, 252), and at another point in the essay he is even more direct: "The last Indian of Nantucket, who died a few years ago, was very properly represented in a painting which I saw there, with a basket full of huckleberries in his hand, as if to hint at the employment of his last days. I trust that I may not outlive the last of the huckleberries" (H, 237). On the one hand, then, his desire to conserve wild fruits and other wild things, and to write about them, was the expression of his desire to see himself as caretaker, protector, and loving elegist also of Indians and those other significant men he had survived only with guilt and anxiety. To keep in public hands a mountaintop such as Mount Washington—"even to the minds of the Indians a sacred place"—rather than make it "only accessible through private grounds" (J, XIV:305) was to preserve access to, even keep alive in a way, those people with whom he wished to commune. Thoreau speaks often with the air of one who alone has survived briefly to tell the tale for posterity of those people and things that have passed from the scene. His employment in his last days was, like the "last Indian" in Nantucket, partly to gather huckleberries—into an essay; he could also be "very properly represented" as the "last Indian," the unambitious, soon-to-be-extinct huckleberry gatherer. In a sense, it was his task to evoke, keep alive, the memory and dream of Eden, of a golden age on earth. On the other hand, however, he perceived that it was unlikely the golden age he evoked could ever actually be restored; society was rushing headlong in another direction. "Young America," he writes in "Huckleberries," "has become Old America" (H, 247).[10] Thus the only means to achieve reconciliation and redemption was ultimately to die and thereby join all those who had already passed away. It was more important that his *works* survive him and be a fitting memorial to all that had been lost. If the golden age was in the distant past—and in remembering his huckleberrying adventures as a boy ("a lad of ten" [H, 246–47]) he is able to regress briefly to that more innocent age—it was now accessible through death. At the same time, the partaking of berries (both literally and as translated into literature) provided access to the pure "mother" and "lover," the feminine principle in nature that was linked with being moored at last at home, another component of the pre-Fall golden age he sought: "We pluck and eat [berries] in remembrance of her [Nature]. It is a sort of sacrament—a communion—the *not* forbidden fruits, which no serpent tempts us to eat" (H, 241).

On September 20, 1860, Thoreau gave a lecture in Concord for the Middlesex Agricultural Society called "The Succession of Forest Trees," a subject integral to his investigations of the dispersion of seeds which were so consuming an interest in these final days of relative health and mobility. In the lecture, as in his journal of 1860, he revels in the discovery of what he very much wanted to confirm: the ingenious ways nature has provided for the dispersal and germination of seeds. He is thus able indirectly to assert his faith that his own seeds are, and will remain, viable, will be propagated and take root in the fertile soil of the future. He remarks in the lecture, "I have great faith in a seed," and in the final paragraph he speaks of "other seeds I have which will find other things in that corner of my garden, in like fashion, almost any fruit you wish, every year for ages, until the crop more than fills the whole garden. . . . Perfect alchemists I keep, who can transmute substances without end; and thus the corner of my garden is an inexhaustible treasure-chest" (E, 160). One suspects that the garden to which he is referring is not only a plot of land but also that creative "inner garden" that was so essential to his sense of generativity. It was, moreover, a garden of perennials. Just as his creative seeds had been an alternative to the producing of human progeny, so, as he says on January 14, 1861, nature's seeds "have many other uses than to reproduce their kind" (J, XIV:312). And if there had been the inevitable times when he, too, had been artistically fallow, there was, in the end, no reason for fear or self-reproach; after all, "If every acorn of this year's crop is destroyed, never fear! she has more years to come. It is not necessary that a pine or an oak should bear fruit every year. . . . If Nature has a pine or an oak wood to produce, she manifests no haste about it" (J, XIV:312). Only the insensitive and unappreciative could say that the squirrel planting acorns, like himself planting his seeds and nurturing them, has not at least "a transient thought for its posterity" (J, XIV:312). As with wild fruits, seeds furnished a link with the Indians; indeed, on October 31 he portrays arrowheads as another kind of enduring seed: "Consider what a demand for arrowheads there must be, that the surface of the earth should be thus sprinkled with them, —the arrowhead and all the disposition it implies toward both man and brute. There they lie, pointed still, making part of the sands of almost every field" (J, XIV:201). Thus, in focusing on the seeds he is again contemplating his relation to those who have preceded him. Not surprisingly, given his need to avoid any hint of direct competition with his elders, he is delighted to find, again and again, that most seeds can only prosper when transported some distance from their "parent stems" (J, XIV: 333–34).

Among the most dramatic instances of self-tracking in late 1860 and early 1861 related to Thoreau's consideration of trees, the succession of trees, and woodlots. As with his studies of wild fruits and the dispersion of seeds (of which the tree and woodlot studies were in many ways a part), he was able to review his life and affirm his virtues, ponder and resolve issues related to the succession of generations, reconnect with those things and people he had survived, discover those truths he so much needed to find. In a long and imploring letter of October 14, Ricketson, who had received no answer from a January 1860 letter, expressed "disappointment and hurt" at Thoreau's "sepulchral silence" toward him (C, 593); in Thoreau's November 4 reply he remarks, "Infer from it [his silence] what you might from the silence of a dense pine wood. It is its natural condition, except when the winds blow, and the jays scream, & the chickadee winds up his clock. My silence is just as inhuman as that, and no more." Explaining that he "never promised to correspond with" him, that "life is short, and there are other things also to be done," and that he has been "very busy," Thoreau advises Ricketson that he should not "regard" him "as a regular diet, but at most only as acorns, which too are not to be despised, which, at least, we love to think are edible in a bracing walk" (C, 599–600). Clearly, Thoreau had deeply immersed himself in the nature that he was studying and that he knew would continue after his departure. He was identifying more strongly than ever with trees and seeds, "pines" and "acorns," as he came to sense just how short his life would be.[11] He was constantly amazed at the persistent vitality in the "stumps and roots" (J, XIV:93–94) of trees and was no doubt also thinking of how he, too, had persisted and remained vital all these years, even if it had sometimes seemed that his creative forest was becoming a wasteland. While his hold on life was now precarious, he had reason to be encouraged in his belief that, even after he was "cut down," his words and deeds would have a persistent vitality. It was, as it had frequently been, comforting to see how "rapidly" nature "recover[s] herself" after a forest fire; the "vivacious roots" have "survived perhaps several burnings or cuttings" (J, XIV:105). He, too, had survived many fires, both literal (most notably the 1844 fire) and figurative—the many trials by fire he had encountered as he had striven to live a life of creativity and integrity. And his actions and words would, he hoped, stand the test of time and be recovered by future generations. His "leaves" would be seen in a different, more favorable light with the perspectives of time and distance:

> You cannot judge a tree by seeing it from one side only. As you go round or away from it, it may overcome you with its mass of glowing scarlet or yellow light. You need to stand where the greatest number of leaves will transmit or reflect to you most favorably. The tree which looked comparatively lifeless, cold, and merely parti-colored, seen in a more favorable light as you are floating away from it, may affect you wonderfully as a warm, glowing drapery." (J, XIV:107–8)

In the history of the oak he could see his own problematic but ultimately triumphant history and destiny:

> They have commonly met with accidents and seen a good deal of the world already. They have learned to endure and bide their time. When you see an oak fully grown and of fair proportions, you little suspect what difficulties it may have encountered in its early youth, what sores it has overgrown, how for years it was a feeble layer lurking under the leaves and scarcely daring to show its head above them, burnt and cut, and browsed by rabbits. Driven back to earth again twenty times, —as often as it aspires to the heavens. The soil of the forest is crowded with a mass of these old and tough fibres, annually sending up their shoots here and there. The underground part survives and holds its own, though the top meets with countless accidents; so that, although seeds were not to be supplied for many years, there would still spring up shoots enough to stock it. (J, XIV:121–22)

In such a description, even without making the analogy explicit, Thoreau has invoked metaphors of metamorphosis and rebirth after apparent death that are different from, but every bit as forceful as, those used in *Walden*. In these instances, though, Thoreau is speaking not only of a person's ability to create new life and worlds of "fair proportions" after many accidents, moratoria, and "little deaths" but also of the manner in which a person's legacy may provide him with "new life" even after he has literally died. The pitch pines may have a "feeble beginning" but will become "lofty trees which will endure two hundred years" (J, XIV:270).

Sometimes he would make the analogy between trees and human life more explicit, as he does the day after writing the letter to Ricketson:

I am struck by the fact that the more slowly trees grow at first, the sounder they are at the core, and I think that the same is true of human beings. We do not wish to see children precocious, making great strides in their early years like sprouts, producing a soft and perishable timber, but better if they expand slowly at first, as if contending with difficulties, and so are solidified and perfected. (J, XIV:217)

Himself a late bloomer whose continued growth had been spurred by "contending with difficulties," he could vouch firsthand for this correspondence between tree and human being.

On December 1, just prior to coming down with his severe cold, he again had the opportunity to review his life and anticipate the future life of his work. He rejoiced in how much the hickories "had endured and prevailed over"; trying to determine the age of young hickories, he "sawed off two or three inches below the surface, and also higher up" and found that each tree had "died down once at least, years ago." Like these hickories, he too bore subterranean scars and had died down more than once in preceding years. But in the end he had "endured and prevailed." Thoreau expands on the analogy, and finally makes it explicit, when he notes that these hardwood trees

are often of such fantastic form and so diseased that they seem to be wholly dead at a little distance, and yet evidently many of them make erect, smooth, and sound trees at last, all defects smoothed over or obliterated. Some which have thus died down and sprung up again are in the form of rude harps and the like. These had great tap-roots considerably larger just beneath the surface than the stock above, and they were so firmly set to the ground that . . . it was impossible to pull one up. . . . They are iron trees so rigid and firm set are they. . . . It will be very suggestive to a novice just to go and dig up a dozen seedling oaks and hickories and see what they have had to contend with. Theirs is like the early career of genius. (J, XIV:286–87)

Clearly the hickories provide perspective on his own early and troubled "career"; he has been a "tap-root man" whose own defects, deformities, and disease—perhaps more in his art than in his life—have been "smoothed over or obliterated." In the end, he feels that he can "stand tall," and it is in the words and deeds by which he will be remembered that he will stand tallest of all—his weaknesses "smoothed over or obliterated" with the passage of time and by the transforming powers of genius and imagination.

As with seeds and fruits, his calls for the conservation of forests were also ways to confirm his generativity and immortality. Just as the trees with which he identified were in themselves generative—and should be introduced to "a school of children" before "they are all gone" and it is "too late" (J, XIV:210)—so was safeguarding and nurturing them a generative act and a means of expressing his desire that his own educative leavings not be cut off. "Why not control our own woods and destiny more?" (J, XIV:127), he asks. The trees were jeopardized by poor forest management and the profit motive; and the "noblest trees and those which it took the longest to produce . . . are the first to become extinct" (J, XIV:135). Once more, as with huckleberries, there was reason for Thoreau to "despair of my trees," to feel that the old, statuesque pines and oaks "are now extinct in this town, and the present generation are not acquainted with" them (J, XIV:141–42). "The woods within my recollection," he remarks a bit later, "have gradually withdrawn further from the village" (J, XIV:161). He once more positions and defines himself as the surviving elder who alone can testify and transmit to his "children" regarding the generations that preceded them, thereby preventing them from being cut off from their rightful heritage. He is the historian, archeologist, and genealogist of the woods with which he so closely associated himself; if his father had been a historian of the town's center (J, XI:436–38), it fell especially to him to bear witness to, to record for posterity, the history of generations of woodlots:

> Thus I can easily find in countless numbers in our forests, frequently in the third succession, the stumps of the oaks which were cut near the end of the last century. Perhaps I can recover thus generally the oak woods of the beginning of the last century, if the land has remained woodland. I have an advantage over the geologist, for I can not only detect the order of events but the time during which they elapsed, by counting the rings on the stumps. Thus you can unroll the rotten papyrus on which the history of the Concord forest is written. (J, XIV:152)

As one who has survived, he is a mourner of all the forest that has already been lost and feels duty-bound to visit the graves almost daily and pay his respects: "It is with the graves of trees as with those of men, —at first an upright stump (for a monument), in course of time a mere mound, and finally, when the corpse has decayed and shrunk, a depression in the soil" (J, XIV:158).

In standing before these graves, he eulogizes the trees as he had eulogized Brown. And, indeed, the trees were linked, as had been the berries and seeds, with the Indians and noble others who were now gone. He imagines the Indians weaving their way through the ancient forests and notes that people often could see the stumps of trees that had been there before the advent of the white man.[12] He speculates as well on how the Indians' practices have led to the contemporary forest:

> Who knows but the fires or clearings of the Indians may have had to do with the presence of these trees there? They regularly cleared extensive tracts for cultivation, and these were always level tracts where the soil was light—such as they could turn over with their rude hoes. Such was the land which they are known to have cultivated extensively in this town.... It is in such places chiefly that you find their relics in any part of the county. (J, XIV:272)

The November woods, peopled with the spirits of those who once inhabited the forest, "are your companions, as if it were an iron age, yet in simplicity, innocence, and strength a golden one" (J, XIV:259). His forest studies, then, helped Thoreau "recover" in some measure the "golden age" by binding and bonding him to all those—Indians, his brother, his father, Brown—who had disappeared from the scene and made the present seem so bleak by their absence. While he could seek to keep them alive, honor them, pay homage to them, and evoke in language and imagination the golden age that had been lost, he sensed that in the end it was only by joining, sharing the fate of, these now hoary and noble ancestors, rather than by surviving them, that he could retrieve the blessed peace and purity of that golden age. He was prepared, like the noble trees that had become stumps, to have his life truncated, so long as his survival (and theirs) through memory and art was assured.

In his scrutiny of the succession of forest trees, Thoreau was clearly working through private familial and generational issues. It is thus indicative that he often uses parent-child imagery in his discussions of trees. Apparently the discovery that was most welcome for Thoreau—one that he *wanted* to find and that he kept coming back to, reconfirming almost obsessively in the fall and early winter 1860–61—was that seedlings and young trees rarely, if ever, could flourish in the shadow of parent trees; nature had, in "her" infinite wisdom, devised various means whereby the younger generation would not be pitted against the older. To be sure, Thoreau would sometimes see, "amid or beside a pitch or white pine grove, though thirty years old, a few yet larger and older trees, from which they came, rising above them, like patriarchs surrounded by their children" (J, XIV:142–43). At least in such cases as these, the "patriarch" still loomed assertively over "his" offspring; the younger generation had not done away with, or superseded, the patriarch in their effort to grow, to garner sunlight or nourishing soil. But far more preferable for one who was tracking himself, who wanted to see those facts that were most compatible with his psychological needs, was the prevalent observation—

registered, with the same imagery, on several occasions—that, for instance, the "pine woods are a natural nursery of oaks" (J, XIV:139). Thoreau, himself a "nurse" of pines, oaks, and all other trees, admits that this is not only what he does see but also what he *wishes* to see:

> For aught that I know, I would much rather have a young oak wood which has succeeded to pines than one that has succeeded to oaks, for they will make better trees, not only because the soil is new to them, but because they are all seedlings, while in the other case far the greater part are sprouts; just as I would prefer apple trees five or six years from the seed for my orchard to suckers from those which have come to maturity or decayed. Otherwise your young oaks will soon, when half grown, have the diseases of old trees, —warts and decay. (J, XIV:145)

Just as "it is very important that the little oaks, when they are tenderest, should have the shelter of pines and other trees as long as they can bear it," so is it crucial for healthy development that young pitch pines not try to spring up under older pitch pines: "there are countless white pines springing up under the pitch pines (as well as many oaks), and very few or scarcely any little pitch pines, and they are sickly" (J, XIV:147, 162). Certainly these observations suggested to Thoreau that human children are far better off not growing up in their parents' shadows and not aspiring to supplant them, to compete with them for available space, light, air, warmth, and nourishment. The same probably applied, at least to some extent, to such parent surrogates as Emerson. Examining an oak seedling that has died down but sent up two slender shoots under older oaks in, significantly, Emerson's woodlot, he reflects, "The root was probably ten years old when the seedling first died down, and is now some sixteen years old. Yet, as I say, the oak is only ten inches high. This shows how it endures and gradually pines and dies" (J, XIV:169–70). Such children growing up in the shadows of their elders are likely to be enfeebled, seeking to grow up in a soil exhausted by tradition and expectation, already tired and worn through their seniors' long reliance upon it. Their growth is liable to be stunted, as they attempt to find their own places in the sun but are threatened by the overbearing, overhanging boughs and leaves of their parents. Thoreau had sought to carve out his own personal space away from his parents (and, after a time, from Emerson), even if he had also depended upon their proximity. On another, oedipal and survivor level, his discoveries about trees meshed with his need to deny the wish to supplant or harm the father and elder brother—a denial even more necessary given his survival, supersession, and surpassing of them. Of course, he *had* been "sickened," "diseased" by oedipally related anxieties and guilt, however much he might have repressed or suppressed the insight. But to the extent that he could claim—partly through his study of trees—that he had avoided growing up in the shadows of parents or parent figures and that this avoidance was wise and fortunate—following the same natural laws the trees did—he both shored up his sense of himself as autonomous and alleviated anxiety and guilt.

He, like the trees, obeyed the natural order. Presiding over this natural order, caring benignly for her "nursery" (J, XIV:103), was nature herself, an alternative mother he could trust. That "mother" had provided him with a means to distance himself from his parents and parent figures and thereby insure growth. Success and succession were all too connected in Thoreau's mind, and thus it was only in the context of a peaceful and benevolent succession of generations that he could entertain the prospect of "success"—of a noncompetitive variety. One way of envisioning the natural order that offered him the opportunity to deny any intentions to surpass is suggested in a journal entry of October 13:

> In the true natural order the order or system is not insisted on. Each is first, and each last. That which presents itself to us this moment occupies the whole of the present and rests on the very topmost point of the sphere, under the zenith. The species and individuals of all the natural kingdoms ask our attention and admiration in a round robin. We make straight lines, putting a captain at their head and a lieutenant at their tails, with sergeant and corporals all along the line and a flourish of trumpets near the beginning, insisting on a particular uniformity where Nature has made curves to which belongs their own sphere-music. (J, XIV:119–20)

As one who saw himself as having marched to his own drummer, he had curved or veered off the beaten path and was not competing for space on that path; in another sense, the natural order was a circular "round robin" in which nothing is ever supplanted. In either case, imaged as curve or circle, his wish for *symbolic* forms of immortality was not tainted by competitive or hostile motivations. However, insofar as he could not—and he could not—discard a more linear view of succession, one entailing an acknowledgment of mortality, Thoreau, too, as a "pioneer" and trailblazer, had to be prepared, like the pines that were the "nurses" of oaks, to take his place in a "regular" order (J, XIII:68) and eventually yield to the oaks, lay down his life:

> Thus this double forest was advancing to conquer new (or old) land, sending forward their children on the wings of the wind, while already the oak seedlings from the oak wood had established themselves beneath the old pines

ready to supplant them. The pines were the vanguard. They stood up to fire with their children before them, while the little oaks kneeled behind and between them. The pine is the pioneer, the oak the more permanent settler who lays out his improvements. (J, XIV: 130)

Counting rings and examining stumps of trees enabled Thoreau to speculate on the quality and longevity not only of tree life but also of his own. Studying a large chestnut stump on October 28, he determined that the tree "had grown very fast till the last fifty years of its existence, but since comparatively slowly" (J, XIV: 185). The next day he concluded that rapid growth can "make large trees in comparatively few years, but they will be decaying[?] as fast at the core as they are growing at the circumference." "It is," he adds, "with men as with trees; you must grow slowly to last long" (J, XIV: 190, 191). In one respect, he saw himself as such a slow-growing tree, one who, in avoiding premature commitments and patiently developing, had prevented quick decay at the core. But "lasting long" might be a mixed blessing if growth was *too* slow, *too* feeble, in the later years. "The growth of very old trees," he observes on November 17, "as appears by calculating the bulk of wood formed, is feebler at last than when in middle age" (J, XIV: 251). Scrutinizing the pitch pines on November 10, he speculated that they

> grew in the first decade more than in any decade after their fiftieth year, and continued to grow with pretty regularly accelerated growth up to about the end of the third decade. . . . They continued to grow at nearly the same rate through the fourth decade, and then their rate of growth very suddenly decreased, —i.e., in the fifth decade or from the fortieth to the fiftieth years, when they grew only about the same as in the first decade. (J, XIV:234–35)

Thoreau, in his own fifth decade, may well have been contemplating the prospect of his own decreasing growth and increasing feebleness if he continued to live on for very long. Faced with the prospect of atrophy and entropy, he may have sensed that death would be a not unwelcome way to head off a period of steadily decreasing growth. In any event, and for other reasons already discussed, Thoreau was on some level increasingly "ready to receive" death and meditated often on it immediately preceding the fact of his final illness. Those old pines that lay on their sides—which, in a sense, accepted their deaths—decayed much less rapidly than those "upright in the ground"; the former were "almost indestructible," presumably suggesting to Thoreau that if he emulated the pines "lying on their sides" his own legacy would be virtually indestructible (J, XIV:198–99). He, too, would leave his monument behind. Even in their decomposition, his "leaves" would "enrich" the "soil" of the future (J, XIV: 123). It was, indeed, more comforting to contemplate being physically buried in an earth that was a crucible for new life. As he says on November 25, "I confess that I love to be convinced of this inextinguishable vitality in Nature. I would rather that my body should be buried in a soil thus wide-awake than in a mere inert and dead earth" (J, XIV: 268).

On December 1 Thoreau had detected that hickories bore scars below the surface; on December 2, the first anniversary of Brown's trip to the gallows, he found it difficult to ignore the scars left by that infamous event. The emphasis, in his further consideration of the hickories, was on the survival and persistence of hickory seedlings in the face of "fire, cultivation, and frost." Unlike other trees, which are "exterminated," the "hickories are tough and stubborn and do not give up the ground" (J, XIV: 289–90). Clearly, in some respects Thoreau viewed Brown—and himself—as "old hickory," prepared to make a last stand, perhaps futile in the short run, against all odds in defense of their principles. But, as he had indicated the previous year, it was Brown's—and his own—"*immortal*" life that would be the most resilient and memorable. In October 1859 he had said that he "almost feared" that he would hear of Brown's "deliverance," for he was skeptical that "a prolonged life, if any life, can do as much good as his death" (J, XII: 429). Apparently, Thoreau was inclined to apply similar criteria to the prolongation of his life. In what can be considered a case of astonishing coincidence or premonition, he examined an old chestnut stump on this fateful day commemorating Brown's death and determined that the "old stump was cut there forty-five years ago" (J, XIV: 289–90). It hardly needs to be pointed out that Thoreau, the man who so intimately identified with trees, would be cut down in his forty-fifth year, only about two months shy of his forty-fifth birthday.

The very next day, December 3, Thoreau was beset by the illness that would lead inexorably to his death.[13] On March 22, 1861, he would write to Ricketson that, as he recollected it, he "took a severe cold about the 3 of Dec. which at length resulted in a kind of bronchitis, so that I have been confined to the house ever since, excepting a very few experimental trips as far as the P.O. in some particularly mild noons" (C, 609). The December 3 context in which he developed this cold is highly suggestive. On this "bitterly cold day,"[14] Thoreau nevertheless proceeded to Fair Haven Hill where he counted rings and reflected on the succession of forests. What he did find might have been momentarily disconcerting or even ominous: a hickory that had been "blown down by the wall" and "cut up into lengths." Also, he was not able to find any "young hickories springing up on the *open* hillside." "Yet," he asks, "if they do so elsewhere, why should they not here, where nuts are abundant?" Seeing "many small hickories" "under and about" what may have been a parent hickory "amid the birches and pines, —the largest of which birches and pines have been lately cut off," may have called briefly into question his wished-for conception of proper succession. He does, however, manage to come up with an observation that satisfies him: "both oaks and hickories are occasionally planted in open land a rod or two or more beyond the edge of a pine or other wood, but . . . the hickory roots are more persistent under these circumstances and hence oftener succeed there." He goes on to consider the prospects for white oak acorns, all the "soundest" of which "have now sent down their radicle under these circumstances, though, no doubt, far the greatest part of them will be killed this winter" (J, XIV:290, 291).

Immediately following is Thoreau's discussion and defense of "radicals," including one who had been killed the preceding December. His defense was provoked by a fierce argument he had had that evening with Sam Staples and Walcott:

> Talking with Walcott and Staples to-day, they declared that John Brown did wrong. When I said that I thought he was right, they agreed in asserting that he did wrong because he threw his life away, and that no man had a right to undertake anything which he knew would cost him his life. I inquired if Christ did not foresee that he would be crucified if he preached such doctrines as he did, but they both, though as if it was their only escape, asserted that they did not believe that he did. Upon which a third party threw in, "You do not think that he had so much foresight as Brown." Of course, they as good as said that, if Christ *had* foreseen that he would be crucified, he would have "backed out." Such are the principles and the logic of the mass of men. (J, XIV:291–92)

Thus, on the same day he described himself as having first developed his illness, almost a year to the day after Brown's death, here he was, defending Brown, Christ, and himself, arguing that the other two radicals had foreseen their martyrdom, their crucifixion, but were absolutely justified not only in preaching their principles but also in accepting the fatal consequences of their beliefs and actions. In a very real sense, Thoreau was himself prepared to lay down his life in defense of these men with whom he identified; indeed, Harding suggests that he undertook this defense in lieu of "taking care of himself" after his day of exposure to the harsh cold.[15] If his cold, which would quickly become a bronchitis,[16] was precipitated or worsened by this sacrificing of his own health concerns in order to stand up for Brown and Christ, then it might be said that he literally did lay down his life for them, that he was himself inviting martyrdom for the cause. Surely there seems to have been a certain reckless, self-abandoning willingness to risk sickness in his behavior. Without question, the argument with Staples and Walcott, coming on the heels of the anniversary of Brown's death, was very likely to have stirred up all those powerful emotions that had accompanied his defense of Brown the previous year, emotions that had contributed to his increasing predilection to death. The stress and affect of this day, December 3, seems to have lowered even further his resistance to illness and death. Already so ripe for a fall to earth, he was easy prey to the illness that would mark the beginning of the end, that would develop into the "family infection,"[17] tuberculosis. If his grip on life was more tenuous, this radical was reassured that, like other radicals such as Brown and Christ, his "radicles," like those sent out by the "soundest acorns," would survive, promising him the "immortal life" that both Brown and Christ had achieved. In the final part of his journal entry for December 3, he writes, "It is to be remembered that by good deeds or words you encourage yourself, who always have need to witness or hear them" (J, XIV:292). He had been "encouraged" by the "good deeds or words" of his heroic predecessors; it was, moreover, by his own "good deeds or words" that he would be remembered. They would live forever as encouragement to those of succeeding generations. He had borne witness, and others would "have need to witness" or hear him.

The first snow fell, appropriately, the next day, almost a sign that Thoreau, too, was bound inexorably toward his own winter. On December 11 he went—against the advice of both doctor and friends—to Waterbury, Connecticut, to deliver, in lackluster fashion, "Autumnal Tints"; and the "strain of the journey worsened Thoreau's condition and he returned to Concord a seriously ill man."[18] Adding to the strain, no doubt, was that his mother, as he reports in a letter of December 17, was "confined to bed" at the same time that he was kept inside by "influenza" (C, 602). But for a few inspired entries on slavery and huckleberries, the quality and quantity of his journal writing declined along with his health over the winter; many would be the day, in the following months, when there would be no entry at all. On January 3, Thoreau unquestionably compares his condition to that of white pine trees bent under the burden of snow: "As I was confined to the house by sickness, and the tree had already been four or five days in that position, I despaired of its ever recovering itself." Although, to his surprise, the tree was "almost perfectly upright again" after the snow had melted (J, XIV:307–8), he could not say the same for himself. The snow would never entirely melt again. On January 11, the anniversary of his brother's death, he started to write an introduction for his elegiac lecture on huckleberries (J, XIV:310), but the lecture would never be completed. The Indians, he notes on January 8, "made a much greater account of wild fruits," and they had enjoyed huckleberry cake "before our ancestors heard of Indian meal or huckleberries" (J, XIV:308–9). Now, as he contemplated huckleberries, he was taking communion with them and thereby approaching even closer to communion with the Indians whom he had survived.

Friend Alcott discovered Thoreau in February at work "classifying and arranging his papers by subjects, as if he had a new book in mind," a book Alcott hoped would be a "book of Concord."[19] But the sickly Thoreau explained that he had "other projects in mind."[20] The overriding "project" of this final era, suggested by the tasks of classifying and arranging in which he was engaged, was to put his house in order, compose himself for death, and invest his ebbing energies into what would survive him. The deaths in February of both Miss Minott and Miss Porter were an additional indication of what was in store for him. Late in the month, and early in March, he was able to take short walks and perhaps briefly thought he would at least be able to saunter with relative ease through one more spring. It was inspiriting to him, who in any case knew how precarious his health and life now were, to identify himself and his creations with the "buoyant" seeds of the willow. "No sterile weeping willows have been introduced into this country," he writes on March 11, and he expresses his delight in seeing willow seeds "fill[ing] the air with their lint," proving that nature was "so lavish and persevering . . . that her purpose is completely answered" (J, XIV:327). On March 16 there was a heavy late-winter snowstorm, however, and Thoreau was again kept inside. On March 18, though, he was not prevented from continuing his meditations on the weeping willow which, rather than being the "emblem of despairing love," should "be the emblem of love and sympathy with all nature. It may droop, —it is so lithe, supple, and pliant, —but it never weeps. . . . It is not only soft and pliant but tough and resilient . . . not splitting at the first blow, but closing its wounds at once and refusing to transmit its hurts" (J, XIV:328–29). For one who had fought a protracted pitched battle with despair and who, as his last days neared, urgently sought to assert the triumph of integrity over despair, the weeping willow was one of his last and most poignant symbols and models. Yet he was not entirely immune to flare-ups of despair and melancholy as he surveyed his waning life and the world in which he had lived. On March 18 he confesses, "Ah, willow! willow! Would that I always possessed thy good spirits" (J, XIV:329), and he added, in his notes on the dispersion of seeds, that he wished he were more like the willow, that he had as strong a hold on life and could recover as speedily from his "hurts."[21]

Unquestionably contributing to whatever despair, conscious or unconscious, Thoreau felt, and perhaps even tipping the balance unalterably
toward death, were the gathering storm clouds of the imminent Civil War
and then, on April 12, 1861, the attack on Fort Sumter. He had, in fact,
once said, "Sickness is civil war";[22] and with his health deteriorating
rapidly and the Civil War raging, Thoreau told Channing that he "could
never recover while the war lasted."[23] Marble says that he was "sick for his
country."[24] The Civil War was traumatic for many northern intellectuals
who, as George Frederickson puts it, experienced an "inner Civil War."[25]
Thoreau would himself in part be a casualty of that war. Few experienced
the "inner Civil War" with more intensity than Thoreau, who had for so
long waged an inner civil war in which brother had been pitted against
brother, in which he was "cursed" and besieged by such inward foes
as guilt and anxiety. Both the patricidal and fratricidal rhetoric of the
Civil War—and the imagery of the "house divided"[26]—and its violent
realities were too much for Thoreau, summoning to the emotional front
line his own anxieties and guilt—partly oedipal, partly connected to survivorship—relating to real and imagined conflicts with, and the deaths of,
his brother and father. To survive such a war was at best a Pyrrhic victory;
indeed, the only way he could resolve the inner turmoil and anguish was to
die himself, thereby gaining release and restoring the union which alone
would bring peace.

But there were other reasons why the Civil War provoked such mortification. On the one hand, of course, Thoreau could not fail to support the
North in the conflict, fighting as it was against the slavery he so despised.
He could not avoid wishing that the North would be victorious and end
the "purgatory"[27] as quickly as possible, thus not only abolishing slavery
but also mercifully ending the fratricidal-patricidal hostilities that unnerved him, even if many brothers and fathers were killed in the process.
His support of the war was emotionally problematic, however. The "only
resort of justice," he writes on December 4, 1860, is "not where the judges
are, but where the mob is, where human hearts are beating, and hands
move in obedience to their impulses" (J, XIV:293). That "justice" could
only be gained by the collective action of a "mob," while it met certain generative needs to get quick and lasting results in the public sphere, also
aroused guilt in that it was a call to violence (on some level against brothers
and fathers) and in that it contradicted his earlier dedication to individual-
ism. Thus, even supporting the war fervently put Thoreau in a bind, aggra-
vated stress and distress.

Moreover, his attitudes toward the North were far too complex for an unambivalent response to the war and its possible outcome. On December 4, 1860, he writes, "Talk about slavery! It is not the peculiar institution of the South. It exists wherever men are bought and sold, wherever a man allows himself to be made a mere thing or a tool, and surrenders his inalienable rights of reason and conscience" (J, XIV:292). This theme had been a recurrent one in his writings, including *Walden*. While the North was finally refusing to compromise on the issue of the bondage of human beings in the South, to root for or identify with the North was in some manner to tolerate or endorse the forms of slavery that still existed in the North. And, after all, had not many in the North, including many Concordians, been implicated in the hanging of Brown in Charlestown, Virginia? The prospect of joining Brown, rather than supporting those in the North who had condemned him, must have been inviting. Furthermore, the North's victory would, in some respects, insure the perpetuation and proliferation of northern forms of slavery and the triumph of a commercialism and industrialization that made "tools" of men and would permeate and further corrupt the very core of American life. Thoreau's deathbed dream of "being a railroad cut, where they were digging through and laying down the rails, —the place being in his lungs,"[28] suggests the link between his own health and his sense that America was to be permanently ravaged by the machine, which would emerge definitively victorious along with the North. The victory of the North, then, would represent in part the triumph of a "new," but fallen, America and the final death knell of the "old" America he had so often elegized, eulogized, and romanticized. The Civil War brought home ugly and incontrovertible realities; its aftermath would dramatize and embody the end of a world he had known, loved, and had high hopes for. For one who had dreamed so idealistically of an America whose youth would give way to a noble adulthood, it was a cruel blow to see what America had made, or would probably make, of its opportunities for maturity. The Civil War was the most emphatic shattering of the dream for Thoreau. That he had himself partaken of the secessionary impulse throughout his life,[29] and even tended to identify— however uneasily—with the more agrarian orientation of the South, made the war even more emotionally stressful. In the end, the only escape or refuge from these emotions would be death, the ultimate secession from both North and South.

In early spring 1861, Thoreau's health was unsteady at best. "To tell the truth," he writes to Ricketson on March 22, "I am not on the alert for the signs of Spring, not having had any winter yet" (C, 609). In April his health did not rebound with the spring, and in early May he defined himself in a letter to Blake as an "invalid," aware of the danger that "the cold weather may come again, before I get over my bronchitis." His doctor prescribed that he "clear out" to the West Indies or southern Europe, but the patient objected to these locales, the former due to "their muggy heat in summer" and the latter due to "the expense of time & money." As he indicated to Blake, he had decided instead that he would travel to Minnesota and be away for three months (c, 615). Harding suggests that he may have been influenced by the testimonial of a distant relative whose lung difficulties had diminished there and by the publicity put out by Minnesotans concerning the supposedly rejuvenating qualities of their dry climate.[30] Yet, unquestionably, his motives for choosing to go to Minnesota—which now at least, as Sayre comments, "may seem like a less than perfect place for someone with bronchitis and tuberculosis"[31]—were mixed. One wonders, indeed, if his decision to journey to Minnesota for three months—a temporary and partial solution for one with an increasingly severe and chronic affliction—did not contain an element of resignation. If not a self-destructive move (and, in light of how his health declined by the end of the strenuous trip, one cannot fully discount the possibility that he was in some way courting danger), it was not the action of one committed above all else to recovery. On the other hand, heading west—farther than he had ever been—did offer a potentially therapeutic mode of secession, short of death, to a man who was anxious to flee from the tumult, tensions, and trauma generated by the Civil War, who had remarked in a letter to Parker Pillsbury on April 10, "As for my prospective reader, I hope that he *ignores* Fort Sumpter, & Old Abe, & all that, for that is just the most fatal and indeed the only fatal, weapon you can direct against evil ever. . . . I do not so much regret the present condition of things in this country (provided I regret it at all) as I do that I ever heard of it" (c, 611). Clearly, the selection of Minnesota represented another attempt at tracking himself and a quest for reunion. Minnesota, or at least the *idea* of the American frontier, held out the promise that he would find what he wanted and needed to find: wildness, the West, the Indians.[32] The prospect of getting geographically—and psychologically—closer to the West and the wild than he had ever been before, and of reasserting his kinship with his Indian brothers (and, with his own "Indian" brother) who lived there, was at once exciting and soothing. If, as he could not help suspecting, this was to be his final prolonged excursion, it would be a grand and fitting finale, a prelude to a journey even farther west; and, to the extent that he could purge and redeem himself in the uncontaminated West, America's and his own last best hope, he might even recover sufficiently to make other excursions.

After unsuccessfully soliciting Channing and then Blake to accompany him, Thoreau settled—fortuitously, it must have seemed to him—on Horace Mann, Jr., as his traveling companion. In the seventeen-year-old Mann, who was "already an accomplished naturalist,"[33] he found someone who could not fail to remind him of his brother at a younger age, and in this sense the trip might enable Thoreau to re-create the halcyon days when he and John were fast friends rather than rivals. He could assert his generativity, his care and affection for his brother, by passing on to Mann all that he knew; and Mann would himself take on the role of elder brother, watching over him and his health, sharing his enthusiasm for nature. Throughout the trip, begun on May 11, Mann would monitor Thoreau's health and, in letters to his own mother, report on the status of his charge's condition.

Despite its promise, the trip to Minnesota did not ultimately prove to be therapeutic, let alone creatively fruitful, for Thoreau. Hoping to track himself, he found the Minnesota expedition in many ways leading him off the track. To be sure, as they made their way through Albany, Niagara Falls, Detroit, Chicago, and on into Minnesota, Mann wrote home that Thoreau was doing either "pretty well" or "very well" and showed some vacillating signs of improvement.[34] It was, perhaps, an augury to him that when he called on a distant cousin, Col. Samuel Thatcher, in Saint Anthony, he learned that his cousin had "been recently thrown from a carriage, —so as to have had watchers within a few nights past" (C, 617). Thatcher would die before the end of the summer.[35] Probably the inspirational highlight of the first month of the journey was his discovery and touching of the "half-fabulous" wild crab-apple tree to which he would refer in "Wild Apples"; traveling through Michigan by rail, he had first caught sight of it. "But," he would write in his essay, "the cars never stopped before one, and so I was launched on the bosom of the Mississippi without having touched one, experiencing the fate of Tantalus" (E, 280–81). Clearly he was tracking himself, that most "wild" part of himself, in his search for the tantalizing but elusive crab apple. Finally, on June 11, he "succeeded in finding it about eight miles west of the [Saint Anthony's] Falls; touched it and smelled it, and secured a lingering corymb of flowers for my herbarium" (E, 281). What he does not mention in his account of communion with the crab apple in "Wild Apples" is that the one he discovered was not entirely wild but rather had been transplanted and cared for by Jonathan Grimes, a nurseryman whom Thoreau consulted.[36] Thus, even on the frontier, pure wildness was becoming increasingly difficult to find.

The moments of inspiration and exultation were few and far between.

His notebook, "Notes of a Journey West," would consist primarily of undigested narrative, facts, lists, and descriptions. Not only was his feeble literary performance symptomatic of flagging health, it also quite possibly confirmed to him that he could not expect much more in the way of spontaneous or sustained outbursts of creativity. Even his handwriting, which, says Harding, "for most of his adult life was little more than a scrawl," had by 1861 "degenerated into almost indecipherable chaos"—nowhere more so than in his disorganized notes on the western journey.[37]

During his stay in Minnesota, Thoreau no doubt became acutely aware that, even in the West, he could not escape civilization or history, could not leave behind him the troubling conflicts partly engendered by the Civil War, could not discard the emotional baggage he brought with him. It was indicative that, as he writes in a long and revealing letter to Sanborn from Redwing, Minnesota, on June 25, "It has chanced that about half the men whom I have spoken with in Minnesota, whether travellers or settlers, were from Massachusetts." In the letter to Sanborn he displays some telltale ambivalence about the Civil War. On the one hand, he seems pleased and relieved about his relative detachment from the day-to-day news of the war: "I am not even so well informed as to the progress of the war as you suppose. I have seen but one eastern paper . . . for 5 weeks. I have not taken much pains to get them; but, necessarily, I have not seen any paper at all for more than a week at a time." On the other hand, he speaks disapprovingly of the Minnesotans, who "*seemed* to be more cold—to feel less implicated in this war, than the people of Massachusetts," and was "glad" when informed "that there was a good deal of weeping here at Redwing the other day, when the volunteers stationed at Fort Snelling followed the regulars to the seat of the war." Surely Thoreau was divided and torn as he contemplated the war, his own "implication" in the hostilities, and the conflicts stemming from it. And even if Massachusetts was to be praised for "doing much more than her share" in "carrying on" the war, he could not forget how many people in his native state had condemned John Brown and how, in general, he had fought against all those forms of "slavery in Massachusetts"—smugness, conventionality, pettiness, commercialism, industrialization—over the years. Moreover, the people of Massachusetts had managed to defeat and supplant the Indians, and he now witnessed the Minnesotans waging war on his Indian brothers. He comments disparagingly to Sanborn, "They [Minnesotans] do not weep when their children go *up* the river to occupy the deserted forts, though they *may* have to fight the Indians there" (C, 618–19). Thus, in Minnesota, he was confronted with the distressing paradox that the same people who could fight against slaveholders were also bent on vanquishing the Indians, and he was forced to consider the extent to which he, too, was implicated in the war against the Indians.

Thoreau had gone to Minnesota hoping, among other things, to re-assert his kinship with the Indians and his brother, but his experience there put into threatening relief how divided and contradictory his allegiances and sympathies really were. Here he was unable to find an Indian guide like Polis who would confirm his closeness to Indians and help him re-create in the best possible light his friendship with John Jr.[38] Instead, he and Mann had to resort, on June 17, to a journey 300 miles up the Minnesota River on the steamboat *Frank Steele* to ceremonies organized around the federal government's regular payments to the Sioux. Included among the approximately 100 passengers were "the Governor of Min-nesota, (Ramsay) —the superintendent of Ind. Affairs in this quarter, —& the newly appointed Ind. agent . . . also a German band from St. Paul, a small cannon for salutes." Also aboard was "the money for the Indians (aye and the gamblers, it was said, who were to bring it back in another boat). Many of the passengers were from St. Paul, and more or less recently from the N. Eastern states; also half a dozen young educated Englishmen" (C, 621). This assemblage of curious tourists, officials, and gamblers (per-haps bringing to mind the motley group aboard the *Fidèle* in Melville's *Confidence Man*) was a far cry from the small, unpretentious travel parties of his Maine excursions. And, as Sayre notes, his account in the letter to Sanborn of the trip upriver "shows little development of this experience as an instance of the coarseness and violence of conquest. Instead, he seems to share in the passengers' frontier humor, their laughter and jokes about the clumsy, tedious journey."[39] His description to Sanborn of the Indians at the village of Redwood is short but revealing:

> A regular council was held with the Indians, who had come in on their ponies, and speeches were made on both sides thro' an interpreter, quite in the de-scribed mode; the Indians, as usual, having the advantage in point of truth and earnestness, and therefore of eloquence. The most prominent chief was named Little Crow. They were quite dissatisfied with the white man's treatment of them & probably have reason to be so. . . .
>
> In the afternoon the half naked Indians performed a dance, at the request of the Governor, for our amusement & their own benefit & then we took leave of them & of the officials who had come to treat with them. (C, 621–22)

In his notebook he amplifies briefly on the Indians, observing, for exam-ple, "Indians hungry, not sleek & round-faced. 'Ugh' at the promise of meat and flour."[40] There is an underlying poignancy in these relatively few observations of the Sioux that Thoreau was able to make. The Indians, though their speeches had "the advantage in point of truth and earnestness, and therefore of eloquence," were clearly beaten people, brought to their knees, dependent on the largesse of the government, willing to be put on tawdry display for tourists and officials and subject to being duped by gamblers, hungry and physically far from the "sleek" ideal of the proud and fearless hunter. They knew they were oppressed, downtrodden, plundered, and said so. And here was Thoreau, himself reduced to the role of tourist and onlooker who participated, by his presence and acquiescence, in this sorry situation.

Not only was he, no doubt, sorely disappointed by this, his final encounter with Indians, but he was also susceptible to feelings of guilt. As much as he wished to identify with the Indians, in part as it affirmed his sympathy and solidarity with his brother and the other vanished male figures he had survived, he found himself in Minnesota also identifying with the white men who had complicity, acknowledged or not, in their demise. Sayre observes, in referring to the Minnesota experience, that Thoreau's "Indian sympathy was moral, but his white sympathy was broader, more spontaneous, and fraternal. It was implicit in the kinship of language and humor, in the jokes about the *Frank Steele* and even in the language used to describe the Indians. Thoreau was not alone in his awareness that the Indians were wronged. Other passengers knew that too; but what could be done? . . . There was no response but pity, censure, and to relieve the horror, a certain amount of humor." Indeed, in the letter to Sanborn Thoreau reveals his "equal if not greater sympathy with the whole epic of white American expansion,"[41] an expansion that could be purchased only through the loss of innocence, the destruction of primitive forests, the extinction of the buffalo and other wild things, the triumph of technology, and the conquest of the red man. Thus Thoreau's divided kinship and allegiances were painfully underscored in the trip to Redwood. In search of reunion, he had been haunted by evidence that he was still a "house divided"; the inner Indian and civil wars could be touched off by experiences and observations that did not track. The Minnesota journey seems to have dramatized that, no matter how far west he went in his life, he could not go far enough: he could escape neither the strong undertow of a problematic personal history that was a perpetual plague on his house nor the tragic burdens of national history. If the West represented whatever remained of the opportunity for American salvation, Thoreau could not have felt entirely comfortable with it. If America's "manifest destiny" hinged on expansionism, imperialism, internecine strife, the plundering of land and people, then in some sense his own manifest destiny could only be the purifying and redemptive escape of death. Certainly, though he wanted very much to hold on to his positive vision of the future as associated with the West (E, 183), the trip called into question that vision and further reinforced his inclination to redefine the West not so much as a place where the country's destiny would be played out but rather, as he put it in "Walking," as "but another name for the Wild" (E, 185).

In the remarkable letter to Sanborn, Thoreau describes himself as having "performed this journey in a very dead and alive manner" (C, 618). His sense of aliveness had been a flickering candle even as he embarked on the journey; but it was especially after the anxiety-provoking and anticlimactic excursion to see the Sioux that Mann's relatively positive and optimistic reports home about Thoreau's health status virtually came to a halt. Indeed, according to Harding, it was just after returning to Saint Paul after visiting the Sioux that it became "obvious that Thoreau's health was not improving" and "that the two started their journey home eastward,"[42] fully a month earlier than a return had previously been contemplated. By early July, in Mackinaw City (at that time the name of a settlement on Mackinaw Island), his "health had so deterioated [*sic*] that he spent much time sitting close to the fire."[43] On July 10, less than two months after setting out, the two returned to Concord. Thus an odyssey supposedly designed to improve his condition had, quite possibly due to the emotional as well as physical strain it had imposed, further weakened his hold on life. Thoreau undoubtedly had some sense that he was coming back home to die.

As if to make amends for his recent show of apathy toward Ricketson, Thoreau initiated and was able to martial his strength for one last, brief trip away from Concord, to New Bedford from August nineteenth to the twenty-fourth. Although he took some abbreviated walks and did some botanizing with Ricketson, "his invalidism restricted his activities"; he "refused to go swimming and at night requested a secluded bedroom so that his coughing would not disturb the others."[44] In an extract from his journal, Ricketson reported, "In relation to my friend Thoreau's health my impression is that his case is a very critical one as to recovery; he has a bad cough and expectorates a good deal, is emaciated considerably; his spirits, however, appear as good as usual, his appetite good. Unless some favorable symptom shows itself soon I fear that he will gradually decline."[45] It was during this final excursion that, at the urging of Ricketson, Thoreau had two ambrotypes made by Dunshee,[46] both of which suggest a drawn, frail, philosophical, and resigned man, no longer fully "to be identified with the state of things." This visit to Ricketson's appears to have repaired much of the damage he had caused by virtually ignoring his friend for so long, and Ricketson himself, though so preoccupied with and frightened by health and death issues that he stayed away from Thoreau's bedside in the final stages of his illness, would nevertheless be, along with Sophia and Channing, a devoted chronicler of his friend's last days.

Perhaps responding, as he so often did, to the arrival of autumn, Thoreau had a short period of partial remission of his disease in September and October; still, he could not accept Ricketson's invitation to visit New Bedford in October. "I suspect," he explains, "that it must still be warmer here than there, that, indeed, New Bedford is warmer than Concord only in the winter, & so I abide by Concord" (c, 628). But he would not get to go to New Bedford in the winter. He would "abide by Concord" the rest of his days. In November his condition took a turn for the worse. When George William Curtis visited Thoreau, he found him "much wasted," "his doom clear," even though he "talked in the old strain of wise gravity without either sentiment or sadness."[47] As winter approached, his symptoms grew progressively more severe, with increased coughing and a mid-December "attack of pleurisy" that kept him indoors. George Minott's death in the last month of 1861 must have seemed another indication of what was coming for him.[48]

Fittingly, it was on November 3, as the fall began to give way to winter, that Thoreau made the last entry in his journal, a journal that had been almost bare of entries in the immediately preceding months. His observations on kittens suggest how domestic and circumscribed his life was by then (J, XIV:344–45). The concluding paragraphs are devoted to how the marks left in the gravel by the rain made it possible to determine from which direction the wind had been blowing during the rainstorm. The last short paragraph remarks, "All this is perfectly distinct to an observant eye, and yet could easily pass unnoticed by most. Thus each wind is self-registering" (J, XIV:346). It was quite likely not by chance that he chose to end his journal in this way. Instead of viewing it as part of a "broken task" (Emerson's characterization in his funeral oration for Thoreau [E, 33]), he seemed to be accepting the end of his journal, such a significant part of his life and of himself. Even if he would not get the opportunity to complete any other large-scale, massive projects drawn from or based on it, the *Journal* could stand on its own as a meaningful, inclusive work to all those with a patient and "observant eye." He had probably come to realize that the *Journal* was, more than anything he could now glean from it in the time remaining, his Kalendar and book of Concord, communicating in a most organic way what he had learned regarding the natural and human seasons, and his own. It was particularly through the medium of his journal that he had been able to capture and convey most eloquently and evocatively the richness, multiplicity, subtleties, textures, sequences, patterns, transitions, time sense, and experiential realities of these seasons. In its own way, the *Journal* incorporated and communicated more of his truth than any other form, even if in the process of tracking himself he had covered some of his tracks (though he had done so to an even greater extent in his essays and books). In making his final entry, he seems to be giving instructions, proffering an invitation and challenge, to those who would come upon and read the *Journal* after his own "wind," or breath, was stilled. Like the wind, his journal was itself self-registering, its own excuse for being. In it he had etched his most revealing and detailed imprints in the snow, which he now trusted would be noticed and traced by the "observant." Though his journal was his most uninterrupted and unmediated trail, it would remain an arduous and elusive task, for the observant trying to understand him fully, to trace his footsteps and not lose the trail where it had been covered, intentionally and unintentionally. If even those with an observant eye have had to accept that some mysteries and riddles remain, so did Thoreau himself. Having, in his search for the truth, journeyed toward the sun, he had to acknowledge in "Walking" that, finally, no one "can look serenely and with impunity in the face of the sun" (E, 204).[49] Mystery was itself part of the truth.

Although still a middle-aged man, Thoreau had sensed for an uncommonly extended period that death was imminent; his suspicions had become a near-absolute conviction by the winter of 1861–62. In March he would write to Myron Benton, "I *suppose* that I have not many months to live" (C, 641). The final stage of his life cycle came earlier than for most and, like middle age itself, it was condensed and telescoped. His remaining days numbered, he sought to emulate and identify with the falling leaves eulogized so movingly first in his journal and then in "Autumnal Tints":

> How beautifully they go to their graves. . . . They that soared so loftily, how contentedly they return to dust again, and are laid low, resigned to lie and decay at the foot of the tree, and afford nourishment to new generations of their kind, as well as to flutter on high! They teach us how to die. One wonders if the time will ever come when men, with their boasted faith in immortality, will lie down as gracefully and as ripe, —with such an Indian-summer serenity will shed their bodies, as they do their hair and nails. (E, 241)

For several years he had been seeking to learn not only how to live but also—perhaps the ultimate lesson—how to die. Both consciously and unconsciously, he had been preparing for his death. Now came the final test. As a man who had divined for some time that he was ripe for the fall, he had become, as previously indicated, more and more preoccupied with an identity issue so urgent to those in life's later stages, "I am what survives of me."[50] And it seems likely that, if Thoreau made any resolutions with the coming of 1862, the most crucial involved a determination that his last days, like those of the Johns he had known, would be a final, triumphant capstone legacy to future generations, a concluding chapter in close harmony with his life as he wished to see it. In the few months remaining to him, Thoreau would, by his conduct, write a chapter that might aptly be called, "The Last Days of Henry Thoreau."

Testimonials abound concerning his behavior during his last days. By all accounts he was serene, cheerful, brave, and committed to working on his manuscripts until he drew his final breath. For instance, Sam Staples commented that "he never saw a man dying with so much pleasure and peace."[51] Channing remarks, "His patience was unfailing; assuredly he knew not aught but resignation; he did mightily cheer and console those whose strength was less.[52] He suffered from pain and sleeplessness but, refusing any opiates, "preferred to endure with a clear mind the worst penalties of suffering."[53] Theo Brown remembered that, when he visited Thoreau with Blake in January 1862, "He seemed to be in an exalted state of mind. . . . He said it was just as good to have a poor time as a good time."[54] Sophia reported to Ricketson that she "never before saw such a manifestation of the power of spirit over matter. . . . When he had wakeful nights, he would ask me to arrange the furniture so as to make fantastic shadows on the wall, and he wished his bed was in the form of a shell, that he might curl up in it."[55] Thoreau's sense of humor also stayed with him to the end.

Clearly, to understand how and why Thoreau was able to face death with such apparent courage and equanimity is to learn an invaluable lesson. Harding suggests that one clue may be found in an article by Dr. Arthur Jacobson, "Tuberculosis and the Creative Mind," which indicates that victims of consumption tend to "bear the burdens of disease most cheerfully." "Every practitioner," Jacobson continues, "is familiar with the extraordinary trait which enables the advanced consumptive to declare that he feels 'bully' when his temperature is 104°. . . . In no other disease *with equally extensive lesions* is the psychical and consequently the physical status equally exalted."[56] By late 1861 and early 1862 Thoreau manifested the characteristics of advanced tuberculosis. A family friend observed that "by evening a flush had come to his cheeks and an ominous brightness and beauty to his eyes, painful to behold. His conversation was unusually brilliant, and we listened with a charmed attention which perhaps stimulated him to continue talking until the weak voice could no longer articulate."[57] It is quite possible, then, that the nature of the illness itself had some sort of benign, if intermittent, impact on Thoreau's state of mind. Marble suggests that not only his elation but whatever dejection asserted itself could be attributed to the nature of his illness: "From the time of his return, July 1861 [from Minnesota], until his death the following May, Thoreau experienced those alternates of hope and despair which accompany all bronchial diseases."[58] One might, of course, be led here to draw another conclusion. When a person is in the throes of a painful, debilitating illness, particularly one that threatens or promises to be terminal, there is often an accompanying feeling that death would be welcome, preferable to the suffering, disability, and anxiety associated with the illness. In some cases, it is perhaps only when one experiences the ravages of a severe disease or injury—or the infirmities of age—that one can perceive (if even then) death as an inviting alternative and accept it. There may well have been times when Thoreau partook of this perception. The afflictions of the body thus may help convince us that we are ready to die. Of course, another consideration is that when we are old, or at least feel that we have lived a full life, we may find ourselves prepared to die in ways that we cannot imagine when we are younger or have not had those experiences that constitute for us a full life. While he was not old, and while much would remain unfinished, Thoreau, who said he had gone to Walden so that when he died he would not "discover that [he] had not lived" (w, 90), was able to convince himself, to a great extent at least, that he had lived a full and rounded life.

Whatever the impact of the tuberculosis itself, it should be abundantly evident by now—though it bears further summary and amplification in this context—that a crucial reason why Thoreau was able to confront death so valiantly was that, to a considerable degree, he had a predilection to it, was ripe for it. He had been ripening toward death for some years, and now the stem holding him to the tree of life had atrophied to the point where he was almost ready to let go. Due to a convergence and accumulation of factors, life and death no longer pulled so hard in opposite directions. For him, death was increasingly appropriate. In their important and influential essay, "Predilection to Death," Avery D. Weisman and Thomas P. Hackett propose that an "appropriate death" must meet four main requirements: "(1) conflict is reduced; (2) compatibility with the ego ideal is achieved; (3) continuity of important relations is preserved or restored; (4) consummation of a wish is brought about."[59] Death did satisfy, by and large, these interlocking requirements for Thoreau.

Dying was on track; death was finally compatible with, in line with, Thoreau's psychological needs. The process of dying reconciled ambivalence and helped reduce those conflicts, the civil and Indian wars within and without, that had aroused such guilt and anxiety over the years. Death itself would be the ultimate release from the increasingly intolerable burdens of survivorship, oedipally related guilt, and the relentless pressures of continuously productive authorship. Justice was being served. A weight was being lifted from him. Aside from the critical but manageable demands of dying well and gaining assurance of his generativity, integrity, and symbolic immortality, he had little else to prove, no one else to compete with, combat, or supplant. Death would foreclose or preempt the possibility of further crises in his life, which might conclusively defeat his spirit and constitute a fate worse than death; now he need not fear that he would be menaced or overwhelmed by the sense of stagnation and desperation that had been such a threat in previous crises, such as that which followed *Walden*'s completion and publication. A noble, early death was, moreover, entirely in keeping with his ego ideal of purity, stoic bravery, and autonomy. In serenely renouncing the world and the worldly, he was embracing the ultimate form of purification. And he was following in the footsteps of his own personal heroes who had died young and of venerated elders who had "given up the ghost" with such valor and honor. He could even sense that, like Brown, he was dying for a cause. As he would have appreciated, Channing portrays him at one point as the gallant martyr: "Never at any time at all communicative as to his own physical condition (having caught that Indian trick of superlative reticence), he calmly bore his fatal torture, this dying at the stake, and was torn limb from limb in silence."[60]

In light of his illness, furthermore, there was no need to feel so defensive or apologetic about being dependent and nurtured. He was the intrepid soldier, bloody but unbowed, who had marched faithfully to the beat of a different drummer. Imminent death thus conferred on him a status that lifted him far above any suspicions that he was a tame and dependent "mother's son." While he could satisfy his need to be in charge and control many of the conditions under which he would die, he could nevertheless more safely put himself in others' tender hands. Channing was almost constantly at his bedside, ministering to him, and Alcott could even be permitted to "stoop over and kiss his brow" in benediction.[61] Of course, his mother and sister attended solicitously to his needs. In a way, the fact that he could be mothered with impunity in his parents' home in native Concord was also a step toward reestablishing continuity with his past; with one foot in the grave, he could now, without excuse or rebellion, come home to mother and mothering.

More profoundly, death offered him continuity, reunion, with the "mother" and "home" he most fully trusted: nature. Sophia wrote to

Ricketson of her brother's "childlike trust" in his last days.[62] As it was in the womb and at the breast, so would it be in the tomb; he would be merged with nature again. And he would even be translated by, and reborn in, the elements. Marble reports him saying, "For joy I would embrace the earth. I shall delight to be buried in it."[63] In death, too, he would rejoin permanently and completely, and restore an ideal relationship with, those who had gone off into the winter woods before him: most especially his brother, father, and John Brown but also his sister Helen, Uncle Charles, the Indians, all those human and natural representatives of the Old America that he held dear, and those he loved who would before long be consumed in time's fire.[64] As he was gradually but inexorably being consumed by consumption, he was on the brink of having some of his deepest yearnings and wishes consummated: to restore a tranquil, pure, timeless golden age, immune from the tragic and painful realities of personal and suprapersonal history.

It is unlikely that Thoreau was consciously aware of many of these reasons why the prospect of death was such a balm to his psyche, though he probably had *some* insight. To be sure, he was predisposed to deny or repress much of the conflict, guilt, and anxiety that propelled him toward death. But on a conscious level, it was still necessary to come to terms with his death, and this difficult feat must not be minimized. The equanimity and dignity with which he faced death, though attributable in significant measure to unconscious, subconscious, and partially conscious forces and factors, cannot be adequately explained or appreciated without reference to Thoreau's positive strengths and virtues. Viewed in this light, his conduct during his last days cannot fail to inspire respect and admiration. He was, after all, dying young and painfully; however much he was in some ways inclined toward death, an integral part of him loved life deeply and intensely, savored it, took joy in it and in the beauty of the world surrounding him, and the prospect of leaving this life and world, prematurely at that, was no doubt a bitter pill to swallow. Despair, grief, dejection, fear: these emotions must have threatened him at least occasionally. It was in many ways the supreme test of his faith, fortitude, and seasoning. While unconscious and subconscious factors helped reconcile him to his fate, it was also by sheer effort of the will, by all the more conscious intellectual and emotional preparations for death, and by dint of that mysterious entity we call character that Thoreau met and passed the test in such estimable style, a style consistent with his ego ideal, convictions, and values.[65] His profound grounding in nature and the seasons, and his well-evolved belief and involvement in symbolic forms of immortality, stood him in good stead through this grueling final crisis. Drawing deep on his conscious reserves and resources, and lulled and lured toward death by more subterranean urgings, Thoreau made the outward serenity and integrity of his last days an inspiring part—though just a part—of his bequest to the future.

More than many people, Thoreau was able to orchestrate the manner of his dying. He had said of Brown's death scene, "No theatrical manager could have arranged things so wisely to give effect to his behavior and words" (RP, 151). Now he was making a concerted effort to write and direct the script of his final act. It would be an act in accordance with the edited version of his life and self in which he wished to believe. It was a tour de force in which everything seemed to fall into place. Not only was he able to maintain a firm grip on himself, he was also able to control, to a considerable extent, the environment and people around him who were anxious to follow his script and to accommodate his every need. Control itself had always been crucial for him, and now—paradoxically, as his health, body, and very life careened out of control—that desire was largely satisfied. Thoreau had a captive audience, and he brought off his own performance with élan, with just the right mixture of reverence and irreverence. "As long as he could possibly sit up," Channing tells us, "he insisted on his chair at the family-table."[66] His room, his mother said, "did not look like a sick-room. . . . and he was always so cheerful and wished others to be so while about him."[67] When he no longer had the strength to go upstairs to his room, "he requested that the little cane bed he had used at Walden be brought down and placed in the front parlor."[68]

On April 6, 1862, Sophia wrote to Ricketson that her brother was "the embodiment of weakness; still, he enjoys seeing his friends, and every bright hour he devotes to his manuscripts which he is preparing for publication. . . . Henry . . . is so happy that I feel as if he were being translated rather than dying in the ordinary way of most mortals."[69] As has been stressed, it was particularly through his writing that Thoreau was able to "translate" himself—with Sophia, a genuine heroine in her own right, providing much of the transcription—from mortal to immortal. As an artist he had the good fortune, once provided on a daily basis by the *Journal*, of being able to gain composure through composition. Poring and working over his manuscripts in the final months of his life, and immersing himself in the symbols that represented much of his eternal life, afforded him the chance to compose, collect, and complete himself; to work through and transcend grief; to put his house, papers, and identity in order through writings which were his last will and testament, his last words on those matters which were of ultimate concern to him. When a neighbor found him working on his manuscripts, Thoreau whispered, "You know it's respectable to leave an estate to one's neighbors."[70]

At the beginning of February 1862, he was asked by James T. Fields of Ticknor and Fields, now the owner of the *Atlantic Monthly*, to send on some of his essays for inclusion in the magazine.[71] On the condition, so important to a man intent on composing and imposing his will, that "no sentiment or sentence be altered or omitted without my consent" (C, 636), Thoreau readily agreed to the arrangement, and he worked feverishly—both literally and figuratively—on these manuscripts. Aided by his absolutely devoted sister, who copied over his rough drafts and who, as he grew weaker, took dictation from him, he reaped a final harvest. Over the remaining months, he sent to Fields revised versions of lectures he had previously given: "Autumnal Tints," "Life without Principle," "Wild Apples," "Night and Moonlight," and "Walking." He did not live to see any of these essays published; "Walking" would be the first to appear, in the *Atlantic Monthly*, two weeks after his death, and the others would follow. In 1863 the essays he worked on while on his deathbed, except for "Life without Principle," would be published as part of *Excursions*.[72]

Few passages from the completed essays were new; there is no need to consider them in detail here, as I have already considered many of them in the context of Thoreau's own life passages. Suffice it to say that, as essays, they all have, to a greater or lesser extent, an autumnal aura and a recognition of the inevitability and appropriateness of the coming of winter and night. Moreover, except possibly for "Life without Principle," they all may be taken, among other things, as last words on the human seasons.[73] Even "Night and Moonlight," probably the least consequential of these works and one whose origins went back to 1850, remarks on "How insupportable would be the days, if the night with its dews and darkness did not come to restore the drooping world"; it was even possible for Thoreau to identify with the moon, which the "Hindoos compare . . . to a saintly being who has reached the last stage of bodily existence" (E, 316–17). "Life without Principle," born as a lecture in 1854, took on the urgency, authority, and emphasis of one who, with no time to waste, wants to set forth, once and for all, his testimony about how to live a life—and how not to live it: "As the time is short, I will leave out all the flattery, and retain all the criticism" (RP, 156).

"Walking," too, has that quality of wishing to set the record straight on what he deems important, of wishing "to make an extreme statement, if so I may make an emphatic one," on behalf of "absolute freedom and wildness" (E, 161). In the essay he retraces the steps he has taken toward some ultimate home in the wild and the West, and he ponders the final stage of the journey on which he has embarked. To be sure, the essay contains the contradictions born out of Thoreau's ambivalence about literal wilderness. But it is clear that a less literal, more symbolic "wildness" asserts itself strongly in the final version of "Walking." No longer able to walk himself, he acknowledges that, in the end, it is the human mind, heart, and spirit more than the feet that promise to take the saunterer where he wants to go: "We would fain take that walk, never yet taken by us through this actual world, which is perfectly symbolical of the path which we love to travel in the interior and ideal world; and sometimes, no doubt, we find it difficult to choose our direction, because it does not yet exist distinctly in our idea" (E, 175). In "Walking," Thoreau is ultimately a spiritual "pathfinder,"[74] who takes us as far as he has gone, and who, in bidding us well and adieu, points back to the course he has taken and points ahead to where he is bound. While in the first part of life—"Half the walk is but retracing our steps" (E, 162)—"we go eastward to realize history and study the works of art and literature, retracing the steps of the race," he directs his readers—who, in reading him, will be retracing *his* steps before striking out entirely on their own on a genuinely autonomous walk—finally, in their more mature years, to "go westward as into the future, with a spirit of enterprise and adventure" (E, 177). The walk he has in mind can be taken only by the person who has "paid [his] debts and made [his] will, and settled all [his] affairs" (E, 162–63). The direction he points to is off the beaten track and even above it: "The outline which would bound my walks would be, not a circle, but a parabola, or rather like one of those cometary orbits which have been thought to be non-returning curves, in this case opening westward, in which my house occupies the place of the sun" (E, 176). This image, like that in *Walden* of a "tangent to this sphere," suggests a realm accessible only to the symbol-making human being, transcending in its own way even the immortal sphere, cycles, and circles of nature. The human being may, by being remembered by the people, deeds, and art that survive him, become a sort of eternal star in the sky, or a planet permanently in orbit, watching over and watched by generations to come, who will be illuminated by him and even, perhaps, fall under his orbit. This was a key part of Thoreau's sense of destination and destiny. "Walking," which makes the case that "in Wildness is the preservation of the World" (E, 185), is also an eloquent plea for the preservation of the Word—of the language, symbols, imagination, and memory that make us human and, in a sense, able to transcend our own mortality. In particular, it is a statement of faith regarding the conservation of Thoreau's word. The end of the essay depicts an apparently assured and tranquil Thoreau ready to saunter into the radiant sunset and the Holy Land (E, 214).

"Autumnal Tints" and "Wild Apples" were, of course, the most explicitly autumnal of the essays, testimonies to and chronicles of the ripeness of his later years and, as man and tree were identified with each other, statements of Thoreau's convictions about his generativity and integrity. Even more than he could have imagined, he would, as he suggests in "Autumnal Tints," be a "sugar maple man" whose "sap" would be tapped by each new generation, whose "leaves" would "educate" the children of the future (E, 244, 251); he was, as he puts it in "Wild Apples," one of those "poets and philosophers and statesmen" who, like the wild apple, had sprung up "in the country pastures" and whose "perfect fruit" would "outlast the hosts of unoriginal men" (E, 287).

Not surprisingly, Thoreau was anxious that some of his most perfect fruit, *A Week* and, even more critically, *Walden*, would be readily available to posterity; when Fields suggested that *Walden* be reprinted in a new edition, he quickly and gratefully assented and, in the same letter, noted how many copies of *A Week* he had in his attic (C, 637–38), "an obvious hint," Harding remarks, "that he would like to see the earlier book republished too."[75] Both books, so significant to his claim to immortality, would in fact be republished soon after his death. Perhaps realizing the true nature of *Walden*, he requested that the subtitle, "Life in the Woods," be omitted from the new edition. In the last weeks of his life, Thoreau worked also on his Maine woods manuscripts; with less than two weeks left, he was frustrated by his inability to see well enough to make corrections in his "Allegash and East Branch" essay.[76] Now that he was dying, it was at least permissible to try to complete the manuscript that memorialized his Indian "brother," Polis; no one could accuse him of trying to exploit Polis, Indians, or his brother when he was on the verge of laying down his life, renouncing conclusively any worldly ambitions. Sensing that the leaving behind of an estate was serious business, he sought to excise from his manuscripts what he perceived as cheap frivolity. As Channing says, "He rubbed out as perfectly as he could the more humorous part of those articles, originally a relief to their sterner features, and said to me, 'I cannot bear the levity I find.'"[77]

Though he had not had children of his own, Thoreau was able, on his deathbed, to assert and gain assurance of his real-life generativity. One woman, remembering her childhood, recalled that in "his last illness it did not occur to us that he would care to see us, but his sister told my mother that he watched us from the window as we passed, and said: 'Why don't they come to see me? I love them as if they were my own.' After that we

went often, and he always made us so welcome that we liked to go. I remember our last meetings with as much pleasure as the old play-days."[78]
Popular with children, including Emerson's, until the end, he was able to
perceive himself as "father," paternal but not paternalistic, to a wider,
more inclusive family. He *had* had children, after all. Moreover, he could
believe himself a caretaker of the nature that was so very much a part of his
extended family and that would live on after him. Marble informs us that
"one of his latest interviews, only a few days before his death, was with a
party of boys who had been robbing birds' nests. He touched their deepest
feelings, even to tears, as he described the 'wail of sorrow and anguish'
which they had caused their 'little brothers of the air,' to borrow the poetic
phrase of a later ornithologist."[79] Thoreau would no doubt have approved
of that phrase; his own brother had been a fine amateur ornithologist, and
in watching over his "little brothers of the air" as his life slipped away, he
was affirming the extent to which he had cared for his brother and was
paying final homage to him.

Of course, his words, his writings, were his most prized offspring, and
they would, he could anticipate, afford nurturance and education for generations of children and adults yet unborn. He contemplated, and sought
to provide for, their future well-being with all the tenderness and commitment of a parent. Thoreau had made special preparations to house his
journals and other manuscripts; he had constructed a chest of driftwood
for them.[80] But this treasure chest would not be buried with him. Notwithstanding the public's relative apathy or hostility toward his works in his
own lifetime, he was reassured by others, and ultimately came to believe
firmly, that his "children" had not been conceived in vain and would be fitting, enduring, and treasured memorials, along with the manner in which
he would be inscribed and enshrined in the memory of those who had seen
him as a wise mentor, a friend, and kin. On April 13, Ricketson, who
found it too painful actually to be in attendance at Thoreau's bedside,
wrote to him:

> Although you number fewer years than many who have lived wisely before
> you, yet I know of no one, either in the past or present times, who has drank so
> deeply from the sempiternal spring of truth and knowledge, or who in the
> poetry and beauty of every-day life has enjoyed more or contributed more to
> the happiness of others. Truly you have not lived in vain—your works, and
> above all, your brave and truthful life, will become a precious treasure to those
> whose happiness it has been to have known you, and who will continue to up-
> hold though with feebler hands the fresh and instructive philosophy you have
> taught them. (c, 649)

Published in the April *Atlantic* was Alcott's moving anticipatory eulogy for his friend, "The Forester," which contained an affirmation of Thoreau's "greatness":

> I know of nothing more creditable to his greatness than the thoughtful regard, approaching to reverence, by which he has held for many years some of the best persons of his time, living at a distance, and wont to make their annual pilgrimage, usually on foot, to the master, —a devotion very rare in these times of personal indifference, if not of confessed unbelief in persons and ideas.[81]

Early in 1862, Myron Benton, "a young poet from Leedsville, New York,"[82] wrote him after learning of his illness and paid him the tribute that he had "read and re-read" his books "with ever fresh delight" (C, 632). Replying in March, Thoreau noted how "encouraged" he was "to know that, so far as you are concerned, I have not written my books in vain" (C, 641). After visiting Concord with Blake in January 1862, Theo Brown confessed to Thoreau in a letter, "I have long desired to acknowledge my indebtedness to you for them [his books] & to tell you that through them the value of everything seems infinitely enhanced to me" (C, 634). Channing was a faithful attendant at his bedside and undoubtedly made frequent allusions to his friend's lasting contributions; indeed, he would be among those who would immortalize him in a biography. After his friend's death, Channing would say, "Just half the world died for me when I lost Mr. Thoreau."[83]

There is no record of what tribute, if any, Emerson paid to Thoreau while he was still alive, though he did visit him often "to talk of chickadees, the behavior of the river, the ice on Walden Pond, and the arrival of the spring birds."[84] After his death, Emerson "insisted that it [the funeral] be held in the First Parish Church, though many of his [Thoreau's] friends protested that he would have felt such a service inappropriate after his 'signing-off' from the church as a young man."[85] In the eulogy delivered at his friend's funeral (and later incorporated into *Excursions*), Emerson did acknowledge that

> The country knows not yet, or in the least part, how great a son it has lost. . . . His soul was made for the noblest society; he had in a short life exhausted the capabilities of this world; wherever there is knowledge, wherever there is virtue, wherever there is beauty, he will find a home. (E, 33)

Walking away from the newly filled grave, he murmured, "He had a beautiful soul, he had a beautiful soul."[86] But as heartfelt as his sentiments were and as, in many ways, frank and judicious as his evaluations were, his funeral oration still bore the marks of a mentor disappointed with, mystified by, and critical of his former protégé, referring to him as a "protestant à l'outrance" and as one who left "in the midst his broken task" (E, 9, 33). He also severely downplayed and underestimated such artistic achievements as *A Week*, *Walden*, and "Civil Disobedience" and the extent to which Thoreau, though often content to be "captain of a huckleberry party," did aspire, especially in his later years, to "engineering for all America" (E, 29).[87]

Thoreau lived to see—through the windows at least—the bursting forth of one more spring, but, almost as if he deemed it preferable, he would be spared the haze and heat of any more summers. On the "beautiful spring morning" of May 6, 1862,[88] soon after smelling a bouquet of hyacinths and requesting that he be raised in his own bed, his breathing became progressively shallower; at nine o'clock he died peacefully, at the age of forty-four, with his mother, sister, and Aunt Louisa in attendance.[89] According to Sophia's inscribed copy of *A Week*, from which she had been reading to her brother, Thoreau's last spoken sentence was "Now comes good sailing," uttered as the brothers "entered Massachusetts on their homeward voyage to Concord."[90] Channing reported that his last distinct words were "'moose' and 'Indian.'"[91]

Sophia would comment, in a May 20 letter to Ricketson, "I feel as if something very beautiful had happened, not death; although Henry is with us no longer, yet the memory of his sweet and virtuous soul must ever cheer and comfort me."[92] Louisa May Alcott, who attended his May 9 funeral, planned fittingly by her father along the same lines used for the John Brown memorial service, and his subsequent interment—next to his brother, father, and sister—in the New Burying Ground, wrote,

> It seemed as if Nature wore her most benignant aspect to welcome her dutiful & loving son to his long sleep in her arms. As we entered the church yard birds were singing, early violets blooming in the grass & the pines singing their softest lullaby, & there between his father & his brother we left him, feeling that though his life seemed too short, it would blossom & bear fruit for us long after he was gone, & that perhaps we should know a closer relationship now than even while he lived.[93]

Her words were far more prophetic than she, and perhaps Thoreau himself, could ever have conceived.

Ricketson had sent Thoreau a letter on May 4—perhaps the last letter he received—in which he had stated, "I do not look for a speedy termination of the war, although matters look more hopeful, but I cannot doubt but that slavery will soon find its exodus. What a glorious country this will be for the next generation should this *curse* be removed!" (C, 651–52). For Thoreau, the civil war, both inner and outer, was now emphatically over and the curse removed. Like the leaves, he was finally content to "return to dust again." With death came peace, reconciliation, redemption. He was conclusively reunited with John Jr., his Indian companion and fellow sailor, and with John Sr., John Brown, and all those others, Indians and murdered moose alike, that he had so uneasily survived. For years he had been sauntering toward the Holy Land, a pure and golden place and age, where and when the "sun shall shine more brightly than ever he has done . . . and light up our whole lives with a great awakening light, as warm and serene and golden as on a bank-side in autumn" (E, 214). Nearing this bankside and already bathing in the warmth and blessing of that radiant light, he had been ready to die. Now, after the challenging odyssey whose end had been prefigured in *A Week*, he had come all the way home again, moored at last as at first in the native, natal, and nurturing soil, communing again with the nature and people he loved, recovering all that had been lost in the going out and the coming back.

But in the course of his journey, Thoreau had left indelible tracks, to be traced by each generation in its own way, by each person in his or her own way. Even in death he still had several more lives to live. He would always be in season.

Notes

1 Week of a Man's Life

1 Walter Harding, *The Days of Henry Thoreau* (New York: Alfred A. Knopf, 1965), p. 88. An enlarged, corrected republication of the sixth printing (1970) of *Days* has recently appeared (New York: Dover Publications, Inc., 1982).

2 Linck C. Johnson, "Historical Introduction," *A Week on the Concord and Merrimack Rivers*, ed. Carl F. Hovde, William L. Howarth, and Elizabeth Hall Witherell (Princeton: Princeton University Press, 1980), pp. 434–42.

3 Ibid., pp. 445, 433–34.

4 Cf. Sherman Paul, *The Shores of America: Thoreau's Inward Exploration* (Urbana: University of Illinois Press, 1958), p. 218, and Linck C. Johnson, "'A Natural Harvest': The Writing of *A Week on the Concord and Merrimack Rivers*, with the Text of the First Draft" (Diss., Princeton University, 1975), pp. 219–20. Paul says that "the chapters of Thoreau's journey unfolded his spiritual course from youth to maturity, and each chapter carried the weight of the preceding ones." Johnson indicates that *A Week* "is not simply about an excursion on the Concord and Merrimack; it also concerns the voyage of life." Of course, even if there is agreement that *A Week* depicts a "journey . . . from youth to maturity" or "the voyage of life," there is certainly room for more than one interpretation of the "Picture of Human Life" which unfolds in the book. See, for instance, Paul, pp. 191–233 and Johnson, pp. 212–67.

5 Harding, *Days*, pp. 26–27.

6 See *Early Essays and Miscellanies*, ed. Joseph J. Moldenhauer and Edwin Moser, with Alexander C. Kern (Princeton: Princeton University Press, 1975), p. 3.

7 Ibid., pp. 26–36.

8 Ralph Waldo Emerson, "Nature," *The Collected Works of Ralph Waldo Emerson*, vol. 1: *Nature, Addresses, and Lectures*, ed. Robert E. Spiller and Alfred R. Ferguson (Cambridge: Harvard University Press, 1971), pp. 17, 19.

9 Thoreau's portrayal of the human seasons is clearly oriented more toward men's than women's lives.

10 Erik Erikson is one student of the life cycle emphasized in this chapter. See especially Erikson's "The Life Cycle: Epigenesis of Identity" and "Identity Confusion in Life His-

tory and Case History," in *Identity: Youth and Crisis* (New York: W. W. Norton and Co., 1968), pp. 91–207; "Growth and Crises of the Healthy Personality," in *Identity and the Life Cycle* (New York: W. W. Norton and Co., 1980), pp. 51–107; and "Human Strength and the Cycle of Generations," in *Insight and Responsibility* (New York: W. W. Norton and Co., 1964), pp. 111–57. Other "students" I have prominently in mind are Daniel Levinson et al., in *The Seasons of a Man's Life* (New York: Ballantine Books, 1978), and William Bridges, in *Transitions* (Reading, Mass.: Addison-Wesley Publishing Co., 1980). Other works concerning the life cycle that I have found to be helpful and pertinent are Charlotte Buhler, "The Curve of Life as Studied in Biographies," *Journal of Applied Psychology* 19 (1955):405–9; Roger Gould, *Transformations* (New York: Simon and Schuster, 1978); Elliott Jaques, "Death and the Mid-Life Crisis," *International Journal of Psychoanalysis* 46 (1965):502–14; Clark Moustakas, *Turning Points* (Englewood Cliffs, N.J.: Prentice-Hall, 1979); Ira Progoff, *At a Journal Workshop* (New York: Dialogue House Library, 1975); Gail Sheehy, *Passages* (New York: E. P. Dutton and Co., 1976), and *Pathfinders* (New York: William Morrow and Co., 1981); and George Vaillant, *Adaptation to Life* (Boston: Little, Brown and Co., 1977). These works, especially but by no means exclusively those of Erikson, Levinson, and Bridges, have provided insights and have suggested approaches that have contributed much to the interpretation not only in this chapter but throughout the book.

11 This and all subsequent citations in the text of this chapter, unless otherwise indicated, refer to the edition of *A Week on the Concord and Merrimack Rivers* cited in n. 2; reference is to page number.

12 Thomas Blanding has discovered that John Jr. was born not in 1815 but on July 5, 1814. Henry was born on July 12, 1817. See "Beans Baked and Half-Baked," *Concord Saunterer* 15 (1980):16–18.

13 For a fuller discussion, see my *Young Man Thoreau* (Amherst: University of Massachusetts Press, 1977), esp. chap. 6. Harding writes, "For several years he dreamed tragic dreams on the anniversary of John's death. And many years later he still choked and tears came into his eyes at the mention of John's name" (*Days*, p. 136).

14 See *Young Man Thoreau*, esp. pp. 69–71, 186–87. Cf. Robert Sayre, *Thoreau and the American Indians* (Princeton: Princeton University Press, 1977), pp. 45, 202–3. For Sayre's enlightening interpretation of *A Week*, which emphasizes its "images and history of Indians," see pp. 28–58.

15 Robert Jay Lifton, *The Broken Connection* (New York: Simon and Schuster, 1979), p. 171. This book, and Lifton's *The Life of the Self* (New York: Simon and Schuster, 1976), have been important influences on my thinking about Thoreau.

16 Blanding, "Beans Baked and Half-Baked," pp. 16–18.

17 Erikson, "Growth and Crises of the Healthy Personality," p. 53.

18 Ibid., p. 107.

19 Lifton, *Broken Connection*, p. 178.

20 Ibid.

21 Bridges, *Transitions*, p. 11.

22 Erikson, "Human Strength and the Cycle of Generations," p. 116.

23 Erikson, "The Life Cycle," pp. 96–107. Erikson identifies the first fundamental conflict of life as "trust" vs. "mistrust."

24 Erikson, "Human Strength and the Cycle of Generations," p. 117. See "Mother-Nature," in Raymond D. Gozzi, "Tropes and Figures: A Psychological Study of David Henry Thoreau" (Diss., New York University, 1957), pp. 228–51. A recent summary by

Gozzi of his significant Freudian study can be found in *Thoreau's Psychology: Eight Essays*, ed. Raymond D. Gozzi (Lanham, Md.: University Press of America, 1983), pp. 1–18.

25 See Johnson, "'A Natural Harvest,'" pp. 215–16.

26 Erikson, "Human Strength and the Cycle of Generations," p. 118.

27 Ibid., p. 116.

28 Erikson, "The Life Cycle," pp. 107–14.

29 Erikson, "Human Strength and the Cycle of Generations," pp. 118–19.

30 For a detailed discussion of Cynthia and John Thoreau and their influence on Henry, see *Young Man Thoreau*, esp. chap. 2.

31 Priscilla Rice Edes, as quoted in Raymond Adams, "Thoreau and His Neighbors," *Thoreau Society Bulletin* 44 (1953):2.

32 Harding, *Days*, pp. 8, 246. It should be noted that Mrs. Thoreau once "signed off" from the Unitarian Church and tried to join the Trinitarian Church in 1827. However, as Harding indicates, "the Trinitarians refused to accept her; apparently either she was unwilling to accept verbatim their orthodoxy or they were unwilling to accept her staunch independence." See *Days*, pp. 24–25.

33 Ellery Channing, *Thoreau, the Poet-Naturalist*, ed. F. B. Sanborn (Boston: Charles E. Goodspeed, 1902), p. 5.

34 Erikson, "The Life Cycle," pp. 111, 115–22.

35 Harding, *Days*, p. 8. See also *Young Man Thoreau*, chap. 2.

36 Erikson, "Human Strength and the Cycle of Generations," p. 122.

37 Erikson, "The Life Cycle," pp. 122–28.

38 Erikson, "Human Strength and the Cycle of Generations," p. 122.

39 Erikson, "The Life Cycle," p. 124. Erikson speaks of the conflict between a sense of "industry" and "inferiority."

40 For a full discussion of Thoreau's prolonged moratorium, see *Young Man Thoreau*, esp. chaps. 3–6. For a discussion of the moratorium concept, of "identity crisis," and of the "identity vs. identity confusion" stage, see Erikson, "The Life Cycle," pp. 128–35, and "Identity Confusion in Life History and Case History," pp. 142–207.

41 Erikson, "The Life Cycle," p. 128.

42 See *Young Man Thoreau*, esp. chap. 1.

43 See Erik Erikson, *Young Man Luther* (New York: W. W. Norton and Co., 1958), esp. p. 41.

44 Erikson, "Human Strength and the Cycle of Generations," p. 125.

45 For an interesting alternative interpretation, see Frederick Garber, "A Space for Saddleback," *Centennial Review* 24 (1980):322–37, and also Garber's *Thoreau's Redemptive Imagination* (New York: New York University Press, 1977), pp. 192–98.

46 Bridges, *Transitions*, p. 95.

47 Cf. Paul, *Shores of America*, p. 221.

48 Johnson, "Historical Introduction," p. 434.

49 See Levinson, *Seasons*, pp. 78–84, 139–49. Vaillant, in *Adaptation to Life* (p. 202), points out that Erikson gives short shrift to career consolidation as an issue and stage of adult development.

50 See Levinson, *Seasons*, pp. 144–49.

51 Erikson, "The Life Cycle," pp. 135–38.

52 Johnson, "'A Natural Harvest,'" p. 318.

53 See chapter 3.

54   In his 1842–44 "Long Book," soon after stating that the "death of friends will inspire us as much as their lives," he writes, "Wherever I go I am still on the trail of the Indian" (PJ, 2:38, 39).

55   See Sayre's discussion in *Thoreau and the American Indians*, pp. 43–46. Leslie Fiedler, in *The Return of the Vanishing American* (New York: Stein and Day Publishers, 1968), calls this story "a fable of Pagan Paradise Regained" (p. 115).

56   See Erikson, "The Life Cycle," p. 136.

57   See *Young Man Thoreau*, p. 118.

58   See Levinson, *Seasons*, pp. 195–97, 335–36. The concept of "individuation" owes much to Jung's perspectives on the "second half of life." Also pertinent in this context is Abraham Maslow's "self-actualization" (and "peak experience").

59   Bridges, *Transitions*, p. 52.

60   See Johnson, "'A Natural Harvest,'" pp. 309–10, for a discussion of the possible connections between the 1846 Katahdin experience and the short account of the White Mountains expedition in *A Week*.

61   Erikson, "The Life Cycle," pp. 138–39.

62   That he began drafting the Dustan story in early 1847 (Johnson, "'A Natural Harvest,'" p. 313) may suggest that he was coming to feel some anxiety about his mother as he contemplated leaving Walden Pond.

63   Cf. Sayre, *Thoreau and the American Indians*, pp. 145–48. Eric J. Sundquist's *Home as Found: Authority and Genealogy in Nineteenth-Century American Literature* (Baltimore: Johns Hopkins University Press, 1979) contains an intriguing psychoanalytic interpretation of the Dustan story (pp. 61–63) and other aspects of *A Week* (pp. 41–85).

64   Erikson, "The Life Cycle," pp. 139–41.

65   See Jaques, "Death and the Mid-Life Crisis," pp. 502–14, and Sheehy's discussion of "The Creative Crisis" in *Passages*, pp. 255–57.

66   I am indebted to Robert Lifton's discussion of "symbolic immortality" in *Broken Connection* and to Ernest Becker's exploration of the human condition and the quest for immortality in *The Denial of Death* (New York: Free Press, 1973). See subsequent chapters for further development of the issues discussed in this paragraph.

67   See Lifton, *Broken Connection*, esp. pp. 13–23.

68   Erikson defines such wisdom as "the detached concern with life itself, in the face of death itself." See "Human Strength and the Cycle of Generations," p. 133.

69   Cf. Lawrence Buell, *Literary Transcendentalism* (Ithaca: Cornell University Press, 1973), p. 235. For Buell's analysis of *A Week*, see pp. 208–38.

70   See discussion in later chapters, and "Wild Apples," in *Excursions* (1863; reprint ed., New York: Corinth Books, 1962), pp. 266–306.

2   Spring Growth

1   Harding, *Days*, p. 181.

2   Gay Wilson Allen, *Waldo Emerson* (New York: Viking Press, 1981), p. 449.

3   See *Young Man Thoreau*, pp. 209–13.

4   Levinson, *Seasons*, pp. 80, 79.

5   Ibid., p. 80.

6   Ibid., pp. 98–99.

7   Ibid., pp. 41–43.

8   This and all subsequent citations in the text of this chapter, unless otherwise indicated, refer to the "First Version of *Walden*," in J. Lyndon Shanley, *The Making of Walden* (Chicago: University of Chicago Press, 1957).

9   See Harding, *Days*, pp. 13–14.

10 See Ethel Seybold, *Thoreau: The Quest and the Classics* (New Haven: Yale University Press, 1951), esp. pp. 48–63.

11 Harding, *Days*, p. 197.

12 See G. Thomas Couser, *American Autobiography: The Prophetic Mode* (Amherst: University of Massachusetts Press, 1979), pp. 62–79, esp. pp. 71–72.

13 See *Young Man Thoreau*, p. 75.

14 Harding, *Days*, p. 186.

15 See D. Gordon Rohman, "Second Growth in *Walden*," *Papers of the Michigan Academy of Science, Arts, and Letters* 47 (1962):565–70.

16 J. Lyndon Shanley, "Historical Introduction," in *Walden*, ed. J. Lyndon Shanley (Princeton: Princeton University Press, 1971), p. 362.

17 Levinson, *Seasons*, pp. 49, 54.

18 Ibid., p. 85.

19 *Journal 2* transcription, provided by the Thoreau Textual Center, Princeton University, Princeton, N.J.

20 For a detailed discussion of the "civil disobedience" episode, see Harding, *Days*, pp. 199–206.

21 See chapter 3 for a further consideration of this episode and of the "Civil Disobedience" essay.

22 Walter Harding and Carl Bode, eds., in *Correspondence* (New York: New York University Press, 1958), p. 167.

23 Harding, *Days*, p. 184; also Annie Russell Marble, *Thoreau: His Home, Friends and Books* (1902; reprint ed., New York: AMS Press, 1969), p. 129. Some have considered these facts to reveal a gaping flaw. See, for instance, Leon Edel, *Henry D. Thoreau* (Minneapolis: University of Minnesota Press, 1970), esp. pp. 23–26. For a more recent version, see Edel's "The Mystery of Walden Pond," in *Stuff of Sleep and Dreams* (New York: Harper and Row, 1982), pp. 47–65.

24 Harding, *Days*, p. 184.

25 Richard Bridgman, in *Dark Thoreau* (Lincoln: University of Nebraska Press, 1982), suggestively indicates that "almost all the instances of anger and metaphorical destructiveness were added after the initial version of *Walden* was composed" (p. 80).

26 See *Young Man Thoreau*, pp. 188–90.

27 Cf. Bridgman, *Dark Thoreau*, pp. 195–96.

28 *Journal 2* transcription, provided by the Thoreau Textual Center.

29 Ibid.

30 Cf. Bridgman, *Dark Thoreau*, pp. 196–97.

31 *Journal 2* transcription, provided by the Thoreau Textual Center.

32 See James McIntosh, *Thoreau as Romantic Naturalist* (Ithaca: Cornell University Press, 1974), for an excellent discussion of these issues.

33 See Sundquist, *Home as Found*, pp. 41–85.

34 Levinson, *Seasons*, p. 53.

35 Johnson, "Historical Introduction," p. 434, and " 'A Natural Harvest,' " p. 269.

36   Levinson, *Seasons*, pp. 140, 141.

37   I have found very helpful Erik S. Lunde's *Horace Greeley* (Boston: Twayne Publishers, 1981).

38   Harding, *Days*, p. 197.

39   Ibid.

40   Johnson, " 'A Natural Harvest,' " pp. 314–15.

41   This comparison with Emerson may also be taken as an early sign of competition with him. See Bridgman, *Dark Thoreau*, p. 159.

42   Harding, *Days*, p. 245.

43   See *Young Man Thoreau*, chap. 5.

3   *A Sojourner in Civilized Life Again*

1   Ronald Clapper, "The Development of *Walden*: A Genetic Text" (Diss., University of California at Los Angeles, 1967), p. 142.

2   Harding, *Days*, p. 220.

3   Evidence of tensions in their relationship appears earlier than many biographers have noted.

4   See my article, "Emerson's Young Adulthood: From Patienthood to Patiencehood," *ESQ: A Journal of the American Renaissance* 25 (1979):203–10.

5   See Levinson, *Seasons*, pp. 251–56.

6   Allen, *Waldo Emerson*, p. 500.

7   Harding, *Days*, p. 299.

8   Allen, *Waldo Emerson*, p. 492.

9   Ibid., p. 497.

10   See *Correspondence*, pp. 120, 123–25; *Young Man Thoreau*, p. 232 n.

11   See Allen's discussion of Emerson's marriage to Lidian in *Waldo Emerson*.

12   See Gozzi, "Tropes and Figures," esp. pp. 321–400.

13   Harding, *Days*, pp. 222–24.

14   See Paul Hourihan, "Crisis in the Emerson-Thoreau Friendship: the Symbolic Function of 'Civil Disobedience,' " in Gozzi, *Thoreau's Psychology*, pp. 109–22; see esp. 115–16.

15   See Johnson, " 'A Natural Harvest,' " pp. 115–29.

16   Wendell Glick, "Textual Introduction" to "Resistance to Civil Government," in *Reform Papers*, ed. Wendell Glick (Princeton: Princeton University Press, 1973), pp. 313–14.

17   Harding, *Days*, p. 205.

18   Hourihan, "Crisis," pp. 113–14.

19   Cf. Hourihan, "Crisis," esp. pp. 119–20.

20   Clapper, "Development of *Walden*," p. 45.

21   See Gozzi, "Tropes and Figures," pp. 251–68.

22   See Glick, "Textual Introduction," p. 325.

23   Harding, *Days*, pp. 205–6.

24   See *Young Man Thoreau*, pp. 176–78.

25   Erik Erikson, *Gandhi's Truth* (New York: W. W. Norton and Co., 1969), p. 129.

26   See *Young Man Thoreau*, p. 70.

27   Cf. Hourihan, "Crisis," pp. 118–18a.

28   Hourihan contends (p. 121) that this passage shows Thoreau "thanking Emerson for his lectures in the tone of a suddenly *matured* disciple."

29 Ellen Tucker Emerson, *The Life of Lidian Jackson Emerson*, ed. Dolores Bird Carpenter (Boston: Twayne Publishers, 1980), p. 108.

30 Hourihan, "Crisis," p. 121, refers to it as a "skeleton in their closet."

31 Ruth Hallingby Frost, "Thoreau's Worcester Associations" (Worcester, Mass.: American Antiquarian Society, 1943), pp. 32–33.

32 Ibid., pp. 37, 43.

33 See my article, "Emerson's Young Adulthood."

34 Frost, "Thoreau's Worcester Associations," p. 44.

35 Ibid., pp. 55–56.

36 Ibid., p. 52.

37 Thoreau's letter of March 31 is not in the *Correspondence* but is referred to in Greeley's April 3 letter to Thoreau (c, 217). Its contents can be inferred from Greeley's April 3 response.

38 Allen, *Waldo Emerson*, p. 505; Harding, *Days*, p. 224.

39 Cf. Hourihan, "Crisis," p. 121.

40 Harding, *Days*, pp. 234, 235; see also Allen, *Waldo Emerson*, p. 520.

41 Allen, *Waldo Emerson*, pp. 519–20.

42 Harding, *Days*, p. 234.

43 Ibid., p. 233.

44 Ibid., p. 234.

45 Johnson, "'A Natural Harvest,'" p. 318.

46 I have found Tillie Olsen's *Silences* (New York: Delacorte Press, 1978) very helpful in considering the creative "silences" of both female and male writers.

47 Allen, *Waldo Emerson*, p. 520.

48 Harding, *Days*, p. 236.

49 See Johnson, "'A Natural Harvest,'" p. 319.

50 Allen, *Waldo Emerson*, p. 522.

51 Harding, *Days*, pp. 236–37.

52 James Russell Lowell, "From *A Fable for Critics*," as quoted in *The Recognition of Henry David Thoreau*, ed. Wendell Glick (Ann Arbor: University of Michigan Press, 1969), p. 3; see also Harding, *Days*, p. 299.

53 Harding, *Days*, p. 230.

54 Ibid., p. 246.

55 Ibid., pp. 238–39.

56 Ibid., pp. 240–41.

57 Thoreau did receive an intimation of things to come in a *Worcester Palladium* review, and "Aunt Maria Thoreau, having heard about the *Palladium* account, was sure that Worcester had had enough of her nephew, and confessed that she was as disgusted with what he had to say as the *Palladium* had been" (Harding, *Days*, p. 242).

58 See Lunde, *Horace Greeley*, p. 19.

59 Transcription of letter to Thatcher of February 9, 1849, Thoreau Textual Center, Princeton University, Princeton, NJ. This letter, along with other letters not in the *Correspondence*, will be published in the new Princeton Edition of Thoreau's correspondence.

60 See Johnson, "'A Natural Harvest,'" p. 321.

61 Letter to Prudence Ward of February 28, 1849, in Henry Seidel Canby, *Thoreau* (Boston: Houghton Mifflin Co., 1939), pp. 248–49.

62 Letter to Thatcher of February 9, 1849, Thoreau Textual Center.

63 Canby, *Thoreau*, p. 249.

64   Harding, *Days*, p. 246.

65   Ibid., p. 258.

66   Ibid., p. 248.

67   Ibid., p. 249.

68   Ibid., p. 250.

69   See Johnson, " 'A Natural Harvest,' " p. 324.

70   Harding, *Days*, pp. 250–51.

71   Anonymous review of *A Week* in *London Athenaeum*, October 27, 1849, in Glick, *Recognition*, pp. 4–5.

72   Levinson, *Seasons*, pp. 144, 147.

73   See Levinson, *Seasons*, pp. 100–101.

74   See Levinson, *Seasons*, p. 148. Obviously, this analysis refers to male mentoring relationships. Male-female or female-female mentoring relationships, though they may have much in common with the exclusively male relationship, surely have other dimensions and dynamics.

75   See Levinson, *Seasons*, pp. 99–100; see also *Young Man Thoreau*, esp. pp. 79–98.

76   See *Young Man Thoreau*, esp. pp. 79–98, and "Emerson's Young Adulthood."

77   Levinson, *Seasons*, p. 148. For other interpretations and dimensions of the Emerson-Thoreau relationship, see Joel Porte, *Emerson and Thoreau: Transcendentalists in Conflict* (Middletown, Conn.: Wesleyan University Press, 1966); Paul, *Shores of America*; Joel Porte, *Representative Man* (New York: Oxford University Press, 1979), esp. pp. 300–313, 316–17; Mary Elkins Moller, *Thoreau in the Human Community* (Amherst: University of Massachusetts Press, 1980); and Leonard Neufeldt, *The House of Emerson* (Lincoln: University of Nebraska Press, 1982), pp. 123–40.

78   Levinson, *Seasons*, pp. 100–101.

79   Harding, *Days*, pp. 253–54.

80   See chapters 4, 5, and 6. Thoreau had completed two revised versions of *Walden* (the second and third versions) in 1849. Shanley says, "The effect and apparent intention of his work in these versions was to tidy up and to increase the clarity and force of the first version, which he had written at the pond. And so he could properly write in III: 'At the time the following pages were written I lived alone, in the woods.' " See Shanley, *The Making of Walden*, pp. 27–30, and Clapper, "Development of *Walden*," pp. 30–31.

4   Seedtime

1   Levinson, *Seasons*, pp. 54–56.

2   Harding, *Days*, p. 254.

3   Ibid., p. 235.

4   Cf. William Howarth, *The Book of Concord: Thoreau's Life as a Writer* (New York: Viking Press, 1982), esp. pp. 59–63. See this book for an illuminating analysis and evaluation of the *Journal*.

5   Cf. Howarth, *Book of Concord*, p. 62. Howarth says that Thoreau "no longer shared Emerson's notions of a literary career. When they talked in late October [1850], Emerson praised England while Thoreau defended the obscurity and independence of American scholars."

6   Cf. Howarth, *Book of Concord*, p. 9.

7   If, as Edel says in *Henry D. Thoreau*, Thoreau's "works were the anchor of his days"

(p. 43), the *Journal* was the most consistently crucial anchor.

8 See Howarth, *Book of Concord.*

9 Cf. Bridges, *Transitions*, esp. pp. 2–56, 90–159. Significantly, Bridges (and other humanistic psychologists), like Thoreau, often uses natural, organic imagery, metaphors, and analogies (as well as mythological references) to characterize human developmental processes. According to Bridges, the transition process, which occurs at many points and crises in the life cycle, includes an ending, a "neutral zone," and a new beginning. Cf. also Levinson, *Seasons*, esp. pp. 6–7, and Sheehy's discussion in *Passages* of "Rooting and Extending" in the early thirties, esp. pp. 213–14.

10 See Bridges, *Transitions*, p. 45.

11 Levinson, *Seasons*, p. 145.

12 See Howarth, *Book of Concord*, p. 60.

13 Harding, *Days*, p. 255.

14 Ibid., p. 263.

15 Ibid., pp. 264–65. See also Howarth's vivid description of the attic room (*Book of Concord*, pp. 61–62).

16 See *The Journal of Henry D. Thoreau*, ed. Bradford Torrey and Francis H. Allen (1906; reprint ed., New York: Dover Publications, 1962), II:21–35; hereafter cited as J.

17 See *Young Man Thoreau*, pp. 199–204.

18 See Mitchell Robert Breitweiser, "Thoreau and the Wrecks of Cape Cod," *Studies in Romanticism* 20 (1981):3–20.

19 Harding, *Days*, p. 277.

20 There have even been some apocryphal, and highly unlikely, suggestions that there was some kind of romantic link between Thoreau and Fuller; see Harding, *Days*, pp. 68–69.

21 See *Young Man Thoreau*, pp. 162–66.

22 See Bridges, *Transitions*, pp. 87, 111–31.

23 Channing was one person Thoreau did sometimes allow to accompany him on his walks; see Moller, *Thoreau in the Human Community*, pp. 41–47.

24 Again, the reader is referred to McIntosh, *Thoreau as Romantic Naturalist.*

25 Cf. Garber, *Thoreau's Redemptive Imagination*, pp. 61–65.

26 Harding, *Days*, p. 283.

27 See chapter 5 and the discussion of "Walking" in chapter 9.

28 Moller, in *Thoreau in the Human Community*, indicates that Channing was apparently a fellow traveler on some of these walks by night (p. 46).

29 See Moller, *Thoreau in the Human Community*, for some valuable discussion of what she calls Thoreau's "nocturnes."

30 As will be seen, only when he went to Maine in 1857 would he come upon phosphorescent wood; and soon thereafter he would see glowworms; see chapter 7.

31 See Robert Sattelmeyer, "Introduction," *Henry David Thoreau: The Natural History Essays* (Salt Lake City: Peregrine Smith, 1980), pp. vii–xxxiv; see also Harding and Bode, in *Correspondence*, p. 317.

32 By May 1851 (J, II:198–99), Thoreau was intermittently using extensive scientific nomenclature.

33 Cf. Howarth, *Book of Concord*, p. 7; Channing, *Thoreau, the Poet-Naturalist*, pp. 67–68.

34 Cf. Moller, *Thoreau in the Human Community*, pp. 28–30.

35 Cf. Moller's interpretation of the dream (*Thoreau in the Human Community*, p. 29).

5 Second Spring

1 Shanley, "Historical Introduction," pp. 362–64; Clapper, "Development of *Walden*," pp. 23–24.

2 See Shanley, *Making of Walden*, p. 31.

3 Clapper, "Development of *Walden*," p. 534.

4 Shanley, "Historical Introduction," pp. 363–64.

5 See chapter 2.

6 Clapper, "Development of *Walden*," p. 525.

7 Jaques, "Death and the Mid-Life Crisis," p. 512.

8 Shanley, *Making of Walden*, pp. 67–68 n.

9 See Leo Marx, "The Two Thoreaus," *New York Review of Books*, October 26, 1978, p. 42. See also Leo Marx, "Introduction," in *Excursions*, and Shanley, *Making of Walden*.

10 F. B. Sanborn, *Henry D. Thoreau* (Boston: Houghton Mifflin Co., 1882), p. 231.

11 Cf. Clapper, "Development of *Walden*," pp. 25–26.

12 Ibid., p. 256.

13 Cf. Garber, *Thoreau's Redemptive Imagination*.

14 Shanley, *Making of Walden*, p. 67.

15 Clapper, "Development of *Walden*," p. 863. Clapper refers to Thoreau's evolving "defiant optimism" in this period (p. 26).

16 Shanley, "Historical Introduction," pp. 363–64.

17 Clapper, "Development of *Walden*," p. 31.

18 See Levinson, *Seasons*, pp. 144–49.

19 Shanley, *Making of Walden*, p. 67.

20 See Levinson, *Seasons*, esp. pp. 191–208.

21 See, for instance, Levinson, *Seasons*, pp. 222–23; Sheehy, *Passages*, pp. 350–64; Gould, *Transformations*, pp. 218–19, 305–6.

22 Cf. Bridgman, *Dark Thoreau*, esp. pp. 284–87.

23 See Levinson, *Seasons*, p. 193.

24 Levinson writes that while illusions "can be tremendously harmful," they "can also inspire nobility and accomplishment. . . . Some reduction in illusions is now appropriate and beneficial, but it is neither possible nor desirable to overcome *all* illusions in the Mid-life Transition or even by the end of middle adulthood. Illusion continues to have its place—a mixed blessing, or a mixed curse—all through the life cycle" (ibid., p. 193).

25 See Clapper, "Development of *Walden*," p. 26.

26 Levinson, *Seasons*, p. 225.

27 Cf. Moller, *Thoreau in the Human Community*, pp. 30–37.

28 Clapper, "Development of *Walden*," p. 248.

29 See Becker, *Denial of Death*, esp. pp. 225–85.

30 See Howarth, *Book of Concord*, p. 78, and Harding, *Days*, pp. 111–12.

31 See James Armstrong, "Thoreau, Chastity, and the Reformers," in Gozzi, *Thoreau's Psychology*. Armstrong contends (p. 125) that "Thoreau's attitudes and behavior with regard to sex and sensuality were . . . consistent with the advice and philosophy of the most popular moral reformers of his time. . . . the basic motive for Thoreau's asceticism, both dietary and sexual, was his desire to reduce the threats to his uncertain health that the reformers maintained were offered by gastric and genital excitement." See the entire essay, pp. 123–39. In any case, such notions could well have instilled anxiety and guilt about masturbation and sexual desire.

32 See Gozzi, "Tropes and Figures." See also Walter Harding, "Afterword: Some Random Thoughts on Thoreau's Personality," in *Henry David Thoreau: A Profile*, ed. Walter Harding (New York: Hill and Wang, 1971), pp. 246–47; Harding's "Thoreau and Eros," a bold yet tactful essay on Thoreau's possible homoerotic orientation, in Gozzi, *Thoreau's Psychology*, pp. 145–59; Jonathan Katz, *Gay American History* (New York: Crowell, 1976); *Young Man Thoreau*, p. 236 n.

33 See Gozzi, "Tropes and Figures," pp. 334–35. Even if this particular possibility is remote, in general I have found Gozzi's discussion of Thoreau's sexuality, especially of oedipal factors, very helpful and illuminating. Also insightful is Moller's discussion of Thoreau's sexuality in *Thoreau in the Human Community*.

34 See *Young Man Thoreau*, esp. chap. 4.

35 Cf. Gozzi, "Tropes and Figures," p. 67.

36 Shanley, *Making of Walden*, p. 67.

37 Cf. Vaillant, *Adaptation to Life*, in which sublimation is identified as one of the "healthy," "mature" defenses and adaptive styles. He says, "unlike the case with 'neurotic' defenses, with *sublimation* instincts are channeled rather than dammed or diverted. Successful artistic expression remains the classic example" (p. 386).

38 See Sayre, *Thoreau and the American Indians*, pp. 166–72.

39 Ibid., p. 168.

40 See Levinson, *Seasons*, p. 193. "De-illusionment" is Levinson's term.

41 See chapter 6 for a full discussion of these issues.

42 Shanley, *Making of Walden*, pp. 66–69; Shanley, "Historical Introduction," pp. 366–67.

43 Shanley, *Making of Walden*, p. 67.

44 Ibid., pp. 66–67; Shanley, "Historical Introduction," p. 366.

45 Shanley, *Making of Walden*, pp. 67–68.

46 Clapper, "Development of *Walden*," p. 245.

47 Ibid., p. 263.

48 Ibid., p. 25.

49 Ibid., p. 24.

50 See chapter 6 and subsequent chapters for a full discussion of Thoreau's anxieties about ripening and his ambivalence about accepting his own autumn.

51 Perhaps by this time he recognized that he would have to do another, sixth, draft of a *Walden* still in the process of being matured.

52 Shanley, "Historical Introduction," p. 364.

53 Ibid.

6   But a Morning Star

1 Harding, *Days*, p. 331.

2 After all, one of the primary reasons why Thoreau had gone to Walden Pond was to write *A Week*, which was to be in some way a memorial and elegy for his brother; going to Walden was itself a form of penitence. As previously suggested, one can imagine that he would have felt uneasy, for all his ambitions, had the book achieved substantial success; he would, in a sense, have been profiting by having "used" or exploited his brother. Similarly, Thoreau may well have suspected that *Walden* could never have been the same book (if it had been written at all) if it had not been for his brother. Thus, in this respect,

the possibility of gaining fame through *Walden* may well have aroused guilt.

3   Harding, *Days*, p. 134.

4   Ibid., p. 332.

5   Cf. Garber's discussion in *Thoreau's Redemptive Imagination* of Thoreau's line, circle, and tangent-parabola imagery.

6   Quite possibly this is one reason why he simply could not make progress on "October Hues" during this period. He still did not feel "*well in*" October, still could not accept fully his own autumn or feel entirely in correspondence with October. Another reason why he could not make progress was that he was so busy (J, VII:46).

7   Harding, *Days*, p. 317.

8   See Leo Marx, *The Machine in the Garden* (New York: Oxford University Press, 1964), including his consideration of *Walden*, pp. 242–65.

9   Cf. Howarth, *Book of Concord*, p. 93; and see his discussion of *Walden*, pp. 92–99. For other interpretations of *Walden*, see, for instance, Paul, *Shores of America*, pp. 293– 353; Stanley Cavell, *The Senses of Walden* (New York: Viking Press, 1972); Charles R. Anderson, *The Magic Circle of Walden* (New York: Holt, Rinehart and Winston, 1968); Bridgman, *Dark Thoreau*, pp. 75–157; Sayre, *Thoreau and the American Indians*, pp. 59–100; Buell, *Literary Transcendentalism*, pp. 296–311. See also Buell's discussion of "World and Word," esp. pp. 141–44.

10   See Howarth, *Book of Concord*, p. 96.

11   Becker, *Denial of Death*, p. 257; see Becker's provocative discussion of the "problems" of the artist, esp. pp. 171–75, 255–85.

12   See Lifton, *Broken Connection*, p. 403.

13   As Levinson uses the term (and as I do), "midlife crisis" refers only to "that one which occurs within the Mid-life Transition" (*Seasons*, p. 159).

14   See Vaillant, *Adaptation to Life*.

15   See Jaques, "Death and the Mid-Life Crisis," and Sheehy, *Passages*, esp. pp. 255–57. Truman Nelson, "Thoreau and John Brown," in *Thoreau in Our Season*, ed. John Hicks (Amherst: University of Massachusetts Press, 1962), speaks (with reference to *Walden*) of "that black despair and hopelessness that comes to a serious writer when a book he *knows* is the best work he will ever perform, falls flat and becomes, in a month or so, stale and unprofitable" (p. 145).

16   Letter of September 11, 1854, transcription, Thoreau Textual Center. For an important and provocative account of the "sentimental" culture which flourished in America at this time, and how it developed, see Ann Douglas, *The Feminization of American Culture* (New York: Alfred A Knopf, 1977).

17   See my articles, "An Unpublished Letter to Russell," *Thoreau Society Bulletin* 151 (1980):3–4, and "Thoreau's Scientific Phase: Thoreau and John Russell," *Concord Saunterer* 15 (1980):1–5.

18   See Lifton, *Broken Connection*, p. 21.

19   See Lifton, *Broken Connection*.

20   Harding, *Days*, p. 335.

21   Thoreau had initially given a copy of *Walden* to Mrs. Emerson (Harding, *Days*, p. 338). Emerson's own copy of *Walden*, whenever he got it, has come to light only recently and is now, Harding indicates, in the Concord Free Public Library.

22   Cf. Gozzi, "Tropes and Figures," pp. 137–48.

23   Harding, *Days*, p. 335.

24   See Harding, *Days*, pp. 334–38, and Gary Scharnhorst, "Five Uncollected Contem-

porary Reviews of *Walden*," *Thoreau Society Bulletin* 160 (1982):1–3.

25 Harding, *Days*, p. 336.

26 Letter of August 31, 1854, transcription, Thoreau Textual Center.

27 Cf. Moller, *Thoreau in the Human Community*, p. 114.

28 Harding, *Days*, p. 341.

29 See Harding, *Days*, pp. 351–52, and Thomas Blanding and Walter Harding, *A Thoreau Iconography* (Geneseo, N.Y.: Thoreau Society Booklet 30, 1980).

30 Harding, *Days*, p. 346.

31 Ibid., p. 341.

32 Ibid., pp. 341–43.

33 Ibid., p. 346.

34 Ibid., pp. 344–45.

35 Ibid., p. 342.

36 See Sayre, *Thoreau and the American Indians*, pp. 101–22.

37 See Marble, *Thoreau*, p. 48.

38 Howarth, *Book of Concord*, p. 110.

39 James Russell Lowell, "Thoreau," *North American Review* 101 (1865), in Glick, *Recognition*, said, "His whole life was a search for the doctor" (p. 41).

40 Harding, *Days*, p. 340. Harding informs us, "On September 29, 1855, Ticknor & Fields sent him a check for $51.60 for the sale of 344 copies and on February 16, 1857, $45.00 for the sale of 240 copies plus 12 copies of *A Week*."

41 See Harding, *Days*, p. 359. Possibly these activities served partly as an attempt to prop up generativity at a time when there was little evidence of it.

42 Gozzi, "Tropes and Figures," p. 141. Gozzi characterizes the "breakdown" of 1855–57 as "the response of his unconscious to the success of *Walden* and his assertion of maturity."

43 See Lifton, *Broken Connection*, p. 402. Leon Edel, referring to Thoreau's summer 1853 headaches (but also suggesting a wider application to Thoreau's health problems), indicates that suppressed rage may have been a causative factor. "We know," he says, "that suppressed rage of this kind does drain energy and in a sense dries one up"; See "Journals of a Narcissist," *New Republic* 187 (1982):35–36.

44 As Bridges says in *Transitions*, "transition takes its toll on us physically as well as mentally and socially" (p. 24).

45 See Erikson's discussion of the symptoms of severe identity confusion in "Identity Confusion in Life History and Case History," pp. 142–207.

46 Erikson, "The Life Cycle," p. 138.

47 Sheehy, *Passages*, p. 255; according to Sheehy, Jaques may have coined the term "midlife crisis."

48 Ibid.; see pp. 252–59, and Jaques, "Death and the Mid-Life Crisis."

49 For contrasting views, see, for instance, Paul, *Shores of America*, and J. Lyndon Shanley, "'Years of Decay and Disappointment?'" in *Henry David Thoreau*, ed. Harding, pp. 188–98. Shanley's essay is in part a response to Paul's interpretation of Thoreau's post-*Walden* years. See also Marx, "Introduction," *Excursions*, pp. v–xiv; Leo Stoller, *After Walden: Thoreau's Changing Views on Economic Man* (Stanford: Stanford University Press, 1957); and Howarth, *Book of Concord*.

50 See Bridges, *Transitions*, esp. pp. 46–56, 149–50.

51 Paul, in *Shores of America*, speaks of Thoreau's "agonies of assimilation" (p. 114).

52 In a conversation, Joseph Lichtenberg, M.D., Institute of Psychoanalysis, Baltimore–

District of Columbia, spoke of the phenomenon in artists (particularly in middle age and beyond) of a "generativity gone crazy."

53 Harding, *Days*, p. 358. See J, VII:365–67.

54 Harding, *Days*, p. 357.

55 Ibid., p. 344.

56 Ibid., pp. 343–44.

57 Letter of December 4, 1855, transcription, Thoreau Textual Center.

58 Harding, *Days*, pp. 343–44.

59 Gozzi, "Tropes and Figures," p. 314.

60 Letter of December 22, 1855, transcription, Thoreau Textual Center.

7   Sugar Maple Man

1   See Howarth, *Book of Concord.*

2   See Gozzi's discussion, in "Tropes and Figures," of Thoreau's early life, pp. 1–52. One may surmise that Thoreau, being ill, rambled less, spent more time with his family talking about the past, and often felt a sort of cabin fever.

3   See chapters 8 and 9.

4   Letter of May 5, 1856, transcription, Thoreau Textual Center.

5   Harding, *Days*, p. 366.

6   See chapter 8.

7   Gozzi, "Tropes and Figures," p. 179.

8   See my articles, "An Unpublished Letter to Russell" and "Thoreau's Scientific Phase," for the full text of this letter.

9   See Ruth Frost's description of this trip (and other trips to Worcester) in "Thoreau's Worcester Associations."

10 See Blanding and Harding, *A Thoreau Iconography.*

11 Harding, *Days*, p. 367.

12 Cf. Gozzi on the "lure of swamps," in "Tropes and Figures," pp. 197–201.

13 Cf. Sayre, *Thoreau and the American Indians*, p. 188.

14 Harding, *Days*, p. 370. Alcott had encouraged him to take this trip.

15 Ibid., p. 376. Perhaps Emerson did not mention Whitman's name because some in the audience *would* have known of him. When Emerson, Alcott, and Thoreau contemplated inviting Whitman to Concord at one point, "Mrs. Emerson, Mrs. Alcott, and Sophia Thoreau were all so strongly prejudiced against him for his outspoken verse that they joined in vetoing the invitation before it could be extended" (ibid., p. 376). When Sophia learned that the person "not known to this audience" in Emerson's funeral oration was Whitman, "she strongly protested and the sentence was dropped when the eulogy was printed" (p. 376). For an illuminating recent consideration of the Emerson-Whitman relationship, see Jerome Loving, *Emerson, Whitman, and the American Muse* (Chapel Hill: University of North Carolina Press, 1982).

16 Thoreau met Whitman's mother and conversed with the poet in his cluttered, unkempt bedroom; later, the conversation moved downstairs to the living room. Their discussion tended to center on Whitman's interests, schedule, and writing; Whitman was eager for feedback on the 1855 *Leaves of Grass.* They discussed their differing views of politics and the common man. Before parting, the two writers exchanged copies of books, the 1856 edition of *Leaves of Grass* and *A Week* (ibid., pp. 372–74; for more details of their meeting, see pp. 372–74).

17 Ibid., p. 374.

18 Ibid.

19 See my essay, "Walt Whitman and His Poems, 1856–1860: The Quest for Intimacy and Generativity," *Walt Whitman Review* 25 (1979):146–63.

20 Canby, *Thoreau*, pp. 151–52, and Moller, *Thoreau in the Human Community*, p. 37, think that Lidian was probably the friend to whom Thoreau was referring; Harding, in *Days*, p. 303, thinks it was most likely Waldo.

21 On March 18, 1857, Thoreau would compare Emerson unfavorably with Goodwin (J, IX:296).

22 Harding, *Days*, pp. 378–79.

23 Sanborn says that he "never heard Henry speak of his brother except by the parable of this sea-song"; see F. B. Sanborn, *The Personality of Thoreau* (1901; reprint ed., Folcroft, Pa.: Folcroft Press, 1969), pp. 38–39. See also *Young Man Thoreau*, pp. 197–98, 200–1.

24 Erikson, "The Life Cycle," p. 138.

25 Harding, *Days*, p. 382.

26 Ibid., p. 384.

27 Ibid., pp. 350–51.

28 Letter of July 11, 1857, transcription, Thoreau Textual Center.

29 Harding, *Days*, p. 385.

30 Sayre describes Polis as a "thoroughly bi-cultural individual"; see *Thoreau and the American Indians*, pp. 172–87. See also Robert Sayre, "Charles Bird King's Joseph Porus and Thoreau's Maine Woods Guide," *Thoreau Journal Quarterly* 13 (1981):10–14. This article includes a copy of a painting that Sayre believes (with good evidence) is of Joe Polis.

　　Polis told Thoreau that his mother was a white woman and his father a pure-blooded Indian; Thoreau says, however, "I saw no trace of white blood in his face, and others, who knew him well and also his father, were confident that his mother was an Indian" (J, IX:497). It seemed important for Thoreau to believe that Polis was "pure-blooded" (or at least a "real" Indian), but he was also clearly happy and comfortable with Polis's "civilized" qualities.

31 Sayre, *Thoreau and the American Indians*, p. 178.

32 Harding, *Days*, p. 386.

33 As Robert Sayre, for instance, shows, there were many instances of tension between Thoreau and Polis regarding religion, hunting, eating habits, Polis's disposition and occasionally incomprehensible or unresponsive behavior (*Thoreau and the American Indians*, pp. 174–87). Infrequently, Thoreau takes a questioning or superior attitude toward the Indian.

　　Perhaps the most disturbing occurrence was when, soon after traversing some burnt lands (with Hoar as a companion, could the anxiety-provoking remembrance of their complicity in the 1844 woodsburning be avoided?), Hoar became separated from the other two men and Thoreau feared his nearsighted friend might have walked over a precipice. Although Polis offered some suggestions and tried to reassure Thoreau or calm him down, he was troubled by the Indian's relative lack of concern or effort in finding Hoar and reports that he "lay awake a good deal from anxiety." Considering the anxiety and guilt he was subject to regarding the loss of his own brother, we may surmise that his uneasy feelings in this situation were all the more intense. When, the next morning, the search continued, the Indian fell into the water while portaging, and Thoreau "hastily stepped forward to help him, asking if he was much hurt, but after a moment's pause, he sprang up and went forward. He was all the way subject to taciturn fits, but they were harmless ones." Finally Hoar answered one of Thoreau's shouts, and they found him, smoking his pipe. Just before Thoreau saw Hoar, he "naturally shouted again and again, but the Indian curtly remarked, 'He hears you.' " There may be some overtones here of a rivalry among brothers—with Polis apparently wanting to keep Thoreau to himself. However, the anxiety of the event was soon dispelled with the reunion: "The beauty of the scene may have been enhanced to our eyes by the fact that we had just come together again after a night of some anxiety." The fear of loss accentuated the feeling of relief upon their "coming together," and before long the uneasy residue of the incident seems to disappear. *The Maine Woods* (MW), ed. Joseph J. Moldenhauer (Princeton: Princeton University Press, 1972), pp. 259–64.

8   Ripe for the Fall

1   See the articles by Lauriat Lane, Jr., on Thoreau's autumnal vision, "Thoreau's Autumnal, Archetypal Hero: Captain John Brown," *Ariel* 6 (1975):41–48, and "Thoreau's Autumnal Indian," *Canadian Review of American Studies* 6 (1975):228–36; Stoller, *After Walden*; Howarth, *Book of Concord*, pp. 161–219; Paul, *Shores of America*, pp. 392–417.

2   See the discussion of "Walking" in chapter 9. See also Garber, *Thoreau's Redemptive Imagination*.

3   The reader is once more referred to Lifton's discussion of "symbolic immortality" in *Broken Connection*.

4   Harding, *Days*, p. 397.

5   Ibid. Edward Emerson, in *Henry Thoreau as Remembered by a Young Friend* (1917; reprint ed., Concord, Mass.: Thoreau Foundation, 1968), contends that Thoreau's exposure, more common during this period, to "irritant" pencil dust may have been a factor in "render[ing] him more susceptible to pulmonary disease" (pp. 37–38). Thus his father's debilitation, and his taking over for him, may have put him more at risk in terms of occupational health hazards.

6   Harding, *Days*, p. 393.

7   See chapter 5.

8   Harding, *Days*, pp. 396–97.

9   Ibid., p. 406.

10   Cf. Sattelmeyer, "Introduction," *Natural History Essays*, pp. xxviii–ix.

11   Harding, *Days*, p. 409.

12   Ibid., p. 408.

13   See Gozzi, "Tropes and Figures," pp. 401–37 ("The John Brown Principle"). See also Carl Bode, "The Half-Hidden Thoreau," in Hicks, *Thoreau in Our Season*, pp. 104–16.

14   See *Young Man Thoreau*, pp. 176–77.

15   Mary Hosmer Brown, as quoted in Gozzi, "Tropes and Figures," p. 63.

16   Though in many ways Thoreau defined himself, in contrast to his father, as "historian" and chronicler of the margins of Concord—the forests, fields, etc.—his interest in Concord history was in some way an attempt to identify with his father and carry on John Sr.'s task.

17   It must be stressed that Thoreau, in spite of the uneasiness and embarrassment he had

sometimes caused his parents and other family members, was a good and dutiful son who usually "came through" when his family most needed him.

18 Harding, *Days*, p. 409.

19 Ibid., p. 411.

20 See Stoller, *After Walden*, for a fine discussion of Thoreau's developing concern for conservation.

21 Harding, *Days*, p. 412.

22 See later in this chapter and chapter 9. As Lifton observes in *Broken Connection*, the sense of living on through the collectivity, as well as through the ongoingness of nature and the natural environment, is an important form of symbolic immortality. The concern with conservation combines and affords modes of symbolic immortality related to living on through both the human collectivity and the nature that remains.

23 See Avery D. Weisman and Thomas P. Hackett, "Predilection to Death," in *Death and Identity*, ed. Robert Fulton (New York: John Wiley and Sons, 1965), pp. 293–329; reprinted from *Psychosomatic Medicine* 23 (1961):232–56. This is, says Lifton (who discusses it in *Broken Connection*, pp. 107–8), a "classic" article, and it had an important influence (partly a confirming influence) on my thinking.

24 That Emerson, as Thoreau reported to Blake on September 26, 1859, had been "seriously lame for 2 or three months past— Sprained his foot and does not yet get better" (C, 559), could well have heightened his uneasiness about aspiring to such "success." It had been, as Thoreau put it, a "bad business" for Emerson, and it most likely made Thoreau feel "bad," or at least ambivalent, about the "business" of pursuing literary ripeness.

25 See the discussion of "Huckleberries" in chapter 9.

26 See chapter 9.

27 Harding, *Days*, p. 411.

28 Channing, *Thoreau, the Poet-Naturalist*, p. 262.

29 See Michael Meyer's excellent and provocative essay, "Thoreau's Rescue of John Brown from History," *Studies in the American Renaissance, 1980*, ed. Joel Myerson (Boston: Twayne Publishers, 1980), pp. 301–16.

30 Cf. Gozzi, "Tropes and Figures," pp. 401–37.

31 Channing, *Thoreau, the Poet-Naturalist*, p. 16.

32 Cf. Gozzi, "Tropes and Figures," p. 432 (and pp. 401–37). In defending Brown so forcefully, Thoreau was, in Gozzi's view, seeking to turn outward his aggressive feelings toward authority and, specifically, toward his father. But when Brown was judged guilty and hanged by the state, Thoreau's unconscious perceived it as a just judgment on himself for attacking authority and, at bottom, his father. I do not see the judgment to execute Brown as the one most significant factor in inclining Thoreau toward death. As I have argued, before the Brown affair he was already "less to be identified with the state of things." But the Brown controversy did strongly exacerbate his inclination toward death, and the judgment on Brown, and Brown's hanging, constituted one more turn of the screw. For other factors involved, see the rest of this chapter and chapter 9.

33 Harding, *Days*, p. 417.

34 See *Young Man Thoreau*, pp. 178–79, 209–13.

35 Harding, *Days*, p. 417.

36 Refer back to chapter 4.

37 Harding, *Days*, pp. 415–16.

38   Cf. Meyer, "Thoreau's Rescue of Brown," pp. 301–16, and Howarth, *Book of Concord*, pp. 177–81.

39   See *Young Man Thoreau*, p. 179.

40   Meyer, "Thoreau's Rescue of Brown."

41   Cf. Lane, "Thoreau's Autumnal, Archetypal Hero."

42   See chapter 9.

43   Erikson, "The Life Cycle," pp. 139–41. See the previous discussion of integrity in chapter 1.

44   Erikson, "The Life Cycle," p. 139.

45   Harding, *Days*, p. 421. See "Martyrdom of John Brown," in Glick, *Reform Papers*, pp. 139–43, and "Sir Walter Raleigh," in Moldenhauer and Moser, *Early Essays and Miscellanies*, pp. 178–218.

46   Harding, *Days*, p. 421.

47   A year to the day later, December 3, 1860, Thoreau would come down with the cold that would develop into tuberculosis.

9   Tracks in the Snow

1   Cf. Meyer, "Thoreau's Rescue of Brown," esp. pp. 310–12.

2   On different forms of "symbolic immortality," see Lifton, *Broken Connection*, esp. pp. 18–23.

3   Erikson, "The Life Cycle," p. 139.

4   Ibid., p. 141.

5   Ibid., p. 140.

6   Harding, *Days*, p. 441.

7   Milton Meltzer, ed., *Thoreau: People, Principles, and Politics* (New York: Hill and Wang, 1963), p. 182.

8   "Wild Fruits," transcription, Thoreau Textual Center. Leo Stoller reconstructed the "Huckleberry" lecture.

9   Ibid.

10   Cf. Howarth, *Book of Concord*, pp. 161–211.

11   In another sense, counting tree rings was also a way to be a more detached observer who transcends time. As Vaillant says, in *Adaptation to Life*, "By studying the cross-section of a redwood tree, we can discern a milennium of forest history—in minutes. In our view of a thousand concentric rings we stand outside time" (pp. 199–200).

12   "The Dispersion of Seeds," transcription, Thoreau Textual Center.

13   Cf. Gozzi, "Tropes and Figures," p. 418. Gozzi argues that guilt may have helped precipitate the " 'severe cold' that developed into tuberculosis."

14   Harding, *Days*, p. 441.

15   Ibid. Edward Emerson, in *Thoreau as Remembered*, says, "Even his health could not throw off a chill got by long stooping in a wet snow storm counting the growth-rings on the stumps of some old trees" (pp. 116–17).

16   Harding, *Days*, p. 441.

17   Edward Emerson, *Thoreau as Remembered*, pp. 116–17.

18   Harding, *Days*, p. 441.

19   Ibid., p. 443. See Howarth, *Book of Concord*.

20   Harding, *Days*, p. 443.

21   "The Dispersion of Seeds," Thoreau Textual Center.

22   Perry Miller, *Consciousness in Concord* (Boston: Houghton Mifflin Co., 1958), p. 215. See also *Journal: The Writings of Henry D. Thoreau* (PJ), ed. John C. Broderick et al. (Princeton: Princeton University Press, 1981–), 1:223.

23   Channing, *Thoreau, the Poet-Naturalist*, p. 16.

24   Marble, *Thoreau*, p. 176.

25   See George M. Frederickson, *The Inner Civil War: Northern Intellectuals and the Crisis of the Union* (New York: Harper and Row Publishers, 1965).

26   See George B. Forgie, *Patricide in the House Divided*, including the chapter, "The Literature of Fratricide" (New York: W. W. Norton and Co., 1979). For two recent suggestive interpretations partly concerning Lincoln's psychology and the Civil War (which may be related to Thoreau's dilemmas), see Dwight G. Anderson, *Abraham Lincoln: The Quest for Immortality* (New York: Alfred A. Knopf, 1982), and Charles B. Strozier, *Lincoln's Quest for Union: Public and Private Meanings* (New York: Basic Books, 1982).

27   Letter to Thatcher of March 31, 1861, transcription, Thoreau Textual Center.

28   Channing, *Thoreau, the Poet-Naturalist*, p. 339.

29   I am indebted for this suggestion to Prof. James Cox, in a commentary on a paper I delivered at the American Studies Association Convention in Minneapolis, October 1979. Of course, the prospect of the South winning the war would have been horrifying for Thoreau, however ambivalent he was about the North and however drawn he was to some sort of agrarian orientation. Psychologically speaking, whatever the war's outcome, Thoreau could not be a clear winner.

30   Harding, *Days*, p. 445.

31   Sayre, *Thoreau and the American Indians*, p. 193.

32   Sayre asks, "Did Thoreau now so clearly equate wildness and Indians with health and renewal that Minnesota would have been his first choice whatever the doctor ordered or economy dictated?" (ibid.).

33   *Thoreau's Minnesota Journey: Two Documents—Thoreau's Notes on the Journey West and the Letters of Horace Mann, Jr.*, ed. Walter Harding (Geneseo, N.Y.: Thoreau Society Booklet 16, 1962), p. i.

34   Ibid., pp. 47–54.

35   Ibid., p. ii.

36   Harding, *Days*, p. 448.

37   Harding, *Thoreau's Minnesota Journey*, p. v.

38   See Sayre, *Thoreau and the American Indians*, p. 199.

39   Ibid., p. 200.

40   Harding, *Thoreau's Minnesota Journey*, p. 22.

41   Sayre, *Thoreau and the American Indians*, pp. 201–2.

42   Harding, *Thoreau's Minnesota Journey*, p. ii.

43   Ibid.

44   Harding, *Days*, p. 452.

45   *Daniel Ricketson and His Friends*, ed. Anna and Walton Ricketson (Boston: Houghton Mifflin Co., 1902), p. 318.

46   See Blanding and Harding, *A Thoreau Iconography*.

47   Harding, *Days*, p. 455.

48   Ibid., pp. 455–56.

49   Cf. Seybold, *Thoreau*, p. 88.

50   Erikson, "The Life Cycle," p. 141.

51   Edward Emerson, *Thoreau as Remembered*, p. 117.

52   Channing, *Thoreau, the Poet-Naturalist*, p. 340.

53   Ibid., p. 337.

54   Ricketson and Ricketson, *Daniel Ricketson and His Friends*, p. 214.

55   Ibid., p. 141.

56   Harding, "Afterword," in *Henry David Thoreau*, p. 252.

57   Harding, *Days*, p. 455.

58   Marble, *Thoreau*, p. 175.

59   Weisman and Hackett, "Predilection to Death," p. 321.

60   Channing, *Thoreau, the Poet-Naturalist*, p. 340.

61   Harding, *Days*, p. 465.

62   Ricketson and Ricketson, *Daniel Ricketson and His Friends*, pp. 136–37.

63   Marble, *Thoreau*, p. 179. Clearly, Thoreau's pantheistic impulses and inclinations (related in part to his steeping not only in nature but in transcendentalism and oriental philosophy) contributed to and supplemented these feelings.

64   Though a reverent man in many ways, Thoreau does not seem to have leaned on a conventional concept of God; there was little reference to God in his last days. He indicated to one friend that "a snow-storm was more to him than Christ" (Harding, *Days*, p. 464). But to any extent that Thoreau did hold onto an anthropomorphic concept of God (he referred to "God" frequently, for instance, after his brother's death [see *Young Man Thoreau*, pp. 183–86]), it is likely that "God" was closely linked, psychologically, with such figures as his father and brother. For a classic discussion of God as father, see Sigmund Freud, *The Future of an Illusion*, trans. W. D. Robson-Scott, ed. James Strachey (Garden City, N.Y.: Doubleday and Co., 1964). Erikson explains (see, for example, *Gandhi's Truth*, p. 129) that God is first experienced by infants in the image of the personal father, and it seems probable that there was some transference between God's image and that of the father—and the brother who was an elder-brother–father figure for Thoreau (cf. Gozzi, "Father-God," in "Tropes and Figures," pp. 202–27). He answered Aunt Maria's question about whether he had made his peace with God by saying, "I did not know we had ever quarrelled, Aunt" (Edward Emerson, *Thoreau as Remembered*, pp. 117–18). In one sense, this appears to be a statement of acceptance. In another sense, however, it was clearly important for him to deny that he had ever quarreled with a God he on some level identified with his father and brother. In any event, death would allow him to atone, make peace with, and gain the conclusive blessings of such a God.

65   Joseph Wood Krutch, in *Henry David Thoreau* (New York: William Sloan Associates, 1948), says "There were many ways during a long, enervating illness in which he might have weakened or relented. He might at least have ceased to regret his 'good behavior.' Without so much as hinting anything that could be called a recantation, he might have exhibited some mere failure of nerve. Men who are sick and dying cannot always find the courage to hold out against the insistent human temptation to regret and sentimentalize. But Thoreau did more than merely hold out. He found . . . the courage and the strength to choose mocking, aphoristic words in which to reiterate, with all their pristine pungency, both his fundamental convictions and his acceptance of the universe" (pp. 243–44).

66   Channing, *Thoreau, the Poet-Naturalist*, p. 340.

67   Harding, *Days*, p. 463.

68   Ibid.

69   Ricketson and Ricketson, *Daniel Ricketson and His Friends*, pp. 136–37.

70 Edward Emerson, *Thoreau as Remembered*, p. 117.

71 Harding, *Days*, p. 457.

72 Ibid., p. 469.

73 Ethel Seybold, in *Thoreau*, argues that "Autumnal Tints," "Night and Moonlight," and "Wild Apples" were "chapters from that half-seriously projected book about the phenomena of nature and the thoughts of man to show the pattern of life" (p. 86). See also the discussion of the "Excursion" essays in Paul, *Shores of America*; Howarth, *Book of Concord*; and Sattelmeyer, "Introduction," *Natural History Essays*.

74 See Sheehy, *Pathfinders*. Thoreau must surely qualify in many respects as one of Sheehy's "pathfinders."

75 Harding, *Days*, p. 458.

76 Ibid., pp. 461–62.

77 Channing, *Thoreau, the Poet-Naturalist*, p. 40.

78 Sanborn, *Henry D. Thoreau*, pp. 270–73.

79 Marble, *Thoreau*, p. 269.

80 Channing, *Thoreau, the Poet-Naturalist*, p. 14. See also Carl Bode, ed. *The Portable Thoreau*, rev. ed. (New York: Penguin Books, 1977), p. 573. Bode describes it as a "sturdy wooden box."

81 Harding, *Days*, p. 459.

82 Ibid., p. 457.

83 Ibid., p. 466.

84 Ibid., p. 460.

85 Ibid., p. 466.

86 Ibid., p. 468.

87 See Stoller, *After Walden*, for the ways in which Thoreau did, in fact, aspire to do some "engineering for all America." For a helpful analysis of Emerson's funeral oration, see Neufeldt, *House of Emerson*, pp. 127–40.

88 Channing, *Thoreau, the Poet-Naturalist*, p. 336.

89 Harding, *Days*, p. 466.

90 Howarth, *Book of Concord*, p. 219. See also Thomas Blanding, "A Last Word from Thoreau," *Concord Saunterer* 11 (1976):16–17; Thomas Woodson, "Another Word on Thoreau's Last 'Good Sailing,' " ibid., 12 (1977):17; and Sayre, *Thoreau and the American Indians*, pp. 214–15.

91 Channing, *Thoreau, the Poet-Naturalist*, p. 336.

92 Ricketson and Ricketson, *Daniel Ricketson and His Friends*, p. 141.

93 Harding, *Days*, pp. 467–68. As Harding informs us, in his "Afterword" to the 1982 Dover edition of *Days*, "ten years or so later his body was removed from the New Burying Ground to its present resting place on Authors' Ridge in the adjacent Sleepy Hollow Cemetery" (p. 474).

Index

Library of Congress Cataloging in Publication Data
Lebeaux, Richard, 1946–
Thoreau's seasons.
(New England writers series)
Includes index.
1. Thoreau, Henry David, 1817–1862—Biography—
Psychology. 2. Seasons in literature. 3. Authors,
American—19th century—Biography. I. Title. II. Series.
PS3053.L35   1984   818'.309 [B]   83–17982
ISBN 0–87023–401–3